Words That Make America Great

JEROME AGEL

Section Introductions by Milton J. Cantor, Ph.D.

RANDOM HOUSE
New York

Words That Make America Great

Copyright © 1999, 1997 by Jerome B. Agel

Grateful acknowledgment is made to the following for permission to reprint previously published material:

American Civil Liberties Union: ACLU Original Creed of 1929. Reprinted courtesy of the Seeley G. Mudd Manuscript Library, Department of Rare Books and Special Collections, Princeton University Libraries.

Association of American Publishers, Inc.: Executive summary of AAP's February 8, 1996 Congressional Testimony. Reprinted by permission of Association of American Publishers.

The Estate of Martin Luther King, Jr. c/o Writer's House, Inc.: "I have a dream", speech given by Dr. Martin Luther King, Jr. Copyright © 1963 by Martin Luther King, Jr. Copyright renewed 1991 by Coretta Scott King. Reprinted by arrangement with The Heirs to the Estate of Martin Luther King, Jr., c/o Writer's House, Inc. as agent for the proprietor.

Newton N. Minow: Excerpt from "The Vast Wasteland" by Newton N. Minow. Reprinted courtesy of the author.

Franklin D. Roosevelt Library: Letter from Albert Einstein to Franklin Delano Roosevelt. Reprinted by permission of Franklin D. Roosevelt Library.

Times Books, a division of Random House, Inc.: Excerpt from CONTRACT WITH AMERICA by Rep. Newt Gingrich, Rep. Dick Armey and The House Republicans. Copyright © 1994 by Republican National Committee. Reprinted by permission of Times Books, a division of Random House, Inc.

Interior Illustrations:

First Landing, 1620. Engraving by T. Phillibrown, N.Y. Public Library Picture Collection.

The Signing of the Constitution in 1787. From a painting by Sterns in the Smithsonian Institute in Washington D.C. Courtesy CORBIS-BETTMAN.

E Pluribus Unum. National Archives of Canada. C-021765/C-021764/C-039581/C-039582.

Let Freedom Ring: A Ballad of Martin Luther King. Reprinted by permission of Samual Byrd.

Immigrants Passing the Statue of Liberty from Frank Leslie's Illustrated Newspaper, Museum of the City of New York.

The Gallant Charge of the Fifty Fourth Massachusetts (Colored) Regiment. Publisher: Currier & Ives, 1863 Museum of the City of NewYork, 56.300.460 The Harry T. Peters Collection.

The Road Builders, Wm. Wolfson. Howard Simon, *500 Years of Art and Illustration from Albrect Dürer to Rockwell Kent,* World Publishing, Cleveland, 1942. N.Y. Public Library Picture Collection.

The Prayer at Valley Forge, A Pictorial History of the World's Greatest Nations, from Earliest Dates to Present Time, Charlotte Mary Yonge, Hess, N.Y. 1882, N.Y. Public Library Picture Collection.

Georgetown, Federal City or City of Washington, Library of Congress.

Uncle Sam Cartoon. Courtesy Houghton-Mifflin.

The Wright's First Plane at Kitty Hawk, North Carolina. N.Y. Public Library Picture Collection. Courtesy CORBIS-BETTMAN

Originally published in hardcover by Random House, Inc. in 1997.

Library of Congress Cataloging-in-Publication Data
Words that make America great / [compiled by] Jerome Agel. ; category
    essays by Milton J. Cantor. — 1st pbk. ed.
        p.   cm.
    Includes index.
    ISBN 0-679-44959-0 (HC); 0-375-70651-8 (PB)
    1. United States—History Sources.   I. Agel, Jerome. II. Cantor, Milton.
E173.W87   1999
973—dc21   99-21543
                                                           CIP

ISBN 0-679-44959-0 (HC)
ISBN 0-375-70651-8 (PB)

Typeset and printed in the United States of America

Cover Design: Maria Ilardi
Interior Book Design: Charlotte Staub
Page Composition: Allentown Digital Services, an R.R. Donnelley & Sons Company

First Paperback Edition
0 9 8 7 6 5 4 3 2 1
June 1999

New York   Toronto   London   Sydney   Auckland

Contents

E PLURIBUS UNUM 69

CERTAIN UNALIENABLE RIGHTS 103

THE AMERICAN DREAM 147

YEARNING TO BREATHE FREE 173

THE WAR BETWEEN THE STATES:
THE HOUSE DIVIDED 185

WE THE PEOPLE 221

"I DO SOLEMNLY SWEAR (OR AFFIRM)" 267

Contents

THE FIRST AMERICANS 341

POWER TO THE PEOPLE 383

THIS LAND IS YOUR LAND 415

FOREIGN AFFAIRS 435

A FIRE WITHIN: REALLY NEW IDEAS 477

HOME OF THE BRAVE 541

Chronological Index

Preface

America's Big Red, White, and Blue Book

A half century ago, a three-car railroad train emblazoned in red, white, and blue displayed in nearly 350 cities around the United States a collection of 130 or so documents relating to the establishment and the preservation of American liberties and the Federal government. A teen memory of the compiler of this volume is of spending many hours on the train, which rested on spur track of the Rutland Railroad station, at the foot of Main Street, near Lake Champlain, in Burlington, Vermont. The train bypassed segregated cities, such as Memphis, Tennessee, and Birmingham, Alabama. Some communities lifted Jim Crow laws so that the train could stop there.

We Americans flocked to the exhibition. The Freedom Train was a spectacular success.

So much has happened since the late 1940s:

A President was shot to death.

A President quit under fire.

Twelve Americans walked on the Moon.

Schools were integrated.

Organized baseball—America's pastime—let black men play for the first time.

Two states joined the Union.

The U.S. warred in Korea, southeast Asia, Central America, Africa, and the Persian Gulf.

The U.S. transferred control of the Panama Canal and struck up diplomatic relations with the billion people of the People's Republic of China.

Microsoft became a billion-dollar business.

The air and the water became cleaner.

The Federal government sponsored culture big time.

The nearly 200 documents in this volume, which include hallowed texts displayed on the Freedom Train, span nearly 400 variegated years—the Iroquois Federation Constitution (c. 1570) and the Mayflower Compact (1620), manifest destiny, the Civil War (more than 600,000 dead), two world wars and the 40-year cold war, voting rights, civil rights, women's rights, gays in the military, Senate majority leader Bob Dole's decision to run for the Presidency (1996). Not all of the documents are governments'. Not all were composed by Americans.

Fifty years ago, most of us would not have predicted the sometimes controversial documents, revolutionary and evolutionary, that would burst forth as the United States became the world's indispensable nation. Legal decisions, speeches, and reports revealed the innards of a fast-paced, highly charged, unique democratic society which probes itself, takes its temperature, and feels its pulse seemingly every day. We the

People are heard in songs, treaties, executive orders, and Congressional investigations which expose our attitudes and spirit—illuminating, inspiring, sometimes shocking but always reflecting the representative-democracy's dialogue we've had. Our sacred texts bang around in the American consciousness. They presage and echo governance in the eras of sailing ships and horse-drawn carriages, supersonic jets and the electric technology of the global village.

You may wish to consider the documents in this volume as signposts along the highways and byways of American history. Directionals and destinations. U.S. history unfolds as you breeze along.

Some editing here and there prompts intense reader involvement. (There *are* surprises.) Keen assistance in harvesting some of the documents was rendered by Mary Mortensen, of Lawrence, Kansas.

This is America's big red, white, and blue book.

—JEROME AGEL

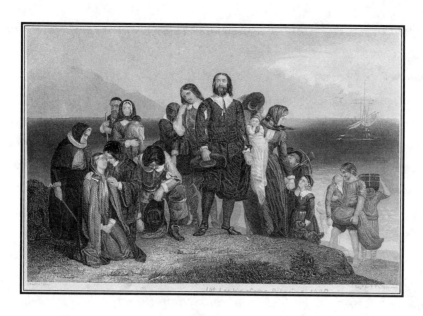

IN THE BEGINNING

The law, said Oliver Wendell Holmes, is a magic mirror in which we see reflected not only our own lives but also the lives of those who went before us. Never did the wise Supreme Court Justice utter a sounder, more discerning observation. Those settlers who fled Old England for the New World in the seventeenth century brought with them explicit convictions about law and governance. One of their propositions, the idea of government under law, rather than under men, meant that not even the King of England could ignore the law of the land or deny accepted legal practices. Another was a belief in the common law, the law developed over centuries by English judges. It, too, made a smooth passage to America's shores, guided our first judges and lawmakers, and included fundamental liberties. From the outset of settlement, with the charter granted the Virginia settlers in 1606, the colonists understood their rights and liberties to be those granted to all Englishmen, and the Crown assumed as much. Hence, the laws and liberties enjoyed in the motherland governed in the colonies. Direct democracy, the freedom of the frontier, and the face-to-face town meeting guaranteed their continuance.

Colonial rights, however, could not be entirely recreated in a wilderness society. Assumptions about governmental power over daily life had to be reconsidered. Views on toleration required reexamination and rationalization when dealing with slaves, Indians, religious dissenters, etc. The line between freedom and authority needed to be established. The Puritans brought over the idea of covenant, which was virtually synonymous with the words "contract" and "compact" and ran deep in English political thought. The idea of a body of consensually agreed-upon governors, first expressed in the Mayflower Compact, embodied a conviction that the people themselves, without guidance from outside agencies, could compact together to create a self-governing community. To be sure, they were applying customary church practices to meet the need of a raw frontier, but, germane for us, they also were establishing the rudiments of representative government. While not a true constitution, the Compact drew on the long tradition of contractual thought, and marked the recognition that governments ruled by consent of the governed.

That such political theory did not apply to Indians, slaves, or religious dissenters suggests only that there is more than one version of our history to reconstruct. Though the selections here reflect only one side of the historical pact, that of the emergence of individual liberty in the first 150 years, they confirm the openness and pluralism of American society. Even when the demand was that of a specific religious body for "true doctrine," it became a demand for freedom and contributed to an atmosphere of liberty and toleration. That this demand would gradually spill over into Anglo-American relations was inevitable. The campaign for liberty in one area became demands for liberty in all. The "home rule" campaign in the colonies became at the same time a dispute over who should rule at home. The professed loyalty to the

Crown, refusal to obey parliamentary measures, and denial of its jurisdiction in certain areas had a dialectical outcome, namely, successive political crises. They began with the Stamp Act, one of a series of British measures designed to extend imperial power. The break with England accelerated the emergence of democratic political theory and led inexorably to the Declaration of Independence, which itself evolved out of colonial familiarity with representative government, the efficacy of consent of the governed, egalitarian social attitudes, and Enlightenment doctrines such as the existence of natural rights and man's capacity to reason. The rupture also confirmed the colonies' rejection of a belief in the efficacy of government that ruled from afar, which became associated with tyrannical rule and with highly centralized authority. Experiences, then, led them to the principle of federalism and the conviction that it was both wise and feasible to distribute powers among governments, giving local powers to local governments and general powers to the central government. Reacting against strong central governmental authority, the states invented a "firm league of friendship." It was something new under the sun, a government of parts, not of a whole, a form of government unprecedented in history, a decentralized system in which the states were the major political entities.

"Just and equal laws"

The Mayflower Compact
1620

More than a century after metal-clad Spanish conquistadores first trooped through sun-stroked deserts in southwestern North America, a three-masted former wine ship, the *Mayflower*, ferried 35 Christian dissenters (Separatists) from Church of England authority and 66 fortune-seeking, sometimes obstreperous other men and women westward across the vast and furious North Atlantic to the unknowns of New England. Eight days before a "good harbor and pleasant" bay sheltered by Cape Cod, Massachusetts, was sighted, 51 of the men assembled in a cabin to plan for the unity and authority of their proposed colony. Modeling a social contract on church covenants that the dissenters had known in England, they established a "Civil Body Politic" to frame and enact "just and equal Laws, Ordinances, Acts, Constitutions, (and) Offices . . . for the general good of the Colony." The Mayflower Compact, dated November 11, 1620, was government by consent. Foreshadowing ideas and ideals of democratic governance, it went into force as the immigrants established Plimoth Plantation on deserted land of disease-plagued Wampanoag Indians at the end of the year. When the *Mayflower* lifted anchor, on April 7, 1621, none of the survivors of that first winter chose to return to England. The colony lasted until King James II ordered it merged into the Dominion of New England, in 1686. (Former Vice President Dan Quayle is a Mayflower descendant.)

IN THE NAME OF GOD, AMEN. We whose names are underwritten, the loyal subjects of our dread Sovereign Lord King James, by the Grace of God, of Great Britain, France, and Ireland King, Defender of the Faith, etc.

Having undertaken, for the Glory of God, and advancement of the Christian Faith, and Honour of our King and Country, a Voyage to plant the First Colony in the Northern Parts of Virginia, do by these presents solemnly and mutually in the presence of God and one of another, Covenant, and Combine ourselves together into a Civil Body Politic, for our better ordering and preservation, and furtherance of the ends aforesaid; and by virtue hereof to enact, constitute, and frame such just and equal Laws, Ordinances, Acts, Constitutions, Offices, from time to time, as shall be thought most meet and convenient for the general good of the Colony: unto which we promise all due submission and obedience. In witness whereof we have hereunder subscribed our names; Cape Cod, the 11th of November, in the year of the reign of our Sovereign Lord King James, of England, France and Ireland the eighteenth, and of Scotland the fifty-fourth. Anno Domini 1620.

"Shall be punished with death"

THE MARYLAND ACT OF TOLERATION
1649

The first proprietor of Maryland, Cecilius Calvert (1605–1675), the second Lord Baltimore, established the colony as a refuge for Roman Catholics. He feared an influx of Virginian Puritans—a Protestant majority—when Puritans took power in England. The Maryland Assembly's so-called Act of Toleration was a step towards establishing freedom of conscience, but it did not recognize the principle of toleration for everybody: It granted liberty of conscience only to people who believed in the divinity of Jesus Christ. Blasphemers faced severe punishment. In 1654, a Puritan law forbade Catholics to practice their faith openly. It was not until the mid-1820s that Jews were permitted to hold public office in Maryland. Maryland's law requiring a belief in God as a condition for holding public office held until 1961.

Be it therefore . . . enacted. . . . That whatsoever person or persons within this Province . . . shall from henceforth blaspheme God, . . . or shall deny our Saviour Jesus Christ to bee the sonne of God, or shall deny the holy Trinity the ffather sonne and holy Ghost, or the Godhead of any of the said Three persons of the Trinity or the Unity of the Godhead . . . shall be punished with death and confiscation or forfeiture of all his or her lands. . . . Be it Therefore . . . enacted (except as in this present Act is before Declared and sett forth) that noe person or persons whatsoever within this Province, or the Islands, Ports, Harbors, Creekes, or havens thereunto belonging professing to believe in Jesus Christ, shall from henceforth bee any waies troubled, Molested or discountenanced for or in respect of his or her religion nor in the free exercise thereof within this Province or the Islands thereunto belonging nor any way compelled to the beleife or exercise of any other Religion against his or her consent, soe as they be not unfaithful to the Lord Proprietary, or molest or conspire against the civil Government established or to bee established in this Province under him or his heires.

"Each colony may retain its constitution"

BENJAMIN FRANKLIN'S PLAN OF UNION

1754

In the first year of the French and Indian War (1754–1763), delegates from seven of England's thirteen North American colonies met in Albany, New York. Benjamin Franklin (1706–1790), of Pennsylvania, proposed a common-cause scheme for uniting the colonies against the Indians and for providing mutual defense. Appealing to the "weak noodles" of the delegates, the polymath argued that it would be "a strange thing if Six Nations of ignorant savages should be capable for forming . . . a union . . . , yet a like union should be impracticable for ten or a dozen English colonies." Although the delegates adopted Franklin's proposal, both the colonial legislatures (believing the plan would weaken their power) and the English (fearing dimunition of both monarchical and parliamentary powers) turned thumbs down.

It is proposed that humble application be made for an act of Parliament of Great Britain, by virtue of which one general government may be formed in America, including all the said colonies, within and under which government each colony may retain its present constitution, except in the particulars wherein a change may be directed by the said act, as hereafter follows.

1. That the said general government be administered by a President-General, to be appointed and supported by the crown; and a Grand Council, to be chosen by the representatives of the people of the several Colonies met in their respective assemblies.

2. That within——months after the passing such act, the House of Representatives that happen to be sitting within that time, or that shall be especially for that purpose convened, may and shall choose members for the Grand Council, in the following proportion, that is to say,

Massachusetts Bay	7
New Hampshire	2
Connecticut	5
Rhode Island	2
New York	4
New Jersey	3
Pennsylvania	6
Maryland	4
Virginia	7
North Carolina	4
South Carolina	4
	48

5. That after the first three years, when the proportion of money arising out of each Colony to the general treasury can be known, the number of members to be chosen for each Colony shall, from time to time, in all ensuing elections, be regulated by that proportion, yet so as that the number to be chosen by any one Province be not more than seven, nor less than two.

6. That the Grand Council shall meet once in every year, and oftener if occasion require, at such time and place as they shall adjourn to at the last preceding meeting, or as they shall be

called to meet at by the President-General on any emergency; he having first obtained in writing the consent of seven of the members to such call, and sent duly and timely notice to the whole.

10. That the President-General, with the advice of the Grand Council, hold or direct all Indian treaties, in which the general interest of the Colonies may be concerned; and make peace or declare war with Indian nations.

11. That they make such laws as they judge necessary for regulating all Indian trade.

12. That they make all purchases from Indians, for the crown, of lands not now within the bounds of particular Colonies, or that shall not be within their bounds when some of them are reduced to more convenient dimensions.

15. That they raise and pay soldiers and build forts for the defence of any of the Colonies, and equip vessels of force to guard the coasts and protect the trade on the ocean, lakes, or great rivers; but they shall not impress men in any Colony, without the consent of the Legislature.

16. That for these purposes they have power to make laws, and lay and levy such general duties, imposts, or taxes, as to them shall appear most equal and just (considering the ability and other circumstances of the inhabitants in the several Colonies), and such as may be collected with the least inconvenience to the people; rather discouraging luxury, than loading industry with unnecessary burdens.

19. That the general accounts shall be yearly settled and reported to the several Assemblies.

21. That the laws. . .shall not be repugnant, but, as near as may be, agreeable to the laws of England, and shall be transmitted to the King in Council for approbation, as soon as may be after their passing; and if not disapproved within three years after presentation, to remain in force.

25. That the particular military as well as civil establishments in each Colony remain in their present state, the general constitution notwithstanding; and that on sudden emergencies any Colony may defend itself, and lay the accounts of expense thence arising before the President-General and General Council, who may allow and order payment of the same, as far as they judge such accounts just and reasonable.

"Rights and grievances"

THE STAMP ACT CONGRESS
1765

The English Parliament, eager to defray the escalating cost of quartering British troops defending the North American colonies against Indian forays, imposed a stamp tax on purchases in the colonies of legal and commercial documents, licenses, newspapers, pamphlets, almanacs, playing cards, dice, and liquor permits. It was England's first direct tax on the colonies. The Stamp Act Congress–conservative delegates from nine colonies meeting in New York–mildly asserted the right of the colonies to freedom from taxation without representation. Parliament rejected the petition, but Americans boycotted British goods and refused to buy the revenue stamp. The tax was repealed after one year.

THE CONGRESS MET according to adjournment, and resumed, etc., upon mature deliberation agreed to the following declarations of the rights and grievances of the colonists, in America, which were ordered to be inserted. . . . the present and impending misfortunes of the British colonies on this continent, having considered as maturely as time will permit the circumstances of the said colonies, esteem it our indispensable duty to make the following declarations of our humble opinion, respecting the most essential rights and liberties of the colonists, and of the grievances under which they labor, by reason of several late acts of Parliament.

1. That His Majesty's subjects in these colonies owe the same allegiance to the Crown of Great Britain that is owing from his subjects born within the Realm, and all due subordination to that august body, the Parliament of Great Britain.

2. That His Majesty's liege subjects in these colonies are entitled to all the inherent rights and liberties of his natural-born subjects within the Kingdom of Great Britain.

3. That it is inseparably essential to the freedom of a people, and the undoubted right of Englishmen, that no taxes be imposed on them but with their own consent, given personally or by their representatives.

4. That the people of these colonies are not, and, from their local circumstances, cannot be represented in the House of Commons in Great Britain.

5. That the only representatives of the people of these colonies are persons chosen therein by themselves, and that no taxes ever have been or can be constitutionally imposed on them but by their respective legislature.

6. That all supplies to the Crown being free gifts of the people, it is unreasonable and inconsistent with the principles and spirit of the British constitution for the people of Great Britain to grant to His Majesty the property of the colonists.

7. That trial by jury is the inherent and invaluable right of every British subject in these colonies.

8. That the late act of Parliament entitled "An

act for granting and applying certain stamp duties, and other duties, in the British colonies and plantations in America, etc.," by imposing taxes on the inhabitants of these colonies, and the said act and several other acts by extending the jurisdiction of the Courts of Admiralty beyond its ancient limits, have a manifest tendency to subvert the rights and liberties of the colonists.

9. That the duties imposed by several late acts of Parliament, from the peculiar circumstances of these colonies, will be extremely burdensome and grievous; and from the scarcity of specie, the payment of them absolutely impracticable.

10. That as the profits of the trade of these colonies ultimately center in Great Britain to pay for the manufactures which they are obliged to take from thence, they eventually contribute very largely to all supplies granted there to the Crown.

11. That the restrictions imposed by several late acts of Parliament on the trade of these colonies will render them unable to purchase the manufactures of Great Britain.

12. That the increase, prosperity, and happiness of these colonies depend on the full and free enjoyment of their rights and liberties, and an intercourse with Great Britain mutually affectionate and advantageous.

13. That it is the right of the British subjects in these colonies to petition the King or either house of Parliament.

Lastly. That it is the indispensable duty of these colonies, to the best of sovereigns, to the mother country, and to themselves, to endeavor by a loyal and dutiful address to His Majesty and humble applications to both houses of Parliament, to procure the repeal of the act for granting and applying certain stamp duties, of all clauses of any other acts of Parliament whereby the jurisdiction of the Admiralty is extended as aforesaid, and of the other late acts for the restriction of American commerce.

"Give me liberty, or give me death!"

PATRICK HENRY

1775

Revolutionary figure, Virginia governor (1776–1779, 1784–1786), and acid-tongued orator Patrick Henry (1736–1799) talked his way into prominence in the English colonies along the Atlantic seaboard: "I am not a Virginian, I am an American." He vigorously opposed the Stamp Act. He was a delegate to the First and Second Continental Congresses. (Virginia was, by far, the largest colony; it included today's West Virginia and Kentucky.) Smelling "a rat," he did not attend the Federal Convention in Philadelphia, in 1787, which composed the charter that would replace the weak-kneed, states-oriented Articles of Confederation (1781), then furiously opposed ratification because, he said, the Constitution would interfere with rights of the states and the people. Years earlier, Henry had delivered his memorable "give me liberty, or give me death!" speech at the Virginia Convention of Delegates. Advocating war rather than negotiation, he impassionedly asked Virginia's second revolutionary conclave, "Is life so dear or peace so sweet as to be purchased at the price of chains and slavery?" Three weeks later, the first shots were fired in the war for independence.

Different men often see the same subject in different lights; and, therefore, I hope that it will not be thought disrespectful to those gentlemen, if, entertaining as I do, opinions of a character very opposite to theirs, I shall speak forth my sentiments freely and without reserve. This is no time for ceremony. The question before the House is one of awful moment to this country. For my own part I consider it as nothing less than a question of freedom or slavery; and in proportion to the magnitude of the subject ought to be the freedom of the debate. It is only in this way that we can hope to arrive at truth, and fulfil the great responsibility which we hold to God and our country. Should I keep back my opinions at such a time, through fear of giving offence, I should consider myself as guilty of treason towards my country, and of an act of dis-

loyalty towards the majesty of heaven, which I revere above all earthly kings.

. . . it is natural to man to indulge in the illusions of hope. We are apt to shut our eyes against a painful truth, and listen to the song of that siren, till she transforms us into beasts. Is this the part of wise men, engaged in a great and arduous struggle for liberty? Are we disposed to be of the number of those who, having eyes, see not, and having ears, hear not, the things which so nearly concern their temporal salvation? For my part, whatever anguish of spirit it may cost, I am willing to know the whole truth; to know the worst and to provide for it.

I have but one lamp by which my feet are guided; and that is the lamp of experience. I know of no way of judging of the future but by the past. And judging by the past, I wish to know what there has been in the conduct of the British ministry for the last ten years, to justify those hopes with which gentlemen have been pleased to solace themselves and the House? Is it that insidious smile with which our petition has been lately received? Trust it not, sir; it will prove a snare to your feet. Suffer not yourselves to be betrayed with a kiss. Ask yourselves how this gracious reception of our petition comports with these war-like preparations which cover our waters and darken our land. Are fleets and armies necessary to a work of love and reconciliation? Have we shown ourselves so unwilling to be reconciled, that force must be called in to win back our love? Let us not deceive ourselves, sir. These are the implements of war and subjugation; the last arguments to which kings resort. I ask gentlemen, sir, what means this martial array, if its purpose be not to force us to submission? Can gentlemen assign any other possible motives for it? Has Great Britain any enemy, in this quarter of the world, to call for all this accumulation of navies and armies? No, sir, she has none. They are meant for us; they can be meant for no other. They are sent over to bind and rivet upon us those chains which the British ministry have been so long forging. And what have we to oppose to them? Shall we try argument? Sir, we have been trying that for the last ten years. Have we anything new to offer on the subject? Nothing. We have held the subject up in every light of which it is capable; but it has been all in vain. Shall we resort to entreaty and humble supplication? What terms shall we find which have not been already exhausted? Let us not, I beseech you, sir, deceive ourselves longer. Sir, we have done everything that could be done, to avert the storm which is now coming on. We have petitioned; we have remonstrated; we have supplicated; we have prostrated ourselves before the throne, and have implored its interposition to arrest the tyrannical hands of the ministry and Parliament. Our petitions have been slighted; our remonstrances have produced additional violence and insult; our supplications have been disregarded; and we have been spurned, with contempt, from the foot of the throne. In vain, after these things, may we indulge the fond hope of peace and reconciliation. There is no longer any room for hope. If we wish to be free—if we mean to preserve inviolate those inestimable privileges for which we have been so long contending—if we mean not basely to abandon the noble struggle in which we have been so long engaged, and which we have pledged ourselves never to abandon until the glorious object of our contest shall be obtained, we must fight! I repeat it, sir, we must fight! An appeal to arms and to the God of Hosts is all that is left us!

They tell us, sir, that we are weak; unable to cope with so formidable an adversary. But when shall we be stronger? Will it be the next week, or the next year? Will it be when we are totally disarmed, and when a British guard shall be stationed in every house? Shall we gather strength by irresolution and inaction? Shall we acquire the means of effectual resistance, by lying supinely on our backs, and hugging the delusive phantom of hope, until our enemies shall have bound us hand and foot? Sir, we are not weak, if we make a proper use of the means which the God of nature hath placed in our power. Three millions of people, armed in the holy cause of liberty, and in such a country as that which we possess, are invincible by any force which our enemy can send against us. Besides, sir, we shall not fight our battles alone. There is a just God who presides over the destinies of nations; and who will raise up friends to fight our battles for us. The battle, sir, is not to the strong alone; it is to the vigilant, the active, the brave. Besides, sir, we have no election. If we were base enough to desire it, it is now too late to retire from the contest. There is no retreat, but in submission and slavery! Our chains are forged! Their clanking may be heard on the plains of Boston! The war is inevitable—and let it come! I repeat it, sir, let it come!

It is in vain, sir, to extenuate the matter. Gentlemen may cry peace, peace—but there is no peace. The war is actually begun! The next gale that sweeps from the north will bring to our ears the clash of resounding arms! Our brethren are already in the field! Why stand we here idle? What is it that gentlemen wish? What would they have? Is life so dear, or peace so sweet, as to be purchased at the price of chains and slavery? Forbid it, Almighty God! I know not what course others may take; but as for me, give me liberty, or give me death!

"We are determined to foment a rebelion"

ABIGAIL ADAMS WRITES HER HUSBAND

1776

During the American Revolution, she was the best-known woman in America. In the first decades of the nascent United States, she was its most important woman. Abigail Smith Adams (1744–1818) was the captivating, self-possessed wife of the political philosopher John Adams (1735–1826), who was a lawyer of integrity and courage (he defended the British soldiers tried for the Boston Massacre of 1770); he masterminded the colonies' break with England, represented the U.S. in France and England, and served as the first Vice President and the second President. Possessed of the country's history and its seminal events, Abigail Adams called over and over again for the colonies to declare their independence. Although they were apart for years at a time, the Adamses were an enduring partnership. More than 300 letters passed between them. Writing from their home in Braintree, Massachusetts, Abigail Adams urged her husband and his fellow delegates shaping the new government at the Continental Congress, in Philadelphia, to "Remember the Laidies."

Braintree March 31, 1776

I wish you would ever write me a Letter half as long as I write you; and tell me if you may where your Fleet are gone? What sort of Defence Virginia can make against our common Enemy? Whether it is so situated as to make an able Defence? Are not the Gentery Lords and the common people vassals, are they not like the uncivilized Natives Brittain represents us to be? I hope their Riffel Men who have shewen themselves very savage and even Blood thirsty; are not a specimen of the Generality of the people.

I am willing to allow the Colony great merrit for having produced a Washington but they have been shamefully duped by a Dunmore.

I have sometimes been ready to think that the passion for Liberty cannot be Eaquelly Strong in the Breasts of those who have been accustomed to deprive their fellow Creatures of theirs. Of this I am certain that it is not founded upon that generous and christian principal of doing to others as we would that others should do unto us.

Do not you want to see Boston; I am fearfull of the small pox, or I should have been in before this time. I got Mr. Crane to go to our House and see what state it was in. I find it has been occupied by one of the Doctors of a Regiment, very dirty, but no other damage has been done to it. The few things which were left in it are all gone. Cranch has the key which he never deliverd up. I have wrote to him for it and am determined to get it cleand as soon as possible and shut it up. I look upon it a new acquisition of property, a property which one month ago I did not value at a single Shilling, and could with pleasure have seen it in flames.

The Town in General is left in a better state than we expected, more oweing to a percipitate flight than any Regard to the inhabitants, tho some individuals discovered a sense of honour and justice and have left the rent of the Houses in which they were, for the owners and the furniture unhurt, or if damaged suffcent to make it good.

Others have committed abominable Ravages. The Mansion House of your President is safe and the furniture unhurt whilst both the House and Furniture of the Solisiter General have fallen a prey to their own merciless party. Surely the very Fiends feel a Reverential awe for Virtue and patriotism, whilst they Detest the particle and traitor.

I feel very differently at the approach of spring to what I did a month ago. We knew not then whether we could plant or sow with safety, whether when we had toild we could reap the fruits of our own industery, whether we could rest in our own Cottages, or whether we should not be driven from the sea coasts to seek shelter in the wilderness, but now we feel as if we might sit under our own vine and eat the good of the land.

I feel a gaieti de Coar to which before I was a stranger. I think the Sun looks brighter, the Birds sing more melodiously, and Nature puts on a more chearfull countenance. We feel a temporary peace, and the poor fugitives are returning to their deserted habitations.

Tho we felicitate ourselves, we sympathize with those who are trembling least the Lot of Boston should be theirs. But they cannot be in similar circumstances unless pusilanimity and cowardise should take possession of them. They have time and warning given them to see the Evil and shun it.—I long to hear that you have declared an independancy—and by the way in the new Code of Laws which I suppose it will be necessary for you to make I desire you would Remember the Ladies, and be more generous and favourable to them than your ancestors. Do not put such unlimited power into the hands of the Husbands. Remember all Men would be tyrants if they could. If perticuliar care and attention is not paid to the Laidies we are determined to foment a Rebelion, and will not hold ourselves bound by any Laws in which we have no voice, or Representation.

That your Sex are Naturally Tyrannical is a Truth so thoroughly established as to admit of no dispute, but such of you as wish to be happy willingly give up the harsh title of Master for the more tender and endearing one of Friend. Why then, not put it out of the power of the vicious and the Lawless to use us with cruelty and indignity with impunity. Men of Sense in all Ages abhor those customs which treat us only as the vassals of your Sex. Regard us then as Beings placed by providence under your protection and in immitation of the Supreem Being make use of that power only for our happiness.

"All power is . . . derived from the people"

THE VIRGINIA DECLARATION OF RIGHTS
1776

Virginia's eloquent Declaration of Rights, prefixed to the colony's constitution, was the most famous doctrine of inalienable rights before the Constitution's Bill of Rights (1791). Composed a month before the Declaration of Independence, the first enumeration of rights to be part of a constitutional framework was authored by George Mason (1725–1792), Virginia's largest landowner (and reluctant public servant), who believed in the "great rights of human nature." As the historian Richard B. Bernstein (born 1956) has noted, "rights" included not just individual rights safeguarded from government intrusion but "right things" and standards of conduct. Mason's restatement of English principles of individual rights and liberties "has an honored place in the history of human liberty."

A declaration of rights made by the representatives of the good people of Virginia, assembled in full and free convention; which rights do pertain to them and their posterity, as the basis and foundation of government.

1. That all men are by nature equally free and independent, and have certain inherent rights, of which, when they enter into a state of society, they cannot by any compact deprive or divest their posterity; namely, the enjoyment of life and liberty, with the means of acquiring and possessing property, and pursuing and obtaining happiness and safety.

2. That all power is vested in, and consequently derived from, the people; that magistrates are their trustees and servants, and at all times amenable to them.

3. That government is or ought to be instituted for the common benefit, protection, and security of the people, nation, or community; of all the various modes and forms of government, that is best which is capable of producing the greatest degree of happiness and safety, and is most effectually secured against the danger of maladministration; and that when any government shall be found inadequate or contrary to these purposes, a majority of the community hath an indubitable, unalienable and indefeasible right to reform, alter or abolish it, in such manner as shall be judged most conducive to the public weal.

4. That no man, or set of men, are entitled to exclusive or separate emoluments or privileges from the community, but in consideration of publick services; which, not being descendible, neither ought the offices of magistrate, legislator or judge to be hereditary.

5. That the legislative and executive powers of the state should be separate and distinct from the judiciary; and that the members of the two first may be restrained from oppression, by feeling and participating the burthens of the people, they should, at fixed periods, be reduced to a private station, return into that body from which they were originally taken, and the vacancies be supplied by frequent, certain, and regular elec-

tions, in which all, or any part of the former members to be again eligible or ineligible, as the laws shall direct.

6. That elections of members to serve as representatives of the people in assembly, ought to be free; and that all men having sufficient evidence of permanent common interest with, and attachment to the community, have the right of suffrage, and cannot be taxed or deprived of their property for publick uses, without their own consent, or that of their representatives so elected, nor bound by any law to which they have not, in like manner, assented for the public good.

7. That all power of suspending laws, or the execution of laws, by any authority without consent of the representatives of the people, is injurious to their rights, and ought not to be exercised.

8. That in all capital or criminal prosecutions a man hath a right to demand the cause and nature of his accusation, to be confronted with the accusers and witnesses, to call for evidence in his favour, and to a speedy trial by an impartial jury of his vicinage, without whose unanimous consent he cannot be found guilty; nor can he be compelled to give evidence against himself; that no man be deprived of his liberty, except by the law of the land or the judgment of his peers.

9. That excessive bail ought not to be required, nor excessive fines imposed, nor cruel and unusual punishments inflicted.

10. That general warrants, whereby an officer or messenger may be commanded to search suspected places without evidence of a fact committed, or to seize any person or persons not named, or whose offence is not particularly described and supported by evidence, are grievous and oppressive, and ought not to be granted.

11. That in controversies respecting property, and in suits between man and man, the ancient trial by jury is preferable to any other, and ought to be held sacred.

12. That the freedom of the press is one of the great bulwarks of liberty, and can never be restrained but by despotick governments.

13. That a well-regulated militia, composed of the body of the people trained to arms, is the proper, natural and safe defence of a free state; that standing armies in time of peace should be avoided as dangerous to liberty; and that in all cases the military should be under strict subordination to, and governed by, the civil power.

14. That the people have a right to uniform government; and, therefore, that no government separate from, or independent of the government of Virginia, ought to be erected or established within the limits thereof.

15. That no free government, or the blessings of liberty, can be preserved to any people, but by a firm adherence to justice, moderation, temperance, frugality and virtue, and by frequent recurrence to fundamental principles.

16. That religion, or the duty which we owe to our Creator, and the manner of discharging it, can be directed only by reason and conviction, not by force or violence; and therefore all men are equally entitled to the free exercise of religion, according to the dictates of conscience; and that it is the mutual duty of all to practise Christian forbearance, love, and charity towards each other.

"We hold these truths to be self-evident"

THE DECLARATION OF INDEPENDENCE

1776

America's Revolutionary War was in its second year when the Second Continental Congress decided that the uprising would fail unless independence was identified as its goal: "The colonies are, and of right ought to be, free and independent States." The Declaration of Independence, enumerating grievances against the British Crown, was the U.S. "birth certificate." The taciturn, shy Thomas Jefferson (1743–1826), who had a happy talent for composition and a peculiar felicity of expression, drew up the document between June 11 and June 28, 1776, on a custom-made portable desk on the second floor of his temporary lodgings in Philadelphia. His purpose, he said, was to express the American mind, "not to find new principles, or new arguments, never before thought of, not merely to say things which had never been said before; but to place before mankind the common sense of the subject, in terms so plain and firm as to command their assent, and to justify ourselves in the independent stand we are compelled to take . . ." (Congress deleted Jefferson's indictment of King George III for trafficking in slaves.) On July 2, twelve of the thirteen colonies voted in favor of independence. (The thirteenth, New York, abstained, awaiting approval from its newly elected convention.) The Declaration of Independence was printed during the night of July 4. The capstone of the ocean-wide, decade-long war of words that the colonists had been waging with Britain, the Declaration has become the great American symbol of independence, revolution, and liberty. In 1858, Senatorial candidate Abraham Lincoln (1809–1865) described the Founding Fathers' stirring call to throw off the bonds of tyranny as "the electric cord . . . that links the hearts of patriotic and liberty-loving men together . . . "

WHEN IN THE COURSE OF HUMAN EVENTS, it becomes necessary for one people to dissolve the political bands which have connected them with another, and to assume among the Powers of the earth, the separate and equal station to which the Laws of Nature and of Nature's God entitle them, a decent respect to the opinions of mankind requires that they should declare the causes which impel them to the separation.

We hold these truths to be self-evident, that all men are created equal, that they are endowed by their Creator with certain unalienable Rights, that among these are Life, Liberty and the pursuit of Happiness. That to secure these rights, Governments are instituted among Men, deriving their just powers from the consent of the governed. That whenever any Form of Government becomes destructive of these ends, it is the Right of the People to alter or to abolish it, and to institute new Government, laying its foundation on such principles and organizing its powers in such form, as to them shall seem most likely to effect their Safety and Happiness. Prudence, indeed, will dictate that Governments long established should not be changed for light and transient causes; and accordingly all experience hath shown, that mankind are more disposed to suffer, while evils are sufferable, than to right themselves by abolishing the forms to which they are accustomed. But when a long train of abuses and usurpations, pursuing invariably the same Object evinces a design to reduce them under absolute Despotism, it is their right, it is their duty, to throw off such Government, and to provide new Guards for their future security.— Such has been the patient sufferance of these Colonies; and such is now the necessity which constrains them to alter their former Systems of Government. The history of the present King of Great Britain is a history of repeated injuries and usurpations, all having in direct object the establishment of an absolute Tyranny over these States. To prove this, let Facts be submitted to a candid world.

He has refused his Assent to Laws, the most wholesome and necessary for the public good.

He has forbidden his Governors to pass Laws of immediate and pressing importance, unless suspended in their operation till his Assent should be obtained; and when so suspended, he has utterly neglected to attend to them.

He has refused to pass other Laws for the accommodation of large districts of people, unless those people would relinquish the right of Representation in the Legislature, a right inestimable to them and formidable to tyrants only.

He has called together legislative bodies at places unusual, uncomfortable, and distant from the depository of their Public Records, for the sole purpose of fatiguing them into compliance with his measures.

He has dissolved Representative Houses repeatedly, for opposing with manly firmness his invasions on the rights of the people.

He has refused for a long time, after such dissolutions, to cause others to be elected; whereby the Legislative Powers, incapable of Annihilation, have returned to the People at large for their exercise; the State remaining in the mean time exposed to all the dangers of invasion from without, and convulsions within.

He has endeavoured to prevent the population of these States; for that purpose obstructing the Laws of Naturalization of Foreigners; refusing to pass others to encourage their migration hither, and raising the conditions of new Appropriations of Lands.

He has obstructed the Administration of Justice, by refusing his Assent to Laws for establishing Judiciary Powers.

He has made Judges dependent on his Will alone, for the tenure of their offices, and the amount and payment of their salaries.

He has erected a multitude of New Offices, and sent hither swarms of Officers to harass our People, and eat out their substance.

He has kept among us, in times of peace, Standing Armies without the Consent of our legislature.

He has affected to render the Military independent of and superior to the Civil Power.

He has combined with others to subject us to a jurisdiction foreign to our constitution, and unacknowledged by our laws; giving his Assent to their acts of pretended legislation:

For quartering large bodies of armed troops among us:

For protecting them, by a mock Trial, from

Punishment for any Murders which they should commit on the Inhabitants of these States:

For cutting off our Trade with all parts of the world:

For imposing taxes on us without our Consent:

For depriving us in many cases, of the benefits of Trial by Jury:

For transporting us beyond Seas to be tried for pretended offences:

For abolishing the free System of English Laws in a neighbouring Province, establishing therein an Arbitrary government, and enlarging its Boundaries so as to render it at once an example and fit instrument for introducing the same absolute rule into these Colonies:

For taking away our Charters, abolishing our most valuable Laws, and altering fundamentally the Forms of our Governments:

For suspending our own Legislature, and declaring themselves invested with Power to legislate for us in all cases whatsoever.

He has abdicated Government here, by declaring us out of his Protection and waging War against us.

He has plundered our seas, ravaged our Coasts, burnt our towns, and destroyed the lives of our people.

He is at this time transporting large armies of foreign mercenaries to compleat the works of death, desolation and tyranny, already begun with circumstances of Cruelty & perfidy scarcely paralleled in the most barbarous ages, and totally unworthy the Head of a civilized nation.

He has constrained our fellow Citizens taken Captive on the high Seas to bear Arms against their Country, to become the executioners of their friends and Brethren, or to fall themselves by their Hands.

He has excited domestic insurrections amongst us, and has endeavoured to bring on the inhabitants of our frontiers, the merciless Indian Savages, whose known rule of warfare, is an undistinguished destruction of all ages, sexes and conditions.

In every stage of these Oppressions We have Petitioned for Redress in the most humble terms: Our repeated Petitions have been answered only by repeated injury. A Prince, whose character is thus marked by every act which may define a Tyrant, is unfit to be the ruler of a free People.

Nor have We been wanting in attention to our British brethren. We have warned them from time to time of attempts by their legislature to extend an unwarrantable jurisdiction over us. We have reminded them of the circumstances of our emigration and settlement here. We have appealed to their native justice and magnanimity, and we have conjured them by the ties of our common kindred to disavow these usurpations, which, would inevitably interrupt our connections and correspondence. They too have been deaf to the voice of justice and of consanguinity. We must, therefore, acquiesce in the necessity, which denounces our Separation, and hold them, as we hold the rest of mankind, Enemies in War, in Peace Friends.

We, therefore, the Representatives of the United States of America, in General Congress, Assembled, appealing to the Supreme Judge of the world for the rectitude of our intentions, do, in the Name, and by Authority of the good People of these Colonies, solemnly publish and declare, That these United Colonies are, and of Right ought to be Free and Independent States; that they are Absolved from all Allegiance to the British Crown, and that all political connection between them and the State of Great Britain, is and ought to be totally dissolved; and that as Free and Independent States, they have full

Power to levy War, conclude Peace, contract Alliances, establish Commerce, and to do all other Acts and Things which Independent States may of right do. And for the support of this Declaration, with a firm reliance on the Protection of Divine Providence, we mutually pledge to each other our Lives, our Fortunes and our sacred Honor.

JOHN HANCOCK

New Hampshire
JOSIAH BARTLETT
WM. WHIPPLE
MATTHEW THORNTON

Massachusetts-Bay
SAML. ADAMS
JOHN ADAMS
ROBT. TREAT PAINE
ELBRIDGE GERRY

Rhode Island
STEP. HOPKINS
WILLIAM ELLERY

Connecticut
ROGER SHERMAN
SAM'EL HUNTINGTON
WM. WILLIAMS
OLIVER WOLCOTT

New York
WM. FLOYD
PHIL. LIVINGSTON
FRANS. LEWIS
LEWIS MORRIS

Pennsylvania
ROBT. MORRIS
BENJAMIN RUSH
BENJA. FRANKLIN
JOHN MORTON
GEO. CLYMER
JAS. SMITH
GEO. TAYLOR
JAMES WILSON
GEO. ROSS

Delaware
CAESAR RODNEY
GEO. READ
THO. M'KEAN

North Carolina
WM. HOOPER
JOSEPH HEWES
JOHN PENN

South Carolina
EDWARD RUTLEDGE
THOS. HEYWARD, JUNR.
THOMAS LYNCH, JUNR.
ARTHUR MIDDLETON

New Jersey
RICHD. STOCKTON
JNO. WITHERSPOON
FRAS. HOPKINSON
JOHN HART
ABRA. CLARK

Georgia
BUTTON GWINNETT
LYMAN HALL
GEO. WALTON

Maryland
SAMUEL CHASE
WM. PACA
THOS. STONE
CHARLES CARROLL
OF CARROLLTON

Virginia
GEORGE WYTHE
RICHARD HENRY LEE
TH. JEFFERSON
BENJA. HARRISON
THS. NELSON, JR.
FRANCIS LIGHTFOOT LEE
CARTER BRAXTON

"Sovereignty, freedom, and independence"

THE ARTICLES OF CONFEDERATION
1781

The states took four years (1777–1781)—the heart of the eight-year Revolutionary War—to ratify their first charter. Under the Articles of Confederation, the thirteen former English colonies were to form a league of friendship, a loose but perpetual union, more of a diplomatic body than a direct government. The President was merely a figurehead. Congress, with only one chamber, was the central government but subordinate to the disunited, sovereign, selfish, feuding states. Each state, regardless of population, had one vote; measures required a supermajority of nine states (hamstringing Congressional action on critical problems, e.g., revenue). There was no federal court system. The Confederation's most significant piece of legislation, the Northwest Ordinance of 1787, was enacted while Founding Fathers were replacing the Articles with a new charter for the nation—the Constitution.

To ALL TO WHOM these Presents shall come, we the undersigned Delegates of the States affixed to our Names send greeting.

Whereas the Delegates of the United States of America in Congress assembled did on the fifteenth day of November in the Year of our Lord One Thousand Seven Hundred and Seventy seven, and in the Second Year of the Independence of America agree to certain articles of Confederation and perpetual Union between the States of Newhampshire, Massachusetts-bay, Rhodeisland and Providence Plantations, Connecticut, New York, New Jersey, Pennsylvania, Delaware, Maryland, Virginia, North-Carolina, South-Carolina and Georgia in the Words following, viz. "Articles of Confederation and perpetual Union between the States of Newhampshire, Massachusetts-bay, Rhodeisland and Providence Plantations, Connecticut, New-York, New-Jersey, Pennsylvania, Delaware,

Maryland, Virginia, North-Carolina, South-Carolina and Georgia."

Article I. The Stile of this confederacy shall be "The United States of America."

Article II. Each state retains its sovereignty, freedom and independence, and every Power, Jurisdiction and right, which is not by this confederation expressly delegated to the United States, in Congress assembled.

Article III. The said states hereby severally enter into a firm league of friendship with each other, for their common defence, the security of their Liberties, and their mutual and general welfare, binding themselves to assist each other, against all force offered to, or attacks made upon them, or any of them, on account of religion, sovereignty, trade or any other pretence whatever.

Article IV. The better to secure and perpetuate mutual friendship and intercourse among the people of the different states in this union, the free inhabitants of each of these states, paupers, vagabonds and fugitives from Justice excepted, shall be entitled to all privileges and immunities of free citizens in the several states; and the people of each state shall have free ingress and regress to and from any other state, and shall enjoy therein all the privileges of trade and commerce, subject to the same duties, impositions and restrictions as the inhabitants thereof respectively, provided that such restriction shall not extend so far as to prevent the removal of property imported into any state, to any other state of which the Owner is an inhabitant; provided also that no imposition, duties or restriction shall be laid by any state, on the property of the united states, or either of them.

If any Person guilty of, or charged with treason, felony, or other high misdemeanor in any state, shall flee from justice, and be found in any of the united states, he shall upon demand of the Governor or executive power, of the state from which he fled, be delivered up and removed to the state having jurisdiction of his offence.

Full faith and credit shall be given in each of these states to the records, acts and judicial proceedings of the courts and magistrates of every other state.

Article V. For the more convenient management of the general interests of the united states, delegates shall be annually appointed in such manner as the legislature of each state shall direct, to meet in Congress on the first Monday in November, in every year, with a power reserved to each state, to recall its delegates, or any of them, at any time within the year, and to send others in their stead, for the remainder of the Year.

No state shall be represented in Congress by less than two, nor by more than seven Members; and no person shall be capable of being a dele-

gate for more than three years in any term of six years; nor shall any person, being a delegate, be capable of holding any office under the united states, for which he, or another for his benefit receives any salary, fees or emolument of any kind.

Each state shall maintain its own delegates in a meeting of the states, and while they act as members of the committee of the states.

In determining questions in the united states, in Congress assembled, each state shall have one vote.

Freedom of speech and debate in Congress shall not be impeached or questioned in any Court, or place out of Congress, and the members of congress shall be protected in their persons from arrests and imprisonments, during the time of their going to and from, and attendance on congress, except for treason, felony, or breach of the peace.

Article VI. No state without the Consent of the united states in congress assembled, shall send any embassy to, or receive any embassy from, or enter into any conference, agreement, alliance or treaty with any King, prince or state; nor shall any person holding any office of profit or trust under the united states, or any of them, accept of any present, emolument, office or title of any kind whatever from any king, prince or foreign state, nor shall the united states in congress assembled, or any of them, grant any title of nobility.

No two or more states shall enter into any treaty, confederation or alliance whatever between them, without the consent of the united states in congress assembled, specifying accurately the purposes for which the same is to be entered into, and how long it shall continue.

No state shall lay any imposts or duties, which may interfere with any stipulations in treaties, entered into by the united states in congress assembled, with any king, prince or state, in pursuance of any treaties already proposed by congress, to the courts of France and Spain.

No vessels of war shall be kept up in time of peace by any state, except such number only, as shall be deemed necessary by the united states in congress assembled, for the defence of such state, or its trade; nor shall any body of forces be kept up by any state, in time of peace, except such number only, as in the judgment of the united states, in congress assembled, shall be deemed requisite to garrison the forts necessary for the defence of such state; but every state shall always keep up a well regulated and disciplined militia, sufficiently armed and accoutred, and shall provide and constantly have ready for use, in public stores, a due number of field pieces and tents, and a proper quantity of arms, ammunition and camp equipage.

No state shall engage in any war without the consent of the united states in congress assembled, unless such state be actually invaded by enemies, or shall have received certain advice of a resolution being formed by some nation of Indians to invade such state, and the danger is so imminent as not to admit of a delay, till the united states in congress assembled can be consulted: nor shall any state grant commissions to any ships or vessels of war, nor letters of marque or reprisal, except it be after a declaration of war by the united states in congress assembled, and then only against the kingdom or state and the subjects thereof, against which war has been so declared, and under such regulations as shall be established by the united states in congress assembled, unless such state be infested by pirates, in which case vessels of war may be fitted out for that occasion, and kept so long as the danger shall continue, or until the united states in congress assembled shall determine otherwise.

Article VII. When land-forces are raised by any state of the common defence, all officers of or under the rank of colonel, shall be appointed by the legislature of each state respectively by whom such forces shall be raised, or in such manner as such state shall direct, and all vacancies shall be filled up by the state which first made the appointment.

Article VIII. All charges of war, and all other expences that shall be incurred for the common defence or general welfare, and allowed by the united states in congress assembled, shall be defrayed out of a common treasury, which shall be supplied by the several states, in proportion to the value of all land within each state, granted to or surveyed for any Person, as such land and the buildings and improvements thereon shall be estimated according to such mode as the united states in congress assembled, shall from time to time direct and appoint. The taxes for paying that proportion shall be laid and levied by the authority and direction of the legislatures of the several states within the time agreed upon by the united states in congress assembled.

Article IX. The united states in congress assembled, shall have the sole and exclusive right and power of determining on peace and war, except in the cases mentioned in the sixth article— of sending and receiving ambassadors—entering into treaties and alliances, provided that no treaty of commerce shall be made whereby the legislative power of the respective states shall be restrained from imposing such imposts and duties on foreigners, as their own people are subjected to, or from prohibiting the exportation or importation of and species of goods or commodities whatsoever—of establishing rules for deciding in all cases, what captures on land or water shall be legal, and in what manner prizes taken by land or naval forces in the service of the united states shall be divided or appropriated— of granting letters of marque and reprisal in times of peace—appointing courts for the trial of piracies and felonies committed on the high seas and establishing courts for receiving and determining finally appeals in all cases of captures, provided that no member of congress shall be appointed a judge of any of the said courts.

The united states in congress assembled shall also be the last resort on appeal in all disputes and differences now subsisting or that thereafter may arise between two or more states concerning boundary, jurisdiction or any other cause whatever; which authority shall always be exercised in the manner following. Whenever the legislative or executive authority or lawful agent of any state in controversy with another shall present a petition to congress stating the matter in question and praying for a hearing, notice thereof shall be given by order of congress to the legislative or executive authority of the other state in controversy, and a day assigned for the appearance of the parties by their lawful agents, who shall then be directed to appoint by joint consent, commissioners or judges to constitute a court for hearing and determining the matter in question: but if they cannot agree, congress shall name three persons out of each of the united states, and from the list of such persons each party shall alternately strike out one, the petitioners beginning, until the number shall be reduced to thirteen; and from that number not less than seven, nor more than nine names as congress shall direct, shall in the presence of congress be drawn out by lot, and the persons whose names shall be so drawn or any five of them, shall be commissioners or judges, to hear and finally determine the controversy, so always as a major part of the judges who shall hear the cause shall agree in the determination: and if either party shall neglect to attend at the day appointed, without shewing reasons, which congress shall judge sufficient, or being present shall refuse to strike, the congress shall proceed to nominate three persons out of

each state, and the secretary of congress shall strike in behalf of such party absent or refusing; and the judgment and sentence of the court to be appointed, in the manner before prescribed, shall be final and conclusive; and if any of the parties shall refuse to submit to the authority of such court, or to appear or defend their claim or cause, the court shall nevertheless proceed to pronounce sentence, or judgment, which shall in like manner be final and decisive, the judgment or sentence and other proceedings being in either case transmitted to congress, and lodged among the acts of congress for the security of the parties concerned: provided that every commissioner, before he sits in judgment, shall take an oath to be administered by one of the judges of the supreme or superior court of the state, where the cause shall be tried, "well and truly to hear and determine the matter in question, according to the best of his judgment, without favour, affection or hope of reward:" provided also that no state shall be deprived of territory for the benefit of the united states.

All controversies concerning the private right of soil claimed under different grants of two or more states, whose jurisdictions as they may respect such lands, and the states which passed such grants are adjusted, the said grants or either of them being at the same time claimed to have originated antecedent to such settlement of jurisdiction, shall on the petition of either party to the congress of the united states, be finally determined as near as maybe in the same manner as is before prescribed for deciding disputes respecting territorial jurisdictions between different states.

The united states in congress assembled shall also have the sole and exclusive right and power of regulating the alloy and value of coin struck by their own authority, or by that of the respective states—fixing the standard of weights and measures throughout the united states—regulating the trade and managing all affairs with the Indians, not members of any of the states, provided that the legislative right of any state within its own limits be not infringed or violated—establishing and regulating post-offices from one state to another, throughout all of the united states, and exacting such postage on the papers passing thro' the same as may be requisite to defray the expences of the said office—appointing all officers of the land forces, in the service of the united states, excepting regimental officers—appointing all the officers of the naval forces, and commissioning all officers whatever in the service of the united states—making rules for the government and regulation of the said land and naval forces, and directing their operations.

The united states in congress assembled shall have authority to appoint a committee, to sit in the recess of congress, to be denominated "A Committee of the States," and to consist of one delegate from each state; and to appoint such other committees and civil officers as may be necessary for managing the general affairs of the united states under their direction—to appoint one of their number to preside, provided that no person be allowed to serve in the office of president more than one year in any term of three years; to ascertain the necessary sums of Money to be raised for the service of the united states, and to appropriate and apply the same for defraying the public expences—to borrow money, or emit bills on the credit of the united states, transmitting every half year to the respective states an account of the sums of money so borrowed or emitted,—to build and equip a navy—to agree upon the number of land forces, and to make requisitions from each State for its quota, in proportion to the number of white inhabitants in such state; which requisition shall be binding, and thereupon the legislature of each state shall appoint the regimental officers, raise the men and cloath, arm and equip them in a soldier like manner, at the expence of the united states, and the officers and men so cloathed, armed and equipped shall march to the place appointed, and within the time agreed on by the united states in congress assembled: But if the united states in congress assembled shall, on consideration of circumstances judge proper that any state should not raise men, or should raise a smaller number than its quota, and that any other state should raise a greater number of men than the quota thereof, such extra number shall be raised, officered, cloathed, armed and equipped in the same manner as the quota of such state, unless the legislature of such state shall judge that such extra number cannot be safely spared out of the same, in which case they shall raise officer, cloath, arm and equip as many of such extra number as they judge can be safely spared. And the officers and men so cloathed, armed and equipped, shall march to the place appointed, and within the time agreed on by the united states in congress assembled.

The united states in congress assembled shall never engage in a war, nor grant letters of marque and reprisal in time of peace, nor enter into any treaties or alliances, nor coin money, nor regulate the value thereof, nor ascertain the sums and expences necessary for the defence and welfare of the united states, or any of them, nor emit bills, nor borrow money on the credit of the united states, nor appropriate money, nor agree upon the number of vessels of war, to be built or purchased, or the number of land or sea forces to be raised, nor appoint a commander in chief of the army or navy, unless nine states assent to the same: nor shall a question on any other point, except for adjourning from day to day be determined, unless by the votes of a majority of the united states in congress assembled.

The congress of the united states shall have power to adjourn to any time within the year, and to any place within the united states, so that no period of adjournment be for a longer duration than the space of six Months, and shall publish the Journal of their proceedings monthly, except such parts thereof relating to treaties, alliances or military operations, as in their judgment require secresy; and the yeas and nays of the delegates of each state on any question shall be entered on the Journal, when it is desired by any delegate; and the delegates of a state, or any of them, at his or their request shall be furnished with a transcript of the said Journal, except such parts as are above excepted, to lay before the Legislatures of the several states.

Article X. The committee of the states, or any nine of them, shall be authorized to execute, in the recess of congress, such of the powers of congress as the united states in congress assembled, by the consent of nine states, shall from time to time think expedient to vest them with; provided that no power be delegated to the said committee, for the exercise of which, by the articles of confederation, the voice of nine states in the congress of the united states assembled is requisite.

Article XI. Canada acceding to this confederation, and joining in the measures of the united states, shall be admitted into, and entitled to all the advantages of this union: but no other colony shall be admitted into the same, unless such admission be agreed to by nine states.

Article XII. All bills of credit emitted, monies borrowed and debts contracted by, or under the authority of congress, before the assembling of the united states, in pursuance of the present confederation, shall be deemed and considered as a charge against the united states, for payment and satisfaction whereof the said united states, and the public faith are hereby solemnly pledged.

Article XIII. Every state shall abide by the determinations of the united states in congress assembled, on all questions which by this confederation are submitted to them. And the Articles of this confederation shall be inviolably observed by every state, and the union shall be perpetual; nor shall any alteration at any time hereafter be made in any of them; unless such alteration be agreed to in a congress of the united states, and be afterwards confirmed by the legislatures of every state.

And WHEREAS it hath pleased the Great Governor of the World to incline the hearts of the legislatures we respectively represent in congress, to approve of, and to authorize us to ratify the said articles of confederation and perpetual union. KNOW YE that we the undersigned delegates, by virtue of the power and authority to us given for that purpose, do by these presents, in the name and in behalf of our respective constituents, full and entirely ratify and confirm each and every of the said articles of confederation and perpetual union, and all and singular the matters and things therein contained: And we do further solemnly plight and engage the faith of our respective constituents, that they shall abide by the determinations of the united states in congress assembled, on all questions, which by the said confederation are submitted to them. And that the articles thereof shall be inviolably observed by the states we respectively represent, and that the union shall be perpetual.

In Witness whereof we have hereunto set our hands in Congress. Done at Philadelphia in the state of Pennsylvania the ninth Day of July in the Year of our Lord one Thousand seven Hundred and Seventy-eight, and in the third year of the independence of America.

"Acknowledges . . . free, sovereign, and independent States"

THE PARIS PEACE TREATY
1783

Twenty-three months after British General Charles Cornwallis (1738–1805) surrendered British forces at Yorktown, Virginia, to American General George Washington (1732–1799) in the last great battle of the War of Independence, the United States and Great Britain signed the Treaty of Paris. England acknowledged the independence of its thirteen former colonies across the Atlantic. The northern boundary of the United States was fixed at approximately where it is today; the western boundary was placed at the Mississippi River; the southern border, at Spanish Florida. Negotiators for the United States were Benjamin Franklin (1706–1790), John Adams (1735–1826), Henry Laurens (1724–1792), and John Jay (1745–1829).

• • • ART. I.—His Britannic Majesty acknowledges the said United States, viz. New Hampshire, Massachusetts Bay, Rhode Island, and Providence Plantations, Connecticut, New York, New Jersey, Pennsylvania, Delaware, Maryland, Virginia, North Carolina, South Carolina, and Georgia, to be free, sovereign and independent States; that he treats with them as such, and for himself, his heirs and successors, relinquishes all claims to the Government, proprietary and territorial rights of the same, and every part thereof.

ART. II.—And that all disputes which might arise in future, on the subject of the boundaries of the said United States may be prevented, it is hereby agreed and declared, that the following are, and shall be their boundaries, viz.: From the northwest angle of Nova Scotia, viz.: that angle which is formed by a line drawn due north from the source of Saint Croix River to the Highlands; along the said Highlands which divide those rivers that empty themselves into the river St. Lawrence, from those which fall into the Atlantic Ocean, to the northwesternmost head of Connecticut River; thence down along the middle of that river, to the forty-fifth degree of north latitude; from thence, by a line due west on said latitude, until it strikes the river Iroquois or Cataraquy; thence along the middle of said river into Lake Ontario, through the middle of said lake until it strikes the communication by water between that lake and Lake Erie; thence along the middle of said communication into Lake Erie, through the middle of said lake until it arrives at the water communication between that lake and Lake Huron; thence along the middle of said water communication into the Lake Huron; thence through the middle of said lake to the water communication between that lake and Lake Superior; thence through Lake Superior northward of the Isles Royal and Phelipeaux, to the Long Lake; thence through the middle of said Long Lake, and the water communication between it and the Lake of the Woods, to the said Lake of the Woods; thence through the said lake to the most northwestern point thereof, and from thence on a due west course to the river Mississippi; thence by a line to be drawn along the middle of the said river Mississippi until it shall intersect the northernmost part of the thirty-first degree of north latitude. South, by a line to be drawn due east from the determination of the line last mentioned, in the latitude of thirty-one degrees north of the Equator, to the middle of the river Appalachicola or Cata-houche; thence along the middle thereof to its junction with the Flint River; thence straight to the head of St. Mary's River; and thence down along the middle of St. Mary's River to the Atlantic Ocean. East, by a line to be drawn along the middle of the river St. Croix, from its mouth in the Bay of Fundy to its source, and from its source directly north to the aforesaid Highlands, which divide the rivers that fall into the Atlantic Ocean from those which fall into the river St. Lawrence; comprehending all islands within twenty leagues of any part of the shores of the United States, and lying between lines to be drawn due east from the points where the aforesaid boundaries between Nova Scotia on the one part, and East Florida on the other, shall respectively touch the Bay of Fundy and the Atlantic Ocean; excepting such islands as now are, or heretofore have been, within the limits of the said province of Nova Scotia.

ART. III.—It is agreed that the people of the United States shall continue to enjoy unmolested the right to take fish of every kind on the Grand Bank, and on all the other banks of Newfoundland; also in the Gulph of Saint Lawrence, and at all other places in the sea where the inhabitants of both countries used at any time heretofore to fish. And also that the inhabitants of the United States shall have liberty to take fish of every kind on such part of the coast of Newfoundland as British fishermen shall use (but not to dry or cure the same on that island) and also on the coasts, bays and creeks of all other of His Britannic Majesty's dominions in America; and that the American fishermen shall have liberty to dry and cure fish in any of the unsettled bays, harbours and creeks of Nova Scotia, Magdalen Islands, and Labrador, so long as the same shall remain unsettled; but so soon as the same or either of them shall be settled, it shall not be lawful for the said fishermen to dry or cure fish at such settlements, without a previous agreement for that purpose with the inhabitants, proprietors or possessors of the ground.

ART. IV.—It is agreed that creditors on either side shall meet with no lawful impediment to the recovery of the full value in sterling money, of all *bona fide* debts heretofore contracted.

ART. V.—It is agreed that the Congress shall earnestly recommend it to the legislatures of the respective States, to provide for the restitution of all estates, rights and properties which have been confiscated, belonging to real British subjects, and also of the estates, rights and properties of persons resident in districts in the possession of His Majesty's arms, and who have not borne arms against the said United States. And that persons of any other description shall have free liberty to go to any part or parts of any of the thirteen United States, and therein to remain twelve months, unmolested in their endeavours to obtain the restitution of such of their estates, rights and properties as may have been confiscated; and that Congress shall also earnestly recommend to the several States a reconsideration and revision of all acts or laws regarding the premises, so as to render the said laws or acts perfectly consistent, not only with justice and equity, but with that spirit of conciliation which, on the return of the blessings of peace, should universally prevail. And that Congress shall also earnestly recommend to the several States, that the estates, rights and properties of such last mentioned persons, shall be restored to them, they refunding to any persons who may be now in possession, the *bona fide* price (where any has been given) which such persons may have paid on purchasing any of the said lands, rights or properties, since the confiscation. And it is agreed, that all persons who have any interest in confiscated lands, either by debts, marriage settlements or otherwise, shall meet with no lawful impediment in the prosecution of their just rights.

ART. VI.—That there shall be no future confiscations made, nor any prosecutions commenced against any person or persons for, or by reason of the part which he or they may have taken in the present war; and that no person shall, on that account, suffer any future loss or damage, either in his person, liberty, or property; and that those who may be in confinement on such charges, at the time of the ratification of the treaty in America, shall be immediately set at liberty, and the prosecutions so commenced be discontinued.

ART. VII.—There shall be a firm and perpetual peace between His Britannic Majesty and the said States, and between the subjects of the one and the citizens of the other, wherefore all hostilities, both by sea and land, shall from hence-forth cease; All prisoners on both sides shall be set at liberty, and His Britannic Majesty shall, with all convenient speed, and without causing any destruction, or carrying away any negroes or other property of the American inhabitants, withdraw all his armies, garrisons and fleets from the said United States, and from every post, place and harbour within the same; leaving in all fortifications the American artillery that may be therein; And shall also order and cause all archives, records, deeds and papers, belonging to any of the said States, or their citizens, which, in the course of the war, may have fallen into the hands of his officers, to be forthwith restored and deliver'd to the proper States and persons to whom they belong.

ART. VIII.—The navigation of the river Mississippi, from its source to the ocean, shall forever remain free and open to the subjects of Great Britain, and the citizens of the United States.

ART. IX.—In case it should so happen that any place or territory belonging to Great Britain or to the United States, should have been conquer'd by the arms of either from the other, before the arrival of the said provisional articles in America, it is agreed, that the same shall be restored without difficulty, and without requiring any compensation. . . .

"To advance the interests of the Union"

THE ANNAPOLIS CONVENTION
1786

The U.S. was a crippled ship of state. Floundering at home and all but ignored abroad, the young nation in the view of George Washington (1732–1799) was "tottering at every step." He warned that "without some alteration in our political creed the superstructure we have been raising at the expense of so much blood and treasure must fall: We are fast verging to anarchy and confusion." Virginia issued an invitation to all states to meet and discuss matters of commerce. Originally, nine states accepted. But when the gathering met in Annapolis, Maryland, on September 11, 1786, representatives from only five states attended—New York, New Jersey, Pennsylvania, Delaware, and Virginia. Among the attendees were John Dickinson (1732–1808), James Madison (1751–1836), and Alexander Hamilton (1755–1804). Hamilton, a delegate from New York and a dedicated advocate of strong Federal government, drafted a resolution that called for all thirteen states to gather the following year. His proposed agenda called for the states to: "to take into consideration the trade and commerce of the United States" and to address all issues necessary "to render the Constitution of the Federal government adequate to the exigencies of the Union." Rebellious farmers had to be curbed, the states unified, and order maintained. The nation needed a strong authority to help carry out the public business. "Let us have [a government] by which our lives and liberties and properties will be served," the revered Washington affirmed, "or let us know the worst at once." Though attendance at the Annapolis Convention was poor and many issues remained unresolved, Hamilton's proposal laid the groundwork for the historic Constitutional Convention that was held in Philadelphia, in 1787.

To THE HONORABLE, THE LEGISLATURES of Virginia, Delaware, Pennsylvania, New Jersey, and New York, the commissioners from the said states, respectively assembled at Annapolis, humbly beg leave to report:

That, pursuant to their several appointments, they met at Annapolis in the state of Maryland on the 11th day of September instant, and having proceeded to a communication of their powers, they found that the states of New York, Pennsylvania, and Virginia had, in substance and nearly in the same terms, authorized their respective commissioners to meet such other commissioners as were, or might be, appointed by the other states in the Union, at such time and place as should be agreed upon by the said commissioners, to take into consideration the trade and commerce of the United States, to consider how far a uniform system in their commercial intercourse and regulations might be necessary to their common interest and permanent harmony, and to report to the several states such an act, relative to this great object, as when unanimously ratified by them would enable the United States in Congress assembled effectually to provide for the same.

That the state of Delaware had given similar powers to their commissioners, with this difference only, that the act to be framed in virtue of these powers is required to be reported "to the United States in Congress assembled, to be agreed to by them, and confirmed by the legislatures of every state."

That the state of New Jersey had enlarged the object of their appointment, empowering their commissioners "to consider how far a uniform system in their commercial regulations and *other important matters* might be necessary to the common interest and permanent harmony of the several states," and to report such an act on the subject, as when ratified by them, "would enable the United States in Congress assembled effectually to provide for the exigencies of the Union."

That appointments of commissioners have also been made by the states of New Hampshire, Massachusetts, Rhode Island, and North Carolina, none of whom, however, have attended; but that no information has been received by your commissioners of any appointment having been made by the states of Connecticut, Maryland, South Carolina, or Georgia.

That the express terms of the powers of your commissioners supposing a deputation from all the states, and having for object the trade and commerce of the United States, your commissioners did not conceive it advisable to proceed on the business of their mission under the circumstance of so partial and defective a representation.

Deeply impressed, however, with the magnitude and importance of the object confided to them on this occasion, your commissioners cannot forbear to indulge an expression of their earnest and unanimous wish that speedy measures be taken to effect a general meeting of the states in a future convention, for the same and such other purposes as the situation of public affairs may be found to require.

If, in expressing this wish, or in intimating any other sentiment, your commissioners should seem to exceed the strict bounds of their appointment, they entertain a full confidence that a conduct, dictated by an anxiety for the welfare of the United States, will not fail to receive an indulgent construction.

In this persuasion, your commissioners submit an opinion that the idea of extending the powers of their deputies to other objects than those of commerce, which has been adopted by the state of New Jersey, was an improvement on the original plan, and will deserve to be incorporated into that of a future convention. They are the more naturally led to this conclusion as in the course of their reflections on the subject they have been induced to think that the power of regulating trade is of such comprehensive extent, and will enter so far into the general system of the federal government, that to give it efficacy and to obviate questions and doubts concerning its precise nature and limits may require a correspondent adjustment of other parts of the federal system.

That there are important defects in the system of the federal government is acknowledged by the acts of all those states which have concurred in the present meeting; that the defects, upon a closer examination, may be found greater and more numerous than even these acts imply is at least so far probable, from the embarrassments which characterize the present state of our national affairs, foreign and domestic, as may reasonably be supposed to merit a deliberate and candid discussion, in some mode, which will unite the sentiments and councils of all the states. In the choice of the mode, your commissioners are of opinion that a convention of deputies from the different states, for the special and sole purpose of entering into this investigation and digesting a plan for supplying such defects as may be discovered to exist, will be entitled to a preference from considerations which will occur without being particularized.

Your commissioners decline an enumeration of those national circumstances on which their opinion respecting the propriety of a future convention, with more enlarged powers, is founded; as it would be a useless intrusion of facts and observations, most of which have been frequently the subject of public discussion, and none of which can have escaped the penetration of those to whom they would in this instance be addressed. They are, however, of a nature so serious as, in the view of your commissioners, to render the situation of the United States delicate and critical, calling for an exertion of the united virtue and wisdom of all the members of the Confederacy.

Under this impression, your commissioners, with the most respectful deference, beg leave to suggest their unanimous conviction that it may essentially tend to advance the interests of the Union if the states, by whom they have been respectively delegated, would themselves concur and use their endeavors to procure the concurrence of the other states in the appointment of commissioners, to meet at Philadelphia on the second Monday in May next, to take into consideration the situation of the United States, to devise such further provisions as shall appear to them necessary to render the Constitution of the federal government adequate to the exigencies of the Union; and to report such an act for that purpose to the United States in Congress assembled, as when agreed to by them, and afterward confirmed by the legislatures of every state, will effectually provide for the same.

Though your commissioners could not with propriety address these observations and sentiments to any but the states they have the honor to represent, they have nevertheless concluded from motives of respect to transmit copies of this report to the United States in Congress assembled, and to the executives of the other states.

FORMING
A MORE PERFECT UNION

Though the defects of the Articles outweighed its virtues, the document was one more step toward creating the constitutional policy that became America's great contribution to political theory. It was another document that sought to develop fundamental law and to limit government and its powers. The earliest, we have seen, was the Mayflower Compact; it was followed by the Fundamental Orders of Connecticut in 1639 and the Massachusetts Body of Liberties in 1641. These and other governmental texts sought to protect individual rights and liberties. The Revolution produced a period of feverish constitution-making by the states, and the frenetic two decades after the conflict were yet another remarkable period in our history. Rarely had the future seemed so promising and the problems more profound. Having severed ties with the motherland, Americans were entering upon un-

explored and unknown territory. They considered themselves as somewhat in a state of nature, at a turning point. It was time to write a new compact, to design a new governmental structure. By the end of the eighteenth century, all the states except Rhode Island and Connecticut had adopted new plans of government, with Massachusetts leading the way in 1780. The Articles, seemingly feeble and inadequate, almost immediately inspired calls for revision. Its weaknesses, combined with hard times and the social turbulence triggered by debtor unrest, prompted the politically and economically prominent to reconsider the feasibility of the states' initial experiment in radical polity. Eventually, led to a gathering of fifty-five delegates in Philadelphia in the hot summer months of 1787. Meeting in secrecy, the men early decided not to be confined to a mere revision of the Articles. Agreeing upon an entirely new constitutional text, they submitted it to the states, which excited vigorous and critical debate over ratification. In some states, such as Virginia and New York, the opposition was powerful and determined, the outcome uncertain; the central dispute, as a number of the following selections suggest, turned on questions of Federal jurisdiction and power, that is, on the issue of whether the states or the central government was sovereign. Ratification by a necessary majority of states hung in the balance and the friends of the Constitution secured ratification only after significant concessions were made, especially the future addition of a bill of rights, although nothing was said about contents.

Once ratification was secured, the constitutional system, with the single exception of a bill of rights, was in place. The basic structure of government, with occasional (27) amendments, is the one under which we live today. It set forth three distinct branches of government, legislative, executive, judiciary, which, while not entirely separate, insured that each of the three great powers essential to government would be effectively distributed and exercised. One branch, the judiciary, was embodied in a Supreme Court, which Alexis de Tocqueville asserted "is placed higher than any known tribunal. The peace, the prosperity, and the very existence of the Union are vested in the hands of the seven Federal judges." The presence of this tribunal, however, did not entirely fulfill the vital role of the judicial power. Indeed, the Court, as Alexander Hamilton understood, was "weakest of the three departments of power." Something more was needed for the new nation, namely a federal court system; this was secured by the 1789 Judiciary Act, which established a three-tier court structure which virtually duplicated the states' judiciary structure and guaranteed that all the great questions of constitutionalism would eventually come before the High Court for review. The fact of a fully-coordinate third branch of government finally became a reality with this statute and with the Chief Justice, John Marshall, who, in 1803, established the Supreme Court's power to rule on the constitutionality of a congressional measure. With ratification of the Constitution, the basic principles had been established but by no means vindicated. That would come with Marshall, whose contributions to judicial power and to the arsenal of nationalism are unequaled in our history.

"To form a more perfect Union"

THE CONSTITUTION OF THE UNITED STATES
(Literal Text, with Amendments)
1787–1992

The feckless, states-oriented Articles of Confederation (1781) wasn't working. George Washington (1732–1799) declared, "I can foresee no evil greater than disunion." It took 42 of the nation's "better sort" with sticktoitiveness—"well-bred, well-fed, well-read, and well-wed" white men—from twelve of the thirteen states (obdurate Rhode-Island and Providence Plantations didn't send a delegate to the Federal Convention in centrally-located Philadelphia) nearly four months to create a strong national government to help carry out the public business: Four prescient parchment pages, which still protect all 260,000,000 Americans in their beliefs, thoughts, emotions, and sensations. Meeting in secret, with sentries posted at the doors, and with the unanimously chosen Washington presiding, the "superpatriots" wrote an inherently ambiguous document, a "bundle of compromises" (Alexander Hamilton's description) paradoxically entrenching both liberty and slavery. "We the People" were the source of all power. The promise of democracy was incorporated into new political institutions. Since ratification (1788), Congresspersons have proposed more than 10,000 amendments (such as direct election of the President, a balanced Federal budget, prohibition of dueling and flag-burning); 33 have been formalized (for example, equality of rights regardless of gender and non-Congressional interference in slavery) and sent to the states for ratification; 27 have been adopted.

WE THE PEOPLE of the United States, in Order to form a more perfect Union, establish Justice, insure domestic Tranquility, provide for the common defence, promote the general Welfare, and secure the Blessings of Liberty to ourselves and our Posterity, do ordain and establish this Constitution for the United States of America.

ARTICLE. I.

Section. 1. All legislative Powers herein granted shall be vested in a Congress of the United States, which shall consist of a Senate and House of Representatives.

Section. 2. The House of Representatives shall be composed of Members chosen every second Year by the People of the several States, and the Electors in each State shall have the Qualifications requisite for Electors of the most numerous Branch of the State Legislature.

No Person shall be a Representative who shall not have attained to the Age of twenty five Years, and been seven Years a Citizen of the United States, and who shall not, when elected, be an Inhabitant of that State in which he shall be chosen.

[Representatives and direct Taxes shall be apportioned among the several States which may be included within this Union, according to their respective Numbers, which shall be determined by adding to the whole Number of free Persons, including those bound to Service for a Term of Years, and excluding Indians not taxed, three fifths of all other Persons.] The actual Enumeration shall be made within three Years after the first Meeting of the Congress of the United States, and within every subsequent Term of ten Years, in such Manner as they shall by Law direct. The number of Representatives shall not exceed one for every thirty Thousand, but each State shall have at Least one Representative; and until such enumeration shall be made, the State of New Hampshire shall be entitled to chuse three, Massachusetts eight, Rhode-Island and Providence Plantations one, Connecticut five, New-York six, New Jersey four, Pennsylvania eight, Delaware one, Maryland six, Virginia ten, North Carolina five, South Carolina five, and Georgia three.

When vacancies happen in the Representation from any State, the Executive Authority thereof shall issue Writs of Election to fill such Vacancies.

The House of Representatives shall chuse their Speaker and other Officers; and shall have the sole Power of Impeachment.

Section. 3. The Senate of the United States shall be composed of two Senators from each State, [chosen by the Legislature thereof,] for six Years; and each Senator shall have one Vote.

Immediately after they shall be assembled in Consequence of the first Election, they shall be divided as equally as may be into three Classes. The Seats of the Senators of the first Class shall be vacated at the Expiration of the second Year, of the second Class at the Expiration of the fourth Year, and of the third Class at the Expira-

tion of the sixth Year, so that one third may be chosen every second Year; [and if Vacancies happen by Resignation, or otherwise, during the Recess of the Legislature of any State, the Executive thereof may make temporary Appointments until the next Meeting of the Legislature, which shall then fill such Vacancies.]

No Person shall be a Senator who shall not have attained to the Age of thirty Years, and been nine Years a Citizen of the United States, and who shall not, when elected, be an Inhabitant of that State for which he shall be chosen.

The Vice President of the United States shall be President of the Senate, but shall have no Vote, unless they be equally divided.

The Senate shall chuse their other Officers, and also a President pro tempore, in the Absence of the Vice President, or when he shall exercise the Office of President of the United States.

The Senate shall have the sole Power to try all Impeachments. When sitting for that Purpose, they shall be on Oath or Affirmation. When the President of the United States is tried, the Chief Justice shall preside: And no Person shall be convicted without the Concurrence of two thirds of the Members present.

Judgment in Cases of Impeachment shall not extend further than to removal from Office, and disqualification to hold and enjoy any Office of honor, Trust or Profit under the United States: but the Party convicted shall nevertheless be liable and subject to Indictment, Trial, Judgment and Punishment, according to Law.

Section. 4. The Times, Places and Manner of holding Elections for Senators and Representatives, shall be prescribed in each State by the Legislature thereof; but the Congress may at any time by Law make or alter such Regulations, except as to the Places of chusing Senators.

The Congress shall assemble at least once in every Year, and such Meeting shall be [on the first Monday in December,] unless they shall by Law appoint a different Day.

Section. 5. Each House shall be the Judge of the Elections, Returns and Qualifications of its own Members, and a Majority of each shall constitute a Quorum to do Business; but a smaller Number may adjourn from day to day, and may be authorized to compel the Attendance of absent Members, in such Manner, and under such Penalties as each House may provide.

Each House may determine the Rules of its Proceedings, punish its Members for disorderly Behaviour, and, with the Concurrence of two thirds, expel a Member.

Each House shall keep a Journal of its Proceedings, and from time to time publish the same, excepting such Parts as may in their Judgment require Secrecy; and the Yeas and Nays of the Members of either House on any question shall, at the desire of one-fifth of those present, be entered on the journal.

Neither House, during the Session of Congress, shall, without the Consent of the other, adjourn for more than three days, nor to any other Place than that in which the two Houses shall be sitting.

Section. 6. The Senators and Representatives shall receive a Compensation for their Services, to be ascertained by Law, and paid out of the Treasury of the United States. They shall in all Cases, except Treason, Felony and Breach of the Peace, be privileged from Arrest during their Attendance at the Session of their respective Houses, and in going to and returning from the same; and for any Speech or Debate in either House, they shall not be questioned in any other Place.

No Senator or Representative shall, during the Time for which he was elected, be appointed to any civil Office under the Authority of the United States, which shall have been created, or the Emoluments whereof shall have been encreased during such time; and no Person holding any Office under the United States, shall be a Member of either House during his Continuance in Office.

Section. 7. All Bills for raising Revenue shall originate in the House of Representatives; but the Senate may propose or concur with Amendments as on other Bills.

Every Bill which shall have passed the House of Representatives and the Senate, shall, before it becomes a Law, be presented to the President of the United States; If he approve he shall sign it, but if not he shall return it, with his Objections to that House in which it shall have originated, who shall enter the Objections at large on their Journal, and proceed to reconsider it. If after such Reconsideration two thirds of that House shall agree to pass the Bill, it shall be sent, together with the Objections, to the other House, by which it shall likewise be reconsidered, and if approved by two thirds of that House, it shall become a Law. But in all such Cases the Votes of both Houses shall be determined by yeas and Nays, and the Names of the Persons voting for and against the Bill shall be entered on the Journal of each House respectively. If any Bill shall not be returned by the President within ten Days (Sundays excepted) after it shall have been presented to him, the Same shall be a Law, in like Manner as if he had signed it, unless the Congress by their Adjournment prevent its Return, in which Case it shall not be a Law.

Every Order, Resolution, or Vote to which the Concurrence of the Senate and House of Representatives may be necessary (except on a question of Adjournment) shall be presented to the President of the United States; and before the Same shall take Effect, shall be approved by him, or being disapproved by him, shall be repassed by two thirds of the Senate and House of Representatives, according to the Rules and Limitations prescribed in the Case of a Bill.

Section. 8. The Congress shall have Power To lay and collect Taxes, Duties, Imposts and Excises, to pay the Debts and provide for the common Defence and general Welfare of the United States; but all Duties, Imposts and Excises shall be uniform throughout the United States;

To borrow Money on the credit of the United States;

To regulate Commerce with foreign Nations, and among the several States, and with the Indian Tribes;

To establish an uniform Rule of Naturalization, and uniform Laws on the subject of Bankruptcies throughout the United States;

To coin Money, regulate the Value thereof, and of foreign Coin, and fix the Standard of Weights and Measures;

To provide for the Punishment of counterfeiting the Securities and current Coin of the United States;

To establish Post Offices and post Roads;

To promote the Progress of Science and useful Arts, by securing for limited Times to Authors and Inventors the exclusive Right to their respective Writings and Discoveries;

To constitute Tribunals inferior to the supreme Court;

To define and punish Piracies and Felonies committed on the high Seas, and Offenses against the Law of Nations;

To declare War, grant Letters of Marque and Reprisal, and make Rules concerning Captures on Land and Water;

To raise and support Armies, but no Appropriation of Money to that Use shall be for a longer Term than two Years;

To provide and maintain a Navy;

To make Rules for the Government and Regulation of the land and naval Forces;

To provide for calling forth the Militia to execute the Laws of the Union, suppress Insurrections and repel Invasions;

To provide for organizing, arming, and disciplining, the Militia, and for governing such Part of them as may be employed in the Service of the United States, reserving to the States respectively, the Appointment of the Officers, and the Authority of training the Militia according to the discipline prescribed by Congress;

To exercise exclusive Legislation in all Cases whatsoever, over such District (not exceeding ten Miles square) as may, by Cession of particular States, and the Acceptance of Congress, become the Seat of the Government of the United States, and to exercise like Authority over all Places purchased by the Consent of the Legislature of the State in which the Same shall be, for the Erection of Forts, Magazines, Arsenals, dock-Yards and other needful Buildings;—And

To make all Laws which shall be necessary and proper for carrying into Execution the foregoing Powers, and all other Powers vested by this Constitution in the Government of the United States, or in any Department or Officer thereof.

Section. 9. The Migration or Importation of such Persons as any of the States now existing shall think proper to admit, shall not be prohibited by the Congress prior to the Year one thousand eight hundred and eight, but a Tax or duty may be imposed on such Importation, not exceeding ten dollars for each Person.

The Privilege of the Writ of Habeas Corpus shall not be suspended, unless when in Cases of Rebellion or Invasion the public Safety may require it.

No Bill of Attainder or ex post facto Law shall be passed.

[No Capitation, or other direct, Tax shall be laid, unless in Proportion to the Census or Enumeration herein before directed to be taken.]

No Tax or Duty shall be laid on Articles exported from any State.

No Preference shall be given by any Regulation of Commerce or Revenue to the Ports of one State over those of another: nor shall Vessels bound to, or from, one State, be obliged to enter, clear, or pay Duties in another.

No Money shall be drawn from the Treasury, but in Consequence of Appropriations made by Law; and a regular Statement and Account of the Receipts and Expenditures of all public Money shall be published from time to time.

No Title of Nobility shall be granted by the United States: And no Person holding any Office of Profit or Trust under them, shall, without the Consent of the Congress, accept of any present, Emolument, Office, or Title, of any kind whatever, from any King, Prince, or foreign State.

Section. 10. No State shall enter into any Treaty, Alliance, or Confederation; grant Letters of Marque and Reprisal; coin Money; emit Bills of Credit; make any Thing but gold and silver Coin a Tender in Payment of Debts; pass any Bill of Attainder, ex post facto Law, or Law impairing the Obligation of Contracts, or grant any Title of Nobility.

No State shall, without the Consent of the Congress, lay any Imposts or Duties on Imports or Exports, except what may be absolutely necessary for executing it's inspection Laws: and the net Produce of all Duties and Imposts, laid by any State on Imports or Exports, shall be for the Use of the Treasury of the United States; and all such Laws shall be subject to the Revision and Controul of the Congress.

No State shall, without the Consent of Congress, lay any Duty of Tonnage, keep Troops, or Ships of War in time of Peace, enter into any Agreement or Compact with another State, or with a foreign Power, or engage in War, unless actually invaded, or in such imminent Danger as will not admit of delay.

ARTICLE. II.

Section. 1. The executive Power shall be vested in a President of the United States of America. He shall hold his Office during the Term of four Years, and, together with the Vice President, chosen for the same Term, be elected, as follows

Each State shall appoint, in such Manner as the Legislature thereof may direct, a Number of Electors, equal to the whole Number of Senators and Representatives to which the State may be entitled in the Congress: but no Senator or Representative, or Person holding an Office of Trust or Profit under the United States, shall be appointed an Elector.

[The Electors shall meet in their respective States, and vote by Ballot for two Persons, of whom one at least shall not be an Inhabitant of the same State with themselves. And they shall make a List of all the Persons voted for, and of the Number of Votes for each; which List they shall sign and certify, and transmit sealed to the Seat of the Government of the United States, directed to the President of the Senate. The President of the Senate shall, in the Presence of the Senate and House of Representatives, open all the Certificates, and the Votes shall then be counted. The Person having the greatest Number of Votes shall be the President, if such Number be a Majority of the whole Number of Electors appointed; and if there be more than one who have such Majority, and have an equal Number of Votes, then the House of Representatives shall immediately chuse by Ballot one of them for President; and if no Person have a Majority, then from the five highest on the List the said House shall in like Manner chuse the President. But in chusing the President, the Votes shall be taken by States, the Representation from each State having one Vote; A quorum for this Purpose shall consist of a Member or Members from two thirds of the States, and a Majority of all the States shall be necessary to a Choice. In every Case, after the Choice of the President, the Person having the greatest Number of Votes of the Electors shall be the Vice President. But if there should remain two or more who have equal Votes, the Senate shall chuse from them by Ballot the Vice President.]

The Congress may determine the Time of chusing the Electors, and the Day on which they shall give their Votes; which Day shall be the same throughout the United States.

No Person except a natural born Citizen, or a Citizen of the United States, at the time of the Adoption of this Constitution, shall be eligible to the Office of the President; neither shall any person be eligible to that Office who shall not have attained to the Age of thirty five Years, and been fourteen Years a Resident within the United States.

[In Case of the Removal of the President from Office, or of his Death, Resignation, or Inability to discharge the Powers and Duties of the said Office, the Same shall devolve on the Vice President, and the Congress may by Law provide for the Case of Removal, Death, Resignation or Inability, both of the President and Vice President, declaring what Officer shall then act as President, and such Officer shall act accordingly, until the Disability be removed, or a President shall be elected.]

The President shall, at stated Times, receive for his Services, a Compensation, which shall neither be increased nor diminished during the Period for which he shall have been elected, and he shall not receive within that Period any other Emolument from the United States, or any of them.

Before he enter on the Execution of his Office, he shall take the following Oath or Affirmation:—"I do solemnly swear (or affirm) that I will faithfully execute the Office of President of the United States, and will to the best of my Ability, preserve, protect and defend the Constitution of the United States."

Section. 2. The President shall be Commander in Chief of the Army and Navy of the United States, and of the Militia of the several States, when called into the actual Service of the United States; he may require the Opinion, in writing, of the principal Officer in each of the executive Departments, upon any Subject relating to the Duties of their respective Offices, and he shall have Power to grant Reprieves and Pardons for Offenses against the United States, except in Cases of Impeachment.

He shall have Power, by and with the Advice and Consent of the Senate, to make Treaties, provided two thirds of the Senators present concur; and he shall nominate, and by and with the Advice and Consent of the Senate, shall appoint Ambassadors, other public Ministers and Consuls, Judges of the supreme Court, and all other Officers of the United States, whose Appointments are not herein otherwise provided for, and which shall be established by Law: but the Congress may by Law vest the Appointment of such inferior Officers, as they think proper, in the President alone, in the Courts of Law, or in the Heads of Departments.

The President shall have Power to fill up all Vacancies that may happen during the Recess of the Senate, by granting Commissions which shall expire at the End of their next Session.

Section. 3. He shall from time to time give to the Congress Information of the State of the Union, and recommend to their Consideration such Measures as he shall judge necessary and expedient; he may, on extraordinary Occasions, convene both Houses, or either of them, and in Case of Disagreement between them, with Respect to the Time of Adjournment, he may adjourn them to such Time as he shall think proper; he shall receive Ambassadors and other public Ministers; he shall take Care that the Laws be faithfully executed, and shall Commission all the Officers of the United States.

Section. 4. The President, Vice President and all civil Officers of the United States, shall be removed from Office on Impeachment for, and Conviction of, Treason, Bribery, or other high Crimes and Misdemeanors.

ARTICLE. III.

Section. 1. The judicial Power of the United States, shall be vested in one supreme Court, and in such inferior Courts as the Congress may from time to time ordain and establish. The Judges, both of the supreme and inferior Courts, shall hold their Offices during good Behaviour, and shall, at stated Times, receive for their Services, a Compensation, which shall not be diminished during their Continuance in Office.

Section. 2. The judicial Power shall extend to all Cases, in Law and Equity, arising under this Constitution, the Laws of the United States, and Treaties made, or which shall be made, under their Authority;—to all Cases affecting Ambassadors, other public Ministers and Consuls;—to all Cases of admiralty and maritime Jurisdiction;—to Controversies to which the United States shall be a Party;—to Controversies between two or more States; [between a State and Citizens of another State;—] between Citizens of different States—between Citizens of the same State claiming Lands under Grants of different States, [and between a State, or the Citizens thereof, and foreign States, Citizens or Subjects.]

In all Cases affecting Ambassadors, other pub-lic Ministers and Consuls, and those in which a State shall be Party, the supreme Court shall have original Jurisdiction. In all the other Cases before mentioned, the supreme Court shall have appellate Jurisdiction, both as to Law and Fact, with such Exceptions, and under such Regulations as the Congress shall make.

The Trial of all Crimes, except in Cases of Impeachment; shall be by Jury; and such Trial shall be held in the State where the said Crimes shall have been committed; but when not committed within any State, the Trial shall be at such Place or Places as the Congress may by Law have directed.

Section. 3. Treason against the United States, shall consist only in levying War against them, or in adhering to their Enemies, giving them Aid and Comfort. No Person shall be convicted of Treason unless on the Testimony of two Witnesses to the same overt Act, or on Confession in open Court.

The Congress shall have Power to declare the Punishment of Treason, but no Attainder of Treason shall work Corruption of Blood, or Forfeiture except during the Life of the Person attainted.

ARTICLE. IV.

Section. 1. Full Faith and Credit shall be given in each State to the public Acts, Records, and judicial Proceedings of every other State; And the Congress may by general Laws prescribe the Manner in which such Acts, Records and Proceedings shall be proved, and the Effect thereof.

Section. 2. The Citizens of each State shall be entitled to all Privileges and Immunities of Citizens in the several States.

A Person charged in any State with Treason, Felony, or other Crime, who shall flee from Justice, and be found in another State, shall on Demand of the executive Authority of the State from which he fled, be delivered up, to be removed to the State having Jurisdiction of the Crime.

[No Person held to Service or Labour in one State, under the Laws thereof, escaping into another, shall, in Consequence of any Law or Regulation therein, be discharged from such Service or Labour, but shall be delivered up on Claim of the Party to whom such Service or Labour may be due.]

Section. 3. New States may be admitted by the Congress into this Union; but no new State shall be formed or erected within the Jurisdiction of any other State; nor any State be formed by the Junction of two or more States, or Parts of States, without the Consent of the Legislatures of the States concerned as well as of the Congress.

The Congress shall have Power to dispose of and make all needful Rules and Regulations respecting the Territory or other Property belonging to the United States; and nothing in this Constitution shall be so construed as to Prejudice any Claims of the United States, or of any particular State.

Section. 4. The United States shall guarantee to every State in this Union a Republican Form of Government, and shall protect each of them against Invasion; and on Application of the Legislature, or of the Executive (when the Legislature cannot be convened) against domestic Violence.

ARTICLE. V.

The Congress, whenever two thirds of both Houses shall deem it necessary, shall propose Amendments to this Constitution, or, on the Application of the Legislatures of two thirds of the several States, shall call a Convention for proposing Amendments, which, in either Case, shall be valid to all Intents and Purposes, as Part of this Constitution, when ratified by the Legislatures of three fourths of the several States, or by

Conventions in three fourths thereof, as the one or the other Mode of Ratification may be proposed by the Congress; Provided that no Amendment which may be made prior to the Year One thousand eight hundred and eight shall in any Manner affect the first and fourth Clauses in the Ninth Section of the first Article; and that no State, without its Consent, shall be deprived of it's equal Suffrage in the Senate.

ARTICLE. VI.

All Debts contracted and Engagements entered into, before the Adoption of this Constitution, shall be as valid against the United States under this Constitution, as under the Confederation.

This Constitution, and the Laws of the United States which shall be made in Pursuance thereof; and all Treaties made, or which shall be made, under the Authority of the United States, shall be the supreme Law of the Land; and the Judges in every State shall be bound thereby, any Thing in the Constitution or Laws of any State to the Contrary notwithstanding.

The Senators and Representatives before mentioned, and the Members of the several State Legislatures, and all executive and judicial Officers, both of the United States and of the several States, shall be bound by Oath or Affirmation, to support this Constitution; but no religious Test shall ever be required as a Qualification to any Office or public Trust under the United States.

ARTICLE. VII.

The Ratification of the Conventions of nine States, shall be sufficient for the Establishment of this Constitution between the States so ratifying the Same.

done in Convention by the Unanimous Consent of the States present the Seventeenth Day of September in the Year of our Lord one thousand seven hundred and Eighty seven and of the Independence of the United States of America the Twelfth In Witness whereof We have hereunto subscribed our Names,

G°. WASHINGTON—*Presidt.*
and deputy from Virginia

New Hampshire
JOHN LANGDON
NICHOLAS GILMAN

Massachusetts
NATHANIEL GORHAM
RUFUS KING

Connecticut
WM: SAML. JOHNSON
ROGER SHERMAN

New York
ALEXANDER HAMILTON

New Jersey
WIL: LIVINGSTON
DAVID BREARLEY
WM. PATERSON
JONA: DAYTON

Pennsylvania
B FRANKLIN
THOMAS MIFFLIN
ROBT MORRIS
GEO. CLYMER
THOS. FITZSIMONS
JARED INGERSOLL
JAMES WILSON
GOUV. MORRIS

Delaware
GEO: READ
GUNNING BEDFORD JUN
JOHN DICKINSON
RICHARD BASSETT
JACO: BROOM

Maryland
JAMES MCHENRY
DAN OF ST THOS. JENIFER
DANL CARROLL

Virginia
JOHN BLAIR—
JAMES MADISON JR.

North Carolina
WM. BLOUNT
RICHD. DOBBS SPAIGHT
HU WILLIAMSON

South Carolina
J. RUTLEDGE
CHARLES COTESWORTH
PINCKNEY
CHARLES PINCKNEY
PIERCE BUTLER

Georgia
WILLIAM FEW
ABR BALDWIN

Attest WILLIAM
JACKSON—*Secretary*

IN CONVENTION MONDAY SEPTEMBER 17TH 1787

Present The States of New Hampshire, Massachusetts, Connecticut, Mr. Hamilton from New York, New Jersey, Pennsylvania, Delaware, Maryland, Virginia, North Carolina, South Carolina and Georgia.

RESOLVED,

That the preceding Constitution be laid before the United States in Congress assembled, and that it is the Opinion of this Convention, that it should afterwards be submitted to a Convention of Delegates, chosen in each State by the People thereof, under the Recommendation of its Legislature, for their Assent and Ratification; and that each Convention assenting to, and ratifying the Same, should give Notice thereof to the United States in Congress assembled. Resolved, That it is the Opinion of this Convention, that as soon as the Conventions of nine States shall have ratified this Constitution, the United States in Congress assembled should fix a Day on which Electors should be appointed by the States which shall have ratified the same, and a Day on which the Electors should assemble to vote for the President, and the Time and Place for commencing Proceedings under this Constitution.

That after such Publication the Electors

should be appointed, and the Senators and Representatives elected: That the Electors should meet on the Day fixed for the Election of the President, and should transmit their Votes certified, signed, sealed and directed, as the Constitution requires, to the Secretary of the United States in Congress assembled, that the Senators and Representatives should convene at the Time and Place assigned; that the Senators should appoint a President of the Senate, for the sole Purpose of receiving, opening and counting the Votes for President; and, that after he shall be chosen, the Congress, together with the President, should, without Delay, proceed to execute this Constitution.

By the unanimous Order of the Convention
G°. Washington—*Presidt.*
W. Jackson—*Secretary*

Amendments to the Constitution of The United States of America

Articles in Addition to, and Amendment of, the Constitution of the United States of America, Proposed by Congress, and Ratified by the Several States, Pursuant to the Fifth Article of the Original Constitution.

Amendment I. (1791)

Congress shall make no law respecting an establishment of religion, or prohibiting the free exercise thereof; or abridging the freedom of speech, or of the press, or the right of the people peaceably to assemble, and to petition the Government for a redress of grievances.

Amendment II. (1791)

A well regulated Militia, being necessary to the security of a free State, the right of the people to keep and bear Arms, shall not be infringed.

Amendment III. (1791)

No Soldier shall, in time of peace be quartered in any house, without the consent of the Owner, nor in time of war, but in a manner to be prescribed by law.

Amendment IV. (1791)

The right of the people to be secure in their persons, houses, papers, and effects, against unreasonable searches and seizures, shall not be violated, and no Warrants shall issue, but upon probable cause, supported by Oath or affirmation, and particularly describing the place to be searched, and the persons or things to be seized.

Amendment V. (1791)

No person shall be held to answer for a capital, or otherwise infamous crime, unless on a presentment or indictment of a Grand Jury, except in cases arising in the land or naval forces, or in the Militia, when in actual service in time of War or public danger; nor shall any person be subject for the same offence to be twice put in jeopardy of life or limb, nor shall be compelled in any criminal case to be a witness against himself, nor be deprived of life, liberty, or property, without due process of law; nor shall private property be taken for public use without just compensation.

Amendment VI. (1791)

In all criminal prosecutions, the accused shall enjoy the right to a speedy and public trial, by an impartial jury of the State and district wherein the crime shall have been committed; which district shall have been previously ascertained by law, and to be informed of the nature and cause of the accusation; to be confronted with the witnesses against him; to have compulsory process for obtaining witnesses in his favor, and to have the assistance of counsel for his defence.

Amendment VII. (1791)

In Suits at common law, where the value in controversy shall exceed twenty dollars, the right of trial by jury shall be preserved, and no fact tried by a jury shall be otherwise re-examined in any Court of the United States, than according to the rules of the common law.

Amendment VIII. (1791)

Excessive bail shall not be required, nor excessive fines imposed, nor cruel and unusual punishments inflicted.

Amendment IX. (1791)

The enumeration in the Constitution of certain rights shall not be construed to deny or disparage others retained by the people.

Amendment X. (1791)

The powers not delegated to the United States by the Constitution, nor prohibited by it to the States, are reserved to the States respectively, or to the people.

Amendment XI. (1798)

The Judicial power of the United States shall not be construed to extend to any suit in law or equity, commenced or prosecuted against one of the United States by Citizens of another State, or by Citizens or Subjects of any Foreign State.

Amendment XII. (1804)

The Electors shall meet in their respective states, and vote by ballot for President and Vice President, one of whom, at least, shall not be an inhabitant of the same state with themselves; they shall name in their ballots the person voted for as President, and in distinct ballots the person voted for as Vice-President, and they shall make distinct lists of all persons voted for as President, and of all persons voted for as Vice-President, and of the number of votes for each, which lists they shall sign and certify, and transmit sealed to the seat of the government of the United States, directed to the President of the Senate;—The President of the Senate shall, in the presence of the Senate and House of Representatives, open all the certificates and the votes shall then be counted;—The person having the greatest number of votes for President, shall be the President, if such number be a majority of the whole number of Electors appointed; and if no person have such majority, then from the persons having the highest numbers not exceeding three on the list of those voted for as President, the House of Representatives shall choose immediately, by ballot, the President. But in choosing the President, the votes shall be taken by states, the representation from each state having one vote; a quorum for this purpose shall consist of a member or members from two-thirds of the states, and a majority of all the states shall be necessary to a choice. [And if the House of Representatives shall not choose a President whenever the right of choice shall devolve upon them, before the fourth day of March next following, then the Vice-President shall act as President, as in the case of the death or other constitutional disability of the President—] The person having the greatest number of votes as Vice-President, shall be the Vice-President, if such number be a majority of the whole number of Electors appointed, and if no person have a majority, then from the two highest numbers on the list, the Senate shall choose the Vice-President; a quorum for the purpose shall consist of two-thirds of the whole number of Senators, and a majority of the whole number shall be necessary to a choice. But no person constitutionally ineligible to the office of President shall be eligible to that of Vice-President of the United States.

Amendment XIII. (1865)

Section 1. Neither slavery nor involuntary servitude, except as a punishment for crime whereof the party shall have been duly convicted, shall exist within the United States, or any place subject to their jurisdiction.

Section 2. Congress shall have power to enforce this article by appropriate legislation.

Amendment XIV. (1868)

Section 1. All persons born or naturalized in the United States and subject to the jurisdiction thereof, are citizens of the United States and of the State wherein they reside. No State shall make or enforce any law which shall abridge the privileges or immunities of citizens of the United States; nor shall any State deprive any person of life, liberty, or property, without due process of law; nor deny to any person within its jurisdiction the equal protection of the laws.

Section 2. Representatives shall be apportioned among the several States according to their respective numbers, counting the whole number of persons in each State, excluding Indians not taxed. But when the right to vote at any election for the choice of electors for President and Vice President of the United States, Representatives in Congress, the Executive and Judicial officers of a State, or the members of the Legislature thereof, is denied to any of the male inhabitants of such State, being twenty-one years of age, and citizens of the United States, or in any way abridged, except for participation in rebellion, or other crime, the basis of representation therein shall be reduced in the proportion which the number of such male citizens shall bear to the whole number of male citizens twenty-one years of age in such State.

Section 3. No person shall be a Senator or Representative in Congress, or elector of President and Vice President, or hold any office, civil or military, under the United States, or under any State, who, having previously taken an oath, as a member of Congress, or as an officer of the United States, or as a member of any State legislature, or as an executive or judicial officer of any State, to support the Constitution of the United States, shall have engaged in insurrection or rebellion against the same, or given aid or comfort to the enemies thereof. But Congress may by a vote of two-thirds of each House, remove such disability.

Section 4. The validity of the public debt of the United States, authorized by law, including debts incurred for payment of pensions and bounties for services in suppressing insurrection or rebellion, shall not be questioned. But neither the United States nor any State shall assume or pay any debt or obligation incurred in aid of insurrection or rebellion against the United States, or any claim for the loss or emancipation of any slave; but all such debts, obligations and claims shall be held illegal and void.

Section 5. The Congress shall have power to enforce, by appropriate legislation, the provisions of this article.

Amendment XV. (1870)

Section 1. The right of citizens of the United States to vote shall not be denied or abridged by the United States or by any State on account of race, color, or previous condition of servitude.

Section 2. The Congress shall have power to enforce this article by appropriate legislation.

Amendment XVI. (1913)

The Congress shall have power to lay and collect taxes on incomes, from whatever source derived, without apportionment among the several States, and without regard to any census or enumeration.

Amendment XVII. (1913)

The Senate of the United States shall be composed of two Senators from each State, elected by the people thereof, for six years; and each Senator shall have one vote. The electors in each State shall have the qualifications requisite for electors of the most numerous branch of the State legislatures.

When vacancies happen in the representation of any State in the Senate, the executive authority of such State shall issue writs of election to fill such vacancies: *Provided,* That the legislature of any State may empower the executive thereof to make temporary appointments until the people fill the vacancies by election as the legislature may direct.

This amendment shall not be so construed as to affect the election or term of any Senator chosen before it becomes valid as part of the Constitution.

Amendment XVIII. (1919)

[Section 1. After one year from the ratification of this article the manufacture, sale, or transportation of intoxicating liquors within, the importation thereof into, or the exportation thereof from the United States and all territory subject to the jurisdiction thereof for beverage purposes is hereby prohibited.

Section 2. The Congress and the several States shall have concurrent power to enforce this article by appropriate legislation.

Section 3. This article shall be inoperative unless it shall have been ratified as an amendment to the Constitution by the legislatures of the several States, as provided in the Constitution, within seven years from the date of the submission hereof to the States by the Congress.]

Amendment XIX. (1920)

The right of citizens of the United States to vote shall not be denied or abridged by the United States or by any State on account of sex.

Congress shall have power to enforce this article by appropriate legislation.

Amendment XX. (1933)

Section 1. The terms of the President and Vice President shall end at noon on the 20th day of January, and the terms of Senators and Representatives at noon on the 3d day of January, of the years in which such terms would have ended if this article had not been ratified; and the terms of their successors shall then begin.

Section 2. The Congress shall assemble at least once in every year, and such meeting shall begin at noon on the 3d day of January, unless they shall by law appoint a different day.

Section 3. If, at the time fixed for the beginning of the term of the President, the President elect shall have died, the Vice President elect shall become President. If a President shall not have been chosen before the time fixed for the beginning of his term, or if the President elect shall have failed to qualify, then the Vice President elect shall act as President until a President shall have qualified; and the Congress may by law provide for the case wherein neither a President elect nor a Vice President elect shall have qualified, declaring who shall then act as President, or the manner in which one who is to act shall be selected, and such person shall act accordingly until a President or Vice President shall have qualified.

Section 4. The Congress may by law provide for the case of the death of any of the persons from whom the House of Representatives may choose a President whenever the right of choice shall have devolved upon them, and for the case of the death of any of the persons from whom the Senate may choose a Vice President whenever the right of choice shall have devolved upon them.

FORMING A MORE PERFECT UNION

Section 5. Sections 1 and 2 shall take effect on the 15th day of October following the ratification of this article.

Section 6. This article shall be inoperative unless it shall have been ratified as an amendment to the Constitution by the legislatures of three-fourths of the several States within seven years from the date of its submission.

Amendment XXI. (1933)

Section 1. The eighteenth article of amendment to the Constitution of the United States is hereby repealed.

Section 2. The transportation or importation into any State, Territory, or possession of the United States for delivery or use therein of intoxicating liquor in violation of the laws thereof, is hereby prohibited.

Section 3. This article shall be inoperative unless it shall have been ratified an amendment to the Constitution by conventions in the several States, provided in the Constitution, within seven years from the date of the submission hereof to the States by the Congress.

Amendment XXII. (1951)

Section 1. No person shall be elected to the office of the President more than twice, and no person who has held the office of President, or acted as President, for more than two years of a term to which some other person was elected President shall be elected to the office of the President more than once. But this Article shall not apply to any person holding the office of President when this Article was proposed by the Congress, and shall not prevent any person who may be holding the office of President, or acting as President, during the term within which this Article becomes operative from holding the office of President or acting as President during the remainder of such term.

Section 2. This article shall be inoperative unless it shall have been ratified as an amendment to the Constitution by the legislatures of three-fourths of the several States within seven years from the date of its submission to the States by the Congress.

Amendment XXIII. (1961)

Section 1. The District constituting the seat of Government of the United States shall appoint in such manner as the Congress may direct:

A number of electors of President and Vice President equal to the whole number of Senators and Representatives in Congress to which the District would be entitled if it were a State, but in no event more than the least populous State; they shall be in addition to those appointed by the States, but they shall be considered, for the purposes of the election of President and Vice President, to be electors appointed by a State; and they shall meet in the District and perform such duties as provided by the twelfth article of amendment.

Section 2. The Congress shall have power to enforce this article by appropriate legislation.

Amendment XXIV. (1964)

Section 1. The right of citizens of the United States to vote in any primary or other election for President or Vice President, for electors for President or Vice President, or for Senator or Representative in Congress, shall not be denied or abridged by the United States or any State by reason of failure to pay any poll tax or other tax.

Section 2. The Congress shall have power to enforce this article by appropriate legislation.

Amendment XXV. (1967)

Section 1. In case of the removal of the President from office or of his death or resignation, the Vice President shall become President.

Section 2. Whenever there is a vacancy in the office of the Vice President, the President shall nominate a Vice President who shall take office upon confirmation by a majority vote of both Houses of Congress.

Section 3. Whenever the President transmits to the President pro tempore of the Senate and the Speaker of the House of Representatives his written declaration that he is unable to discharge the powers and duties of his office, and until he transmits to them a written declaration to the contrary, such powers and duties shall be discharged by the Vice President as Acting President.

Section 4. Whenever the Vice President and a majority of either the principal officers of the executive departments or of such other body as Congress may by law provide, transmit to the President pro tempore of the Senate and the Speaker of the House of Representatives their written declaration that the President is unable to discharge the powers and duties of his office, the Vice President shall immediately assume the powers and duties of the office as Acting President.

Thereafter, when the President transmits to the President pro tempore of the Senate and the Speaker of the House of Representatives his written declaration that no inability exists, he shall resume the powers and duties of his office unless the Vice President and a majority of either the principal officers of the executive department or

of such other body as Congress may by law provide, transmit within four days to the President pro tempore of the Senate and the Speaker of the House of Representatives their written declaration that the President is unable to discharge the powers and duties of his office. Thereupon Congress shall decide the issue, assembling within forty-eight hours for that purpose if not in session. If the Congress, within twenty-one days after receipt of the latter written declaration, or, if Congress is not in session, within twenty-one days after Congress is required to assemble, determines by two-thirds vote of both Houses that the President is unable to discharge the powers and duties of his office, the Vice President shall continue to discharge the same as Acting President; otherwise, the President shall resume the powers and duties of his office.

Amendment XXVI. (1971)

Section 1. The right of citizens of the United States, who are eighteen years of age or older, to vote shall not be denied or abridged by the United States or by any State on account of age.

Section 2. The Congress shall have power to enforce this article by appropriate legislation.

Amendment XXVII (1992)

No law, varying the compensation for the services of the Senators and Representatives, shall take effect, until an election of Representatives shall have intervened.

"It is your interest to adopt it"

THE FEDERALIST NUMBER 1

1787

The reluctant Confederation Congress, prodded by the fatigued "father of the Constitution," James Madison (1751–1836), submitted the proposed replacement for the Articles of Confederation to ratifying conventions called by each state legislature. Federalists, conceding that the new charter might need some changes, suggested that the conventions adopt the Constitution and submit suggestions for amendments. It was a master stroke. To assuage the fears of the people, "rights" amendments—the sacred fire of liberty—*would be* proposed in the First Congress. Three heavy Federalist guns, Madison, John Jay (1745–1829), and Alexander Hamilton (1755–1804), laid down a comprehensive, reasoned, and candid defense of the Constitution. Writing under the pen name of Publius, they promulgated 85 newspaper letters favoring adoption. The Federalist papers have been hailed as America's greatest contribution to political thought. Hamilton, celebrating the American Union and invoking the challenge of experimenting with free government in behalf of all mankind, composed a capsule introduction to the series. Federalist #1 was published on October 27, 1787, in *The Independent Journal* and addressed to the People of the State of New-York, where anti-Federalists, or Grumbletonians, aggressively opposed the proposed Constitution.

After an unequivocal experience of the inefficacy of the subsisting Fœderal Government, you are called upon to deliberate on a new Constitution for the United States of America. The subject speaks its own importance; comprehending in its consequences, nothing less than the existence of the UNION, the safety and welfare of the parts of which it is composed, the fate of an empire, in many respects, the most interesting in the world. It has been frequently remarked, that it seems to have been reserved to the people of this country, by their conduct and example, to decide the important question, whether societies of men are really capable or not, of establishing good government from reflection and choice, or whether they are forever destined to depend, for their political constitutions, on accident and force. If there be any truth in the remark, the crisis, at which we are arrived, may with propriety be regarded as the æra in which that decision is to be made; and a wrong election of the part we shall act, may, in this view, deserve to be considered as the general misfortune of mankind.

This idea will add the inducements of philanthropy to those of patriotism to heighten the sollicitude, which all considerate and good men must feel for the event. Happy will it be if our choice should be decided by a judicious estimate of our true interests, unperplexed and unbiassed by considerations not connected with the public good. But this is a thing more ardently to be wished, than seriously to be expected. The plan offered to our deliberations, affects too many particular interests, innovates upon too many local institutions, not to involve in its discussion a variety of objects foreign to its merits, and of views, passions and prejudices little favourable to the discovery of truth.

Among the most formidable of the obstacles which the new Constitution will have to encounter, may readily be distinguished the obvious interest of a certain class of men in every State to resist all changes which may hazard a diminution of the power, emolument and consequence of the offices they hold under the State-establishments—and the perverted ambition of another class of men, who will either hope to aggrandise themselves by the confusions of their country, or will flatter themselves with fairer prospects of elevation from the subdivision of the empire into several partial confederacies, than from its union under one government.

It is not, however, my design to dwell upon observations of this nature. I am well aware that it would be disingenuous to resolve indiscriminately the opposition of any set of men (merely because their situations might subject them to suspicion) into interested or ambitious views: Candour will oblige us to admit, that even such men may be actuated by upright intentions; and it cannot be doubted, that much of the opposition which has made its appearance, or may hereafter make its appearance, will spring from sources, blameless at least, if not respectable, the honest errors of minds led astray by preconceived jealousies and fears. So numerous indeed and so powerful are the causes, which serve to give a false bias to the judgment, that we upon many occasions, see wise and good men on the wrong as well as on the right side of questions, of the first magnitude to society. This circumstance, if duly attended to, would furnish a les-

son of moderation to those, who are ever so much persuaded of their being in the right, in any controversy. And a further reason for caution, in this respect, might be drawn from the reflection, that we are not always sure, that those who advocate the truth are influenced by purer principles than their antagonists. Ambition, avarice, personal animosity, party opposition, and many other motives, not more laudable than these, are apt to operate as well upon those who support as upon those who oppose the right side of a question. Were there not even these inducements to moderation, nothing could be more ill-judged than that intolerant spirit, which has, at all times, characterised political parties. For, in politics as in religion, it is equally absurd to aim at making proselytes by fire and sword. Heresies in either can rarely be cured by persecution.

And yet however just these sentiments will be allowed to be, we have already sufficient indications, that it will happen in this as in all former cases of great national discussion. A torrent of angry and malignant passions will be let loose. To judge from the conduct of the opposite parties, we shall be led to conclude, that they will mutually hope to evince the justness of their opinions, and to increase the number of their converts by the loudness of their declamations, and by the bitterness of their invectives. An enlightened zeal for the energy and efficiency of government will be stigmatised, as the off-spring of a temper fond of despotic power and hostile to the principles of liberty. An overscrupulous jealousy of danger to the rights of the people, which is more commonly the fault of the head than of the heart, will be represented as mere pretence and artifice; the bait for popularity at the expence of public good. It will be forgotten, on the one hand, that jealousy is the usual concomitant of violent love, and that the noble enthusiasm of liberty is too apt to be infected with a spirit of narrow and illiberal distrust. On the other hand, it will be equally forgotten, that the vigour of government is essential to the security of liberty; that, in the contemplation of a sound and well informed judgment, their interest can never be separated; and that a dangerous ambition more often lurks behind the specious mask of zeal for the rights of the people, than under the forbidding appearance of zeal for the firmness and efficiency of government. History will teach us, that the former has been found a much more certain road to the introduction of despotism, than the latter, and that of those men who have overturned the liberties of republics the greatest number have begun their career, by paying an obsequious court to the people, commencing Demagogues and ending Tyrants.

In the course of the preceeding observations I have had an eye, my Fellow Citizens, to putting you upon your guard against all attempts, from whatever quarter, to influence your decision in a matter of the utmost moment to your welfare by any impressions other than those which may result from the evidence of truth. You will, no doubt, at the same time, have collected from the general scope of them that they proceed from a source not unfriendly to the new Constitution. Yes, my Countrymen, I own to you, that, after having given it an attentive consideration, I am clearly of opinion, it is your interest to adopt it. I am convinced, that this is the safest course for your liberty, your dignity, and your happiness.

"We behold a . . . remedy"

THE FEDERALIST NUMBER 10
1788

Virginia's James Madison (1751–1836) had served as indefatigable secretary and chief warhorse of the Constitutional Convention. His notes of the proceedings and deliberations, first published after his death—he was the last surviving delegate—are a guide to the four-month convention. He prompted his fellow delegates (55 were present in the beginning, only 42 at the end) to disregard Congress's mandate merely to fix the Articles of Confederation. Later, he labored tirelessly to "sell" the Constitution to his countrymen. He helped to head off the second convention desired by anti-Federalists, believing it would "give opportunities to designing men which it might be impossible to counteract." In his first Federalist paper, Madison masterfully notes that factions are the product and the price of liberty, and looks to "the extent and proper structure of the Union" for a "republican remedy for the diseases most incident to republican government."

AMONG the numerous advantages promised by a well-constructed Union, none deserves to be more accurately developed than its tendency to break and control the violence of faction. The friend of popular governments never finds himself so much alarmed for their character and fate as when he contemplates their propensity to this dangerous vice. He will not fail, therefore, to set a due value on any plan which, without violating the principles to which he is attached, provides a proper cure for it. The instability, injustice, and confusion introduced into the public councils have, in truth, been the mortal diseases under which popular governments have everywhere perished, as they continue to be the favorite and fruitful topics from which the adversaries to liberty derive their most specious declamations. The valuable improvements made by the American constitutions on the popular models, both ancient and modern, cannot certainly be too much admired; but it would be an unwarrantable partiality to contend that they have as effectually obviated the danger on this side, as was wished and expected. Complaints are everywhere heard from our most considerate and virtuous citizens, equally the friends of public and private faith and of public and personal liberty, that our governments are too unstable, that the public good is disregarded in the conflicts of rival parties, and that measures are too often decided, not according to the rules of justice and the rights of the minor party, but by the superior force of an interested and overbearing majority. However anxiously we may wish that these complaints had no foundation, the evidence of known facts will not permit us to deny that they are in some degree true. It will be found, indeed, on a candid review of our situation, that some of the distresses under which we labor have been erroneously charged on the operation of our governments; but it will be found, at the same time, that other causes will not alone account for many of our heaviest misfortunes; and, particularly, for that prevailing and increasing distrust of public engagements and alarm for private rights which are echoed from one end of the continent to the other. These must be chiefly, if not wholly, effects of the unsteadiness and injustice with which a factious spirit has tainted our public administration.

By a faction I understand a number of citizens, whether amounting to a majority or minority of the whole, who are united and actuated by some common impulse of passion, or of interest, adverse to the rights of other citizens, or to the permanent and aggregate interests of the community.

There are two methods of curing the mischiefs of faction: the one, by removing its causes; the other, by controlling its effects.

There are again two methods of removing the causes of faction: the one, by destroying the liberty which is essential to its existence; the other, by giving to every citizen the same opinions, the same passions, and the same interests.

It could never be more truly said than of the first remedy that it was worse than the disease. Liberty is to faction what air is to fire, an ailment without which it instantly expires. But it could not be a less folly to abolish liberty, which is essential to political life, because it nourishes faction than it would be to wish the annihilation of air, which is essential to animal life, because it imparts to fire its destructive agency.

The second expedient is as impracticable as the first would be unwise. As long as the reason of man continues fallible, and he is at liberty to exercise it, different opinions will be formed. As long as the connection subsists between his reason and his self-love, his opinions and his passions will have a reciprocal influence on each other; and the former will be objects to which the latter will attach themselves. The diversity in the faculties of men, from which the rights of property originate, is not less an insuperable obstacle to a uniformity of interests. The protection of these faculties is the first object of government. From the protection of different and unequal faculties of acquiring property, the possession of different degrees and kinds of property immediately results; and from the influence of these on the sentiments and views of the respective proprietors ensues a division of the society into different interests and parties.

The latent causes of faction are thus sown in the nature of man; and we see them everywhere brought into different degrees of activity, according to the different circumstances of civil society. A zeal for different opinions concerning religion, concerning government, and many other points, as well of speculation as of practice; an attachment to different leaders ambitiously contending for pre-eminence and power; or to persons of other descriptions whose fortunes have been interesting to the human passions, have, in turn, divided mankind into parties, inflamed them with mutual animosity, and rendered them much more disposed to vex and oppress each other than to co-operate for their common good. So strong is this propensity of mankind to fall into mutual animosities that where no substantial occasion presents itself the most frivolous and fanciful distinctions have been sufficient to kindle their unfriendly passions and excite their most violent conflicts. But the most common and durable source of factions has been the verious and unequal distribution of property. Those who hold and those who are without property have ever formed distinct interests in society. Those who are creditors, and those who are debtors, fall under a like discrimination. A landed interest, a manufacturing interest, a mercantile interest, a moneyed interest, with many lesser interests, grow up of necessity in civilized nations, and divide them into different classes, actuated by different sentiments and views. The regulation of these various and interfering interests forms the principal task of modern legislation and involves the spirit of party and faction in the necessary and ordinary operations of government.

No man is allowed to be a judge in his own cause, because his interest would certainly bias his judgment, and, not improbably, corrupt his integrity. With equal, nay with greater reason, a body of men are unfit to be both judges and parties at the same time; yet what are many of the most important acts of legislation but so many judicial determinations, not indeed concerning the rights of single persons, but concerning the rights of large bodies of citizens? And what are the different classes of legislators but advocates and parties to the causes which they determine? Is a law proposed concerning private debts? It is a question to which the creditors are parties on one side and the debtors on the other. Justice ought to hold the balance between them. Yet the parties are, and must be, themselves the judges; and the most numerous party, or in other words, the most powerful faction must be expected to prevail. Shall domestic manufacturers be encouraged, and in what degree, by restrictions on foreign manufacturers? are questions which would be differently decided by the landed and the manufacturing classes, and probably by neither with a sole regard to justice and the public good. The apportionment of taxes on the various descriptions of property is an act which seems to require the most exact impartiality; yet there is, perhaps, no legislative act in which greater opportunity and temptation are given to a predominant party to trample on the rules of justice. Every shilling with which they overburden the inferior number is a shilling saved to their own pockets.

It is in vain to say that enlightened statesmen will be able to adjust these clashing interests and render them all subservient to the public good. Enlightened statesmen will not always be at the helm. Nor, in many cases, can such an adjustment be made at all without taking into view indirect and remote considerations, which will rarely prevail over the immediate interest which one party may find in disregarding the rights of another or the good of the whole.

The inference to which we are brought is that the *causes* of faction cannot be removed and that relief is only to be sought in the means of controlling its *effects*.

If a faction consists of less than a majority, relief is supplied by the republican principle, which enables the majority to defeat its sinister views by regular vote. It may clog the administration, it may convulse the society; but it will be unable to execute and mask its violence under the forms of the Constitution. When a majority is included in a faction, the form of popular government, on the other hand, enables it to sacrifice to its ruling passion or interest both the public good and the rights of other citizens. To secure the public good and private rights against the danger of such a faction, and at the same time to preserve the spirit and the form of popular government, is then the great object to which our inquiries are directed. Let me add that it is the great desideratum by which alone this form of government can be rescued from the opprobrium under which it has so long labored and be recommended to the esteem and adoption of mankind.

By what means is this object attainable? Evidently by one of two only. Either the existence of the same passion or interest in a majority at the same time must be prevented, or the majority, having such coexistent passion or interest, must be rendered, by their number and local situation, unable to concert and carry into effect schemes of oppression. If the impulse and the opportunity be suffered to coincide, we well know that neither moral nor religious motives can be relied on as an adequate control. They are not found to be such on the injustice and violence of individuals, and lose their efficacy in proportion to the number combined together, that is, in proportion as their efficacy becomes needful.

From this view of the subject it may be concluded that a pure democracy, by which I mean a society consisting of a small number of citizens, who assemble and administer the government in person, can admit of no cure for the mischiefs of faction. A common passion or interest will, in almost every case, be felt by a majority of the whole; a communication and concert results from the form of government itself; and there is nothing to check the inducements to sacrifice the weaker party or an obnoxious individual. Hence it is that such democracies have ever been spectacles of turbulence and contention; have ever been found incompatible with personal security or the rights of property; and have in general been as short in their lives as they have been violent in their deaths. Theoretic politicians, who have patronized this species of government, have erroneously supposed that by reducing mankind to a perfect equality in their political rights, they would at the same time be perfectly equalized and assimilated in their possessions, their opinions, and their passions.

A republic, by which I mean a government in which the scheme of representation takes place, opens a different prospect and promises the cure for which we are seeking. Let us examine the points in which it varies from pure democracy, and we shall comprehend both the nature of the cure and the efficacy which it must derive from the Union.

The two great points of difference between a democracy and a republic are: first, the delegation of the government, in the latter, to a small number of citizens elected by the rest; secondly, the greater number of citizens and greater sphere of country over which the latter may be extended.

The effect of the first difference is, on the one hand, to refine and enlarge the public views by passing them through the medium of a chosen body of citizens, whose wisdom may best discern the true interest of their country and whose patriotism and love of justice will be least likely to sacrifice it to temporary or partial considerations. Under such a regulation it may well happen that the public voice, pronounced by the representatives of the people, will be more consonant to the public good than if pronounced by the people themselves, convened for the purpose. On the other hand, the effect may be inverted. Men of factious tempers, of local prejudices, or of sinister designs, may, by intrigue, by corruption, or by other means, first obtain the suffrages, and then betray the interests of the people. The question resulting is, whether small or extensive republics are most favorable to the election of proper guardians of the public weal; and it is clearly decided in favor of the latter by two obvious considerations.

In the first place it is to be remarked that however small the republic may be the representatives must be raised to a certain number in order to guard against the cabals of a few; and that however large it may be they must be limited to a certain number in order to guard against the confusion of a multitude. Hence, the number of representatives in the two cases not being in proportion to that of the constituents, and being proportionally greatest in the small republic, it follows that if the proportion of fit characters be not less in the large than in the small republic, the former will present a greater option, and consequently a greater probability of a fit choice.

In the next place, as each representative will be chosen by a greater number of citizens in the large than in the small republic, it will be more difficult for unworthy candidates to practise with success the vicious arts by which elections are too often carried; and the suffrages of the people being more free, will be more likely to center on men who possess the most attractive merit and the most diffusive and established characters.

It must be confessed that in this, as in most other cases, there is a mean, on both sides of which inconveniencies will be found to lie. By enlarging too much the number of electors, you render the representative too little acquainted with all their local circumstances and lesser interests; as by reducing it too much, you render him unduly attached to these, and too little fit to comprehend and pursue great and national objects. The federal Constitution forms a happy combination in this respect; the great and aggregate interests being referred to the national, the local and particular to the State legislatures.

The other point of difference is the greater number of citizens and extent of territory which may be brought within the compass of republican than of democratic government; and it is this circumstance principally which renders factious combinations less to be dreaded in the former than in the latter. The smaller the society, the fewer probably will be the distinct parties and interests composing it; the fewer the distinct parties and interests, the most frequently will a majority be found of the same party; and the smaller the number of individuals composing a majority, and the smaller the compass within which they are placed, the more easily will they concert and execute their plans of oppression. Extend the sphere and you take in a greater variety of parties and interests; you make it less probable that a majority of the whole will have a common motive to invade the rights of other citizens; or if such a common motive exists; it will be more difficult for all who feel it to discover their own strength and to act in unison with each other. Besides other impediments, it may be remarked that, where there is a consciousness of unjust or dishonorable purposes, communication is always checked by distrust in proportion to the number whose concurrence is necessary.

Hence, it clearly appears that the same advantage which a republic has over a democracy in controlling the effects of faction is enjoyed by a large over a small republic—is enjoyed by the Union over the States composing it. Does this advantage consist in the substitution of representatives whose enlightened views and virtuous sentiments render them superior to local prejudices and to schemes of injustice? It will not be denied that the representation of the Union will be most likely to possess these requisite endowments. Does it consist in the greater security afforded by a greater variety of parties, against the event of any one party being able to outnumber and oppress the rest? In an equal degree does the increased variety of parties comprised within the Union increase this security. Does it, in fine, consist in the greater obstacles opposed to the concert and accomplishment of the secret wishes of an unjust and interested majority? Here again the extent of the Union gives it the most palpable advantage.

The influence of factious leaders may kindle a flame within their particular States but will be unable to spread a general conflagration through the other States. A religious sect may degenerate into a political faction in a part of the Confederacy; but the variety of sects dispersed over the entire face of it must secure the national councils against any danger from that source. A rage for paper money, for an abolition of debts, for an equal division of property, or for any other improper or wicked project, will be less apt to pervade the whole body of the Union than a particular member of it, in the same proportion as such a malady is more likely to taint a particular county or district than an entire State.

In the extent and proper structure of the Union, therefore, we behold a republican remedy for the diseases most incident to republican government. And according to the degree of pleasure and pride we feel in being republicans ought to be our zeal in cherishing the spirit and supporting the character of federalists.

"Happiness depends . . . much on the modes of government"

MERCY WARREN, A COLUMBIAN PATRIOT
1788

It wasn't until 1930 that family papers proved that the playwright, historian (three volumes on the War of Independence, with intimate comments on the important personages of the day), and Grumbletonian Mercy Otis Warren (1728–1814) was "A Columbian Patriot," who had argued heatedly against ratification of the Constitution, the "fraudulent usurpation" by a secret, dark cabal that would "draw blood from every pore by taxes, impositions, and illegal restrictions." Trading the Articles of Confederation for a new charter without a bill of rights was preposterous; the people didn't want thirteen pillars struck down in favor of one colossus. Mercy Warren's husband was a prominent anti-Federalist and the Speaker of the Massachusetts House of Representatives. A month after the Bay State convention ratified the Constitution (February 6, 1788), "A Columbian Patriot" published a nineteen-page pamphlet in Boston entitled "Observations on the New Constitution, and on the Federal and State Conventions."

THE PROPOSED CONSTITUTION appears contradictory to the first principles which ought to govern mankind; and it is equally so to enquire into the motives that induced to so bold a step as the annihilation of the independence and sovereignty of the thirteen distinct states.—They are but too obvious through the whole progress of the business, from the first shutting up the doors of the federal convention and resolving that no member should correspond with gentlemen in the different states on the subject under discussion; till the trivial proposition of *recommending* a few amendments was artfully ushered into the convention of the Massachusetts. The questions that were then before that honorable assembly were profound and important, they were of such magnitude and extent, that the consequences may run parallel with the existence of the country; and to see them waved and hastily terminated by a measure too absurd to require a serious refutation, raises the honest indignation of every true lover of his country. Nor are they less grieved that the ill policy and arbitrary disposition of some of the sons of America has thus precipitated to the contemplation and discussion of questions that no one could rationally suppose would have been agitated among us, till time had blotted out the principles on which the late revolution was grounded; or till the last traits of the many political tracts, which defended the seperation from Britain, and the rights of men were consigned to everlasting oblivion. After the severe conflicts this country has suffered, it is presumed that they are disposed to make every reasonable sacrifice before the altar of peace.— But when we contemplate the nature of men and consider them originally on an equal footing, subject to the same feelings, stimulated by the same passions, and recollecting the struggles they have recently made, for the security of their civil rights; it cannot be expected that the inhabitants of the Massachusetts, can be easily lulled into a fatal security, by the declamatory effusions of gentlemen, who, contrary to the experience of all ages would perswade them there is no danger to be apprehended, from vesting discretionary powers in the hands of man, which he may, or may not abuse. The very suggestion, that we ought to trust to the precarious hope of amendments and redress, after we have voluntarily fixed the shackles on our own necks should have awakened to a double degree of caution.—This people have not forgotten the artful insinuations of a former Governor, when pleading the unlimited authority of parliament before the legislature of the Massachusetts; nor that his arguments were very similar to some lately urged by gentlemen who boast of opposing his measure, *"with halters about their necks. . . ."*

The banners of freedom were erected in the wilds of America by our ancestors, while the wolf prowled for his prey on the one hand, and more savage man on the other; they have been since rescued from the invading hand of foreign power, by the valor and blood of their posterity; and there was reason to hope they would continue for ages to illumine a quarter of the globe, by nature kindly separated from the proud monarchies of Europe, and the infernal darkness of Asiatic slavery.—And it is to be feared we shall soon see this country rushing into the extremes of confusion and violence, in consequence of the proceedings of a set of gentlemen, who disregarding the purposes of their appointment, have assumed powers unauthorised by any commission, have unnecessarily rejected the confederation of the United States, and annihilated the sovereignty and independence of the individual governments.—The causes which have inspired a few men assembled for very different purposes with such a degree of temerity as to break with a single stroke the union of America, and disseminate the seeds of discord through the land may be easily investigated, when we survey the pa[r]tizans of monarchy in the state conventions, urging the adoption of a mode of government that militates with the former professions and exertions of this country, and with all ideas of republicanism, and the equal rights of men. . . .

It is presumed the great body of the people unite in sentiment with the writer of these observations, who most devoutly prays that public credit may rear her declining head, and remunerative justice pervade the land; nor is there a doubt if a free government is continued, that time and industry will enable both the public and private debtor to liquidate their arrearages in the most equitable manner. They wish to see the Confederated States bound together by the most indissoluble union, but without renouncing their separate sovereignties and independence, and becoming tributaries to a consolidated fabrick of aristocratick tyranny.—They wish to see government established, and peaceably holding the reins with honour, energy, and dignity; but they wish for no *federal city* whose *"cloud cap't towers"* may screen the state culprit from the hand of justice; while its exclusive jurisdiction may protect the riot of armies encamped within its limits.—They deprecate discord and civil convulsions, but they are not yet generally prepared with the ungrateful Israelites to ask a King, nor are their spirits sufficiently broken to yield the best of their olive grounds to his servants, and to see their sons appointed to run before his chariots—It has been observed by a zealous advocate for the new system, that most governments are the result of fraud or violence, and this with design to recommend its acceptance—but has not almost every step towards its fabrication been fraudulent in the extreme? Did not the prohibition strictly enjoined by the general Convention, that no member should make any communication to his Constituents, or to gentlemen of consideration and abilities in the other States, bear evident marks of fraudulent designs?—This circumstance is regretted in strong terms by Mr. Martin, a member from Maryland, who acknowledges "He had no idea that all the wisdom, integrity, and virtue of the States was contained in that Convention, and that he wished to have corresponded with gentlemen of eminent political characters abroad, and to give their sentiments due weight"—he adds, "so extremely solicitous were they, that their proceedings should not transpire, that the members were prohibited from taking copies of their resolutions, or extracts from the Journals, without express permission, by vote."—And the hurry with which it has been urged to the acceptance of the people, without giving time, by adjournments, for better information, and more unanimity has a deceptive appearance; and if finally driven to resistance, as the only alternative between that and servitude, till in the confusion of discord, the reins should be seized by the violence of some enterprizing genius, that may sweep down the last barrier of liberty, it must be added to the score of criminality with which the fraudulent usurpation at Philadelphia, may be chargeable.—Heaven avert such a tremendous scene! and let us still hope a more happy termination of the present ferment:—may the people be calm, and wait a legal redress; may the mad transport of some of our infatuated capitals subside; and every influential character through the States, make the most prudent exertions for a new general Convention, who may vest adequate powers in Congress, for all national purposes, without

annihilating the individual governments, and drawing blood from every pore by taxes, impositions and illegal restrictions.—This step might again re-establish the Union, restore tranquility to the ruffled mind of the inhabitants, and save America from distresses, dreadful even in contemplation. . . .

By the chicanery, intrigue, and false colouring of those who plume themselves, more on their education and abilities, than their political, patriotic, or private virtues—by the imbecility of some, and the duplicity of others, a majority of the Convention of Massachusetts have been flattered with the ideas of amendments, when it will be too late to complain—While several very worthy characters, too timid for their situation, magnified the hopeless alternative, between the dissolution of the bands of all government, and receiving the proffered system *in toto,* after long endeavouring to reconcile it to their consciences, swallowed the indigestible penacea, and in a kind of sudden desperation lent their signature to the dereliction of the honorable station they held in the Union, and have broken over the solemn compact, by which they were bound to support their own excellent constitution till the period of revision. . . .

The happiness of mankind depends much on the modes of government, and the virtues of the governors; and America may yet produce characters who have genius and capacity sufficient to form the manners and correct the morals of the people, and virtue enough to lead their country to freedom. Since her dismemberment from the British empire, America has, in many instances, resembled the conduct of a restless, vigorous, luxurious youth, prematurely emancipated from the authority of a parent, but without the experience necessary to direct him to act with dignity or discretion. Thus we have seen her break the shackles of foreign dominion, and all the blessings of peace restored on the most honourable terms: She acquired the liberty of framing her own laws, choosing her own magistrates, and adopting manners and modes of government the most favourable to the freedom and happiness of society. But how little have we availed ourselves of these superior advantages: The glorious fabric of liberty successfully reared with so much labour and assiduity totters to the foundation, and may be blown away as the bubble of fancy by the rude breath of military combinations, and politicians of yesterday.

It is true this country lately armed in opposition to regal despotism—impoverished by the expences of a long war, and unable immediately to fulfil their public or private engagements, have appeared in some instances, with a boldness of spirit that seemed to set at defiance all authority, government, or order, on the one hand; while on the other, there has been, not only a secret wish, but an open avowal of the necessity of drawing the reins of government much too taught, not only for republicanism, but for a wise and limited monarchy.—But the character of this people is not averse to a degree of subordination: the truth of this appears from the easy restoration of tranquility, after a dangerous insurrection in one of the states; this also evinces the little necessity of a complete revolution of government throughout the union. But it is a republican principle that the majority should rule; and if a spirit of moderation could be cultivated on both sides, till the voice of the people at large could be fairly heard it should be held sacred.—And if, on such a scrutiny, the proposed constitution should appear repugnant to their character and wishes; if they, in the language of a late elegant pen, should acknowledge that "no confusion in my mind, is more terrible to them than the stern disciplined regularity and vaunted police of arbitrary governments, where every heart is depraved by fear, where mankind dare not assume their natural characters, where the free spirit must crouch to the slave in office, where genius must repress her effusions, or like the Egyptian worshippers, offer them in sacrifice to the calves in power, and where the human mind, always in shackles, shrinks from every generous effort." Who would then have the effrontery to say, it ought not to be thrown out with indignation, however some respectable names have appeared to support it.—But if after all, on a dispassionate and fair discussion, the people generally give their voice for a voluntary dereliction of their privileges, let every individual who chooses the active scenes of life, strive to support the peace and unanimity of his country, though every other blessing may expire—And while the statesman is plodding for power, and the courtier practising the arts of dissimulation without check—while the rapacious are growing rich by oppression, and fortune throwing her gifts into the lap of fools, let the sublimer characters, the philosophic lovers of freedom who have wept over her exit, retire to the calm shades of contemplation, there they may look down with pity on the inconsistency of human nature, the revolutions of states, the rise of kingdoms, and the fall of empires.

Source: State Historical Society of Wisconsin and the Documentary History of the Ratification of the Constitution.

"Courts shall have power to issue writs"

THE JUDICIARY ACT
1789

The Constitution details and circumscribes the legislative and executive branches of the new government but sets out only the barest of outlines for the new judiciary: Article III, Section 1 vests the judicial power of the United States "in one Supreme Court, and in such inferior courts as the Congress may from time to time ordain and establish." In one of the most important enactments it has undertaken, Congress, in the first Judiciary Act, organized and laid out the composition of the judicial branch of the Federal government: a three-tiered hierarchical structure—the Supreme Court, circuit courts, district courts. There also would be federal judicial review over state legislation—an influential, far-reaching doctrine. More akin to a constitutive act (like constitutional amendments) than to ordinary legislation, the Act has been the enduring blueprint for America's judicial structure.

Section 1. *Be it enacted by the Senate and House of Representatives of the United States of America in Congress assembled,* that the Supreme Court of the United States shall consist of a chief justice and five associate justices, any four of whom shall be a quorum and shall hold annually at the seat of government two sessions: the one commencing the first Monday of February, and the other the first Monday of August. That the associate justices shall have precedence according to the date of their commissions, or when the commissions of two or more of them bear date on the same day according to their respective ages.

Section 2. *And be it further enacted,* that the United States shall be, and they hereby are, divided into thirteen districts. . . .

Section 3. *And be it further enacted,* that there be a court called a District Court in each of the aforementioned districts, to consist of one judge, who shall reside in the district for which he is appointed, and shall be called a district judge, and shall hold annually four sessions. . . .

Section 14. *And be it further enacted,* that all the beforementioned courts of the United States shall have power to issue writs of *scire facias,* habeas corpus, and all other writs not specially provided for by statute, which may be necessary for the exercise of their respective jurisdictions, and agreeable to the principles and usages of law. And that either of the justices of the Supreme Court, as well as judges of the district courts, shall have power to grant writs of habeas corpus for the purpose of an inquiry into the cause of commitment. *Provided,* that writs of habeas corpus shall in no case extend to prisoners in gaol, unless where they are in custody, under or by color of the authority of the United States, or are committed for trial before some court of the same, or are necessary to be brought into court to testify.

Section 17. *And be it further enacted,* that all the said courts of the United States shall have power to grant new trials in cases where there has been a trial by jury for reasons for which new trials have usually been granted in the courts of law; and shall have power to impose and administer all necessary oaths or affirmations, and to punish by fine or imprisonment, at the discretion of said courts, all contempts of authority in any case or hearing before the same; and to make and establish all necessary rules for the orderly conducting of business in the said courts, provided such rules are not repugnant to the laws. . . .

Section 29. *And be it further enacted,* that, in cases punishable with death, the trial shall be had in the county where the offense was committed, or where that cannot be done without great inconvenience, twelve petit jurors at least shall be summoned from thence. . . .

Section 30. *And be it further enacted,* that the mode of proof by oral testimony and examination of witnesses in open court shall be the same in all the courts of the United States, as well in the trial of cases in equity and of Admiralty and maritime jurisdiction, as of actions at common law. . . .

"A law repugnant to the Constitution is void"

MARBURY V. MADISON
1803

In this historic, fundamental decision, the Supreme Court applied the emergent doctrine of judicial review to a Congressional statute for the first time. John Marshall (1755–1835), Chief Justice of the United States, opined for the unanimous court of five Justices that the section of the Judiciary Act of 1789 under which William Marbury had brought suit for his district judgeship (he had been appointed by John Adams [1735–1826] in the last hours of the Adams Presidency but never officially commissioned) was unconstitutional. Only in certain special cases did the Supreme Court, according to the Constitution, have original jurisdiction; the Court could not help Marbury. For the first time an act of Congress was held to be unconstitutional. By declaring that the Court had the power of judicial review, and by establishing the power of the Court to declare Acts of Congress unconstitutional, Marshall extended the Court's authority by limiting it. (The "Madison" in Marbury v. Madison was James Madison [1751–1836], serving as President Thomas Jefferson's Secretary of State.)

• • • It is apparent that the framers of the Constitution contemplated that instrument as a rule for the government of *courts* as well as of the legislature.

Why, otherwise, does it direct the judges to take an oath to support it? This oath certainly applies, in an especial manner, to their conduct in their official character. How immoral to impose it on them if they were to be used as the instruments, and the knowing instruments, for violating what they swear to support!

The oath of office, too, imposed by the legislature is completely demonstrative of the legislative opinion on this subject. It is in these words:

I do solemnly swear that I will administer justice without respect to persons, and do equal right to the poor and to the rich; and that I will faithfully and impartially discharge all the duties incumbent on me as _____, according to the best of my abilities and understanding, agreeably to the Constitution and laws of the United States.

Why does a judge swear to discharge his duties agreeably to the Constitution of the United States if that Constitution forms no rule for his government? If it is closed upon him and cannot be inspected by him? If such be the real state of things, this is worse than solemn mockery. To prescribe, or to take this oath, becomes equally a crime.

It is also not entirely unworthy of observation that in declaring what shall be the supreme law of the land, the Constitution itself is first mentioned, and not the laws of the United States generally, but those only which shall be made in pursuance of the Constitution have that rank.

Thus, the particular phraseology of the Constitution of the United States confirms and strengthens the principle, supposed to be essential to all written constitutions, that a law repugnant to the Constitution is void and that courts, as well as other departments, are bound by that instrument.

E Pluribus Unum

By the 1783 Treaty of Paris, the boundaries of the new nation had been set. The Constitution of four years later coincided with the end of a serious post-Revolutionary economic depression; a vigorous economic and political life characterized the decade. Equally energetic, settlers moved over the plains and prairies and rolling foothills to the Rockies and the legendary Pacific, and greatly extended the territories of the United States. Jefferson, in his first inaugural, described the country as "a rising nation, spread over a wide and fertile land, advancing rapidly to destinies beyond the reach of mortal eye." The third President was certainly accurate. If the United States was born along the Eastern seaboard, it grew up moving West, cheap farmland being the chief lure. The first census in 1790 counted less than four-million people; the 1820 census, six years before Jefferson's death, counted ten-million—as restless Americans pushed rapidly over the Appalachians. When Jefferson spoke, in 1801, the nation was limited to 900,000 square miles; within three years, he had increased the country's area to 1,700,000 square miles with the purchase of Louisiana, which came after the Northwest Ordinance of 1787, one of the most enlightened measures in our history, and after 1791, the year Vermont entered the Union. With Jefferson's encouragement, explorers went across the Rockies, and within the lifetime of many people who had known Jefferson in their youth the country's size doubled again, with Texas, Florida, California, Oregon, and Alaska. Thus, within fifty years of Jefferson's death, the United States had become, second to Russia, the largest nation on the planet.

This breathtaking acquisition of new lands had a profound impact upon the national character. Not simply a frontier line, the West became a social process. It bred a spirit of local self-determination coupled with respect for national government. It helped shape the nation's identity, though the states carved out of the territories took on the governing structure of the settled states "back East." Improbably, the addition of Western territories, peoples, and government produced nationalistic rather than divisive impulses. Yet the West was also the venue for bitterly divisive conflict over the extension of slavery. Witness, for example, the opposition to Missouri's admission as a slave state, which threatened to destroy the delicate balance of power between the two sections. The controversy was "like a fire bell in the night," Jefferson declared. It "awakened and filled me with terror. I considered it at once as the knell of the Union." Compromise hushed the fire bell, but he knew it was "a reprieve only, not a final sentence."

Though the West spawned a spread-eagle nationalism, the result was, paradoxically, a greater pluralism than in the past, a heterogeneity reflected in language, politics, and social life. Individual liberty and toleration was a function of this openness unlike two centuries earlier when, with a few exceptions like Pennsylvania, an open society was dotted with closed enclaves. The Europeans who had come to America's shores in the 1600s were deeply *familiar with the denial of religious freedom in the homeland; the First Amendment in the Bill of Rights was the product of this legacy. It not only prohibited the Government from taking actions favoring one religion over another, it forbid assistance to any religion. The Northwest Ordinance and the 1819 treaty with Spain were among a host of documents that reflected this legacy.*

The variables in regional culture, politics, and society also had a down-side, which became more pronounced in the 1820s than it had forty years earlier. Northern and Southern sections developed distinctly different social and economic features, each hoping for support from the rapidly growing trans-Appalachian West. One section was plantation, the other farm; one was slave labor, the other free; one produced a landed aristocracy, the other lawyers and entrepreneurs; one grew increasingly conservative and fearful of change in the status quo, the other generated widespread social reforms, strange cults, and a great religious revival. The Northeast was undergoing constant and profound change owing to industrialization, urbanization, and, accompanying them, the rise of a wage-earning labor force. The emergence of this labor force produced deep fissures not only between the sections but within them as well. To the urban North came unskilled Irish Protestant labor and then, after 1846, the overwhelmingly-Catholic famine Irish, who triggered a Protestant nativist crusade against the Catholic newcomers. It warned of a Papist conspiracy and urged immigrant restrictionism. A rough parallel would appear a half century later, especially on the West coast, with the arrival of Chinese labor, who, it was feared, would not only take the jobs of Anglo-Saxon Protestants but also result in racial pollution.

And in yet another, even more profound example of the dark side of American history there was the fact of slavery, which also prompted anxieties about the mongrelization of the pure stock. The slave system, however, did more. Among other things, it produced a large defensive literature that rationalized human bondage by testifying to the inferiority of blacks and by affirming that God, nature, and history destined blacks to be slaves. An extensive set of measures buttressed these claims. They would restrict the slaves' freedom, frustrate their efforts to become freemen, and hedge in and control a potentially dangerous but immensely important workforce. The struggle over slavery became entangled with controversy raised by westward expansion. It was more than a conflict between very different sectional social and economic interests. There was a profound moral issue. Slavery itself gave the lie to the contention that men were born equal, that they were equal in the eyes of God and equal before the law. In sum, growing toleration could take the form of a majoritarian tolerance of racism and oppression—in both North and South—resulting in a passionate moral struggle that threatened the American Union.

"No person . . . shall ever be molested on account of his mode of worship or religious sentiments"

THE NORTHWEST ORDINANCE
1787

As the Constitutional Convention (1787) was dismantling the Articles of Confederation and drafting a new charter for the United States that would put the Confederation Congress out of business, Congress was recording its most significant achievement. The Northwest Ordinance led to the creation of five states (and a part of a sixth) in U.S. territory northwest of the Ohio River (states had ceded the land to the nation). The new states would share all powers of government equally with the original thirteen states. The Ordinance established an orderly procedure for surveying and selling land in the public domain and reserved part of the land for development of public education. It also banned slavery and put forth the first Federal bill of rights guaranteeing freedom of religion, speech, and press.

BE IT ORDAINED by the United States in Congress assembled, That the said territory, for the purposes of temporary government, be one district, subject, however, to be divided into two districts, as future circumstances may, in the opinion of Congress, make it expedient. . . .

Be it ordained by the authority aforesaid, That there shall be appointed from time to time by Congress, a governor, whose commission shall continue in force for the term of three years, unless sooner revoked by Congress; he shall reside in the district, and have a freehold estate therein in 1,000 acres of land, while in the exercise of his office.

There shall be appointed from time to time by Congress, a secretary, whose commission shall continue in force for four years unless sooner revoked; he shall reside in the district, and have a freehold estate therein in 500 acres of land, while in the exercise of his office. It shall be his duty to keep and preserve the acts and laws passed by the legislature, and the public records of the district, and the proceedings of the governor in his executive department, and transmit authentic copies of such acts and proceedings, every six months, to the Secretary of Congress: There shall also be appointed a court to consist of three judges, any two of whom to form a court, who shall have a common law jurisdiction, and reside in the district, and have each therein a freehold estate in 500 acres of land while in the exercise of their offices, and their commissions shall continue in force during good behavior.

The governor and judges, or a majority of them, shall adopt and publish in the district such laws of the original States, criminal and civil, as may be necessary and best suited to the circumstances of the district, and report them to Congress from time to time: which laws shall be in force in the district until the organization of the General Assembly therein, unless disapproved of by Congress; but afterwards the Legislature shall have authority to alter them as they shall think fit.

The governor, for the time being, shall be commander-in-chief of the militia, appoint and commission all officers in the same below the rank of general officers; all general officers shall be appointed and commissioned by Congress.

Previous to the organization of the general assembly, the governor shall appoint such magistrates and other civil officers in each county or township, as he shall find necessary for the preservation of the peace and good order in the same: After the general assembly shall be organized, the powers and duties of the magistrates and other civil officers shall be regulated and defined by the said assembly; but all magistrates and other civil officers not herein otherwise directed, shall, during the continuance of this temporary government, be appointed by the governor.

For the prevention of crimes and injuries, the laws to be adopted or made shall have force in all parts of the district, and for the execution of process, criminal and civil, the governor shall make proper divisions thereof; and he shall proceed from time to time as circumstances may require, to lay out the parts of the district in which the Indian titles shall have been extinguished, into counties and townships, subject however to such alterations as may thereafter be made by the legislature.

So soon as there shall be five thousand free male inhabitants of full age in the district, upon giving proof thereof to the governor, they shall receive authority, with time and place, to elect representatives from their counties or townships to represent them in the general assembly: Pro-

vided, That, for every five hundred free male inhabitants, there shall be one representative, and so on progressively with the number of free male inhabitants shall the right of representation increase, until the number of representatives shall amount to twenty-five; after which, the number and proportion of representatives shall be regulated by the legislature: *Provided,* That no person be eligible or qualified to act as a representative unless he shall have been a citizen of one of the United States three years, and be a resident in the district, or unless he shall have resided in the district three years; and, in either case, shall likewise hold in his own right, in fee simple, two hundred acres of land within the same: *Provided, also,* That a freehold in fifty acres of land in the district, having been a citizen of one of the states, and being resident in the district, or the like freehold and two years residence in the district, shall be necessary to qualify a man as an elector of a representative.

The representatives thus elected, shall serve for the term of two years; and, in case of the death of a representative, or removal from office, the governor shall issue a writ to the county or township for which he was a member, to elect another in his stead, to serve for the residue of the term.

The general assembly or legislature shall consist of the governor, legislative council, and a house of representatives. The Legislative Council shall consist of five members, to continue in office five years, unless sooner removed by Congress; any three of whom to be a quorum: and the members of the Council shall be nominated and appointed in the following manner, to wit: As soon as representatives shall be elected, the Governor shall appoint a time and place for them to meet together; and, when met, they shall nominate ten persons, residents in the district, and each possessed of a freehold in five hundred acres of land, and return their names to Congress; five of whom Congress shall appoint and commission to serve as aforesaid; and, whenever a vacancy shall happen in the council, by death or removal from office, the house of representatives shall nominate two persons, qualified as aforesaid, for each vacancy, and return their names to Congress; one of whom Congress shall appoint and commission for the residue of the term. And every five years, four months at least before the expiration of the time of service of the members of council, the said house shall nominate ten persons, qualified as aforesaid, and return their names to Congress; five of whom Congress shall appoint and commission to serve as members of the council five years, unless sooner removed. And the governor, legislative council, and house of representatives, shall have authority to make laws in all cases, for the good government of the district, not repugnant to the principles and articles in this ordinance established and declared. And all bills, having passed by a majority in the house, and by a majority in the council, shall be referred to the governor for his assent; but no bill, or legislative act whatever, shall be of any force without his assent. The governor shall have power to convene, prorogue, and dissolve the general assembly, when, in his opinion, it shall be expedient.

The governor, judges, legislative council, secretary, and such other officers as Congress shall appoint in the district, shall take an oath or affirmation of fidelity and of office; the governor before the president of congress, and all other officers before the Governor. As soon as a legislature shall be formed in the district, the council and house assembled in one room, shall have authority, by joint ballot, to elect a delegate to Congress, who shall have a seat in Congress, with a right of debating but not of voting during this temporary government.

And, for extending the fundamental principles of civil and religious liberty, which form the basis whereon these republics, their laws and constitutions are erected; to fix and establish those principles as the basis of all laws, constitutions, and governments, which forever hereafter shall be formed in the said territory: to provide also for the establishment of States, and permanent government therein, and for their admission to a share in the federal councils on an equal footing with the original States, at as early periods as may be consistent with the general interest:

It is hereby ordained and declared by the authority aforesaid, That the following articles shall be considered as articles of compact between the original States and the people and States in the said territory and forever remain unalterable, unless by common consent, to wit:

ART. 1. No person, demeaning himself in a peaceable and orderly manner, shall ever be molested on account of his mode of worship or religious sentiments, in the said territory.

ART. 2. The inhabitants of the said territory shall always be entitled to the benefits of the writ of *habeas corpus,* and of the trial by jury; of a proportionate representation of the people in the legislature; and of judicial proceedings according to the course of the common law. All persons shall be bailable, unless for capital offences, where the proof shall be evident or the presumption great. All fines shall be moderate; and no cruel or unusual punishments shall be inflicted. No man shall be deprived of his liberty or property, but by the judgment of his peers or the law of the land; and, should the public exigencies make it necessary, for the common preservation, to take any person's property, or to demand his particular services, full compensation shall be made for the same. And, in the just preservation of rights and property, it is understood and declared, that no law ought ever to be made, or have force in the said territory, that shall, in any manner whatever, interfere with or affect private contracts or engagements, *bona fide,* and without fraud, previously formed.

ART. 3. Religion, morality, and knowledge, being necessary to good government and the happiness of mankind, schools and the means of education shall forever be encouraged. The utmost good faith shall always be observed towards the Indians; their lands and property shall never be taken from them without their consent; and, in their property, rights, and liberty, they shall never be invaded or disturbed, unless in just and lawful wars authorized by Congress; but laws founded in justice and humanity, shall from time to time be made for preventing wrongs being done to them, and for preserving peace and friendship with them.

ART. 4. The said territory, and the States which may be formed therein, shall forever remain a part of this Confederacy of the United States of America, subject to the Articles of Confederation, and to such alterations therein as shall be constitutionally made; and to all the acts and ordinances of the United States in Congress assembled, conformable thereto. The inhabitants and settlers in the said territory shall be subject to pay a part of the federal debts contracted or to be contracted, and a proportional part of the expenses of government, to be apportioned on them by Congress according to the same common rule and measure by which apportionments thereof shall be made on the other States; and the taxes for paying their proportion shall be laid and levied by the authority and direction of the legislatures of the district or districts, or new States, as in the original States, within the time agreed upon by the United States in Congress assembled. The legislatures of those districts or new States, shall never interfere

with the primary disposal of the soil by the United States in Congress assembled, nor with any regulations Congress may find necessary for securing the title in such soil to the *bona fide* purchasers. No tax shall be imposed on lands the property of the United States; and, in no case, shall non-resident proprietors be taxed higher than residents. The navigable waters leading into the Mississippi and St. Lawrence, and the carrying places between the same, shall be common highways and forever free, as well to the inhabitants of the said territory as to the citizens of the United States, and those of any other States that may be admitted into the confederacy, without any tax, impost, or duty therefor.

ART. 5. There shall be formed in the said territory, not less than three nor more than five States; and the boundaries of the States, as soon as Virginia shall alter her act of cession, and consent to the same, shall become fixed and established as follows, to wit: The western State in the said territory, shall be bounded by the Mississippi, the Ohio, and Wabash Rivers; a direct line drawn from the Wabash and Post Vincents, due North, to the territorial line between the United States and Canada; and, by the said territorial line, to the Lake of the Woods and Mississippi. The middle State shall be bounded by the said direct line, the Wabash from Post Vincents to the Ohio, by the Ohio, by a direct line, drawn due north from the mouth of the Great Miami, to the said territorial line, and by the said territorial line. The eastern State shall be bounded by the last mentioned direct line, the Ohio, Pennsylvania, and the said territorial line: *Provided, however,* and it is further understood and declared, that the boundaries of these three States shall be subject so far to be altered, that, if Congress shall hereafter find it expedient, they shall have authority to form one or two States in that part of the said territory which lies north of an east and west line drawn through the southerly bend or extreme of lake Michigan. And, whenever any of the said States shall have sixty thousand free inhabitants therein, such State shall be admitted, by its delegates, into the Congress of the United States, on an equal footing with the original States in all respects whatever, and shall be at liberty to form a permanent constitution and State government: *Provided,* the constitution and government so to be formed, shall be republican, and in conformity to the principles contained in these articles; and, so far as it can be consistent with the general interest of the confederacy, such admission shall be allowed at an earlier period, and when there may be a less number of free inhabitants in the State than sixty thousand.

ART. 6. There shall be neither slavery nor involuntary servitude in the said territory, otherwise than in the punishment of crimes whereof the party shall have been duly convicted: *Provided, always,* That any person escaping into the same, from whom labor or service is lawfully claimed in any one of the original States, such fugitive may be lawfully reclaimed and conveyed to the person claiming his or her labor or service as aforesaid.

Be it ordained by the authority aforesaid, That the resolutions of the 23rd of April 1784, relative to the subject of this ordinance, be, and the same are hereby repealed and declared null and void.

"A new and entire member of the United States of America"

VERMONT ADOPTS THE CONSTITUTION
1791

Article IV of the Constitution establishes procedures, but no hard and fast require-ments, for creating new states as equal parts of the Union with the original thirteen states—equal in power, dignity, and authority. Admission to the Union is on a state-by-state basis: "New States may be admitted by the Congress into this Union; but no new State shall be formed or erected within the jurisdiction of any other State; nor any State be formed by the junction of two or more States, or parts of States, without the consent of the legislatures of the States concerned, as well as of the Congress." Article IV requires the Federal government to protect all states against invasion. Less than two years after George Washington (1732–1799) was sworn as first President, the first state beyond the original thirteen was admitted. For fourteen years, green-mountained Vermont had governed itself as an independent republic, coining money, carrying on foreign trade, running a postal service, maintaining a militia, and abolishing slavery. Congress admitted Vermont after the states of Massachusetts (in 1781), New Hamp-shire (1782), and New York (1790) had surrendered claims to any territory in Ver-mont.

In Convention of the Delegates of the People of the State of Vermont.

Whereas, by an Act of the Commissioners of the State of New York, done at New York, the Seventh day of October, in the fifteenth year of the Independence of the United States of Amer-ica, one thousand seven hundred and ninety, every impediment, as well on the part of the State of New York, as on the part of the State of Vermont, to the admission of the State of Ver-mont into the Union of the United States of America, is removed;—In full faith and assur-ance that the same will stand approved and rati-fied by Congress;—

This Convention, having impartially deliber-ated upon the Constitution of the United States of America, as now established, submitted to us by an Act of the General Assembly of the State of Vermont passed October the twenty seventh one thousand seven hundred and ninety, DO, in virtue of the power and authority to us given, for that purpose, fully and entirely approve of, as-sent to, and ratify the said Constitution; and de-clare that immediately from, and after, this state shall be admitted by the Congress into the Union, and to a full participation of the benefits of the government now enjoyed by the states in the Union, the same shall be binding on us and the people of the State of Vermont forever.

Done at Bennington, in the County of Bennington, the tenth day of January, in the 15. year of the Independence of the United States of America, one thousand seven hundred and ninety one.—In testimony whereof we have hereunto subscribed our Names—

THOS. CHITTENDEN,
President,

MOSES ROBINSON,
Vice President

State of Vermont fr. Bennington Jany 10th 1791

The foregoing ratification was agreed to, and signed by one hundred and five, and dissented to, by four, which is a majority of one hundred and one.

THOS. CHITTENDEN,
President

ATTEST, ROSL. HOPKINS,
Sec^y of Convention

STATE OF VERMONT

In Convention Bennington Jany 10th 1791

Resolved (the Governor of this State being President) that the Vice President be and hereby is directed to transmit to his Excellency the Governor Duplicates of the act of this Convention ratifying the Constitution of the United States of America to be by him transmitted to the President of the United States and the Legislature of this State.

ATTEST, ROSL. HOPKINS, *Sec^y*

CONGRESS OF THE UNITED STATES

At the Third Session,

Begun and held at the City of Philadelphia, on Monday the fifth of December, one thousand seven hundred and ninety.

An ACT for the Admission of the State of Vermont into this Union.

THE State of Vermont having petitioned the Congress to be admitted a member of the United States, Be it enacted by the SENATE and HOUSE OF REPRESENTATIVES of the United States of America in Congress assembled, and it is hereby enacted and declared, That on the fourth day of March, one thousand seven hundred and ninety-one, the said State, by the name and title of "the State of Vermont," shall be received and admitted into the Union, as a new and entire member of the United States of America.

FREDERICK AUGUSTUS MUHLENBERG,
Speaker of the House of Representatives.

JOHN ADAMS,
Vice-President of the United States, and President of the Senate

APPROVED, February the eighteenth, 1791

GEORGE WASHINGTON,
President of the United States

"A strong proof of . . . friendship"

THE LOUISIANA PURCHASE
1803

It was the greatest real estate deal in history: the Louisiana Purchase nearly doubled the size of the United States, and precluded British, English, and Russian influence in the west. President Thomas Jefferson (1743–1826) had originally planned to buy only the Isle of Orleans, that is, New Orleans and West Florida, from France to help farmers shipping through the Gulf of Mexico to East Coast ports and to Europe. But French Emperor Napoleon (1769–1821) unexpectedly offered to sell the Louisiana Territory, which Spain had secretly retroceded to France. Recognizing that it couldn't hang on to such vast lands far across the ocean, France preferred that the United States, rather than its bitter-enemy, Great Britain, take possession. After Jefferson cast "metaphysical subtleties" behind him, deciding that a Constitutional amendment was not necessary for the purchase, the U.S. seized the opportunity: only $15-million for 883,072 square miles of land west of the Mississippi River—from the Mississippi to the Rocky Mountains, from the Gulf of Mexico to the Canadian border—an area seven times larger than England, Scotland, and Ireland combined, or the areas of France, Germany, Italy, Spain, and Portugal combined. Jefferson got what he wanted, land and empire. "Let the Land rejoice, for you have bought Louisiana for a Song," U.S. General Horatio Gates (c.1727–1806) wrote to the President.

The President of the United States of America, and the First Consul of the French Republic, in the name of the French people, desiring to remove all source of misunderstanding relative to objects of discussion mentioned in the second and fifth articles of the convention of the 8th Vendémiaire, an 9 (30th September, 1800) relative to the rights claimed by the United States, in virtue of the treaty concluded at Madrid, the 27th of October, 1795, between his Catholic Majesty and the said United States, and willing to strengthen the union and friendship which at the time of the said convention was happily reestablished between the two nations, have respectively named their Plenipotentiaries, to wit: the President of the United States, by and with the advice and consent of the Senate of the said States, Robert R. Livingston, Minister Plenipotentiary of the United States, and James Monroe, Minister Plenipotentiary and Envoy Extraordinary of the said States, near the Government of the French Republic; and the First Consul, in the name of the French people, Citizen Francis Barbé Marbois, Minister of the Public Treasury; who, after having respectively exchanged their full powers, have agreed to the following articles:

ARTICLE I.

Whereas by the article the third of the treaty concluded at St. Idelfonso, the 9th Vendemiaire, an 9 (1st October, 1800,) between the First Consul of the French Republic and His Catholic Majesty, it was agreed as follows: "His Catholic Majesty promises and engages on his part, to cede to the French Republic, six months after the full and entire execution of the conditions and stipulations herein relative to His Royal Highness the Duke of Parma, the colony or province of Louisiana, with the same extent that it now has in the hands of Spain, and that it had when France possessed it, and such as it should be after the treaties subsequently entered into between Spain and other States." And whereas, in pursuance of the treaty, and particularly of the third article, the French Republic has an incontestable title to the domain and to the possession of the said territory: The First Consul of the French Republic desiring to give to the United States a strong proof of his friendship, doth hereby cede to the said United States, in the name of the French Republic, forever and in full sovereignty, the said territory, with all its rights and appurtenances, as fully and in the same manner as they have been acquired by the French Republic, in virtue of the above-mentioned treaty, concluded with His Catholic Majesty.

ARTICLE II.

In the cession made by the preceding article are included the adjacent islands belonging to Louisiana, all public lots and squares, vacant lands, and all public buildings, fortifications, barracks, and other edifices which are not private property. The archives, papers, and documents, relative to the domain and sovereignty of Louisiana and its dependences, will be left in the possession of the commissaries of the United States, and copies will be afterwards given in due form to the magistrates and municipal officers of such of the said papers and documents as may be necessary to them.

ARTICLE III.

The inhabitants of the ceded territory shall be incorporated in the Union of the United States, and admitted as soon as possible, according to the principles of the Federal constitution, to the enjoyment of all the rights, advantages, and immunities of citizens of the United States; and in the mean time they shall be maintained and protected in the free enjoyment of their liberty, property, and the religion which they profess.

ARTICLE IV.

There shall be sent by the Government of France a commissary to Louisiana, to the end that he do every act necessary, as well to receive from the officers of His Catholic Majesty the said country and its dependences, in the name of the French Republic, if it has not been already done, as to transmit it in the name of the French Republic to the commissary or agent of the United States.

ARTICLE V.

Immediately after the ratification of the present treaty by the President of the United States, and in case that of the First Consul shall have been previously obtained, the commissary of the French Republic shall remit all military posts of New Orleans, and other parts of the ceded territory, to the commissary or commissaries named by the President to take possession; the troops, whether of France or Spain, who may be there, shall cease to occupy any military post from the time of taking possession, and shall be embarked as soon as possible, in the course of three months after the ratification of this treaty.

ARTICLE VI.

The United States promise to execute such treaties and articles as may have been agreed between Spain and the tribes and nations of Indians, until, by mutual consent of the United States and the said tribes or nations, other suitable articles shall have been agreed upon.

ARTICLE VII.

As it is reciprocally advantageous to the commerce of France and the United States to encourage the communication of both nations for a limited time in the country ceded by the present treaty, until general arrangements relative to the commerce of both nations may be agreed on; it has been agreed between the contracting parties, that the French ships coming directly from France or any of her colonies, loaded only with the produce and manufactures of France or her said colonies: and the ships of Spain coming directly from Spain or any of her colonies, loaded only with the produce or manufactures of Spain or her colonies, shall be admitted during the space of twelve years in the port of New Orleans, and in all other legal ports of entry within the ceded territory, in the same manner as the ships of the United States coming directly from France or Spain, or any of their colonies, without being subject to any other or greater duty on merchandise, or other or greater tonnage than that paid by the citizens of the United States.

During the space of time above mentioned, no other nation shall have a right to the same privileges in the ports of the ceded territory; the twelve years shall commence three months after the exchange of ratifications, if it shall take place in France, or three months after it shall have been notified at Paris to the French Government, if it shall take place in the United States; it is however

well understood that the object of the above article is to favor the manufactures, commerce, freight, and navigation of France and of Spain, so far as relates to the importations that the French and Spanish shall make into the said ports of the United States, without in any sort affecting the regulations that the United States may make concerning the exportation of the produce and merchandise of the United States, or any right they may have to make such regulations.

ARTICLE VIII.

In future and forever after the expiration of the twelve years, the ships of France shall be treated upon the footing of the most favored nations in the ports above mentioned.

ARTICLE IX.

The particular convention signed this day by the respective ministers, having for its object to provide for the payment of debts due to the citizens of the United States by the French Republic prior to the 30th Septr., 1800, (8th Vendémiaire, an 9,) is approved, and to have its execution in the same manner as if it had been inserted in this present treaty; and it shall be ratified in the same form and in the same time, so that the one shall not be ratified distinct from the other.

Another particular convention signed at the same date as the present treaty relative to a definitive rule between the contracting parties is in the like manner approved, and will be ratified in the same form, and in the same time, and jointly.

ARTICLE X.

The present treaty shall be ratified in good and due form and the ratifications shall be exchanged in the space of six months after the date of the signature by the Ministers Plenipotentiary, or sooner if possible.

In faith whereof, the respective Plenipotentiaries have signed these articles in the French and English languages; declaring nevertheless that the present treaty was originally agreed to in the French language; and have thereunto affixed their seals.

"An ample journal . . . must afford much intelligence"

LEWIS & CLARK

1806

Until astronauts first walked on the Moon, in 1969, America's most spectacular odyssey was the two-year Lewis and Clark expedition into the unexplored American northwest. With a secret Congressional grant of $2,500, the soldier Meriwether Lewis (1774–1809), who had been President Thomas Jefferson's private secretary for two years (he was tutored geographically and scientifically by the President), the land-holding William Clark (1770–1838), and their party of 30-odd men boldly went where no U.S. citizen had been before. Armed with the best cartographic concepts of the western portion of North America, they paddled north from St. Louis "under a jentle brease up the Missouri" and hiked across the just-purchased Louisiana Territory, over the Rocky Mountains, to the Pacific Ocean—and back again—for the purpose of commerce. With the loss of only one man (ruptured appendix) the Corps of Discovery was a triumph and set the stage for the westward expansion of the United States. Lewis and Clark discovered 24 Indian tribes (with whom they showed an unmatched record of decency), 178 plants, and 122 animals previously unknown to Americans back east. Intelligence, critics agreed, was the principal reason that the unprecedented adventure was successful. Because the commanders were unable to make a post-odyssey report, their illustrated journals became their official report to the President.

A letter from St. Louis (Upper Louisiana), dated Sept. 23, 1806, announced the arrival of Captains Lewis and Clark, from their expedition into the interior.

They went to the Pacific Ocean, have brought some of the natives and curiosities of the countries through which they paddled, and only lost one man. They left the Pacific Ocean 23d March, 1806, where they arrived in November, 1805;—and where some Americans had been just before.—They state the Indians to be as numerous on the Columbia river, which empties into the Pacific, as the whites in any part of the U.S. They brought a family of the Mandan Indians with them. The winter was very mild on the Pacific.—They have kept an ample journal of their tour, which will be published, and must afford much intelligence.

———

Here we remained during the day, the wind having risen at twelve so high that we could not proceed. It continued to blow violently all night, with occasional springklings of rain from sunset till midnight. On both sides of the river the country is rough and broken, the low grounds becoming narrower; the tops of the hills on the north exhibits some scattered pine and cedar, on the south the pine has not yet commenced, though there is some cedar on the sides of the hills and in the little ravines. The chokecherry, the wild hyssop, sage, fleshy-leafed thorn, and particularly the aromatic herb on which the antelope and hare feed, are to be found on the plains and hills. The soil of the hills has now altered its texture considerably: their bases, like that of the river plains, is as usual a rich, black loam, while from the middle to the summits they are composed of a light brown-coloured earth, poor and sterile, and intermixed with a coarse white sand.

"Free exercise of their religion"

ADAMS-ONIS TREATY: U.S. TITLE TO THE FLORIDAS
1819

Spanish explorers, thirsting for the legendary fountain of youth, scouted the Florida peninsula as early as 1513. Legal ownership of the region passed from Spain to Great Britain in 1763. Twenty years later, Florida passed back to Spain under the Treaty of Paris. By the 1810s, Spain realized that it no longer could defend or maintain control of the territory, some 3,000 miles across the Atlantic. In 1819, Spain ceded the territory to the expansive United States, ending "all differences and pretensions." The U.S. treaty negotiator was the ardent nationalist Secretary of State John Quincy Adams (1767–1848). The Spanish negotiator was Ambassador Luis de Onis (1762–1827). Three years later, in 1822, President James Monroe (1758–1831) directed General Andrew Jackson (1767–1845) to organize a territorial government. Jackson had twice (1814, 1818) led military campaigns to quell disturbances in the Spanish territory. Florida had become a refuge for runaway slaves and a base for Indian (Seminole) attacks on new settlers. Jackson provided the leadership allowing for the creation of a civil government which divided Florida into two counties (Escambia and St. Johns) and established a court system with five justices in each county. To preserve the balance between free and slave states, Florida (a slave state) was not admitted to the Union until March 4, 1845, when Iowa (a free territory) applied for statehood.

The United States of America and his Catholic Majesty, desiring to consolidate, on a permanent basis, the friendship and good correspondence which happily prevails between the two parties, have determined to settle and terminate all their differences and pretensions, by a Treaty, which shall designate, with precision, the limits of their respective bordering territories in North America.

ARTICLE I.

There shall be a firm and inviolable peace and sincere friendship between the United States and their citizens, and his Catholic Majesty, his suc-cessors and subjects, without exception of persons or places.

ARTICLE II.

His Catholic Majesty cedes to the United States, in full property and sovereignty, all the territories which belong to him, situated to the eastward of the Mississippi, known by the name of East and West Florida. The adjacent islands dependent on said provinces, all public lots and squares, vacant lands, public edifices, fortifications, barracks, and other buildings, which are not private property, archives and documents, which relate directly to the property and sovereignty of the said provinces, are included in this article.

ARTICLE III.

The boundary line between the two countries, west of the Mississippi, shall begin on the Gulf of Mexico, at the mouth of the river Sabine, in the sea, continuing north along the western bank of that river, to the 32d degree of latitude; thence, by a line due north, to the degree of latitude where it strikes the Rio Roxo of Nachitoches, or Red River; then following the course of the Rio Roxo westward, to the degree of longitude 100 west from London and 23 from Washington; then crossing the said Red River, and running thence, by a line due north to the river Arkansas; thence, following the course of the southern bank of the Arkansas, to its source, in latitude 42 north; and thence, by that parallel of latitude, to the South Sea, The whole being, as laid down in Melish's map of the United States, published at Philadelphia, improved to the first of January, 1818. But, if the source of the Arkansas River shall be found to fall north or south of latitude 42, then the line shall run from the said source due south or north, as the case may be, till it meets the said parallel of latitude 42, and thence, along the said parallel, to the South Sea: All the islands in the Sabine, and the said Red and Arkansas rivers, throughout the course thus described, to belong to the United States; but the use of the waters, and the navigation of the Sabine to the sea, and of the said rivers Roxo and Arkansas, throughout the extent of the said boundary, on their respective banks, shall be common to the respective inhabitants of both nations.

The two high contracting parties agree to cede and renounce all their rights, claims, and pretensions, to the territories prescribed by the said line; that is to say, the United States cede to his Catholic Majesty, and renounce forever, all their rights, claims, and pretensions to the territories lying west and south of the above-described line; and, in like manner, his Catholic Majesty cedes to the said United States, all his rights, claims, and pretensions, to any territories east and north of the said line; and for himself, his heirs, and successors, renounces all claim to the said territories forever.

ARTICLE IV.

To fix this line with more precision, and to place the landmarks which shall designate exactly the limits of both nations, each of the contracting parties shall appoint a Commissioner and a Surveyor, who shall meet before the termination of one year, from the date of the ratification of this treaty, at Nachitoches, on the Red River, and proceed to run and mark the said line, from the mouth of the Sabine to the Red River, and from the Red River to the river Arkansas, and to ascertain the latitude of the source of the said river Arkansas, in conformity to what is above agreed upon and stipulated, and the line of latitude 42, to the South Sea; they shall make out plans, and keep journals of their proceedings, and the result agreed upon by them shall be considered as part of this treaty, and shall have the same force as if it were inserted therein. . . .

ARTICLE V.

The inhabitants of the ceded territories shall be secured in the free exercise of their religion, without any restriction; and all those who may desire to remove to the Spanish dominions, shall be permitted to sell or export their effects, at any time whatever, without being subject, in either case, to duties.

ARTICLE VI.

The inhabitants of the territories which his Catholic Majesty cedes to the United States, by this Treaty, shall be incorporated in the Union of the United States, as soon as may be consistent with the principles of the Federal Constitution, and admitted to the enjoyment of all the privileges, rights, and immunities, of the citizens of the United States.

ARTICLE VII.

The officers and troops of his Catholic Majesty, in the territories hereby ceded by him to the United States, shall be withdrawn, and possession of the places occupied by them shall be given within six months after the exchange of the ratifications of this Treaty, or sooner, if possible, by the officers of his Catholic Majesty, to the commissioners or officers of the United States, duly appointed to receive them; and the United States shall furnish the transports and escort necessary to convey the Spanish officers and troops, and their baggage, to the Havana.

ARTICLE VIII.

All the grants of land made before the 24th of January, 1818, by his Catholic Majesty, or by his lawful authorities, in the said territories ceded by his Majesty to the United States, shall be ratified and confirmed to the persons in possession of the lands, to the same extent that the same grants would be valid if the territories had remained under the dominion of his Catholic Majesty. But the owners in possession of such lands, who, by reason of the recent circumstances of the Spanish nation, and the revolutions in Europe, have been prevented from fulfilling all the conditions of their grants, shall complete them within the terms limited in the same, respectively, from the date of this treaty; in default of which, the said grants shall be null and void. All grants made since the said 24th of January, 1818, when the first proposal, on the part of his Catholic Majesty, for the cession of the Floridas, was made, are hereby declared, and agreed to be, null and void.

ARTICLE IX.

The two high contracting parties, animated with the most earnest desire of conciliation, and with the object of putting an end to all the differences which have existed between them, and of confirming the good understanding which they wish to be forever maintained between them, reciprocally renounce all claims for damages or injuries which they, themselves, as well as their respective citizens and subjects, may have suffered until the time of signing this Treaty. . . .

The United States will cause satisfaction to be made for the injuries, if any, which, by process of law, shall be established to have been suffered by the Spanish officers, and individual Spanish inhabitants, by the late operations of the American army in Florida.

ARTICLE XI.

The United States, exeronerating Spain from all demands in future, on account of the claims of their citizens to which the renunciations herein contained extend, and considering them entirely cancelled, undertake to make satisfaction for the same, to an amount not exceeding five millions of dollars.

ARTICLE XII.

With respect to the 15th article of the same Treaty of Friendship, Limits, and Navigation, of

1795, in which it is stipulated that the flag shall cover the property, the two high contracting parties agree that this shall be so understood with respect to those powers who recognize this principle; but, if either of the two contracting parties shall be at war with a third party, and the other neutral, the flag of the neutral shall cover the property of enemies whose government acknowledges this principle, and not of others.

ARTICLE XIII.

Both contracting parties, wishing to favor their mutual commerce, by affording in their ports every necessary assistance to their respective merchant vessels, have agreed, that the sailors who shall desert from their vessels in the ports of the other, shall be arrested and delivered up, at the instance of the consul, who shall prove, nevertheless, that the deserters belonged to the vessels that claim them, exhibiting the document that is customary in their nation; that is to say, the American consul in a Spanish port, shall exhibit the document known by the name of articles; and the Spanish consul in American ports, the roll of the vessel; and if the name of the deserter or deserters, who are claimed, shall appear in the one or the other, they shall be arrested, held in custody, and delivered to the vessel to which they shall belong.

ARTICLE XIV.

The United States hereby certify that they have not received any compensation from France, for the injuries they suffered from her privateers, consuls, and tribunals, on the coasts and in the ports of Spain, for the satisfaction of which provision is made by this Treaty; and they will present an authentic statement of the prizes made, and of their true value, that Spain may avail herself of the same, in such manner as she may deem just and proper.

ARTICLE XV.

The United States, to give to his Catholic Majesty a proof of their desire to cement the relations of amity subsisting between the two nations, and to favor the commerce of the subjects of his Catholic Majesty, agree that Spanish vessels, coming laden only with productions of Spanish growth or manufacture, directly from the ports of Spain, or of her colonies, shall be admitted, for the term of twelve years, to the ports of Pensacola and St. Augustine, in the Florida, without paying other or higher duties on their cargoes, or of tonnage, than will be paid by the vessels of the United States. During the said term, no other nation shall enjoy the same privileges within the ceded Territories. . . .

"Such fugitive may be . . . reclaimed"

THE MISSOURI COMPROMISE
1820

In 1819, when there were eleven slave states and eleven free states, the territory of Missouri, acquired by the United States in the Louisiana Purchase (1803), applied for admission to the Union as a slave state. This would result in changing the balance of Senatorial voting in favor of slavery. What if it were admitted as a free state! The bitterly debated Missouri Enabling Act, or Missouri Compromise, revealed the deep division in the nation over the issue of slavery. Missouri would be admitted as a slave state. Maine (once part of Massachusetts) would come in as a free state. Slavery would be prohibited in the remaining parts of the Louisiana Territory above 36°30´, the southern boundary of Missouri. To former President Thomas Jefferson (1743–1826), the Compromise was "like a firebell in the night . . . I considered it at once as the knell of the Union. It is hushed, indeed, for the moment. But this is a reprieve only, not a final sentence. A geographical line, coinciding with a marked principle, moral and political, once conceived and held up to the angry passions of men, will never be obliterated; and every new irritation will mark it deeper and deeper." To John Quincy Adams (1767–1848), President James Monroe's Secretary of State, the present was "mere preamble—a title page to a great, tragic volume."

Be it enacted by the Senate and House of Representatives of the United States of America, in Congress assembled, That the inhabitants of that portion of the Missouri territory included within the boundaries hereinafter designated, be, and they are hereby, authorized to form for themselves a constitution and state government, and to assume such name as they shall deem proper; and the said state, when formed, shall be admitted into the Union, upon an equal footing with the original states, in all respects whatsoever.

SEC. 2. *And be it further enacted,* That the said state shall consist of all the territory included within the following boundaries, to wit: Beginning in the middle of the Mississippi river, on the parallel of thirty-six degrees of north latitude; thence west, along that parallel of latitude, to the St. Francois river; thence up, and following the course of that river, in the middle of the main channel thereof, to the parallel of latitude of thirty-six degrees and thirty minutes; thence west, along the same, to a point where the said parallel is intersected by a meridian line passing through the middle of the mouth of the Kansas river, where the same empties into the Missouri river, thence, from the point aforesaid north, along the said meridian line, to the intersection of the parallel of latitude which passes through the rapids of the river Des Moines, making the said line to correspond with the Indian boundary line; thence east, from the point of intersection last aforesaid, along the said parallel of latitude, to the middle of the channel of the main fork of the said river Des Moines; thence down and along the middle of the main channel of the said river Des Moines, to the mouth of the same, where it empties into the Mississippi river; thence, due east, to the middle of the main channel of the Mississippi river; thence down, and following the course of the Mississippi river, in the middle of the main channel thereof, to the place of beginning: *Provided,* The said state shall ratify the boundaries aforesaid; *And provided also,* That the said state shall have concurrent jurisdiction on the river Mississippi, and every other river bordering on the said state, so far as the said rivers shall form a common boundary to the said state; and any other state or states, now or hereafter to be formed and bounded by the same, such rivers to be common to both; and that the river Mississippi, and the navigable rivers and waters leading into the same, shall be common highways, and for ever free, as well to the inhabitants of the said state as to other citizens of the United States, without any tax, duty, impost, or toll, therefor, imposed by the said state.

SEC. 4. *And be it further enacted,* That the members of the convention thus duly elected, shall be, and they are hereby authorized to meet at the seat of government of said territory on the second Monday of the month of June next; and the said convention, when so assembled, shall have power and authority to adjourn to any other place in the said territory, which to them shall seem best for the convenient transaction of their business; and which convention, when so met, shall first determine by a majority of the whole number elected, whether it be, or be not,

expedient at that time to form a constitution and state government for the people within the said territory, as included within the boundaries above designated. . . .

SEC. 5. *And be it further enacted,* That until the next general census shall be taken, the said state shall be entitled to one representative in the House of Representatives of the United States.

Second. That all salt springs, not exceeding twelve in number, with six sections of land adjoining to each, shall be granted to the said state for the use of said state. . . .

Fifth. That thirty-six sections, or one entire township, which shall be designated by the President of the United States, together with the other lands heretofore reserved for that purpose, shall be reserved for the use of a seminary of learning, and vested in the legislature of said state, to be appropriated solely to the use of such seminary by the said legislature. . . .

SEC. 8. *And be it further enacted,* That in all that territory ceded by France to the United States, under the name of Louisiana, which lies north of thirty-six degrees and thirty minutes north latitude, not included within the limits of the state, contemplated by this act, slavery and involuntary servitude, otherwise than in the punishment of crimes, whereof the parties shall have been duly convicted, shall be, and is hereby, forever prohibited: *Provided always,* That any person escaping into the same, from whom labour or service is lawfully claimed, in any state or territory of the United States, such fugitive may be lawfully reclaimed and conveyed to the person claiming his or her labour or service as aforesaid.

"Said State to be formed"

THE U.S. ANNEXES TEXAS
1845

Fifteen years after Mexico had gained independence from Spain (Texas was Mexican territory) and two months after Texans under Sam Houston (1793–1863) had revenged Mexican General Santa Anna's massacre at the San Antonio mission ("Remember the Alamo"), Texas gained its independence from Mexico and was recognized as a republic by the United States. In the 1844 Presidential campaign, the first dark-horse candidate, the Democratic expansionist James K. Polk (1795–1849), called for annexing Texas. Three days before Polk was sworn as the eleventh President, a joint resolution of Congress consented to Texas's admission into the Union as the twenty-eighth, and a slave, state— the only internationally recognized nation ever to enter the Union. In his inaugural, Polk declared that foreign powers should look on the annexation of Texas not as the conquest of a nation seeking to extend its dominions by arms and violence but as the peaceful acquisition of a territory once its own, by adding another member to the confederation with the consent of that member, thereby diminishing the chances of war and opening new and ever increasing markets for their products: "To Texas the reunion is important because the strong protecting arm of our government would be extended over her, and the vast resources of her fertile soil and genial climate would be speedily developed. . ."

Resolved by the Senate and House of Representatives of the United States of America in Congress assembled, That Congress doth consent that the territory properly included within, and rightfully belonging to the Republic of Texas, may be erected into a new State, to be called the State of Texas, with a republican form of government, to be adopted by the people of said republic, by deputies in convention assembled, with the consent of the existing government, in order that the same may be admitted as one of the States of this Union.

2. *And be it further resolved,* That the foregoing consent of Congress is given upon the following conditions, and with the following guarantees, to wit: *First,* Said State to be formed, subject to the adjustment by this government of all questions of boundary that may arise with other governments; and the constitution thereof, with the proper evidence of its adoption by the people of said Republic of Texas, shall be transmitted to the President of the United States, to be laid before Congress for its final action, on or before the first day of January, one thousand eight hundred and forty-six. *Second.* Said State, when admitted into the Union, after ceding to the United States, all public edifices, fortifications, barracks, ports and harbors, navy and navy-yards, docks, magazines, arms, armaments, and all other property and means pertaining to the public defence belonging to said Republic of Texas, shall retain all the public funds, debts, taxes, and dues of every kind,

which may belong to or be due and owing said republic; and shall also retain all the vacant and unappropriated lands lying within its limits, to be applied to the payment of the debts and liabilities of said Republic of Texas, and the residue of said lands, after discharging said debts and liabilities, to be disposed of as said State may direct; but in no event are said debts and liabilities to become a charge upon the Government of the United States. *Third.* New States, of convenient size, not exceeding four in number, in addition to said State of Texas, and having sufficient population, may hereafter, by the consent of said State, be formed out of the territory thereof, which shall be entitled to admission under the provisions of the federal constitution. And such States as may be formed out of that portion of said territory lying south of thirty-six degrees thirty minutes north latitude, commonly known as the Missouri compromise line, shall be admitted into the Union with or without slavery, as the people of each State asking admission may desire. And in such State or States as shall be formed out of said territory north of said Missouri compromise line, slavery, or involuntary servitude, (except for crime,) shall be prohibited.

3. *And be it further resolved,* That if the President of the United States shall in his judgment and discretion deem it most advisable, instead of proceeding to submit the foregoing resolution to the Republic of Texas, as an overture on the part of the United States for admission, to negotiate with that Republic; then,

Be it resolved, That a State, to be formed out of the present Republic of Texas, with suitable extent and boundaries, and with two representatives in Congress, until the next apportionment of representation, shall be admitted into the Union, by virtue of this act, on an equal footing with the existing States, as soon as the terms and conditions of such admission, and the cession of the remaining Texian territory to the United States shall be agreed upon by the Governments of Texas and the United States: And that the sum of one hundred thousand dollars be, and the same is hereby, appropriated to defray the expenses of missions and negotiations, to agree upon the terms of said admission and cession, either by treaty to be submitted to the Senate, or by articles to be submitted to the two houses of Congress, as the President may direct.

"The forty-ninth parallel of north latitude"

THE OREGON TREATY

1846

Russia, Great Britain, Spain, and the United States held disputed claims on the Oregon Territory, which extended from Alaska to northern California. Spain withdrew its claim in 1819; Russia, most of its claim in 1824. Settlers emigrating over the Oregon Trail began living in the area in 1842. In the 1844 Presidential campaign, the victorious Democratic candidate, James K. Polk (1795–1849), pledged to "reoccupy Oregon," as he pledged to annex Texas. The Oregon Treaty terminated joint U.S.–British occupancy of the territory between the 42nd and 54th parallels and amicably drew the disputed boundary line between the U.S. and Canada along the 49th parallel. Western Democrats, who had been Polk yeomen, clamored for a boundary at fifty-four forty "or fight."

ART. I. From the point on the forty-ninth parallel of north latitude, where the boundary laid down in existing treaties and conventions between the United States and Great Britain terminates, the line of boundary between the territories of the United States and those of her Britannic Majesty shall be continued westward along the said forty-ninth parallel of north latitude to the middle of the channel which separates the continent from Vancouver's Island, and thence southerly through the middle of the said channel, and of Fuca's Straits, to the Pacific Ocean: *Provided, however,* That the navigation of the whole of the said channel and straits, south of the forty-ninth parallel of north latitude, remain free and open to both parties.

ART. II. From the point at which the forty-ninth parallel of north latitude shall be found to intersect the great northern branch of the Columbia River, the navigation of the said branch shall be free and open to the Hudson's Bay Company, and to all British subjects trading with the same. . .always understood that nothing in this article shall be construed as preventing, or intended to prevent, the government of the United States from making any regulations respecting the navigation of the said river or rivers not inconsistent with the present treaty.

ART. III. . . .the possessory rights of the Hudson's Bay Company, and of all British subjects who may be already in the occupation of land or other property lawfully acquired within the said territory, shall be respected.

ART. IV. The farms, lands, and other property of every description, belonging to the Puget's Sound Agricultural Company, on the north side of the Columbia River, shall be confirmed to the said company. . . .

"The U.S. engages to pay . . . the sum of $15-million."

THE TREATY OF GUADALUPE-HIDALGO
1848

Ulysses S. Grant (1822–1885), the 18th President, who was a second lieutenant in the Mexican War (1846–1848), described the war as "the most unjust" in American history. Annexation of Texas by the U.S. in 1845 had inflamed relations with Mexico, which refused to negotiate Americans' claims for injuries and property damages. When the Mexican army attacked U.S. troops in a disputed area between the Nueces River and the Rio Grande, President James K. Polk (1795–1849) asked Congress for a declaration of war. Nicholas Trist (1800–1874), who had studied law with Thomas Jefferson (and married the former President's granddaughter), disobeyed the President's recall and negotiated with Mexican moderates the treaty ending the war after the U.S. had captured Mexico City. Trist's was clearly an act of insubordination but he believed he knew the situation in Mexico better than Washington officials. He was *there* and he *knew* that there was the possibility that Mexico would dissolve into anarchy. Many officials in Washington were seeking harsh terms, including annexation of all of Mexico—*even* the extinction of the Mexican people. Polk accepted the treaty because it conformed to his publicly announced goals. It set the southern boundary of Texas at the Rio Grande. Trist's minimum territorial demands added an area from Texas to California, which now includes the states of Colorado, Utah, Nevada, New Mexico, and Arizona.

IN THE NAME OF ALMIGHTY GOD:
The United States of America and the United Mexican States, animated by a sincere desire to put an end to the calamities of the war which unhappily exists between the two Republics, and to establish upon a solid basis relations of peace and friendship, which shall confer reciprocal benefits upon the citizens of both, and assure the concord, harmony, and mutual confidence wherein the two peoples should live, as good neighbours, have for that purpose appointed their respective plenipotentiaries,

ARTICLE I.

There shall be firm and universal peace between the United States of America and the Mexican Republic, and between their respective countries, territories, cities, towns, and people, without exception of places or persons.

ARTICLE V.

The boundary line between the two Republics shall commence in the Gulf of Mexico, three leagues from land, opposite the mouth of the Rio Grande, otherwise called Rio Bravo del Norte, or opposite the mouth of its deepest branch, if it should have more than one branch emptying directly into the sea; from thence up the middle of that river, following the deepest channel, where it has more than one, to the point where it strikes the southern boundary of New Mexico; thence, westwardly, along the whole southern boundary of New Mexico (which runs north of the town called *Paso*) to its western termination; thence, northward, along the western line of New Mexico, until it intersects the first branch of the River Gila; (or if it should not intersect any branch of that river, then to the point on the said line nearest to such branch, and thence in a direct line to the same;) thence down the middle of the said branch and of the said river, until it empties into the Rio Colorado; thence across the Rio Colorado, following the division line between Upper and Lower California, to the Pacific Ocean. . . .

ART. VIII. Mexicans now established in territories previously belonging to Mexico, and which remain for the future within the limits of the United States, as defined by the present treaty, shall be free to continue where they now reside, or to remove at any time to the Mexican republic, retaining the property which they possess in the said territories, or disposing thereof, and removing the proceeds wherever they please, without their being subjected, on this account, to any contribution, tax, or charge whatever. . . .

ART. XII. In consideration of the extension acquired by the boundaries of the United States, as defined in the fifth article of the present treaty, the Government of the United States engages to pay to that of the Mexican Republic the sum of fifteen millions of dollars. . . .

"Seven million two hundred thousand dollars in gold"

THE U.S. BUYS ALASKA

1867

"Seward's folly" or "Seward's icebox"—persistent opponents, envisaging little financial return, ridiculed Secretary of State William Henry Seward's enthusiastic purchase of Russian America—Alaska—for $7.2-million, or less than two cents an acre. A Congressman weighed in: "Alaska is utterly worthless, and even if it were otherwise we have no earthly use for it." Russia had acquired the vast territory by right of discovery, and held it for more than a century. When it seemed that Great Britain, an inveterate Russian foe, would seize the far-removed land, Russia made it known that it would be interested in cession to the United States, the most constant and grateful of Russia's friends. Secretary Seward (1801–1872) literally burned the midnight oil to get signatures to parchment. Alaska turned out to be a gold mine, obliterating any negative public sentiment. It is extraordinarily wealthy in natural resources. In 1959, Alaska became the forty-ninth state and the first non-contiguous state, the largest U.S. political division by far. It is one-fifth the size of the other forty-nine states *combined*. It also is thinly populated; every resident could have a square mile all to himself. Alaska enjoys a state holiday on Seward's birthday, May 16th.

The United States of America and his Majesty the Emperor of all the Russias, being desirous of strengthening, if possible, the good understanding which exists between them, have, for that purpose, appointed as their plenipotentiaries: the President of the United States, William H. Seward, Secretary of State; and his Majesty the Emperor of all the Russias, the privy counsellor Edward de Stoeckl, his envoy extraordinary and minister plenipotentiary to the United States.

And the said plenipotentiaries, having exchanged their full powers, which were found to be in due form, have agreed upon and signed the following articles:—

ARTICLE I.—His Majesty the Emperor of all the Russias agrees to cede to the United States, by this convention, immediately upon the exchange of the ratifications thereof, all the territory and dominion now possessed by his said Majesty on the continent of America and in the adjacent islands, the same being contained within the geographical limits herein set forth, to wit: the eastern limit is the line of demarcation between the Russian and the British possessions in North America, as established by the convention between Russia and Great Britain, of February 28–16, 1825, and described in Articles III. and IV. of said convention, in the following terms:—

Commencing from the southernmost point of the island called Prince of Wales Island, which point lies in the parallel of 54 degrees 40 minutes north latitude, and between the 131st and 133d degree of west longitude (meridian of Greenwich), the said line shall ascend to the north along the channel called Portland Channel, as far as the point of the continent where it strikes the 56th degree of north latitude; from this last-mentioned point the line of demarcation shall follow the summit of the mountains situated parallel to the coast as far as the point of intersection of the 141st degree of west longitude (of the same meridian); and finally, from the said point of intersection, the said meridian line of the 141st degree, in its prolongation as far as the Frozen Ocean.

IV. With reference to the line of demarcation laid down in the preceding article, it is understood—

1st. That the island called Prince of Wales Island shall belong wholly to Russia (now by this cession to the United States).

2d. That whenever the summit of the mountains which extend in a direction parallel to the coast from the 56th degree of north latitude to the point of intersection of the 141st degree of west longitude shall prove to be at the distance of more than ten marine leagues from the ocean, the limit between the British possessions and the line of coast which is to belong to Russia as above mentioned (that is to say, the limit to the possessions ceded by this convention) shall be formed by a line parallel to the winding of the coast, and which shall never exceed the distance of ten marine leagues therefrom.

The western limit within which the territories and dominion conveyed are contained passes through a point in Behring's Straits on the parallel of 65 degrees 30 minutes north latitude, at its intersection by the meridian which passes midway between the islands of Krusenstern, or Ignalook, and the island of Ratmanoff, or

Noonarbook, and proceeds due north, without limitation, into the same Frozen Ocean. The same western limit, beginning at the same initial point, proceeds thence in a course nearly southwest, through Behring's Straits and Behring's Sea, so as to pass midway between the northwest point of the island of St. Lawrence and the southeast point of Cape Choukotski, to the meridian of 172 west longitude; thence, from the intersection of that meridian, in a southwesterly direction, so as to pass midway between the island of Attou and the Copper Island of the Kormandorski couplet or group in the North Pacific Ocean, to the meridian of 193 degrees west longitude, so as to include in the territory conveyed the whole of the Aleutian Islands east of that meridian.

ARTICLE II.—In the cession of territory and dominion made by the preceding article are included the right of property in all public lots and squares, vacant lands, and all public buildings, fortifications, barracks, and other edifices which are not private individual property. It is, however, understood and agreed that the churches which have been built in the ceded territory by the Russian government shall remain the property of such members of the Greek Oriental Church resident in the territory as may choose to worship therein. Any government archives, papers, and documents relative to the territory and dominion aforesaid, which may be now existing there, will be left in the possession of the agent of the United States; but an authenticated copy of such of them as may be required will be at all times given by the United States to the Russian government, or to such Russian officers or subjects as they may apply for.

ARTICLE III.—The inhabitants of the ceded territory, according to their choice, reserving their natural allegiance, may return to Russia within three years; but, if they should prefer to remain in the ceded territory, they, with the exception of uncivilized native tribes, shall be admitted to the enjoyment of all the rights, advantages, and immunities of citizens of the United States, and shall be maintained and protected in the free enjoyment of their liberty, property, and religion. The uncivilized tribes will be subject to such laws and regulations as the United States may from time to time adopt in regard to aboriginal tribes of that country. . . .

ARTICLE V.—Immediately after the exchange of the ratifications of this convention, any fortifications or military posts which may be in the ceded territory shall be delivered to the agent of the United States, and any Russian troops which may be in the territory shall be withdrawn as soon as may be reasonably and conveniently practicable.

ARTICLE VI.—In consideration of the cession aforesaid the United States agree to pay at the treasury in Washington, within ten months after the exchange of the ratifications of this convention, to the diplomatic representative or other agent of his Majesty the Emperor of all the Russias, duly authorized to receive the same, seven million two hundred thousand dollars in gold. . . .

"No further immigration of Chinese"

ANNEXING THE HAWAIIAN ISLANDS
1898

The 122 lush, tropical, volcanic, and coral Hawaiian islands—the 50th U.S. state—are the peaks of an emerging mountain range. Forty-million years ago, the 1,600-mile-long chain was two miles under the waters of the north-central Pacific Ocean. About 2,500 years ago, Polynesian voyagers settled the islands, arriving in huge outrigger canoes from 2,400 miles to the south. England's intrepid Captain James Cook (1727–1779) discovered the islands in 1778 and dubbed them the Sandwich Islands. (He was murdered there a year later.) A little more than a century ago, American settlers, fearing that Queen Lili'uokalani (1838–1917) was about to break their political and business stranglehold on her kingdom, instigated a bloodless revolution. One hundred sixty-eight Marines, dispatched from a U.S. gunboat offshore, helped to depose the monarchy. The U.S. recognized Hawaii as a republic in 1894, then annexed the islands (1898) and established a Federal territory (1900). Hawaii was an extensively developed U.S. naval and military base when it was struck by Japanese bombers in December, 1941. Congress had not voted for Hawaiian statehood in 1937 because of anti-Asian sentiments and because the "Paradise of the Pacific" was deemed to be too far away from the continental U.S.—it's more than 2,000 Pacific miles southwest of California. Hawaii became the Aloha State in 1959. The population is 59.1 percent Asian.

Whereas the Government of the Republic of Hawaii having, in due form, signified its consent, in the manner provided by its constitution, to cede absolutely and without reserve to the United States of America all rights of sovereignty of whatsoever kind in and over the Hawaiian Islands and their dependencies, and also to cede and transfer to the United States the absolute fee and ownership of all public, Government, or Crown lands, public buildings or edifices, ports, harbors, military equipment, and all other public property of every kind and description belonging to the Government of the Hawaiian Islands, together with every right and appurtenance thereunto appertaining; Therefore

Resolved by the Senate and House of Representatives of the United States of America in Congress Assembled, That said cession is accepted, ratified, and confirmed, and that the said Hawaiian Islands and their dependencies be, and they are hereby, annexed as a part of the territory of the United States and are subject to the sovereign dominion thereof, and that all and singular the property and rights hereinbefore mentioned are vested in the United States of America.

The existing laws of the United States relative to public lands shall not apply to such lands in the Hawaiian Islands; but the Congress of the United States shall enact special laws for their management and disposition: *Provided,* That all revenue from or proceeds of the same, except as regards such part thereof as may be used or occupied for the civil, military, or naval purposes of the United States, or may be assigned for the use of the local government, shall be used solely for the benefit of the inhabitants of the Hawaiian Islands for educational and other public purposes.

Until Congress shall provide for the government of such islands all the civil, judicial, and military powers exercised by the officers of the existing government in said islands shall be vested in such person or persons and shall be exercised in such manner as the President of the United States shall direct; and the President shall have the power to remove said officers and fill the vacancies so occasioned.

The existing treaties of the Hawaiian Islands with foreign nations shall forthwith cease and determine, being replaced by such treaties as may exist, or as may be hereafter concluded, between the United States and such foreign nations. The municipal legislation of the Hawaiian Islands, not enacted for the fulfillment of the treaties so extinguished, and not inconsistent with this joint resolution nor contrary to the Constitution of the United States nor to any existing treaty of the United States, shall remain in force until the Congress of the United States shall otherwise determine.

Until legislation shall be enacted extending the United States customs laws and regulations to the Hawaiian Islands the existing customs relations of the Hawaiian Islands with the United States and other countries shall remain unchanged.

The public debt of the Republic of Hawaii, lawfully existing at the date of the passage of this joint resolution, including the amounts due to depositors in the Hawaiian Postal Savings Bank, is hereby assumed by the Government of the United States; but the liability of the United States in this regard shall in no case exceed four million dollars. So long, however, as the existing Government and the present commercial relations of the Hawaiian Islands are continued as hereinbefore provided said Government shall continue to pay the interest on said debt.

There shall be no further immigration of Chinese into the Hawaiian Islands, except upon such conditions as are now or may hereafter be allowed by the laws of the United States; no Chinese, by reason of anything herein contained, shall be allowed to enter the United States from the Hawaiian Islands.

CERTAIN UNALIENABLE RIGHTS

Antipathy to blacks, in the North as well as in the South, was a fact of national life. The South was very aware that an almost insoluble race problem underlay the slavery problem. Racism "had the wolf by the ears," as Jefferson observed, and "could neither hold him nor let him go." It led to mail censorship—of antislavery tracts sent out of Abolitionist strongholds in the North—and to a new defensive/aggressive formulation that claimed slavery was not an evil, which some Southerners had admitted before the 1830s. Rather, it was "a positive good"—and a form of property protected by the Constitution. In reaction, many Northerners assumed an antislavery stance (which is not to deny their racism) that was expressed in Abolitionist sentiments. Agitation against slavery took other forms. It ranged from the views of moderates like Lincoln, who would not interfere with slavery in the states where it existed but feared that radical Southerners—the so-called "fire-eaters"—would try to spread slavery over the entire nation, to the convictions of editors, clergymen, and politicians, who engaged in endless harangues about the evils of slavery and the intentions of slave owners. Abolitionists generally went beyond immediate anxiety over slavery expansion to a passionate concern for the overriding moral issue. Thus, "extremists" like Garrison arraigned slavery in uncompromising and apocalyptic terms, and eventually were prepared for violence if that were the only way to end the system of human bondage.

The Civil War, of course, brought a heavy cost in casualties and psychic health for the nation. The systemic antebellum racism, however, was not destroyed—indeed, it retained its viability. Lincoln was entirely too optimistic when contending that the abolition of slavery repudiated the heresy that "all men are created equal, except Negroes." The vigorous reweaving of the social fabric and a transformed economic landscape seemingly did not affect popular perceptions of the black man's status or the low regard in which he was held by the overwhelmingly majority of his countrymen. Nor did the epochal provisions of the Fourteenth Amendment, which became law on July 28, 1868. They expressly guaranteed a right of equality for the freedman and federalized his civil rights which, until the end of hostilities, left protection of these rights to the states alone; after 1868, the guarantees of the Bill of Rights were incorporated into this Amendment, which thus directly applied to the states. But the Supreme Court, the putative guardian of these rights, was disappointingly unresponsive and unhelpful in the period after the Confederacy surrendered at Appomattox Courthouse. From the outset, it kept blacks insulated from the Fourteenth Amendment; indeed, from the entire Bill of Rights. In 1883, for instance, the Court struck down the 1875 Bill of Rights Act, holding that the enforcement clause of the Fourteenth Amendment was limited to state actions; that is, Congress could not effect discriminatory action that was purely private in character. And the legal formula of "separate but equal" gave the states an acceptable juridical principle for compulsory segregation of the races. (Justice Henry Brown agreed that the aim of the Fourteenth Amendment "was undoubtedly to enforce the absolute equality of the two races before the law, but in the nature of things it could not have been intended to abolish distinctions based on color, or to enforce social, as distinguished from political, equality or a commingling of the two races upon terms unsatisfactory to either.") In decisions that underlined a boundless cynicism, the judicial majority argued that Federal laws and amendments could not eradicate racism, yet it ignored the fact that state measures had helped maintain it. This opinion (in Plessy) gave the lie to the American ideal that Justice John Harlan so eloquently expressed in dissent: "Our Constitution is color-blind." It turned the "equal protection of the law" clause in the Fourteenth Amendment into an empty slogan. The passage of so-called "Jim Crow" laws by Southern states proceeded unhampered, having tacit Federal court assent. Their entire purpose was to reaffirm white supremacy and to brand blacks as inferior, barring them from inclusion in white society. The Court chose to close its eyes to state-enforced racial segregation.

The near total loss of fundamental civil liberties for blacks had its parallel in the struggle for women's rights. In pre-Civil War society, both blacks and women were roughly in the same category, outside the select circle of those granted full citizenship and outside the protections of the Bill of Rights. Women were believed to be second-class citizens at best. The governing social consensus considered them to be the property of their husbands, a view reflected even in the Constitution. The Declaration of Independence itself had been dominated by an exclusionary view: "All men are created equal." Four decades later, the Jackson-period campaign for women's rights—in law, politics, the professions—absorbed a dozen reformers, Theodore Parker, Wendell Phillips, Thomas Wentworth Higginson, among them, but efforts were unavailing. Continuing into the post-war years, reformers fixed on the primary goal of female suffrage. But much as with blacks, the High Court found the states, in the case of Myra Bradwell, were free to deny legal equality to their citizens, regardless of the mandates of the Fourteenth Amendment. In rejecting her claim—to be admitted to the Illinois state bar—the Justices took a narrow view of the Fourteenth Amendment and withheld from women access to Federal authority to challenge state restrictions on their political and social rights. They added gratuitous comments that reflected the discriminatory attitudes confronting women at the time— and, for that matter, a century later: "The paramount destiny and mission of a woman is to fulfill the noble and benign offices of wife and mother. This is the law of the Creator." Two years later, they found that state measures that denied some citizens (women) the franchise did not violate the Fourteenth Amendment; from then on, it became clear that a constitutional amendment would be needed if women were to be granted suffrage—it didn't happen until 1920, with the Nineteenth Amendment. But the court cases up to then, as we have seen, revealed popular attitudes toward a woman's role and rights. Her proper place was in the private sphere of the home, caring for her husband, rearing their children, while men were to go out and do the rough work of the world.

The Nineteenth Amendment failed to accomplish more than its limited objective. The explosion of women's rights, as well as those of blacks, did not occur until the second half of this century. Proponents of women's rights urged sexual equality, to the point of eliminating discrimination in hiring practices, equal pay for equal work, and privacy. The last was expanded into a fundamental and all-inclusive guarantee that extended to the right of a woman to control her own body; this became the core argument for those who rejected state anti-abortion statutes. Of course, when a woman became pregnant, not only her body was involved but that of the fetus, and this became ethical and religious issues, perhaps the most volatile and divisive ones of recent decades. The Court settled them on schematic grounds of fetus development over trimesters rather than what would have been arguably the more legally sound proposition of equal protection and sex discrimination. It failed to resolve the basic controversy. The abortion question has been subject to a seemingly interminable push-pull of religious groups and political leaders.

"Speaking and writing truth"

FREEDOM OF THE PRESS
1735

Under British law, a printed attack on a Crown official was libelous. The legal doctrine that truth is a defense against libel was successfully argued after Governor William Cosby (c.1690–c.1735), of New York, had imprisoned John Peter Zenger (1697–1746), printer and publisher of the anti-government *New York Weekly Journal.* The defense lawyer Andrew Hamilton (c.1676–1741), of Philadelphia, convinced the jury to ignore the existing law and, instead, baffle "the attempt of tyranny": A statement, even if defamatory, he argued, is not libelous if it is proved to be true. Three huzzas greeted the verdict, and wide popular sentiment was aroused in favor of freedom of the press. The verdict, however, did not set a precedent; it did not establish that truth could be a defense in a libel case.

But to conclude. The question before the Court and you gentlemen of the jury is not of small or private concern; it is not the cause of a poor printer, nor of New York alone, which you are now trying. No! It may in its consequence affect every freeman that lives under a British government on the main of America. It is the best cause. It is the cause of liberty; and I make no doubt but your upright conduct this day will not only entitle you to the love and esteem of your fellow citizens, but every man who prefers freedom to a life of slavery will bless and honor you as men who have baffled the attempt of tyranny; and by an impartial and uncorrupt verdict, have laid a noble foundation for securing to ourselves, our posterity, and our neighbors that to which nature and the laws of our country have given us a right—the liberty—both of exposing and opposing arbitrary power (in these parts of the world, at least) by speaking and writing truth.

"All inhabitants are entitled"

New Jersey Women and Blacks Can Vote
1776

With the American Revolution looming, petitions were drawn calling for a wider electorate—let more than freeholders vote. Two days before U.S. independence from the
Crown was declared, New Jersey adopted a constitution whose Section IV granted all
qualified inhabitants—men, women, free blacks—the franchise. There was a modest
property qualification. Their right to vote was reaffirmed three years later in an act
regulating the election of members of the Legislative Council and General Assembly,
Sheriffs and Coroners: ". . . every voter shall openly, and in full view deliver his or her
ballot . . ." Women voted occasionally from 1776 to 1797, then in considerable numbers until 1807. Election law, not an amended constitution, denied them the vote. Allegations of fraud by some women voters in an election concerning the placement of
a courthouse prompted a bipartisan legislature to issue Laws of 1807:

> "Whereas doubts have been raised, the great diversities in practice obtained throughout
> the state in regard to the admission of aliens, females, and persons of color, or negroes to
> vote in elections . . . Section I: Be it enacted, by the council and general assembly of this
> state, and it is hereby enacted by the authority of the same, That from and after the pass-
> ing of this act, no person shall vote in any state or county election . . . unless such person
> be a free, white, male citizen of this state . . ."

WHEREAS all the constitutional authority
ever possessed by the Kings of Great
Britain over these Colonies, or their other dominions, was, by compact, derived from the people, and held of them, for the common interest
of the whole society; allegiance and protection
are, in the nature of things, reciprocal ties, each
equally depending upon the other, and liable to
be dissolved by the others being refused or withdrawn. And whereas George the Third, King of
Great Britain, has refused protection to the good
people of these Colonies; and, by assenting to
sundry acts of the British Parliament, attempting
to subject them to the absolute dominion of that
body; and has also made war upon them, in the
most cruel and unnatural manner, for no other
cause, than asserting their just rights—all civil
authority under him is necessarily at an end, and
a dissolution of government in each Colony has
consequently taken place.

And whereas, in the present deplorable situation of these Colonies, exposed to the fury of a
cruel and relentless enemy, some form of government is absolutely necessary, not only for the
preservation of good order, but also the more effectually to unite the people, and enable them to
exert their whole force in their own necessary defence: and as the honorable the Continental
Congress, the supreme council of the American
Colonies, has advised such of the Colonies as

have not yet gone into measures, to adopt for themselves, respectively, such government as shall best conduce to their own happiness and safety, and the well-being of America in general:—We, the representatives of the Colony of New Jersey, having been elected by all the Counties, in the freest manner, and in congress assembled, have, after mature deliberations, agreed upon a set of charter rights and the form of a Constitution, in manner following, viz. . . .

IV. That all inhabitants of this Colony, of full age, who are worth fifty pounds proclamation money, clear estate in the same, and have resided within the County in which they claim a vote for twelve months immediately preceding the election, shall be entitled to vote for Representatives in Council and Assembly; and also for all other public officers, that shall be elected by the people of the County at large.

"I will be as harsh as truth"

GARRISON PUBLISHES *THE LIBERATOR*
1831

Demanding complete and immediate emancipation for the millions of slaves, the pacifist William Lloyd Garrison (1805–1879) published his radical anti-slavery newspaper, *The Liberator,* for 34 years, until 1865, the end of the Civil War and the ratification of the Thirteenth Amendment to the Constitution abolishing slavery: "I am in earnest—I will not equivocate—I will not excuse—I will not retreat a single inch—*and I will be heard." The Liberator's* motto was "Our country is the world. Our countrymen are mankind." There was a price on Garrison's head; Georgia offered a $5,000 reward for his arrest and conviction. He founded the American Anti-Slavery Society (1833) and drew up its Declaration of Sentiments. In 1854, he burned a facsimile of the Constitution, decrying the "supreme law of the land" as "a covenant with death and an agreement with hell . . . a compromise with tyranny." In his judgement, "and in the judgement of the nation ever since adoption" of the Constitution, not one of his "sincere and true friends will ever reproach me for the deed—the light of which shall be seen long after this mortal shall have put on immortality." Freedom, Garrison declared, must rule a rescued land. Relying on moral pressure and the mobilization of public opinion, he also pressed for prohibition, woman suffrage, and better treatment for Indians.

TO THE PUBLIC.

In the month of August, I issued proposals for publishing "THE LIBERATOR" in Washington city; but the enterprise, though hailed in different sections of the country, was palsied by public indifference. Since that time, the removal of the Genius of Universal Emancipation to the Seat of Government has rendered less imperious the establishment of a similar periodical in that quarter.

During my recent tour for the purpose of exciting the minds of the people by a series of discourses on the subject of slavery, every place that I visited gave fresh evidence of the fact, that a greater revolution in public sentiment was to be effected in the free states—*and particularly in New-England*—than at the south. I found contempt more bitter, opposition more active, detraction more relentless, prejudice more stubborn, and apathy more frozen, than among slave owners themselves. Of course, there were individual exceptions to the contrary. This state of things afflicted, but did not dishearten me. I determined, at every hazard, to lift up the standard of emancipation in the eyes of the nation, *within sight of Bunker Hill and in the birth place of liberty.* That standard is now unfurled; and long may it float, unhurt by the spoliations of time or the missiles of a desperate foe—yea, till every chain be broken, and every bondman set free! Let southern oppressors tremble—let their secret abettors tremble—let their northern apologists tremble—let all the enemies of the persecuted blacks tremble.

I deem the publication of my original Prospectus unnecessary, as it has obtained a wide circulation. The principles therein inculcated will be steadily pursued in this paper, excepting that I shall not array myself as the political partisan of any man. In defending the great cause of human rights, I wish to derive the assistance of all religions and of all parties.

Assenting to the 'self-evident truth' maintained in the American Declaration of Independence, 'that all men are created equal, and endowed by their Creator with certain inalienable rights—among which are life, liberty and the pursuit of happiness,' I shall strenuously contend for the immediate enfranchisement of our slave population. In Park-street Church, on the Fourth of July, 1829, in an address on slavery, I unreflectingly assented to the popular but pernicious doctrine of *gradual* abolition. I seize this opportunity to make a full and unequivocal recantation, and thus publicly to ask pardon of my God, of my country, and of my brethren the poor slaves, for having uttered a sentiment so full of timidity, injustice and absurdity. A similar recantation, from my pen, was published in the Genius of Universal Emancipation at Baltimore, in September, 1829. My conscience is now satisfied.

I am aware, that many object to the severity of my language; but is there not cause for severity? I *will be* as harsh as truth, and as uncompromising as justice. On this subject, I do not wish to think, or speak, or write, with moderation. No! no! Tell a man whose house is on fire, to give a moderate alarm; tell him to moderately rescue his wife from the hands of the ravisher; tell the mother to gradually extricate her babe from the fire into which it has fallen;—but urge me not to use moderation in a cause like the present. I am in earnest—I will not equivocate—I will not excuse—I will not retreat a single inch—AND I WILL BE HEARD. The apathy of the people is enough to make every statue leap from its pedestal, and to hasten the resurrection of the dead.

It is pretended, that I am retarding the cause of emancipation by the coarseness of my invective, and the precipitancy of my measures. *The charge is not true.* On this question my influence,—humble as it is,—is felt at this moment to a considerable extent, and shall be felt in coming years—not perniciously, but beneficially— not as a curse, but as a blessing; and posterity will bear testimony that I was right. I desire to thank God, that he enables me to disregard 'the fear of man which bringeth a snare,' and to speak his truth in its simplicity and power.

And here I close with this fresh dedication:

'Oppression! I have seen thee, face to face,
And met thy cruel eye and cloudy brow;
But thy soul-withering glance I fear not now—
For dread to prouder feelings doth give place
Of deep abhorrence! Scorning the disgrace
Of slavish knees that at thy footstool bow,
I also kneel—but with far other bow
Do hail thee and thy herd of hirelings base:—
I swear, while life-blood warms my throbbing veins,
Still to oppose and thwart, with heart and hand,
Thy brutalizing sway—till Afric's chains
Are burst, and Freedom rules the rescued land,—
Trampling Oppression and his iron rod:
Such is the vow I take—SO HELP ME GOD!'

"Woman is man's equal"

WOMEN'S RIGHTS
1848

To many Americans, including women, the emancipation of women was a radical notion. Inspired by the anti-slavery crusade, the convention that launched the women's rights movement attracted interested women and sympathetic men (including the celebrated abolitionist, orator, and former slave Frederick Douglass [1817–1895]), to Seneca Falls, New York. It called for extensive reforms, particularly changes in the political, economic, and domestic positions of women. The Declaration of Sentiments was modeled on the U.S. Declaration of Independence. Co-organizer Elizabeth Cady Stanton (1815–1902), who had insisted that the word "obey" be dropped from her wedding ceremony (she married a prominent abolitionist), argued that natural rights extended to women, who could gain social rights through the franchise. Seventy-two years later, the Nineteenth Amendment to the Constitution extended the vote to women: "The right of citizens of the United States to vote shall not be denied or abridged by the United States or by any State on account of sex." With a flourish of his ordinary steel pen, Secretary of State Bainbridge Colby (1869–1950) signed the certificate of ratification, declaring, "I say to the women of America, you may fire when you are ready." The ceremony was not witnessed either by a photographer or by a woman. The United States was the sixteenth nation to give women the vote nationally. The proposed Equal Rights Amendment, circulated to the states in 1972, fell three states shy of adoption.

1. Declaration of Sentiments

When, in the course of human events, it becomes necessary for one portion of the family of man to assume among the people of the earth a position different from that which they have hitherto occupied, but one to which the laws of nature and of nature's God entitle them, a decent respect to the opinions of mankind requires that they should declare the causes that impel them to such a course.

We hold these truths to be self-evident: that all men and women are created equal; that they are endowed by their Creator with certain inalienable rights; that among these are life, liberty, and the pursuit of happiness; that to secure these rights governments are instituted, deriving their just powers from the consent of the governed. Whenever any form of government becomes destructive of these ends, it is the right of those who suffer from it to refuse allegiance to it, and to insist upon the institution of a new government, laying its foundation on such principles, and organizing its powers in such form, as to them shall seem most likely to effect their safety and happiness. Prudence, indeed, will dictate that governments long established should not be changed for light and transient causes; and accordingly all experience hath shown that mankind are more disposed to suffer while evils are sufferable, than to right themselves by abolishing the forms to which they were accustomed. But when a long train of abuses and usurpations, pursuing invariably the same object, evinces a design to reduce them under absolute despotism, it is their duty to throw off such government, and to provide new guards for their future security. Such has been the patient sufferance of the women under this government, and such is now the necessity which constrains them to demand the equal station to which they are entitled.

The history of mankind is a history of repeated injuries and usurpations on the part of man toward woman, having in direct object the establishment of an absolute tyranny over her. To prove this, let facts be submitted to a candid world.

He has never permitted her to exercise her inalienable right to the elective franchise.

He has compelled her to submit to laws, in the formation of which she had no voice.

He has withheld from her rights which are given to the most ignorant and degraded men—both natives and foreigners.

Having deprived her of this first right of a citizen, the elective franchise, thereby leaving her without representation in the halls of legislation, he has oppressed her on all sides.

He has made her, if married, in the eye of the law, civilly dead.

He has taken from her all right in property, even to the wages she earns.

He has made her, morally, an irresponsible being, as she can commit many crimes with impunity, provided they be done in the presence of her husband. In the covenant of marriage, she is compelled to promise obedience to her husband,

he becoming, to all intents and purposes, her master—the law giving him power to deprive her of her liberty, and to administer chastisement.

He has so framed the laws of divorce, as to what shall be the proper causes, and in case of separation, to whom the guardianship of the children shall be given, as to be wholly regardless of the happiness of women—the law, in all cases, going upon a false supposition of the supremacy of man, and giving all power into his hands.

After depriving her of all rights as a married woman, if single, and the owner of property, he has taxed her to support a government which recognizes her only when her property can be made profitable to it.

He has monopolized nearly all the profitable employments, and from those she is permitted to follow, she receives but a scanty remuneration. He closes against her all the avenues to wealth and distinction which he considers most honorable to himself. As a teacher of theology, medicine, or law, she is not known.

He has denied her the facilities for obtaining a thorough education, all colleges being closed against her.

He allows her in Church, as well as State, but a subordinate position, claiming Apostolic authority for her exclusion from the ministry, and, with some exceptions, from any public participation in the affairs of the Church.

He has created a false public sentiment by giving to the world a different code of morals for men and women, by which moral delinquencies which exclude women from society, are not only tolerated, but deemed of little account in man.

He has usurped the prerogative of Jehovah himself, claiming it as his right to assign for her a sphere of action, when that belongs to her conscience and to her God.

He has endeavored, in every way that he

could, to destroy her confidence in her own powers, to lessen her self-respect and to make her willing to lead a dependent and abject life.

Now, in view of this entire disfranchisement of one-half the people of this country, their social and religious degradation—in view of the unjust laws above mentioned, and because women do feel themselves aggrieved, oppressed, and fraudulently deprived of their most sacred rights, we insist that they have immediate admission to all the rights and privileges which belong to them as citizens of the United States.

In entering upon the great work before us, we anticipate no small amount of misconception, misrepresentation, and ridicule; but we shall use every instrumentality within our power to effect our object. We shall employ agents, circulate tracts, petition the State and National legislatures, and endeavor to enlist the pulpit and the press in our behalf. We hope this Convention will be followed by a series of Conventions embracing every part of the country.

2. Resolutions

Whereas, The great precept of nature is conceded to be, that "man shall pursue his own true and substantial happiness." Blackstone in his *Commentaries* remarks, that this law of Nature being coeval with mankind, and dictated by God himself, is of course superior in obligation to any other. It is binding over all the globe, in all countries and at all times; no human laws are of any validity if contrary to this, and such of them as are valid, derive all their force, and all their validity, and all their authority, mediately and immediately, from this original; therefore,

Resolved, That all laws which prevent woman from occupying such a station in society as her conscience shall dictate, or which place her in a position inferior to that of man, are contrary to the great precept of nature, and therefore of no force or authority.

Resolved, That woman is man's equal—was intended to be so by the Creator, and the highest good of the race demands that she should be recognized as such.

Resolved, That the women of this country ought to be enlightened in regard to the laws under which they live, that they may no longer publish their degradation by declaring themselves satisfied with their present position, nor their ignorance, by asserting that they have all the rights they want.

Resolved, That inasmuch as man, while claiming for himself intellectual superiority, does accord to woman moral superiority, it is pre-eminently his duty to encourage her to speak and teach, as she has an opportunity, in all religious assemblies.

Resolved, That the same amount of virtue, delicacy, and refinement of behavior that is required of woman in the social state, should also be required of man, and the same transgressions should be visited with equal severity on both man and woman.

Resolved, That the objection of indelicacy and impropriety, which is so often brought against woman when she addresses a public audience, comes with a very ill-grace from those who encourage, by their attendance, her appearance on the stage, in the concert, or in feats of the circus.

Resolved, That woman has too long rested satisfied in the circumscribed limits which corrupt customs and a perverted application of the Scriptures have marked out for her, and that it is time she should move in the enlarged sphere which her great Creator has assigned her.

Resolved, That it is the duty of the women of this country to secure to themselves their sacred right to the elective franchise.

Resolved, That the equality of human rights

results necessarily from the fact of the identity of the race in capabilities and responsibilities.

Resolved, That the speedy success of our cause depends upon the zealous and untiring efforts of both men and women, for the overthrow of the monopoly of the pulpit, and for the securing to women an equal participation with men in the various trades, professions, and commerce.

Resolved, therefore, That, being invested by the creator with the same capabilities, and the same consciousness of responsibility for their exercise, it is demonstrably the right and duty of woman, equally with man, to promote every righteous cause by every righteous means; and especially in regard to the great subjects of morals and religion, it is self-evidently her right to participate with her brother in teaching them, both in private and in public, by writing and by speaking, by any instrumentalities proper to be used, and in any assemblies proper to be held; and this being a self-evident truth growing out of the divinely implanted principles of human nature, any custom or authority adverse to it, whether modern or wearing the hoary sanction of antiquity, is to be regarded as a self-evident falsehood, and at war with mankind.

"Right of property in a slave is distinctly and expressly affirmed in the Constitution"

THE DRED SCOTT DECISION
1857

With *Dred Scott*, abolitionists sought to force national law to deal with slavery. The scheme backfired. Legal and constitutional scholars consider the Supreme Court decision to be the worst ever rendered—it crystallized attitudes that rang in the Civil War. Scott (1795–1858), a black man born into slavery in Virginia, thought he had gained his freedom when he moved with his owner into the free state of Illinois and later into free Wisconsin Territory. When Scott returned to a state that permitted slavery, he was declared by local courts still to be a slave. A New York abolitionist seeking freedom for all slaves took Scott's case to the Supreme Court. The Ultimate Arbiter, the Supreme Court, ruled (7–2) that a slave did not automatically become free by moving into a free state; therefore, Scott had *never* been free. Blacks were not U.S. citizens, anyway, and therefore not competent to sue in Federal courts. Chief Justice Roger Brooke Taney (1777–1864) declared that blacks "had no right which the white man was bound to respect; the right of property in a slave is distinctly and expressly affirmed in the Constitution." *Scott* unleashed irreconcilable partisan passions. Anti-slavery forces feared legalization of slavery everywhere. (A slave *could* be freed by the mere stroke of the owner's pen. When Scott's owner gave him his freedom, Scott went to work as a janitor in a boardinghouse in St. Louis.) The Fourteenth Amendment to the Constitution (1868) would vouchsafe citizenship on all persons born in the United States. (As Chief Justice, Taney swore Abraham Lincoln, the Great Liberator, as the sixteenth President, in 1861.)

There are two leading questions presented by the record:

1. Had the Circuit Court of the United States jurisdiction to hear and determine the case between these parties? And,

2. If it had jurisdiction, is the judgment it has given erroneous or not?

The plaintiff in error, who was also the plaintiff in the court below, was, with his wife and children, held as slaves by the defendant, in the State of Missouri, and he brought this action in the Circuit Court of the United States for that district, to assert the title of himself and his family to freedom.

The declaration is . . . that he and the defendant are citizens of different States; that is, that he is a citizen of Missouri, and the defendant a citizen of New York.

The defendant pleaded in abatement to the jurisdiction of the court, that the plaintiff was not a citizen of the State of Missouri, as alleged in his declaration, being a negro of African descent whose ancestors were of pure African blood, and who were brought into this country and sold as slaves.

To this plea the plaintiff demurred, and the defendant joined in demurrer. . . .

The question is simply this: Can a negro, whose ancestors were imported into this country, and sold as slaves, become a member of the political community formed and brought into existence by the Constitution of the United States, and as such become entitled to all the rights, and privileges, and immunities, guarantied by that instrument to the citizen? One of which rights is the privilege of suing in a court of the United States in the cases specified in the Constitution.

It will be observed, that the plea applies to that class of persons only whose ancestors were negroes of the African race, and imported into this country, and sold and held as slaves. The only matter in issue before the court, therefore, is, whether the descendants of such slaves, when they shall be emancipated, or who are born of parents who had become free before their birth, are citizens of a State, in the sense in which the word citizen is used in the Constitution of the United States. And this being the only matter in dispute on the pleadings, the court must be understood as speaking in this opinion of that class only, that is of persons who are the descendants of Africans who were imported into this country and sold as slaves. . . .

We proceed to examine the case as presented by the pleadings.

The words "people of the United States" and "citizens" are synonymous terms, and mean the same thing. They both describe the political body who, according to our republican institutions, form the sovereignty, and who hold the power and conduct the government through their representatives. They are what we familiarly call the "sovereign people," and every citizen is one of this people, and a constituent member of this sovereignty. The question before us is, whether the class of persons described in the plea in abatement compose a portion of this people, and are constituent members of this sovereignty? We think they are not, and that they are not included, and were not intended to be included, under the word "citizens" in the Constitution, and can, therefore, claim none of the rights and privileges which that instrument provides for and secures to citizens of the United States. On the contrary, they were at that time considered as a subordinate and inferior class of beings, who had been subjugated by the dominant race, and whether emancipated or not, yet remained subject to their authority, and had no rights or privileges but such as those who held the power and the government might choose to grant them. . . .

In discussing this question, we must not confound the rights of citizenship which a state may confer within its own limits, and the rights of citizenship as a member of the Union. It does not by any means follow, because he has all the rights and privileges of a citizen of a State, that he must be a citizen of the United States. He may have all of the rights and privileges of the citizen of a State, and yet not be entitled to the rights and privileges of a citizen in any other State. For, previous to the adoption of the Constitution of the United States, every State had the undoubted right to confer on whomsoever it pleased the character of a citizen, and to endow him with all its rights. But this character, of course, was confined to the boundaries of the State, and gave him no rights or privileges in other States beyond those secured to him by the laws of nations and the comity of States. Nor have the several States surrendered the power of conferring these rights and privileges by adopting the Constitution of the United States. Each State may still confer them upon an alien, or any one it thinks proper, or upon any class or description of persons; yet he would not be a citizen in the sense in which that word is used in the Constitution of the United States, nor entitled to sue as such in one of its courts, nor to the privileges and immunities of a citizen in the other States. The rights which he would acquire would be restricted to the State which gave them. . . .

It is very clear, therefore, that no State can, by any Act or law of its own, passed since the adoption of the Constitution, introduce a new member into the political community created by the Constitution of the United States. It cannot make him a member of this community by making him a member of its own. And for the same reason it cannot introduce any person, or description of persons, who were not intended to be embraced in this new political family, which the Constitution brought into existence, but were intended to be excluded from it.

The question then arises, whether the provisions of the Constitution, in relation to the personal rights and privileges to which the citizen of a State should be entitled, embraced the negro African race, at that time in this country, or who might afterwards be imported, who had then or should afterwards be made free in any State; and to put it in the power of a single State to make him a citizen of the United States, and endue him with the full rights of citizenship in every other State without their consent. Does the Constitution of the United States act upon him whenever he shall be made free under the laws of a State, and raised there to the rank of a citizen, and immediately clothe him with all the privileges of a citizen in every other State, and in its own courts?

The court think the affirmative of these propositions cannot be maintained. And if it cannot, the plaintiff in error could not be a citizen of the State of Missouri, within the meaning of the Constitution of the United States, and, consequently, was not entitled to sue in its courts.

It is true, every person, and every class and description of persons, who were at the time of the adoption of the Constitution recognized as citizens in the several States, became also citizens of this new political body; but none other; it was formed by them, and for them and their posterity, but for no one else. And the personal rights and privileges guarantied to citizens of this new sovereignty were intended to embrace those only who were then members of the several state communities, or who should afterwards, by birthright or otherwise, become members, according to the provisions of the Constitution and the principles on which it was founded. . . .

It becomes necessary, therefore, to determine who were citizens of the several States when the Constitution was adopted. And in order to do this, we must recur to the governments and institutions of the thirteen Colonies, when they separated from Great Britain and formed new sovereignties. . . . We must inquire who, at that time, were recognized as the people or citizens of a State. . . .

In the opinion of the court, the legislation and histories of the times, and the language used in the Declaration of Independence, show, that neither the class of persons who had been imported as slaves, nor their descendants, whether they had become free or not, were then acknowledged as a part of the people, nor intended to be included in the general words used in that memorable instrument. . . .

There are two clauses in the Constitution which point directly and specifically to the negro race as a separate class of persons, and show clearly that they were not regarded as a portion of the people or citizens of the Government then formed.

One of these clauses reserves to each of the thirteen States the right to import slaves until the year 1808, if he thinks it proper. And the importation which it thus sanctions was unquestionably of persons of the race of which we are speaking, as the traffic in slaves in the United States had always been confined to them. And by the other provision the States pledge themselves to each other to maintain the right of property of the master, by delivering up to him any slave who may have escaped from his service, and be found within their respective territories. . . . And these two provisions show, conclusively, that neither the description of persons therein referred to, nor their descendants, were embraced in any of the other provisions of the Constitution: for certainly these two clauses were not intended to confer on them or their posterity the blessings of liberty, or any of the personal rights so carefully provided for the citizen. . . .

Indeed, when we look to the condition of this race in the several States at the time, it is impossible to believe that these rights and privileges were intended to be extended to them. . . .

Undoubtedly, a person may be a citizen, that is, a member of the community who form the sovereignty, although he exercises no share of the political power, and is incapacitated from holding particular offices. . . .

So, too, a person may be entitled to vote by the law of the State, who is not a citizen even of the State itself. And in some of the States of the Union foreigners not naturalized are allowed to vote. And the State may give the right to free negroes and mulattoes, but that does not make them citizens of the State, and still less of the United States. And the provision in the Constitution giving privileges and immunities in other States, does not apply to them.

Neither does it apply to a person who, being the citizen of a State, migrates to another State. For then he becomes subject to the laws of the State in which he lives, and he is no longer a citizen of the State from which he removed. And the State in which he resides may then, unquestionably, determine his *status* or condition, and place him among the class of persons who are not recognized as citizens, but belong to an inferior and subject race; and may deny him the privileges and immunities enjoyed by its citizens. . . .

. . . But if he ranks as a citizen of the State to which he belongs, within the meaning of the Constitution of the United States, then, whenever he goes into another State, the Constitution clothes him, as to the rights of person, with all the privileges and immunities which belong to citizens of the State. And if persons of the African race are citizens of a state, and of the United States, they would be entitled to all of these privileges and immunities in every State, and the State could not restrict them; for they would hold these privileges and immunities, under the paramount authority of the Federal Government, and its courts would be bound to maintain and enforce them, the Constitution and laws of the State to the contrary notwithstanding. . . .

And upon a full and careful consideration of the subject, the court is of opinion that, upon the facts stated in the plea in abatement, Dred Scott was not a citizen of Missouri within the meaning of the Constitution of the United States, and not entitled as such to sue in its courts; and, consequently, that the Circuit Court had no jurisdiction of the case, and that the judgment on the plea in abatement is erroneous. . . .

We proceed, therefore, to inquire whether the facts relied on by the plaintiff entitled him to his freedom. . . .

In considering this part of the controversy, two questions arise: 1st. Was he, together with his family, free in Missouri by reason of the stay in the territory of the United States hereinbefore mentioned? And 2d, If they were not, is Scott himself free by reason of his removal to Rock Island, in the State of Illinois, as stated in the above admissions?

The Act of Congress, upon which the plaintiff relies, declares that slavery and involuntary servitude, except as a punishment for crime, shall be forever prohibited in all that part of the territory ceded by France, under the name of Louisiana, which lies north of thirty-six degrees thirty minutes north latitude, and not included within the limits of Missouri. And the difficulty which meets us at the threshold of this part of the inquiry is, whether Congress was authorized to pass this law under any of the powers granted to it by the Constitution; for if the authority is not given by that instrument, it is the duty of this court to declare it void and inoperative, and incapable of conferring freedom upon any one who is held as a slave under the laws of any one of the States.

The counsel for the plaintiff has laid much stress upon that article in the Constitution which confers on Congress the power "to dispose of and make all needful rules and regulations respecting the territory or other property belonging to the United States;" but, in the judgment of the court, that provision has no bearing on the present controversy, and the power there given, whatever it may be, is confined, and was intended to be confined, to the territory which at that time belonged to, or was claimed by, the United States, and was within their boundaries as settled by the treaty with Great Britain, and can have no influence upon a territory afterwards acquired from a foreign Government. It was a special provision for a known and particular territory, and to meet a present emergency, and nothing more. . . .

If this clause is construed to extend to territory acquired by the present Government from a foreign nation, outside of the limits of any charter from the British Government to a colony, it would be difficult to say, why it was deemed necessary to give the Government the power to sell any vacant lands belonging to the sovereignty which might be found within it; and if this was necessary, why the grant of this power should precede the power to legislate over it and establish a Government there; and still more difficult to say, why it was deemed necessary so specially and particularly to grant the power to make needful rules and regulations in relation to any personal or movable property it might acquire there. For the words, *other property* necessarily, by every known rule of interpretation, must mean property of a different description from territory or land. And the difficulty would perhaps be insurmountable in endeavoring to account for the last member of the sentence, which provides that "nothing in this Constitution shall be so construed as to prejudice any claims of the United States or any particular State," or to say how any particular State could have claims in or to a territory ceded by a foreign Government, or to account for associating this provision with the preceding provisions of the clause, with which it would appear to have no connection. . . .

The rights of private property have been guarded with equal care. Thus the rights of property are united with the rights of person, and placed on the same ground by the fifth amendment to the Constitution. . . . An Act of Congress which deprives a person of the United States of his liberty or property merely because he came himself or brought his property into a particular Territory of the United States, and who had committed no offense against the laws, could hardly be dignified with the name of due process of law. . . .

. . . if the Constitution recognizes the right of property of the master in a slave, and makes no distinction between that description of property and other property owned by a citizen, no tribunal, acting under the authority of the United States, whether it be legislative, executive, or judicial, has a right to draw such a distinction, or deny to it the benefit of the provisions and guarantees which have been provided for the protection of private property against the encroachments of the Government.

Now . . . the right of property in a slave is distinctly and expressly affirmed in the Constitution. The right to traffic in it, like an ordinary article of merchandise and property, was guaranteed to the citizens of the United States, in every State that might desire it, for twenty years. And the Government in express terms is pledged to protect it in all future time, if the slave escapes from his owner. . . . And no word can be found in the Constitution which gives Congress a greater power over

slave property, or which entitles property of that kind to less protection than property of any other description. The only power conferred is the power coupled with the duty of guarding and protecting the owner in his rights.

Upon these considerations, it is the opinion of the court that the Act of Congress which prohibited a citizen from holding and owning property of this kind in the territory of the United States north of the line therein mentioned, is not warranted by the Constitution, and is therefore void; and that neither Dred Scott himself, nor any of his family, were made free by being carried into this territory; even if they had been carried there by the owner, with the intention of becoming a permanent resident. . . .

Upon the whole, therefore, it is the judgment of this court, that it appears by the record before us that the plaintiff in error is not a citizen of Missouri, in the sense in which that word is used in the Constitution; and that the Circuit Court of the United States, for that reason, had no jurisdiction in the case, and could give no judgment in it.

Its judgment for the defendant must, consequently, be reversed, and a mandate issued directing the suit to be dismissed for want of jurisdiction.

"Be it enacted"

FEMALE SUFFRAGE IN WYOMING
1869

Four years after the Civil War, Wyoming Territory granted women "of the age of twenty-one years" the right of suffrage. Women also could hold public office. The first states to grant women permanent suffrage were four western states: Wyoming, the Equality State (which was admitted into the Union in 1890) in 1869; Colorado, in 1893; Utah, in 1895; and Idaho, in 1896. The Supreme Court, in 1875, had unanimously decided the right of suffrage must result from explicit legislation or Constitutional amendment rather than through interpretation of the Constitution. Three years later, Congressmen began introducing Constitutional amendments extending suffrage to women. By the time the Nineteenth Amendment extended the vote in 1920, the following states also had full suffrage: Montana, Texas, South Dakota, Kansas, Oklahoma, Nevada, Arizona, California, Oregon, Washington, Arkansas, New York, and Michigan. Some other states let women vote in Presidential elections.

An Act to grant to the women of Wyoming Territory the right of suffrage and to hold office. Be it enacted by the Council and House of Representatives of the Territory of Wyoming. Section 1. That every woman of the age of twenty-one years residing in this Territory may at every election to be holden under the laws thereof, cash her vote, and her rights to the elective Franchise, and to hold office, shall be the same under the election laws of the Territory as those of electors. Section 2. This act shall take effect and be in force from and after its passage.

"Social equality is the extremest folly"

BOOKER T. WASHINGTON REPRESENTS THE NEGRO RACE

1895

The educator Booker Taliaferro Washington (1856–1915) was the most prominent American black man in his day. Born a slave, he worked in a salt furnace and a coal mine while becoming an exceptional student. Washington later became both an outstanding teacher and administrator. He transformed Tuskegee (Alabama) Normal and Industrial School, a simple vocational school, into The Tuskegee Institute, a leading center for the practical training of hard-working blacks in trades and professions. Washington also was a leader in social reform. He stressed the value of education and jobs as tools for advancement for black Americans in battles to win political and civil rights. Because Washington derived power from white support, and accepted racial segregation and discrimination, many other black leaders saw his philosophy as the guarantee of continued servility. But there was considerable cheering from blacks when "the representative of Negro enterprise and Negro civilization" rose to deliver his "Compromise" speech at the Atlanta Exposition in 1895. Washington saw thousands of eyes looking intently into his face. "The thing that was uppermost in his mind," he later related about himself and the occasion, "was the desire to say something that would cement the friendship of the races and bring about hearty cooperation between them." He declared that "in all things that are purely social we can be as separate as the fingers, yet one as the hand in all things essential to mutual progress." Georgia's governor rushed across the platform to congratulate the speaker. President Grover Cleveland (1837–1908) wrote to Washington: "Your words cannot fail to delight and encourage all who wish well for your race . . . "

One-third of the population of the South is of the Negro race. No enterprise seeking the material, civil, or moral welfare of this section can disregard this element of our population and reach the highest success. . . .

To those of my race who depend on bettering their condition in a foreign land or who underestimate the importance of cultivating friendly relations with the Southern white man, who is their next-door neighbour, I would say: "Cast down your bucket where you are"—cast it down in making friends in every manly way of the people of all races by whom we are surrounded.

Cast it down in agriculture, mechanics, in commerce, in domestic service, and in the professions. And in this connection it is well to bear in mind that whatever other sins the South may be called to bear, when it comes to business, pure and simple, it is in the South that the Negro is given a man's chance in the commercial world, and in nothing is this Exposition more eloquent than in emphasizing this chance. Our greatest danger is that in the great leap from slavery to freedom we may overlook the fact that the masses of us are to live by the productions of our hands, and fail to keep in mind that we shall prosper in proportion as we learn to dignify and glorify common labour and put brains and skill into the common occupations of life; shall prosper in proportion as we learn to draw the line between the superficial and the substantial, the ornamental gewgaws of life and the useful. No race can prosper till it learns that there is as much dignity in tilling a field as in writing a poem. It is at the bottom of life we must begin, and not at the top. Nor should we permit our grievances to overshadow our opportunities.

To those of the white race who look to the incoming of those of foreign birth and strange tongue and habits for the prosperity of the South, were I permitted I would repeat what I say to my own race, "Cast down your bucket where you are." Cast it down among the eight millions of Negroes whose habits you know, whose fidelity and love you have tested in days when to have proved treacherous meant the ruin of your firesides. Cast down your bucket among these people who have, without strikes and labour wars, tilled your fields, cleared your forests, builded your railroads and cities, and brought forth treasures from the bowels of the earth, and helped make possible this magnificent representation of the progress of the South. Casting down your bucket among my people, helping and encouraging them as you are doing on these grounds, and to education of head, hand, and heart, you will find that they will buy your surplus land, make blossom the waste places in your fields, and run your factories. While doing this, you can be sure in the future, as in the past, that you and your families will be surrounded by the most patient, faithful, law-abiding, and unresentful people that the world has seen. As we have proved our loyalty to you in the past, in nursing your children, watching by the sick-bed of your mothers and fathers, and often following them with tear-dimmed eyes to their graves, so in the future, in our humble way, we shall stand by you with a devotion that no foreigner can approach, ready to lay down our lives, if need be, in defence of yours, interlacing our industrial, commercial, civil, and religious life with yours in a way that shall make the interests of both races one. In all things that are purely social we can be as separate as the fingers, yet one as the hand in all things essential to mutual progress.

There is no defence or security for any of us except in the highest intelligence and development of all. If anywhere there are efforts tending to curtail the fullest growth of the Negro, let these efforts be turned into stimulating, encouraging, and making him the most useful and intelligent citizen. Effort or means so invested will pay a thousand per cent interest. These efforts will be twice blessed—"blessing him that gives and him that takes."

There is no escape through law of man or God from the inevitable:

> The laws of changeless justice bind
> Oppressor with oppressed;
> And close as sin and suffering joined
> We march to fate abreast.

Nearly sixteen millions of hands will aid you in pulling the load upward, or they will pull against you the load downward. We shall constitute one-third and more of the ignorance and crime of the South, or one-third its intelligence and progress; we shall contribute one-third to the business and industrial prosperity of the South, or we shall prove a veritable body of death, stagnating, depressing, retarding every effort to advance the body politic. . . .

The wisest among my race understand that the agitation of questions of social equality is the extremest folly, and that progress in the enjoyment of all the privileges that will come to us must be the result of severe and constant struggle rather than of artificial forcing. No race that has anything to contribute to the markets of the world is long in any degree ostracized. It is important and right that all privileges of the law be ours, but it is vastly more important that we be prepared for the exercises of these privileges. The opportunity to earn a dollar in a factory just now is worth infinitely more than the opportunity to spend a dollar in an opera-house. . . .

I pledge that in your effort to work out the great and intricate problem which God has laid at the doors of the South, you shall have at all times the patient, sympathetic help of my race; only let this be constantly in mind, that, while from representations in these buildings of the product of field, of forest, of mine, of factory, letters, and art, much good will come, yet far above and beyond material benefits will be that higher good, that, let us pray God, will come, in a blotting out of sectional differences and racial animosities and suspicions, in a determination to administer absolute justice, in a willing obedience among all classes to the mandates of law. This, this, coupled with our material prosperity, will bring into our beloved South a new heaven and a new earth.

"Legislation is powerless to eradicate racial instincts"

PLESSY V. FERGUSON
1896

Private railroad companies did not want to continue segregating passengers according to race. Hoping for a favorable constitutional precedent, they financed the public-interest litigation *Plessy v. Ferguson.* In 1892, Homer Adolph Plessy (died 1925), a light-complexioned black man, a shoemaker, was arrested and forcibly ejected when he refused to sit in the designated "black" coach of a train in Louisiana. (Ferguson was Judge John H. Ferguson, a segregationist, of New Orleans.) The United States Supreme Court (8–1) upheld Louisiana's "Jim Crow" law requiring railway companies carrying passengers to provide equal but separate accommodations for the white and the colored races: Enforced racial segregation was constitutional under the Thirteenth and Fourteen Amendments to the Constitution; separation of the races was natural; it did not stamp blacks with a badge of inferiority; government could classify people on the basis of race. (Even drinking fountains were segregated in parts of the U.S.) In a blistering dissent, Justice John Marshall Harlan (1833–1911) affirmed the principle of equal rights: "There is no caste here. Our Constitution is color-blind, and neither knows nor tolerates classes among citizens . . . The law regards man as man, and takes no account of his surroundings or his color when his civil rights as guaranteed by the supreme law of the land are involved." (The "separate but equal" doctrine reigned until the Warren Court's unanimous ruling in *Brown v. Board of Education* [1954]).

This case turns upon the constitutionality of an act of the general assembly of the state of Louisiana, passed in 1890, providing for separate railway carriages for the white and colored races. . . .

The constitutionality of this act is attacked upon the ground that it conflicts both with the 13th Amendment of the Constitution, abolishing slavery, and the 14th Amendment, which prohibits certain restrictive legislation on the part of the states.

1. That it does not conflict with the 13th Amendment, which abolished slavery and involuntary servitude, except as a punishment for crime, is too clear for argument. . . .

A statute which implies merely a legal distinction between the white and colored races—a distinction which is founded in the color of the two races, and which must always exist so long as white men are distinguished from the other race by color—has no tendency to destroy the legal equality of the two races, or re-establish a state of involuntary servitude. . . .

Laws permitting, and even requiring their

separation in places where they are liable to be brought into contact do not necessarily imply the inferiority of either race to the other, and have been generally, if not universally, recognized as within the competency of the state legislatures in the exercise of their police power. The most common instance of this is connected with the establishment of separate schools for white and colored children, which have been held to be a valid exercise of the legislative power even by courts of states where the political rights of the colored race have been longest and most earnestly enforced. . . .

It is claimed by the plaintiff in error that, in any mixed community, the reputation of belonging to the dominant race, in this instance the white race is *property,* in the same sense that a right of action, or of inheritance, is property. Conceding this to be so, for the purposes of this case, we are unable to see how this statute deprives him of, or in any way affects his right to, such property. . . .

So far, then, as a conflict with the 14th Amendment is concerned, the case reduces itself to the question whether the statute of Louisiana is a reasonable regulation, and with respect to this there must necessarily be a large discretion on the part of the legislature. In determining the question of reasonableness it is at liberty to act with reference to the established usages, customs, and traditions of the people, and with a view to the promotion of their comfort, and the preservation of the public peace and good order. Gauged by this standard, we cannot say that a law which authorizes or even requires the separation of the two races in public conveyances is unreasonable or more obnoxious to the 14th Amendment than the acts of Congress requiring separate schools for colored children in the District of Columbia, the constitutionality of which does not seem to have been questioned, or the corresponding acts of state legislatures.

We consider the underlying fallacy of the plaintiff's argument to consist in the assumption that the enforced separation of the two races stamps the colored race with a badge of inferiority. If this be so, it is not by reason of anything found in the act, but solely because the colored race chooses to put that construction upon it. . . .

The argument assumes that social prejudice may be overcome by legislation, and that equal rights cannot be secured to the Negro except by an enforced commingling of the two races. We cannot accept this proposition. If the two races are to meet on terms of social equality, it must be the result of natural affinities, a mutual appreciation of each other's merits and a voluntary consent of individuals. . . . Legislation is powerless to eradicate racial instincts or to abolish distinctions based upon physical differences, and the attempt to do so can only result in accentuating the difficulties of the present situation. If the civil and political right of both races be equal, one cannot be inferior to the other civilly or politically. If one race be inferior to the other socially, the Constitution of the United States cannot put them upon the same plane. . . .

"All mothers welcome"

MARGARET SANGER'S "DODGER"
1916

Margaret Higgins Sanger (1883–1966) was the tenth child in a family of eleven. A trained maternity nurse, the birth-control pioneer was determined to open a clinic in New York City in order "to disseminate information where it was poignantly required by human beings. Our inspiration was the mothers of the poor; our object, to help them." The "curse of Eve" must be lifted:

> "with a small bundle of handbills and a large amount of zeal, we fared forth each morning in a house-to-house canvass of the district in which the clinic was located. Every family . . . received a 'dodger' printed in English, Yiddish, and Italian. Nothing, not even the ghost of Anthony Comstock, could have stopped the people from coming! All day long and far into the evening, in ever-increasing numbers, they came. A hundred women and a score of men sought our help on the opening day."

"The First Lady of Contraception" was arrested for sending birth-control information through the mail, and sentenced to a month in a workhouse for opening a clinic in Brooklyn. Before she could claim that the battle for birth control had been brought to ultimate victory, Sanger said that she had to "enlist in this army every enlightened and intelligent voter of this republic. Together we shall march to the gates of victory."

MOTHERS!

Can you afford to have a large family?
Do you want any more children?
If not, why do you have them?

DO NOT KILL, DO NOT TAKE LIFE, BUT PREVENT

Safe, Harmless Information can be obtained of trained Nurses at

46 AMBOY STREET
NEAR PITKIN AVE. — BROOKLYN.

Tell Your Friends and Neighbors.   All Mothers Welcome

A registration fee of 10 cents entitles any mother to this information.

מומערס!

זייט איהר פערמעגליך צו האבען א גרויסע פאמיליע?

ווילט איהר האבען נאך קינדער?

אויב ניט, ווארום האט איהר זיי?

מערדערט ניט, נעהמט ניט קיין לעבען, נור פערהיט זיך.

זיכערע, אונשעדליכע אויסקינפטע קענט איהר באקומען פון ערפארענע נוירסעס אין

46 אמבאי סטריט ניער פיטקין עוועניו ברוקלין

מאכט דאס באקאנט צו אייערע פריינד און שכנות.   יעדער מומער איז וועלקאמען

פיר 10 סענט איינשרייב־געלד זיינט איהר בערעכטיגט צו דיעזע אינפארמיישאן.

MADRI!

Potete permettervi il lusso d'avere altri bambini?
Ne volete ancora?
Se non ne volete piu', perche' continuate a metterli al mondo?

NON UCCIDETE MA PREVENITE!

Informazioni sicure ed innocue saranno fornite da infermiere autorizzate a

46 AMBOY STREET   Near Pitkin Ave. Brooklyn

a cominciare dal 12 Ottobre. Avvertite le vostre amiche e vicine.

Tutte le madri sono ben accette. La tassa d'iscrizione di 10 cents da diritto a qualunque madre di ricevere consigli ed informazioni gratis.

Margaret Sanger's "Dodger"

"Thought . . . should be freely expressed"

AMERICAN CIVIL LIBERTIES UNION CREED

1929

The American Civil Liberties Union (A.C.L.U.), successor to the National Civil Liberties Bureau, was formed to maintain throughout the United States and its possessions the rights of free speech, free press, free assemblage, and other civil rights, and to take all legitimate action in furtherance of such purposes. The first directors included the celebrated liberals Roger M. Baldwin (1884–1981), Morris Ernst (1888–1976), Walter Frank (1882–1969), Elizabeth Gurley Flynn (1890–1964), Arthur Garfield Hays (1881–1954), Rex Stout (1886–1975), and Norman M. Thomas (1884–1968). The national committee included Jane Addams (1860–1935), a social reformer whom "superpatriots" labeled a traitor and the most dangerous woman in America (she opposed war); in 1931, Addams became the first American woman to be honored with the Nobel Peace Prize.

We stand on the general principle that all thought on matters of public concern should be freely expressed without interference. Orderly social progress is promoted by unrestricted freedom of opinion. The punishment of mere opinion, without overt acts, is never in the interest of orderly progress. Suppression of opinion makes for violence and bloodshed.

The principle of freedom of speech, press and assemblage, embodied in our constitutional law, must be reasserted in its application to American conditions today. That application must deal with various methods now used to repress new ideas and democratic movements. The following paragraphs cover the most significant of the tactics of repression in the United States today.

1. Free Speech. There should be no control whatever in advance over what any person may say. The right to meet and to speak freely without permit should be unquestioned.

There should be no prosecutions for the mere expression of opinion on matters of public concern, however radical, however violent. The ex-pression of all opinions, however radical, should be tolerated. The fullest freedom of speech should be encouraged by setting aside special places in streets or parks and in the use of public buildings, free of charge, for public meetings of any sort.

2. Free Press. There should be no censorship over the mails by the post-office or any other agency at any time or in any way. Privacy of communication should be inviolate. Printed matter should never be subject to a political censorship. The granting or revoking of second class mailing privileges should have nothing whatever to do with a paper's opinions and policies.

If libelous, fraudulent, or other illegal matter is being circulated, it should be seized by proper warrant through the prosecuting authorities, not by the post-office department. The business of the post-office department is to carry the mails, not to investigate crime or to act as censors.

There should be no control over the distribution of literature at meetings or hand to hand in public or in private places. No system of licenses for distribution should be tolerated.

3. Freedom of Assemblage. Meetings in public places, parades and processions should be freely permitted, the only reasonable regulation being the advance notification to the police of the time and place. No discretion should be given the police to prohibit parades or processions, but merely to alter routes in accordance with the imperative demands of traffic in crowded cities. There should be no laws or regulations prohibiting the display of red flags or other political emblems.

The right of assemblage is involved in the right to picket in time of strike. Peaceful picketing, therefore, should not be prohibited, regulated by injunction, by order of court or by police edict. It is the business of the police in places where picketing is conducted merely to keep traffic free and to handle specific violations of law against persons upon complaint.

4. The Right to Strike. The right of workers to organize in organizations of their own choosing, and to strike, should never be infringed by law.

Compulsory arbitration is to be condemned not only because it destroys the workers' right to strike, but because it lays emphasis on one set of obligations alone, those of workers to society.

5. Law Enforcement. The practice of deputizing privately paid police as general police officers should be opposed. So should the attempts of private company employes to police the streets or property other than that of the company.

The efforts of private associations to take into their own hands the enforcement of law should be opposed at every point. Public officials, employes of private corporations, and leaders of mobs, who interfere with the exercise of the constitutionally established rights of free speech and free assembly, should be vigorously proceeded against.

The sending of troops into areas of industrial conflict to maintain law and order almost inevitably results in the government taking sides in an industrial conflict in behalf of the employer. The presence of troops, whether or not martial law is declared, very rarely affects the employer adversely, but it usually results in the complete denial of civil rights to the workers.

6. Search and Seizure. It is the custom of certain federal, state and city officials, particularly in cases involving civil liberty, to make arrests without warrant, to enter upon private property, and to seize papers and literature without legal process. Such practices should be contested. Officials so violating constitutional guarantees should be proceeded against.

7. The Right to a Fair Trial. Every person charged with an offense should have the fullest opportunity for a fair trial, for securing counsel and bail in a reasonable sum. In the case of a poor person, special aid should be organized to secure a fair trial, and when necessary, an appeal. The legal profession should be alert to defend cases involving civil liberty. The resolutions of various associations of lawyers against taking cases of radicals are wholly against the traditions of American liberty.

8. Immigration, Deportation and Passports. No person should be refused admission to the United States on the ground of holding objectionable opinions. The present restrictions against radicals of various beliefs is wholly opposed to our tradition of political asylum.

No alien should be deported merely for the expression of opinion or for membership in a radical or revolutionary organization. This is as un-American a practice as the prosecution of citizens for expression of opinion.

The attempt to revoke naturalization papers in order to declare a citizen an alien subject to deportation is a perversion of a law which was intended to cover only cases of fraud.

Citizenship papers should not be refused to any alien because of the expression of radical views, or activities in the cause of labor.

The granting of passports to or from the United States should not be dependent merely upon the opinions of citizens or membership in radical or labor organizations.

9. Liberty in Education. The attempts to maintain a uniform orthodox opinion among teachers should be opposed. The attempts of educational authorities to inject into public school and college instruction propaganda in the interest of any particular theory of society to the exclusion of others should be opposed.

10. Race Equality. Every attempt to discriminate between races in the application of all principles of civil liberty here set forth should be opposed.

HOW TO GET CIVIL LIBERTY

We realize that these standards of civil liberty cannot be attained as abstract principles or as constitutional guarantees. Economic or political power is necessary to assert and maintain all "rights". In the midst of any conflict they are not granted by the side holding the economic and political power, except as they may be forced by the strength of the opposition. However, the mere public assertion of the principle of freedom of opinion in the words or deeds of individuals, or weak minorities, helps win it recognition, and in the long run makes for tolerance and against resort to violence.

Today the organized movements of labor and of the farmers are waging the chief fight for civil liberty throughout the United States as part of their effort for increased control of industry. Publicity, demonstrations, political activities and legal aid are organized nationally and locally. Only by such an aggressive policy of insistence can rights be secured and maintained. The union of organized labor, the farmers, radical and liberal movements is the most effective means to this.

It is these forces which the American Civil Liberties Union serves in their efforts for civil liberty. The practical work of free speech demonstrations, publicity and legal defense is done primarily in the struggles of the organized labor and farmers movements.

Source: Archives of the American Civil Liberties Union, Reel 63, Seeley G. Mudd Manuscript Library, Department of Rare Books and Special Collections, Princeton University Libraries.

CERTAIN UNALIENABLE RIGHTS

"Such segregation is a denial of the equal protection of the laws"

BROWN V. BOARD OF EDUCATION
1954

Chief Justice Earl Warren (1891–1974) read the unanimous landmark decision of the Supreme Court: Separate was not equal. "Separate educational facilities are inherently unequal," even though buildings, transportation, curricula, and qualifications of teachers were substantially equal. Racial segregation in public schools denied black students their rights under the Fourteenth Amendment, which defines citizenship and restrains state governments from violating civil rights. Thurgood Marshall (1908–1993), counsel for the National Association for the Advancement of Colored People, who, in 1967, would be appointed to the Supreme Court by President Lyndon B. Johnson (1908–1973), had argued that the Constitution denies "any power to make any racial classification in any governmental field. That the Constitution is color-blind is our dedicated belief." The desegregation decision overturned 58-year-old *Plessy v. Ferguson* allowing separate but equal transportation facilities. In that 1896 case, which had backfired on the litigates, the Court held that the Fourteenth Amendment was "not intended to abolish distinctions based upon color that were 'reasonable.' "

• • • **M**inors of the Negro race, through their legal representatives, seek the aid of the courts in obtaining admission to the public schools of their community on a nonsegregated basis. In each instance, they had been denied admission to schools attended by white children under laws requiring or permitting segregation according to race. This segregation was alleged to deprive the plaintiffs of the equal protection of the laws under the Fourteenth Amendment. In each of the cases other than the Delaware case, a three-judge federal District Court denied relief to the plaintiffs on the so-called "separate but equal" doctrine announced by this Court in *Plessy v. Ferguson*, 163 U.S. 537. Under that doctrine, equality of treatment is accorded when the races are provided substantially equal facilities, even though these facilities be separate. In the Delaware case, the Supreme Court of Delaware adhered to that doctrine, but ordered that the plaintiffs be admitted to the white schools because of their superiority to the Negro schools.

The plaintiffs contend that segregated public schools are not "equal" and cannot be made "equal," and that hence they are deprived of the equal protection of the laws. . . .

Reargument was largely devoted to the circumstances surrounding the adoption of the Fourteenth Amendment in 1868. It covered exhaustively consideration of the amendment in Congress, ratification by the states, then-existing practices in racial segregation, and the views of proponents and opponents of the amendment.

This discussion and our own investigation convince us that, although these sources cast some light, it is not enough to resolve the problem with which we are faced. At best, they are inconclusive. . . .

The doctrine of "separate but equal" did not make its appearance in this Court until 1896 in the case of *Plessy v. Ferguson, supra,* involving not education but transportation. American courts have since labored with the doctrine for over half a century. . . .

Our decision, therefore, cannot turn on merely a comparison of these tangible factors in the Negro and white schools involved in each of the cases. We must look instead to the effect of segregation itself on public education.

In approaching this problem, we cannot turn the clock back to 1868 when the amendment was adopted, or even to 1896 when *Plessy v. Ferguson* was written. We must consider public education in the light of its full development and its present place in American life throughout the nation. Only in this way can it be determined if segregation in public schools deprives these plaintiffs of the equal protection of the laws.

Today, education is perhaps the most important function of state and local governments. Compulsory school-attendance laws and the great expenditures for education both demonstrate our recognition of the importance of education to our democratic society. It is required in the performance of our most basic public responsibilities, even service in the armed forces. It

is the very foundation of good citizenship. Today it is a principal instrument in awakening the child to cultural values, in preparing him for later professional training, and in helping him to adjust normally to his environment. In these days, it is doubtful that any child may reasonably be expected to succeed in life if he is denied the opportunity of an education. Such an opportunity, where the state has undertaken to provide it, is a right which must be made available to all on equal terms. . . .

We conclude that in the field of public education the doctrine of "separate but equal" has no place. Separate educational facilities are inherently unequal. Therefore, we hold that the plaintiffs and others similarly situated for whom the actions have been brought are, by reason of the segregation complained of, deprived of the equal protection of the laws guaranteed by the Fourteenth Amendment. This disposition makes unnecessary any discussion whether such segregation also violates the due process clause of the Fourteenth Amendment.

Because these are class actions, because of the wide applicability of this decision, and because of the great variety of local conditions, the formulation of decrees in these cases presents problems of considerable complexity. On reargument, the consideration of appropriate relief was necessarily subordinated to the primary question—the constitutionality of segregation in public education. We have now announced that such segregation is a denial of the equal protection of the laws. . . .

"No . . . qualification . . . shall be imposed or applied"

VOTING RIGHTS
1965

"The most difficult domestic issue we have ever faced" is how President Lyndon B. Johnson (1908–1973) described the "civil rights problem." The more it was grappled with, "the more we realize that the position of minorities in American society is defined not merely by law, but by social, education, and economic conditions." An "ideal America" would not need to seek new laws guaranteeing the rights of citizens. In the 1960s, the civil rights movement shamed most white Americans into exploring ways to uphold the civil rights of black citizens. President John F. Kennedy (1917–1963) made civil rights legislation a high priority. President Johnson, in his first address to Congress after the assassination of President Kennedy, urged action. The Voting Rights Act of 1965 provided for effective Federal protection enabling blacks to register and vote; the Supreme Court alone cannot always protect constitutionally guaranteed rights. President Johnson called the Act a "triumph as huge as any victory that has ever been won on any battlefield;" it was "a great challenge" to black leadership, which must teach blacks their responsibilities and lead them to exercise their rights. In 1996, the Supreme Court voided race-based plans for redistricting, or gerrymandering. The Court's precedents "acknowledge voters as more than mere racial statistics," Justice Sandra Day O'Connor (born 1930) asserted.

SEC. 2. No voting qualification or prerequisite to voting, or standard, practice, or procedure shall be imposed or applied by any State or political subdivision to deny or abridge the right of any citizen of the United States to vote on account of race or color. . . .

SEC. 4. (a) To assure that the right of citizens of the United States to vote is not denied or abridged on account of race or color, no citizen shall be denied the right to vote in any Federal, State, or local election because of his failure to comply with any test or device in any State with respect to which the determinations have been made under subsection (b) or in any political subdivision with respect to which such determinations have been made as a separate unit, unless the United States District Court for the District of Columbia in an action for a declaratory judgment brought by such State or subdivision against the United States has determined that no such test or device has been used during the five years preceding the filing of the action for the purpose or with the effect of denying or abridging the right to vote on account of race or color: *Provided,* That no such declaratory judgment shall issue with respect to any plaintiff for a period of five years after the entry of a final judgment of any court of the United States, other than the denial of a declaratory judgment under this section, whether entered prior to or after the enactment of this Act, determining that denials or abridgments of the right to vote on account of race or color through the use of such tests or devices have occurred anywhere in the territory of such plaintiff.

(d) . . . no State or political subdivision shall be determined to have engaged in the use of tests or devices for the purpose or with the effect of denying or abridging the right to vote on account of race or color if (1) incidents of such use have been few in number and have been promptly and effectively corrected by State or local action, (2) the continuing effect of such incidents has been eliminated, and (3) there is no reasonable probability of their recurrence in the future.

(e)(1) Congress hereby declares that to secure the rights under the fourteenth amendment of persons educated in American-flag schools in which the predominant classroom language was other than English, it is necessary to prohibit the States from conditioning the right to vote of such persons on ability to read, write, understand, or interpret any matter in the English language.

(2) No person who demonstrates that he has successfully completed the sixth primary grade in a public school in, or a private school accredited by, any State or territory, the District of Columbia, or the Commonwealth of Puerto Rico in which the predominant classroom language was other than English, shall be denied the right to vote in any Federal, State, or local election because of his inability to read, write, understand, or interpret any matter in the English language except that in States in which State law provides that a different level of education is presumptive of literacy, he shall demonstrate that he has successfully completed an equivalent level of education in a public school in, or a private school accredited by, any State or territory, the District of Columbia, or the Commonwealth of Puerto Rico in which the predominant classroom language was other than English. . . .

"Riot means a public disturbance involving an act or acts of violence"

CIVIL RIGHTS ACT
1968

The first piece of Congressional civil rights legislation, enacted a year after Appomattox, was designed to recognize the 4,000,000 or so freed slaves and free African-Americans as citizens on an equal basis with whites. A century later, Congress was still enacting civil rights legislation. Two days after the funeral of the assassinated civil rights leader Dr. Martin Luther King, Jr. (1929–1968), and propelled by the forceful leadership of a southern President, Lyndon B. Johnson (1908–1973), Congress passed its fifth civil rights bill in eleven years. The Civil Rights Act of 1968 prohibited discrimination on the basis of race, religion, or national origin in selling or renting houses; it affected 80 percent of the country's housing. President Johnson affirmed that "it is not just Negroes, but really it is all of us who must overcome the crippling legacy of bigotry and injustice." The legislation also prescribed penalties for certain acts of violence or intimidation.

SEC. 2101.

(a) (1.) Whoever travels in interstate or foreign commerce or uses any facility of interstate or foreign commerce, including, but not limited to, the mail, telegraph, telephone, radio, or television, with intent—

(A) to incite a riot; or

(B) to organize, promote, encourage, participate in, or carry on a riot; or

(C) to commit any act of violence in furtherance of a riot; or

(D) to aid or abet any person in inciting or participating in or carrying on a riot or committing any act of violence in furtherance of a riot;

and who either during the course of any such travel or use or thereafter performs or attempts to perform any other overt act for any purpose specified [above]—

Shall be fined not more than $10,000, or imprisoned not more than five years, or both.

(b) In any prosecution under this section, proof that a defendant engaged or attempted to engage in one or more of the overt acts described [above] and (1) has traveled in interstate or foreign commerce, or (2) has use of or used any facility of interstate or foreign commerce, including but not limited to, mail, telegraph, telephone, radio, or television, to communicate with or broadcast to any person or group of persons prior to such overt acts, such travel or use shall be admissible proof to establish that such defendant traveled in or used such facility of interstate or foreign commerce.

SEC. 2102.

(a) As used in this chapter, the term "riot" means a public disturbance involving (1) an act or acts of violence by one or more persons part of an assemblage of three or more persons, which act or acts shall constitute a clear and present danger of, or shall result in, damage or injury to the property of any other person or to the person of any other individual or (2) a threat or threats of the commission of an act or acts of violence by one or more persons part of an assemblage of three or more persons having, individually or collectively, the ability of immediate execution of such threat or threats, where the performance of the threatened act or acts of violence would constitute a clear and present danger of, or would result in, damage or injury to the property of any other person or to the person of any other individual.

(b) As used in this chapter, the term "to incite a riot," or "to organize, promote, encourage, participate in, or carry on a riot," includes, but is not limited to, urging or instigating other persons to riot, but shall not be deemed to mean the mere oral or written (1) advocacy of ideas or (2) expression of belief, not involving advocacy of any act or acts of violence or assertion of the rightness of, or the right to commit, any such act or acts.

TITLE X

CIVIL OBEDIENCE

Civil Disorders

(a)(1) Whoever teaches or demonstrates to any other person the use, application, or making of any firearm or explosive or incendiary device, or technique capable of causing injury or death to persons, knowing or having reason to know or intending that the same will be unlawfully employed for use in, or in furtherance of, a civil disorder which may in any way or degree obstruct, delay, or adversely affect commerce or the movement of any article or commodity in commerce or the conduct or performance of any federally protected function; or

(2) Whoever transports or manufactures for transportation in commerce any firearm, or explosive or incendiary device, knowing or having reason to know or intending that the same will be used unlawfully in furtherance of a civil disorder; or

(3) Whoever commits or attempts to commit any act to obstruct, impede, or interfere with any fireman or law enforcement officer lawfully engaged in the lawful performance of his official duties incident to and during the commission of a civil disorder which in any way or degree obstructs, delays, or adversely affects commerce or the movement of any article or commodity in commerce or the conduct or performance of any federally protected function—

Shall be fined not more than $10,000 or imprisoned not more than five years, or both.

"On behalf of herself and all other women similarly situated"

ROE V. WADE

1973

The Supreme Court of the United States limited the power of the state to regulate abortion. Justice Harry A. Blackmun (born 1908), writing for the majority (7–2), held that the Constitution's mention of personal liberty is broad enough to include the right to privacy; it includes a woman's decision whether to bear a child. In _Roe v. Wade,_ the Court did not resolve the question of when life begins. States have some valid interests in regulating abortion; however, they cannot decide, for instance, that fetuses have the same rights as newborn infants. States _could_ place increasing restrictions on abortions as the period of pregnancy lengthens. "Jane Roe" (her real name is Norma McCorvey) was a pregnant single woman who, after a failed relationship, had challenged the constitutionality of the severely restrictive Texas abortion law. (Henry Wade [born 1914], who was the father of three daughters and two sons, had investigated the assassination of President John F. Kennedy and was the long-time District Attorney of Dallas County.) After the District Court found partially for _Roe,_ both sides appealed to the Supreme Court for its opinion on constitutional challenges to state criminal abortion legislation. The _Roe_ decision energized the substantial "right to life" constituency.

This Texas federal appeal and its Georgia companion, _Doe_ v. _Bolton, post,_ p. 179, present constitutional challenges to state criminal abortion legislation. The Texas statutes under attack here are typical of those that have been in effect in many States for approximately a century. The Georgia statutes, in contrast, have a modern cast and are a legislative product that, to an extent at least, obviously reflects the influences of recent attitudinal change, of advancing medical knowledge and techniques, and of new thinking about an old issue.

We forthwith acknowledge our awareness of the sensitive and emotional nature of the abortion controversy, of the vigorous opposing views, of the deep and seemingly absolute convictions that the subject inspires. One's philosophy, one's experiences, one's exposure to the raw edges of human existence, one's religious training, one's attitudes toward life and family and their values, and the moral standards one establishes and seeks to observe, are all likely to influence and to color one's thinking and conclusions about abortion.

In addition, population growth, pollution, poverty, and racial overtones tend to complicate and not to simplify the problem.

Our task, of course, is to resolve the issue by

constitutional measurement, free of emotion and of predilection.

II

Jane Roe, a single woman who was residing in Dallas County, Texas, instituted this federal action in March 1970 against the District Attorney of the county. She sought a declaratory judgment that the Texas criminal abortion statutes were unconstitutional on their face, and an injunction restraining the defendant from enforcing the statutes.

Roe alleged that she was unmarried and pregnant; that she wished to terminate her pregnancy by an abortion "performed by a competent, licensed physician, under safe, clinical conditions"; that she was unable to get a "legal" abortion in Texas because her life did not appear to be threatened by the continuation of her pregnancy; and that she could not afford to travel to another jurisdiction in order to secure a legal abortion under safe conditions. She claimed that the Texas statutes were unconstitutionally vague and that they abridged her right of personal privacy, protected by the First, Fourth, Fifth, Ninth, and Fourteenth Amendments. By an amendment to her complaint Roe purported to sue "on behalf of herself and all other women" similarly situated. . . .

1. *Ancient attitudes.* These are not capable of precise determination. We are told that at the time of the Persian Empire abortifacients were known and that criminal abortions were severely punished. We are also told, however, that abortion was practiced in Greek times as well as in the Roman Era, and that "it was resorted to without scruple." The Ephesian, Soranos, often described as the greatest of the ancient gynecologists, appears to have been generally opposed to Rome's prevailing free-abortion practices. He found it necessary to think first of the life of the mother, and he resorted to abortion when, upon this standard, he felt the procedure advisable. Greek and Roman law afforded little protection to the unborn. If abortion was prosecuted in some places, it seems to have been based on a concept of a violation of the father's right to his offspring. Ancient religion did not bar abortion.

. . .This right of privacy, whether it be founded in the Fourteenth Amendment's concept of personal liberty and restrictions upon state action, as we feel it is, or, as the District Court determined, in the Ninth Amendment's reservation of rights to the people, is broad enough to encompass a woman's decision whether or not to terminate her pregnancy. The detriment that the State would impose upon the pregnant woman by denying this choice altogether is apparent. Specific and direct harm medically diagnosable even in early pregnancy may be involved. Maternity, or additional offspring, may force upon the woman a distressful life and future. Psychological harm may be imminent. Mental and physical health may be taxed by child care. There is also the distress, for all concerned, associated with the unwanted child, and there is the problem of bringing a child into a family already unable, psychologically and otherwise, to care for it. In other cases, as in this one, the additional difficulties and continuing stigma of unwed motherhood may be involved. All these are factors the woman and her responsible physician necessarily will consider in consultation.

On the basis of elements such as these, appellant and some *amici* argue that the woman's right is absolute and that she is entitled to terminate her pregnancy at whatever time, in whatever way, and for whatever reason she alone chooses. With this we do not agree. Appellant's arguments that Texas either has no valid interest at all in regulating the abortion decision, or no interest strong enough to support any limitation upon the woman's sole determination, are unpersuasive. The Court's decisions recognizing a right of privacy also acknowledge that some state regulation in areas protected by that right is appropriate. As noted above, a State may properly assert important interests in safe-guarding health, in maintaining medical standards, and in protecting potential life. At some point in pregnancy, these respective interests become sufficiently compelling to sustain regulation of the factors that govern the abortion decision. The privacy right involved, therefore, cannot be said to be absolute. In fact, it is not clear to us that the claim asserted by some *amici* that one has an unlimited right to do with one's body as one pleases bears a close relationship to the right of privacy previously articulated in the Court's decisions. The Court has refused to recognize an unlimited right of this kind in the past. *Jacobson* v. *Massachusetts,* 197 U. S. 11 (1905) (vaccination); *Buck* v. *Bell,* 274 U.S. 200 (1927) (sterilization).

We, therefore, conclude that the right of personal privacy includes the abortion decision, but that this right is not unqualified and must be considered against important state interests in regulation.

We note that those federal and state courts that have recently considered abortion law challenges have reached the same conclusion. A majority, in addition to the District Court in the present case, have held state laws unconstitutional, at least in part, because of vagueness or because of overbreadth and abridgment of rights. . . .In a recent development, generally opposed by the commentators, some States permit the parents of a stillborn child to maintain an action for wrongful death because of prenatal injuries. Such an action, however, would appear to be one to vindicate the parents' interest and is thus consistent with the view that the fetus, at most, represents only the potentiality of life. Similarly, unborn children have been recognized as acquiring rights or interests by way of inheritance or other devolution of property, and have been represented by guardians *ad litem.* Perfection of the interests involved, again, has generally been contingent upon live birth. In short, the unborn have never been recognized in the law as persons in the whole sense.

X

In view of all this, we do not agree that, by adopting one theory of life, Texas may override the rights of the pregnant woman that are at stake. We repeat, however, that the State does have an important and legitimate interest in preserving and protecting the health of the pregnant woman, whether she be a resident of the State or a nonresident who seeks medical consultation and treatment there, and that it has still *another* important and legitimate interest in protecting the potentiality of human life. These interests are separate and distinct. Each grows in substantiality as the woman approaches term and, at a point during pregnancy, each becomes "compelling."

With respect to the State's important and legitimate interest in the health of the mother, the "compelling" point, in the light of present medical knowledge, is at approximately the end of the first trimester. This is so because of the now-established medical fact, referred to above at 149, that until the end of the first trimester mortality in abortion may be less than mortality in normal childbirth. It follows that, from and after this point, a State may regulate the abortion procedure to the extent that the regulation reasonably relates to the preservation and protection of maternal health. Examples of permissible state regulation in this area are requirements as to the qualifications of the person who is to perform the abortion; as to the licensure of that person; as to the facility in which the procedure is to be performed, that is, whether it must be a hospital or may be a clinic or some other place of less-than-hospital status; as to the licensing of the facility; and the like.

This means, on the other hand, that, for the period of pregnancy prior to this "compelling" point, the attending physician, in consultation with his patient, is free to determine, without regulation by the State, that, in his medical judgment, the patient's pregnancy should be terminated. If that decision is reached, the judgment may be effectuated by an abortion free of interference by the State.

With respect to the State's important and legitimate interest in potential life, the "compelling" point is at viability. This is so because the fetus then presumably has the capability of meaningful life outside the mother's womb. State regulation protective of fetal life after viability thus has both logical and biological justifications. If the State is interested in protecting fetal life after viability, it may go so far as to proscribe abortion during that period, except when it is necessary to preserve the life or health of the mother.

Measured against these standards, Art. 1196 of the Texas Penal Code, in restricting legal abortions to those "procured or attempted by medical advice for the purpose of saving the life of the mother," sweeps too broadly. The statute makes no distinction between abortions performed early in pregnancy and those performed later, and it limits to a single reason, "saving" the mother's life, the legal justification for the procedure. The statute, therefore, cannot survive the constitutional attack made upon it here.

This conclusion makes it unnecessary for us to consider the additional challenge to the Texas statute asserted on grounds of vagueness. See *United States* v. *Vuitch,* 402 U. S., at 67-72.

XI

To summarize and to repeat:

1. A state criminal abortion statute of the current Texas type, that excepts from criminality only a *life-saving* procedure on behalf of the mother, without regard to pregnancy stage and without recognition of the other interests involved, is violative of the Due Process Clause of the Fourteenth Amendment.

(a) For the stage prior to approximately the end of the first trimester, the abortion decision and its effectuation must be left to the medical judgment of the pregnant woman's attending physician.

(b) For the stage subsequent to approximately the end of the first trimester, the State, in promoting its interest in the health of the mother, may, if it chooses, regulate the abortion procedure in ways that are reasonably related to maternal health.

(c) For the stage subsequent to viability, the State in promoting its interest in the potentiality of human life may, if it chooses, regulate, and even proscribe, abortion except where it is necessary, in appropriate medical judgment, for the preservation of the life or health of the mother.

2. The State may define the term "physician," as it has been employed in the preceding paragraphs of this Part XI of this opinion, to mean only a physician currently licensed by the State, and may proscribe any abortion by a person who is not a physician as so defined.

In *Doe* v. *Bolton, post,* p. 179, procedural requirements contained in one of the modern abortion statutes are considered. That opinion and this one, of course, are to be read together.

This holding, we feel, is consistent with the relative weights of the respective interests involved, with the lessons and examples of medical and legal history, with the lenity of the common law, and with the demands of the profound problems of the present day. The decision leaves the State free to place increasing restrictions on abortion as the period of pregnancy lengthens, so long as those restrictions are tailored to the recognized state interests. The decision vindicates the right of the physician to administer medical treatment according to his professional judgment up to the points where important state interests provide compelling justifications for intervention. Up to those points, the abortion decision in all its aspects is inherently, and primarily, a medical decision, and basic responsibility for it must rest with the physician. If an individual practitioner abuses the privilege of exercising proper medical judgment, the usual remedies, judicial and intra-professional, are available.

XII

Our conclusion that Art. 1196 is unconstitutional means, of course, that the Texas abortion statutes, as a unit, must fall. The exception of Art. 1196 cannot be struck down separately, for then the State would be left with a statute proscribing all abortion procedures no matter how medically urgent the case.

Although the District Court granted appellant Roe declaratory relief, it stopped short of issuing an injunction against enforcement of the Texas statutes. The Court has recognized that different considerations enter into a federal court's decision as to declaratory relief, on the one hand, and injunctive relief, on the other. *Zwickler* v. *Koota,* 389 U. S. 241, 252–255 (1967); *Dombrowski* v. *Pfister,* 380 U. S. 479 (1965). We are not dealing with a statute that, on its face, appears to abridge free expression, an area of particular concern under *Dombrowski* and refined in *Younger* v. *Harris,* 401 U. S., at 50.

We find it unnecessary to decide whether the District Court erred in withholding injunctive relief, for we assume the Texas prosecutorial authorities will give full credence to this decision that the present criminal abortion statutes of that State are unconstitutional.

"Human rights are women's rights"

HILLARY RODHAM CLINTON IN BEIJING

1995

The First Lady identified herself as "a wife and mother and daughter. I am a friend. I am a Christian. I am an advocate on behalf of causes I care deeply about. I am a lawyer by training. I am someone who likes to have fun with her friends. I'm a mediocre athlete who wishes I were better. I'm a terrible singer who wants to sing anyway. I'm a devotee of old movies and good books. I'm all of these things." At the behest of the Secretary General of the United Nations, Hillary Rodham Clinton (born 1947) flew to the besieged Fourth World Conference on Women and vigorously advocated a cause she cared deeply about. Despite the host nation's attempts to limit free and open discussion, Mrs. Clinton recited a catalog of abuse that afflicts women around the globe. *The New York Times* editorialized that her "unflinching speech" in China "may have been her finest moment in public life. She demonstrated that a clear and forthright speech makes a far more powerful point than staying home in sullen protest." The First Lady became an icon to many American women.

This is truly a celebration—a celebration of the contributions women make in every aspect of life: in the home, on the job, in their communities, as mothers, wives, sisters, daughters, learners, workers, citizens, and leaders.

It is also a coming together, much the way women come together every day in every country.

We come together in fields and in factories. In village markets and supermarkets. In living rooms and board rooms.

Whether it is while playing with our children in the park, or washing clothes in a river, or taking a break at the office water cooler, we come together and talk about our aspirations and concerns. And time and again, our talk turns to our children and our families. . . .

By gathering in Beijing, we are focusing world attention on issues that matter most in the lives of women and their families: access to education, health care, jobs, and credit, the chance to enjoy basic legal and human rights and participate fully in the political life of their countries. . . .

It is conferences like this that compel governments and peoples everywhere to listen, look and face the world's most pressing problems.

Wasn't it after the women's conference in Nairobi ten years ago that the world focused for the first time on the crisis of domestic violence?

. . .What we are learning around the world is that, if women are healthy and educated, their families will flourish. If women are free from violence, their families will flourish. If women have a chance to work and earn as full and equal partners in society, their families will flourish.

And when families flourish, communities and nations will flourish.

Women comprise more than half the world's population. Women are 70 percent of the world's poor, and two-thirds of those are not taught to read and write.

Women are the primary caretakers for most of the world's children and elderly. Yet much of the work we do is not valued—not by economists, not by historians, not by popular culture, not by government leaders.

At this very moment, as we sit here, women around the world are giving birth, raising children, cooking meals, washing clothes, cleaning houses, planting crops, working on assembly lines, running companies, and running countries.

Women also are dying from diseases that should have been prevented or treated; they are watching their children succumb to malnutrition caused by poverty and economic deprivation; they are being denied the right to go to school by their own fathers and brothers; they are being forced into prostitution, and they are being barred from the ballot box and the bank lending office.

Those of us who have the opportunity to be here have the responsibility to speak for those who could not. . . .

The truth is that most women around the world work both inside and outside the home, usually by necessity.

We need to understand that there is no formula for how women should lead their lives. That is why we must respect the choices that each woman makes for herself and her family. Every woman deserves the chance to realize her God-given potential.

We also must recognize that women will never gain full dignity until their human rights are respected and protected.

The international community has long acknowledged . . . that both women and men are entitled to a range of protections and personal freedoms, from the right of personal security to the right to determine freely the number and spacing of the children they bear.

No one should be forced to remain silent for fear of religious or political persecution, arrest, abuse or torture.

Tragically, women are most often the ones whose human rights are violated. Even in the late 20th century, the rape of women continues to be used as an instrument of armed conflict. Women and children make up a large majority of the world's refugees. And when women are excluded from the political process, they become even more vulnerable to abuse.

I believe that, on the eve of a new millennium, it is time to break our silence. . . .

It is a violation of *human* rights when babies are denied food, or drowned, or suffocated, or their spines broken, simply because they are born girls.

It is a violation of *human* rights when women and girls are sold into the slavery of prostitution.

It is a violation of *human* rights when women are doused with gasoline, set on fire and burned to death because their marriage dowries are deemed too small.

It is a violation of *human* rights when individual women are raped in their own communities and when thousands of women are subjected to rape as a tactic or prize of war.

It is a violation of *human* rights when a leading cause of death worldwide among women ages 14 to 44 is the violence they are subjected to in their own homes.

It is a violation of *human* rights when young girls are brutalized by the painful and degrading practice of genital mutilation.

It is a violation of *human* rights when women are denied the right to plan their own families, and that includes being forced to have abortions or being sterilized against their will.

If there is one message that echoes forth from this conference, it is that human rights are women's rights. . . . And women's rights are human rights. . . .

THE AMERICAN DREAM

Writing in an age of great democratic upheaval and social change, *Ralph Waldo Emerson observed in 1841: "In the history of the world, the doctrine of Reform had never such scope as at the present hour." All earlier reforms had respected some institutions—the church or the state tradition it-self—but, Emerson contended, "now all these things and all things else hear the trumpet and must rush to judgment—Christianity, the laws, commerce, schools, the farm, the laboratory; and not a kingdom, town, statute, rite, call-ing, man, or woman, but is threatened by this new spirit." The reform move-ment, he averred, might pull out of its waistcoat pocket some petition, some protest, some plan for Utopia. Granted some allowance for Emersonian hy-perbole, he was not an inaccurate observer of the social scene. Consider, for one, Brook Farm, a prominent Utopian experiment near Boston, where*

Emerson and a number in his circle visited or resided. Others outside of Cambridge and Concord became eager recruits to Owenite and Fourierite communities which dotted the landscape and, it was hoped, would serve as a model for a brave new world, a more just social order. Still others succumbed to this remarkable outburst of reform activity by taking up different causes. They formed countless societies and organizations crusading for the elimination of social or economic abuses and the betterment of individuals. Men like Emerson and women joined the pacifist movement, abolition crusade, or anti-war campaign; entered the campaign of criminals, orphans, or the poor; enlisted in efforts to improve factory conditions and the educational system.

Many believed that reform could best be achieved by local and state institutions that care for the insane and mentally incompetent. Utopians frequently went further than reform and urged a transformed state as well as government assistance to all in need. The idea that any government—municipal, state, or Federal—be given such a role ran counter to the Jeffersonian fear of government and faith in voluntarism, in the individual—in the individual's ability to fend for self and kin. Generally, Americans have been conservative in the economic realm, even when faced with national disaster. They had placed their fate in the negative state contending that government should not meddle in economic and social affairs. This conviction, that the government should not have an intrusive presence—laissez faire, in effect—and that it should not intervene to help the poor or regulate the economy, had its most extreme expression in the propositions of men like Herbert Spencer and William Graham Sumner; many of our best thinkers paid indiscreet obeisance to their views. But in the 1930s a hungry and impoverished society demanded boldness and experimentation. Significant minorities were ready to try virtually any innovation or experimentation that might lift the nation out of the Depression, be it pension-plan proposals or often cruel measures to eliminate grain surpluses—anything to relieve the visible suffering of the people. These changes took the form of a new role for government. A quantum leap in its efforts and in the distribution of its largesse took place, *and new agencies and new institutions arose that would regulate virtually every aspect of economic life—regardless of the Tenth Amendment, states rights, and the reserved-power clause. The urgent need to protect individuals from economic loss and the vicissitudes of life, such as old age, illness, and unemployment, took precedence over theoretical models dictating that the state should keep its hands off. A far-reaching program was undertaken by the New Deal to assist farmers, workers, young people, small businessmen, writers, and artists. Reform measures in banking, water power, agriculture, public utilities, labor conditions, social security, indeed virtually all aspects of economic life, became permanent features of the national scene. They suggest how far Franklin Roosevelt had departed from Wilson. It was a quantum leap from 1913 when Wilson reformed the nation's banking system, a most limited governmental action, to March, 1933, when Roosevelt kept the banks closed, a harbinger of the vast transformation that was to come.*

Roosevelt's New Deal, however, did not help blacks; they remained second-class citizens even as the centenary of the Civil War and emancipation approached. They were placed in segregated and inferior schools, denied admission to universities, required to sit in segregated public transport, eat at segregated lunch counters, play in segregated recreational facilities, even worship in segregated churches. They received inferior pay at inferior employment, and lived in areas that bred crime and delinquency. Rumblings began across the nation at mid-century—with the rise of interracial sporting events, beginning in baseball; mounting protests against segregation in street cars, luncheonettes, and movie theaters. The Supreme Court unanimously struck down school segregation in 1954, generating a contagious drive for civil rights which evolved into one of the most significant social movements of the twentieth century. A decade later, these rumblings evolved into a vigorous interracial crusade for equal rights. Protests, boycotts, demonstrations, non-violent actions like sit-ins and freedom rides, and white resistance and confrontations awoke the nation, which watched marches like that of midsummer, 1963. President Lyndon Johnson skillfully translated social turbu-

lence into congressional measures, such as the Civil Rights Act of 1964 and the Voting Rights Act of 1965. In sum, black Americans, after two centuries of discrimination and oppression, began to gain a measure of economic, political, and social equality. Prefigured in the twentieth century by DuBois's Niagara Movement and the founding of the NAACP and the Urban League, Martin Luther King's efforts, abetted by CORE and SNCC, were the capstone of two centuries of struggle. The civil-rights movement become one of the most significant social movements of the twentieth century, and equal rights, eddying out from black protest, became a rallying cry for minority groups—Asian, Hispanic, Native American, homosexual, alien, prisoner— which has persisted down to the present.

"To prevent the exercise of worldly anxiety"

BROOK FARM
1841

The most famous of the 130 or so communitarian experiments in the United States between 1663 and 1858 was founded by the ecstatic literary critic and reformer George Ripley (1802–1880), an 1826 graduate of Harvard Divinity School. A 200-acre cooperative institute of agriculture and education nine miles south of Boston, Brook Farm attempted to put Transcendentalist ideals into practice: Intuition, rather than experience or logic, would reveal the most profound truths. There should be leisure to live in all the faculties of the soul. Life should be refined, its meaning exalted. A perfect Earth would bear on her bosom a race of men worthy of the name. Celebrated Transcendentalists from literary Boston and Concord visited Brook Farm. The venture in individual reformation became a phalanx for Fourierism, named for the French socialist writer and reformer François Marie Charles Fourier (1772–1837). Ripley little understood or sympathized with the new philosophy, which organized society in serial divisions of labor: Physical and intellectual work was paid the same rate; a part-time boarder exchanged services as a baker for instruction in German philosophy. The idealists failed to carry through on plans for societal reformation, and the experiment dissolved after fire had destroyed the main building, the phalanstery (1846). The novelist Nathaniel Hawthorne (1804–1864), a disenchanted member of Brook Farm, satirized the venture in *The Blithedale Romance.*

In order more effectually to promote the great purposes of human culture; to establish the external relations of life on a basis of wisdom and purity; to apply the principles of justice and love to our social organization in accordance with the laws of Divine Providence; to substitute a system of brotherly coöperation for one of selfish competition; to secure to our children, and to those who may be entrusted to our care, the benefits of the highest physical, intellectual and moral education in the present state of human knowledge, the resources at our command will permit; to institute an attractive, efficient and productive system of industry; to prevent the exercise of worldly anxiety by the competent supply of our necessary wants; to diminish the desire of excessive accumulation by making the acquisition of individual property subservient to upright and disinterested uses; to guarantee to each other the means of physical support and of spiritual progress, and thus to impart a greater freedom, simplicity, truthfulness, refinement and moral dignity to our mode of life,—

ARTICLE I. The name and style of the Association shall be "(The Brook Farm) Institute of Agriculture and Education." All persons who shall hold one or more shares in the stock of the Association, and shall sign the articles of agreement, or who shall hereafter be admitted by the pleasure of the Association, shall be members thereof.

ART. 2. No religious test shall ever be required of any member of the Association; no authority assumed over individual freedom of opinion by the Association, nor by any member over another; nor shall anyone be held accountable to the Association except for such acts as violate rights of the members, and the essential principles on which the Association is founded; and in such cases the relation of any member may be suspended, or discontinued, at the pleasure of the Association.

ART. 3. The members of this Association shall own and manage such real and personal estate, in joint stock proprietorship, as may, from time to time, be agreed on, and establish such branches of industry as may be deemed expedient and desirable. . . .

ART. 5. The members of this Association shall be paid for all labor performed under its direction and for its advantage, at a fixed and equal rate, both for men and women. This rate shall not exceed one dollar per day, nor shall more than ten hours in the day be paid for as a day's labor.

ART. 6. The Association shall furnish to all its members, their children and family dependents, house-rent, fuel, food and clothing, and all other comforts and advantages possible, at the actual cost, as nearly as the same can be ascertained; but no charge shall be made for education, medical or nursing attendance, or the use of the library, public rooms or baths to the members; nor shall any charge be paid for food, rent or fuel by those deprived of labor by sickness, nor for food of children under ten years of age, nor for anything on members over seventy years of age, unless at the special request of the individual by whom the charges are paid, or unless the credits in his favor exceed, or equal, the amount of such charges. . . .

ART. 8. Every child over ten years of age shall be charged for food, clothing, and articles furnished at cost, and shall be credited for his labor, not exceeding fifty cents per day, and on the completion of his education in the Association at the age of twenty, shall be entitled to a certificate of stock, to the amount of credits in his favor, and may be admitted a member of the Association. . . .

ART. 11. All payments may be made in certificates of stock at the option of the Association; *but in any case of need,* to be decided by himself, every member may be permitted to draw on the funds of the treasury to an amount not exceeding the credits in his favor.

ART. 12. The Association shall hold an annual meeting for the choice of officers, and such other necessary business as shall come before them. . . .

"A more effective supervision of banking"

THE FEDERAL RESERVE SYSTEM
1913

The Bank of England has existed since the 1600s. Napoleon established the Banque de France in 1800. Congress founded the central bank of the United States, the Federal Reserve System, hailed as a rational solution to real problems, in the second decade of the twentieth century. Periodic financial panics plaguing the nation had contributed to bank failures, business bankruptcies, and general economic downturns. A particularly severe crisis (1907) prompted Congress to establish the National Monetary Commission, which put forth proposals to create an institution that would counter financial disruptions. Congress, after much debate, passed the Federal Reserve Act, which had been promoted by President Woodrow Wilson (1856-1924) when he revived the custom, abandoned in 1801, of addressing Congress in person. The Federal Reserve is independent within the government; its decisions do not have to be ratified by the President or by anyone else in the executive branch. Because the Constitution gives Congress the power to coin money and set its value, a power that, in the 1913 Act, Congress delegated to the Federal Reserve, the entire system *is* subject to Congressional oversight. The Federal Reserve must work within the framework of the overall objectives of economic and financial policy established by the government; description of the System as "independent within the government" is more accurate. Duties include conducting the nation's monetary policy by influencing the money and credit conditions in the economy in pursuit of full employment and stable prices.

* * * To provide for the establishment of Federal reserve banks, to furnish an elastic currency, to afford means of rediscounting commercial paper, to establish a more effective supervision of banking in the United States, and for other purposes.

"Reflected the spirit of the American people"

HERBERT HOOVER ON REPUBLICANISM
1928

There were only a couple of weeks before the American electorate would choose a new President. The Republican candidate was Herbert Clark Hoover (1874–1964), "Bert" to his friends, a mining engineer, director of the American Relief Administration after the First World War, and Secretary of Commerce since 1921. The Democratic standardbearer, New York Governor Alfred Emanuel Smith (1873–1944), known as "Al" and the "Happy Warrior" to his friends on the sidewalks of New York, was the first Catholic nominated by a major political party for the highest political office in the nation. In this late October, 1928, speech, in New York, Mr. Hoover discussed fundamental principles and ideals of government conduct, offering voters the opportunity to cast their ballot for the "American system of rugged individualism." Hoover rolled to victory on the tide of continuing "Republican prosperity": 444 electoral votes to Smith's 87. Within a few months of the inauguration, the nation's financial structure collapsed. A Republican wouldn't win the White House for another 24 years.

• • • The Republican party has even been a party of progress. . . . It has always reflected the spirit of the American people. Never has it done more for the advancement of fundamental progress than during the past seven and a half years since we took over the Government amidst the ruin left by war.

It detracts nothing from the character and energy of the American people, it minimizes in no degree the quality of their accomplishments to say that the policies of the Republican party have played a large part in recuperation from the war and the building of the magnificent progress which shows upon every hand today. I say with emphasis that without the wise policies which the Republican Party has brought into action during this period, no such progress would have been possible.

The first responsibility of the Republican Administration was to renew the march of progress from its collapse by the war. That task involved the restoration of confidence in the future and the liberation and stimulation of the constructive energies of our people. It discharged that task. There is not a person within the sound of my voice that does not know the profound progress which our country has made in this period. Every man and woman knows that American comfort, hope and confidence for the future are immeasurably higher this day than they were seven and one-half years ago.

. . . It is sufficient to remind you of the restoration of employment to the millions who walked your streets in idleness; to remind you of the creation of the budget system; the reduction of six billions of national debt which gave the powerful impulse of that vast sum returned to industry and commerce; the four sequent reductions of taxes and thereby the lift to the living of every family; the enactment of adequate protective tariff and immigration laws which have safeguarded our workers and farmers from floods of goods and labor from foreign countries; the creation of credit facilities and many other aids to agriculture; the building up of foreign trade; the care of veterans; the development of aviation, of radio, of our inland waterways, of our highways; the expansion of scientific research, of welfare activities, the making of safer highways, safer mines, better homes; the spread of outdoor recreation; the improvement in public health and the care of children; and a score of other progressive actions.

Nor do I need to remind you that Government today deals with an economic and social system vastly more intricate and delicately adjusted than ever before. That system now must be kept in perfect tune if we would maintain uninterrupted employment and the high standards of living of our people. The Government has come to touch this delicate web at a thousand points. Yearly the relations of Government to national prosperity become more and more intimate. Only through keen vision and helpful cooperation by the Government has stability in business and stability in employment been maintained during this past seven and a half years. There always are some localities, some industries and some individuals who do not share the prevailing prosperity. The task of government is to lessen these inequalities. . . . After the war, when the Republican Party assumed administration of the country, we were faced with the problem of determination of the very nature of our national life. During 150 years we have builded up a form of self-government and a social system which is peculiarly our own. It differs essentially

from all others in the world. It is the American system. It is just as definite and positive a political and social system as has ever been developed on earth. It is founded upon a particular conception of self-government; in which decentralized local responsibility is the very base. Further than this, it is founded upon the conception that only through ordered liberty, freedom and equal opportunity to the individual will his initiative and enterprise spur on the march of progress. And in our insistence upon equality of opportunity has our system advanced beyond all the world. . . .

When the war closed, the most vital of all issues both in our own country and throughout the world was whether Governments should continue their wartime ownership and operation of many instrumentalities of production and distribution. We were challenged with a peace-time choice between the American system of rugged individualism and a European philosophy of diametrically opposed doctrines—doctrines of paternalism and state socialism. The acceptance of these ideas would have meant the destruction of self-government through centralization of government. It would have meant the undermining of the individual initiative and enterprise through which our people have grown to unparalleled greatness.

The Republican Party from the beginning resolutely turned its face away from these ideas and these war practices. A Republican Congress cooperated with the Democratic administration to demobilize many of our war activities. At that time the two parties were accord upon that point. When the Republican Party came into full power it went at once resolutely back to our fundamental conception of the state and the rights and responsibilities of the individual. Thereby it restored confidence and hope in the American people, it freed and stimulated enterprise, it restored the Government to its position as an umpire instead of a player in the economic game. For these reasons the American people have gone forward in progress while the rest of the world has halted, and some countries have even gone backwards. If anyone will study the causes of retarded recuperation in Europe, he will find much of it due to the stifling of private initiative on one hand, and overloading of the Government with business on the other.

There has been revived in this campaign, however, a series of proposals which, if adopted, would be a long step toward the abandonment of our American system and a surrender to the destructive operation of governmental conduct of commercial business. Because the country is faced with difficulty and doubt over certain national problems—that is, prohibition, farm relief and electrical power—our opponents propose that we must thrust government a long way into the businesses which give rise to these problems. In effect, they abandon the tenets of their own party and turn to state socialism as a solution for the difficulties presented by all three. It is proposed that we shall change from prohibition to the state purchase and sale of liquor. If their agricultural relief program means anything, it means that the Government shall directly or indirectly buy and sell and fix prices of agricultural products. And we are to go into the hydro-electric-power business. In other words, we are confronted with a huge program of government in business.

There is, therefore, submitted to the American people a question of fundamental principle. That is: shall we depart from the principles of our American political and economic system, upon which we have advanced beyond all the rest of the world, in order to adopt methods based on principles destructive of its very foundations? And I wish to emphasize the seriousness of these proposals. I wish to make my position clear; for this goes to the very roots of American life and progress.

I should like to state to you the effect that this projection of government in business would have upon our system of self-government and our economic system. That effect would reach to the daily life of every man and woman. It would impair the very basis of liberty and freedom not only for those left outside the fold of expanded bureaucracy but for those embraced within it.

. . . There is no better example of the practical incompetence of government to conduct business than the history of our railways. During the war the government found it necessary to operate the railways. That operation continued until after the war. In the year before being freed from Government operation they were not able to meet the demands for transportation. Eight years later we find them under private enterprise transporting 15 per cent more goods and meeting every demand for service. Rates have been reduced by 15 per cent and net earnings increased from less than 1 per cent on their valuation to about 5 per cent. Wages of employees have improved by 13 per cent. The wages of railway employees are today 121 per cent above pre-war, while the wages of Government employees are today only 65 per cent above pre-war. That should be a sufficient commentary upon the efficiency of Government operation. . . .

Bureaucracy is ever desirous of spreading its influence and its power. You cannot extend the mastery of the government over the daily working life of a people without at the same time making it the master of the people's souls and thoughts. Every expansion of government in business means that government in order to protect itself from the political consequences of its errors and wrongs is driven irresistibly without peace to greater and greater control of the nations' press and platform. Free speech does not live many hours after free industry and free commerce die.

It is a false liberalism that interprets itself into the Government operation of commercial business. Every step of bureaucratizing of the business of our country poisons the very roots of liberalism—that is, political equality, free speech, free assembly, free press, and equality of opportunity. It is the road not to more liberty, but to less liberty. Liberalism should be found not striving to spread bureaucracy but striving to set bounds to it. True liberalism seeks all legitimate freedom first in the confident belief that without such freedom the pursuit of all other blessings and benefits is vain. That belief is the foundation of all American progress, political as well as economic.

Liberalism is a force truly of the spirit, a force proceeding from the deep realization that economic freedom cannot be sacrificed if political freedom is to be preserved. Even if governmental conduct of business could give us more efficiency instead of less efficiency, the fundamental objection to it would remain unaltered and unabated. It would destroy political equality. It would increase rather than decrease abuse and corruption. It would stifle initiative and invention. It would undermine the development of leadership. It would cramp and cripple the mental and spiritual energies of our people. It would extinguish equality and opportunity. It would dry up the spirit of liberty and progress. For these reasons primarily it must be resisted. For a hundred and fifty years liberalism has found its true spirit in the American system, not in the European systems. . . .

Our people have the right to know whether we can continue to solve our great problems without abandonment of our American system. I know we can. We have demonstrated that our system is responsive enough to meet any new and intricate development in our economic and business life. We have demonstrated that we can meet any economic problem and still maintain our democracy as master in its own house and that we can at the same time preserve equality of opportunity and individual freedom. . . .

One of the great problems of government is to determine to what extent the Government shall regulate and control commerce and industry and how much it shall leave it alone. No system is perfect. We have had many abuses in the private conduct of business. That every good citizen resents. It is just as important that business keep out of government as that government keep out of business.

. . . what have been the results of our American system? Our country has become the land of opportunity to those born without inheritance, not merely because of the wealth of its resources and industry but because of this freedom of initiative and enterprise. Russia has natural resources equal to ours. Her people are equally industrious, but she has not had the blessings of 150 years of our form of government and of our social system.

By adherence to the principles of decentralized self-government, ordered liberty, equal opportunity and freedom to the individual our American experiment in human welfare has yielded a degree of well-being unparalleled in all the world. It has come nearer to the abolition of poverty, to the abolition of fear of want, than humanity has ever reached before. Progress of the past seven years is the proof of it. This alone furnishes the answer to our opponents who ask us to introduce destructive elements into the system by which this has been accomplished. . . .

As a nation we came out of the war with great losses. We made no profits from it. The apparent increases in wages were at that time fictitious. We were poorer as a nation when we emerged from the war. Yet during these last eight years we have recovered from these losses and increased our national income by over one-third even if we discount the inflation of the dollar. That there has been a wide diffusion of our gain in wealth and income is marked by a hundred proofs. I know of no better test of the improved conditions of the average family than the combined increase in assets of life and industrial insurance, building and loan associations, and savings deposits. These are the savings banks of the average man. These agencies alone have in seven years increased by nearly 100 per cent to the gigantic sum of over 50 billions of dollars, or nearly one-sixth of our whole national wealth. We have increased in home ownership, we have expanded the investments of the average man.

In addition to these evidences of larger savings, our people are steadily increasing their spending for higher standards of living. Today there are almost 9 automobiles for each 10 families, where seven and a half years ago only enough automobiles were running to average less than 4 for each 10 families. The slogan of progress is changing from the full dinner pail to the full garage. Our people have more to eat, better things to wear, and better homes. We have even gained in elbow room, for the increase of residential floor space is over 25 per cent with less than 10 per cent increase in our number of people. Wages have increased, the cost of living has decreased. The job to every man and woman has been made more secure. We have in this short period decreased the fear of poverty, the fear of unemployment, the fear of old age; and these are fears that are the greatest calamities of human kind.

All this progress means far more than greater creature comforts. It finds a thousand interpretations into a greater and fuller life. A score of new helps save the drudgery of the home. In seven years we have added 70 per cent to the electric power at the elbow of our workers and further promoted them from carriers of burdens to directors of machines. We have steadily reduced the sweat in human labor. Our hours of labor are lessened; our leisure has increased. We have expanded our parks and playgrounds. We have nearly doubled our attendance at games. We pour into outdoor recreation in every direction. The visitors at our national parks have trebled and we have so increased the number of sportsmen fishing in our streams and lakes that the longer time between bites is becoming a political issue. In these seven and one-half years the radio has brought music and laughter, education and political discussion to almost every fireside.

Springing from our prosperity with its greater freedom, its vast endowment of scientific research and the greater resources with which to care for public health, we have according to our insurance actuaries during this short period since the war lengthened the average span of life by nearly eight years. We have reduced infant mortality, we have vastly decreased the days of illness and suffering in the life of every man and woman. We have improved the facilities for the care of the crippled and helpless and deranged.

. . . We have made progress in the leadership of every branch of American life. Never in our history was the leadership in our economic life more distinguished in its abilities than today, and it has grown greatly in its consciousness of public responsibility. Leadership in our professions—and in moral and spiritual affairs of our country was never of a higher order. And our magnificent educational system is bringing forward a host of recruits for the succession to this leadership.

I cannot believe that the American people wish to abandon or in any way to weaken the principles of economic freedom and self-government which have been maintained by the Republican Party and which have produced results so amazing and so stimulating to the spiritual as well as to the material advance of the nation. . . .

We still have great problems if we would achieve the full economic advancement of our country. In these past few years some groups in our country have lagged behind others in the march of progress. I refer more particularly to those engaged in the textile, coal and in the agricultural industries. We can assist in solving these problems by cooperation of our Government. To the agricultural industry we shall need to advance initial capital to assist them to stabilize their industry. But this proposal implies that they shall conduct it themselves, and not by the Government. It is in the interest of our cities that we shall bring agriculture and all industries into full stability and prosperity. I know you will gladly cooperate in the faith that in the common prosperity of our country lies its future. . . .

To me the foundation of American life rests upon the home and the family. I read into these great economic forces, these intricate and delicate relations of the Government with business and with our political and social life, but one supreme end—that we reinforce the ties that bind together the millions of our families, that we strengthen the security, the happiness and the independence of every home.

My conception of America is a land where men and women may walk in ordered freedom in the independent conduct of their occupations; where they may enjoy the advantages of wealth, not concentrated in the hands of the few but spread through the lives of all, where they build and safeguard their homes, and give to their children the fullest advantages and opportunities of American life; where every man shall be respected in the faith that his conscience and his heart direct him to follow; where a contented and happy people, secure in their liberties, free from poverty and fear, shall have the leisure and impulse to seek a fuller life.

Some may ask where all this may lead beyond mere material progress. It leads to a release of the energies of men and women from the dull drudgery of life to a wider vision and a higher hope. It leads to the opportunity for greater and greater service, not alone from man to man in our own land, but from our country to the whole world. It leads to an America, healthy in body, healthy in spirit, unfettered, youthful, eager—with a vision searching beyond the farthest horizons, with an open mind sympathetic and generous. It is to these higher ideals and for these purposes that I pledge myself and the Republican Party.

"Bid depression go"

THE TOWNSEND PLAN
1933

An unemployed physician, Francis Everett Townsend (1867–1960), born in a log cabin in Illinois, had had his fill of America's hard times. He wanted to cure the ills of the Great Depression. "The time has arrived," he said,

> "when the citizenry must take charge of their government and repudiate the philosophy of want and hunger in a land of wealth and abundance. Taking care of people runs against the American grain—against the feeling that everyone ought to hustle for himself. But there comes a time when people can't hustle anymore. I believe that we owe a decent living to the older people. After all, they built our country and made it what it is."

Concerned with the plight of the aged—many had lost savings, jobs, and homes as economic conditions worsened—Dr.Townsend proposed that Washington give each person over sixty and free of criminality a monthly stipend of scrip worth $200, which had to be spent within the month. The program would pump purchasing power into the economy and promote jobs. A national sales tax would finance the $20-billion-a-year scheme. With millions of members, quasi-religious Townsend Clubs sprang up everywhere. Old-Age Revolving Pensions, Ltd. (OARP) became the most notorious crusade of 1935. President Franklin Roosevelt is said to have been quite concerned about the Townsend Plan: too much of a good thing. The U.S. House of Representatives defeated legislation incorporating the Townsend Plan. Rapidly growing popular pressures for far-reaching welfare legislation is believed to have sped passage of Social Security (1935) with inclusion of old-age insurance.

The Townsend Club Fighting Song
Onward, Townsend soldiers,
Marching as to war,
With the Townsend banner
Going on before.

Our devoted leaders
Bid depression go;
Join them in the battle,
Help them fight the foe.

"Will take care of human needs"

F.D.R. Signs Social Security Bill

1935

President Franklin Delano Roosevelt (1882–1945) signed America's first Social Security measure. The historic New Deal bill, establishing Federal responsibility for the security of, and a better life for, the "men, women, and children of the nation," immediately gave some protection to 30,000,000 people floundering in the Great Depression. It was weak legislation, a modest beginning. Benefits were small and there were grave administrative difficulties, but the national government had acted to underpin the future security of Americans. Provisions involved unemployment and old age. There was an appropriation for preventive public health. Today, Social Security, repeatedly amended over the years, is the biggest Federal budget item. Monthly checks are loosely tied to how much the individual paid into the system. The average payee—retiree, survivor, disabled person—receives around $860 a month. Although the System runs an annual $50-billion surplus—a tax on payrolls shared equally by employer and employee supports it—projections indicate that the System will be unable to meet all commitments after the year 2029. The declining birth rate leaves too few workers to support the retirement of the baby-boom generation and those who follow. In addition, Americans are living longer.

Today a hope of many years standing is in large part fulfilled. The civilization of the past hundred years, with its startling industrial changes, has tended more and more to make life insecure. Young people have come to wonder what would be their lot when they came to old age. The man with a job has wondered how long the job would last.

This social security measure gives at least some protection to thirty million of our citizens who will reap direct benefits through unemployment compensation, through old age pensions and through increased services for the protection of children and the prevention of ill health.

We can never insure one hundred per cent of the population against one hundred per cent of the hazards and vicissitudes of life but we have tried to frame a law which will give some measure of protection to the average citizen and to his family against the loss of a job and against poverty-ridden old age.

This law, too, represents a corner stone in a structure which is being built but is by no means complete—a structure intended to lessen the force of possible future depressions, to act as a protection to future Administrations of the Government against the necessity of going deeply into debt to furnish relief to the needy—a law to flatten out the peaks and valleys of deflation and of inflation—in other words, a law that will take care of human needs and at the same time provide for the United States an economic structure of vastly greater soundness. . . .

If the Senate and the House of Representatives in this long and arduous session had done nothing more than pass this Bill, the session would be regarded as historic for all time.

"One citizen has as much right to play as another"

THE MAJORS SIGN A BLACK BASEBALLER
1947

Major league baseball, the national pastime, was exclusively a white man's game until the Brooklyn Dodgers signed the black infielder Jack Roosevelt Robinson (1919–1972), who referred to himself as a "guinea pig." Robinson had been a four-letter athlete at U.C.L.A. and a second lieutenant in the U.S. Army. After a season as the International League's most valuable player (.349 batting average) with the Dodgers' top farm team, the Montreal Royals, Robinson joined the bigs. He was dogged by unrelenting racial cries and slurs. Bench jockeying was cruel, but it cemented teammate support. "I was in two wars," he said. "One against a foreign enemy, the other against prejudice at home." Robinson was National League rookie of the year in 1947 and the league's most valuable player in 1949. He played ten years with the Dodgers, batting .311 and hitting 137 home runs. During the Robinson decade, the Dodgers won the league championship six times. Robby became the first black voted into the National Baseball Hall of Fame.

ANYTOWN, U.S.A.

The sportswriter Dan Daniel (1891–1981) imagined a tonsorial parlor in Anytown, U.S.A.

HIGGLEBOTTOM: I see how the Dodgers have signed a Negro ballplayer. First thing you know, we'll have Old Black Joe McCarthy managing the Yankees.

SNORT: And the club turned into a minstrel show. That MacPhail is always looking for something different, here's his chance.

MIGGS: At 2:30 in the afternoon, or at 8:30 before night games, the umpire won't call "play ball." He will holler "Gentlemen be seated!"

JASPER: The time will come when white players will have to cork up to stay in the major leagues.

CHEERBYL: You men make me sick. You cheer for Negro players on college football teams. You think its okay to have Negro players on National Football League teams. You are willing to let Negro athletes win Olympic championships and you think its great for Joe Louis to be heavyweight champion of the World. Why not Negro ball players?

MOANS: Well, it ain't never been done before.

CHEERBYL: We never threw an atomic bomb before either. Wake up Willie, this is 1945. Negroes helped win the war.

JASPER: Well, if the Negro ball players—granted there are any good enough to make the grade, which they say they ain't—want to put up with the hardships they will run into in the big time, let them take their medicine.

THE AMERICAN DREAM

In what's been described as "the most noble statement ever made by a baseball man," National League President Ford Frick (1894–1978) warned against a threatened players' strike. If you do this you will be suspended from the league. You will find that the friends you think you have in the press box will not support you, that you will be outcasts. I do not care if half the league strikes. Those who do it will encounter quick retribution. They will be suspended, and I don't care if it wrecks the National League for five years. This is the United States of America, and one citizen has as much right to play as another.

The National League will go down the line with Robinson whatever the consequence. You will find that if you go through with your intention that you have been guilty of madness.

Jackie Robinson: His Decade with the Dodgers

Year	Games	BA	SA	AB	H	2B	3B	HR	HR%	R	RBI	BB	SO	SB
1947	151	.297	.427	590	175	31	5	12	2.0	125	48	74	36	29
1948	147	.296	.453	574	170	38	8	12	2.1	108	85	57	37	22
1949	156	.342	.528	593	203	38	12	16	2.7	122	124	86	27	37
1950	144	.328	.500	518	170	39	4	14	2.7	99	81	80	24	12
1951	153	.338	.527	548	185	33	7	19	3.5	106	88	79	27	25
1952	149	.308	.465	510	157	17	3	19	3.7	104	75	106	40	24
1953	136	.329	.502	484	159	34	7	12	2.5	109	95	74	30	17
1954	124	.311	.505	386	120	22	4	15	3.9	62	59	63	20	7
1955	105	.256	.363	317	81	6	2	8	2.5	51	36	61	18	12
1956	117	.275	.412	357	98	15	2	10	2.8	61	43	60	32	12
	1382	.311	.474	4877	1518	273	54	137	2.8	947	734	740	291	197

"*Mississippi and Alabama will be transformed*"

MARTIN LUTHER KING, JR., HAS A DREAM
1963

Dr. Martin Luther King, Jr. (1929–1968), religious leader, civil rights activist, Nobel Peace Prize honoree, led nonviolent crusades throughout the South, including sit-ins, kneel-ins, wade-ins, freedom rides, and prayer meetings. Two hundred thousand people supporting black demands for jobs and freedom heard his "I have a dream" speech before the Lincoln Memorial in the nation's capital. An inspired Congress renewed efforts to deal with the issues of civil rights and poverty. The speech is read at gatherings on Dr. King's birth date, January 15, a national holiday since 1986. Dr. King had been helping Memphis's mostly black city workers improve the conditions of their jobs when he was assassinated by a white sniper, an escaped convict. (In the wake of the murder, there were demonstrations of outrage in 125 cities in 28 states. Washington, D.C., experienced the worst riots in its history; troops guarded the White House. Forty-six persons, most of them blacks, were killed across the nation; 2,600 were injured, 21,270 were arrested; there was an estimated $45-million of property damage.)

Five score years ago, a great American, in whose symbolic shadow we stand, signed the Emancipation Proclamation. This momentous decree came as a great beacon light of hope to millions of Negro slaves who had been seared in the flames of withering injustice. It came as a joyous daybreak to end the long night of captivity.

But one hundred years later, we must face the tragic fact that the Negro is still not free. One hundred years later, the life of the Negro is still sadly crippled by the manacles of segregation and the chains of discrimination. One hundred years later, the Negro lives on a lonely island of poverty in the midst of a vast ocean of material prosperity. One hundred years later, the Negro is still languishing in the corners of American society and finds himself an exile in his own land. So

we have come here today to dramatize an appalling condition.

In a sense we have come to our nation's capital to cash a check. When the architects of our republic wrote the magnificent words of the Constitution and the Declaration of Independence, they were signing a promissory note to which every American was to fall heir. This note was a promise that all men would be guaranteed the inalienable rights of life, liberty, and the pursuit of happiness.

It is obvious today that America has defaulted on this promissory note insofar as her citizens of color are concerned. Instead of honoring this sacred obligation, America has given the Negro people a bad check which has come back marked "insufficient funds." But we refuse to believe that the bank of justice is bankrupt. We refuse to believe that there are insufficient funds in the great vaults of opportunity of this nation. So we have come to cash this check—a check that will give us upon demand the riches of freedom and the security of justice. We have also come to this hallowed spot to remind America of the fierce urgency of now. This is no time to engage in the luxury of cooling off or to take the tranquilizing drug of gradualism. Now is the time to rise from the dark and desolate valley of segregation to the sunlit path of racial justice. Now is the time to open the doors of opportunity to all of God's children. Now is the time to lift our nation from the quicksands of racial injustice to the solid rock of brotherhood.

It would be fatal for the nation to overlook the urgency of the moment and to underestimate the determination of the Negro. This sweltering summer of the Negro's legitimate discontent will not pass until there is an invigorating autumn of freedom and equality. Nineteen sixty-three is not an end, but a beginning. Those who hope that the Negro needed to blow off steam and will now be content will have a rude awakening if the nation returns to business as usual. There will be neither rest nor tranquility in America until the Negro is granted his citizenship rights. The whirlwinds of revolt will continue to shake the foundations of our nation until the bright day of justice emerges.

But there is something that I must say to my people who stand on the warm threshold which leads into the palace of justice. In the process of gaining our rightful place we must not be guilty of wrongful deeds. Let us not seek to satisfy our thirst for freedom by drinking from the cup of bitterness and hatred.

We must forever conduct our struggle on the high plane of dignity and discipline. We must not allow our creative protest to degenerate into physical violence. Again and again we must rise to the majestic heights of meeting physical force with soul force. The marvelous new militancy which has engulfed the Negro community must not lead us to distrust of all white people, for many of our white brothers, as evidenced by their presence here today, have come to realize that their destiny is tied up with our destiny and their freedom is inextricably bound to our freedom. We cannot walk alone.

And as we walk, we must make the pledge that we shall march ahead. We cannot turn back. There are those who are asking the devotees of civil rights, "When will you be satisfied?" We can never be satisfied as long as our bodies, heavy with the fatigue of travel, cannot gain lodging in the motels of the highways and the hotels of the cities. We cannot be satisfied as long as the Negro's basic mobility is from a smaller ghetto to a larger one. We can never be satisfied as long as a Negro in Mississippi cannot vote and a Negro in New York believes he has nothing for which to vote. No, no, we are not satisfied, and we will not be satisfied until justice rolls down like waters and righteousness like a mighty stream.

I am not unmindful that some of you have come here out of great trials and tribulations. Some of you have come fresh from narrow cells. Some of you have come from areas where your quest for freedom left you battered by the storms of persecution and staggered by the winds of police brutality. You have been the veterans of creative suffering. Continue to work with the faith that unearned suffering is redemptive.

Go back to Mississippi, go back to Alabama, go back to Georgia, go back to Louisiana, go back to the slums and ghettos of our northern cities, knowing that somehow this situation can and will be changed. Let us not wallow in the valley of despair.

I say to you today, my friends, that in spite of

the difficulties and frustrations of the moment, I still have a dream. It is a dream deeply rooted in the American dream.

I have a dream that one day this nation will rise up and live out the true meaning of its creed: "We hold these truths to be self-evident: that all men are created equal."

I have a dream that one day on the red hills of Georgia the sons of former slaves and the sons of former slaveowners will be able to sit down together at a table of brotherhood.

I have a dream that one day even the state of Mississippi, a desert state, sweltering with the heat of injustice and oppression, will be transformed into an oasis of freedom and justice.

I have a dream that my four children will one day live in a nation where they will not be judged by the color of their skin but by the content of their character.

I have a dream today.

I have a dream that one day the state of Alabama, whose governor's lips are presently dripping with the words of interposition and nullification, will be transformed into a situation where little black boys and black girls will be able to join hands with little white boys and white girls and walk together as sisters and brothers.

I have a dream today.

I have a dream that one day every valley shall be exalted, every hill and mountain shall be made low, the rough places will be made plain, and the crooked places will be made straight, and the glory of the Lord shall be revealed, and all flesh shall see it together.

This is our hope. This is the faith with which I return to the South. With this faith we will be able to hew out of the mountain of despair a stone of hope. With this faith we will be able to transform the jangling discords of our nation into a beautiful symphony of brotherhood. With this faith we will be able to work together, to pray together, to struggle together, to go to jail together, to stand up for freedom together, knowing that we will be free one day.

This will be the day when all of God's children will be able to sing with a new meaning, "My country, 'tis of thee, sweet land of liberty, of thee I sing. Land where my fathers died, land of the pilgrim's pride, from every mountainside, let freedom ring."

And if America is to be a great nation this must become true. So let freedom ring from the prodigious hilltops of New Hampshire. Let freedom ring from the mighty mountains of New York. Let freedom ring from the heightening Alleghenies of Pennsylvania!

Let freedom ring from the snowcapped Rockies of Colorado!

Let freedom ring from the curvaceous peaks of California!

But not only that; let freedom ring from Stone Mountain of Georgia!

Let freedom ring from Lookout Mountain of Tennessee!

Let freedom ring from every hill and every molehill of Mississippi. From every mountainside, let freedom ring.

When we let freedom ring, when we let it ring from every village and every hamlet, from every state and every city, we will be able to speed up that day when all of God's children, black men and white men, Jews and Gentiles, Protestants and Catholics, will be able to join hands and sing in the words of the old Negro spiritual, "Free at last! free at last! thank God Almighty, we are free at last!"

"Give maximum encouragement"

THE NATIONAL HISTORIC PRESERVATION ACT
1966–1992

Asserting that the spirit and direction of the nation are founded upon and reflected in its historic heritage, Congress established a program for the preservation of historic properties. The Department of the Interior coordinates and supports public and private efforts to identify, evaluate, and protect historic and archeological resources. (The Native American Graves Protection and Repatriation Act has become a significant portion of expanded legislation.)

The Congress finds and declares that—
(1) the spirit and direction of the Nation are founded upon and reflected in its historic heritage;

(2) the historical and cultural foundations of the Nation should be preserved as a living part of our community life and development in order to give a sense of orientation to the American people;

(3) historic properties significant to the Nation's heritage are being lost or substantially altered, often inadvertently, with increasing frequency;

(4) the preservation of this irreplaceable heritage is in the public interest so that its vital legacy of cultural, educational, aesthetic, inspirational, economic, and energy benefits will be maintained and enriched for future generations of Americans;

(5) in the face of ever-increasing extensions of urban centers, highways, and residential, commercial, and industrial developments, the present governmental and nongovernmental historic preservation programs and activities are inadequate to insure future generations a genuine opportunity to appreciate and enjoy the rich heritage of our Nation;

(6) the increased knowledge of our historic resources, the establishment of better means of identifying and administering them, and the encouragement of their preservation will improve the planning and execution of federal and federally assisted projects and will assist economic growth and development; and

(7) although the major burdens of historic preservation have been borne and major efforts initiated by private agencies and individuals, and both should continue to play a vital role, it is nevertheless necessary and appropriate for the Federal Government to accelerate its historic preservation programs and activities, to give maximum encouragement to agencies and individuals undertaking preservation by private means, and to assist State and local governments and the National Trust for Historic Preservation in the United States to expand and accelerate their historic preservation programs and activities.

SEC. 2. It shall be the policy of the Federal Government, in cooperation with other nations and in partnership with the States, local governments, Indian tribes, and private organizations and individuals to—
(1) use measures, including financial and tech-

nical assistance, to foster conditions under which our modern society and our prehistoric and historic resources can exist in productive harmony and fulfill the social, economic, and other requirements of present and future generations;

(2) provide leadership in the preservation of the prehistoric and historic resources of the United States and of the international community of nations and in the administration of the national preservation program in partnership with States, Indian tribes, Native Hawaiians, and local governments;

(3) administer federally owned, administered, or controlled prehistoric and historic resources in a spirit of stewardship for the inspiration and benefit of present and future generations;

(4) contribute to the preservation of nonfederally owned prehistoric and historic resources and give maximum encouragement to organizations and individuals undertaking preservation by private means;

(5) encourage the public and private preservation and utilization of all usable elements of the Nation's historic built environment; and

(6) assist State and local governments, Indian tribes and Native Hawaiian organizations and the National Trust for Historic Preservation in the United States to expand and accelerate their historic preservation programs and activities.

TITLE I

SEC. 101 (a) (1) (A) The Secretary of the Interior is authorized to expand and maintain a National Register of Historic Places composed of districts, sites, buildings, structures, and objects significant in American history, architecture, archaeology, engineering, and culture.

(B) Properties meeting the criteria for National Historic Landmarks established pursuant to paragraph (2) shall be designated as "National Historic Landmarks" and included on the National Register, subject to the requirements of paragraph (6). All historic properties included on the National Register on the date of enactment of the National Historic Preservation Act Amendments of 1980 shall be deemed to be included on the National Register as of their initial listing for purposes of this Act. All historic properties listed in the Federal Register of February 6, 1979, as "National Historic Landmarks" or thereafter prior to the effective date of this Act are declared by Congress to be National Historic Landmarks of national historic significance as of their initial listing as such in the Federal Register for purposes of this Act and the Act of August 21, 1935 (49 Stat.666); except that in cases of National Historic Landmark districts for which no boundaries have been established, boundaries must first be published in the Federal Register and submitted to the Committee on Energy and Natural Resources of the United States Senate and to the Committee on Interior and Insular Affairs of the United States House of Representatives.

(2) The Secretary in consultation with national historic and archaeological associations, shall establish or revise criteria for properties to be included on the National Register and criteria for National Historic Landmarks, and shall also promulgate or revise regulations as may be necessary for—

(A) nominating properties for inclusion in, and removal from, the National Register and the recommendation of properties by certified local governments;

(B) designating properties as National Historic Landmarks and removing such designation;

(C) considering appeals from such recommendations, nomination, removals, and designations (or any failure or refusal by a nominating authority to nominate or designate);

(D) nominating historic properties for inclusion in the World Heritage List in accordance with the terms of the Convention concerning the Protection of the World Cultural and Natural Heritage;

(E) making determinations of eligibility of properties for inclusion on the National Register; and

(F) notifying the owner of a property, and any appropriate local governments, and the general public when the property is being considered for inclusion on the National Register, for designation as a National Historic Landmark or for nomination to the World Heritage List. . . .

"We are . . . in search of a national community"

BARBARA JORDAN: KEYNOTE ADDRESS, DEMOCRATIC CONVENTION 1976

The eloquent Texas Congresswoman Barbara Jordan (1936–1996) was the first black person to keynote the Presidential-nominating convention of a major political party. Asserting that a "nation is formed by the willingness of each of us to share in the responsibility for upholding the common good," she led off the 1976 Democratic conclave in New York's Madison Square Garden which nominated former Governor Jimmy Carter (born 1924), of Georgia, who went on to defeat the incumbent Republican nominee, Gerald R. Ford (born 1913), in the November election.

One hundred and forty-four years ago, members of the Democratic Party first met in convention to select a Presidential candidate. Since that time, Democrats have continued to convene once every four years and draft a party platform and nominate a Presidential candidate. And our meeting this week is a continuation of that tradition.

But there is something different about tonight. There is something special about tonight. What is different? What is special? I, Barbara Jordan, am a keynote speaker.

A lot of years passed since 1832, and during that time it would have been most unusual for any national political party to ask that a Barbara Jordan deliver a keynote address . . . but tonight here I am. And I feel that notwithstanding the past that my presence here is one additional bit of evidence that the American Dream need not forever be deferred. . . .

We are a people in a quandry about the present. We are a people in search of our future. We are a people in search of a national community.

We are a people trying not only to solve the problems of the present: unemployment, inflation . . . but we are attempting on a larger scale to fulfill the promise of America. We are attempting to fulfill our national purpose; to create and sustain a society in which all of us are equal.

. . . what is it about the Democratic Party that makes it the instrument that people use when they search for ways to shape their future? Well, I believe the answer to that question lies in our concept of governing. Our concept of governing is derived from our view of people. It is a concept deeply rooted in a set of beliefs firmly etched in the national conscience, of all of us.

. . . we believe in equality for all and privileges for none. This is a belief that each American regardless of background has equal standing in the public forum, all of us. Because we believe this idea so firmly, we are an inclusive rather than an exclusive party. Let everybody come.

I think it no accident that most of those emigrating to America in the 19th century identified with the Democratic Party. We are a heterogeneous party made up of Americans of diverse backgrounds.

We believe that the people are the source of all governmental power; that the authority of the people is to be extended, not restricted. This can be accomplished only by providing each citizen with every opportunity to participate in the management of the government. They must have that.

We believe that the government which represents the authority of all the people, not just one interest group, but all the people, has an obligation to actively underscore, actively seek to remove those obstacles which would block individual achievement . . . obstacles emanating from race, sex, economic condition. The government must seek to remove them.

We are a party of innovation. We do not reject our traditions, but we are willing to adapt to changing circumstances, when change we must. We are willing to suffer the discomfort of change in order to achieve a better future.

We have a positive vision of the future founded on the belief that the gap between the promise and reality of America can one day be finally closed. We believe that.

This, my friends, is the bedrock of our concept of governing. . . .

Even as I stand here and admit that we have made mistakes I still believe that as the people of America sit in judgement on each party, they will recognize that our mistakes were mistakes of the heart.

And now we must look to the future. Let us heed the voice of the people and recognize their common sense. If we do not, we not only blaspheme our political heritage, we ignore the common ties that bind all Americans.

. . . we must restore our belief in ourselves. We are a generous people so why can't we be generous with each other? We need to take to heart the words spoken by Thomas Jefferson:

Let us restore to social intercourse that harmony and that affection without which liberty and even life are but dreary things.

A nation is formed by the willingness of each of us to share in the responsibility for upholding the common good.

A government is invigorated when each of us is willing to participate in shaping the future of this nation. . . .

If we promise as public officials, we must deliver. If we as public officials propose, we must produce. If we say to the American people it is time for you to be sacrificial; sacrifice. If the public official says that, we (public officials) must be the first to give. We must be. And again, if we make mistakes, we must be willing to admit them. We have to do that. What we have to do is strike a balance between the idea that government should do everything and the idea, the belief, that government ought to do nothing. Strike a balance.

. . . But a spirit of harmony will survive in America only if each of us remembers that we share a common destiny. If each of us remembers when self-interest and bitterness seem to prevail, that we share a common destiny.

I have confidence that we can form this kind of national community. . . .

Now, I began this speech by commenting to you on the uniqueness of a Barbara Jordan making the keynote address. Well I am going to close my speech by quoting a Republican President and I ask you that as you listen to these words of Abraham Lincoln, relate them to the concept of a national community in which every last one of us participates:

As I would not be a slave, so I would not be a master. This expresses my idea of Democracy. Whatever differs from this, to the extent of the difference is no Democracy.

YEARNING TO BREATHE FREE

America was the objective of the largest migration of people ever seen on the planet. This extraordinary flow shaped us as a nation. The newcomers came for different reasons and were very different people who settled in different regions. But most of them considered America a haven, a refuge, a country of the second chance. Certainly those who came in the seventeenth century, say to New England, believed this was so. They showed courage, fortitude, industry, respect for the law, high moral and religious purpose. Indeed, these settlers were driven by religious faith. The Puritan impulse that captured their passions carried the insistent belief that they could be "born again" and the sense of God's majesty and righteousness. Within these convictions was the certainty that they were the Chosen People of God—like the Israelites, they had an errand in the wilderness, that He was with them. After all, He had safely transported them across the waters, thereby making a covenant with them, a bargain to which both contracting parties were bound. Their contractual obligation was to obey all God's ordinances and to be faithful to Him, and to build "a city upon a hill," to borrow the phrase of John Winthrop, first governor of the Bay Colony; that is, to build a godly community of the saints.

Neither this dual sense of an overriding moral impulse nor the conviction that God endowed their enterprise with His purpose was much diminished over the decades. Indeed, it was triumphantly announced in the aftermath of the Revolution, a decade that marked a self-conscious determination to develop an American language, an American literature, and an American law. Educators like Noah Webster compiled American spellers, jurists like Joseph Story transmitted reverence for the Constitution, historians like George Bancroft inculcated a pride in American history, late eighteenth-century Connecticut Wits like Joel Barlow composed national epics celebrating the rise of a providentially-guided nation, and painters from limners to landscapists made Americans conscious of their land. An unabashed nationalism emerged. It appeared whenever American armaments needed blessing or expansionist ideology needed fortifying. Both came into play with the War of 1812, which conflict prompted an exhilarating sense of republican institutions and their viability—surviving hostilities with the mightiest power on Earth; it was twinned with intense nationalism. The latter was embodied in the hymn to the nation's flag, "The Star-Spangled Banner," and inspired by Andrew Jackson's 1815 victory at New Orleans, which gave Americans a new basis for national pride. It was reflected in post-war literature, song, the expansive Western movement, and popular perceptions everywhere. Two centuries earlier, in "News from Virginia," one of the earliest poems about the new land, Richard Rush wrote:

Let England know our willingness, for that our work is good.

We hope to plant a nation, where none before hath stood.

Well might Americans say it with conviction in the 1820s and 1830s.

Transplanted to an unfamiliar country, early nineteenth-century immigrants held to a double consciousness—a powerful attachment to their national and cultural heritage and a growing emotional attachment to their adopted land. The result: a prominent cultural pluralism that recognized the integrity and contribution of different ethnic groups, all the while proclaiming the reality of the "melting pot." The melting pot, by some process of alchemy, took place—especially for the offspring of immigrants—and yet selective new ways and values were resisted. Newcomers frequently held to their pre-migration culture, which enabled Americans to boast of the country's great diversity. But pride in the dizzying mix of peoples, religions, and cultures declined when foreign threats became imminent. At such times, conformity was demanded, the national cause was pronounced good and noble, as the anthem had early documented: "Then conquer we must, for our cause it is just, and this be our motto, in God is our trust"—even if many doubted the righteousness of the War of 1812 or the Mexican War.

Nor was armed conflict the only trigger for insistent demands for ideological and racial homogeneity. When massive numbers of newcomers debarked on America's shores, it was argued that they would take jobs from Americans as well as pollute the pure biological stock, thereby endangering the pure Anglo-Saxon peoples. Thus, these allegedly morally and socially inferior newcomers triggered an ugly nationalism which degenerated into chauvinism and restrictionism. Consider, for example, the flood of famine Irish after 1846, a staggering number of impoverished immigrants. They prompted the Protestant crusade, an unlovely nativist and specifically anti-Catholic episode—much as immigrants from the Far East a half century later encountered bitter opposition and a powerful strain of racism. Nationalism eventually had its way, sweeping aside almost all multi-ethnic distinctions. Nearly every national group made the necessary adjustments, which gave the mythic melting pot greater credibility. Even today, America remains the "promised land," though, as in the past, many contend that it can no longer be such on the same free terms—a haven to the poor and oppressed of other nations.

"O! long may it wave"

"THE STAR-SPANGLED BANNER"
1814

During the War of 1812, Francis Scott Key (1779–1843), a Georgetown lawyer and poet, was so inspired by besieged Fort McHenry's resistance to an intermittent 25-hour bombardment by a British warship in Baltimore harbor that he exultantly composed eyewitness verses. Originally titled "Defense of Fort M'Henry," they were linked to the tune of a popular British drinking song. Within a year they were retitled "The Star-Spangled Banner." In 1889, the U.S. Navy adopted the patriotic ballad; fourteen years later, the Army adopted it. In 1931, Congress (ignoring musical difficulty) designated "The Star-Spangled Banner" the national anthem of the United States by law as it already had been in spirit.

O! SAY can you see, by the dawn's early light,
    What so proudly we hail'd at the twilight's last gleaming,
Whose broad stripes and bright stars through the perilous fight,
O'er the ramparts we watch'd were so gallantly streaming?
And the Rockets' red glare, the Bombs bursting in air,
Gave proof through the night that our Flag was still there;
        O! say, does that star-spangled Banner yet wave,
        O'er the Land of the free, and the home of the brave?

On that shore, dimly seen through the mists of the deep,
    Where the foe's haughty host in dread silence reposes,
What is that, which the breeze o'er the towering steep,
As it fitfully blows, half conceals, half discloses?
Now it catches the gleam of the morning's first beam,
In full glory reflected now shines on the stream.
        'Tis the star-spangled banner. O! long may it wave,
        O'er the land of the free and the home of the brave.

And where is that band who so vauntingly swore,
    That the havoc of war and the battle's confusion
A home and a country should leave us no more?
Their blood has wash'd out their foul footsteps' pollution.
No refuge could save the hireling and slave,
From the terror of flight or the gloom of the grave;

And the star-spangled banner in triumph doth wave,
O'er the land of the free and the home of the brave.

O! thus be it ever when freemen shall stand,
Between their lov'd home, and the war's desolation,
Blest with vict'ry and peace, may the Heav'n-rescued land,
Praise the power that hath made and preserv'd us a nation!

Then conquer we must, when our cause it is just,
And this be our motto—"In God is our Trust!"
And the star-spangled banner in triumph shall wave,
O'er the land of the free and the home of the brave.

"Give me your tired, your poor"

"THE NEW COLOSSUS"

1886

France's delivery of the Statue of Liberty was scheduled for the centennial of the Declaration of Independence, but was delayed a decade by the Franco-Prussian war. Dedicated on Bedloe's Island (renamed Liberty Island), in Upper New York Bay, it quickly became a symbol of liberty and hope for European immigrants flowing through the golden door. The last five lines of Emma Lazarus's sonnet "The New Colossus" were placed on the 150-foot-high pedestal supporting Frédéric Auguste Bartholdi's sculpture. The wealthy Ms. Lazarus (1849–1887), who was born in New York, was an essayist and poet; her first book, *Poems and Translations* (1867), was praised by Ralph Waldo Emerson (1803–1882). She worked for the relief of immigrants, especially Jews fleeing persecution in Russia; with her pen, she scathingly assailed Russian pogroms.

Not like the brazen giant of Greek fame,
With conquering limbs astride from land to land;
Here at our sea-washed, sunset gates shall stand
A mighty woman with a torch, whose flame
Is the imprisoned lightning, and her name
Mother of Exiles. From her beacon-hand
Glows world-wide welcome; her mild eyes command
The air-bridged harbor that twin cities frame.
"Keep, ancient lands, your storied pomp!" cries she
With silent lips. "Give me your tired, your poor,
Your huddled masses yearning to breathe free,
The wretched refuse of your teeming shore.
Send these, the homeless, tempest-tossed to me:
I lift my lamp beside the golden door!"

"God shed His grace on thee"

"AMERICA THE BEAUTIFUL"
1895

The view from the 14,110-foot summit of Colorado's Pikes Peak is awesome. On halcyon days, it is possible to see the Kansas border 165 miles to the east. Gazing upon amber waves of grain and the enameled plain inspired the educator and poet Katharine Lee Bates (1859–1929) to compose the patriotic poem "America the Beautiful" to the melody "Materna," by Samuel A. Ward (1848–1903). "America the Beautiful" has become the unofficial U.S. hymn.

O beautiful for halcyon skies,
For amber waves of grain,
For purple mountain majesties
Above the enameled plain!
America! America!
God shed His grace on thee
Till souls wax fair as earth and air
And music-hearted sea!

O beautiful for Pilgrim feet,
Whose stern, impassioned stress
A thoroughfare for freedom beat
Across the wilderness!
America! America!
God shed His grace on thee
Till paths be wrought through wilds of thought
By Pilgrim foot and knee!

O beautiful for glory tale
Of liberating strife,
When once and twice, far man's avail,
Men lavished precious life!
America! America!
God shed His grace for thee,
Till selfish gain no longer stain
The banner of the free!

O beautiful for patriot dream
That sees beyond the years
Thine alabaster cities gleam
Undimmed by human tears!
America! America!
God shed His grace for thee,
Till nobler men keep once again
Thy whiter jubilee!

"Each search . . . is unique"

HOW TO FIND YOUR IMMIGRANT ANCESTOR'S SHIP
1996

For more than 60 years, Ellis Island, an U.S. immigration station in Upper New York Bay, about a mile southwest of Manhattan, was the first patch of America on which tens of millions of European newcomers first set foot. Between 1820, when records first were kept, and 1890, 15,400,000 immigrants from England, Ireland, Germany, and Scandinavia came ashore. Another 18,200,000 newcomers, mostly from Italy, Austria, Hungary, Romania, and Russia, arrived between 1891 and 1920. Today, Ellis Island is a museum of immigration history run by the National Park Service of the Department of the Interior. A written guide advises visitors how to learn on what ship their ancestors arrived.

Most Americans can discover what ship brought their ancestors to this continent. Each search for ancestor's ship is unique. Your search may be easy and result in quick success. Or it may be a challenge requiring time and persistence. Here are the steps you follow:

YOU MUST KNOW YOUR ANCESTOR'S:

- Full real name
- Approximate age at arrival
- Approximate date of arrival

Where Can You Find This Information?

- Oral family tradition
- Family documents—passports, letters, Bible inscriptions, etc.
- Public records—military service, naturalization, U.S. censuses, etc.
- Published geneologies, local histories

WHAT WILL THE PASSENGER LIST TELL YOU ABOUT YOUR ANCESTOR?

When you find your ancestor's name or the ship's name in the index, use the reference cited in the index to locate the published or microfilmed list. Then read the list line by line to find the name. Double check what you find against your ancestor's real name, approximate age at arrival, and approximate date of arrival, to be certain you have your ancestor! In all cases, the list will give the name of his or her ship the date and port of its arrival in America and usually your ancestor's age and country of origin. Lists to 1893 contain little more than this. You may learn if your ancestor was travelling alone or with family, and how many bags he or she was carrying. From 1893 on lists became increasingly informative, including the above data plus marital status, occupation, last residence, birthplace, final destination in the U.S.A., whether joining a relative (if so, who and where), whether previously in the U.S.A. (if so, when and for how long), and more.

IF YOUR ANCESTOR ARRIVED BETWEEN 1565 AND 1819, SEARCH THE INDEXES OF PUBLISHED LISTS.

The passenger list, if it still exists, might be in any archive, museum, courthouse, basement or attic. But many have been published.

If You Know the Name of Your Ancestor's Ship:

Search for that ship in the indexes compiled by ship name;

or

If You Do Not Know the Ship:

Search for your ancestor in indexes compiled by passenger name;

or

If You Know Your Ancestor's Nationality:

Search in the indexes compiled by nationality;

or

If You Do Not Know the Nationality:

Search in indexes by particular group (such as indentured Servants or Irish Potato Famine Immigrants) or by geographic settlement or ports of entry;

or

If Your Ancestor was a Slave:

He or she was not listed by name in the cargo manifest.

Circumstantial evidence of your ancestor's ship can be obtained, however, if you know where, when and by whom the slave was first sold, then search:

- In the National Archives, manifests of ships importing slaves into the ports of Savannah, Mobile, and New Orleans, 1789–1808, or
- In museums, special collections containing manifests of slave ships, or
- In libraries, published compilations of documents relating to the slave trade in America.

If Your Ancestor Arrived Between 1820 and 1954, Search the National Archives and Indexes.

A copy of the passenger list is probably at the National Archives in Washington, D.C. You will search the indexes there, or, if necessary, in other indexes.

National Archives Indexes

These are compiled by port for most U.S. ports on the Atlantic, Pacific, Great Lakes and Gulf Coast, but they do not cover every year or every port.

- If you know your ancestor's port of entry: search the index to passenger arrivals for that port.
- If your ancestor arrived in New York, 1847–1896; search the Registry of Vessel Arrivals, note which ships arrived when your ancestor did, then search those lines.
- If you do not know the port of entry: search all available indexes to passenger arrivals.
- National Archives staff will search the indexes for you. If you supply a passenger's name, port of entry, and month and year of arrival. Use NATF form 81. More detailed information is needed for staff to search individual lists.

Published Indexes

These are limited in years covered and specialized in passengers included, but they often complement the National Archive indexes.

- Search in indexes compiled by nationality or port of entry.

The Morton-Allan Directory

This book lists the arrival date of every steamship entering New York, 1890–1930, and Baltimore, Boston, and Philadelphia, 1904–1926.

- If you know the name of your ancestor's ship: Note every date when that ship arrived, then search those lists.
- If you know the date when your ancestor arrived: Note which ships arrived on that date, then search those lists.

The Hamburg Emigration Index

If your ancestor emigrated from eastern, northern, or central Europe, he or she may have embarked from Hamburg, Germany. Emigration lists at Hamburg are indexed, 1850–1934.

- Search a microform copy of the index at any branch of the Mormon Genealogical Library.

THE GALLANT CHARGE OF THE FIFTY FOURTH MASSACHUSETTS (COLORED) REGIMENT.
*On the Rebel works at Fort Wagner, Morris Island, near Charleston, July 18*th *1863, and death of Colonel Robt. G. Shaw.*

THE WAR BETWEEN
THE STATES:
THE HOUSE DIVIDED

*E*nduring *the present, the relation between states and nations is probably the most persistent issue in American politics. In the mid-nineteenth century, as earlier with the 1798 Virginia and Kentucky Resolutions and the 1828 Exposition and Protest, nullification derived from two theories: The Constitution was a compact between states and sovereignty was indivisible. The insistent claim that the Constitution was established by the thirteen sovereign states, not by the people, was inseparably tied to the institution of slavery—which, in one of the ironies in constitutional development, appeared almost simultaneously with the institution of representative government. Revivified by the 1820 conflict over Missouri's admission* *to the Union and politicized as never before, slavery resurfaced in the Age of Jackson.*

To one degree or another, many Americans questioned slavery's existence, though they never fell back on Tocqueville's claim that egalitarianism has dominated our history. The Puritans, the Framers, the Jacksonians, etc., the last sotto voce, *surely held otherwise. Whatever their words, formulas, protestations, Americans endorsed the inherent inequality of those outside the select circle of full citizenship. Though considering slavery reprehensible, they thought that blacks, and women, were excluded from this circle. Even those who called for immediate abolition of slavery would grudgingly agree. Certainly John Calhoun did! Indeed, he came around to the view that slavery was a "positive good." In 1832, in the crisis over nullification, he argued for the right of secession as derived from the compact theory of government. By mid-century, he foresaw that the acquisition of new territory would reopen the question of slavery expansion. Although motivated by the imperative necessity to protect slavery where it existed—in the states—Calhoun shifted to the question of slavery in the territories, because expansion was the urgent issue. The territories, he asserted, belonged to the states, not to the United States. Like other Southern Senators, he claimed that slavery followed the flag, that Congress had only superintending power in the territories, that it was limited to the function of trustee, having only a police power to protect property. The bitter 1849-1850 congressional debate, one of the greatest in legislative history, swirled around these issues, triggered by the swelling population of California, owing to the Forty-Niners, and by the imminent admission of the territory to the Union as a free state. In the Senate Calhoun, haggard, emaciated, approaching the grave, addressed these matters. He fearfully declared that "the cords that bind the states together" were snapping, the South could not remain within the Union unless its rights were guaranteed, the North must "do justice by conceding to the South an equal right in the acquired territory" and "cease the agitation of the slave question." Henry Clay and the Senate moderates hoped that his compromise on this and other questions, set forth in an omnibus bill, would settle once and for all this and other vexing questions. His compromise included a number of critical provisions, among them being the admission of California as a free state, organization of New Mexico and Utah as territories without mention of slavery, a fugitive slave law more effective than that of 1793, and the prohibition of slave trade in the District of Columbia.*

A decade later, in the Spring of 1860, Southern political leaders and legislators warned that if the Republicans won in the coming Presidential elections, Southern states would secede. In November, Lincoln captured every free state except New Jersey and, winning in a four-way race, became a minority President. The South promptly made good on its threat. South Carolina led the way at a state convention meeting in Charleston, in December, 1860. It referred to itself as a "nation" and by unanimous vote declared "that the Union now subsisting between South Carolina and other states under the name of 'The United States of America' is hereby dissolved." Ten other Cotton States followed in open defiance of Federal laws and the Constitution, and adopted the Confederate constitution. Nearly identical to the 1787 text, this Southern text differed as expected on the twin issues of slavery and states' rights. No "law denying or impairing the right of property in negro slaves" could be passed by the Confederate congress, and in all new territory "the institution of negro slavery, as it now exists in the Confederate States, shall be recognized and protected." Jefferson Davis, of Mississippi, became president of the new Confederacy, one that never was able to dampen the resistance of individual states to Confederate legislative measures. The old chestnut of states' rights was continually reaffirmed—to the point where it worked against the exigent needs of the Southern armies and against the unity and central government functioning necessary in wartime.

Thus, by the time Lincoln took the oath of office in 1861, secession was a reality. Ironically, he was a moderate, unready to interfere with slavery where it legally existed; that is, let the sovereign states retain the peculiar institution within their own borders. To do otherwise, he believed, would deny to these states their clear constitutional rights. Indeed, at no time in the first years of the war did Lincoln admit it was being fought to abolish slavery: the objective was to preserve the Union, not eliminate the system of bondage in the states. Lincoln affirmed as much in his first inaugural, though reasserting that secession was illegal. Only in 1865, with the second inaugural address, when victory was assured, did he acknowledge the larger reason for the war—in one of the greatest speeches of our literature.

"Time [for] . . . an open and manly avowal"

CALHOUN ON SLAVERY
1850

Historians seem to agree that "perhaps there is, in all the history of American thought, no more brilliantly clear-sighted exposition of the factors leading the slaveowners to make the sane, clear, and deliberate calculation to stake their fate, and the country's fate, upon secession and war" than Senator John C. Calhoun's (1782–1850) opposition to Senator Henry "The Great Compromiser" Clay's (1777–1852) proposed bill. By once again compromising on the sectional differences that threatened the Union, Clay's bill was an attempt to prevent the secession of the South. Calhoun, who had resigned the Vice Presidency in 1832 because he believed he could be more helpful to the South as a South Carolina Senator, saw slavery as a lawful institution. A month before Calhoun died, his colleague James A. Mason (1798–1871) read the once-flamboyant Calhoun's last great speech to a hushed and crowded chamber. The author, emaciated and unable to speak, sat nearby. (Bitter debate produced five laws in Clay's "Omnibus Bill," which held the Union together—temporarily: California's admission to the Union as a free state; a stricter fugitive slave law; prohibition of the slave trade in the District of Columbia; postponement of the decision on slavery in New Mexico and Utah until these territories applied for statehood; the Federal government would assume Texas's debt of $10-million when Texas relinquished much of its western territory to the Federal government.)

I have, Senators, believed from the first that the agitation of the subject of slavery would, if not prevented by some timely and effective measure, end in disunion. I have, on all proper occasions, endeavored to call the attention of both the two great parties which divide the country to adopt some measure to prevent so great a disaster, but without success. The agitation has been permitted to proceed, with almost no attempt to resist it, until it has reached a period when it can no longer be disguised or denied, that the Union is in danger. You have thus had forced upon you the greatest and the gravest question that can ever come under your consideration: how can the Union be preserved? . . .

Indeed, as events are now moving, it will not require the South to secede, to dissolve the Union. Agitation will of itself effect it, of which past history furnishes abundant proof. . . .

It is a great mistake to suppose that disunion can be effected by a single blow. The cords which bind these states together in one common Union are far too numerous and powerful for that. Disunion must be the work of time. It is only through a long process, and successively, that the cords can be snapped, until the whole fabric falls asunder. Already the agitation of the slavery question has snapped some of the most important, and has greatly weakened all the others, as I shall proceed to show.

The cords which bind the states together are not only many, but various in character. Among them, some are spiritual or ecclesiastical; some political; others social. Others pertain to the benefit conferred by the Union, and others to the feelings of duty and obligation.

The strongest of those of a spiritual and ecclesiastical nature consisted in the unity of the great religious denominations, all of which originally embraced the Union. All these denominations, with the exception perhaps of the Catholics, were organized very much upon the principle of our political institutions. Beginning with smaller meetings, corresponding with the political divisions of the country, their organization terminated in one great central assemblage, corresponding very much with the character of Congress. At these meetings the principal clergymen and lay members of the respective denominations from all parts of the Union, met to transact business relating to their common concerns. It was not confined to what appertained to the doctrines and discipline of the respective denominations, but extended to plans for disseminating the Bible, establishing missionaries, distributing tracts, and of establishing presses for the publication of tracts, newspapers, and periodicals, with a view of diffusing religious information and for the support of the doctrines and creeds of the denomination.

All this combined contributed greatly to strengthen the bonds of the Union. The ties which held each denomination together formed a strong cord to hold the whole Union together. But, powerful as they were, they have not been able to resist the explosive effect of slavery agitation. There is but one way by which it [the Union] can with any certainty be saved, and that is a full and final settlement, on the principle of justice, of all the questions at issue between the two sections. The South asks for justice, simple justice, and less she ought not to take. She has no compromise to offer, but the Constitution; and no concession or surrender to make. She has already surrendered so much that she has little left to surrender. Such a settlement would go to the root of the evil, and remove all cause of discontent, and satisfy the South that she could remain honorably and safely in the Union; and thereby restore the harmony and fraternal feelings between the sections, which existed anterior to the Missouri agitation. Nothing else can, with any certainty, finally and forever settle the questions at issue, terminate agitation, and save the Union.

But can this be done? Yes, easily; not by the weaker party, for it can of itself do nothing—not even protect itself—but by the stronger. The North has only to will it, to do justice and perform her duty, in order to accomplish it: to do justice by conceding to the South an equal right in the acquired territory, and to do her duty by causing the stipulations relative to fugitive slaves to be faithfully fulfilled: to cease the agitation of the slave question, and to provide for the insertion of a provision in the Constitution, by an amendment, which will restore to the South in substance the power she possessed of protecting herself, before the equilibrium between the sections was destroyed by the action of this government. There will be no difficulty in devising such a provision. One that will protect the South, and which, at the same time, will improve and strengthen the government, instead of impairing or weakening it.

But will the North agree to do this? It is for her to answer the question. But I will say, she cannot refuse, if she has half the love of the Union which she professes to have, or without justly exposing herself to the charge that her love of power and aggrandizement is far greater than her love of the Union. At all events, the responsibility of saving the Union is on the North and not the South. The South cannot save it by any act of hers, and the North may save it without any sacrifice whatever, unless to do justice and to perform her duties under the Constitution be regarded by her as a sacrifice.

It is time, Senators, that there should be an open and manly avowal on all sides, as to what is intended to be done. If the question is not now settled, it is uncertain whether it ever can hereafter be; and we, as the representatives of the states of this Union, regarded as governments, should come to a distinct understanding as to our respective views, in order to ascertain whether the great questions at issue between the two sections can be settled or not. If you, who represent the stronger portion, cannot agree to settle them on the broad principles of justice and duty, say so; and let the states we both represent agree to separate and part in peace. If you are unwilling we should part in peace, tell us so; and we shall know what to do, when you reduce the question to submission or resistance. If you remain silent, you then compel us to infer what you intend. In that case, California will become the test question. If you admit her, under all the difficulties that oppose her admission, you compel us to infer that you intend to exclude us from the whole of the acquired territories, with the intention of destroying irretrievably the equilibrium between the two sections. We would be blind not to perceive in that case that your real objects are power and aggrandizement, and infatuated not to act accordingly. . . .

I have now, Senators, done my duty in expressing my opinions fully, freely, and candidly, on this solemn occasion. In doing so, I have been governed by the motives which have governed me in all the stages of the agitation of the slavery question since its commencement; and exerted myself to arrest it, with the intention of saving the Union, if it could be done; and, if it cannot, to save the section where it has pleased Providence to cast my lot, and which I sincerely believe has justice and the Constitution on its side. Having faithfully done my duty to the best of my ability, both to the Union and my section, throughout the whole of this agitation, I shall have the consolation, let what will come, that I am free from all responsibility.

"All one thing, or all the other"

LINCOLN'S "HOUSE DIVIDED" SPEECH
1858

Senatorial nominee Abraham Lincoln (1809–1865) delivered his memorable, radical, "house divided" speech at the Illinois Republican State Convention, in Springfield. He shortened the Biblical quotation "If a house be divided against itself, that house cannot stand" to "A house divided against itself cannot stand," and predicted that "this government cannot endure permanently half slave and half free." The Democratic incumbent, Stephen A. Douglas (1813–1861), had to be defeated, Lincoln said, because Douglas contributed to the tendency to nationalize slavery. Many people understood Lincoln's speech to be "an implied pledge on behalf of the Republican party to make war upon the institution in the States where it exists." Because of a gerrymandered legislature, Lincoln lost the election. He defeated Douglas, narrowly, in the 1860 Presidential campaign.

If we could first know where we are, and whither we are tending, we could better judge what to do, and how to do it. We are now far into the fifth year since a policy was initiated with the avowed object and confident promise of putting an end to slavery agitation. Under the operation of that policy, that agitation has not only not ceased, but has constantly augmented. In my opinion, it will not cease until a crisis shall have been reached and passed. "A house divided against itself cannot stand." I believe this government cannot endure permanently half slave and half free. I do not expect the Union to be dissolved; I do not expect the house to fall; but I do expect it will cease to be divided. It will become all one thing, or all the other. Either the opponents of slavery will arrest the further spread of it, and place it where the public mind shall rest in the belief that it is in the course of ultimate extinction, or its advocates will push it forward till it shall become alike lawful in all the States, old as well as new, North as well as South.

Have we no tendency to the latter condition? . . .

The new year of 1854 found slavery excluded from more than half the States by State Constitutions, and from most of the National territory by Congressional prohibition. Four days later, commenced the struggle which ended in repealing that Congressional prohibition. This opened all the National territory to slavery, and was the first point gained. . . .

While the Nebraska Bill was passing through Congress, a *law case,* involving the question of a negro's freedom, by reason of his owner having voluntarily taken him first into a free State, and then into a territory covered by the Congressional prohibition, and held him as a slave for a long time in each, was passing through the United States Circuit Court for the District of Missouri; and both Nebraska Bill and lawsuit were brought to a decision in the same month of May, 1854. The negro's name was "Dred Scott," which name now designates the decision finally made in the case. Before the then next Presidential election, the law case came to, and was argued in, the Supreme Court of the United States; but the decision of it was deferred until after the election. . . .

The several points of the Dred Scott decision are:

Firstly, That no negro slave, imported as such from Africa, and no descendant of such slave, can ever be a citizen of any State, in the sense of that term as used in the Constitution of the United States. This point is made in order to deprive the negro, in every possible event, of the benefit of that provision of the United States Constitution which declares that "The citizens of each State shall be entitled to all privileges and immunities of citizens in the several States."

Secondly, That, "subject to the Constitution of the United States," neither Congress nor a Territorial Legislature can exclude slavery from any United States Territory. This point is made in order that individual men may fill up the Territories with slaves, without danger of losing them as property, and thus to enhance the chances of permanency to the institution through all the future.

Thirdly, That whether the holding a negro in actual slavery in a free State makes him free, as against the holder, the United States courts will not decide, but will leave to be decided by the courts of any slave State the negro may be forced into by the master. This point is made, not to be pressed immediately; but, if acquiesced in for a while, and apparently indorsed by the people at an election, then to sustain the logical conclusion that what Dred Scott's master might lawfully do with Dred Scott, in the free State of Illinois, every other master may lawfully do with any other one, or one thousand slaves, in Illinois, or in any other free State.

Auxiliary to all this, and working hand in hand with it, the Nebraska doctrine, or what is left of it, is to educate and mould public opinion, at least Northern public opinion, not to care whether slavery is voted down or voted up. This shows exactly where we now are; and partially, also, whither we are tending. . . .

"*Early on one frosty mornin'* "
"DIXIE"
1859

The unofficial anthem of the South's rebellion—and, ironically, President Abraham Lincoln's favorite song—was composed by the entertainer Daniel Decatur Emmett (1815–1904) as a "walkaround" or "hooray" song for minstrels. Although it originally referred to Louisiana and New Orleans, "Dixie Land" came to mean the entire South. "Dixie" was an immediate success. It was performed at Jefferson Davis's inauguration as President of the Confederacy:

"Then here's to our Confederacy, strong we are and brave, Like patriots of old we'll fight, Our heritage to save; And rather than submit to shame, to die we would prefer, So cheer for the Bonnie Blue Flag that bears a single star."

I wish I was in the land of cotton,
Old times there are not forgotten,
Look away! Look away! Lookaway!
Dixie Land.
In Dixie Land where I was born in,
early on one frosty mornin',
Look away! Look away! Dixie Land.

"Union . . . is hereby dissolved"

AN ORDINANCE OF SECESSION
1860

Six weeks after Abraham Lincoln (1809–1863) was elected the first Republican President, but more than two months before he was sworn, the secessionist convention in South Carolina unanimously authorized by the legislature voted for the state's immediate withdrawal from the Union. Southern politicians were convinced that slavery, that "peculiar institution" (the late South Carolina Senator John C. Calhoun's coinage), would be destroyed. (President James Buchanan [1791–1868] had no policy for dealing with the crisis; he was convinced he would be the last President.) Talk of secession spread across the Palmetto State as differences over trade, protective tariffs, and slavery further fractured North and South relationships. South Carolina was the first of eleven Southern states to pull out of the Union. In April, 1861, the Confederacy's first cannonballs in the Civil War were fired at the Federal bastion on a rocky shoal in Charleston harbor—a besieged symbol of United States authority, Fort Sumter.

We, the people of the State of South Carolina, in Convention assembled, do declare and ordain, and it is hereby declared and ordained, that the ordinance adopted by us in Convention, on the 23d day of May, in the year of our Lord 1788, whereby the Constitution of the United States of America was ratified, and also all Acts and parts of Acts of the General Assembly of this State ratifying the amendments of the said Constitution, are hereby repealed, and that the union now subsisting between South Carolina and other States under the name of the United States of America is hereby dissolved.

"I have no purpose . . . to interfere with the institution of slavery"

LINCOLN'S FIRST INAUGURAL ADDRESS

1861

Seven slave states had already left the Union and Jefferson Davis (1808–1889) was provisional President of the Confederate States of America when Abraham Lincoln (1809–1865) was inaugurated as the sixteenth President of the United States (he was sworn by Chief Justice Roger Brooke Taney [1777–1864], whose *Dred Scott* decision had decisively sundered the nation on slavery). Lincoln had won a three-candidate race, but was really little known: He had had a disappointing two years in the U.S. House of Representatives, twice had failed to gain a Senate seat, was nominated by the Republican convention after it had passed over two appealing possibilities, and had not campaigned vigorously. Amid heavy protection from assassination, the new Chief Executive proposed that the central idea of secession was the essence of anarchy: "Physically speaking, we cannot separate. We cannot remove our respective sections from each other, nor build an impassable wall between them . . . In *your* hands, my dissatisfied fellow countrymen, and not in *mine*, is the momentous issue of civil war." Lincoln's speech convinced the Confederacy that war was just around the corner. It was! The South's first cannonballs were launched a little more than a month later.

Apprehension seems to exist among the people of the Southern States that by the accession of a Republican Administration their property and their peace and personal security are to be endangered. There has never been any reasonable cause for such apprehension. Indeed, the most ample evidence to the contrary has all the while existed and been open to their inspection. It is found in nearly all the published speeches of him who now addresses you. I do but quote from one of those speeches when I declare that—

I have no purpose, directly or indirectly, to interfere with the institution of slavery in the States where it exists. I believe I have no lawful right to do so, and I have no inclination to do so.

Those who nominated and elected me did so with full knowledge that I had made this and many similar declarations and had never recanted them; and more than this, they placed in the platform for my acceptance, and as a law to themselves and to me, the clear and emphatic resolution which I now read:

Resolved, That the maintenance inviolate of the rights of the States, and especially the right of each State to order and control its own domestic institutions according to its own judgment exclusively, is essential to that balance of power on which the perfection and endurance of our political fabric depend; and we denounce the lawless invasion by armed force of the soil of any State or Territory, no matter under what pretext, as among the gravest of crimes.

I now reiterate these sentiments, and in doing so I only press upon the public attention the most conclusive evidence of which the case is susceptible that the property, peace, and security of no section are to be in any wise endangered by the now incoming Administration. I add, too, that all the protection which, consistently with the Constitution and the laws, can be given will be cheerfully given to all the States when lawfully demanded, for whatever cause—as cheerfully to one section as to another.

There is much controversy about the delivering up of fugitives from service or labor. The clause I now read is as plainly written in the Constitution as any other of its provisions:

> No person held to service or labor in one State, under the laws thereof, escaping into another, shall in consequence of any law or regulation therein be discharged from such service or labor, but shall be delivered up on claim of the party to whom such service or labor may be due.

It is scarcely questioned that this provision was intended by those who made it for the reclaiming of what we call fugitive slaves; and the intention of the lawgiver is the law. All members of Congress swear their support to the whole Constitution—to this provision as much as to any other. To the proposition, then, that slaves whose cases come within the terms of this clause "shall be delivered up" their oaths are unanimous. Now, if they would make the effort in good temper, could they not with nearly equal unanimity frame and pass a law by means of which to keep good that unanimous oath? . . . .

I take the official oath to-day with no mental reservations and with no purpose to construe the Constitution or laws by any hypercritical rules; and while I do not choose now to specify particular acts of Congress as proper to be enforced, I do suggest that it will be much safer for all, both in official and private stations, to conform to and abide by all those acts which stand unrepealed than to violate any of them trusting to find impunity in having them held to be unconstitutional.

It is seventy-two years since the first inauguration of a President under our National Constitution. During that period fifteen different and greatly distinguished citizens have in succession administered the executive branch of the Government. They have conducted it through many perils, and generally with great success. Yet, with all this scope of precedent, I now enter upon the same task for the brief constitutional term of four years under great and peculiar difficulty. A disruption of the Federal Union, heretofore only menaced, is now formidably attempted.

I hold that in contemplation of universal law and of the Constitution the Union of these States is perpetual. Perpetuity is implied, if not expressed, in the fundamental law of all national governments. It is safe to assert that no government proper ever had a provision in its organic law for its own termination. Continue to execute all the express provisions of our National Constitution, and the Union will endure forever, it being impossible to destroy it except by some action not provided for in the instrument itself.

Again: If the United States be not a government proper, but an association of States in the nature of contract merely, can it, as a contract, be peaceably unmade by less than all the parties who made it? One party to a contract may violate it—break it, so to speak—but does it not require all to lawfully rescind it?

Descending from these general principles, we find the proposition that in legal contemplation the Union is perpetual confirmed by the history of the Union itself. The Union is much older than the Constitution. It was formed, in fact, by the Articles of Association in 1774. It was matured and continued by the Declaration of Independence in 1776. It was further matured, and the faith of all the then thirteen States expressly plighted and engaged that it should be perpetual, by the Articles of Confederation in 1778. And finally, in 1787, one of the declared objects for ordaining and establishing the Constitution was *"to form a more perfect Union."*

But if destruction of the Union by one or by a part only of the States be lawfully possible, the Union is *less* perfect than before the Constitution, having lost the vital element of perpetuity.

It follows from these views that no State upon its own mere motion can lawfully get out of the Union; that *resolves* and *ordinances* to that effect are legally void, and that acts of violence within any State or States against the authority of the United States are insurrectionary or revolutionary, according to circumstances.

I therefore consider that in view of the Constitution and the laws the Union is unbroken, and to the extent of my ability I shall take care, as the Constitution itself expressly enjoins upon me, that the laws of the Union be faithfully executed in all the States. Doing this I deem to be only a simple duty on my part, and I shall perform it so far as practicable unless my rightful masters, the American people, shall withhold the requisite means or in some authoritative manner direct the contrary. I trust this will not be regarded as a menace, but only as the declared purpose of the Union that it *will* constitutionally defend and maintain itself.

In doing this there needs to be no bloodshed or violence, and there shall be none unless it be forced upon the national authority. The power confided to me will be used to hold, occupy, and possess the property and places belonging to the Government and to collect the duties and imposts; but beyond what may be necessary for these objects, there will be no invasion, no using of force against or among the people anywhere. Where hostility to the United States in any interior locality shall be so great and universal as to prevent competent resident citizens from holding the Federal offices, there will be no attempt to force obnoxious strangers among the people for that object. While the strict legal right may exist in the Government to enforce the exercise of these offices, the attempt to do so would be so irritating and so nearly impracticable withal that I deem it better to forego for the time the uses of such offices.

The mails, unless repelled, will continue to be furnished in all parts of the Union. So far as possible the people everywhere shall have that sense of perfect security which is most favorable to calm thought and reflection. The course here indicated will be followed unless current events and experience shall show a modification or change to be proper, and in every case and exigency my best discretion will be exercised, according to circumstances actually existing and with a view and a hope of a peaceful solution of the national troubles and the restoration of fraternal sympathies and affections.

That there are persons in one section or another who seek to destroy the Union at all events and are glad of any pretext to do it I will neither affirm nor deny; but if there be such, I need address no word to them. To those, however, who really love the Union may I not speak?

Before entering upon so grave a matter as the destruction of our national fabric, with all its benefits, its memories, and its hopes, would it not be wise to ascertain precisely why we do it?

Will you hazard so desperate a step while there is any possibility that any portion of the ills you fly from have no real existence? Will you, while the certain ills you fly to are greater than all the real ones you fly from, will you risk the commission of so fearful a mistake?

All profess to be content in the Union if all constitutional rights can be maintained. Is it true, then, that any right plainly written in the Constitution has been denied? I think not. Happily, the human mind is so constituted that no party can reach to the audacity of doing this. Think, if you can, of a single instance in which a plainly written provision of the Constitution has ever been denied. If by the mere force of numbers a majority should deprive a minority of any clearly written constitutional right, it might in a moral point of view justify revolution; certainly would if such right were a vital one. But such is not our case. All the vital rights of minorities and of individuals are so plainly assured to them by affirmations and negations, guaranties and prohibitions, in the Constitution that controversies never arise concerning them. But no organic law can ever be framed with a provision specifically applicable to every question which may occur in practical administration. No foresight can anticipate nor any document of reasonable length contain express provisions for all possible questions. Shall fugitives from labor be surrendered by national or by State authority? The Constitution does not expressly say. *May* Congress prohibit slavery in the Territories? The Constitution does not expressly say. *Must* Congress protect slavery in the Territories? The Constitution does not expressly say. . . .

Plainly the central idea of secession is the essence of anarchy. A majority held in restraint by constitutional checks and limitations, and always changing easily with deliberate changes of popular opinions and sentiments, is the only true

sovereign of a free people. Whoever rejects it does of necessity fly to anarchy or to despotism. Unanimity is impossible. The rule of a minority, as a permanent arrangement, is wholly inadmissible; so that, rejecting the majority principle, anarchy or despotism in some form is all that is left. . . .

One section of our country believes slavery is *right* and ought to be extended, while the other believes it is *wrong* and ought not to be extended. This is the only substantial dispute. The fugitive-slave clause of the Constitution and the law for the suppression of the foreign slave trade are each as well enforced, perhaps, as any law can ever be in a community where the moral sense of the people imperfectly supports the law itself. The great body of the people abide by the dry legal obligation in both cases, and a few break over in each. This, I think, can not be perfectly cured, and it would be worse in both cases *after* the separation of the sections than before. The foreign slave trade, now imperfectly suppressed, would be ultimately revived without restriction in one section, while fugitive slaves, now only partially surrendered, would not be surrendered at all by the other.

Physically speaking, we can not separate. We can not remove our respective sections from each other nor build an impassable wall between them. A husband and wife may be divorced and go out of the presence and beyond the reach of each other, but the different parts of our country can not do this. They can not but remain face to face, and intercourse, either amicable or hostile, must continue between them. Is it possible, then, to make that intercourse more advantageous or more satisfactory *after* separation than *before?* Can aliens make treaties easier than friends can make laws? Can treaties be more faithfully enforced between aliens than laws can among friends? Suppose you go to war, you can not fight always; and when, after much loss on both sides and no gain on either, you cease fighting, the identical old questions, as to terms of intercourse, are again upon you.

This country, with its institutions, belongs to the people who inhabit it. Whenever they shall grow weary of the existing Government, they can exercise their *constitutional* right of amending it or their *revolutionary* right to dismember or overthrow it. I can not be ignorant of the fact that many worthy and patriotic citizens are desirous of having the National Constitution amended. While I make no recommendation of amendments, I fully recognize the rightful authority of the people over the whole subject, to be exercised in either of the modes prescribed in the instrument itself; and I should, under existing circumstances, favor rather than oppose a fair opportunity being afforded the people to act upon it. I will venture to add that to me the convention mode seems preferable, in that it allows amendments to originate with the people themselves, instead of only permitting them to take or reject propositions originated by others, not especially chosen for the purpose, and which might not be precisely such as they would wish to either accept or refuse. I understand a proposed amendment to the Constitution—which amendment, however, I have not seen—has passed Congress, to the effect that the Federal Government shall never interfere with the domestic institutions of the States, including that of persons held to service. To avoid misconstruction of what I have said, I depart from my purpose not to speak of particular amendments so far as to say that, holding such a provision to now be implied constitutional law, I have no objection to its being made express and irrevocable. . . .

My countrymen, one and all, think calmly and *well* upon this whole subject. Nothing valuable can be lost by taking time. If there be an object to *hurry* any of you in hot haste to a step which you would never take *deliberately,* that object will be frustrated by taking time; but no good object can be frustrated by it. Such of you as are now dissatisfied still have the old Constitution unimpaired, and, on the sensitive point, the laws of your own framing under it; while the new Administration will have no immediate power, if it would, to change either. If it were admitted that you who are dissatisfied hold the right side in the dispute, there still is no single good reason for precipitate action. Intelligence, patriotism, Christianity, and a firm reliance on Him who has never yet forsaken this favored land are still competent to adjust in the best way all our present difficulty.

In *your* hands, my dissatisfied fellow-countrymen, and not in *mine,* is the momentous issue of civil war. The Government will not assail *you.* You can have no conflict without being yourselves the aggressors. *You* have no oath registered in heaven to destroy the Government, while *I* shall have the most solemn one to "preserve, protect, and defend it."

I am loath to close. We are not enemies, but friends. We must not be enemies. Though passion may have strained it must not break our bonds of affection. The mystic chords of memory, stretching from every battlefield and patriot grave to every living heart and hearthstone all over this broad land, will yet swell the chorus of the Union, when again touched, as surely they will be, by the better angels of our nature.

"Importation of negroes . . . is . . . hereby forbidden"

THE CONSTITUTION OF THE CONFEDERATE STATES OF AMERICA
1861

Modeled on the U.S. Constitution (1787), the breakaway states' charter was promulgated a week after President Abraham Lincoln's (1809–1865) first inauguration. It spoke of "sovereign and independent states" rather than of "We the People," and invoked "the favor and guidance of Almighty God." It protected slavery. The president, who had the power of the line-item veto and the control of appropriations, could serve only one term (six years). New states could be admitted by a vote of two thirds of the House of Representatives and the Senate. At the last session of the Confederate Congress (November, 1864), President Jefferson Davis (1808–1889) proposed a limited form of emancipation.

We, the people of the Confederate States, each State acting in its sovereign and independent character, in order to form a permanent government, establish justice, insure domestic tranquillity, and secure the blessings of liberty to ourselves and our posterity—invoking the favor and guidance of Almighty God—do ordain and establish this Constitution for the Confederate States of America.

ART. I

SEC. I.—All legislative powers herein delegated shall be vested in a Congress of the Confederate States, which shall consist of a Senate and House of Representatives.

SEC. 2. (1) The House of Representatives shall be . . . chosen every second year by the people of the several States; and the electors in each State shall be citizens of the Confederate States, and have the qualifications requisite for electors of the most numerous branch of the State Legislature; but no person of foreign birth, not a citizen of the Confederate States, shall be allowed to vote for any officer, civil or political, State or Federal.

(2) No person shall be a Representative who shall not have attained the age of twenty-five years, and be a citizen of the Confederate States, and who shall not, when elected, be an inhabitant of that State in which he shall be chosen.

(3) Representatives and direct taxes shall be apportioned among the several States which may be included within this Confederacy, according to their respective numbers, which shall be determined by adding to the whole number of free persons, including those bound to service for a term of years, and excluding Indians not taxed, three-fifths of all slaves. The actual enumeration shall be made within three years after the first meeting of the Congress of the Confederate States, and within every subsequent term of ten years, in such manner as they shall by law direct. The number of Representatives shall not exceed

one for every fifty thousand, but each State shall have at least one Representative; and until such enumeration shall be made the State of South Carolina shall be entitled to choose six; the State of Georgia ten; the State of Alabama nine; the State of Florida two; the State of Mississippi seven; the State of Louisiana six; and the State of Texas six.

(4) When vacancies happen in the representation of any State, the Executive authority thereof shall issue writs of election to fill such vacancies.

(5) The House of Representatives shall choose their Speaker and other officers; and shall have the sole power of impeachment; except that any judicial or other federal officer resident and acting solely within the limits of any State, may be impeached by a vote of two-thirds of both branches of the Legislature thereof.

SEC. 3. (1) The Senate of the Confederate States shall be composed of two Senators from each State, chosen for six years by the Legislature thereof, at the regular session next immediately preceding the commencement of the term of service; and each Senator shall have one vote.

(2) Immediately after they shall be assembled, in consequence of the first election, they shall be divided as equally as may be into three classes. The seats of the Senators of the first class shall be vacated at the expiration of the second year; of the second class at the expiration of the fourth year; and of the third class at the expiration of the sixth year; so that one-third may be chosen every second year; and if vacancies happen by resignation or otherwise during the recess of the Legislature of any State, the Executive thereof may make temporary appointments until the next meeting of the Legislature, which shall then fill such vacancies.

(3) No person shall be a Senator, who shall not have attained the age of thirty years, and be a citizen of the Confederate States; and who shall not, when elected, be an inhabitant of the State for which he shall be chosen.

(4) The Vice-President of the Confederate States shall be President of the Senate, but shall have no vote, unless they be equally divided.

(5) The Senate shall choose their other officers, and also a President pro tempore, in the absence of the Vice-President, or when he shall exercise the office of President of the Confederate States.

(6) The Senate shall have sole power to try all impeachments. When sitting for that purpose they shall be on oath or affirmation. When the President of the Confederate States is tried, the Chief Justice shall preside; and no person shall be convicted without the concurrence of two-thirds of the members present.

(7) Judgment in cases of impeachment shall not extend further than removal from office, and disqualification to hold and enjoy any office of honor, trust, or profit, under the Confederate States; but the party convicted shall, nevertheless, be liable and subject to indictment, trial, judgment, and punishment according to law.

SEC. 4. (1) The times, places, and manner of holding elections for Senators and Representatives, shall be prescribed in each State by the Legislature thereof, subject to the provisions of this Constitution; but the Congress may, at any time, by law, make or alter such regulations, except as to the times and places of choosing Senators.

(2) The Congress shall assemble at least once in every year; and such meeting shall be on the first Monday in December, unless they shall, by law, appoint a different day.

SEC. 5. (1) Each House shall be the judge of the elections, returns, and qualifications of its own members, and a majority of each shall constitute a quorum to do business; but a smaller number may adjourn from day to day, and may be authorized to compel the attendance of absent members, in such manner and under such penalties as each House may provide.

(2) Each House may determine the rules of its proceedings, punish its members for disorderly behavior, and, with the concurrence of two-thirds of the whole number, expel a member.

(3) Each House shall keep a journal of its proceedings, and from time to time publish the same, excepting such parts as may in their judgment require secrecy, and the ayes and nays of the members of either House, on any question, shall, at the desire of one-fifth of those present, be entered on the journal.

(4) Neither House, during the session of Congress, shall, without the consent of the other, adjourn for more than three days, nor to any other place than that in which the two Houses shall be sitting.

SEC. 6. (1) The Senators and Representatives shall receive a compensation for their services, to be ascertained by law, and paid out of the Treasury of the Confederate States. They shall, in all cases except treason and breach of the peace, be privileged from arrest during their attendance at the session of their respective Houses, and in going to and returning from the same; and for any speech or debate in either House, they shall not be questioned in any other place.

(2) No Senator or Representative shall, during the time for which he was elected, be appointed to any civil office under the authority of the Confederate States, which shall have been created, or the emoluments whereof shall have been increased during such time; and no person holding any office under the Confederate States shall be a member of either House during his continuance in office. But Congress may, by law, grant to the principal officer in each of the Executive Departments a seat upon the floor of either House, with the privilege of discussing any measure appertaining to his department.

SEC. 7. (1) All bills for raising revenue shall originate in the House of Representatives; but the Senate may propose or concur with amendments as on other bills.

(2) Every bill which shall have passed both Houses shall, before it becomes a law, be presented to the President of the Confederate States; if he approve he shall sign it; but if not, he shall return it with his objections to that House in which it shall have originated, who shall enter the objections at large on their journal, and proceed to reconsider it. If, after such reconsideration, two-thirds of that House shall agree to pass the bill, it shall be sent, together with the objections, to the other House, by which it shall likewise be reconsidered, and if approved by two-thirds of that House, it shall become a law. But in all such cases, the votes of both Houses shall be determined by yeas and nays, and the names of the persons voting for and against the bill shall be entered on the journal of each House respectively. If any bill shall not be returned by the President within ten days (Sundays excepted) after it shall have been presented to him, the same shall be a law, in like manner as if he had signed it, unless the Congress, by their adjournment, prevent its return; in which case it shall not be a law. The President may approve any appropriation and disapprove any other appropriation in the same bill. In such case he shall, in signing the bill, designate the appropriations disapproved; and shall return a copy of such appropriations, with his objections, to the House in which the bill shall have originated; and the same proceedings shall then be had as in case of other bills, disapproved by the President.

(3) Every order, resolution, or vote, to which the concurrence of both Houses may be necessary (except on a question of adjournment) shall be presented to the President of the Confederate

States; and before the same shall take effect shall be approved by him; or being disapproved by him, shall be repassed by two-thirds of both Houses, according to the rules and limitations prescribed in case of a bill.

Sec. 8.—The Congress shall have power—(1) To lay and collect taxes, duties, imposts, and excises, for revenue necessary to pay the debts, provide for the common defence, and carry on the Government of the Confederate States; but no bounties shall be granted from the treasury; nor shall any duties or taxes on importations from foreign nations be laid to promote or foster any branch of industry; and all duties, imposts, and excises shall be uniform throughout the Confederate States.

(2) To borrow money on the credit of the Confederate States.

(3) To regulate commerce with foreign nations, and among the several States, and with the Indian tribes; but neither this nor any other clause contained in the Constitution shall be construed to delegate the power to Congress to appropriate money for any internal improvement intended to facilitate commerce; except for the purpose of furnishing lights, beacons, and buoys, and other aids to navigation upon the coasts, and the improvement of harbors, and the removing of obstructions in river navigation, in all which cases, such duties shall be laid on the navigation facilitated thereby, as may be necessary to pay the costs and expenses thereof.

(4) To establish uniform laws of naturalization, and uniform laws on the subject of bankruptcies throughout the Confederate States, but no law of Congress shall discharge any debt contracted before the passage of the same.

(5) To coin money, regulate the value thereof, and of foreign coin, and fix the standard of weights and measures.

(6) To provide for the punishment of counterfeiting the securities and current coin of the Confederate States.

(7) To establish post-offices and post-routes; but the expenses of the Post-office Department, after the first day of March, in the year of our Lord eighteen hundred and sixty-three, shall be paid out of its own revenues.

(8) To promote the progress of science and useful arts, by securing for limited times to authors and inventors the exclusive right to their respective writings and discoveries.

(9) To constitute tribunals inferior to the Supreme Court.

(10) To define and punish piracies and felonies committed on the high seas, and offences against the law of nations.

(11) To declare war, grant letters of marque and reprisal, and make rules concerning captures on land and water.

(12) To raise and support armies; but no appropriation of money to that use shall be for a longer term than two years.

(13) To provide and maintain a navy.

(14) To make rules for government and regulation of the land and naval forces.

(15) To provide for calling forth the militia to execute the laws of the Confederate States; suppress insurrections, and repel invasions.

(16) To provide for organizing, arming, and disciplining the militia, and for governing such part of them as may be employed in the service of the Confederate States; reserving to the States, respectively, the appointment of the officers, and the authority of training the militia according to the discipline prescribed by Congress.

(17) To exercise exclusive legislation, in all cases whatsoever, over such district (not exceeding ten miles square) as may, by cession of one or more States, and the acceptance of Congress, become the seat of the Government of the Confederate States; and to exercise a like authority over

all places purchased by the consent of the Legislature of the State in which the same shall be, for the erection of forts, magazines, arsenals, dockyards, and other needful buildings, and

(18) To make all laws which shall be necessary and proper for carrying into execution the foregoing powers, and all other powers vested by this Constitution in the Government of the Confederate States, or in any department or officer thereof.

SEC. 9. (1) The importation of negroes of the African race, from any foreign country, other than the slaveholding States or Territories of the United States of America, is hereby forbidden; and Congress is required to pass such laws as shall effectually prevent the same.

(2) Congress shall also have power to prohibit the introduction of slaves from any State not a member of, or Territory not belonging to, this Confederacy.

(3) The privilege of the writ of habeas corpus shall not be suspended, unless when in cases of rebellion or invasion the public safety may require it.

(4) No bill of attainder, ex post facto law, or law denying or impairing the right of property in negro slaves shall be passed.

(5) No capitation or other direct tax shall be laid unless in proportion to the census or enumeration hereinbefore directed to be taken.

(6) No tax or duty shall be laid on articles exported from any State, except by a vote of two-thirds of both Houses.

(7) No preference shall be given by any regulation of commerce or revenue to the ports of one State over those of another.

(8) No money shall be drawn from the treasury but in consequence of appropriations made by law; and a regular statement and account of the receipts and expenditures of all public money shall be published from time to time.

(9) Congress shall appropriate no money from the treasury except by a vote of two-thirds of both Houses, taken by yeas and nays, unless it be asked and estimated for by some one of the heads of departments, and submitted to Congress by the President; or for the purpose of paying its own expenses and contingencies; or for the payment of claims against the Confederate States, the justice of which shall have been judicially declared by a tribunal for the investigation of claims against the Government, which it is hereby made the duty of Congress to establish.

(10) All bills appropriating money shall specify in federal currency the exact amount of each appropriation and the purposes for which it is made; and Congress shall grant no extra compensation to any public contractor, officer, agent, or servant, after such contract shall have been made or such service rendered.

(11) No title of nobility shall be granted by the Confederate States; and no person holding any office of profit or trust under them shall, without the consent of the Congress, accept of any present, emolument, office, or title of any kind whatever, from any king, prince, or foreign state.

(12) Congress shall make no law respecting an establishment of religion, or prohibiting the free exercise thereof; or abridging the freedom of speech or of the press; or the right of the people peaceably to assemble and petition the Government for a redress of grievances.

(13) A well-regulated militia being necessary to the security of a free State, the right of the people to keep and bear arms shall not be infringed.

(14) No soldier shall, in time of peace, be quartered in any house without the consent of the owner; nor in time of war, but in a manner to be prescribed by law.

(15) The right of the people to be secure in their persons, houses, papers, and effects, against unreasonable searches and seizures, shall not be violated; and no warrant shall issue but upon

probable cause, supported by oath or affirmation, and particularly describing the place to be searched, and the person or things to be seized.

(16) No person shall be held to answer for a capital or otherwise infamous crime, unless on a presentment or indictment of a grand jury, except in cases arising in the land or naval forces, or in the militia, when in actual service, in time of war, or public danger; nor shall any person be subject for the same offence to be twice put in jeopardy of life or limb; nor be compelled in any criminal case to be a witness against himself; nor be deprived of life, liberty, or property, without due process of law; nor shall private property be taken for public use without just compensation.

(17) In all criminal prosecutions the accused shall enjoy the right to a speedy and public trial, by an impartial jury of the State and district wherein the crime shall have been committed, which district shall have been previously ascertained by law, and to be informed of the nature and cause of the accusation; to be confronted with the witnesses against him; to have compulsory process for obtaining witnesses in his favor; and to have the assistance of counsel for his defence.

(18) In suits at common law, where the value in controversy shall exceed twenty dollars, the right of trial by jury shall be preserved; and no fact so tried by a jury shall be otherwise reexamined in any court of the Confederacy, than according to the rules of common law.

(19) Excessive bail shall not be required, nor excessive fines imposed, nor cruel and unusual punishment inflicted.

(20) Every law, or resolution having the force of law, shall relate to but one subject, and that shall be expressed in the title.

Sec. 10. (1) No State shall enter into any treaty, alliance, or confederation; grant letters of marque and reprisal; coin money; make any thing but gold and silver coin a tender in payment of debts; pass any bill of attainder, or ex post facto law, or law impairing the obligation of contracts; or grant any title of nobility.

(2) No State shall, without the consent of Congress, lay any imposts or duties on imports or exports, except what may be absolutely necessary for executing its inspection laws; and the net produce of all duties and imposts, laid by any State on imports or exports, shall be for the use of the Treasury of the Confederate States; and all such laws shall be subject to the revision and control of Congress.

(3) No State shall, without the consent of Congress, lay any duty on tonnage, except on sea-going vessels, for the improvement of its rivers and harbors navigated by the said vessels; but such duties shall not conflict with any treaties of the Confederate States with foreign nations; and any surplus revenue, thus derived, shall, after making such improvement, be paid into the common treasury; nor shall any State keep troops or ships of war in time of peace, enter into any agreement or compact with another State, or with a foreign power, or engage in war, unless actually invaded, or in such imminent danger as will not admit of delay. But when any river divides or flows through two or more States, they may enter into compacts with each other to improve the navigation thereof.

ART. II

Sec. 1. (1) The Executive power shall be vested in a President of the Confederate States of America. He and the Vice-President shall hold their offices for the term of six years; but the President shall not be reeligible. The President and Vice-President shall be elected as follows:

(2) Each State shall appoint, in such manner as the Legislature thereof may direct, a number of electors equal to the whole number of Sena-

tors and Representatives to which the State may be entitled in the Congress; but no Senator or Representative, or person holding an office of trust or profit under the Confederate States, shall be appointed an elector.

(3) The electors shall meet in their respective States and vote by ballot for President and Vice-President, one of whom, at least shall not be an inhabitant of the same State with themselves; they shall name in their ballots the person voted for as President, and in distinct ballots the person voted for as Vice-President, and they shall make distinct lists of all persons voted for as President, and of all persons voted for as Vice-President, and of the number of votes for each; which list they shall sign, and certify, and transmit, sealed, to the . . . government of the Confederate States, directed to the President of the Senate. The President of the Senate shall, in the presence of the Senate and House of Representatives, open all the certificates, and the votes shall then be counted; the person having the greatest number of votes for President shall be the President, if such number be a majority of the whole number of electors appointed; and if no person shall have such a majority, then, from the persons having the highest numbers, not exceeding three, on the list of those voted for as President, the House of Representatives shall choose immediately, by ballot, the President. But, in choosing the President, the votes shall be taken by States, the representation from each State having one vote; a quorum for this purpose shall consist of a member or members from two-thirds of the States, and a majority of all the States shall be necessary to a choice. And if the House of Representatives shall not choose a President, whenever the right of choice shall devolve upon them, before the fourth day of March next following, then the Vice-President shall act as President, as in case of the death, or other constitutional disability of the President.

(4) The person having the greatest number of votes as Vice-President shall be the Vice-President, if such number be a majority of the whole number of electors appointed; and if no person have a majority, then from the two highest numbers on the list, the Senate shall choose the Vice-President; a quorum for the purpose shall consist of two-thirds of the whole number of Senators, and a majority of the whole number shall be necessary for a choice.

(5) But no person constitutionally ineligible to the office of President shall be eligible to that of Vice-President of the Confederate States.

(6) The Congress may determine the time of choosing the electors, and the day on which they shall give their votes; which day shall be the same throughout the Confederate States.

(7) No person except a natural born citizen of the Confederate States, or a citizen thereof, at the time of the adoption of this Constitution, or a citizen thereof born in the United States prior to the 20th of December, 1860, shall be eligible to that office of President; neither shall any person be eligible to that office who shall not have attained the age of thirty-five years, and been fourteen years a resident within the limits of the Confederate States, as they may exist at the time of his election.

(8) In case of the removal of the President from office, or of his death, resignation, or inability to discharge the powers and duties of the said office, the same shall devolve on the Vice-President; and the Congress may, by law, provide for the case of the removal, death, resignation, or inability both of the President and the Vice-President, declaring what officer shall then act as President, and such officer shall then act accordingly until the disability be removed or a President shall be elected.

(9) The President shall, at stated times, receive for his services a compensation, which shall nei-

ther be increased nor diminished during the period for which he shall have been elected; and he shall not receive within that period any other emolument from the Confederate States, or any of them.

(10) Before he enters on the execution [of the duties] of his office, he shall take the following oath or affirmation:

"I do solemnly swear (or affirm) that I will faithfully execute the office of President of the Confederate States, and will, to the best of my ability, preserve, protect, and defend the Constitution thereof."

Sec. 2. (1) The President shall be commander-in-chief of the army and navy of the Confederate States, and of the militia of the several States, when called into the actual service of the Confederate States; he may require the opinion, in writing, of the principal officer in each of the Executive Departments, upon any subject relating to the duties of their respective offices; and he shall have power to grant reprieves and pardons for offences against the Confederate States, except in cases of impeachment.

(2) He shall have power, by and with the advice and consent of the Senate, to make treaties, provided two-thirds of the Senators present concur; and he shall nominate, and, by and with the advice and consent of the Senate, shall appoint ambassadors, other public ministers, and consuls, Judges of the Supreme Court, and all other officers of the Confederate States, whose appointments are not herein otherwise provided for, and which shall be established by law; but the Congress may by law vest the appointment of such inferior officers, as they think proper, in the President alone, in the courts of law, or in the heads of departments.

(3) The principal officer in each of the Executive Departments, and all persons connected with the diplomatic service, may be removed from office at the pleasure of the President. All other civil officers of the Executive Departments may be removed at any time by the President, or other appointing power, when their services are unnecessary, or for dishonesty, incapacity, inefficiency, misconduct, or neglect of duty; and when so removed, the removal shall be reported to the Senate, together with the reasons therefor.

(4) The President shall have power to fill all vacancies that may happen during the recess of the Senate, by granting commissions which shall expire at the end of the next session; but no person rejected by the Senate shall be reappointed to the same office during their ensuing recess.

Sec. 3. (1) The President shall, from time to time, give to the Congress information of the state of the Confederacy, and recommend to their consideration such measures as he shall judge necessary and expedient; he may, on extraordinary occasions, convene both Houses, or either of them; and, in case of disagreement between them, with respect to the time of adjournment he may adjourn them to such time as he shall think proper; he shall receive ambassadors and other public ministers; he shall take care that the laws be faithfully executed, and shall commission all the officers of the Confederate States.

Sec. 4. (1) The President and Vice-President, and all Civil officers of the Confederate States, shall be removed from office on impeachment for, or conviction of, treason, bribery, or other high crimes and misdemeanors.

ART. III

Sec. 1. (1) The judicial power of the Confederate States shall be vested in one Supreme Court, and in such inferior courts as the Congress may from time to time ordain and establish. The judges, both of the Supreme and inferior courts, shall hold their offices during good behavior, and shall, at stated times, receive for their services a compensation, which shall not be diminished during their continuance in office. . . .

ART. IV

SEC. I. (1) Full faith and credit shall be given in each State to the public acts, records, and judicial proceedings of every other State. And the Congress may, by general laws, prescribe the manner in which such acts, records, and proceedings shall be proved, and the effect thereof.

SEC. 2. (1) The citizens of each State shall be entitled to all the privileges and immunities of citizens of the several States, and shall have the right of transit and sojourn in any State of this Confederacy, with their slaves and other property; and the right of property in said slaves shall not be thereby impaired.

(2) A person charged in any State with treason, felony, or other crime against the laws of such State, who shall flee from justice, and be found in another State, shall, on demand of the executive authority of the State from which he fled, be delivered up to be removed to the State having jurisdiction of the crime.

(3) No slave or other person held to service or labor in any State or Territory of the Confederate States, under the laws thereof, escaping or [un]lawfully carried into another, shall, in consequence of any law or regulation therein, be discharged from such service or labor; but shall be delivered up on claim of the party to whom such slave belongs, or to whom such service or labor may be due.

SEC. 3. (1) Other States may be admitted into this Confederacy by a vote of two-thirds of the whole House of Representatives, and two-thirds of the Senate, the Senate voting by States; but no new State shall be formed or erected within the jurisdiction of any other State; nor any State be formed by the junction of two or more States, or parts of States, without the consent of the Legislatures of the States concerned as well as of the Congress.

(2) The Congress shall have power to dispose of and make all needful rules and regulations concerning the property of the Confederate States, including the lands thereof.

(3) The Confederate States may acquire new territory; and Congress shall have power to legislate and provide governments for the inhabitants of all territory belonging to the Confederate States, lying without the limits of the several States, and may permit them, at such times, and in such manner as it may by law provide, to form States to be admitted into the Confederacy. In all such territory, the institution of negro slavery, as it now exists in the Confederate States, shall be recognized and protected by Congress and by the territorial government; and the inhabitants of the several Confederate States and Territories shall have the right to take to such territory any slaves lawfully held by them in any of the States or Territories of the Confederate States.

(4) The Confederate States shall guarantee to every State that now is or hereafter may become a member of this Confederacy, a Republican form of Government, and shall protect each of them against invasion; and on application of the Legislature, (or of the Executive when the Legislature is not in session,) against domestic violence.

ART. V

SEC. I. (1) Upon the demand of any three States, legally assembled in their several Conventions, the Congress shall summon a Convention of all the States, to take into consideration such amendments to the Constitution as the said States shall concur in suggesting at the time when the said demand is made; and should any of the proposed amendments to the Constitution be agreed on by the said Convention—voting by States—and the same be ratified by the Legislatures of two-thirds thereof—as the one or the other mode of ratification may be proposed by the general convention—they shall thenceforward form a part of this Constitution. But no State shall, without its consent, be deprived of its equal representation in the Senate.

ART. VI

1.—The Government established by this Constitution is the successor of the Provisional Government of the Confederate States of America, and all the laws passed by the latter shall continue in force until the same shall be repealed or modified; and all the officers appointed by the same shall remain in office until their successors are appointed and qualified, or the offices abolished.

2. All debts contracted and engagements entered into before the adoption of this Constitution, shall be as valid against the Confederate States under this Constitution as under the Provisional Government.

3. This Constitution, and the laws of the Confederate States, made in pursuance thereof, and all treaties made, or which shall be made, under the authority of the Confederate States, shall be the supreme law of the land; and the judges in every State shall be bound thereby, any thing in the Constitution or laws of any State to the contrary notwithstanding.

4. The Senators and Representatives before mentioned, and the members of the several State Legislatures, and all executive and judicial officers, both of the Confederate States and of the several States, shall be bound, by oath or affirmation, to support this Constitution; but no religious test shall ever be required as a qualification to any office or public trust under the Confederate States.

5. The enumeration, in the Constitution, of certain rights, shall not be construed to deny or disparage others retained by the people of the several States.

6. The powers not delegated to the Confederate States by the Constitution, nor prohibited by it to the States, are reserved to the States, respectively, or to the people thereof.

ART. VII

1.—The ratification of the conventions of five States shall be sufficient for the establishment of this Constitution between the States so ratifying the same.

2. When five States shall have ratified this Constitution in the manner before specified, the Congress, under the provisional Constitution, shall prescribe the time for holding the election of President and Vice-President, and for the meeting of the electoral college, and for counting the votes and inaugurating the President. They shall also prescribe the time for holding the first election of members of Congress under this Constitution, and the time for assembling the same. Until the assembling of such Congress, the Congress under the provisional Constitution shall continue to exercise the legislative powers granted them; not extending beyond the time limited by the Constitution of the Provisional Government.

Adopted unanimously by the Congress of the Confederate States of South Carolina, Georgia, Florida, Alabama, Mississippi, Louisiana, and Texas, sitting in convention at the capitol, in the city of Montgomery, Alabama, on the Eleventh day of March, in the year Eighteen Hundred and Sixty-One.

HOWELL COBB
President of the Congress

"The most eventful year"

JEFFERSON DAVIS'S INAUGURAL ADDRESS
1862

The author and humorist Mark Twain (1835–1910) described Jefferson Davis (1808–1889) as "the head, the heart, and soul of the mightiest rebellion of modern times." As Secretary of War in Franklin Pierce's Administration (1853–1857), Davis built up the Union Army that would shatter his Confederacy. As a Mississippi Senator (1847–1851) he was popular in the North. Reluctantly, Davis helped to set up the Confederate States of America, becoming its president after serving for a year as provisional president. The Civil War (1861–1865) had been underway for nearly a year when Davis delivered his inaugural address. On that same day, U.S. President (and Commander-in-Chief) Abraham Lincoln (1809–1865) gave General Order No. 1, directing the Union military to undertake a general advance. During the last year of the war, Davis was often in the field with General Robert E. Lee (1807–1870). He was captured in Georgia a month after Appomattox, and held in irons in a Federal military prison in Virginia. Because of legal maneuverings, Davis was never brought to trial.

On this the birthday of the man most identified with the establishment of American independence, and beneath the monument erected to commemorate his heroic virtues and those of his compatriots, we have assembled to usher into existence the Permanent Government of the Confederate States. Through this instrumentality, under the favor of Divine Providence, we hope to perpetuate the principles of our revolutionary fathers. The day, the memory, and the purpose seem fitly associated. . . .

When a long course of class legislation, directed not to the general welfare, but to the aggrandizement of the Northern section of the Union, culminated in a warfare on the domestic institutions of the Southern States—when the dogmas of a sectional party, substituted for the provisions of the constitutional compact, threatened to destroy the sovereign rights of the States, six of those States, withdrawing from the Union, confederated together to exercise the right and perform the duty of instituting a Government which would better secure the liberties for the preservation of which that Union was established.

Whatever of hope some may have entertained that a returning sense of justice would remove the danger with which our rights were threatened, and render it possible to preserve the Union of the Constitution, must have been dispelled by the malignity and barbarity of the Northern States in the prosecution of the existing war. The confidence of the most hopeful among us must have been destroyed by the disregard they have recently exhibited for all the time-honored bulwarks of civil and religious liberty. Bastiles filled with prisoners, arrested without civil process or indictment duly found; the writ of *habeas corpus* suspended by Executive mandate; a State Legislature controlled by the imprisonment of members whose avowed principles suggested to the Federal Executive that there might be another added to the list of seceded States; elections held under threats of a military power; civil officers, peaceful citizens, and gentlewomen incarcerated for opinion's sake—proclaimed the incapacity of our late associates to administer a Government as free, liberal, and humane as that established for our common use.

For proof of the sincerity of our purpose to maintain our ancient institutions, we may point to the Constitution of the Confederacy and the laws enacted under it, as well as to the fact that through all the necessities of an unequal struggle there has been no act on our part to impair personal liberty or the freedom of speech, of thought, or of the press. The courts have been open, the judicial functions fully executed, and every right of the peaceful citizen maintained as securely as if a war of invasion had not disturbed the land.

The people of the States now confederated became convinced that the Government of the United States had fallen into the hands of a sectional majority, who would pervert that most sacred of all trusts to the destruction of the rights which it was pledged to protect. They believed that to remain longer in the Union would subject them to a continuance of a disparaging discrimination, submission to which would be inconsistent with their welfare, and intolerable to a proud people. They therefore determined to sever its bonds and establish a new Confederacy for themselves.

The experiment instituted by our revolutionary fathers, of a voluntary Union of sovereign States for purposes specified in a solemn compact, had been perverted by those who, feeling power and forgetting right, were determined to respect no law but their own will. The Government had ceased to answer the ends for which it was ordained and established. To save ourselves from a revolution which, in its silent but rapid progress, was about to place us under the despotism of numbers, and to preserve in spirit, as well as in form, a system of government we believed to be peculiarly fitted to our condition, and full of promise for mankind, we determined to make a new association, composed of States homogeneous in interest, in policy, and in feeling. . . .

The first year in our history has been the most eventful in the annals of this continent. A new Government has been established, and its machinery put in operation over an area exceeding seven hundred thousand square miles. The great principles upon which we have been willing to hazard everything that is dear to man have made conquests for us which could never have been achieved by the sword. Our Confederacy has grown from six to thirteen States; and Maryland, already united to us by hallowed memories and material interests, will, I believe, when able to speak with unstifled voice, connect her destiny with the South. Our people have rallied with unexampled unanimity to the support of the great principles of constitutional government, with firm resolve to perpetuate by arms the right which they could not peacefully secure. A million of men, it is estimated, are now standing in hostile array, and waging war along a frontier of thousands of miles. . . .

The period is near at hand when our foes must sink under the immense load of debt which they have incurred, a debt which in their effort to subjugate us has already attained such fearful dimensions as will subject them to burdens which must continue to oppress them for generations to come. . . .

It is a satisfaction that we have maintained the war by our unaided exertions. We have neither asked nor received assistance from any quarter. Yet the interest involved is not wholly our own. The world at large is concerned in opening our markets to its commerce. When the independence of the Confederate States is recognized by the nations of the earth, and we are free to follow our interests and inclinations by cultivating foreign trade, the Southern States will offer to manufacturing nations the most favorable markets which ever invited their commerce. Cotton, sugar, rice, tobacco, provisions, timber, and naval stores will furnish attractive exchanges. Nor would the constancy of these supplies be likely to be disturbed by war. . . .

The tyranny of an unbridled majority, the most odious and least responsible form of despotism, has denied us both the right and the remedy. Therefore we are in arms to renew such sacrifices as our fathers made to the holy cause of constitutional liberty. At the darkest hour of our struggle the Provisional gives place to the Permanent Government.

To show ourselves worthy of the inheritance bequeathed to us by the patriots of the Revolution, we must emulate that heroic devotion which made reverse to them but the crucible in which their patriotism was refined.

"Shall be . . . forever free"

THE EMANCIPATION PROCLAMATION
1863

Preservation of the Union was President Abraham Lincoln's goal in the Civil War (1861–1865). It was "not either to save or to destroy slavery. If I could save the Union without freeing *any* slave," he said, "I would do it, and if I could save it by freeing *all* the slaves I would do it; and if I could save it by freeing some and leaving others alone I would also do that." Between 1835 and 1844, the U.S. House of Representatives had argued whether Congress could even discuss the subject of slavery. By the time (New Year's Day, 1863) Lincoln (1809–1865) signed the proclamation freeing all slaves in any territory in rebellion, there were well over 3,000,000 slaves in the Confederacy, and he had determined that his forces would be an army of liberation and moral crusaders. (Excluded from emancipation were the 4,350,000 slaves in Delaware, Kentucky, Maryland, and Missouri, border states that had remained within the Union; the 275,000 slaves in Union-occupied Tennessee; and the myriad in portions of Virginia and Louisiana under the control of Federal armies.) Emancipation transformed the character of the war, and boosted Northern morale tremendously. There was no chance that slavery would survive a Union victory. The Thirteenth Amendment to the Constitution (1865) abolishing slavery everywhere was necessary, because the Emancipation Proclamation did not prevent Southern states, on re-admission to the Union, from reinstituting slavery. (Around 180,000 blacks had joined the Union military toward war's end.)

WHEREAS on the 22d day of September, A.D. 1862, a proclamation was issued by the President of the United States, containing, among other things, the following, to wit:

"That on the 1st day of January, A.D. 1863, all persons held as slaves within any State or designated part of a State the people whereof shall then be in rebellion against the United States shall be then, thenceforward, and forever free; and the executive government of the United States, including the military and naval authority thereof, will recognize and maintain the freedom of such persons and will do no act or acts to repress such persons, or any of them, in any efforts they may make for their actual freedom.

"That the executive will on the 1st day of January aforesaid, by proclamation, designate the States and parts of States, if any, in which the people thereof, respectively, shall then be in rebellion against the United States; and the fact that any State or the people thereof shall on that day be in good faith represented in the Congress of the United States by members chosen thereto at elections wherein a majority of the qualified voters of such States shall have participated shall, in the absence of strong countervailing testimony, be deemed conclusive evidence that such

State and the people thereof are not then in rebellion against the United States."

Now, therefore, I, Abraham Lincoln, President of the United States, by virtue of the power in me vested as Commander-in-Chief of the Army and Navy of the United States in time of actual armed rebellion against the authority and government of the United States, and as a fit and necessary war measure for suppressing said rebellion, do, on this 1st day of January, A.D. 1863, and in accordance with my purpose so to do, publicly proclaimed for the full period of one hundred days from the first day above mentioned, order and designate as the States and parts of States wherein the people thereof, respectively, are this day in rebellion against the United States the following, to wit:

Arkansas, Texas, Louisiana (except the parishes of St. Bernard, Plaquemines, Jefferson, St. John, St. Charles, St. James, Ascension, Assumption, Terrebonne, Lafourche, St. Mary, St. Martin, and Orleans, including the city of New Orleans), Mississippi, Alabama, Florida, Georgia, South Carolina, North Carolina, and Virginia (except the forty-eight counties designated as West Virginia, and also the counties of Berkeley, Accomac, Northampton, Elizabeth City, York, Princess Anne, and Norfolk, including the cities of Norfolk and Portsmouth), and which excepted parts are for the present left precisely as if this proclamation were not issued.

And by virtue of the power and for the purpose aforesaid, I do order and declare that all persons held as slaves within said designated States and parts of States are, and henceforward shall be, free; and that the Executive Government of the United States, including the military and naval authorities thereof, will recognize and maintain the freedom of said persons.

And I hereby enjoin upon the people so declared to be free to abstain from all violence, unless in necessary self-defense; and I recommend to them that, in all cases when allowed, they labor faithfully for reasonable wages.

And I further declare and make known that such persons of suitable condition will be received into the armed service of the United States to garrison forts, positions, stations, and other places, and to man vessels of all sorts in said service.

And upon this act, sincerely believed to be an act of justice, warranted by the Constitution upon military necessity, I invoke the considerate judgment of mankind and the gracious favor of Almighty God.

"That these dead shall not have died in vain"

LINCOLN'S GETTYSBURG ADDRESS
1863

Only 272 words—but what words! Only 10 sentences—but what sentences! The historian Garry Wills (born 1934) has written about President Abraham Lincoln's brief speech at the formal dedication of the 17-acre National Soldiers' Cemetery, in Gettysburg, Pennsylvania:

> "The crowd departed with a new thing in its ideological luggage, that new constitution Lincoln had substituted for the one they brought there with them. They walked off, from those curving graves on the hillside, under a changed sky, into a different America. Lincoln had revolutionized the Revolution, giving people a new past to live with that would change their future indefinitely."

In early July, 1863, General Robert E. Lee's army, driving to split the United States in two, had been turned back by the Union soldiers at Gettysburg. Seven thousand Union and Confederate soldiers gave their "last full measure of devotion" in the decisive three-day battle. The Union had "a new birth of freedom," the Southern cause was broken. The Confederate army, thrown into a defensive war, realized it would never win. The nation, "conceived in liberty and dedicated to the proposition that all men are created equal," had endured. Lincoln (1809–1865) worked on the speech the night before delivery and on the platform while waiting hours to be introduced. He spoke it slowly, clearly, and, with his Kentucky accent, in a high voice. It was over so fast that photographers missed it.

FOUR SCORE AND SEVEN YEARS AGO our fathers brought forth on this continent a new nation, conceived in liberty and dedicated to the proposition that all men are created equal.

Now we are engaged in a great civil war, testing whether that nation or any nation so conceived and so dedicated can long endure. We are met on a great battlefield of that war. We have come to dedicate a portion of that field as a final resting place for those who here gave their lives that that nation might live. It is altogether fitting and proper that we should do this.

But, in a larger sense, we cannot dedicate—we cannot consecrate—we cannot hallow—this ground. The brave men, living and dead, who struggled here have consecrated it far above our poor power to add or detract. The world will little note nor long remember what we say here, but it can never forget what they did here. It is for us, the living, rather, to be dedicated here to the unfinished work which they who fought here have thus far so nobly advanced.

It is rather for us to be here dedicated to the great task remaining before us—that from these honored dead we take increased devotion to that cause for which they gave the last full measure of devotion; that we here highly resolve that these dead shall not have died in vain; that this nation, under God, shall have a new birth of freedom; and that government of the people, by the people, for the people shall not perish from the earth.

"Achieve and cherish a just, and a lasting peace"

LINCOLN'S SECOND INAUGURAL
1865

It was a time of "dis-Union" when President Abraham Lincoln (1809–1865) delivered his first Inaugural Address, a brief for the Northern position. It was a time of great triumph—the Civil War was all but over—when he delivered his second Inaugural Address. Washington was wet and windy, knee-deep in late winter mud. Lincoln's face was heavily lined, his cheeks sunken; he was exhausted. The Chief Executive was concerned with reconciliation and reconstruction; moral absolutes would serve the nation poorly. Reading from a half sheet of foolscap, he strove to bind the nation's wounds. To applause, he exhorted "malice toward none, charity for all." Although it was one of the shortest (703 words) inaugural addresses, it was one of the most memorable. Lincoln thought there was "lots of wisdom in that document, I suspect." It would "wear as well as—perhaps better than—anything" he had produced, "but I believe it is not immediately popular." The President took to bed for a few days. The Civil War ended one month later. ("If the Confederacy falls," its president, Jefferson Davis, had said privately, "there should be written on its tombstone: *Died of a Theory*.") Less than a week after Appomattox (April 9), the 56-year-old President was murdered by a Southern conspirator, an actor whom Lincoln had once invited to the White House.

At this second appearing to take the oath of the presidential office, there is less occasion for an extended address than there was at the first. Then a statement, somewhat in detail, of a course to be pursued, seemed fitting and proper. Now, at the expiration of four years, during which public declarations have been constantly called forth on every point and phase of the great contest which still absorbs the attention, and engrosses the energies of the nation, little that is new could be presented. The progress of our arms, upon which all else chiefly depends, is as well known to the public as to myself; and it is, I trust, reasonably satisfactory and encouraging to all. With high hope for the future, no prediction in regard to it is ventured.

On the occasion corresponding to this four years ago, all thoughts were anxiously directed to an impending civil-war. All dreaded it—all sought to avert it. While the inaugural address was being delivered from this place, devoted altogether to *saving* the Union without war, insurgent agents were in the city seeking to *destroy* it without war—seeking to dissol[v]e the Union, and divide effects, by negotiation. Both parties deprecated war; but one of them would *make* war rather than let the nation survive; and the other would *accept* war rather than let it perish. And the war came.

One eighth of the whole population were colored slaves, not distributed generally over the Union, but localized in the Southern part of it. These slaves constituted a peculiar and powerful interest. All knew that this interest was, somehow, the cause of the war. To strengthen, perpetuate, and extend this interest was the object for which the insurgents would rend the Union, even by war; while the government claimed no right to do more than to restrict the territorial enlargement of it. Neither party expected for the war, the magnitude, or the duration, which it has already attained. Neither anticipated that the *cause* of the conflict might cease with, or even before, the conflict itself should cease. Each looked for an easier triumph, and a result less fundamental and astounding. Both read the same Bible, and pray to the same God; and each invokes His aid against the other. It may seem strange that any men should dare to ask a just God's assistance in wringing their bread from the sweat of other men's faces; but let us judge not that we be not judged. The prayers of both could not be answered; that of neither has been answered fully. The Almighty has His own purposes. "Woe unto the world because of offences! for it must needs be that offences come; but woe to that man by whom the offence cometh!" If we shall suppose that American Slavery is one of those offences which, in the providence of God, must needs come, but which, having continued through His appointed time, He now wills to remove, and that He gives to both North and South, this terrible war, as the woe due to those by whom the offence came, shall we discern therein any departure from those divine attributes which the believers in a Living God always ascribe to Him? Fondly do we hope—fervently do we pray—that this mighty scourge of war may speedily pass away. Yet, if God wills that it continue, until all the wealth piled by the bond-man's two hundred and fifty years of unrequited toil shall be sunk, and until every drop of blood drawn with the lash, shall be paid by another drawn with the sword, as was said three thousand years ago, so still it must be said "the judgments of the Lord, are true and righteous altogether."

With malice toward none; with charity for all; with firmness in the right, as God gives us to see the right, let us strive on to finish the work we are in; to bind up the nation's wounds; to care for him who shall have borne the battle, and for his widow, and his orphan—to do all which may achieve and cherish a just, and a lasting peace, among ourselves, and with all nations.[4]

WE THE PEOPLE

Any discussion of immigration inevitably suggests something of the wonderful diversity of the American scene—the mix of races and people, cultures and religions that would define the national character. While wary of such normative generalizations as the "American mind," we may still ask how and what shaped its distinctiveness, a question preoccupying observers ever since Crèvecoeur. What can be certain is that it did not spring fully blown, like Pallas Athena from the brow of Zeus. It was the victim and possessor of the past, a past that antedated settlement in America. This "American mind" took some of its shape in the early national period from the non-American characteristics of the immigrant's country of origin. It partook as well of the dominant norms and activities of the new nation, once the land had time to catch its breath.

Fourteen years after the Declaration of Independence, after the colonies declared "to a candid world" that they were "and of right ought to be free and independent states," Americans, their writings suggest, were aware that they dwelt in a land of plenty, that the Old World claims of social rank and deference to a gentry were irrelevant, that an independent yeomanry, in an overwhelmingly agrarian order, was the best and freest of conditions. National cohesion was lacking, the states would develop intense rivalries, and the industrial revolution, transportation revolution, educational and humanitarian movements, and demographic changes would result in two distinct societies. The population tripled between 1790 and 1830, in the midst of Jackson's first administration, and by the Civil War it roughly equaled England's and France's. An exploding population encouraged westward expansion, fueled economic growth, provided a growing workforce, and offered an increasing demand for housing, food, banking, and consumer goods.

The quantum leap in manufacturing, transportation, technology, even mechanized agriculture helped define Americans as a brash, ambitious people who enjoyed high expectations and intense individualism—for whom no speculation was too reckless, no experiment too bold. An emergent middle class was guided by norms of competition, increasingly demonstrating an insouciant disregard for the old reciprocity and traditional face-to-face community values. It ignored the plight of the craftsman whose skills were increasingly obsolete, thought little of discarding those who didn't "make it"; and, fearing a new factory workforce composed of those alien to consensual middle-class norms, placed great faith in schools as the agency that would maintain a stable and orderly society. No other people ever demanded so much of its schools. They were central to thinking and to the transmission of discipline, obedience, acculturation to consensual values. Schools, it was hoped, would create homogeneity out of diversity. From the early national period to the 1944 G.I. Bill for returning Second World War veterans—and their education in colleges and vocational schools—a continuous concern for education is apparent. Schooling became the national religion. Americans put their faith in it, recognizing that conveying enlightenment to the people was the first duty of a democracy.

The rising middle class also found time for entertainment. Sports, like baseball and football, became part of the mass culture, associated with dominant values of manliness and competitiveness. Workers now could join in such recreation, because the shorter work week allowed time for leisure activities. This cross-class popular culture had an enormous impact upon American attitudes and tastes, especially after the late nineteenth century. Pre-Civil War society was a harbinger, with its minstrel shows, vaudeville, touring professional troupes, and "rough" culture of spectators, who were notoriously rowdy. They whistled, hooted stage villains, identified with heroes, responded to images of the ideal American, the immigrant "greenhorn," and the humble, shuffling black man. In the 1880s and 1890s, recreational venues were appropriated by merchants of leisure who advertised their vaudeville shows, dance halls, and nickelodeons. The last were extraordinarily successful, and in tandem with the radio, which reached into the homes of millions after 1920, shaped peoples' expectations and produced a "flattening out" of the culture. Of all the popular arts, they had the greatest influence on national tastes and attitudes.

This growing popular appreciation of the vehicles of mass culture continued into the twentieth century and even received considerable government support after the Second World War. Federal funding is a relatively modern development, with only one significant exception, when the Works Project Administration (W.P.A.) supported arts projects. Until 1965, when the National Endowment for the Arts and the National Endowment for the Humanities were founded, the arts and humanities in America had received no governmental subventions. They remained a private venture of imaginative entrepreneurs. Over 200 Federal programs were quickly sponsored by the NEA and NEH, in the belief that these were integral to the preservation of a national heritage and a sense of national identity. Congress did not interfere for twenty-five years, relying on the neutrality and professionalism of the directors. In recent years, however, pressured by moralistic politicians and their religious Fundamentalist allies, Congress began to interfere with Endowment decisions owing to a small number of controversial projects, and prohibited grants involving material considered "obscene."

This conflict illustrates a basic ambiguity in the so-called "American mind"; namely, the continuous tension between liberty and order, and the contrary tendencies to which they give expression. The contradictions are apparent in the issue over public funding. They appear earlier when Hollywood is threatened by state and Federal obscenity laws. Here, too, the threat of censorship of artistic expression led the movie industry to engage in self-censoring practices under the former United States Postmaster General Will Hays. That is, responding to growing pressure from political forces and the Catholic Church's League of Decency, Hollywood abided by the "Don'ts and Be Carefuls" Hays Code, which banned any criticism of organized religion and prohibited depiction of nudity, interracial love, "excessive and lustful kissing," "adultery and illicit sex," or "dances suggesting or representing sexual actions."

Many instances of these fundamental ambiguities inherent in American values and perceptions come to mind, and they all suggest how we as a nation have been torn between liberty and order; moral restraints and freedom of expression; paeans to individualism and the nonconformity flowing from it and tendencies toward suspicion of nonconformity and suppression of dissent; professions of egalitarianism and intolerant practices. Consider, for example, familiar slave scenes, which included multiple forms of resistance to bondage, including runaways, conscious or subconscious sabotage, labor slowdowns in the cotton fields, feigned illness to avoid work, individual rebelliousness, group rebellion, mutinies on slave vessels. And yet blacks, not categorically repudiating the world of the Northern racists and Southern slaveholders, simply wanted citizenship and freedom within their society.

Contradictory strains exist for freedmen after the late 1870s. Denuded of their traditional culture and victimized by all sorts of brutalities and injustices, many were ready to become what the Swedish sociologist Gunnar Myrdal termed an "exaggerated American," to accept the dominant culture of the dominant group. There is no wish to deny campaigns to develop a distinct black culture or the separatist movements among blacks, such as the pan-African movement of the late 1880s, the black nationalism of Marcus Garvey, or the late 1960s–early 1970s Black Power cry of rage. Yet most blacks endorse Myrdal's assertion: "In practically all its divergences, American Negro culture is not something independent of general American culture;" or, as the American sociologists Nathan Glazer and Daniel Moynihan have concluded: "The Negro is only an American, and nothing else." The larger contention is that, notwithstanding his immiserization and despondency, the black man is accepting of the hegemonic culture and economy; he wants to work, to enter the competitive order, to have a level playing field in employment, to vote and elect legislators responsive to his needs; that is, he wants nothing more than justice within the existing social system.

Yet another instance of the divided character of the "American mind" is seen in the Populist movement of the late nineteenth century. Small farmers of the South and Midwest joined the National Grange during the serious depression of the 1870s and then joined the Northwest and Southern Alliances—in response to the discriminatory railroad freight rates and the power of the Eastern banks to freeze them into interminable indebtedness. The Alliances evolved into the Populist Party, the most colorful of American political parties, and a farm revolt swept the hot, dusty prairies and the sun-baked cotton fields. It was "fanaticism like the Crusades," one observer wrote. But this fanaticism and this revolt sought nothing more than justice. The farmers had suffered a quarter century of repeated injustices, but, not losing faith in political democracy, they only wanted their men in the statehouses and the staid halls of Congress. They'd not change the political system and only modestly reform current economic practices.

The clash of power and liberty affords yet another example of dissonant and contradictory responses. Americans have generally mistrusted power, which includes all governmental processes—even democratic ones—and believed that government would inevitably and aggressively seek to restrict liberty. After the mid-1960s, this conflict was resolved in favor of liberty, when the Supreme Court found—in Griswold v. Connecticut *(1965)—that a Connecticut law prohibiting the purchase of contraceptives in a pharmacy was an intolerable legislative intrusion. The Justices affirmed a right of privacy, a non-enumerated right inherent in the enumerated liberties of the Bill of Rights. In opposing restrictions on individual liberty, the Court established a precedent—in which "privacy" became an expanding legal concept, to be applied creatively to other kinds of privacy, such as individual freedom of choice, roughly translated in this context as the right to an abortion, then becoming an important moral and legal right. But the counter tendency, the readiness to use the power of government to prohibit abortion, is ironically embraced by those who are usually suspicious of any government regulation of individual liberties. In sum, diametrically opposed tendencies suggest the heterogeneity of the "American mind."*

3,893,635

THE FIRST CENSUS
1790

Article I, Section II of the U.S. Constitution called for enumeration of "We the People of the United States" within three years after the first meeting of the Congress, and "within every subsequent term of ten years." Composition of the House of Representatives depended on the number of people in each state; there would be one Representative for every 33,000. The first Congress began work in 1789 and the first census was underway a year later. U.S. marshals and their assistants, travelling by boat and horse, canvassed the 13 states, the districts of Vermont, Kentucky, and Maine, and the Southwest Territory (the Northwest Territory was not surveyed). The law required six inquiries: the name of the head of the family, the number of free white males of 16

(continued on following page)

DISTICTS	Free white Males of 16 years and upwards, including heads of families.	Free white Males under sixteen years.	Free white Females, including heads of families.	All other free persons.	Slaves.	Total.
Vermont	22435	22328	40505	255	16	85539
N. Hampshire	36086	34851	70160	630	158	141885
Maine	24384	24748	46870	538	NONE	96540
Massachusetts	95453	87289	190582	5463	NONE	378787
Rhode Island	16019	15799	32652	3407	948	68825
Connecticut	60523	54403	117448	2808	2764	237946
New York	83700	78122	152320	4654	21324	340120
New Jersey	45251	41416	83287	2762	11423	184139
Pennsylvania	110788	106948	206363	6537	3737	434373
Delaware	11783	12143	22384	3899	8887	59094
Maryland	55915	51339	101395	8043	103036	319728
Virginia	110936	116135	215046	12866	292627	747610
Kentucky	15154	17057	28922	114	12430	73677
N. Carolina	69988	77506	140710	4975	100572	393751
S. Carolina	35576	37722	66880	1801	107094	249073
Georgia	13103	14044	25739	398	29264	82548
	807094	791850	1541263	59150	694280	3893635

Total number of Inhabitants of the United States exclusive of S. Western and N. Territory.	Free white Males of 21 years and upwards.	Free Males under 21 years of age.	Free white Females.	All other persons.	Slaves.	Total
S.W. territory	6271	10277	15365	361	3417	35691
N. Ditto	—	—	—	—	—	—

years of age and upward, including the head of the family (in order to ascertain the nation's industrial and military potential); free white males under 16; free white females, including heads of families; all other free persons (by sex and color); and slaves. Virginia was the most populated state (747,610); Pennsylvania, the second most populated (434,373). The new nation's three largest cities were New York City (just over 30,000), Philadelphia (28,522), and Boston (18,320).

Note: The census of 1790, published in 1791, reported 16 slaves in Vermont. Subsequently, and up to 1860, the number was given as 17. An examination of the original manuscript returns showed that there were never any slaves in Vermont. The original error occurred in preparing the results for publication, when 16 persons returned as "Free colored" were classified as "Slave."

Corrected figures are 85,425, or 114 less than figures published in 1790 due to an error of addition in the returns for each of the Vermont towns of Fairfield, Milton, Shelburne, and Williston, in the county of Chittenden; Brookfield, Newbury, Randolph, and Strafford, in the county of Orange; Castleton, Clarendon, Hubbardton, Poultney, Rutland, Shrewsbury, and Wallingford, in the county of Rutland; Dummerston, Guilford, Halifax, and Westminster, in the county of Windham; and Woodstock, in the county of Windsor.

Corrected figures for Delaware were 59,096 or two more than figures published in 1790, due to error of addition.

"Fitting up a suitable apartment"

THE LIBRARY OF CONGRESS
1800

As Congress prepared to move from Philadelphia to permanent quarters in the new, swampy city of Washington, it appropriated a sum of $5,000 "for the purchase of such books as may be necessary for the use of Congress . . . and for fitting up a suitable apartment for containing them . . ." Congress already had acquired a few standard references: Blackstone's *Commentaries*, Vattel's *Law of Nature and Nations*, Hume's *History of England*, Morse's *American Geography*—some 50 titles in all—plus subscriptions to a few periodicals. After British troops had burned the first library (3,000 volumes), in 1814, former President Thomas Jefferson (1743–1826) offered a replacement—his personal library accumulated over a half century: "I do not know that it contains any branch of science which Congress would wish to exclude from their collection; there is, in fact, no subject to which a Member of Congress may not have occasion to refer." Congress appropriated $23,950 for Jefferson's 6,487 books, laying the foundation for the great national library. A fire in 1851 destroyed two-thirds of the holdings, some 35,000 volumes, including a substantial portion of the Jefferson collection. Today, the "nation's library" includes more than 16,000,000 books and 100,000,000 other items, ranging from a cuneiform (from 2040 B.C.) to compact disks. There are some 532 miles of shelves in three buildings. The library, the memory bank of the nation, receives about 1,000,000 new items each year. It plans to have 5,000,000 items accessible electronically by the turn of the century.

That for the purchase of such books as may be necessary for the use of Congress at the said city of Washington, and for fitting up a suitable apartment for containing them and for placing them therein the sum of five thousand dollars shall be, and hereby is, appropriated; and that the said purchase shall be made by the Secretary of the Senate and Clerk of the House of Representatives, pursuant to such directions as shall be given, and such catalogue as shall be furnished by a joint committee of both Houses of Congress to be appointed for that purpose; and that the said books shall be placed in one suitable apartment in the Capitol in the said city, for the use of both Houses of Congress and the members thereof, according to such regulations as the committee aforesaid shall devise and establish.

"Appeal to the friends of humanity"

THE AMISTAD AFFAIR

1839

The *Amistad* incident created serious problems in international relations and raised complicated legal questions. It brought all factions of the antislavery movement together in common cause, at least temporarily. The current President and a former President were involved. The concerned sought the rescue of the Amistaders, 53 African slaves imprisoned in New London, Connecticut, after they had murdered the captain and three crewmen of the Spanish schooner *La Amistad,* which was transporting slaves from Cuba to the United States. When the schooner was boarded in Long Island waters by U.S. Navy officers, the *La Amistad* was, the United States Supreme Court later ruled, in the possession of the mutineers (who, obviously, had not come to sell themselves as slaves). The slaves, of course, had been kidnapped; they were entitled to their liberty and were to be discharged at once. They received no compensation for either having been snatched from their African homes and held for more than two years or for the suffering they experienced in captivity. The 35 survivors sailed to Freetown, Sierra Leone.

Thirty-eight fellow-men from Africa, after having been piratically kidnapped from their native land, transported across the seas, and subjected to atrocious cruelties, have been thrown upon our shores, and are now incarcerated in jail to await their trial for crimes alleged by their oppressors to have been committed by them. They are ignorant of our language, of the usages of civilized society, and the obligations of Christianity. Under these circumstances, several friends of human rights have met to consult upon the case of these unfortunate men, and have appointed the undersigned a Committee to employ interpreters and able counsel, and take all the necessary means to secure the rights of the accused. It is intended to employ three legal gentlemen of distinguished abilities, and to incur other needful expenses. The poor prisoners being destitute of clothing, and several having scarcely a rag to cover them, immediate steps will be taken to provide what may be necessary. The undersigned, therefore, make this appeal to the friends of humanity to contribute for the above objects. Donations may be sent to either of the Committee, who will acknowledge the same, and make a public report of all their disbursements.

"The ball must be pitched"

BASEBALL'S ORIGINAL RULES

1845

In a park called Elysian Fields in Hoboken, New Jersey, directly across the North River from Manhattan, Alexander J. Cartwright (1820–1892), a surveyor and an amateur athlete, laid out the perfect baseball diamond—four bases 90 feet apart. He based the rules of the new sport on the English game of rounders. The very first game, played on June 19, 1846, was between a squad of gentlemen doctors, lawyers, and businessmen, whose sedentary habits required recreation—the New York Knickerbockers—and a team of clerks and blue-collar workers, the New York Nine. Cartwright was the umpire. The game ended after four innings, the New York Nine winning by the score of 23–1. The second organized game wasn't recorded for another five years.

1st. Members must strictly observe the time agreed upon for exercise, and be punctual in their attendance.

2nd. When assembled for exercise, the President, or in his absence, the Vice-President, shall appoint an Umpire, who shall keep the game in a book provided for that purpose, and note all violations of the By-Laws and Rules during the time of exercise.

3rd. The presiding officer shall designate two members as Captains, who shall retire and make the match to be played, observing at the same time that the players opposite to each other should be as nearly equal as possible, the choice of sides to be then tossed for, and the first in hand to be decided in like manner.

4th. The bases shall be from "home" to second base, forty-two paces; from first to third base, forty-two paces, equidistant.

5th. No stump match shall be played on a regular day of exercise.

6th. If there should not be a sufficient number of members of the Club present at the time agreed upon to commence exercise, gentlemen not members may be chosen in to make up the match, which shall not be broken up to take in members that may afterwards appear; but in all cases, members shall have the preference, when present, at the making of a match.

7th. If members appear after the game is commenced, they may be chosen in if mutually agreed upon.

8th. The game to consist of twenty-one counts, or aces; but at the conclusion an equal number of hands must be played.

9th. The ball must be pitched, not thrown, for the bat.

10th. A ball knocked out of the field, or outside the range of the first or third base, is foul.

11th. Three balls being struck at and missed and the last one caught, is a hand out; if not caught is considered fair, and the striker bound to run.

12th. If a ball be struck, or tipped, and caught, either flying or on the first bound, it is a hand out.

13th. A player running the bases shall be out, if the ball is in the hands of an adversary on the base, or the runner is touched with it before he makes his base; it being understood, however, that in no instance is a ball to be thrown at him.

14th. A player running who shall prevent an adversary from catching or getting the ball before making his base, is a hand out.

15th. Three hands out, all out.

16th. Players must take their strike in regular turn.

17th. All disputes and differences relative to the game, to be decided by the Umpire, from which there is no appeal.

18th. No ace or base can be made on a foul strike.

19th. A runner cannot be put out in making one base, when a balk is made by the pitcher.

20th. But one base allowed when a ball bounds out of the field when struck.

RULES FOR BASEBALL'S FIRST GAME

Section 1. The bases shall be from "home" to second base, 42 paces, from first to third base 42 paces, equidistant.

Section 2. The game shall consist of 21 counts or aces, but at the end an equal number of hands must be played. (First team to score 21 runs in equal opportunities wins. Changed to 9 innings in May 1857.)

Section 3. The ball must be pitched and not thrown for the bat. (The ball had to be thrown underhand.)

Section 4. A ball knocked outside the range of first or third base is foul.

Section 5. The three balls being struck at and missed and the last one caught is a hand out; if not caught is considered fair and the striker bound to run.

Section 6. A ball being struck or tipped and caught either flying or on the first bounce is a hand out.

Section 7. A player running the bases shall be out if the ball is in the hands of an adversary on the base, and the runner is touched by it before he makes the base; it being understood, however, that in no instance is a ball to be thrown at him.

Section 8. A player running who shall prevent an adversary from catching or getting the ball before making his base is a hand out.

Section 9. If two hands are already out, a player running home at the time a ball is struck cannot make an ace if the striker is caught out.

Section 10. Three hands out, all out. (Three outs and the inning is over.)

Section 11. Players must take their strike in regular turn.

Section 12. No ace or base can be made on a foul strike.

Section 13. A runner cannot be put out on making one base when a balk is made by the pitcher.

Section 14. But one base allowed when the ball bounds out of the field when struck.

Section 15. All disputes and differences related to the game to be decided by the umpire, from which there is no appeal.

"Restore the government to 'the plain people'"

THE POPULIST PARTY PLATFORM
1892

The nation was in the midst of moral, political, and material crises. Prices were falling. Farms were foreclosed. Meeting in Omaha, Nebraska, on the 116th anniversary of the Declaration of Independence, the new People's Party of America, or Populist Party, put forth in the name and on behalf of the people of the United States, and with the "blessing of Almighty God," a platform of grassroots principles that would assuage angry farm organizations, the principal sponsors of the meeting, which were disappointed in the major political parties and the corporate state. Its Declaration of Independence, calling for free coinage of silver and a graduated income tax, was intended to curb the "money power" in the East. It also called for nationalization of the telegraph, telephone, and railroads and for creation of postal savings banks. The Populists' Presidential candidate, former Iowa Congressman James B. Weaver (1833–1912), won slightly more than one million of the votes cast in the 1892 election and 22 electoral votes (Colorado, Idaho, Kansas, and Nevada). Although the largest democratic mass movement in U.S. history gained Congressional representation, it was never a threat to the major political parties while arguing that new rules of commerce were working against (at least) the huge number of farmers.

The conditions which surround us best justify our co-operation; we meet in the midst of a nation brought to the verge of moral, political, and material ruin. Corruption dominates the ballot box, the legislatures, the Congress, and touches even the ermine of the bench. The people are demoralized; most of the states have been compelled to isolate the voters at the polling places to prevent universal intimidation and bribery. The newspapers are largely subsidized or muzzled, public opinion silenced, business prostrated, homes covered with mortgages, labor impoverished, and the land concentrating in the hands of capitalists. The urban workmen are denied the right to organize for self-protection, imported pauperized labor beats down their wages, a hireling standing army, unrecognized by our laws, is established to shoot them down, and they are rapidly degenerating into European conditions. The fruits of the toil of millions are boldly stolen to build up colossal fortunes for a few, unprecedented in the history of mankind; and the possessors of those, in turn, despise the Republic and endanger liberty. From the same prolific womb of governmental injustice we breed the two great classes—tramps and millionaires.

The national power to create money is appropriated to enrich bondholders; a vast public debt payable in legal tender currency has been funded into gold-bearing bonds, thereby adding millions to the burdens of the people.

Silver, which has been accepted as coin since the dawn of history, has been demonetized to add to the purchasing power of gold by decreasing the value of all forms of property as well as human labor, and the supply of currency is purposely abridged to fatten usurers [moneylenders], bankrupt enterprise, and enslave industry. A vast conspiracy against mankind has been organized on two continents, and it is rapidly taking possession of the world. If not met and overthrown at once, it forebodes terrible social convulsions, the destruction of civilization, or the establishment of an absolute despotism.

We have witnessed for more than a quarter of a century the struggles of the two great political parties for power and plunder, while grievous wrongs have been inflicted upon the suffering people. We charge that the controlling influences dominating both these parties have permitted the existing dreadful conditions to develop without serious effort to prevent or restrain them. Neither do they now promise us any substantial reform. They have agreed together to ignore, in the coming campaign, every issue but one. They propose to drown the outcries of a plundered people with the uproar of a sham battle over the tariff, so that capitalists, corporations, national banks, rings, trusts, watered stock, the demonetization of silver, and the oppressions of the usurers may all be lost sight of. They propose to sacrifice our homes, lives, and children on the altar of mammon; to destroy the multitude in order to secure corruption funds from the millionaires.

. . . we seek to restore the government of the Republic to the hands of "the plain people," with which class it originated. We assert our purposes to be identical with the purposes of the national Constitution; to form a more perfect union and establish justice, insure domestic tranquillity, provide for the common defense, promote the general welfare, and secure the blessings of liberty for ourselves and our posterity.

We declare that this Republic can only endure as a free government while built upon the love of the people for each other and for the nation; that it cannot be pinned together by bayonets; that the Civil War is over, and that every passion and resentment which grew out of it must die with it, and that we must be in fact, as we are in name, one united brotherhood of free men.

Our country finds itself confronted by conditions for which there is no precedent in the history of the world; our annual agricultural productions amount to billions of dollars in value, which must, within a few weeks or months, be exchanged for billions of dollars' worth of commodities consumed in their production; the existing currency supply is wholly inadequate to make this exchange; the results are falling prices, the formation of combines and rings, the impoverishment of the producing class. We pledge ourselves that if given power we will labor to correct these evils by wise and reasonable legislation, in accordance with the terms of our platform.

We believe that the power of government—in other words, of the people—should be expanded (as in the case of the postal service) as rapidly and as far as the good sense of an intelligent people and the teachings of experience shall justify, to the end that oppression, injustice, and poverty shall eventually cease in the land.

. . . we ask all men to first help us to determine whether we are to have a republic to administer [manage] before we differ as to the conditions upon which it is to be administered, believing that the forces of reform this day organized will never cease to move forward until every wrong is righted and equal rights and equal privileges securely established for all the men and women of this country.

We declare, therefore:

First: That the union of the labor forces of the United States this day consummated shall be permanent and perpetual. . . .

Second: Wealth belongs to him who creates it, and every dollar taken from industry without an equivalent is robbery. "If any will not work, neither shall he eat." The interests of rural and civic labor are the same; their enemies are identical.

Third: We believe that the time has come when the railroad corporations will either own the people or the people must own the railroads, and should the government enter upon the work of owning and managing all railroads, we should favor an amendment to the Constitution by which all persons engaged in the government service shall be placed under a civil service regulation of the most rigid character, so as to prevent the increase of the power of the national administration by the use of such additional government employees.

Finance: We demand a national currency, safe, sound, and flexible, issued by the general government only, a full legal tender for all debts, public and private, and that without the use of banking corporations, [and] a just, equitable, and efficient means of distribution direct to the people. . . .

Transportation: Transportation being a means of exchange and a public necessity, the government should own and operate the railroads in the interest of the people. The telegraph and telephone, like the post-office system, being a necessity for the transmission of news, should be owned and operated by the government in the interest of the people.

Land: The land, including all the natural sources of wealth, is the heritage of the people, and should not be monopolized for speculative purposes, and alien ownership of land should be prohibited. All land now held by railroads and other corporations in excess of their actual needs, and all lands now owned by aliens should be reclaimed by the government and held for actual settlers only.

. . . . 1. *Resolved,* That we demand a free ballot and a fair count in all elections, and pledge ourselves to secure it . . . [for] every legal voter without federal intervention, through the adoption by the states of the unperverted Australian, or secret ballot, system.

2. *Resolved,* That the revenue derived from a graduated income tax should be applied to the reduction of the burden of taxation now levied upon the domestic industries of this country.

3. *Resolved,* That we pledge our support to fair and liberal pensions to ex-Union soldiers and sailors.

4. *Resolved,* That we condemn the fallacy of protecting American labor under the present system, which opens our ports to the pauper and criminal classes of the world and crowds out our wage earners; and we denounce the present ineffective laws against contract labor, and demand the further restriction of undesirable emigration.

5. *Resolved,* That we cordially sympathize with the efforts of organized workingmen to shorten the hours of labor, and demand a rigid enforcement of the existing eight-hour law on government work, and ask that a penalty clause be added to the said law.

6. *Resolved,* That we regard the maintenance of a large standing army of mercenaries, known as the Pinkerton system, as a menace to our liberties, and we demand its abolition; and we condemn the recent invasion of the territory of Wyoming by the hired assassins of plutocracy [influentially wealthy people], assisted by federal officers.

7. *Resolved,* That we commend to the favorable consideration of the people and the reform press the legislative system known as the initiative and referendum.

8. *Resolved,* That we favor a constitutional provision limiting the office of President and Vice-President to one term, and providing for the election of Senators of the United States by a direct vote of the people.

9. *Resolved,* That we oppose any subsidy or national aid to any private corporation for any purpose.

10. *Resolved,* That this convention sympathizes with the Knights of Labor and their righteous contest with the tyrannical combine of clothing manufacturers of Rochester, and declare it to be the duty of all who hate tyranny and oppression to refuse to purchase the goods made by the said manufacturers, or to patronize any merchants who sell such goods.

"*Maintain the highest . . . moral . . . standards*"

THE HAYS FORMULA
1924

Hollywood decided to get its act together. As president of the Motion Picture Producers and Distributors of America (1922–1945), the former chairman of the Republican National Committee Will H. Hays (1879–1954) administered the motion picture moral code, popularly called the Hays Formula (or Hays Code), which prompted a guideline for producers.

"WHEREAS, The members of the Motion Picture Producers and Distributors of America, Inc., in their continuing effort 'to establish and maintain the highest possible moral and artistic standards of motion picture production' are engaged in a special effort to prevent the prevalent type of book and play from becoming the prevalent type of picture; to exercise every possible care that only books or plays which are of the right type are used for screen presentation; to avoid the picturization of books or plays which can be produced after such chances as to leave the producer subject to a charge of deception; to avoid using titles which are indicative of a kind of picture which should not be produced, or by their suggestiveness seek to obtain attendance by deception, a thing equally reprehensible; and to prevent misleading, salacious or dishonest advertising:

"*Now, therefore, be it resolved* by the board of directors of the Motion Picture Producers and Distributors of America, Inc., That said Association does hereby reaffirm its determination to carry out its purposes above set out; and does hereby repledge the best efforts of the members of the Association to that end; and does hereby further declare that they will not produce or promote the production, distribute or promote the distribution, exhibit or promote the exhibition, or aid in any way whatsoever in the production, distribution or exhibition by the members of this Association or by companies subsidiary to said members or by any other person, firm or corporation producing, distributing or exhibiting pictures, of any picture or pictures by whomsoever produced, distributed or exhibited, which because of the unfit character of title, story, exploitation or picture itself, do not meet the requirements of this preamble and resolution or hinder the fulfillment of the purposes of the Association set out herein."

List of "Don'ts and Be Carefuls" adopted by California Association for guidance of producers: (1927)

Resolved, That those things which are included in the following list shall not appear in pictures produced by the members of this Association, irrespective of the manner in which they are treated:

1. Pointed profanity—by either title or lip—this includes the words "God," "Lord," "Jesus," "Christ" (unless they be used reverently

in connection with proper religious ceremonies), "hell," "damn," "Gawd," and every other profane and vulgar expression however it may be spelled;

2. Any licentious or suggestive nudity—in fact or in silhouette; and any lecherous or licentious notice thereof by other characters in the picture;

3. The illegal traffic in drugs;

4. Any inference of sex perversion;

5. White slavery;

6. Miscegenation (sex relationships between the white and black races);

7. Sex hygiene and veneral diseases;

8. Scenes of actual childbirth—in fact or in silhouette;

9. Children's sex organs;

10. Ridicule of the clergy;

11. Willful offense to any nation, race or creed:

And be it further

Resolved, That special care be exercised in the manner in which the following subjects are treated, to the end that vulgarity and suggestiveness may be eliminated and that good taste may be emphasized:

1. The use of the flag;

2. International relations (avoiding picturizing in an unfavorable light another country's religion, history, institutions, prominent people, and citizenry);

3. Arson;

4. The use of firearms;

5. Theft, robbery, safe-cracking, and dynamiting of trains, mines, buildings, etc. (having in mind the effect which a too-detailed description of these may have upon the moron);

6. Brutality and possible gruesomeness;

7. Technique of committing murder by whatever method;

8. Methods of smuggling;

9. Third-degree methods;

10. Actual hangings or electrocutions as legal punishment for crime;

11. Sympathy for criminals;

12. Attitude toward public characters and institutions;

13. Sedition;

14. Apparent cruelty to children and animals;

15. Branding of people or animals;

16. The sale of women, or of a woman selling her virtue;

17. Rape or attempted rape;

18. First-night scenes;

19. Man and woman in bed together;

20. Deliberate seduction of girls;

21. The institution of marriage;

22. Surgical operations;

23. The use of drugs;

24. Titles or scenes having to do with the law enforcement or law-enforcing officers;

25. Excessive or lustful kissing, particularly when one character or the other is a "heavy": . . .

"A maximum of employment in all localities"

W.P.A.

1935

The Great Depression was seriously taxing Americans when President Franklin Delano Roosevelt (1882–1945) established and ordered the Works Progress Administration (W.P.A.) "to move from the relief rolls to work on such projects or in private employment the maximum number of persons in the shortest time possible." Over eight years, at an outlay of $11-billion, W.P.A. provided work for 8,000,000 people, who supported 30,000,000 other people. This New Deal creation, which salvaged self-respect, included the construction of waterworks, sewage plants, streets, highways, bridges, schools, and power plants. Murals were painted; histories, novels, and plays were written. W.P.A. restored the Dock Street Theater in Charleston, South Carolina, erected a magnificent ski lodge atop Oregon's Mount Hood, conducted art classes for the insane in a Cincinnati, Ohio, hospital, drew a Braille map for the blind at Watertown, Massachusetts, and ran a library in the Kentucky hills. W.P.A. was given an "honorable discharge" during full employment in the Second World War. The last check was distributed in April, 1943.

By virtue of and pursuant to the authority vested in me under the "Emergency Relief Appropriation Act of 1935", approved April 8, 1935 (Public Resolution No. 11, 74th Congress), and of all other authority vested in me, it is hereby ordered as follows:

I. I hereby establish within the Government certain agencies, and prescribe their respective functions and duties, as follows:

(A) The Division of Applications and Information of the National Emergency Council, to be under the general supervision of the Executive Director of the National Emergency Council. Such Division shall receive all applications for projects, cause the applications to be examined and reviewed, obtaining when necessary aid and assistance of governmental departments or agencies, and transmit such applications to the Advisory Committee on Allotments hereinafter established. The Division shall furnish information to the public on allotments made and on the progress of all projects as they are initiated and carried forward.

(B) The Advisory Committee on Allotments, which shall be composed of:

The Secretary of the Interior, Chairman
The Secretary of Agriculture
The Secretary of Labor
The Executive Director of the National
    Emergency Council
The Administrator of the Works Progress
    Administration
The Director of Procurement

The Director of the Bureau of the Budget

The Chief of Engineers, U. S. Army

The Commissioner of Reclamation

The Director of Soil Erosion

The Chief of the Forest Service

The Director of Emergency Conservation Work

The Chief of the Bureau of Public Roads

The Administrator of the Resettlement Administration

The Administrator of the Rural Electrification Administration

The Federal Emergency Relief Administrator

The Director, Housing Division

The Vice-Chairman, National Resources Board and a representative of

    (*a*) the Business Advisory Council

    (*b*) organized labor

    (*c*) farm organizations

    (*d*) the American Bankers' Association, and

    (*e*) the United States Conference of Mayors

Such Committee shall make recommendations to the President with respect to the allotments of funds for such projects covered by the applications submitted by the Division of Applications and Information as will constitute a co-ordinated and balanced program of work under the said Act.

(C) A Works Progress Administration, which shall be responsible to the President for the honest, efficient, speedy, and coordinated execution of the work relief program as a whole, and for the execution of that program in such manner as to move from the relief rolls to work on such projects or in private employment the maximum number of persons in the shortest time possible.

To this end, the Works Progress Administration shall have the following powers and duties:

1. To establish and operate a division of progress investigation, and to coordinate the per-tinent work of existing investigative agencies of the Government, so as to insure the honest execution of the work relief program.

2. To formulate, and, with the approval of the President, to require uniform periodic reports of progress on all projects; and, where any avoidable delay appears, forthwith to recommend to the President appropriate measures for eliminating such delay, and, similarly, to recommend the termination of projects where it develops that they are not affording the amount of employment warranting their continuance.

3. With the approval of the President, to prescribe rules and regulations:

    a. To assure that as many of the persons employed on all work projects as is feasible shall be persons receiving relief; and

    b. To govern the selection of such persons for such employment.

4. To formulate and administer a system of uniform periodic reports of the employment on such projects of persons receiving relief.

5. To investigate wages and working conditions and to make and submit to the President such findings as will aid the President in prescribing working conditions and rates of pay on projects.

In addition to the foregoing powers and duties, the Works Progress Administration shall:

1. Provide for the coordination of such data compiling projects as form a part of the work relief program and of such portions of other research activities as may be necessary or useful in carrying out such program.

2. Coordinate all requests for opinions and decisions addressed to the Executive departments or independent establishments of the Government on questions affecting the administration of the Act or of orders issued thereunder.

3. Recommend and carry on small useful pro-

jects designed to assure a maximum of employment in all localities.

The Federal Emergency Relief Administrator shall serve also as Administrator of the Works Progress Administration.

II. I hereby direct:

(A) The Secretary of the Treasury, (1) through the disbursing and accounting facilities under the Commissioner of Accounts and Deposits of the Treasury Department, to make provision for all disbursements from the funds appropriated by the "Emergency Relief Appropriation Act of 1935", subject only to such exceptions as the Secretary may authorize, and to maintain a system of accounts necessary to enable the President (*a*) to exercise Executive control over such funds, (*b*) to provide current financial and accounting information for governmental agencies concerned, and (*c*) to make a complete report to the Congress concerning expenditures made and obligations incurred, by classes and amounts; and (2) through the Director of Procurement, to purchase, or to provide a system for the purchase of all materials, supplies and equipment to be procured with the said funds.

(B) The Director of the Bureau of the Budget to pass upon all requests for allotment of funds for administrative expenses.

III. All permanent and emergency agencies of the Government will afford full cooperation to the agencies herein established or designated and make available such personnel and facilities as may aid in carrying out the provisions of the said Act. . . .

"To all it is a trouble"

"AN AMERICAN DILEMMA"
1944

The Swedish economist and sociologist Gunnar Myrdal's (1898–1987) exhaustively detailed two-volume *An American Dilemma: The Negro Problem and Modern Democracy* (48 writers and researchers, with financing by the Carnegie Corporation of America) was a bombshell: Racial problems in the United States were inextricably entwined with the democratic functioning of American society. America's dilemma lay in the disparity between its high democratic ideals and its abusive, discriminatory treatment of blacks. If the police and the courts enforced the Constitution, Myrdal believed, there would be less discrimination, particularly in the South, where a majority of African-Americans were living. He predicted that the democratic principles inherent in the legal system would triumph and racism would eventually disappear. "It is a book that nobody who tries to face the Negro problem with any honesty can afford to miss," said *The New York Times Book Review*. *Time* magazine concluded that Myrdal "will make U.S. citizens either nod or squirm."

There is a "Negro problem" in the United States and most Americans are aware of it, although it assumes varying forms and intensity in different regions of the country and among diverse groups of the American people. Americans have to react to it, politically as citizens and, where there are Negroes present in the community, privately as neighbors.

To the great majority of white Americans the Negro problem has distinctly negative connotations. It suggests something difficult to settle and equally difficult to leave alone. It is embarrassing. It makes for moral uneasiness. The very presence of the Negro in America; his fate in this country through slavery, Civil War and Reconstruction; his recent career and his present status; his accommodation; his protest and his aspiration; in fact his entire biological, historical and social existence as a participant American represent to the ordinary white man in the North as well as in the South an anomaly in the very structure of American society. To many, this takes on the proportion of a menace—biological, economic, social, cultural, and, at times, political. This anxiety may be mingled with a feeling of individual and collective guilt. A few see the problem as a challenge to statesmanship. To all it is a trouble.

"Shall be entitled to vocational rehabilitation"

THE G.I. BILL
1944

Two weeks after Allied troops had successfully invaded Nazi-occupied western Europe, Congress established the Servicemen's Readjustment Act (Public Law 346)—the G.I. Bill of Rights. Called "the best deal ever made by Uncle Sam," 8,000,000 men and women in the U.S. armed forces would be eligible for Federal aid intended to help veterans readjust to civilian life. Legislation authorized a broad program of benefits, including: Up to 52 weeks of unemployment compensation, guaranteed loans financing new housing and education or technical training (veterans flooded college campuses), authorized construction of additional hospital facilities, and strengthened the authority of the Veterans Administration. When President Franklin Delano Roosevelt (1882–1945) signed the bill, he said that "a sound post-war economy is a major present responsibility." Later, Congressional legislation provided educational and economic assistance to veterans of the Korean and Vietnam wars.

TITLE I

CHAPTER I—HOSPITALIZATION, CLAIMS, AND PROCEDURES

SEC. 100. The Veterans' Administration is hereby declared to be an essential war agency and entitled, second only to the War and Navy Departments, to priorities in personnel, equipment, supplies, and material under any laws, Executive orders, and regulations pertaining to priorities, and in appointments of personnel from civil-service registers the Administrator of Veterans' Affairs is hereby granted the same authority and discretion as the War and Navy Departments and the United States Public Health Service: *Provided,* That the provisions of this section as to priorities for materials shall apply to any State institution to be built for the care or hospitalization of veterans. . . .

SEC. 104. No person shall be discharged or released from active duty in the armed forces until his certificate of discharge or release from active duty and final pay, or a substantial portion thereof, are ready for delivery to him or to his next of kin or legal representative; and no person shall be discharged or released from active service on account of disability until and unless he has executed a claim for compensation, pension, or hospitalization, to be filed with the Veterans' Administration or has signed a statement that he has had explained to him the right to file such claim: *Provided,* That this section shall not preclude immediate transfer to a veterans' facility for necessary hospital care, nor preclude the discharge of any person who refuses to sign such claim or statement: *And provided further,* That refusal or failure to file a claim shall be without prejudice to any right the veteran may subsequently assert.

Any person entitled to a prosthetic appliance shall be entitled, in addition, to necessary fitting and training, including institutional training, in the use of such appliance, whether in a Service or a Veterans' Administration hospital, or by out-patient treatment, including such service under contract.

SEC. 105. No person in the armed forces shall be required to sign a statement of any nature relating to the origin, incurrence, or aggravation of any disease or injury he may have, and any such statement against his own interest signed at any time, shall be null and void and of no force and effect. . . .

SEC. 300. The discharge or dismissal by reason of the sentence of a general court martial of any person from the military or naval forces, or the discharge of any such person on the ground that he was a conscientious objector who refused to perform military duty or refused to wear the uniform or otherwise to comply with lawful orders of competent military authority, or as a deserter, or of an officer by the acceptance of his resignation for the good of the service, shall bar all rights of such person, based upon the period of service from which he is so discharged or dismissed, under any laws administered by the Veterans' Administration: *Provided,* That in the case of any such person, if it be established to the satisfaction of the Administrator that at the time of the commission of the offense such person was insane, he shall not be precluded from benefits to which he is otherwise entitled under the laws administered by the Veterans' Administration: *And provided further,* That this section shall not apply to any war risk, Government (converted) or national service life-insurance policy. . . .

TITLE II

SEC. 400. (a) Subsection (f) of section 1, title I, Public Law Numbered 2, Seventy-third Con-gress, added by the Act of March 24, 1943 (Public Law Numbered 16, Seventy-eighth Congress), is hereby amended to read as follows:

"(f) Any person who served in the active military or naval forces on or after September 16, 1940, and prior to the termination of hostilities in the present war, shall be entitled to vocational rehabilitation subject to the provisions and limitations of Veterans Regulation Numbered 1 (a), as amended, part VII, or to education or training subject to the provisions and limitations of part VIII."

(b) Veterans Regulation Numbered 1 (a), is hereby amended by adding a new part VIII as follows:

PART VIII

"1. Any person who served in the active military or naval service on or after September 16, 1940, and prior to the termination of the present war, and who shall have been discharged or released therefrom under conditions other than dishonorable, and whose education or training was impeded, delayed, interrupted, or interfered with by reason of his entrance into the service, or who desires a refresher or retraining course, and who either shall have served ninety days or more, exclusive of any period he was assigned for a course of education or training under the Army specialized training program or the Navy college training program, which course was a continuation of his civilian course and was pursued to completion, or as a cadet or midshipman at one of the service academies, or shall have been discharged or released from active service by reason of an actual service-incurred injury or disability, shall be eligible for and entitled to receive education or training under this part: *Provided,* That such course shall be initiated not later than two years after either the date of his discharge or the termination of the present war, whichever is the later: *Provided further,* That no such education or training shall be afforded beyond seven years after the termination of the present war: *And provided further,* That any such person who was not over 25 years of age at the time he entered the service shall be deemed to have had his education or training impeded, delayed, interrupted, or interfered with.

"2. Any such eligible person shall be entitled to education or training, or a refresher or retraining course, at an approved educational or training institution, for a period of one year (or the equivalent thereof in continuous part-time study), or for such lesser time as may be required for the course of instruction chosen by him. Upon satisfactory completion of such course of education or training, according to the regularly prescribed standards and practices of the institutions, except a refresher or retraining course, such person shall be entitled to an additional period or periods of education or training, not to exceed the time such person was in the active service on or after September 16, 1940, and before the termination of the war, exclusive of any period he was assigned for a course of education or training under the Army specialized training program or the Navy college training program, which course was a continuation of his civilian course and was pursued to completion, or as a cadet or midshipman at one of the service academies, but in no event shall the total period of education or training exceed four years: *Provided,* That his work continues to be satisfactory throughout the period, according to the regularly prescribed standards and practices of the institution: *Provided, however,* That wherever the additional period of instruction ends during a quarter or semester and after a major part of such quarter or semester has expired, such period of instruction shall be extended to the termination of such unexpired quarter or semester.

"3. Such person shall be eligible for and entitled to such course of education or training as he may elect, and at any approved educational or training institution at which he chooses to enroll, whether or not located in the State in which he resides, which will accept or retain him as a student or trainee in any field or branch of knowledge which such institution finds him qualified to undertake or pursue: *Provided,* That, for reasons satisfactory to the Administrator, he may change a course of instruction: *And provided further,* That any such course of education or training may be discontinued at any time, if it is found by the Administrator that, according to the regularly prescribed standards and practices of the institution, the conduct or progress of such person is unsatisfactory.

"4. From time to time the Administrator shall secure from the appropriate agency of each State a list of the educational and training institutions (including industrial establishments), within such jurisdiction, which are qualified and equipped to furnish education and training (including apprenticeship and refresher or retraining training), which institutions, together with such additional ones as may be recognized and approved by the Administrator, shall be deemed qualified and approved to furnish education or training to such persons as shall enroll under this part: *Provided,* That wherever there are established State apprenticeship agencies expressly charged by State laws to administer apprentice training, whenever possible, the Administrator shall utilize such existing facilities and services in training on the job when such training is of one year's duration or more.

"5. The Administrator shall pay to the educational or training institution, for each person enrolled in full time or part time course of education or training, the customary cost of tuition, and such laboratory, library, health, infirmary, and other similar fees as are customarily charged, and may pay for books, supplies, equipment, and other necessary expenses, exclusive of board, lodging, other living expenses, and travel, as are generally required for the successful pursuit and completion of the course by other students in the institution: *Provided,* That in no event shall such payments, with respect to any person, exceed $500 for an ordinary school year: *Provided further,* That no payments shall be made to institutions, business or other establishments furnishing apprentice training on the job: *And provided further,* That if any such institution has no established tuition fee, or if its established tuition fee shall be found by the Administrator to be inadequate compensation to such institution for furnishing such education or training, he is authorized to provide for the payment, with respect to any such person, of such fair and reasonable compensation as will not exceed $500 for an ordinary school year.

"6. While enrolled in and pursuing a course under this part, such person, upon application to the Administrator, shall be paid a subsistence allowance of $50 per month, if without a dependent or dependents, or $75 per month, if he has a dependent or dependents, including regular holidays and leave not exceeding thirty days in a calendar year. Such person attending a course on a part-time basis, and such person receiving compensation for productive labor performed as part of their apprentice or other training on the job at institutions, business or other establishments, shall be entitled to receive such lesser sums, if any, as subsistence or dependency allowances, as may be determined by the Administrator: *Provided,* That any such person eligible under this part, and within the limitations thereof, may pursue such full time or part-time

course or courses as he may elect, without subsistence allowance.

"7. Any such person eligible for the benefits of this part, who is also eligible for the benefit of part VII, may elect which benefit he desires: *Provided,* That, in the event of such election, subsistence allowance hereunder shall not exceed the amount of additional pension payable for training under said part VII.

"8. No department, agency, or officer of the United States, in carrying out the provisions of this part, shall exercise any supervision or control, whatsoever, over any State educational agency, or State apprenticeship agency, or any educational or training institution: *Provided,* That nothing in this section shall be deemed to prevent any department, agency, or officer of the United States from exercising any supervision or control which such department, agency, or officer is authorized, by existing provisions of law, to exercise over any Federal educational or training institution, or to prevent the furnishing of education or training under this part in any institution over which supervision or control is exercised by such other department, agency, or officer under authority of existing provisions of law.

"9. The Administrator of Veterans' Affairs is authorized and empowered to administer this title, and, insofar as he deems practicable, shall utilize existing facilities and services of Federal and State departments and agencies on the basis of mutual agreements with them. Consistent with and subject to the provisions and limitations set forth in this title, the Administrator shall, from time to time, prescribe and promulgate such rules and regulations as may be necessary to carry out its purposes and provisions.

"10. The Administrator may arrange for educational and vocational guidance to persons eligible for education and training under this part.

At such intervals as he deems necessary, he shall make available information respecting the need for general education and for trained personnel in the various crafts, trades, and professions: *Provided,* That facilities of other Federal agencies collecting such information shall be utilized to the extent he deems practicable.

"11. As used in this part, the term 'educational or training institutions' shall include all public or private elementary, secondary, and other schools furnishing education for adults, business schools and colleges, scientific and technical institutions, colleges, vocational schools, junior colleges, teachers colleges, normal schools, professional schools, universities, and other educational institutions, and shall also include business or other establishments providing apprentice or other training on the job, including those under the supervision of an approved college or university or any State department of education, or any State apprenticeship agency or State board of vocational education, or any State apprenticeship council or the Federal Apprentice Training Service established in accordance with Public, Numbered 308, Seventy-fifth Congress, or any agency in the executive branch of the Federal Government authorized under other laws to supervise such training."

Sec. 401. Section 3, Public Law Numbered 16, Seventy-eighth Congress, is hereby amended to read as follows:

"Sec. 3. The appropriation for the Veterans' Administration, 'Salaries and expenses, medical and hospital, and compensation and pensions', shall be available for necessary expenses under part VII, as amended, or part VIII of Veterans Regulation Numbered 1 (a), and there is hereby authorized to be appropriated such additional amount or amounts as may be necessary to accomplish the purposes thereof. Such expenses may include, subject to regulations issued by the Administrator and in addition to medical care, treatment, hospitalization, and prosthesis, otherwise authorized, such care, treatment, and supplies as may be necessary to accomplish the purposes of part VII, as amended, or part VIII of Veterans Regulation Numbered 1 (a)."

Sec. 402. Public Law Numbered 16, Seventy-eighth Congress, is hereby amended by adding thereto to a new section 4 to read as follows:

"Sec. 4. Any books, supplies, or equipment furnished a trainee or student under part VII or part VIII of Veterans Regulation Numbered 1 (a) shall be deemed released to him: *Provided,* That if he fail, because of fault on his part to complete the course of training or education afforded thereunder, he may be required, in the discretion of the Administrator, to return any or all of such books, supplies, or equipment not actually expended or to repay the reasonable value thereof."

Sec. 403. Paragraph 1, part VII, Veterans Regulation Numbered 1 (a) (Public Law Numbered 16, Seventy-eighth Congress), is hereby amended by inserting after the word "time" the words "on or" and deleting the date "December 6, 1941" and substituting therefor the date "September 16, 1940".

TITLE III—LOANS FOR THE PURCHASE OR CONSTRUCTION OF HOMES, FARMS, AND BUSINESS PROPERTY

Chapter V—General Provisions for Loans

Sec. 500. (a) Any person who shall have served in the active military or naval service of the United States at any time on or after September 16, 1940, and prior to the termination of the present war and who shall have been discharged or released therefrom under conditions other than dishonorable after active service of ninety days or more, or by reason of an injury or disability incurred in service in line of duty, shall be eligible for the benefits of this title. Any such veteran may apply within two years after separation from the military or naval forces, or two years after termination of the war, whichever is the later date, but in no event more than five years after the termination of the war, to the Administrator of Veterans' Affairs for the guaranty by the Administrator of not to exceed 50 per centum of a loan or loans for any of the purposes specified in sections 501, 502 and 503: *Provided,* That the aggregate amount guaranteed shall not exceed $2,000. If the Administrator finds that the veteran is eligible for the benefits of this title and that the loan applied for appears practicable, the Administrator shall guarantee the payment of the part thereof as set forth in this title. . . .

PURCHASE OR CONSTRUCTION OF HOMES

SEC. 501. (a) Any application made by a veteran under this title for the guaranty of a loan to be used in purchasing residential property or in constructing a dwelling on unimproved property owned by him to be occupied as his home may be approved by the Administrator of Veterans' Affairs if he finds—

(1) that the proceeds of such loans will be used for payment for such property to be purchased or constructed by the veteran;

(2) that the contemplated terms of payment required in any mortgage to be given in part payment of the purchase price or the construction cost bear a proper relation to the veteran's present and anticipated income and expenses; and that the nature and condition of the property is such as to be suitable for dwelling purposes; and

(3) that the purchase price paid or to be

paid by the veteran for such property or the construction cost, including the value of the unimproved lot, does not exceed the reasonable normal value thereof as determined by proper appraisal.

(b) Any application for the guaranty of a loan under this section for the purpose of making repairs, alterations, or improvements in, or paying delinquent indebtedness, taxes, or special assessments on, residential property owned by the veteran and used by him as his home, may be approved by the Administrator if he finds that the proceeds of such loan will be used for such purpose or purposes.

(c) No first mortgage shall be ineligible for insurance under the National Housing Act, as amended, by reason of any loan guaranteed under this title, or by reason of any secondary lien upon the property involved securing such loan.

PURCHASE OF FARMS AND FARM EQUIPMENT

SEC. 502. Any application made under this title for the guaranty of a loan to be used in purchasing any land, buildings, livestock, equipment, machinery, or implements, or in repairing, altering, or improving any buildings or equipment, to be used in farming operations conducted by the applicant, may be approved by the Administrator of Veterans' Affairs if he finds—

(1) that the proceeds of such loan will be used in payment for real or personal property purchased or to be purchased by the veteran, or for repairing, altering, or improving any buildings or equipment, to be used in bona fide farming operations conducted by him;

(2) that such property will be useful in and reasonably necessary for efficiently conducting such operations;

(3) that the ability and experience of the veteran, and the nature of the proposed farming operations to be conducted by him, are such that there is a reasonable likelihood that such operations will be successful; and

(4) that the purchase price paid or to be paid by the veteran for such property does not exceed the reasonable normal value thereof as determined by proper appraisal. . . .

TITLE IV

CHAPTER VI—EMPLOYMENT OF VETERANS

SEC. 600. (a) In the enactment of the provisions of this title Congress declares as its intent and purpose that there shall be an effective job counseling and employment placement service for veterans, and that, to this end, policies shall be promulgated and administered, so as to provide for them the maximum of job opportunity in the field of gainful employment. . . .

TITLE V

CHAPTER VII—READJUSTMENT ALLOWANCES FOR FORMER MEMBERS OF THE ARMED FORCES WHO ARE UNEMPLOYED

SEC. 700. (a) Any person who shall have served in the active military or naval service of the United States at any time after September 16, 1940, and prior to the termination of the present war, and who shall have been discharged or released from active service under conditions other than dishonorable, after active service of ninety days or more, or by reason of an injury or disability incurred in service in line of duty, shall be entitled, in accordance with the provisions of this title and regulations issued by the Administrator of Veterans' Affairs pursuant thereto, to receive a readjustment allowance as provided herein for each week of unemployment, not to exceed a total of fifty-two weeks, which (1) begins after the first Sunday of the third calendar month after the date of enactment hereof, and (2) occurs not later than two years after discharge or release or the termination of the war, whichever is the later date: *Provided,* That no such allowance shall be paid for any period for which he receives increased pension under part VII of Veterans Regulation 1 (a) or a subsistence allowance under part VIII of such regulation: *Provided further,* That no readjustment allowance shall be payable for any week commencing more than five years after the termination of hostilities in the present war. . . .

"One of the most publicized tragedies"

INVESTIGATING PEARL HARBOR
1946

Japan's sneak attack on the American military base at Pearl Harbor, in the territory of Hawaii, on Sunday dawn, December 7, 1941 (while peace negotiations were going on in Washington), destroyed or damaged 19 naval vessels, including eight battleships, destroyed 188 aircraft, and killed 2,280 servicemen and 68 civilians. It was a day that President Franklin Delano Roosevelt (1882–1945) declared "would live in infamy." (Germany's Adolf Hitler [1889–1945] was also stunned by the Japanese raid; the Führer had been trying to keep the U.S. out of his war.) Although Harvard-educated Isoroku Yamamoto (1884–1943)—"the sword of my emperor"—planned the strike, he was opposed to war with the U.S. After Pearl Harbor, he argued that Japan should negotiate peace with the crippled U.S. Revengeful U.S. P-38s, with the approval of Commander-in-Chief Roosevelt, ambushed and shot down Yamamoto over Bougainville, in the Solomon Islands. After V-J Day, still another investigatory Congressional committee, "in a much better position to form proper estimates and conclusions concerning responsibilities relating to the disaster than has heretofore been possible because of the proper and necessary restrictions within which other inquiries and investigations were conducted during wartime," submitted its verdict.

We have not presumed to pass judgment on the nature of or charges of unfairness with respect to seven prior inquiries and investigations of the Pearl Harbor attack, feeling that by conducting a full and impartial hearing our report to the Congress along with the Committee's record would present to the American people the material and relevant facts of the disaster. . . . Prior investigations were conducted during the course of the most devastating war in history and within the necessary limitations of secrecy imposed by war and the national security. Public hearings concerning the disaster were properly deferred until the cessation of hostilities; to have done otherwise would have been to imperil the entire war effort. . . .

On the morning of December 7, 1941, Admiral Kimmel and General Short were catapulted by the Empire of Japan into the principal roles in one of the most publicized tragedies of all time. That improper and incorrect deductions were drawn by some members of the public, with consequent suffering and mental anguish to both officers, cannot be questioned, just as erroneous conclusions were made by others with respect to the extent and nature of responsibility in Washington. But this is the result of the magnitude of public interest and speculation inspired by the disaster and not the result of mistreatment of anyone. The situation prevailing at Pearl Harbor on the morning of December 7 in the wake of the Japanese attack cast everyone, whether immediately or remotely concerned, beneath the white light of world scrutiny.

CONCLUSIONS WITH RESPECT TO RESPONSIBILITIES

1. The December 7, 1941, attack on Pearl Harbor was an unprovoked act of aggression by the Empire of Japan. The treacherous attack was planned and launched while Japanese ambassadors, instructed with characteristic duplicity, were carrying on the pretense of negotiations with the Government of the United States with a view to an amicable settlement of differences in the Pacific.

2. The ultimate responsibility for the attack and its results rests upon Japan, an attack that was well planned and skillfully executed. Contributing to the effectiveness of the attack was a powerful striking force, much more powerful than it had been thought the Japanese were able to employ in a single tactical venture at such distance and under such circumstances.

3. The diplomatic policies and actions of the United States provided no justifiable provocation whatever for the attack by Japan on this Nation. The Secretary of State fully informed both the War and Navy Departments of diplomatic developments and, in a timely and forceful manner, clearly pointed out to these Departments that relations between the United States and Japan had passed beyond the stage of diplomacy and were in the hands of the military.

4. The committee has found no evidence to support the charges, made before and during the hearings, that the President, the Secretary of State, the Secretary of War, or the Secretary of Navy tricked, provoked, incited, cajoled, or coerced Japan into attacking this Nation in order that a declaration of war might be more easily obtained from the Congress. On the contrary, all evidence conclusively points to the fact that they discharged their responsibilities with distinction, ability, and foresight and in keeping with the highest traditions of our fundamental foreign policy.

5. The President, the Secretary of State, and high Government officials made every possible effort, without sacrificing our national honor and endangering our security, to avert war with Japan.

6. The disaster of Pearl Harbor was the failure, with attendant increase in personnel and material losses, of the Army and the Navy to institute measures designed to detect an approaching hostile force, to effect a state of readiness commensurate with the realization that war was at hand, and to employ every facility at their command in repelling the Japanese.

7. Virtually everyone was surprised that Japan struck the Fleet at Pearl Harbor at the time that she did. Yet officers, both in Washington and Hawaii, were fully conscious of the danger from air attack; they realized this form of attack on Pearl Harbor by Japan was at least a possibility; and they were adequately informed of the imminence of war.

8. Specifically, the Hawaiian commands failed—

(a) To discharge their responsibilities in the light of the warnings received from Washington, other information possessed by them, and the principle of command by mutual cooperation.

(b) To integrate and coordinate their facilities for defense and to alert properly the Army and Navy establishments in Hawaii, particularly in the light of the warnings and intelligence available to them during the period November 27 to December 7, 1941.

(c) To effect liaison on a basis designed to acquaint each of them with the operations of the other, which was necessary to their joint security, and to exchange fully all significant intelligence.

(*d*) To maintain a more effective reconnaissance within the limits of their equipment.

(*e*) To effect a state of readiness throughout the Army and Navy establishments designed to meet all possible attacks.

(*f*) To employ the facilities, matériel, and personnel at their command, which were adequate at least to have greatly minimized the effects of the attack, in repelling the Japanese raiders.

(*g*) To appreciate the significance of intelligence and other information available to them.

9. The errors made by the Hawaiian commands were errors of judgment and not derelictions of duty.

10. The War Plans Division of the War Department failed to discharge its direct responsibility to advise the commanding general he had not properly alerted the Hawaiian Department when the latter, pursuant to instructions, had reported action taken in a message that was not satisfactorily responsive to the original directive.

11. The Intelligence and War Plans Divisions of the War and Navy Departments failed:

(*a*) To give careful and thoughtful consideration to the intercepted messages from Tokyo to Honolulu of September 24, November 15, and November 20 (the harbor berthing plan and related dispatches) and to raise a question as to their significance. Since they indicated a particular interest in the Pacific Fleet's base this intelligence should have been appreciated and supplied the Hawaiian commanders for their assistance, along with other information available to them, in making their estimate of the situation.

(*b*) To be properly on the *qui vive* to receive the "one o'clock" intercept and to recognize in the message the fact that some Japanese military action would very possibly occur somewhere at 1 P.M., December 7. If properly appreciated, this intelligence should have suggested a dispatch to all Pacific outpost commanders supplying this information, as General Marshall attempted to do immediately upon seeing it.

12. Notwithstanding the fact that there were officers on twenty-four hour watch, the Committee believes that under all of the evidence the War and Navy Departments were not sufficiently alerted on December 6 and 7, 1941, in view of the imminence of war.

RECOMMENDATIONS

Based on the evidence in the Committee's record, the following recommendations are respectfully submitted:

That immediate action be taken to insure that unity of command is imposed at all military and naval outposts.

That there be a complete integration of Army and Navy intelligence agencies in order to avoid the pitfalls of divided responsibility which experience has made so abundantly apparent; that upon effecting a unified intelligence, officers be selected for intelligence work who possess the background, penchant, and capacity for such work; and that they be maintained in the work for an extended period of time in order that they may become steeped in the ramifications and refinements of their field and employ this reservoir of knowledge in evaluating material received. . . .

That effective steps be taken to insure that statutory or other restrictions do not operate to the benefit of an enemy or other forces inimical to the Nation's security and to the handicap of our own intelligence agencies. With this in mind, the Congress should give serious study to, among other things, the Communications Act of 1934; to suspension in proper instances of the statute of limitations during war (it was impossible during the war to prosecute violations relating to the "Magic" without giving the secret to the enemy); to legislation designed to prevent unauthorized sketching, photographing, and mapping of military and naval reservations in peacetime; and to legislation fully protecting the security of classified matter. . . .

SUPERVISORY, ADMINISTRATIVE, AND ORGANIZATIONAL DEFICIENCIES IN OUR MILITARY AND NAVAL ESTABLISHMENTS REVEALED BY THE PEARL HARBOR INVESTIGATION

The Committee has been intrigued throughout the Pearl Harbor proceedings by one enigmatical and paramount question: *Why, with some of the finest intelligence available in our history, with the almost certain knowledge that war was at hand, with plans that contemplated the precise type of attack that was executed by Japan on the morning of December 7—Why was it possible for a Pearl Harbor to occur?* The answer to this question and the causative considerations regarded as having any reasonably proximate bearing on the disaster have been set forth in the body of this report. Fundamentally, these considerations reflect supervisory, administrative, and organizational deficiencies which existed in our Military and Naval establishments in the days before Pearl Harbor. *In the course of the Committee's investigation still other deficiencies, not regarded as having a direct bearing on the disaster, have pre-sented themselves.* Otherwise stated, all of these deficiencies reduce themselves to principles which are set forth, not for their novelty or profundity but for the reason that, by their very self-evident simplicity, it is difficult to believe they were ignored.

It is recognized that many of the deficiencies revealed by our investigation may very probably have already been corrected as a result of the experiences of the war. We desire, however, to submit these principles, which are grounded in the evidence adduced by the Committee, for the consideration of our Army and Navy establishments in the earnest hope that something constructive may be accomplished that will aid our national defense and preclude a repetition of the disaster of December 7, 1941. We do this after careful and long consideration of the evidence developed through one of the most important investigations in the history of the Congress.

1. OPERATIONAL AND INTELLIGENCE WORK REQUIRES CENTRALIZATION OF AUTHORITY AND CLEAR-CUT ALLOCATION OF RESPONSIBILITY

Reviewing the testimony of the Director of War Plans and the Director of Naval Intelligence, the conclusion is inescapable that the proper demarcation of responsibility between these two divisions of the Navy Department did not exist. War Plans appears to have insisted that since it had the duty of issuing operational orders it must arrogate the prerogative of evaluating intelligence; Naval Intelligence, on the other hand, seems to have regarded the matter of evaluation as properly its function. It is clear that this intradepartmental misunderstanding and near conflict was not resolved before December 7 and beyond question it prejudiced the effectiveness of Naval Intelligence.

In Hawaii, there was such a marked failure to allocate responsibility in the case of the Fourteenth Naval District that Admiral Bloch testified he did not know whom the commander in chief would hold responsible in the event of shortcomings with respect to the condition and readiness of aircraft. The position of Admiral Bellinger was a wholly anomalous one. He appears to have been responsible to everyone and to no one. The pyramiding of superstructures of organization cannot be conducive to efficiency and endangers the very function of our military and naval services.

2. Supervisory Officials Cannot Safely Take Anything for Granted in the Alerting of Subordinates

The testimony of many crucial witnesses in the Pearl Harbor investigation contains an identical note: "I thought he was alerted"; "I took for granted he would understand"; "I thought he would be doing that." It is the same story—each responsible official seeking to justify his position by reliance upon the fallacious premise that he was entitled to rely upon the assumption that a certain task was being performed or to take for granted that subordinates would be properly vigilant. This tragic theme was particularly marked in Hawaii.

The foregoing was well illustrated in Admiral Kimmel's failure to appreciate the significance of dispatches between December 3 and 6, advising him that Japanese embassies and consulates, including the Embassy in Washington, were destroying their codes. Navy Department officials have almost unanimously testified that instructions to burn codes mean "war in any man's language" and that in supplying Admiral Kimmel

this information they were entitled to believe he would attach the proper significance to this intelligence. Yet the commander in chief of the Pacific Fleet testified that he did not interpret these dispatches to mean that Japan contemplated immediate war on the United States. That the Navy Department was entitled to rely upon the feeling that Admiral Kimmel, as a responsible intelligent commander, should have known what the burning of codes meant appears reasonable; but this is beside the point in determining standards for the future. The simple fact is that the dispatches were not properly interpreted. Had the Navy Department not taken for granted that Kimmel would be alerted by them but instead have given him the benefit of its interpretation, there could now be no argument as to what the state of alertness should have been based on such dispatches. With Pearl Harbor as a sad experience, crucial intelligence should in the future be supplied commanders accompanied by the best estimate of its significance.

3. Any Doubt as to Whether Outposts Should be Given Information Should Always Be Resolved in Favor of Supplying the Information

Admiral Stark hesitated about sending the "one o'clock" intelligence to the Pacific outposts for the reason that he regarded them as adequately alerted and he did not want to confuse them. As has been seen, he was properly entitled to believe that naval establishments were adequately alert but the fact is that one—Hawaii—was not in a state of readiness. This one exception is proof of the principle that any question as to whether information should be supplied the field should always be resolved in favor of transmitting it.

4. The Delegation of Authority or the Issuance of Orders Entails the Duty of Inspection to Determine that the Official Mandate Is Properly Exercised

Perhaps the most signal shortcoming of administration, both at Washington and in Hawaii, was the failure to follow up orders and instructions to insure that they were carried out. The record of all Pearl Harbor proceedings is replete with evidence of this fundamental deficiency in administration. . . .

"The pools . . . shall terminate"

ABOLISHING IMMIGRATION QUOTAS
1965

From the very beginning, when Asian hunters chased their prey eastward across the Bering land mass, America has been an attractive destination for aliens. In 1965, Congress abolished immigration allotments when it amended the Immigration and Nationality Act, ending the 41-year-old national-origins quota system, which had favored northern European countries and, in effect, excluded all Asians (which Japanese bitterly resented). The first restrictions against any particular group were made in 1882: the Chinese Exclusion Act denied entrance to Chinese laborers; thousands of Chinese men had helped to build the transcontinental railroad.) The 1965 law placed an overall limitation on non-western hemisphere nations, and, for the first time, applied restrictions on western hemisphere nations. President Lyndon B. Johnson (1908–1973) signed the measure at the Statue of Liberty. The percentage of the U.S. population that is Hispanic is 9.5; Asian, 3.1; black, 11.8; white, 74. In 1990, 1,536,483 legal immigrants were admitted. (Nearly 200,000 U.S. residents emigrate each year.) The proportion of U.S. population in 1990 that was foreign-born was 7.9 percent. The state where the fewest legal immigrants settled in 1994 was Wyoming, the home state of Senator Alan Simpson (born 1931), who authored a bill to reduce immigration.

B*e it enacted by the Senate and House of Representatives of the United States of America in Congress assembled,* That section 201 of the Immigration and Nationality Act (66 Stat. 175; 8 U.S.C. 1151) be amended to read as follows:

"SEC. 201. (a) Exclusive of special immigrants defined in section 101 (a) (27), and of the immediate relatives of United States citizens specified in subsection (b) of this section, the number of aliens who may be issued immigrant visas or who may otherwise acquire the status of an alien lawfully admitted to the United States for permanent residence, or who may, pursuant to section 203 (a) (7) enter conditionally, (i) shall not in any of the first three quarters of any fiscal year exceed a total of 45,000 and (ii) shall not in any fiscal year exceed a total of 170,000.

"(b) The 'immediate relatives' referred to in subsection (a) of this section shall mean the children, spouses, and parents of a citizen of the United States: *Provided,* That in the case of parents, such citizen must be at least twenty-one years of age. The immediate relatives specified in this subsection who are otherwise qualified for admission as immigrants shall be admitted as such, without regard to the numerical limitations in this Act. . . .

"(e) The immigration pool and the quotas of

quota areas shall terminate June 30, 1968. Thereafter immigrants admissible under the provisions of this Act who are subject to the numerical limitations of subsection (a) of this section shall be admitted in accordance with the percentage limitations and in the order of priority specified in section 203.". . . .

"(b) Each independent country, self-governing dominion, mandated territory, and territory under the international trusteeship system of the United Nations, other than the United States and its outlying possessions shall be treated as a separate foreign state for the purposes of the numerical limitation set forth in the proviso to subsection (a) of this section when approved by the Secretary of State. All other inhabited lands shall be attributed to a foreign state specified by the Secretary of State. . . .

"(27) The term 'special immigrant' means—

"(A) an immigrant who was born in any independent foreign country of the Western Hemisphere or in the Canal Zone and the spouse and children of any such immigrant, if accompanying, or following to join him: *Provided,* That no immigrant visa shall be issued pursuant to this clause until the consular officer is in receipt of a determination made by the Secretary of Labor pursuant to the provisions of section 212 (a) (14);

"(B) an immigrant, lawfully admitted for permanent residence, who is returning from a temporary visit abroad:

"(C) an immigrant who was a citizen of the United States and may, under section 324 (a) or 327 of title III, apply for reacquisition of citizenship;

"(D) (i) an immigrant who continuously for at least two years immediately preceding the time of his application for admission to the United States has been, and who seeks to enter the United States solely for the purpose of carrying on the vocation of minister of a religious denomination, and whose services are needed by such religious denomination having a bona fide organization in the United States: and (ii) the spouse or the child of any such immigrant, if accompanying or following to join him: or

"(E) an immigrant who is an employee, or an honorably retired former employee, of the United States Government abroad, and who has performed faithful service for a total of fifteen years, or more, and his accompanying spouse and children: *Provided,* That the principal officer of a Foreign Service establishment, in his discretion, shall have recommended the granting of special immigrant status to such alien in exceptional circumstances and the Secretary of State approves such recommendation and finds that it is in the national interest to grant such status."

(b) Paragraph (32) of subsection (a) is amended to read as follows:

"(32) The term 'profession' shall include but not be limited to architects, engineers, lawyers, physicians, surgeons, and teachers in elementary or secondary schools, colleges, academies, or seminaries."

(c) Subparagraph (1) (F) of subsection (b) is amended to read as follows:

"(F) a child, under the age of fourteen at the time a petition is filed in his behalf to accord a classification as an immediate relative under section 201 (b), who is an orphan because of the death or disappearance of, abandonment or desertion by, or separation or loss from, both parents, or for whom the sole or surviving parent is incapable of providing the proper care which will be provided the child if admitted to the United States and who has in writing irrevocably released the child for emigration and adoption; who has been adopted abroad by a United States citizen and his spouse who personally saw and observed the child prior to or during the adoption proceedings; or who is coming to the United States for adoption by a United States citizen and spouse who have complied with the preadoption requirements, if any, of the child's proposed residence: *Provided,* That no natural parent or prior adoptive parent of any such child shall thereafter, by virtue of such parentage, be accorded any right, privilege, or status under this Act.". . .

"No vision, the people perish"

THE ARTS AND HUMANITIES ACT
1965

A year before he was sworn as first President, George Washington (1732–1799) said that both "arts and sciences are essential to the prosperity of the state and to the ornament and happiness of human life." The thirty-sixth President, Lyndon B. Johnson (1908–1973), proclaiming art as "a nation's most precious heritage," signed legislation establishing the National Foundation on the Arts and Humanities as the umbrella for the National Endowment for the Arts and the National Endowment for the Humanities and their respective councils. Legislation was the culmination of over 140 years of debate over the proper role of the national government in the permanent encouragement of the arts. Since 1965, the Endowments have awarded more than 100,000 grants to arts organizations and artists. Their first budget totaled $2.5-million. Today's annual budget, following successive cuttings by Congress, is more than $150-million.

Art is a nation's most precious heritage. For it is in our works of art that we reveal ourselves, and to others, the inner vision which guides us as a nation. And where there is no vision, the people perish.

Since 1978, the John F. Kennedy Center for the Performing Arts has annually honored distinguished American talents: *1978* Marian Anderson, Fred Astaire, George Balanchine, Richard Rodgers, Arthur Rubinstein. *1979* Aaron Copland, Ella Fitzgerald, Henry Fonda, Martha Graham, Tennessee Williams. *1980* Leonard Bernstein, James Cagney, Agnes De Mille, Lynn Fontanne, Leontyne Price. *1981* Count Bassie, Cary Grant, Helen Hayes, Jerome Robbins, Rudolf Serkin. *1982* George Abbott, Lillian Gish, Benny Goodman, Gene Kelly, Eugene Ormandy. *1983* Katherine Dunham, Elia Kazan, Frank Sinatra, James Stewart, Virgil Thomson. *1984* Lena Horne, Danny Kaye, Gian Carlo Menotti, Arthur Miller, Isaac Stern. *1985* Merce Cunningham, Irene Dunne, Bob Hope, Alan Jay Lerner, Frederick Loewe, Beverly Sills. *1986* Lucille Ball, Ray Charles, Hume Cronyn, Jessica Tandy, Yehudi Menuhin, Antony Tudor. *1987* Perry Como, Bette Davis, Sammy Davis, Jr., Nathan Milstein, Alwin Nikolais. *1988* Alvin Ailey, George Burns, Myrna Loy, Alexander Schneider, Roger L. Stevens. *1989* Harry Belafonte, Claudette Colbert, Alexandra Danilova, Mary Martin, William Schuman. *1990* Dizzy Gillespie, Katharine Hepburn, Risë Stevens, Jule Styne, Billy Wilder. *1991* Roy Acuff, Betty Comden, Adolph Green, Fayard Nicholas, Harold Nicholas, Gregory Peck, Robert Shaw. *1992* Lionel Hampton, Paul Newman, Joanne Woodward, Ginger Rogers, Mstislav Rostropovich, Paul Taylor. *1993* Johnny Carson, Arthur Mitchell, Sir Georg Solti, Stephen Sondheim, Marion Williams. *1994* Kirk Douglas, Aretha Franklin, Morton Gould, Harold Prince, Pete Seeger. *1995* Jacques d'Amboise, Marilyn Horne, Riley "B.B." King, Sidney Poitier, Neil Simon. *1996* Edward Albee, Benny Carter, Johnny Cash, Jack Lemmon, Maria Tallchief. *1997* Lauren Bacall, Bob Dylan, Charlton Heston, Jessye Norman, Edward Villella. *1998* Bill Cosby, John Kander, Fred Ebb, Willie Nelson, Andre Previn, Shirley Temple (Black).

"Marriage is a coming together"

GRISWOLD V. CONNECTICUT

1965

Just over three decades ago, an 1879 Connecticut law still made the use of any birth control, whether drug or article or instrument preventing conception, a criminal offense. A prominent New Haven physician and Estelle Griswold (1913–1986), executive director of Planned Parenthood of Connecticut, were arrested for giving contraceptive information, instruction, and medical advice to married couples. Criminal charges were pressed, the couple were convicted as accessories to the crime of using birth control, each was fined $100, and the Supreme Court of Connecticut affirmed the conviction. The U.S. Supreme Court (7–2), investing unenumerated rights with full Constitutional status, declared the Connecticut law unconstitutional. Justice Potter Stewart (1915–1985) called it an "uncommonly silly law." Justice William O. Douglas (1898–1980) averred that specific guarantees "have penumbras, formed by emanations from those guarantees that help give them life and substance." The First, Third, Fourth, Fifth, and Ninth Amendments implied "zones of privacy," the basis for the general privacy right affirmed in the case. Justice Arthur Goldberg (1908–1990) concurred.

JUSTICE DOUGLAS: We deal with a right of privacy older than the Bill of Rights—older than our political parties, older than our school system. Marriage is a coming together for better or for worse, hopefully enduring, and intimate to the degree of being sacred. It is an association that promotes a way of life, not causes; a harmony in living, not political faiths; a bilateral loyalty, not commercial or social projects. Yet it is an association for as noble a purpose as any involved in our prior decisions.

JUSTICE GOLDBERG: The makers of our Constitution undertook to secure conditions favorable to the pursuit of happiness. They recognized the significance of man's spiritual nature, of his feelings and of his intellect. They knew that only a part of the pain, pleasure and satisfactions of life are to be found in material things. They sought to protect Americans in their beliefs, their thoughts, their emotions and their sensations. They conferred, as against the Government, the right to be let alone—the most comprehensive of rights and the right most valued by civilized men.

"Reversed"

FEDERAL COMMUNICATIONS COMMISSION
v.
PACIFICA FOUNDATION
1978

The United States Supreme Court upheld the right of the Federal Communications Commission (F.C.C.) to regulate the depiction or description of sexual and excretory activities in a manner that the agency deemed "patently offensive" when children might be watching or listening. Broadcast signals, it ruled, intrude into the privacy of the home. The New York radio station WBAI, a Pacifica Foundation outlet, had broadcast the comedian George Carlin's "seven dirty words" routine. Carlin used the words fuck, shit, piss, cunt, cocksucker, motherfucker, and tit in various broad caricatures and in many idioms. Indecency was not to be confused with obscenity, which the F.C.C. defined as containing an element of prurient appeal. In sum, the Supreme Court reversed a Federal court decision that had overturned the initial F.C.C. ruling against WBAI. In 1996, a Federal panel declared unconstitutional major parts of a new law intended to regulate indecent material on the global computer network and blocked the law's enforcement. The three judges celebrated retrieval as "the most participatory marketplace of speech that this country—and indeed the world—has yet seen."

In response to complaint concerning radio station's broadcast of prerecorded monologue, the Federal Communications Commission determined that language of monologue as broadcast was indecent and was prohibited by statute, and broadcaster sought review. The Court of Appeals, 181 U.S.App.D.C. 132, 556 F.2d 9, reversed, and certiorari was granted. The Supreme Court, Mr. Justice Stevens, held that: (1) focus of review by Supreme Court was on Commission's determination that monologue was indecent as broadcast; (2) Commission's action was not forbidden "censorship" within meaning of section of Communications Act of 1934; (3) Commission properly concluded that indecent language was used in broadcast of monologue, even though monologue was not obscene, and (4) Commission's order did not violate broadcaster's First Amendment rights.

Reversed.

FCC ENFORCEMENT OF PROHIBITION AGAINST OBSCENE AND INDECENT BROADCASTS
(1996)

It is a violation of federal law to broadcast obscene or indecent programming. The prohibition is set forth at Title 18 United States Code, Section 1464 (18 U.S.C. § 1464). Congress has given the Federal Communications Commission the resposibility for administratively enforcing 18

U.S.C. § 1464. In doing so, the Commission may revoke a station license, issue a warning, or impose a monetary forfeiture for the broadcast of obscene or indecent material.

Obscene Broadcasts Prohibited at All Times

Obscene speech is not protected by the First Amendment and cannot be broadcast at any time. To be obscene, material must meet a three-prong test: (1) an average person, applying contemporary community standards, must find that the material, as a whole, appeals to the prurient interest; (2) the material must depict or describe, in a patently offensive way, sexual conduct specifically defined by applicable law; and (3) the material, taken as a whole, must lack serious literary, artistic, political, or scientific value. *See Miller v. California,* 413 U.S. 15 (1973).

Indecent Broadcasts Restricted

The Commission has defined broadcast indecency as

> language or material that, in context, depicts or describes, in terms patently offensive as measured by contemporary community standards for the broadcast medium, sexual or excretory organs or activities.

See Infinity Broadcasting Corporation of Pennsylvania, 2 FCC Rcd 2705 (1987). Indecent programming contains sexual or excretory references that do not rise to the level of obscenity. As such, indecent material is protected by the First Amendment and cannot be banned entirely. It may, however, be restricted in order to avoid its broadcast during times of day when there is a reasonable risk that children may be in the audience. In the wake of decisions rendered by the United States Court of Appeals for the District of Columbia Circuit prior to 1995, the Commis-

sion concluded that it must restrict its enforcement actions to indecent programming aired during daytime hours, i.e., between the hours of 6:00 A.M. and 8:00 P.M. *See Action for Children's Television v. FCC,* 852 F.2d 1332 (D.C. Cir. 1988); *Kansas City Television, Ltd. (KZKC),* 4 FCC Rcd 6706 (1989). In a decision issued June 30, 1995, the United States Court of Appeals for the District of Columbia Circuit, responding to challenges to the FCC's expanded enforcement authority as adopted by Congress, ordered the Commission to revise its rules so that indecent programming from 6:00 A.M. to 10:00 P.M. will be subject to enforcement action. *Action for Children's Television v. FCC,* 58 F.3d 654 (D.C. Cir. 1995). The Commission's new rule, see 47 C.F.R. § 73.3999 adopted pursuant to the Court's mandate, went into effect on August 28, 1995.

As a result, broadcasts—both on television and radio—that fit within the definition and that are aired between 6:00 A.M. and 10:00 P.M. are subject to indecency enforcement action. . . .

The following is part of the verbatim transcript of George Carlin's 1973 comedy album "Filthy Words" prepared by the Federal Communications Commission:

I was thinking about the curse words and the swear words, the cuss words and the words that you can't say, that you're not supposed to say all the time. Some guys like to record your words and sell them back to you if they can, (laughter) listen in on the telephone, write down what words you say. A guy who used to be in Washington, knew that his phone was tapped, used to answer, Fuck Hoover, yes, go ahead. (laughter) Okay, I was thinking one night about the words you couldn't say on the public, ah, airwaves, um, the ones you definitely wouldn't say, ever, [']cause I heard a lady say bitch one night on television, and it was cool like she was talking about, you know, ah, well, the bitch is the first one to notice that in the litter Johnie right (murmur) Right. And, uh, bastard you can say, and hell and damn so I have to figure out which ones you couldn't and ever and it came down to seven but the list is open to amendment, and in fact, has been changed, uh, by now, ha, a lot of people pointed things out to me, and I noticed some myself. The original seven words were, shit, piss, fuck, cunt, cocksucker, motherfucker, and tits. Those are the ones that will curve your spine, grow hair on your hands and (laughter) maybe, even bring us, God help us, peace without honor (laughter). . . .

"To restore the bonds of trust"

CONTRACT WITH AMERICA
1994

Congressional Republican candidates pledged in writing a contract with Americans—an agenda of government reform, respect, and renewal: "Give us majority control of the House of Representatives for the first time in four decades and we will bring to the House floor on the first day real Congressional reforms. In the first 100 days, we will bring to a vote ten bills that would have an immediate and real impact in the lives of ordinary Americans." Two hundred and twenty-four of the candidates were elected. Directing the "revolution" was the new Speaker of the House, the ebullient former backbencher Newt Gingrich (born 1943), of Georgia, described by *Time* magazine as "a chubby repository of the tangled and contradictory hopes held by middle-income Americans who want their federal government to stop meddling in their life, and, at the same time, to improve it." Despite admission of ethics violations, Gingrich won re-election as Speaker in January, 1997. President George W. Bush's 1992 re-election campaign's cool reception to the Gingrich plan had forced a two-year postponement. In 1996, 12 of 70 foot soldiers in the Gingrich revolution were defeated for a second term as President Clinton was re-elected. Speaker Gingrich, admitting shortcomings as a Congressional leader, quit the House after Democratic candidates did better than expected in the November, 1998, elections.

As Republican members of the House of Representatives and as citizens seeking to join that body, we propose not just to change its policies, but even more important to restore the bonds of trust between the people and their elected representatives.

That is why, in this era of official evasion and posturing, we offer instead a detailed agenda for national renewal, a written commitment with no fine print.

This year's election offers the chance, after four decades of one-party control, to bring to the House a new majority that will transform the way Congress works. That historic change would be the end of government that is too big, too in-trusive, and too easy with the public's money. It can be the beginning of a Congress that respects the values and shares the faith of the American family.

Like Lincoln, our first Republican President, we intend to act with firmness in the right, as God gives us to see the right. To restore accountability to Congress. To end its cycle of scandal and disgrace. To make us all proud again of the way free people govern themselves.

On the first day of the 104th Congress, the new Republican majority will immediately pass the following major reforms, aimed at restoring the faith and trust of the American people in their government:

FIRST, require all laws that apply to the rest of the country also apply equally to the Congress;

SECOND, select a major, independent auditing firm to conduct a comprehensive audit of Congress for waste, fraud or abuse;

THIRD, cut the number of House committees, and cut committee staff by one-third;

FOURTH, limit the terms of all committee chairs;

FIFTH, ban the casting of proxy votes in committee;

SIXTH, require committee meetings to be open to the public;

SEVENTH, require a three-fifths majority vote to pass a tax increase;

EIGHTH, guarantee an honest accounting of our Federal Budget by implementing zero baseline budgeting.

Thereafter, within the first 100 days of the 104th Congress, we shall bring to the House floor the following bills, each to be given full and open debate, each to be given a clear and fair vote and each to be immediately available this day for public inspection and scrutiny:

1. The Fiscal Responsibility Act

A balanced budget/tax limitation amendment and a legislative line-item veto to restore fiscal responsibility to an out-of-control Congress, requiring it to live under the same budget constraints as families and businesses.

2. The Taking Back Our Streets Act

An anti-crime package including stronger truth-in-sentencing, "good faith" exclusionary rule exemptions, effective death-penalty provi-

sions, and cuts in social spending from this summer's "crime" bill to fund prison construction and additional law enforcement to keep people secure in their neighborhoods and kids safe in their schools.

3. The Personal Responsibility Act

Discourage illegitimacy and teen pregnancy by prohibiting welfare to minor mothers and denying increased AFDC for additional children while on welfare, cut spending for welfare programs, and enact a tough two-years-and-out provision with work requirements to promote individual responsibility.

4. The Family Reinforcement Act

Child support enforcement, tax incentives for adoption, strengthening rights of parents in their children's education, stronger child pornography laws, and an elderly dependent-care tax credit to reinforce the central role of families in American society.

5. The American Dream Restoration Act

A $500-per-child tax credit; begin repeal of the marriage tax penalty, and creation of American Dream Savings Accounts to provide middle class tax relief.

6. The National Security Restoration Act

No U.S. troops under U.N. command and restoration of the essential parts of our national-security funding to strengthen our national defense and maintain our credibility around the world.

7. THE SENIOR CITIZENS FAIRNESS ACT

Raise the Social Security earnings limit which currently forces seniors out of the work force, repeal the 1993 tax hikes on Social Security benefits, and provide tax incentives for private long-term care insurance to let older Americans keep more of what they have earned over the years.

8. THE JOB CREATION AND WAGE ENHANCEMENT ACT

Small-business incentives, capital-gains cut and indexation, neutral-cost recovery, risk assessment/cost-benefit analysis, strengthening the Regulatory Flexibility Act and unfunded mandate reform to create jobs and raise worker wages.

9. THE COMMON SENSE LEGAL REFORM ACT

"Loser pays" laws, reasonable limits on punitive damages, and reform of product-liability laws to stem the endless tide of litigation.

10. THE CITIZEN LEGISLATURE ACT

A first-ever vote on term limits to replace career politicians with citizen legislators.

Further, we will instruct the House Budget Committee to report to the floor, and we will work to enact additional budget savings beyond the budget cuts specifically included in the legislation described above, to ensure that the Federal budget deficit will be *less* than it would have been without the enactment of these bills.

Respecting the judgment of our fellow citizens as we seek their mandate for reform, we hereby pledge our names to this Contract with America.

"I Do Solemnly Swear (or Affirm)"

It is appropriate to begin commentary on Presidential power with the generation of the Founding Fathers, specifically with George Washington, who considered himself, when President, to be a man above party, devoted exclusively to the national interest in his dealing with foreign powers. Thereafter, it had been asserted that the President, in external affairs, was the "sole organ" of the nation, as Jefferson stated when Secretary of State. "The transaction of business with foreign nations," he said, "is executive altogether." He was on the mark. Though prescribing international agreements in substantive terms was largely a Congressional prerogative, negotiation of agreements was a Presidential monopoly. These agreements, moreover, can be made independent of the Senate, by so-called executive agreements, a practice that has overwhelmed treaty-making, which requires legislative approval and implementation. *The President is also Commander-in-Chief. He endorses America's commitments with other nations. He also provides what is officially indefinable, namely, moral leadership. That is, when the people want to know what they are about, they turn to the Chief Executive for definition.*

These powers cannot be stressed enough. From them effortlessly accrue further influence and control which, borrowing from Patrick Henry, increasingly "squints toward monarchy," or to cite an example, pace *the historian Arthur Schlesinger, the defense treaty with South Korea, with no request for intervention from that government and no call for such intervention from the United Nations. In fact, the initial responses occurred before the UN Security Council met to endorse American intervention and were based, as the State Department observed, on the "traditional power of the President to use the Armed Forces of the United States without consulting Congress." But UN approval is no substitute for Congressional approval. President Truman acted on Presidential prerogative and, notwithstanding the legal argument, dangerously expanded executive power. Jefferson had recognized that he was "unauthorized by the Constitution without sanction of Congress, to go beyond the line of defense"; and that it was the Congressional prerogative to authorize "measures of offense also." Truman, departing from this legal standard, set a precedent for future Presidents to take the United States into a major conflict.*

Russian missiles deployed in Cuba, which presented a more direct threat to United States national security than Korea, prompted President Kennedy's response. Again, no consideration was given to the constitutional prerogatives of Congress. The President simply informed lawmakers about his decision after it had been made. "I have full authority now to take such action" against Cuba, he declared. Though the situation was unique in U.S. history, once again a President invoked his position as Commander-in-Chief. From Presidents Ford through Clinton, Chief Executives have used military force by citing their constitutional authority. Jimmy Carter sent commandos into Teheran—the U.S. embassy rescue operation—without Congressional con-

sultation, informing Congress "at the last minute." Senator Robert Byrd complained that President Reagan, when dispatching U.S. Marines to Lebanon, did not do so pursuant to his "constitutional authority with respect to the conduct of foreign relations and as Commander-in-Chief." This authority as well as inherent Presidential power was again invoked when Grenada was invaded in 1983. Nor did Reagan seek Congressional approval for the air strikes against Libya in 1986 or the military action in the Persian Gulf in 1987. President Bush's action in ordering troops to Panama also fell under these Constitutional rubrics and was undertaken when Congress had recessed. But Bush and Clinton, like Truman, also fell back on treaty obligations, from mutual defense treaties to UN resolutions, as justifications. President Clinton, to be sure, cooperated with lawmakers and worked out Congressional compromises for actions against Baghdad, combat operations in Somalia, sending troops to Haiti, and multilateral plans for Bosnian "peacekeeping," but an administration policy directive stated that the Chief Executive "will never relinquish command of U.S. forces," and claimed sufficient legal authority to use military force without ever seeking Congressional approval. Thus was enshrined, over the long trajectory of Presidential actions, Constitutional argument for independent and unilateral actions by the executive branch of government.

"I was summoned by my country"

First Presidential Inaugural Address
1789

Wearing a dark brown suit of American broadcloth he had bought through an advertisement, white stockings, shoes with silver buckles, and a steel-hilted dress sword, George Washington (1732–1799) took the oath of President of the United States:

> "I do solemnly swear that I will faithfully execute the office of President of the United States, and will to the best of my ability preserve, protect, and defend the Constitution of the United States, so help me God."

Washington had been the electors' unanimous choice to be first Chief Executive. During the War for Independence (1775–1783), Washington had commanded the victorious armies of England's thirteen former North American colonies. Convinced to leave the domestic ease and private enjoyment of his Virginia plantation, Washington presided over the Constitutional Convention, in Philadelphia, in 1787: "To see this country happy," he said, "is so much the wish of my soul." In April, 1789, Washington sailed across New York harbor to his inauguration. He walked on untrodden ground: "There is scarcely any part of my conduct which may not hereafter be drawn into precedent." The skies were cloudy and the nascent nation's future uncertain when Washington was sworn at Federal Hall, in New York City, the nation's temporary capital. In a trembling voice and with shaking hands, he delivered his eight-page inaugural address.

Fellow-Citizens of the Senate and of the House of Representatives:

Among the vicissitudes incident to life no event could have filled me with greater anxieties than that of which the notification was transmitted by your order, and received on the 14th day of the present month. On the one hand, I was summoned by my country, whose voice I can never hear but with veneration and love, from a retreat which I had chosen with the fondest predilection, and, in my flattering hopes, with an immutable decision, as the asylum of my declining years—a retreat which was rendered every day more necessary as well as more dear to me by the addition of habit to inclination, and of frequent interruptions in my health to the gradual waste committed on it by time. On the other hand, the magnitude and difficulty of the trust to which the voice of my country called me, being sufficient to awaken in the wisest and most experienced of her citizens a distrustful scrutiny into his qualifications, could not but overwhelm with despondence one who (inheriting inferior endowments from nature and unpracticed in the duties of civil administration) ought to be peculiarly conscious of his own deficiencies. In this conflict of emotions all I dare aver is that it has been my faithful study to collect my duty from a just appreciation of every circumstance by which it might be affected. All I dare hope is that if, in executing this task, I have been too much swayed by a grateful remembrance of former instances, or by an affectionate sensibility to this transcendent proof of the confidence of my fellow-citizens, and have thence too little consulted my incapacity as well as disinclination for the weighty and untried cares before me, my error will be palliated by the motives which mislead me, and its consequences be judged by my country with some share of the partiality in which they originated.

Such being the impressions under which I have, in obedience to the public summons, repaired to the present station, it would be peculiarly improper to omit in this first official act my fervent supplications to that Almighty Being who rules over the universe, who presides in the councils of nations, and whose providential aids can supply every human defect, that His benediction may consecrate to the liberties and happiness of the people of the United States a Government instituted by themselves for these essential purposes, and may enable every instrument employed in its administration to execute with success the functions allotted to his charge. In tendering this homage to the Great Author of every public and private good, I assure myself that it expresses your sentiments not less than my own, nor those of my fellow-citizens at large less than either. No people can be bound to acknowledge and adore the Invisible Hand which conducts the affairs of men more than those of the United States. Every step by which they have advanced to the character of an independent nation seems to have been distinguished by some token of providential agency; and in the important revolution just accomplished in the system

of their united government the tranquil deliberations and voluntary consent of so many distinct communities from which the event has resulted can not be compared with the means by which most governments have been established without some return of pious gratitude, along with an humble anticipation of the future blessings which the past seem to presage. These reflections, arising out of the present crisis, have forced themselves too strongly on my mind to be suppressed. You will join with me, I trust, in thinking that there are none under the influence of which the proceedings of a new and free government can more auspiciously commence.

By the article establishing the executive department it is made the duty of the President "to recommend to your consideration such measures as he shall judge necessary and expedient." The circumstances under which I now meet you will acquit me from entering into that subject further than to refer to the great constitutional charter under which you are assembled, and which, in defining your powers, designates the objects to which your attention is to be given. It will be more consistent with those circumstances, and far more congenial with the feelings which actuate me, to substitute, in place of a recommendation of particular measures, the tribute that is due to the talents, the rectitude, and the patriotism which adorn the characters selected to devise and adopt them. In these honorable qualifications I behold the surest pledges that as on one side no local prejudices or attachments, no separate views nor party animosities, will misdirect the comprehensive and equal eye which ought to watch over this great assemblage of communities and interests, so, on another, that the foundation of our national policy will be laid in the pure and immutable principles of private morality, and the preeminence of free government be exemplified by all the attributes which can win the affections of its citizens and command the respect of the world. I dwell on this prospect with every satisfaction which an ardent love for my country can inspire, since there is no truth more thoroughly established than that there exists in the economy and course of nature an indissoluble union between virtue and happiness; between duty and advantage; between the genuine maxims of an honest and magnanimous policy and the solid rewards of public prosperity and felicity; since we ought to be no less persuaded that the propitious smiles of Heaven can never be expected on a nation that disregards the eternal rules of order and right which Heaven itself has ordained; and since the preservation of the sacred fire of liberty and the destiny of the republican model of government are justly considered, perhaps, as *deeply,* as *finally,* staked on the experiment intrusted to the hands of the American people.

Besides the ordinary objects submitted to your care, it will remain with your judgment to decide how far an exercise of the occasional power delegated by the fifth article of the Constitution is rendered expedient at the present juncture by the nature of objections which have been urged against the system, or by the degree of inquietude which has given birth to them. Instead of undertaking particular recommendations on this subject, in which I could be guided by no lights derived from official opportunities, I shall again give way to my entire confidence in your discernment and pursuit of the public good; for I assure myself that whilst you carefully avoid every alteration which might endanger the benefits of an united and effective government, or which ought to await the future lessons of experience, a reverence for the characteristic rights of freemen and a regard for the public harmony

will sufficiently influence your deliberations on the question how far the former can be impregnably fortified or the latter be safely and advantageously promoted.

To the foregoing observations I have one to add, which will be most properly addressed to the House of Representatives. It concerns myself, and will therefore be as brief as possible. When I was first honored with a call into the service of my country, then on the eve of an arduous struggle for its liberties, the light in which I contemplated my duty required that I should renounce every pecuniary compensation. From this resolution I have in no instance departed; and being still under the impressions which produced it, I must decline as inapplicable to myself any share in the personal emoluments which may be indispensably included in a permanent provision for the executive department, and must accordingly pray that the pecuniary estimates for the station in which I am placed may during my continuance in it be limited to such actual expenditures as the public good may be thought to require.

Having thus imparted to you my sentiments as they have been awakened by the occasion which brings us together, I shall take my present leave; but not without resorting once more to the benign Parent of the Human Race in humble supplication that, since He has been pleased to favor the American people with opportunities for deliberating in perfect tranquillity, and dispositions for deciding with unparalleled unanimity on a form of government for the security of their union and the advancement of their happiness, so His divine blessing may be equally *conspicuous* in the enlarged views, the temperate consultations, and the wise measures on which the success of this Government must depend. . . .

"Exalt the just pride of patriotism"

WASHINGTON'S FAREWELL ADDRESS
1796

Only the pleas of Secretary of State Thomas Jefferson (1743–1826) and Secretary of the Treasury Alexander Hamilton (1755–1804) persuaded President George Washington (1732–1799) to agree to a second four-year term. But the second term was no picnic. Partisan bickering on many fronts threatened Washington, who was unable to distinguish criticism of his policies from attacks on him personally. Eager to return to his Mount Vernon home, he invited Hamilton to help draft a last message. Washington recast Hamilton's polished version in his own words, but didn't deliver it orally. Two months before the 1796 election, a half year before he was scheduled to retire, Washington asked the printer Claypoole to publish it in his newspaper, in Philadelphia; Claypoole did, as Washington headed south in his carriage for a congenial retirement in Virginia. The Farewell Address—warning Americans against "permanent alliances" with foreign powers, a large public debt, and the devices of a "small, artful, enterprising minority to control or change government"—has become a talisman by which American politics and foreign policy have been measured.

The period for a new election of a citizen to administer the Executive Government of the United States being not far distant, and the time actually arrived when your thoughts must be employed in designating the person who is to be clothed with that important trust, it appears to me proper, especially as it may conduce to a more distinct expression of the public voice, that I should now apprise you of the resolution I have formed to decline being considered among the number of those out of whom a choice is to be made. . . .

The impressions with which I first undertook the arduous trust were explained on the proper occasion. In the discharge of this trust I will only say that I have, with good intentions, contributed toward the organization and administration of the Government the best exertions of

which a very fallible judgment was capable. Not unconscious in the outset of the inferiority of my qualifications, experience in my own eyes, perhaps still more in the eyes of others, has strengthened the motives to diffidence of myself; and every day the increasing weight of years admonishes me more and more that the shade of retirement is as necessary to me as it will be welcome. Satisfied that if any circumstances have given peculiar value to my services they were temporary, I have the consolation to believe that, while choice and prudence invite me to quit the political scene, patriotism does not forbid it. . . .

Here, perhaps, I ought to stop. But a solicitude for your welfare which can not end with my life, and the apprehension of danger natural to that solicitude, urge me on an occasion like the present to offer to your solemn contemplation and to recommend to your frequent review some sentiments which are the result of much reflection, of no inconsiderable observation, and which appear to me all important to the permanency of your felicity as a people. . . .

The unity of government which constitutes you one people is also now dear to you. It is justly so, for it is a main pillar in the edifice of your real independence, the support of your tranquillity at home, your peace abroad, of your safety, of your prosperity, of that very liberty which you so highly prize. But as it is easy to foresee that from different causes and from different quarters much pains will be taken, many artifices employed, to weaken in your minds the conviction of this truth, as this is the point in your political fortress against which the batteries of internal and external enemies will be most constantly and actively (though often covertly and insidiously) directed, it is of infinite moment that you should properly estimate the immense value of your national union to your collective and individual happiness; that you should cherish a cordial, habitual, and immovable attachment to it; accustoming yourselves to think and speak of it as of the palladium of your political safety and prosperity; watching for its preservation with jealous anxiety; discountenancing whatever may suggest even a suspicion that it can in any event be abandoned, and indignantly frowning upon the first dawning of every attempt to alienate any portion of our country from the rest or to enfeeble the sacred ties which now link together the various parts.

. . . The name of American, which belongs to you in your national capacity, must always exalt the just pride of patriotism more than any appellation derived from local discriminations. With slight shades of difference, you have the same religion, manners, habits, and political principles. You have in a common cause fought and triumphed together. The independence and liberty you possess are the work of joint councils and joint efforts, of common dangers, sufferings, and successes.

But these considerations, however powerfully they address themselves to your sensibility, are greatly outweighed by those which apply more immediately to your interest. Here every portion of our country finds the most commanding motives for carefully guarding and preserving the union of the whole.

The *North,* in an unrestrained intercourse with the *South,* protected by the equal laws of a common government, finds in the productions of the latter great additional resources of maritime and commercial enterprise and precious materials of manufacturing industry. The *South,* in the same intercourse, benefiting by the same agency of the *North,* sees its agriculture grow and its commerce expand. Turning partly into its own channels the seamen of the *North,* it finds its particular navigation invigorated; and while it contributes in different ways to nourish and increase the general mass of the national navigation, it looks forward to the protection of a maritime strength to which itself is unequally adapted. The *East,* in a like intercourse with the *West,* already finds, and in the progressive improvement of interior communications by land and water will more and more find, a valuable vent for the commodities which it brings from abroad or manufactures at home. The *West* derives from the *East* supplies requisite to its growth and comfort, and what is perhaps of still greater consequence, it must of necessity owe the *secure* enjoyment of indispensable *outlets* for its own productions to the weight, influence, and the future maritime strength of the Atlantic side of the Union, directed by an indissoluble community of interest as one *nation.* Any other tenure by which the *West* can hold this essential advantage, whether derived from its own separate strength or from an apostate and unnatural connection with any foreign power, must be intrinsically precarious. . . .

Is there a doubt whether a common government can embrace so large a sphere? Let experience solve it. To listen to mere speculation in such a case were criminal. It is well worth a fair and full experiment. With such powerful and obvious motives to union affecting all parts of our country, while experience shall not have demonstrated its impracticability, there will always be reason to distrust the patriotism of those who in any quarter may endeavor to weaken its bands. . . .

To the efficacy and permanency of your union a government for the whole is indispensable. No alliances, however strict, between the parts can be an adequate substitute. They must inevitably experience the infractions and interruptions which all alliances in all times have experienced. Sensible of this momentous truth, you have improved upon your first essay by the adoption of a Constitution of Government better calculated than your former for an intimate union and for the efficacious management of your common concerns. This Government, the offspring of our own choice, uninfluenced and unawed, adopted upon full investigation and mature deliberation, completely free in its principles, in the distribution of its powers, uniting security with energy, and containing within itself a provision for its own amendment, has a just claim to your confidence and your support. Respect for its authority, compliance with its laws, acquiescence in its measures, are duties enjoined by the fundamental maxims of true liberty. The basis of our political systems is the right of the people to make and to alter their constitutions of government. But the constitution which at any time exists till changed by an explicit and authentic act of the whole people is sacredly obligatory upon all. The very idea of the power and the right of the people to establish government presupposes the duty of every individual to obey the established government. . . .

Toward the preservation of your Government and the permanency of your present happy state, it is requisite not only that you steadily discountenance irregular oppositions to its acknowledged authority, but also that you resist with care the spirit of innovation upon its principles, however specious the pretexts. One method of assault may be to effect in the forms of the Constitution alterations which will impair the energy of the system, and thus to undermine what can not be directly overthrown. In all the changes to which you may be invited remember that time and habit are at least as necessary to fix the true character of governments as of other human institutions; that experience is the surest standard by which to test the real tendency of the existing constitution of a country; that facility in changes upon the credit of mere hypothesis and opinion exposes to perpetual change, from the endless variety of hypothesis and opinion; and remember especially that for the efficient management of your common interests in a country so extensive as ours a government of as much vigor as is consistent with the perfect security of liberty is indispensable. Liberty itself will find in such a government, with powers properly distributed and adjusted, its surest guardian. It is, indeed, little else than a name where the government is too feeble to withstand the enterprises of faction, to confine each member of the society within the limits prescribed by the laws, and to maintain all in the secure and tranquil enjoyment of the rights of person and property.

I have already intimated to you the danger of parties in the State, with particular reference to the founding of them on geographical discriminations. Let me now take a more comprehensive view, and warn you in the most solemn manner against the baneful effects of the spirit of party generally.

This spirit, unfortunately, is inseparable from our nature, having its root in the strongest passions of the human mind. It exists under different shapes in all governments, more or less stifled, controlled, or repressed; but in those of the popular form it is seen in its greatest rankness and is truly their worst enemy. . . .

It serves always to distract the public councils and enfeeble the public administration. It agitates the community with ill-founded jealousies and false alarms; kindles the animosity of one part against another: foments occasionally riot and insurrection. It opens the door to foreign influence and corruption, which find a facilitated access to the government itself through the channels of party passion. Thus the policy and the will of one country are subjected to the policy and will of another. . . .

It is important, likewise, that the habits of thinking in a free country should inspire caution in those intrusted with its administration to confine themselves within their respective constitutional spheres, avoiding in the exercise of the powers of one department to encroach upon another. The spirit of encroachment tends to consolidate the powers of all the departments in one, and thus to create, whatever the form of government, a real despotism. . . . If in the opinion of the people the distribution or modification of the constitutional powers be in any particular wrong, let it be corrected by an amendment in the way which the Constitution designates. But let there be no change by usurpation; for though this in one instance may be the instrument of good, it is the customary weapon by which free governments are destroyed. The precedent must always greatly overbalance in permanent evil any partial or transient benefit which the use can at any time yield.

Of all the dispositions and habits which lead to political prosperity, religion and morality are indispensable supports. In vain would that man claim the tribute of patriotism who should labor to subvert these great pillars of human happiness—these firmest props of the duties of men and citizens. The mere politician, equally with the pious man, ought to respect and to cherish them. A volume could not trace all their connections with private and public felicity. Let it simply be asked, Where is the security for property, for reputation, for life, if the sense of religious obligation *desert* the oaths which are the instruments of investigation in courts of justice? And let us with caution indulge the supposition that morality can be maintained without religion. Whatever may be conceded to the influence of refined education on minds of peculiar structure, reason and experience both forbid us to expect that national morality can prevail in exclusion of religious principle.

It is substantially true that virtue or morality is a necessary spring of popular government. The rule indeed extends with more or less force to every species of free government. Who that is a sincere friend to it can look with indifference upon attempts to shake the foundation of the fabric? Promote, then, as an object of primary importance, institutions for the general diffusion of knowledge. In proportion as the structure of a government gives force to public opinion, it is essential that public opinion should be enlightened.

As a very important source of strength and security, cherish public credit. One method of preserving it is to use it as sparingly as possible, avoiding occasions of expense by cultivating peace, but remembering also that timely disbursements to prepare for danger frequently prevent much greater disbursements to repel it; avoiding likewise the accumulation of debt, not only by shunning occasions of expense, but by vigorous exertions in time of peace to discharge the debts which unavoidable wars have occasioned, not ungenerously throwing upon posterity the burthen which we ourselves ought to bear. . . .

Observe good faith and justice toward all nations. Cultivate peace and harmony with all. Religion and morality enjoin this conduct. And can it be that good policy does not equally enjoin it? It will be worthy of a free, enlightened, and at no distant period a great nation to give to mankind the magnanimous and too novel example of a people always guided by an exalted justice and benevolence. Who can doubt that in the course of time and things the fruits of such a plan would richly repay any temporary advantages which might be lost by a steady adherence to it? Can it be that Providence has not connected the permanent felicity of a nation with its virtue? The experiment, at least, is recommended by every sentiment which ennobles human nature. Alas! is it rendered impossible by its vices? . . .

Against the insidious wiles of foreign influence (I conjure you to believe me, fellow-citizens) the jealousy of a free people ought to be *constantly* awake, since history and experience prove that foreign influence is one of the most baneful foes of republican government. But that jealousy, to be useful, must be impartial, else it becomes the instrument of the very influence to be avoided, instead of a defense against it. Excessive partiality for one foreign nation and excessive dislike of another cause those whom they actuate to see danger only on one side, and serve to veil and even second the arts of influence on the other. Real patriots who may resist the intrigues of the favorite are liable to become suspected and odious, while its tools and dupes

usurp the applause and confidence of the people to surrender their interests. . . .

It is our true policy to steer clear of permanent alliances with any portion of the foreign world, so far, I mean, as we are now at liberty to do it; for let me not be understood as capable of patronizing infidelity to existing engagements. I hold the maxim no less applicable to public than to private affairs that honesty is always the best policy. I repeat, therefore, let those engagements be observed in their genuine sense. But in my opinion it is unnecessary and would be unwise to extend them.

Taking care always to keep ourselves by suitable establishments on a respectable defensive posture, we may safely trust to temporary alliances for extraordinary emergencies.

Harmony, liberal intercourse with all nations are recommended by policy, humanity, and interest. But even our commercial policy should hold an equal and impartial hand neither seeking nor granting exclusive favors or preferences; consulting the natural course of things; diffusing and diversifying by gentle means the streams of commerce, but forcing nothing; establishing with powers so disposed, in order to give trade a stable course to define the rights of our merchants, and to enable the Government to support them, conventional rules of intercourse, the best that present circumstances and mutual opinion will permit, but temporary and liable to be from time to time abandoned or varied as experience and circumstances shall dictate; constantly keeping in view that it is folly in one nation to look for disinterested favors from another; that it must pay with a portion of its independence for whatever it may accept under that character; that by such acceptance it may place itself in the condition of having given equivalents for nominal favors, and yet of being reproached with ingratitude for not giving more.

There can be no greater error than to expect or calculate upon real favors from nation to nation. It is an illusion which experience must cure, which a just pride ought to discard. . . .

Relying on its kindness in this as in other things, and actuated by that fervent love toward it which is so natural to a man who views in it the native soil of himself and his progenitors for several generations, I anticipate with pleasing expectation that retreat in which I promise myself to realize without alloy the sweet enjoyment of partaking in the midst of my fellow-citizens the benign influence of good laws under a free government—the ever-favorite object of my heart, and the happy reward, as I trust, of our mutual cares, labors, and dangers.

G°· WASHINGTON.

"The sum of good government"

JEFFERSON'S FIRST INAUGURAL
1801

Thomas Jefferson (1743–1826) wrote his own epitaph: "Here was buried Thomas Jefferson, author of the Declaration of Independence, of the Statute of Virginia for Religious Freedom, and Father of the University of Virginia." He also was the third President of the United States, the only Vice President (John Adams's) to serve two full terms as Chief Executive, a two-term Governor of Virginia, Minister to France during the writing of the Constitution in Philadelphia (he kept in touch by transatlantic post), and Secretary of State under President George Washington. (Jefferson and Aaron Burr [1756–1836] received the same number of votes [73] in the Electoral College in the 1800 election; the House of Representatives needed 36 ballots in February, 1801, to make Jefferson President.) President Jefferson signed legislation barring the importation of slaves after January 1, 1808 (the Continental Congress had eliminated from Jefferson's draft of the Declaration of Independence his criticism of England's support of the slave trade). Jefferson doubled the size of the United States, paying French Emperor Napoleon (1769–1821) two and one-half cents an acre for the Louisiana Purchase. His first Presidential inaugural, marking the rise of Democratic-Republicanism and the fall of Federalism, was the first to be staged in the nation's new, permanent capital city, named for the first President.

• • • A rising nation, spread over a wide and fruitful land, traversing all the seas with the rich productions of their industry, engaged in commerce with nations who feel power and forget right, advancing rapidly to destinies beyond the reach of mortal eye—when I contemplate these transcendent objects, and see the honor, the happiness, and the hopes of this beloved country committed to the issue and the auspices of this day, I shrink from the contemplation, and humble myself before the magnitude of the undertaking.

Let us . . . , fellow citizens, unite with one heart and one mind; let us restore to social intercourse that harmony and affection without which liberty and even life itself are but dreary things. And let us reflect that, having banished from our land that religious intolerance under which mankind so long bled and suffered, we have yet gained little, if we countenance a political intolerance, as despotic, as wicked, and as capable of as bitter and bloody persecutions. During the throes and convulsions of the ancient world, during the agonizing spasms of infuriated man, seeking through blood and slaughter his long-lost liberty, it was not wonderful that the agitation of the billows should reach even this distant and peaceful shore; that this should be more felt and feared by some, and less by others, and should divide opinions as to measures of safety; but every difference of opinion is not a difference of principle. We have called by different names brethren of the same principle. We are all Republicans; we are all Federalists. If there be any among us who wish to dissolve this Union, or to change its republican form, let them stand undisturbed as monuments of the safety with which error of opinion may be tolerated, where reason is left free to combat it. I know, indeed, that some honest men fear that a republican government cannot be strong, that this government is not strong enough. But would the honest patriot, in the full tide of successful experiment, abandon a government which has so far kept us free and firm, on the theoretic and visionary fear, that this government, the world's best hope, may, by possibility, want energy to preserve itself? I trust not. I believe this, on the contrary, the strongest government on earth. I believe it the only one where every man, at the call of the law, would fly to the standard of the law, and would meet invasions of the public order as his own personal concern. Sometimes it is said that man cannot be trusted with the government of himself. Can he, then, be trusted with the government of others? Or have we found angels, in the form of kings, to govern him? Let history answer this question.

Let us, then, with courage and confidence, pursue our own federal and republican princi-ples, our attachment to union and representative government. Kindly separated by nature and a wide ocean from the exterminating havoc of one quarter of the globe; too high-minded to endure the degradation of the others, possessing a chosen country, with room enough for our descendants to the thousandth and thousandth generation, entertaining a due sense of our equal right to the use of our own faculties, to the acquisition of our own industry, to honor and confidence from our fellow citizens, resulting not from birth but from our actions and their sense of them, enlightened by a benign religion, professed in deed and practised in various forms, yet all of them inculcating honesty, truth, temperance, gratitude, and the love of man, acknowledging and adoring an overruling Providence, which, by all its dispensations, proves that it delights in the happiness of man here, and his greater happiness hereafter—with all these blessings, what more is necessary to make us a happy and prosperous people? Still one thing more, fellow citizens, a wise and frugal government, which shall restrain men from injuring one another, shall leave them otherwise free to regulate their own pursuits of industry and improvement, and shall not take from the mouth of labor the bread it has earned. This is the sum of good government, and this is necessary to close the circle of our felicities. . . .

"Dangerous to our peace and safety"

THE MONROE DOCTRINE

1823

The future of the United States was never shinier. The frustrating three-year War of 1812 with Great Britain was over. The "Era of Good Feeling" permeated the early years of President James Monroe's two-term Administration (1817–1825). In the early 1820s, Secretary of State John Quincy Adams (1767–1848) warned an aggressive Russia that the United States would defend the principle that the American continents were no longer subjects of any new European colonial establishment. The Secretary, believing that Spain and France might reassert European rule in Central and South America, urged President Monroe (1758–1831) to affirm in his 1823 message to Congress the doctrine that the Old World and the New World must exist separately, never intervening in the affairs of the other. The Monroe Doctrine became a cornerstone of American foreign policy, but it was a prohibition never used nor, as it turned out, needed.

. . . The occasion has been judged proper for asserting, as a principle in which the rights and interests of the United States are involved, that the American continents, by the free and independent condition which they have assumed and maintain, are henceforth not to be considered as subjects for future colonization by any European powers. . . .

We owe it . . . to candor and to the amicable relations existing between the United States and those powers to declare that we should consider any attempt on their part to extend their system to any portion of this hemisphere as dangerous to our peace and safety.

With the existing colonies or dependencies of any European power we have not interfered and shall not interfere. But with the governments who have declared their independence and maintained it, and whose independence we have, on great consideration and on just principles, acknowledged, we could not view any interposi-

tion for the purpose of oppressing them, or controlling in any other manner their destiny, by any European power in any other light than as the manifestation of an unfriendly disposition toward the United States. In the war between those new governments and Spain we declared our neutrality at the time of their recognition, and to this we have adhered, and shall continue to adhere, provided no change shall occur which, in the judgment of the competent authorities of this government, shall make a corresponding change on the part of the United States indispensable to their security.

Our policy in regard to Europe, which was adopted at an early stage of the wars which have so long agitated that quarter of the globe, nevertheless remains the same, which is not to interfere in the internal concerns of any of its powers; to consider the government de facto as the legitimate government for us; to cultivate friendly relations with it, and to preserve those relations by a frank, firm, and manly policy, meeting in all instances the just claims of every power, submitting to injuries from none. But in regard to those continents, circumstances are eminently and conspicuously different. It is impossible that the allied powers should extend their political system to any portion of either continent without endangering our peace and happiness; nor can anyone believe that our southern brethren, if left to themselves, would adopt it of their own accord.

It is equally impossible, therefore, that we should behold such interposition in any form with indifference. If we look to the comparative strength and resources of Spain and those new governments, and their distance from each other, it must be obvious that she can never subdue them. It is still the true policy of the United States to leave the parties to themselves, in the hope that other powers will pursue the same course.

"Has invaded our territory and shed American blood"

PRESIDENT POLK: WAR WITH MEXICO
1846

The annexation of Texas (December, 1845) made war with Mexico all but inevitable. When President James K. Polk (1795–1849) announced that American blood had been shed on American soil during a skirmish between U.S. and Mexican forces in disputed territory on the border, Congress agreed to a declaration of war. American troops, though vastly outnumbered, won gallant victories. Mexico's sparsely settled province of California declared independence. American naval forces raised the Stars and Stripes at Monterey. Winfield Scott (1786–1866), General-in-Chief of the Army, led a triumphant expeditionary force into Mexico City. The Treaty of Guadalupe-Hidalgo (1848) added a vast area from Texas to California to the "manifest-destinied" United States. (The U.S. watchword in the mid-1840s was "Go ahead." The population was 20,000,000, one sixth in bondage.)

The existing state of the relations between the United States and Mexico renders it proper that I should bring the subject to the consideration of . . . Congress. . . .

The strong desire to establish peace with Mexico on liberal and honorable terms, and the readiness of this Government to regulate and adjust our boundary and other causes of difference with that power on such fair and equitable principles as would lead to permanent relations of the most friendly nature, induced me in September last to seek the reopening of diplomatic relations between the two countries. Every measure adopted on our part had for its object the furtherance of these desired results. In communicating to Congress a succinct statement of the injuries which we had suffered from Mexico, and which have been accumulating during a period of more than twenty years, every expression that

could tend to inflame the people of Mexico or defeat or delay a pacific result was carefully avoided. An envoy of the United States repaired to Mexico with full powers to adjust every existing difference. But though present on the Mexican soil by agreement between the two Governments, invested with full powers, and bearing evidence of the most friendly dispositions, his mission has been unavailing. The Mexican Government not only refused to receive him or listen to his propositions, but after a long-continued series of menaces have at last invaded our territory and shed the blood of our fellow-citizens on our own soil. . . .

In my message at the commencement of the present session I informed you that upon the earnest appeal both of the Congress and convention of Texas I had ordered an efficient military force to take a position "between the Nueces and the Del Norte." This had become necessary to meet a threatened invasion of Texas by the Mexican forces, for which extensive military preparations had been made. The invasion was threatened solely because Texas had determined, in accordance with a solemn resolution of the Congress of the United States, to annex herself to our Union and under these circumstances it was plainly our duty to extend our protection over her citizens and soil.

This force was concentrated at Corpus Christi, and remained there until after I had received such information from Mexico as rendered it probable, if not certain, that the Mexican Government would refuse to receive our envoy.

Meantime Texas, by the final action of our Congress, had become an integral part of our Union. The Congress of Texas, by its act of December 19, 1836, had declared the Rio del Norte to be the boundary of that Republic. Its jurisdiction had been extended and exercised beyond the Nueces. The country between that river and the Del Norte had been represented in the Congress and in the convention of Texas, had thus taken part in the act of annexation itself, and is now included within one of our Congressional districts. Our own Congress had, moreover, with great unanimity, by the act approved December 31, 1845, recognized the country beyond the Nueces as a part of our territory by including it within our own revenue system, and a revenue officer to reside within that district has been appointed by and with the advice and consent of the Senate. It became, therefore, of urgent necessity to provide for the defense of that portion of our country. Accordingly, on the 13th of January last instructions were issued to the general in command of these troops to occupy the left bank of the Del Norte. This river, which is the southwestern boundary of the State of Texas, is an exposed frontier. . . .

The movement of the troops to the Del Norte was made by the commanding general under positive instructions to abstain from all aggressive acts toward Mexico or Mexican citizens and to regard the relations between that Republic and the United States as peaceful unless she should declare war or commit acts of hostility indicative of a state of war. He was specially directed to protect private property and respect personal rights. . . .

The Mexican forces at Matamoras assumed a belligerent attitude, and on the 12th of April General Ampudia, then in command, notified General Taylor to break up his camp within twenty-four hours and to retire beyond the Nueces River, and in the event of his failure to comply with these demands announced that arms, and arms alone, must decide the question. But no open act of hostility was committed until the 24th of April. On that day General Arista, who had succeeded to the command of the Mexican forces, communicated to General Taylor that "he considered hostilities commenced and should prosecute them." A party of dragoons of 63 men and officers were on the same day dispatched from an American camp up the Rio del Norte, on its left bank, to ascertain whether the Mexican troops had crossed or were preparing to cross the river, "became engaged with a large body of these troops, and after a short affair, in which some 16 were killed and wounded, appear to have been surrounded and compelled to surrender."

The grievous wrongs perpetrated by Mexico upon our citizens throughout a long period of years remain unredressed, and solemn treaties pledging her public faith for this redress have been disregarded. A government either unable or unwilling to enforce the execution of such treaties has to perform one of its plainest duties.

. . . . we have tried every effort at reconciliation. The cup of forbearance had been exhausted even before the recent information from the frontier of the Del Norte. But now, after reiterated menaces, Mexico has passed the boundary of the United States, has invaded our territory and shed American blood upon the American soil. She has proclaimed that hostilities have commenced, and that the two nations are now at war.

As war exists, and, notwithstanding all our efforts to avoid it, exists by the act of Mexico herself, we are called upon by every consideration of duty and patriotism to vindicate with decision the honor, the rights, and the interests of our country.

Anticipating the possibility of a crisis like that which has arrived, instructions were given in August last, "as a precautionary measure" against invasion or threatened invasion, authorizing General Taylor, if the emergency required, to accept volunteers, not from Texas only, but from the States of Louisiana, Alabama, Mississippi, Tennessee, and Kentucky, and corresponding letters were addressed to the respective governors of those States. These instructions were repeated, and in January last, soon after the incorporation of "Texas into our Union of States," General Taylor was further "authorized by the President to make a requisition upon the executive of that State for such of its militia force as may be needed to repel invasion or to secure the country against apprehended invasion." . . .

In further vindication of our rights and defense of our territory, I invoke the prompt action of Congress to recognize the existence of the war, and to place at the disposition of the Executive the means of prosecuting the war with vigor, and thus hastening the restoration of peace. To this end I recommend that authority should be given to call into the public service a large body of volunteers to serve for not less than six or twelve months unless sooner discharged. . . .

I deem it proper to declare that it is my anxious desire not only to terminate hostilities speedily, but to bring all matters in dispute between this Government and Mexico to an early and amicable adjustment; and in this view I shall be prepared to renew negotiations whenever Mexico shall be ready to receive propositions or to make propositions of her own. . . .

"General association of nations must be formed"

PRESIDENT WILSON'S FOURTEEN POINTS
1918

The assassination of the heir to the Austrian throne, the extremely vain Archduke Francis Ferdinand (1863–1914), by a teenage Serbian political agitator triggered Europe's Great War—the First World War (1914–1918). President Woodrow Wilson (1856–1924) insisted that the United States wouldn't get involved. However, less than three years later the U.S. joined the Allied forces against Germany and the other Central European powers (Austria-Hungary and the Ottoman Empire). In early 1918, Wilson proposed before a joint session of Congress (given only a half-hour notice) fourteen points for a just and generous peace. (German rapacity made magnanimity impossible.) To gain support for the League of Nations, the President was forced to compromise some of his principles. (By Armistice Day, November 11, 1918, U.S. casualties included 53,402 deaths in the trenches and on the battlefields of Europe.) The Senate blocked both the peace treaty and U.S. membership in the League.

1. Open covenants of peace, openly arrived at, after which there shall be no private international understandings of any kind, but diplomacy shall proceed always frankly and in the public view.

2. Absolute freedom of navigation upon the seas, outside territorial waters, alike in peace and in war, except as the seas may be closed in whole or in part by international action for the enforcement of international covenants.

3. The removal, so far as possible, of all economic barriers and the establishment of an equality of trade conditions among all the nations consenting to the peace and associating themselves for its maintenance.

4. Adequate guarantees given and taken that national armaments will be reduced to the lowest points consistent with domestic safety.

5. A free, open-minded and absolutely impartial adjustment of all colonial claims based upon a strict observance of the principle that in determining all such questions of sovereignty, the interests of the populations concerned must have equal weight with the equitable claims of the government whose title is to be determined.

6. The evacuation of all Russian territory and such a settlement of all questions affecting Russia as will secure the best and freest cooperation of the other nations of the world in obtaining for her an unhampered and unembarrassed opportunity for the independent determination of her own political development and national policy and assure her of a sincere welcome into the society of free nations under institutions of her own choosing; and, more than a welcome, assistance also of every kind that she may need and may herself desire. The treatment accorded Russia by her sister nations in the months to

come will be the acid test of their goodwill, of their comprehension of her needs as distinguished from their own interests, and of their intelligent and unselfish sympathy.

7. Belgium, the whole world will agree, must be evacuated and restored without any attempt to limit the sovereignty which she enjoys in common with all other free nations. No other single act will serve as this will serve to restore confidence among the nations in the laws which they have themselves set and determined for the government of their relations with one another. Without this healing act the whole structure and validity of international law is forever impaired.

8. All French territory should be freed and the invaded portions restored, and the wrong done to France by Prussia in 1871 in the matter of Alsace-Lorraine, which has unsettled the peace of the world for nearly fifty years, should be righted in order that peace may once more be made secure in the interest of all.

9. A readjustment of the frontiers of Italy should be effected along clearly recognizable lines of nationality.

10. The people of Austria-Hungary, whose place among the nations we wish to see safeguarded and assured, should be accorded the freest opportunity of autonomous development.

11. Rumania, [Serbia], and Montenegro should be evacuated; occupied territories restored; Serbia accorded free and secure access to the sea; and the relations of the several Balkan states to one another determined by friendly counsel along historically established lines of allegiance and nationality; and international guarantees of the political and economic independence and territorial integrity of the several Balkan states should be entered into.

12. The Turkish portions of the present Ottoman Empire should be assured a secure sovereignty, but the other nationalities which are now under Turkish rule should be assured an undoubted security of life and an absolutely unmolested opportunity of autonomous development; and the Dardanelles should be permanently opened as a free passage to the ships and commerce of all nations under international guarantees.

13. An independent Polish state should be erected which should include the territories inhabited by indisputably Polish populations, which should be assured a free and secure access to the sea, and whose political and economic independence and territorial integrity should be guaranteed by international covenants.

14. A general association of nations must be formed under specific covenants for the purpose of affording mutual guarantees of political independence and territorial integrity to great and small [states] alike.

"Fear only fear itself"

F.D.R.'s First Inaugural Address
1933

America was mired in the Depression. An exhausted President Herbert C. Hoover cried, "We are at the end of our string." Then, on March 4, 1933, Franklin Delano Roosevelt (1882–1945), Governor of New York, who had trounced President Hoover (1874–1964) in the 1932 election (472–59 in electoral votes), was sworn as the thirty-second President in the last inauguration held in March. Roosevelt believed that the inauguration was the time to "speak the truth, the whole truth, frankly and boldly." On a cloudy and cheerless day, with almost all of the nation's banks closed, a coatless, hatless, and polio-crippled Roosevelt moved out on a high, white, ivy- and flag-bedecked platform at the Capitol and faced the waiting crowd. He asserted his firm belief that the only thing Americans had to fear was fear itself, "namely, nameless, unreasoning, unjustified terror which paralyzes needed efforts to convert retreat into advance." (Working over his speech in a hotel room, Roosevelt had had at hand a copy of Thoreau, who had written, "Nothing is so much to be feared as fear.") The greatest primary task, putting people to work, was "no unsolvable problem if we face it wisely and courageously. It can be accomplished in part by direct recruiting by the Government itself, treating the task as we would treat the emergency of a war, . . . "

This is a day of consecration. I am certain that my fellow Americans expect that on my induction into the Presidency I will address them with a candor and a decision which the present situation of our nation impels. This is preeminently the time to speak the truth, the whole truth, frankly and boldly. Nor need we shrink from honestly facing conditions in our country today. This great nation will endure as it has endured, will revive and will prosper. So first of all let me assert my firm belief that the only thing we have to fear is fear itself,—nameless, unreasoning, unjustified terror which paralyzes needed efforts to convert retreat into advance. In every dark hour of our national life a leadership of frankness and vigor has met with that understanding and support of the people themselves which is essential to victory. I am convinced that you will again give that support to leadership in these critical days.

In such a spirit on my part and on yours we face our common difficulties. They concern, thank God, only material things. Values have shrunken to fantastic levels; taxes have risen; our ability to pay has fallen; government of all kinds is faced by serious curtailment of income; the means of exchange are frozen in the currents of trade; the withered leaves of industrial enterprise lie on every side; farmers find no markets for their produce; the savings of many years in thousands of families are gone.

More important, a host of unemployed citizens face the grim problem of existence, and an equally great number toil with little return. Only a foolish optimist can deny the dark realities of the moment.

Yet our distress comes from no failure of substance. We are stricken by no plague of locusts. Compared with the perils which our forefathers conquered because they believed and were not afraid, we have still much to be thankful for. Nature still offers her bounty and human efforts have multiplied it. Plenty is at our doorstep, but a generous use of it languishes in the very sight of the supply. Primarily, this is because the rulers of the exchange of mankind's goods have failed through their own stubbornness and their own incompetence, have admitted their failure and abdicated. Practices of the unscrupulous money changers stand indicted in the court of public opinion, rejected by the hearts and minds of men.

True, they have tried, but their efforts have been cast in the pattern of an outworn tradition. Faced by failure of credit they have proposed only the lending of more money. Stripped of the lure of profit by which to induce our people to follow their false leadership they have resorted to exhortations, pleading tearfully for restored confidence. They know only the rules of a generation of self-seekers. They have no vision, and when there is no vision the people perish.

The money changers have fled from their high seats in the temple of our civilization. We may now restore that temple to the ancient truths. The measure of the restoration lies in the extent to which we apply social values more noble than mere monetary profit.

Happiness lies not in the mere possession of money; it lies in the joy of achievement, in the thrill of creative effort. The joy and moral stimulation of work no longer must be forgotten in the mad chase of evanescent profits. These dark days will be worth all they cost us if they teach us that our true destiny is not to be ministered unto but to minister to ourselves and to our fellow-men.

Recognition of the falsity of material wealth as the standard of success goes hand in hand with the abandonment of the false belief that public office and high political position are to be valued only by the standards of pride of place and personal profit; and there must be an end to a conduct in banking and in business which too often has given to a sacred trust the likeness of callous and selfish wrongdoing. Small wonder that confidence languishes, for it thrives only on honesty, on honor, on the sacredness of obligations, on faithful protection, on unselfish performance: without them it cannot live.

Restoration calls, however, not for changes in ethics alone. This nation asks for action, and action now.

Our greatest primary task is to put people to work. This is no unsolvable problem if we face it wisely and courageously. It can be accomplished in part by direct recruiting by the government itself, treating the task as we would treat the emergency of a war, but at the same time through this employment accomplishing greatly needed projects to stimulate and reorganize the use of our natural resources.

Hand in hand with this we must frankly recognize the over-balance of population in our industrial centers and, by engaging on a national scale in a redistribution, endeavor to provide a better use of the land for those best fitted for the land. The task can be helped by definite efforts to raise the values of agricultural products and with this the power to purchase the output of our cities. It can be helped by preventing realistically the tragedy of the growing loss through foreclosure, of our small homes and our farms. It can be helped by insistence that the federal, state and local governments act forthwith on the demand that their cost be drastically reduced. It can be helped by the unifying of relief activities which today are often scattered, uneconomical and unequal. It can be helped by national planning for and supervision of all forms of transportation and of communications and other utilities which have a definitely public character. There are many ways in which it can be helped, but it can never be helped merely by talking about it. We must act and act quickly.

Finally, in our progress toward a resumption of work we require two safeguards against a return of the evils of the old order: there must be a strict supervision of all banking and credits and investments; there must be an end to speculation with other people's money, and there must be provision for an adequate but sound currency.

These are the lines of attack. I shall presently urge upon a new Congress in special session detailed measures for their fulfillment, and I shall seek the immediate assistance of the several states.

Through this program of action we address ourselves to putting our own national house in order and making income balance outgo. Our international trade relations though vastly important, are in point of time and necessity secondary to the establishment of a sound national economy. I favor as a practical policy the putting of first things first. I shall spare no effort to restore world trade by international economic readjustment, but the emergency at home cannot wait on that accomplishment.

The basic thought that guides these specific means of national recovery is not narrowly nationalistic. It is the insistence, as a first consideration, upon the interdependence of the various elements in and parts of the United States—a recognition of the old and permanently impor-

tant manifestation of the American spirit of the pioneer. It is the way to recovery. It is the immediate way. It is the strongest assurance that the recovery will endure.

In the field of world policy I would dedicate this nation to the policy of the good neighbor—the neighbor who resolutely respects himself and because he does so, respects the rights of others—the neighbor who respects his obligations and respects the sanctity of his agreements in and with a world of neighbors.

If I read the temper of our people correctly we now realize as we have never realized before our interdependence on each other: that we cannot merely take but we must give as well; that if we are to go forward we must move as a trained and loyal army willing to sacrifice for the good of a common discipline, because without such discipline no progress is made, no leadership becomes effective. We are, I know, ready and willing to submit our lives and property to such discipline because it makes possible a leadership which aims at a larger good. This I propose to offer, pledging that the larger purposes will bind upon us all as a sacred obligation with a unity of duty hitherto evoked only in time of armed strife.

With this pledge taken, I assume unhesitatingly the leadership of this great army of our people dedicated to a disciplined attack upon our common problems. . . .

I am prepared under my constitutional duty to recommend the measures that a stricken nation in the midst of a stricken world may require. These measures, or such other measures as the Congress may build out of its experience and wisdom, I shall seek, within my constitutional authority, to bring to speedy adoption.

But in the event that the Congress shall fail to take one of these two courses, and in the event that the national emergency is still critical, I shall not evade the clear course of duty that will then confront me. I shall ask the Congress for the one remaining instrument to meet the crisis— broad executive power to wage a war against the emergency, as great as the power that would be given to me if we were in fact invaded by a foreign foe.

For the trust reposed in me I will return the courage and the devotion that befit the time. I can do no less. . . .

"We had a bad . . . situation"

PRESIDENT ROOSEVELT ON THE BANKING HOLIDAY
1933

Only two days after his March 4 inauguration, President Franklin Delano Roosevelt (1882–1945) proclaimed a bank holiday, the first step, he said, in the Government's reconstruction of the nation's financial and economic fabric. Roosevelt's first week as Chief Executive was dominated by the banking crisis. The key problem, it seemed, was one of public psychology. The people wanted action and the President promised and delivered it. A Roosevelt biographer noted,

> **"The curious fact was that the important actions already had been taken by the states and by the banks themselves: the banks had closed. Roosevelt played his role of crisis leader with such extraordinary skill that his action in keeping the banks closed in itself struck the country with the bracing effect of a March wind. His action was essentially defensive, negative, and conservative—but he made of it a call to action."**

Late in the evening of March 12, F.D.R. broadcast the first of his celebrated "fireside chats."

I want to talk for a few minutes with the people of the United States about banking—with the comparatively few who understand the mechanics of banking but more particularly with the overwhelming majority who use banks for the making of deposits and the drawing of checks. . . . I owe this in particular because of the fortitude and good temper with which everybody has accepted the inconvenience and hardships of the banking holiday. I know that when you understand what we in Washington have been about I shall continue to have your cooperation as fully as I have had your sympathy and help during the past week.

First of all let me state the simple fact that when you deposit money in a bank the bank does not put the money into a safe deposit vault. It invests your money in many different forms of credit—bonds, commercial paper, mortgages and many other kinds of loans. In other words, the bank puts your money to work to keep the wheels of industry and of agriculture turning around. A comparatively small part of the money you put into the bank is kept in currency—an amount which in normal times is wholly sufficient to cover the cash needs of the average citizen. In other words the total amount of all the currency in the country is only a small fraction of the total deposits in all of the banks.

What, then, happened during the last few days of February and the first few days of March? Because of undermined confidence on the part of the public, there was a general rush by a large portion of our polulation to turn bank deposits into currency or gold. A rush so great that the soundest banks could not get enough currency to meet the demand. The reason for this was that on the spur of the moment it was, of course, impossible to sell perfectly sound assets of a bank and convert them into cash except at panic prices far below their real value.

By the afternoon of March 3 scarcely a bank in the country was open to do business. Proclamations temporarily closing them in whose or in part had been issued by the Governors in almost all the states.

It was then that I issued the proclamation providing for the nation-wide bank holiday, and this was the first step in the Government's reconstruction of our financial and economic fabric.

The second step was the legislation promptly and patriotically passed by the Congress confirming my proclamation and broadening my powers so that it became possible in view of the requirement of time to extend the holiday and lift the ban of that holiday gradually. This law also gave authority to develop a program of rehabilitation of our banking facilities. . . .

The third stage has been the series of regulations permitting the banks to continue their functions to take care of the distribution of food and household necessities and the payment of payrolls.

This bank holiday while resulting in many cases in great inconvenience is affording us the opportunity to supply the currency necessary to meet the situation. No sound bank is a dollar worse off than it was when it closed it doors last Monday. Neither is any bank which may turn out not to be in a position for immediate opening. The new law allows the twelve Federal Reserve banks to issue additional currency on good assets and thus the banks which reopen will be able to meet every legitimate call. The new currency is being sent out by the Bureau of Engraving and Printing in large volume to every part of the country. It is sound currency because it is backed by actual, good assets.

. . . we start tomorrow, Monday, with the opening of banks in the twelve Federal Reserve bank cities—those banks which on first examination by the Treasury have already been found to be all right. This will be followed on Tuesday by the resumption of all their functions by banks already found to be sound in cities where there are recognized clearing houses. That means about 250 cities of the United States.

On Wednesday and succeeding days banks in smaller places all through the country will resume business, subject, of course, to the Government's physical ability to complete its survey. It is necessary that the reopening of banks be extended over a period in order to permit the banks to make applications for necessary loans, to obtain currency needed to meet their requirements and to enable the Government to make common sense checkups.

Let me make it clear to you that if your bank does not open the first day you are by no means justified in believing that it will not open. A bank that opens on one of the subsequent days is in exactly the same status as the bank that opens tomorrow. . . .

I am confident that the state banking departments will be as careful as the National Government in the policy relating to the opening of banks and will follow the same broad policy.

. . . Let me make it clear that the banks will take care of all needs—and it is my belief that hoarding during the past week has become an exceedingly unfashionable pastime. It needs no prophet to tell you that when the people find that they can get their money—that they can get it when they want it for all legitimate purposes—the phantom of fear will soon be laid. People will again be glad to have their money where it will be safely taken care of and where they can use it conveniently at any time. I can assure you that it is safer to keep your money in a reopened bank than under the mattress. . . .

Remember that the essential accomplishment of the new legislation is that it makes it possible for banks more readily to convert their assets into cash than was the case before. . . .

There will be, of course, some banks unable to reopen without being reorganized. The new law allows the Government to assist in making these reorganizations quickly and effectively and even allows the Government to subscribe to at least a part of new capital which may be required. . . .

We had a bad banking situation. Some of our bankers had shown themselves either incompetent or dishonest in their handling of the people's funds. They had used the money entrusted to them in speculations and unwise loans. This was of course not true in the vast majority of our banks but it was true in enough of them to shock the people for a time into a sense of insecurity and to put them into a frame of mind where they did not differentiate, but seemed to assume that the acts of a comparative few had tainted them all. It was the Government's job to straighten out this situation and do it as quickly as possible—and the job is being performed. . . .

"Eliminate the dollar sign"

LEND-LEASE
1940

Hitler (1889–1945) ruled most of Europe. His goose-stepping German war machine appeared invincible. It had blitzkrieged Poland, invaded the Low Countries, and occupied France. The Luftwaffe was blasting England. Most Americans thought that the United States should begin arming to the teeth. During his 1940 campaign for an unprecedented third term, President Franklin Delano Roosevelt (1882–1945) made a deal with the beleaguered, cash-strapped British: The U.S. would exchange 50 over-age destroyers for the rights to construct military bases in Bermuda and the British West Indies. "Lend-Lease" would be part of the President's plan to accustom Americans in supporting allied Europeans in their war with Germany and Italy. The German Führer had pictured the war as a gigantic class struggle between rich, capitalist-ruling nations, with millions of unemployed, and Germany, where all had jobs and work was the supreme value: "The two worlds stand opposed to each other . . . I can beat any other power in the world . . . " By year's end, over 60 percent of the Americans polled favored aid to Britain, even at the risk of war. The following March, Congress enacted Lend-Lease legislation, a milestone in the organization of global resistance to Hitler and his allies. The Commander-in-Chief had tendered a couple of popular notions.

Now, what I am trying to do is to eliminate the dollar sign . . . the silly foolish old dollar sign.

Well, let me give you an illustration: Suppose my neighbor's home catches fire . . . if he can take my garden hose and connect it up with his hydrant, I may help him to put out his fire. Now, what do I do? I don't say to him before that operation, "Neighbor, my garden hose cost me $15; you have got to pay me $15 for it." . . . I don't want $15—I want my garden hose back after the fire is over. . . . In other words, if you lend certain munitions and get the munitions back at the end of the war, . . . you are all right.

"We must have . . . more of everything"

THE ARSENAL OF DEMOCRACY
1940

Expressing the possibility (based on the latest and best data) that the Axis powers could win the war, President Franklin Roosevelt (1882–1945) delivered his most important speech since the banking emergency nearly eight years earlier. Acute interest in the world situation and in national defense prompted the largest radio audience in U.S. history (upwards of 80-million listeners). The Blitz had begun four months earlier. Hitler's "arsonists of the air" were setting London afire. A red glow colored the English sky. The President, interpreting his third-term election as a mandate for the United States to become the "arsenal of democracy," declared a policy of dynamic non-belligerence: The U.S. would send more munitions and supplies to the British, the Greeks, and others in the front lines of democracy's battle.

The nub of the whole purpose of your President is to keep you now, and your children later, and your grandchildren much later out of a last-ditch war for the preservation of American independence.

Never before since Jamestown and Plymouth Rock has our American civilization been in such danger as now.

The Nazi masters of Germany have made it clear that they intend . . . to enslave the whole of Europe, and then to use the resources of Europe to dominate the rest of the world.

The United States has no right or reason to encourage talk of peace until the day shall come when there is a clear intention on the part of the aggressor nations to abandon all thought of dominating or conquering the world.

The experience of the past two years has proven beyond doubt that no nation can appease the Nazis. No man can tame a tiger into a kitten by stroking it.

There is far less chance of the United States getting into war if we do all we can now to sup-port the nations defending themselves against attack by the Axis than if we acquiesce in their defeat, submit tamely to an Axis victory, and wait our turn to be the object of attack in another war later on.

There is no demand for sending an American expeditionary force outside our own borders. There is no intention by any member of your government to send such a force.

The nation expects our defense industries to continue operation without interruption by strikes or lockouts.

All our present efforts are not enough. We must have more ships, more guns, more planes—more of everything.

There will be no "bottlenecks" in our determination to aid Great Britain. No dictator, no combination of dictators, will weaken that determination by threats of how they will construe that determination.

I believe that the Axis powers are not going to win this war. I base that belief on the latest and best information.

"Full participation in the national defense"

BANNING DISCRIMINATION
1941

A week before an estimated 50,000 people were scheduled to participate in the Negro March on Washington for jobs and equal participation in the national defense, President Franklin Roosevelt (1882–1945) issued an executive order banning discrimination in defense industries on account of race, color, creed, or national origin: "The democratic way of life within the Nation can be defended successfully only with the help and support of all groups within its borders." The March committee (its director was the labor leader A. Philip Randolph [1889–1979]) informed the President that his order was "definite, clear, and unmistakable in its meaning and purpose," and called off the protest. Presently, the Fair Employment Practices Committee (F.E.P.C.) was established.

Reaffirming policy of full participation in the defense program by all persons, regardless of race, creed, color, or national origin, and directing certain action in furtherance of said ploicy.

WHEREAS it is the policy of the United States to encourage full participation in the national defense program by all citizens of the United States, regardless of race, creed, color, or national origin, in the firm belief that the democratic way of life within the Nation can be defended successfully only with the help and support of all groups within its borders; and

WHEREAS there is evidence that available and needed workers have been barred from employment in industries engaged in defense production solely because of considerations of race, creed, color, or national origin, to the detriment of workers' morale and of national unity:

NOW, THEREFORE, by virtue of the authority vested in me by the Constitution and the statutes, and as a prerequisite to the successful conduct of our national defense production effort, I do hereby reaffirm the policy of the United States that there shall be no discrimina-

tion in the employment of workers in defense industries or government because of race, creed, color, or national origin, and I do hereby declare that it is the duty of employers and of labor organizations, in furtherance of said policy and of this order, to provide for the full and equitable participation of all workers in defense industries, without discrimination because of race, creed, color, or national origin;

And it is hereby ordered as follows:

1. All departments and agencies of the Government of the United States concerned with vocational and training programs for defense production shall take special measures appropriate to assure that such programs are administered without discrimination because of race, creed, color, or national origin;

2. All contracting agencies of the Government of the United States shall include in all defense contracts hereafter negotiated by them a provision obligating the contractor not to discriminate against any worker because of race, creed, color, or national origin;

3. There is established in the Office of Pro-

duction Management a Committee on Fair Employment Practice, which shall consist of a chairman and four other members to be appointed by the President. The chairman and members of the Committee shall serve as such without compensation but shall be entitled to actual and necessary transportation, subsistence and other expenses incidental to performance of their duties. The Committee shall receive and investigate complaints of discrimination in violation of the provisions of this order and shall take appropriate steps to redress grievances which it finds to be valid. The Committee shall also recommend to the several departments and agencies of the Government of the United States and to the President all measures which may be deemed by it necessary or proper to effectuate the provisions of this order.

"A date which will live in infamy"

U.S. DECLARES WAR AGAINST JAPAN
1941

Japan's conquest of French Indochina, Manchuria, and most of eastern China led to diplomatic recriminations and economic reprisals. British Prime Minister Winston S. Churchill (1874–1965) recalled that "all the great Americans round the President and in his confidence felt, exactly as I did, the awful danger that Japan would attack British or Dutch possessions in the Far East, and would carefully avoid the United States, and that in consequence Congress would not sanction an American declaration of war." On Sunday, December 7, 1941, as Japanese diplomats talked peace with American officials in Washington, D.C., naval and air forces of the Japanese Empire suddenly and unexpectedly roared out of the Pacific dawn and pounded U.S. military and naval bases in the territory of Hawaii, destroying eight battleships and 188 aircraft, and killing 2,280 military personnel. The next day, President Franklin D. Roosevelt (1882–1945) asked a joint session of Congress for a declaration of war against Japan. Thunderous applause greeted the Commander-in-Chief's six-minute address. Two and a half hours later, the President signed Congress's formal declaration of war. Three days later, Germany and Italy—the Axis partners had not been forewarned of the Japanese raid—honored a treaty with their Asian ally and declared war on the U.S.; the U.S. responded with war declarations immediately. The Second World War went on for another 45 months.

Yesterday, December 7, 1941—a date which will live in infamy—the United States of America was suddenly and deliberately attacked by naval and air forces of the Empire of Japan.

The United States was at peace with that nation and, at the solicitation of Japan, was still in conversation with its Government and its Emperor looking toward the maintenance of peace in the Pacific. Indeed, one hour after Japanese air squadrons had commenced bombing in Oahu, the Japanese Ambassador to the United States and his colleague delivered to the Secretary of State a formal reply to a recent American message. While this reply stated that it seemed use-less to continue the existing diplomatic negotiations, it contained no threat or hint of war or armed attack.

It will be recorded that the distance of Hawaii from Japan makes it obvious that the attack was deliberately planned many days or even weeks ago. During the intervening time the Japanese Government has deliberately sought to deceive the United States by false statements and expressions of hope for continued peace.

The attack yesterday on the Hawaiian Islands has caused severe damage to American naval and military forces. Very many American lives have been lost. In addition American ships have been reported torpedoed on the high seas between San Francisco and Honolulu.

Yesterday the Japanese Government also launched an attack against Malaya.

Last night Japanese forces attacked Hong Kong.

Last night Japanese forces attacked Guam.

Last night Japanese forces attacked the Philippine Islands.

Last night the Japanese attacked Wake Island.

This morning the Japanese attacked Midway Island.

Japan has, therefore, undertaken a surprise offensive extending throughout the Pacific area. The facts of yesterday speak for themselves. The people of the United States have already formed their opinions and well understand the implications to the very life and safety of our nation.

As Commander-in-Chief of the Army and Navy I have directed that all measures be taken for our defense.

Always will be remembered the character of the onslaught against us.

No matter how long it may take us to overcome this premeditated invasion, the American people in their righteous might will win through to absolute victory.

I believe I interpret the will of the Congress and of the people when I assert that we will not only defend ourselves to the uttermost but will make very certain that this form of treachery shall never endanger us again.

Hostilities exist. There is no blinking at the fact that our people, our territory and our interests are in grave danger.

With confidence in our armed forces—with the unbounding determination of our people—we will gain the inevitable triumph—so help us God.

I ask that the Congress declare that since the unprovoked and dastardly attack by Japan on Sunday, December seventh, a state of war has existed between the United States and the Japanese Empire.

"Protection against espionage and sabotage"

Excluding Persons from Prescribed Military Areas

1942

Two months into the war, with Japanese military victories mounting throughout the Pacific, President Franklin D. Roosevelt (1882–1945) signed Executive Order No. 9066. It removed all persons of Japanese ancestry (110,000 nationals and naturalized citizens and their children—many were American citizens by birth) from the Pacific coast of the United States and interned them in 10 barbed-wire "relocation centers," or concentration camps, in remote areas of the western mountains and deserts. Although the Government feared espionage and sabotage, relocation was largely the result of racial prejudice. A smaller number of European-Americans—German-Americans and Italian-Americans—also were interned. Federal court justices upheld Executive Order No. 9066 as a valid wartime act. In 1988, the U.S. enacted a statute providing $20,000 in monetary compensation for each of the surviving Japanese internees.

WHEREAS the successful prosecution of the war requires every possible protection against espionage and against sabotage to national-defense material, national-defense premises, and national-defense utilities. . . .

NOW, THEREFORE, by virtue of the authority vested in me as President of the United States, and Commander in Chief of the Army and Navy, I hereby authorize and direct the Secretary of War, and the Military Commanders whom he may from time to time designate, whenever he or any designated Commander deems such action necessary or desirable, to prescribe military areas in such places and of such extent as he or the appropriate Military Commander may determine, from which any or all persons may be excluded, and with respect to which, the right of any person to enter, remain in, or leave shall be subject to whatever restrictions the Secretary of War or the appropriate Military Commander may im-

pose in his discretion. The Secretary of War is hereby authorized to provide for residents of any such area who are excluded therefrom, such transportation, food, shelter, and other accommodations as may be necessary, in the judgment of the Secretary of War or the said Military Commander, and until other arrangements are made, to accomplish the purpose of this order. The designation of military areas in any region or locality shall supersede designations of prohibited and restricted areas by the Attorney General under the Proclamations of December 7 and 8, 1941, and shall supersede the responsibility and authority of the Attorney General under the said Proclamations in respect of such prohibited and restricted areas.

I hereby further authorize and direct the Secretary of War and the said Military Commanders to take such other steps as he or the appropriate Military Commander may deem advisable to enforce compliance with the restrictions applicable to each Military area hereinabove authorized to be designated, including the use of Federal troops and other Federal Agencies, with authority to accept assistance of state and local agencies.

I hereby further authorize and direct all Executive Departments, independent establishments and other Federal Agencies, to assist the Secretary of War or the said Military Commanders in carrying out this Executive Order, including the furnishing of medical aid, hospitalization, food, clothing, transportation, use of land, shelter, and other supplies, equipment, utilities, facilities, and services.

This order shall not be construed as modifying or limiting in any way the authority heretofore granted under Executive Order No. 8972, dated December 12, 1941, nor shall it be construed as limiting or modifying the duty and responsibility of the Federal Bureau of Investigation, with respect to the investigation of alleged acts of sabotage or the duty and responsibility of the Attorney General and the Department of Justice under the Proclamations of December 7 and 8, 1941, prescribing regulations for the conduct and control of alien enemies, except as such duty and responsibility is superseded by the designation of military areas hereunder.

"If the people command me"

THE PRESIDENT WOULD ACCEPT A FOURTH TERM
1944

President Franklin Delano Roosevelt (1882–1945) made it known to the 1940 Democratic National Convention, in Chicago, that he never had any "desire or purpose to continue in the office of President, to be a candidate for that office, or to be nominated by the Convention" for an unprecedented third term. He wished "in all earnestness and sincerity to make it clear" that the delegates were free to vote for any candidate. Accepting the nomination, the President addressed the Convention from the White House's radio broadcasting room at 12:25 A.M. In the face of the public danger, he said, "all those who can be of service to the Republic have no choice but to offer themselves for service in those capacities for which they may be fitted. . . . my conscience will not let me turn my back upon a call to service." Four years later, President Roosevelt said that he owed the Democratic Convention a simple, candid statement of his position: "If the Convention should . . . nominate me for the Presidency, I shall accept. If the people elect me, I will serve . . . if the people command me to continue in this office and in this war, I have as little right to withdraw as the soldier has to leave his post in the line." In the November, 1944, election, he defeated the Republican nominee, New York Governor Thomas E. Dewey (432–99 in electoral votes). The President died in the third month of his fourth term, less than one month before Germany surrendered and four months before Japan surrendered, ending the Second World War.

If the Convention should . . . nominate me for the Presidency, I shall accept. If the people elect me, I will serve.

Every one of our sons serving in this war has officers from whom he takes his orders. Such officers have superior officers. The President is the Commander in Chief and he, too, has his superior officer—the people of the United States.

I would accept and serve, but I would not run, in the usual partisan, political sense. But if the people command me to continue in this office and in this war, I have as little right to withdraw as the soldier has to leave his post in the line.

At the same time, I think I have a right to say to you and to the delegates to the coming Convention something which is personal—purely personal.

For myself, I do not want to run. By next Spring, I shall have been President and Commander in Chief of the Armed Forces for twelve years—three times elected by the people of this country under the American Constitutional system.

From the personal point of view, I believe that our economic system is on a sounder, more human basis than it was at the time of my first inauguration.

It is perhaps unnecessary to say that I have

thought only of the good of the American people. My principal objective, as you know, has been the protection of the rights and privileges and fortunes of what has been so well called the average of American citizens.

After many years of public service, therefore, my personal thoughts have turned to the day when I could return to civil life. All that is within me cries out to go back to my home on the Hudson River, to avoid public responsibilities, and to avoid also the publicity which in our democracy follows every step of the Nation's Chief Executive.

Such would be my choice. But we of this generation chance to live in a day and hour when our Nation has been attacked, and when its fu-

ture existence and the future existence of our chosen method of government are at stake.

To win this war wholeheartedly, unequivocally, and as quickly as we can is our task of the first importance. To win this war in such a way that there be no further world wars in the foreseeable future is our second objective. To provide occupations, and to provide a decent standard of living for our men in the armed forces after the war, and for all Americans, are the final objectives.

Therefore, reluctantly, but as a good soldier, I repeat that I will accept and serve in this office, if I am so ordered by the Commander in Chief of us all—the sovereign people of the United States.

"Total victory"

V-J DAY
1945

The war in Europe had ended in early May, 1945. Hitler (1889–1945) and Mussolini (1883–1945) were dead. Allied armies occupied Berlin and Rome. In the Pacific, half a million American soldiers, sailors, and airmen were preparing to assault Japan's southern beaches. An armada of 300 ships, including 22 battleships and more than 60 aircraft carriers and escort carriers, was armed to the gills. General George C. Marshall (1880–1959), chairman of the combined U.S. chiefs of staff, considered the use of as many as six atomic bombs in the pre-invasion bombardment. (Radiation fallout was still an unknown consequence.) Two days after Hiroshima (the devastating "new-type bomb" prompted the Imperial Government of Japan "to present to the United States Government a protest" via neutral Switzerland), the Soviet Union kept its word: Exactly three months after V-E Day, as promised, it entered the war in the Pacific. One-million Russian soldiers overran Japanese forces in Manchuria. The next day, the U.S. unleashed another atomic bomb, this time on the Japanese city of Nagasaki. On August 15, the Japanese gave up unconditionally—V-J Day. Harry S. Truman (1884–1972), President since Franklin Roosevelt's death in April, went for a swim and then, wearing a crisp double-breasted navy blue suit, blue shirt, and silver-and-blue striped tie with matching handkerchief, announced the appointment of Supreme Allied Commander General Douglas MacArthur (1880–1964) to receive the surrender.

I am speaking to you, the armed forces of the United States, as I did after V Day in Europe, at a high moment of history. The war, to which we have devoted all the resources and all the energy of our country for more than three and a half years, has *now* produced total victory over all our enemies.

This is a time for great rejoicing and a time for solemn contemplation. With the destructive force of war removed from the world, we can turn now to the grave task of preserving the peace which you gallant men and women have won. It is a task which requires our *most urgent* attention. It is one in which we must collaborate with our allies and the other nations of the world. They are as determined as we are that war must be abolished from the earth, if the earth, as *we know* it, is to remain. Civilization cannot survive another total war.

I think you know what is in the hearts of your countrymen on this night. They are thousands of miles away from most of you. Yet they are close to you in deep gratitude and in a solemn sense of obligation. They remember—and I know they will *never* forget—those who have gone from among you, those who are maimed, those who, thank God, are still safe after years of fighting and suffering and danger.

And I know that in this hour of victory their thoughts—like yours—are with your departed Commander-in-Chief, Franklin D. Roosevelt. This is the hour for which he so gallantly fought and so bravely died.

I think I know the American soldier and sailor. He does not want gratitude or sympathy. He had a job to do. He did not *like* it. But he did it. And how he did it!

Now, he wants to come back home and start again the life he loves—a life of peace and quiet, the life of the civilian.

But he wants to know that he can come back to a *good* life. He wants to know that his children will not have to go back to the life of the fox-hole and the bomber, the battleship and the submarine.

I speak in behalf of all your countrymen when I pledge you that we shall do everything in our power to make those wishes come true.

For some of you, I am sorry to say military service must continue for a time. We must keep an occupation force in the Pacific to clean out the militarism of Japan, just as we are cleaning out the militarism of Germany. The United Nations are determined that never again shall either of those countries be able to attack its peaceful neighbors.

But the great majority of you will be returned to civilian life as soon as the ships and planes can get you here. The task of moving so many men and women thousands of miles to their homes is a gigantic one. It will take months to accomplish. You have my pledge that we will do everything possible to speed it up. We want you back with us to make your contribution to our country's welfare and to a new world of peace.

The high tide of victory will carry us forward to great achievements in the era which lies ahead. But we can perform them only in a world which is free from the threat of war. We depend upon you, who have known war in all its horror, to keep this nation aware that only through cooperation among all nations can any nation remain wholly secure.

On this night of total victory, we salute *you* of the armed forces of the United States—wherever you may be. What a job you have done!

We are all waiting for the day when you will be home with us again.

Good luck and God bless you.

"A Jewish state has been proclaimed"

U.S. RECOGNIZES ISRAEL
1948

Two years after the Second World War, the United Nations General Assembly partitioned Palestine, which had been a British mandate since 1922, into two states: one Arab, one Jewish. Recognition of the Jewish state became one of the most divisive issues in the Truman Administration (1945–1953). Secretary of State George C. Marshall (1880–1959), greatly admired by President Harry S. Truman (1884–1972), vigorously and bitterly opposed recognition: The U.S. had overwhelming strategic interests in the Arab world. The President secretly assured the Jewish Agency for Palestine of U.S. support for the partition plan; Chaim Weizmann (1874–1952), president of the Jewish Agency, had told the President, "The choice for our people, Mr. President, is between statehood and extermination." Mr. Truman led from humanitarian considerations—millions of Jews had been murdered by genocidal Nazi Germany and millions of Jewish refugees were seeking sanctuary—but he refused to lift an embargo on arms shipments to the Jewish state.

This Government has been informed that a Jewish state has been proclaimed in Palestine, and recognition has been requested by the provisional government thereof.

The United States recognizes the provisional government as the *de facto* authority of the new State of Israel.

"The highest standards of democracy"

ELIMINATING MILITARY SEGREGATION
1948

Military segregation was a campaign issue in the 1940 and 1944 Presidential elections. In 1947, President Harry S. Truman's (1884–1972) committee on civil rights found military segregation "particularly repugnant" and urged its end. The Commander-in-Chief resolved to use his executive authority to advance civil rights in the face of a recalcitrant Congress and instructed the Secretary of Defense to eliminate military segregation. Predictably, the services resisted. In July, 1948, during the Presidential election campaign, Truman issued Executive Order No. 9981, establishing the President's Committee on Equality of Treatment and Opportunity in the Armed Forces. The Air Force now moved enthusiastically to bring in more black men. The Army resisted and the Navy did little. Ending the ten percent quota on black enlistment spurred integration during the Korean war (1950–1953). Black enlistments, in fact, had expanded beyond the capacity of existing black units to absorb them. Integration proceeded without the dire consequences that had been predicted. By the end of the war, all but ten percent of the Army's units were mixed.

WHEREAS it is essential that there be maintained in the armed services of the United States the highest standards of democracy, with equality of treatment and opportunity for all those who serve in our country's defense:

NOW, THEREFORE, by virtue of the authority vested in me as President of the United States, by the Constitution and the statues of the United States, and as Commander in Chief of the armed services, it is hereby ordered as follows:

1. It is hereby declared to be the policy of the President that there shall be equality of treatment and opportunity for all persons in the armed services without regard to race, color, religion or national origin. This policy shall be put into effect as rapidly as possible, having due regard to the time required to effectuate any necessary changes without impairing efficiency or morale.

2. There shall be created in the National Military Establishment an advisory committee to be known as the President's Committee on Equality of Treatment and Opportunity in the Armed Services, which shall be composed of seven members to be designated by the President.

3. The Committee is authorized on behalf of the President to examine into the rules, procedures and practices of the armed services in order to determine in what respect such rules, procedures and practices may be altered or improved with a view to carrying out the policy of this order. . . .

4. All executive departments and agencies of the Federal Government are authorized and directed to cooperate with the Committee in its work . . . .

"To give . . . cover and support"

TRUMAN ORDERS U.S. INTO THE KOREAN WAR
1950

Political tension permeated the Korean peninsula in the late Spring of 1950. Would South Korea invade North Korea? Would North Korea invade South Korea? Which of the two bitter adversaries would strike first to unite the Asian peninsula? The North Korean military attacked first. With Soviet approval of the invasion, North Koreans swept across the mid-peninsula boundary in late June and did not respond to the U.S.'s and the U.N. Security Council's calls for a cessation of hostilities. President Harry S. Truman (1884–1972), seeking to contain and reduce the spread of Communism, decided to "draw the line" in Korea. He ordered U.S. air and sea forces to give the South Korean government cover and support, then committed U.S. ground troops. He termed his decision a "police action;" through executive power, he bypassed Congress's responsibility for declaring war. North Korean forces made huge advances before Allied forces threw them back to the northern border. Chinese troops entered the war and, with rejuvenated North Korean armies, drove Allied troops reeling southward again. Advantages see-sawed. American bombing left North Korea looking like a moonscape. At least 33,629 Americans died on the battlefield in the "forgotten war;" another 20,617 U.S. military died from other causes. There was no peace treaty. The armistice, signed on July 27, 1953, held the shaky peace into the late 1990s. The two Koreas were divided at the 38th parallel.

In Korea the Government forces, which were armed to prevent border raids and to preserve internal security, were attacked by invading forces from North Korea. The Security Council of the United Nations called upon the invading troops to cease hostilities and to withdraw to the 38th parallel. This they have not done, but on the contrary have pressed the attack. The Security Council called upon all members of the United Nations to render every assistance to the United Nations in the execution of this resolution. In these circumstances I have ordered United States air and sea forces to give the Korean Government troops cover and support.

The attack upon Korea makes it plain beyond all doubt that Communism has passed beyond the use of subversion to conquer independent nations and will now use armed invasion and war. It has defied the orders of the Security Council of the United Nations issued to preserve international peace and security. In these circumstances the occupation of Formosa by Communist forces would be a direct threat to the security of the Pacific area and to the United States forces performing their lawful and necessary functions in that area. Accordingly I have ordered the Seventh Fleet to prevent any attack on Formosa. As a corollary of this action I am calling upon the Chinese Government on Formosa to cease all air and sea operations against the mainland. The Seventh Fleet will see that this is done. The determination of the future status of Formosa must await the restoration of security in the Pacific, a peace settlement with Japan, or consideration by the United Nations.

I have also directed that United States Forces in the Philippines be strengthened and that military assistance to the Philippine Government be accelerated.

I have similarly directed acceleration in the furnishing of military assistance to the forces of France and the Associated States in Indo-China and the dispatch of a military mission to provide close working relations with those forces.

I know that all members of the United Nations will consider carefully the consequences of this latest aggression in Korea in defiance of the Charter of the United Nations. A return to the rule of force in international affairs would have far reaching effects. The United States will continue to uphold the rule of law.

I have instructed Ambassador Austin, as the representative of the United States to the Security Council, to report these steps to the Council.

"With deep regret"

PRESIDENT TRUMAN FIRES GENERAL MACARTHUR
1951

A year into the Korean war (1950–1953), President Harry S. Truman (1884–1972) fired General Douglas MacArthur (1880–1964), chief of the United Nations Command assisting South Korean armies repelling the North Korean invaders. The two had quarrelled over strategic plans since China joined forces with North Korea. MacArthur publicly defied his Commander-in-Chief; Truman, who never tolerated insubordination, believed their differences were irreconcilable. Meeting on a mid-Pacific island, Truman summarily dismissed the popular officer. For a time the President's popularity plummeted (to 24 percent). MacArthur faded into retirement after an emotional address to a joint session of Congress. Later, the U.S. Joint Chiefs of Staff testified that MacArthur's proposed tactics could have led to a third World War.

With deep regret I have concluded that General of the Army Douglas MacArthur is unable to give his wholehearted support to the policies of the United States Government and of the United Nations in matters pertaining to his official duties. In view of the specific responsibilities imposed upon me by the Constitution of the United States and the added responsibility which has been entrusted to me by the United Nations, I have decided that I must make a change of command in the Far East. I have, therefore, relieved General MacArthur of his commands and have designated Lt. Gen. Matthew B. Ridgway as his successor.

Full and vigorous debate on matters of national policy is a vital element in the constitutional system of our free democracy. It is fundamental, however, that military commanders must be governed by the policies and directives issued to them in the manner provided by our laws and Constitution. In time of crisis, this consideration is particularly compelling.

General MacArthur's place in history as one of our greatest commanders is fully established. The nation owes him a debt of gratitude for the distinguished and exceptional service which he has rendered his country in posts of great responsibility. For that reason I repeat my regret at the necessity for the action I feel compelled to take in his case.

"Guard against . . . the military-industrial complex"

IKE'S FAREWELL
1961

Dwight David "Ike" Eisenhower (1890–1969)—known at West Point inexplicably as the "Swedish Jew"—was in the U.S. military for more than four decades. As Supreme Commander of Allied forces, he directed the invasion of Nazi-conquered western Europe during the Second World War. He was ultimately promoted to the rank of five-star general and named General of the Army. In 1952, he barely won the Republican nomination for President on the first ballot, then the general election overwhelmingly. Ike projected moral leadership. His two-term Presidency was what he termed, enigmatically, "dynamic conservatism." In his Farewell Address, he warned the nation about the potential, extraordinary influence of the "military-industrial" alliance on American life.

Three days from now, after half a century in the service of our country, I shall lay down the responsibilities of office as, in traditional and solemn ceremony, the authority of the presidency is vested in my successor.

This evening I come to you with a message of leavetaking and farewell, and to share a few final thoughts with you, my countrymen. . . .

We now stand ten years past the midpoint of a century that has witnessed four major wars among great nations. Three of these involved our own country. Despite these holocausts, America is today the strongest, the most influential, and most productive nation in the world. Understandably proud of this preeminence, we yet realize that America's leadership and prestige depend not merely upon our unmatched material progress, riches, and military strength but on how we use our power in the interests of world peace and human betterment.

Throughout America's adventure in free gov-

ernment our basic purposes have been to keep the peace, to foster progress in human achievement, and to enhance liberty, dignity, and integrity among people and among nations. To strive for less would be unworthy of a free and religious people. Any failure traceable to arrogance or our lack of comprehension or readiness to sacrifice would inflict upon us grievous hurt both at home and abroad. . . .

A vital element in keeping the peace is our military establishment. Our arms must be mighty, ready for instant action, so that no potential aggressor may be tempted to risk his own destruction.

Our military organization today bears little relation to that known by any of my predecessors in peacetime, or indeed by the fighting men of World War II or Korea.

Until the latest of our world conflicts, the United States had no armaments industry. American makers of plowshares could, with time and as required, make swords as well. But now we can no longer risk emergency improvisation of national defense; we have been compelled to create a permanent armaments industry of vast proportions. Added to this, 3.5 million men and women are directly engaged in the defense establishment. We annually spend on military security more than the net income of all United States corporations.

This conjunction of an immense military establishment and a large arms industry is new in the American experience. The total influence—economic, political, even spiritual—is felt in every city, every statehouse, every office of the federal government. We recognize the imperative need for this development. Yet we must not fail to comprehend its grave implications. Our toil, resources, and livelihood are all involved; so is the very structure of our society.

In the councils of government we must guard against the acquisition of unwarranted influence, whether sought or unsought, by the military-industrial complex. The potential for the disastrous rise of misplaced power exists and will persist.

We must never let the weight of this combination endanger our liberties or democratic processes. We should take nothing for granted. Only an alert and knowledgeable citizenry can compel the proper meshing of the huge industrial and military machinery of defense with our peaceful methods and goals so that security and liberty may prosper together. . . .

Today, the solitary inventor, tinkering in his shop, has been overshadowed by task forces of scientists in laboratories and testing fields. In the same fashion, the free university, historically the fountainhead of free ideas and scientific discovery, has experienced a revolution in the conduct of research. Partly because of the huge costs involved, a government contract becomes virtually a substitute for intellectual curiosity. For every old blackboard there are now hundreds of new electronic computers.

The prospect of domination of the nation's scholars by federal employment, project allocations, and the power of money is ever present and is gravely to be regarded. Yet, in holding scientific research and discovery in respect, as we should, we must also be alert to the equal and opposite danger that public policy could itself become the captive of a scientific-technological elite. It is the task of statesmanship to mold, to balance, and to integrate these and other forces, new and old, within the principles of our democratic system—ever aiming toward the supreme goals of our free society. . . .

Down the long lane of the history yet to be written, America knows that this world of ours, ever growing smaller, must avoid becoming a community of dreadful fear and hate, and be, instead, a proud confederation of mutual trust and respect. Such a confederation must be one of equals. The weakest must come to the conference table with the same confidence as do we, protected as we are by our moral, economic, and military strength. That table, though scarred by many past frustrations, cannot be abandoned for the certain agony of the battlefield. . . .

"Space is open to us now"

URGENT NATIONAL NEED: MEN ON THE MOON
1961

Four months into his Presidency, John F. Kennedy (1917–1963) exhorted a joint session of Congress that "if we are to win the battle between freedom and tyranny," the U.S. must take a "clearly leading role in space achievement." Because in many ways space might hold the key to the U.S.'s future, he proposed that within the decade the U.S. land a man on the Moon and, of course, return him safely to Earth. Eight years after Mr. Kennedy's proposal, two American astronauts walked on the powdery surface of Earth's only satellite, planted the Stars and Stripes, hopped around like kangaroos in fine, sandy particles, and returned safely home. Over the next three years, ten more astronauts walked on the cratered Moon, but none have since.

The Constitution imposes upon me the obligation to "from time to time give to the Congress information of the State on the Union." While this has traditionally been interpreted as an annual affair, this tradition has been broken in extraordinary times.

These are extraordinary times. And we face an extraordinary challenge. Our strength as well as our convictions have imposed upon this nation the role of leader in freedom's cause.

No role in history could be more difficult or more important. We stand for freedom. That is our conviction for ourselves—that is our only commitment to others. No friend, no neutral and no adversary should think otherwise. We are not against any man—or any nation—or any system—except as it is hostile to freedom. Nor am I here to present a new military doctrine, bearing any one name or aimed at any one area. I am here to promote the freedom doctrine. . . .

. . . . if we are to win the battle that is now going on around the world between freedom and tyranny, the dramatic achievements in space which occurred in recent weeks should have made clear to us all, as did the Sputnik in 1957, the impact of this adventure on the minds of men everywhere, who are attempting to make a determination of which road they should take. Since early in my term, our efforts in space have been under review. With the advice of the Vice President, who is Chairman of the National Space Council, we have examined where we are strong and where we are not, where we may succeed and where we may not. Now it is time to take longer strides—time for a great new American enterprise—time for this nation to take a clearly leading role in space achievement, which in many ways may hold the key to our future on earth.

I believe we possess all the resources and talents necessary. But the facts of the matter are that we have never made the national decisions or marshalled the national resources required for such leadership. We have never specified long-range goals on an urgent time schedule, or managed our resources and our time so as to insure their fulfillment.

Recognizing the head start obtained by the

Soviets with their large rocket engines, which gives them many months of lead-time, and recognizing the likelihood that they will exploit this lead for some time to come in still more impressive successes, we nevertheless are required to make new efforts on our own. For while we cannot guarantee that we shall one day be first, we can guarantee that any failure to make this effort will make us last. We take an additional risk by making it in full view of the world—but as shown by the feat of astronaut Shepard, this very risk enhances our stature when we are successful. But this is not merely a race. Space is open to us now; and our eagerness to share its meaning is not governed by the efforts of others. We go into space because whatever mankind must undertake, free men must fully share.

I therefore ask the Congress, above and beyond the increases I have earlier requested for space activities, to provide the funds which are needed to meet the following national goals:

First, I believe that this nation should commit itself to achieving the goal, before this decade is out, of landing a man on the moon and returning him safely to the earth. No single space project in this period will be more impressive to mankind, or more important for the long-range exploration of space; and none will be so difficult or expensive to accomplish. We propose to accelerate development of the appropriate lunar space craft. We propose to develop alternate liquid and solid fuel boosters, much larger than any now being developed, until certain which is superior. We propose additional funds for other engine development and for unmanned explo-rations—explorations which are particularly important for one purpose which this nation will never overlook: the survival of the man who first makes this daring flight. But in a very real sense, it will not be one man going to the moon—if we make this judgment affirmatively, it will be an entire nation. For all of us must work to put him there.

Secondly, an additional 23 million dollars, together with 7 million dollars already available, to accelerate development of the ROVER nuclear rocket. This gives promise of some day providing a means for even more exciting and ambitious exploration of space, perhaps beyond the moon, perhaps to the very end of the solar system itself.

Third, an additional 50 million dollars will make the most of our present leadership, by accelerating the use of space satellites for world-wide communications.

Fourth, an additional 75 million dollars—of which 53 million dollars is for the Weather Bureau—will help give us at the earliest possible time a satellite system for world-wide weather observation.

Let it be clear—and this is a judgment which the Members of Congress must finally make—let it be clear that I am asking the Congress and the country to accept a firm commitment to a new course of action—a course which will last for many years and carry very heavy costs of 531 million dollars in fiscal 1962—an estimated seven to nine billion dollars additional over the next five years. If we are to go only half way, or reduce our sights in the face of difficulty, in my judgment it would be better not to go at all. . . .

"The finest men and women"

THE PEACE CORPS
1961

President John F. Kennedy (1917–1963) was especially proud of the Peace Corps and its mostly young men and women volunteers, who were motivated only by the kind of dedication he had urged. These several thousand Americans lived in villages of under-developed nations, mostly in Africa and Central America, that were eager for skilled hands. They filled the gap between technical advisers and local experts on the one hand and relatively unskilled local labor on the other. The compensation: the satisfaction of helping others. At 2 A.M., on October 14, 1960, Presidential candidate Kennedy proposed the Peace Corps, to students on the steps of the Union at the University of Michigan: "On your willingness . . . to serve one year or two years in the service [and] on your willingness to contribute part of your life to this country I think will depend the answer [to] whether a free society can compete." In 1996, there were 6,529 Peace Corps volunteers; average age, 29; 55 percent female—serving in 94 countries.

With the enactment of this legislation, an avenue is provided by which Americans can serve their country in the cause of world peace and understanding and simultaneously assist other nations toward their legitimate goals of freedom and opportunity.

I want particularly to express pleasure at the bipartisan effort and support in the shaping of this new Agency.

Already more than thirteen thousand Americans have offered their services to the Peace Corps. By the end of the year almost one thousand will be serving overseas or completing their training in the United States. By July of next year we hope to have twenty-seven hundred in training or abroad.

These men and women are going overseas at the request of the host nations. They will be doing specific, needed jobs. They will be working at a level and living at a level comparable to the citizens of the foreign nations. They will be farmers and teachers, craftsmen and nurses, doctors and technicians of all kinds. They will be a cross-section of the finest men and women that this nation has to offer.

The sure sign of a good idea is that you can follow it, and I am pleased that several other nations have decided to establish Peace Corps agencies of their own.

Much credit for what has been done must go to Congressional leaders like the men and women in this room, and the scores of other dedicated Americans who have given their advice and counsel.

Also I want to express my esteem for the most effective lobbyist on the Washington scene, Mr. Sargent Shriver.

"I DO SOLEMNLY SWEAR (OR AFFIRM)"

"By whatever means may be necessary."

INTERDICTING SOVIET WEAPONS TO CUBA

1962

When United States surveillance, or photo-spy, planes discovered that the Soviet Union was building long-range offensive-missile sites in Cuba, only 90 miles southeast of Florida, President John F. Kennedy (1917–1963) considered an air raid on the emplacements, but instead ordered interdiction, a strict blockade to halt the delivery of additional offensive weapons. "The purpose of the bases," the President told a tense broadcast audience, "can be none other than to provide a nuclear-strike capability against the western hemisphere: Washington, the Panama Canal, Mexico City, Hudson Bay, Canada, and Lima, Peru." In addition, Soviet bombers capable of carrying nuclear weapons were deployed to Premier Fidel Castro's (born 1926) Caribbean island. Soviet Premier Nikita Khrushchev (1894–1971) blinked; urged by the United States "to move the world back from the abyss of destruction," he ordered Russian marine transports home, withdrew the missiles, and dismantled the launch sites.

WHEREAS the peace of the world and the security of the United States and of all American States are endangered by reason of the establishment by the Sino-Soviet powers of an offensive military capability in Cuba, including bases for ballistic missiles with a potential range covering most of North and South America;

WHEREAS by a Joint Resolution passed by the Congress of the United States and approved on October 3, 1962, it was declared that the United States is determined to prevent by whatever means may be necessary, including the use of arms, the Marxist-Leninist regime in Cuba from extending, by force or the threat of force, its aggressive or subversive activities to any part of this hemisphere, and to prevent in Cuba the creation or use of an externally supported military capability endangering the security of the United States; and

WHEREAS the Organ of Consultation of the American Republics meeting in Washington on October 23, 1962, recommended that the Member States, in accordance with Articles 6 and 8 of the Inter-American Treaty of Reciprocal Assistance, take all measures, individually and collectively, including the use of armed force, which they may deem necessary to ensure that the Government of Cuba cannot continue to receive from the Sino-Soviet powers military material and related supplies which may threaten the peace and security of the Continent and to prevent the missiles in Cuba with offensive capability from ever becoming an active threat to the peace and security of the Continent:

NOW, THEREFORE, I, JOHN F. KENNEDY, President of the United States of America, acting under and by virtue of the authority conferred upon me by the Constitution and statutes of the United States, in accordance with the aforementioned resolutions of the United States Congress and of the Organ of Consultation of the American Republics, and to defend the security of the United States, do hereby proclaim that the forces under my command are ordered, beginning at 2:00 P.M. Greenwich time October 24, 1962, to interdict, subject to the instructions herein contained, the delivery of offensive weapons and associated materiel to Cuba.

For the purposes of this Proclamation, the following are declared to be prohibited materiel:

Surface-to-surface missiles; bomber aircraft; bombs, air-to-surface rockets and guided missiles; warheads for any of the above weapons; mechanical or electronic equipment to support or operate the above items; and any other classes of materiel hereafter designated by the Secretary of Defense for the purpose of effectuating this Proclamation.

To enforce this order, the Secretary of Defense shall take appropriate measures to prevent the delivery of prohibited materiel to Cuba, employing the land, sea and air forces of the United States in cooperation with any forces that may be made available by other American States.

The Secretary of Defense may make such regulations and issue such directives as he deems necessary to ensure the effectiveness of this order, including the designation, within a rea-sonable distance of Cuba, of prohibited or restricted zones and of prescribed routes.

Any vessel or craft which may be proceeding toward Cuba may be intercepted and may be directed to identify itself, its cargo, equipment and stores and its ports of call, to stop, to lie to, to submit to visit and search, or to proceed as directed. Any vessel or craft which fails or refuses to respond to or comply with directions shall be subject to being taken into custody. Any vessel or craft which it is believed is en route to Cuba and may be carrying prohibited materiel or may itself constitute such materiel shall, wherever possible, be directed to proceed to another destination of its own choice and shall be taken into custody if it fails or refuses to obey such directions. All vessels or craft taken into custody shall be sent into a port of the United States for appropriate disposition.

In carrying out this order, force shall not be used except in case of failure or refusal to comply with directions, or with regulations or directives of the Secretary of Defense issued hereunder, after reasonable efforts have been made to communicate them to the vessel or craft, or in case of self-defense. In any case, force shall be used only to the extent necessary.

"I would have preferred to carry through"

PRESIDENT RICHARD M. NIXON RESIGNS

1974

The liberal editor, critic, and columnist Hendrik Hertzberg (born 1943) reminded his *New Yorker* readers that when President Richard M. Nixon (1913–1994) wasn't bombing villages in southeast Asia or bugging "enemies," he was a progressive Republican: Sometimes reluctantly, sometimes enthusiastically, Mr. Nixon established the Environmental Protection Agency and the Occupational Safety and Health Administration; dismantled the dual, segregated public school systems of the South and made affirmative action a central part of civil rights enforcement; signed the landmark Clean Air Act of 1970; indexed Social Security payments to the cost of living; greatly expanded the Food Stamp Program and Federal support for the arts and the humanities; instituted mandatory wage and price controls; proposed a comprehensive health plan based on employer mandates; and proposed to replace the welfare system with a vast Family Assistance Plan, which would have tripled the number of recipients, mostly by extending aid to the working poor. When it was learned that President Nixon had paid only $792.81 in Federal income taxes on an income of $268,777 in 1970 and just $878.03 the following year, the practice of politicians making their tax returns public blossomed. Facing impeachment because of his involvement in the Watergate "second-rate" burglary and cover-up scandal, President Nixon resigned in the second year of his second term. In his last hour in the White House, he addressed his staff and Cabinet.

• • • In all the decisions I have made in my public life, I have always tried to do what was best for the Nation. Throughout the long and difficult period of Watergate, I have felt it was my duty to persevere, to make every possible effort to complete the term of office to which you elected me.

In the past few days, however, it has become evident to me that I no longer have a strong enough political base in the Congress to justify continuing that effort. As long as there was such a base, I felt strongly that it was necessary to see the constitutional process through to its conclusion, that to do otherwise would be unfaithful to the spirit of that deliberately difficult process and a dangerously destabilizing precedent for the future.

But with the disappearance of that base, I now believe that the constitutional purpose has been served, and there is no longer a need for the process to be prolonged.

I would have preferred to carry through to the finish, whatever the personal agony it would have involved, and my family unanimously urged me to do so. But the interests of the Nation must always come before any personal considerations.

THE WHITE HOUSE

WASHINGTON

August 9, 1974

Dear Mr. Secretary:

I hereby resign the Office of President of the
United States.

Sincerely,

s/ Richard Nixon

The Honorable Henry A. Kissinger
The Secretary of State
Washington, D. C. 20520

From the discussions I have had with Congressional and other leaders, I have concluded that because of the Watergate matter, I might not have the support of the Congress that I would consider necessary to back the very difficult decisions and carry out the duties of this office in the way the interests of the Nation will require.

I have never been a quitter. To leave office before my term is completed is abhorrent to every instinct in my body. But as President, I must put the interests of America first. America needs a full-time President and a full-time Congress, particularly at this time with problems we face at home and abroad.

To continue to fight through the months ahead for my personal vindication would almost totally absorb the time and attention of both the President and the Congress in a period when our entire focus should be on the great issues of peace abroad and prosperity without inflation at home.

Therefore, I shall resign the Presidency effective at noon tomorrow. Vice President Ford will be sworn in as President at that hour in this office. . . .

By taking this action, I hope that I will have hastened the start of that process of healing which is so desperately needed in America.

I regret deeply any injuries that may have been

"I Do Solemnly Swear (or Affirm)"

done in the course of the events that led to this decision. I would say only that if some of my judgments were wrong—and some were wrong—they were made in what I believed at the time to be the best interest of the Nation.

To those who have stood with me during these past difficult months—to my family, my friends, to many others who joined in supporting my cause because they believed it was right— I will be eternally grateful for your support.

And to those who have not felt able to give me your support, let me say I leave with no bitterness toward those who have opposed me, because all of us, in the final analysis, have been concerned with the good of the country, however our judgments might differ.

So, let us all now join together in affirming that common commitment and in helping our new President succeed for the benefit of all Americans. . . .

I think the record should show that this is one of those spontaneous things that we always arrange whenever the President comes in to speak, and it will be so reported in the press, and we don't mind, because they have to call it as they see it.

But on our part, believe me, it is spontaneous.

You are here to say goodby to us, and we don't have a good word for it in English—the best is *au revoir*. We will see you again. . . .

This house, for example—I was thinking of it as we walked down this hall, and I was comparing it to some of the great houses of the world that I have been in. This isn't the biggest house. Many, and most, in even smaller countries, are much bigger. This isn't the finest house. Many in Europe, particularly, and in China, Asia, have paintings of great, great value, things that we just don't have here and, probably, will never have until we are 1,000 years old or older.

But this is the best house. It is the best house, because it has something far more important than numbers of people who serve, far more important than numbers of rooms or how big it is, far more important than numbers of magnificent pieces of art.

This house has a great heart, and that heart comes from those who serve. I was rather sorry they didn't come down. We said goodby to them upstairs. But they are really great. And I recall after so many times I have made speeches, and some of them pretty tough, yet, I always come back, or after a hard day—and my days usually have run rather long—I would always get a lift from them, because I might be a little down but they always smiled. . . .

As I pointed out last night, sure, we have done some things wrong in this Administration, and the top man always takes the responsibility, and I have never ducked it. But I want to say one thing: We can be proud of it—5 1/2 years. No man or no woman came into this Administration and left it with more of this world's goods than when he came in. No man or no woman ever profited at the public expense or the public till. That tells something about you. I only wish that I were a wealthy man—at the present time, I have got to find a way to pay my taxes and if I were, I would like to recompense you for the sacrifices that all of you have made to serve in government. . . .

I remember my old man. I think that they would have called him sort of a little man, common man. He didn't consider himself that way. You know what he was? He was a streetcar motorman first, and then he was a farmer, and then he had a lemon ranch. It was the poorest lemon ranch in California, I can assure you. He sold it before they found oil on it. And then he was a grocer. But he was a great man, because he did his job, and every job counts up to the hilt, regardless of what happens.

Nobody will ever write a book, probably, about my mother. Well, I guess all of you would say this about your mother—my mother was a saint. And I think of her, two boys dying of tuberculosis, nursing four others in order that she could take care of my older brother for 3 years in Arizona, and seeing each of them die, and when they died, it was like one of her own.

Yes, she will have no books written about her. But she was a saint. . . .

We think sometimes when things happen that don't go the right way; we think that when you don't pass the bar exam the first time—I happened to, but I was just lucky; I mean, my writing was so poor the bar examiner said, "We have just got to let the guy through." We think that when someone dear to us dies, we think that when we lose an election, we think that when we suffer a defeat that all is ended. We think, as T.R. said, that the light had left his life forever.

Not true. It is only a beginning, always. The young must know it; the old must know it. It must always sustain us, because the greatness comes not when things go always good for you, but the greatness comes and you are really tested, when you take some knocks, some disappointments, when sadness comes, because only if you have been in the deepest valley can you ever know how magnificent it is to be on the highest mountain. . . .

"I cannot prolong the bad dreams"

PRESIDENT FORD PARDONS FORMER PRESIDENT NIXON

1974

One month after President Richard M. Nixon (1913–1994) had resigned because of findings in the Watergate burglary and cover-up investigation—the handwriting was on the wall when leading Republican Congressmen abandoned support—his hand-picked successor, Gerald R. Ford (born 1913), gave the disgraced President a full pardon for all Federal crimes he "committed or may have committed or taken part in" during his Presidency. President Ford declared he had done "the right thing," vowing, "There was no deal, period." Public disapproval of the pardon may have cost Mr. Ford the 1976 Presidential election. In 1973, President Nixon had nominated Congressman Ford to succeed Vice President Spiro T. Agnew (1918-1996), who had quit in an unrelated scandal, accepting monetary kickbacks when he was Governor of Maryland.

I have come to a decision which I felt I should tell you and all of my fellow American citizens, as soon as I was certain in my own mind and in my own conscience that it is the right thing to do.

I have learned already in this office that the difficult decisions always come to this desk. I must admit that many of them do not look at all the same as the hypothetical questions that I have answered freely and perhaps too fast on previous occasions.

My customary policy is to try and get all the facts and to consider the opinions of my countrymen and to take counsel with my most valued friends. But these seldom agree, and in the end, the decision is mine. To procrastinate, to agonize, and to wait for a more favorable turn of events that may never come or more compelling external pressures that may as well be wrong as right, is itself a decision of sorts and a weak and potentially dangerous course for a President to follow.

I have promised to uphold the Constitution, to do what is right as God gives me to see the right, and to do the very best that I can for America.

I have asked your help and your prayers, not only when I became President but many times since. The Constitution is the supreme law of our land and it governs our actions as citizens. Only the laws of God, which govern our consciences, are superior to it.

As we are a nation under God, so I am sworn to uphold our laws with the help of God. And I have sought such guidance and searched my own conscience with special diligence to determine the right thing for me to do with respect to my predecessor in this place, Richard Nixon, and his loyal wife and family.

Theirs is an American tragedy in which we all have played a part. It could go on and on and on, or someone must write the end to it. I have concluded that only I can do that, and if I can, I must.

There are no historic or legal precedents to which I can turn in this matter, none that precisely fit the circumstances of a private citizen who has resigned the Presidency of the United States. But it is common knowledge that serious allegations and accusations hang like a sword over our former President's head, threatening his health as he tries to reshape his life, a great part of which was spent in the service of this country and by the mandate of its people.

After years of bitter controversy and divisive national debate, I have been advised, and I am compelled to conclude that many months and perhaps more years will have to pass before Richard Nixon could obtain a fair trial by jury in any jurisdiction of the United States under governing decisions of the Supreme Court.

I deeply believe in equal justice for all Americans, whatever their station or former station. The law, whether human or divine, is no respecter of persons; but the law is a respecter of reality.

The facts, as I see them, are that a former President of the United States, instead of enjoying equal treatment with any other citizen accused of violating the law, would be cruelly and excessively penalized either in preserving the presumption of his innocence or in obtaining a speedy determination of his guilt in order to repay a legal debt to society.

During this long period of delay and potential litigation, ugly passions would again be aroused. And our people would again be polarized in their opinions. And the credibility of our free institutions of government would again be challenged at home and abroad.

In the end, the courts might well hold that Richard Nixon had been denied due process, and the verdict of history would even more be inconclusive with respect to those charges arising out of the period of his Presidency, of which I am presently aware.

But it is not the ultimate fate of Richard Nixon that most concerns me, though surely it deeply troubles every decent and every compassionate person. My concern is the immediate future of this great country.

In this, I dare not depend upon my personal sympathy as a long-time friend of the former President, nor my professional judgment as a lawyer, and I do not.

As President, my primary concern must always be the greatest good of all the people of the United States whose servant I am. As a man, my first consideration is to be true to my own convictions and my own conscience.

My conscience tells me clearly and certainly that I cannot prolong the bad dreams that continue to reopen a chapter that is closed. My conscience tells me that only I, as President, have the constitutional power to firmly shut and seal this book. My conscience tells me it is my duty, not merely to proclaim domestic tranquillity but to use every means that I have to insure it.

I do believe that the buck stops here, that I cannot rely upon public opinion polls to tell me what is right.

I do believe that right makes might and that if I am wrong, 10 angels swearing I was right would make no difference.

I do believe, with all my heart and mind and spirit, that I, not as President but as a humble servant of God, will receive justice without mercy if I fail to show mercy.

Finally, I feel that Richard Nixon and his loved ones have suffered enough and will continue to suffer, no matter what I do, no matter what we, as a great and good nation, can do together to make his goal of peace come true.

"Now, therefore, I, Gerald R. Ford, President of the United States, pursuant to the pardon power conferred upon me by Article II, Section 2, of the Constitution, have granted and by these presents do grant a full, free, and absolute pardon unto Richard Nixon for all offenses against the United States which he, Richard Nixon, has committed or may have committed or taken part in during the period from July (January) 20, 1969 through August 9, 1974."

"In witness whereof, I have hereunto set my hand this eighth day of September, in the year of our Lord nineteen hundred and seventy-four, and of the Independence of the United States of America the one hundred and ninety-ninth."

"Panama shall . . . maintain military forces"

TREATY CONCERNING THE PERMANENT NEUTRALITY AND OPERATION OF THE PANAMA CANAL
1977

The United States became a two-ocean global power with the completion (1914) of the Panama Canal. An engineering marvel, it was, apart from war efforts and space programs, the largest, most costly single project since antiquity. Its construction was the Moon-shot of its era. President Jimmy Carter (born 1924) was particularly proud of the negotiation that at the turn of the century will transfer control of the canal to the Republic of Panama: "The American people are big enough and strong enough, courageous enough and understanding enough to be proud" as well. He noted that the Canal Treaty of 1903 had been "drafted in a world of manifest destiny so different from ours" that it had "become an obstacle to better relations with Latin America." The U.S. had won its right to a Canal Zone ten miles wide across the Isthmus of Panama through tacit support for a pocket revolution engineered by promoters of the canal and dissidents in Colombia's province of Panama. Senate debate on President Carter's accord was the most dramatic battle of its kind since the Senate had blocked U.S. membership in the League of Nations after the First World War. In his Farewell Address, President Carter reported that the new partnership with Panama was a model for large and small nations; redress of a great wrong had been long overdue.

The United States of America and the Republic of Panama have agreed upon the following:

ARTICLE I

The Republic of Panama declares that the Canal, as an international transit waterway, shall be permanently neutral in accordance with the regime established in this Treaty. The same regime of neutrality shall apply to any other international waterway that may be built either partially or wholly in the territory of the Republic of Panama.

ARTICLE II

The Republic of Panama declares the neutrality of the Canal in order that both in time of peace and in time of war it shall remain secure and open to peaceful transit by the vessels of all nations on terms of entire equality, so that there will be no discrimination against any nation, or its citizens or subjects, concerning the conditions or charges of transit, or for any other reason, and so that the Canal, and therefore the Isthmus of Panama, shall not be the target of reprisals in any armed conflict between other nations of the world. . . .

(c) The requirement that transiting vessels commit no acts of hostility while in the Canal; . . .

ARTICLE III

. . . (e) Vessels of war and auxiliary vessels of all nations shall at all times be entitled to transit the Canal, irrespective of their internal operation, means of propulsion, origin, destination or armament, without being subjected, as a condition of transit, to inspection, search or surveillance. . . .

ARTICLE IV

The United States of America and the Republic of Panama agree to maintain the regime of neutrality established in this Treaty, which shall be maintained in order that the Canal shall remain permanently neutral, notwithstanding the termination of any other treaties entered into by the two Contracting Parties. . . .

ARTICLE V

After the termination of the Panama Canal Treaty, only the Republic of Panama shall operate the Canal and maintain military forces, defense sites and military installations within its national territory.

ARTICLE VI

1. In recognition of the important contributions of the United States of America and of the Republic of Panama to the construction, operation, maintenance, and protection and defense of the Canal, vessels of war and auxiliary vessels of those nations shall, notwithstanding any other provisions of this Treaty, be entitled to transit the Canal irrespective of their internal operation, means of propulsion, origin, destination, armament or cargo carried. Such vessels of war and auxiliary vessels will be entitled to transit the Canal expeditiously.

2. The United States of America, so long as it has responsibility for the operation of the Canal, may continue to provide the Republic of Colombia toll-free transit through the Canal for its troops, vessels and materials of war. Thereafter, the Republic of Panama may provide the Republic of Colombia and the Republic of Costa Rica with the right of toll-free transit. . . .

PROTOCOL TO THE TREATY CONCERNING THE PERMANENT NEUTRALITY AND OPERATION OF THE PANAMA CANAL

Whereas the maintenance of the neutrality of the Panama Canal is important not only to the commerce and security of the United States of America and the Republic of Panama, but to the peace and security of the Western Hemisphere and to the interests of world commerce as well;

Whereas the regime of neutrality which the United States of America and the Republic of Panama have agreed to maintain will ensure permanent access to the Canal by vessels of all nations on the basis of entire equality; and

Whereas the said regime of effective neutrality shall constitute the best protection for the Canal and shall ensure the absence of any hostile act against it; . . . .

"Problems . . . are . . . deeper than gasoline lines"

PRESIDENT CARTER ON AMERICA'S "MALAISE"
1979

During the domestic energy crisis, which was triggered by steep prices for foreign oil, President Jimmy Carter (born 1924) addressed the American public on the nation's "malaise." He had perceived a general crisis in self-confidence and trust in the nation: "Wounds were very deep. They never have been healed." Assassination, Vietnam, Watergate, inflation—he spoke about the need to have faith in the United States, not only in the government but also in one's own ability to solve great problems. He noted growing disrespect for churches, schools, news media, and other institutions. He acknowledged serious problems, but expressed confidence that they could be solved "if we were willing to work together with courage and with concern for one another." Mr. Carter considered it "one of my best speeches, and the response to it was overwhelmingly positive. Intrigued by the mystery of what I would say, about 100-million people had listened, perhaps the largest American audience I ever had." He also proposed alternatives to foreign oil. The President had prepared for the speech by making unannounced trips to private homes near Pittsburgh, Pennsylvania, and Martinsburg, West Virginia, spending a few hours talking with a small group in each community.

• • • It's clear that the true problems of our Nation are much deeper—deeper than gasoline lines or energy shortages, deeper even than inflation or recession. And I realize more than ever that as President I need your help. So, I decided to reach out and listen to the voices of America.

I invited to Camp David people from almost every segment of our society—business and labor, teachers and preachers, Governors, mayors, and private citizens. And then I left Camp David to listen to other Americans, men and women like you. It has been an extraordinary 10 days, and I want to share with you what I've heard.

First of all, I got a lot of personal advice. Let me quote a few of the typical comments that I wrote down.

This from a southern Governor: "Mr. President, you are not leading this Nation—you're just managing the Government."

"You don't see the people enough any more."

"Some of your Cabinet members don't seem loyal. There is not enough discipline among your disciples."

"Don't talk to us about politics or the mechanics of government, but about an understanding of our common good."

"Mr. President, we're in trouble. Talk to us about blood and sweat and tears."

"If you lead, Mr. President, we will follow."

"I Do Solemnly Swear (or Affirm)"

Many people talked about themselves and about the condition of our Nation. This from a young woman in Pennsylvania: "I feel so far from government. I feel like ordinary people are excluded from political power."

And this from a young Chicano: "Some of us have suffered from recession all our lives."

"Some people have wasted energy, but others haven't had anything to waste."

And this from a religious leader: "No material shortage can touch the important things like God's love for us or our love for one another."

And I like this one particularly from a black woman who happens to be the mayor of a small Mississippi town: "The big-shots are not the only ones who are important. Remember, you can't sell anything on Wall Street unless someone digs it up somewhere else first."

This kind of summarized a lot of other statements: "Mr. President, we are confronted with a moral and a spiritual crisis."

Several of our discussions were on energy, and I have a notebook full of comments and advice. . . .

These. . . . confirmed my belief in the decency and the strength and the wisdom of the American people, but it also bore out some of my long-standing concerns about our Nation's underlying problems.

I know, of course, being President, that government actions and legislation can be very important. That's why I've worked hard to put my campaign promises into law—and I have to admit, with just mixed success. But after listening to the American people I have been reminded again that all the legislation in the world can't fix what's wrong with America. So, I want to speak to you first tonight about a subject even more serious than energy or inflation. I want to talk to you right now about a fundamental threat to American democracy.

I do not mean our political and civil liberties. They will endure. And I do not refer to the outward strength of America, a nation that is at peace tonight everywhere in the world, with unmatched economic power and military might.

The threat is nearly invisible in ordinary ways. It is a crisis of confidence. It is a crisis that strikes at the very heart and soul and spirit of our national will. We can see this crisis in the growing doubt about the meaning of our own lives and in the loss of a unity of purpose for our Nation.

The erosion of our confidence in the future is threatening to destroy the social and the political fabric of America. . . .

In a nation that was proud of hard work, strong families, close-knit communities, and our faith in God, too many of us now tend to worship self-indulgence and consumption. Human identity is no longer defined by what one does, but by what one owns. But we've discovered that owning things and consuming things does not satisfy our longing for meaning. We've learned that piling up material goods cannot fill the emptiness of lives which have no confidence or purpose.

The symptoms of this crisis of the American spirit are all around us. For the first time in the history of our country a majority of our people believe that the next 5 years will be worse than the past 5 years. Two-thirds of our people do not even vote. The productivity of American workers is actually dropping, and the willingness of Americans to save for the future has fallen below that of all other people in the Western world.

As you know, there is a growing disrespect for government and for churches and for schools, the news media, and other institutions. This is not a message of happiness or reassurance, but it is the truth and it is a warning.

These changes did not happen overnight. They've come upon us gradually over the last generation, years that were filled with shocks and tragedy. . . .

Looking for a way out of this crisis, our people have turned to the Federal Government and found it isolated from the mainstream of our Nation's life. Washington, D.C., has become an island. The gap between our citizens and our Government has never been so wide. The people are looking for honest answers, not easy answers; clear leadership, not false claims and evasiveness and politics as usual. . . .

Often you see paralysis and stagnation and drift. You don't like it, and neither do I. What can we do?

First of all, we must face the truth, and then we can change our course. We simply must have faith in each other, faith in our ability to govern ourselves, and faith in the future of this Nation. Restoring that faith and that confidence to America is now the most important task we face. It is a true challenge of this generation of Americans.

. . . . I will do my best, but I will not do it alone. Let your voice be heard. Whenever you have a chance, say something good about our country. With God's help and for the sake of our Nation, it is time for us to join hands in America. Let us commit ourselves together to a rebirth of the American spirit. Working together with our common faith we cannot fail.

"Responded to the wishes of its people"

THE BERLIN WALL CRACKS

1989

President George W. Bush (born 1924) admitted that he was surprised that the Berlin Wall, put up (it's been said) with the tacit approval of President John F. Kennedy (1917–1963), fell when it did. Neither he nor anyone else, he confessed, had accurately predicted the speed of the changes that were underway in Eastern Europe. For so much of the four decades since the end of the Second World War, the test of Western resolve, the contest between the free and the unfree, was symbolized by an island of hope behind the Iron Curtain—Berlin, cut in two by The Wall, the notorious artifact of the Cold War. Without The Wall, the 44-year-old Cold War between the Soviet Union and the "free world" came to an end. People and goods flowed between East and West Germany and through Berlin for the first time in 28 years.

• • • Before going into my main remarks, let me just say a word about the momentous events in East Germany. I was moved, as you all were, by the pictures of Berliners from East and West—standing atop the wall with chisels and hammers—celebrating the opening of the most vivid symbol of the Iron Curtain. And then today, just on the plane coming down, I read a report where 18 new border crossings would be made in the wall in the near future.

And to be honest, I doubted that this would happen in the very first year of this administration. Twenty-eight years after the desperate days of 1961, when tanks faced off at Checkpoint Charlie and that terrible barrier was built—now the East German Government has responded to the wishes of its people. And while no one really accurately predicted the speed of the changes underway in Eastern Europe—and certainly I didn't. . . .

"The right thing to do"

GAYS IN THE MILITARY

1993

The new United States policy toward homosexuals in the military was a difficult challenge and "a real step forward." President Bill Clinton (born 1946), speaking at Fort McNair, the National Defense University, in Washington, D.C., insisted that it "provide a sensible balance between the rights of the individual and the needs of our military to remain the world's number-one fighting force."

I have come here today to discuss a difficult challenge and one which has received an enormous amount of publicity and public and private debate over the last several months—our nation's policy toward homosexuals in the military.

I believe the policy I am announcing today represents a real step forward. But I know it will raise concerns in some of your minds. So I wanted you to hear my thinking and my decision directly and in person, because I respect you and because you are among the elite who will lead our Armed Forces into the next century, and because you will have to put this policy into effect and I expect your help in doing it.

The policy I am announcing today is, in my judgment, the right thing to do and the best way to do it. It is right because it provides greater protection to those who happen to be homosexual and want to serve their country honorably in uniform, obeying all the military's rules against sexual misconduct.

It is the best way to proceed because it provides a sensible balance between the rights of the individual and the needs of our military to remain the world's number one fighting force. As President of all the American people, I am pledged to protect and to promote individual rights. As Commander in Chief, I am pledged to protect and

advance our security. In this policy, I believe we have come close to meeting both objectives.

Let me start with this clear fact: Our military is one of our greatest accomplishments and our most valuable assets. It is the world's most effective and powerful fighting force, bar none. . . .

We owe a great deal to the men and women who protect us through their service, their sacrifice and their dedication. And we owe it to our own security to listen hard to them and act carefully as we consider any changes in the military. A force ready to fight must maintain the highest priority under all circumstances.

Let me review the events which bring us here today. Before I ran for President, this issue was already upon us. Some of the members of the military returning from the Gulf War announced their homosexuality in order to protest the ban. The military's policy has been questioned in college ROTC programs. Legal challenges have been filed in court, including one that has since succeeded. In 1991, the Secretary of Defense Dick Cheney was asked about reports that the Defense Department spent an alleged $500 million to separate and replace about 17,000 homosexuals from the military service during the 1980s, in spite of the findings of a government report saying there was no reason to believe that they could not serve effectively and with distinction.

Shortly thereafter, while giving a speech at the Kennedy School of Government at Harvard, I was asked by one of the students what I thought of this report and what I thought of lifting the ban. This question had never before been presented to me, and I had never had the opportunity to discuss it with anyone. I stated then what I still believe: that I thought there ought to be a presumption that people who wish to do so should be able to serve their country if they are willing to conform to the high standards of the military, and that the emphasis should be always on people's conduct, not their status.

For me, and this is very important, this issue has never been one of group rights, but rather of individual ones—of the individual opportunity to serve and the individual responsibility to conform to the highest standards of military conduct. For people who are willing to play by the rules, able to serve, and make a contribution, I believe then and I believe now we should give them the chance to do so.

The central facts of this issue are not much in dispute. First, notwithstanding the ban, there have been and are homosexuals in the military service who serve with distinction. I have had the privilege of meeting some of these men and women, and I have been deeply impressed by their devotion to duty and to country.

Second, there is no study showing them to be less capable or more prone to misconduct than heterosexual soldiers. Indeed, all the information we have indicates that they are not less capable or more prone to misbehavior.

Third, misconduct is already covered by the laws and rules which also cover activities that are improper by heterosexual members of the military.

Fourth, the ban has been lifted in other nations and in police and fire departments in our country with no discernible negative impact on unit cohesion or capacity to do the job, though there is, admittedly, no absolute analogy to the situation we face and no study bearing on this specific issue.

Fifth, even if the ban were lifted entirely, the experience of other nations and police and fire departments in the United States indicates that most homosexuals would probably not declare their sexual orientation openly, thereby, making an already hard life even more difficult in some circumstances.

But as the sociologist Charles Moskos noted after spending many years studying the American military, the issue may be tougher to resolve here in the United States than in Canada, Australia, and in some other nations because of the presence in our country of both vocal gay rights groups and equally vocal antigay rights groups, including some religious groups who believe that lifting the ban amounts to endorsing a lifestyle they strongly disapprove of.

Clearly, the American people are deeply divided on this issue, with most military people opposed to lifting the ban because of the feared impact on unit cohesion, rooted in disapproval of homosexual lifestyles, and the fear of invasion of privacy of heterosexual soldiers who must live and work in close quarters with homosexual military people.

However, those who have studied this issue extensively have discovered an interesting fact. People in this country who are aware of having known homosexuals are far more likely to support lifting the ban. In other words, they are likely to see this issue in terms of individual conduct and individual capacity instead of the claims of a group with which they do not agree; and also to be able to imagine how this ban could be lifted without a destructive impact on group cohesion and morale. . . .

Gays in the Military

For months now, the Secretary of Defense and the service chiefs have worked through this issue in a highly charged, deeply emotional environment, struggling to come to terms with the competing consideration and pressures and, frankly, to work through their own ideas and deep feelings.

During this time many dedicated Americans have come forward to state their own views on this issues. Most, but not all, of the military testimony has been against lifting the ban. But support for changing the policy has come from distinguished combat veterans. . . . It has come from Lawrence Korb, who enforced the gay ban during the Reagan administration; and from former Senator Barry Goldwater, a distinguished veteran, former Chairman of the Senate Arms Services Committee, founder of the Arizona National Guard, and patron saint of the conservative wing of the Republican Party.

Senator Goldwater's statement . . . made it crystal clear that when this matter is viewed as an issue of individual opportunity and responsibility rather than one of alleged group rights, this is not a call for cultural license, but rather a reaffirmation of the American value of extending opportunity to responsible individuals and of limiting the role of government over citizens private lives.

On the other hand, those who oppose lifting the ban are clearly focused not on the conduct of individual gay service members, but on how nongay service members feel about gays in general and, in particular, those in the military service. . . .

I have ordered Secretary Aspin to issue a directive consisting of these essential elements:

One, servicemen and women will be judged based on their conduct, not their sexual orientation.

Two, therefore, the practice, now six months old, of not asking about sexual orientation in the enlistment procedure will continue.

Three, an open statement by a service member that he or she is a homosexual will create a rebuttable presumption that he or she intends to engage prohibited conduct, but the service member will be given an opportunity to refute that presumption; in other words, to demonstrate that he or she intends to live by the rules of conduct that apply in the military service.

And four, all provisions of the Uniform Military Justice will been forced in an even-handed manner as regards both heterosexuals and homosexuals. And, thanks to the policy provisions agreed by the Joint Chiefs, there will be a decent regard to the legitimate privacy and associational rights of all service members.

Just as is the case under current policy, unacceptable conduct, either heterosexual or homosexual, will be unacceptable 24 hours a day, seven days a week, from the time a recruit joins the service until the day he or she is discharged. Now, as in the past, every member of our military will be required to comply with the Uniform Code of Military Justice, which is federal law and military regulations, at all times and in all places.

It is not a perfect solution. It is not identical with some of my own goals. And it certainly will not please everyone, perhaps not anyone, and clearly not those who hold the most adamant opinions on either side of this issue.

But those who wish to ignore the issue must understand that it is already tearing at the cohesion of the military, and it is today being considered by the federal courts in ways that may not be to the liking of those who oppose any change. And those who want the ban to be lifted completely on both status and conduct must understand that such action would have faced certain and decisive reversal by the Congress and the cause for which many have fought for years would be delayed probably for years.

Thus, on grounds of both principle and practicality, this is a major step forward. . . .

"We can bridge this great divide"

PRESIDENT CLINTON ON RACE RELATIONS
1995

As blacks gathered in Washington, D.C., for the Million-Man March, President Bill Clinton (born 1946) declared, solemnly and sternly, that racism must end. In a speech at the University of Texas, he challenged white and black Americans to take responsibility for their attitudes and actions, to reject discord, and to "clean our house of racism." Too many people, black and white, sowed division for their own purposes: "To them I say, 'No more,' we must be one." President Abraham Lincoln (1809–1865) had warned that a "house divided against itself cannot stand." The gulf of mistrust, the 43rd President declared, "must be bridged." Mr. Clinton faced Congressional impeachment, but the Senate, in early 1999, did not convict him.

In recent weeks, every one of us has been made aware of a simple truth—white Americans and black Americans often see the same world in drastically different ways—ways that go beyond and beneath the Simpson trial and its aftermath, which brought these perceptions so starkly into the open.

The rift . . . that is tearing at the heart of America exists in spite of the remarkable progress black Americans have made in the last generation, since Martin Luther King swept America up in his dream, and President Johnson spoke so powerfully for the dignity of man and the destiny of democracy in demanding that Congress guarantee full voting rights to blacks. The rift between blacks and whites exists still in a very special way in America, in spite of the fact that we have become much more racially and ethnically diverse, and that Hispanic Americans—themselves no strangers to discrimination—are now almost 10 percent of our national population.

The reasons for this divide are many. Some are rooted in the awful history and stubborn persistence of racism. Some are rooted in the different ways we experience the threats of modern life to personal security, family values, and strong communities. Some are rooted in the fact that we still haven't learned to talk frankly, to listen carefully, and to work together across racial lines.

Almost 30 years ago, Dr. Martin Luther King took his last march with sanitation workers in Memphis. They marched for dignity, equality, and economic justice. Many carried placards that read simply, "I am a man." The throngs of men marching in Washington today, almost all of them, are doing so for the same stated reason. But there is a profound difference between this march today and those of 30 years ago. Thirty years ago, the marchers were demanding the dignity and opportunity they were due because in the face of terrible discrimination, they had worked hard, raised their children, paid their taxes, obeyed the laws, and fought our wars.

Today's march is also about pride and dignity and respect. But after a generation of deepening social problems that disproportionately impact black Americans, it is also about black men taking renewed responsibility for themselves, their families, and their communities. It's about saying no to crime and drugs and violence. It's about standing up for atonement and reconciliation. It's about insisting that others do the same, and offering to help them. It's about the frank admission that unless black men shoulder their load, no one else can help them or their brothers, their sisters, and their children escape the hard, bleak lives that too many of them still face.

Some of those in the march have a history that is far from its message of atonement and reconciliation. One million men are right to be standing up for personal responsibility. But one million men do not make right one man's message of malice and division. No good house was ever built on a bad foundation. Nothing good ever came of hate. . . .

In the past when we've had the courage to face the truth about our failure to live up to our own best ideals, we've grown stronger, moved forward and restored proud American optimism. At such turning points America moved to preserve the union and abolished slavery; to embrace women's suffrage; to guarantee basic legal rights to America without regard to race, under the leadership of President Johnson. At each of these moments, we looked in the national mirror and were brave enough to say, this is not who we are; we're better than that.

Abraham Lincoln reminded us that a house divided against itself cannot stand. When divisions have threatened to bring our house down, somehow we have always moved together to shore it up. My fellow Americans, our house is the greatest democracy in all human history. And with all its racial and ethnic diversity, it has beaten the odds of human history. But we know that divisions remain, and we still have work to do.

White America must understand and acknowledge the roots of black pain. It began with unequal treatment first in law and later in fact. African Americans indeed have lived too long with a justice system that in too many cases has been and continues to be less than just. The record of abuses extends from lynchings and trumped up charges to false arrests and police brutality. The tragedies of Emmett Till and Rodney King are bloody markers on the very same road. . . .

Blacks are right to think something is terribly wrong when African American men are many times more likely to be victims of homicide than any other group in this country; when there are more African American men in our corrections system than in our colleges; when almost one in three African American men in their 20s are either in jail, on parole or otherwise under the supervision of the criminal justice system—nearly one in three. And that is a disproportionate percentage in comparison to the percentage of blacks who use drugs in our society. I would like every white person here and in America to take a moment to think how he or she would feel if one in three white men were in similar circumstances.

And there is still unacceptable economic disparity between blacks and whites. It is so fashionable to talk today about African Americans as if they have been some sort of protected class. Many whites think blacks are getting more than their fair share in terms of jobs and promotions. That is not true. That is not true.

The truth is that African Americans still make on average about 60 percent of what white people do; that more than half of African American children live in poverty. At the very time our young Americans need access to college more than ever before, black college enrollment is dropping in America.

On the other hand, blacks must understand and acknowledge the roots of white fear in America. There is a legitimate fear of the violence that is too prevalent in our urban areas; often by experience or at least what people see on the news at night, violence for those white people too often has a black face.

It isn't racist for a parent to pull his or her child close when walking through a high-crime neighborhood, or to wish to stay away from neighborhoods where innocent children can be shot in school or standing at bus stops by thugs driving by with assault weapons or toting handguns like old-west desperados.

It isn't racist for parents to recoil in disgust when they read about a national survey of gang members saying that two-thirds of them feel justified in shooting someone simply for showing them disrespect. It isn't racist for whites to say they don't understand why people put up with gangs on the corner or in the projects, or with drugs being sold in the schools or in the open. It's not racist for whites to assert that the culture of welfare dependency, out-of-wedlock pregnancy and absent fatherhood cannot be broken by social programs unless there is first more personal responsibility.

The great potential for this march today, beyond the black community, is that whites will come to see a larger truth—that blacks share their fears and embrace their convictions; openly assert that without changes in the black community and within individuals, real change for our society will not come. . . .

Imagine how you would feel if you were a young parent in your 20s with a young child living in a housing project, working somewhere for $5 an hour with no health insurance, passing every day people on the street selling drugs, making 100 times what you make. Those people are the real heroes of America today, and we should recognize that.

White people too often forget that they are not immune to the problems black Americans face—crime, drugs, domestic abuse, and teen pregnancy. They are too prevalent among whites as well, and some of those problems are growing faster in our white population than in our minority population. Both sides seem to fear deep down inside that they'll never quite be able to see each other as more than enemy faces, all of whom carry at least a sliver of bigotry in their hearts. Differences of opinion rooted in different experiences are healthy, indeed essential, for democracies. But differences so great and so rooted in race threaten to divide the house Mr. Lincoln gave his life to save. As Dr. King said, "We must learn to live together as brothers, or we will perish as fools." . . .

Long before we were so diverse, our nation's motto was E Pluribus Unum—out of many, we are one. We must be one—as neighbors, as fellow citizens; not separate camps, but family—white, black, Latino, all of us, no matter how different, who share basic American values and are willing to live by them. . . .

I ask every governor, every mayor, every business leader, every church leader, every civic leader, every union steward, every student leader—most important, every citizen—in every workplace and learning place and meeting place all across America to take personal responsibility for reaching out to people of different races; for taking time to sit down and talk through this issue; to have the courage to speak honestly and frankly; and then to have the discipline to listen quietly with an open mind and an open heart, as others do the same. . . .

We have to realize that there are some areas of our country—whether in urban areas or poor rural areas like south Texas or eastern Arkansas—where these problems are going to be more prevalent just because there is no opportunity. There is only so much temptation some people can stand when they turn up against a brick wall day after day after day. And if we can spread the benefits of education and free enterprise to those who have been denied them too long and who are isolated in enclaves in this country, then we have a moral obligation to do it. It will be good for our country.

We have to give every child in this country, and every adult who still needs it, the opportunity to get a good education. The people marching in Washington today are right about one fundamental thing—at its base, this issue of race is not about government or political leaders; it is about what is in the heart and the minds and life of the American people. There will be no progress in the absence of real responsibility on the part of all Americans. Nowhere is that responsibility more important than in our efforts to promote public safety and preserve the rule of law. . . .

The single biggest social problem in our society may be the growing absence of fathers from their children's homes, because it contributes to so many other social problems. One child in four grows up in a fatherless home. Without a father to help guide, without a father to care, without a father to teach boys to be men and to teach girls to expect respect from men, it's harder. . . .

Parenting is not easy, and every parent makes mistakes. I know that, too, from my own experi-ence. The point is that we need people to be there for their children day after day. Building a family is the hardest job a man can do, but it's also the most important. . . .

We can only build strong families when men and women respect each other; when they have partnerships; when men are as involved in the homeplace as women have become involved in the workplace. It means, among other things, that we must keep working until we end domestic violence against women and children. . . .

Make no mistake about it, we can bridge this great divide. This is, after all, a very great country. And we have become great by what we have overcome. We have the world's strongest economy, and it's on the move. But we've really lasted because we have understood that our success could never be measured solely by the size of our Gross National Product. . . .

While leaders and legislation may be important, this is work that has to be done by every single one of you. This is the ultimate test of our democracy, for today the house divided exists largely in the minds and hearts of the American people. And it must be united there in the minds and hearts of our people.

There are some who would poison our progress by selling short the great character of our people and our enormous capacity to change and grow. But they will not win the day; we will win the day.

"The President shall restore . . . spending limits"

LINE ITEM VETO
1996

For decades, Presidents from both parties wanted authority to delete spending items in appropriation bills. The Line Item Veto Act allows the Chief Executive to strike individual spending items, special-interest tax breaks, and new entitlement programs in bills otherwise approved. The Act represents a dramatic shift of power from Congress to the President. It will take two-thirds of both the House and the Senate to reverse a Presidential rescission. In June, 1997, the Supreme Court dismissed a challenge to the Act, because there was not yet a genuine "case or controversy."

SECTION 1. SHORT TITLE.
This Act may be cited as the 'The Separate Enrollment and Line Item Veto Act of 1995'.
SEC. 2. STRUCTURE OF LEGISLATION.
(a) APPROPRIATIONS LEGISLATION—
(1) The Committee on Appropriations of either the House or the Senate shall not report an appropriation measure that fails to contain such level of detail on the allocation of an item of appropriation proposed by that House as is set forth in the committee report accompanying such bill.
(2) If an appropriation measure is reported to the House or Senate that fails to contain the level of detail on the allocation of an item of appropriation as required in paragraph (1), it shall not be in order in that House to consider such measure. If a point of order under this paragraph is sustained, the measure shall be recommitted to the Committee on Appropriations of that House. . . .
SEC. 5. DEFINITIONS.
For purposes of this Act:
(1) The term 'appropriation measure' means any general or special appropriation bill or any bill or joint resolution making supplemental, deficiency, or continuing appropriations.
(2) The term 'authorization measure' means any measure other than an appropriations measure that contains a provision providing direct spending or targeted tax benefits.
(3) The term 'direct spending' shall have the same meaning given to such term in section 250(c)(8) of the Balanced Budget and Emergency Deficit Control Act of 1985. . . .
(5) The term 'targeted tax benefit' means any provision:
(A) estimated by the Joint Committee on Taxation as losing revenue for any one of the three following periods—
(1) the first fiscal year covered by the most recently adopted concurrent resolution on the budget;
(2) the period of the 5 fiscal years covered by the most recently adopted concurrent resolution on the budget; or
(3) the period of the 5 fiscal years following the first 5 years covered by the most recently

adopted concurrent resolution on the budget; and

(B) having the practical effect of providing more favorable tax treatment to a particular taxpayer or limited group of taxpayers when compared with other similarly situated taxpayers. . . .

SEC. 8. SAVINGS FROM RESCISSION BILLS USED FOR DEFICIT REDUCTION.

(a) Not later than 45 days of continuous session after the President vetoes an appropriations measure or an authorization measure, the President shall—

(1) with respect to appropriations measures, reduce the discretionary spending limits under section 601 of the Congressional Budget Act of 1974 for the budget year and each outyear by the amount by which the measure would have increased the deficit in each respective year;

(2) with respect to a repeal of direct spending, or a targeted tax benefit, reduce the balances for the budget year and each outyear under section 252(b) of the Balanced Budget and Emergency Deficit Control Act of 1985 by the amount by which the measure would have increased the deficit in each respective year.

(b) Exceptions—

(1) This section shall not apply if the vetoed appropriations measure or authorization measure becomes law, over the objections of the President, before the President orders the reduction required by subsections (a) (1) or (a) (2).

(2) If the vetoed appropriations measure or authorization measure becomes law, over the objections of the President, after the President has ordered the reductions required by subsections (a) (1) or (a) (2), then the President shall restore the discretionary spending limits under section 601 of the Congressional Budget Act of 1974 or the balances under section 252(b) of the Balanced Budget and Emergency Deficit Control Act of 1985 to reflect the positions existing before the reduction ordered by the President in compliance with subsection (a).

SEC. 9. EVALUATION AND SUNSET OF TAX EXPENDITURES

(a) LEGISLATION FOR SUNSETTING TAX EXPENDITURES—The President shall submit legislation for the periodic review, reauthorization, and sunset of tax expenditures with his fiscal year 1997 budget.

(b) BUDGET CONTENTS AND SUBMISSION TO CONGRESS—Section 1105(a) of title 31, United States Code, is amended by adding at the end the following paragraph:

(30) beginning with fiscal year 1999, a Federal Government performance plan for measuring the overall effectiveness of tax expenditures, including a schedule for periodically assessing the effects of specific tax expenditures in achieving performance goals.'. . .

(d) CONGRESSIONAL BUDGET ACT— Title IV of the Congressional Budget Act of 1974 is amended by adding at the end thereof the following:

'TAX EXPENDITURES

'SEC. 409. It shall not be in order in the House of Representatives or the Senate to consider any bill, joint resolution, amendment, motion, or conference report that contains a tax expenditure unless the bill, joint resolution, amendment motion, or conference report provides that the tax expenditure will terminate not later than 10 years after the date of enactment of the tax expenditure.'.

SEC. 10. EFFECTIVE DATE.

The provisions of this Act shall apply to measures passed by the Congress beginning with the date of the enactment of this Act and ending on September 30, 2000.

THE FIRST AMERICANS

A*ny effort to explore the national character must look not only at the European world from which most early Americans came but also to an ancient Indian culture on this side of the ocean. Native Americans have lived on this continent for about 15,000 years, but until recently they have been largely invisible. Yet they have their own complex culture and traditions, which rapidly came into conflict with that of white settlers resulting in terrible consequences.*

When the first Europeans arrived, they did not find an empty wasteland. Probably about 200,000 Indians lived east of the Mississippi and a little more than a half million on the entire continent, grouped into roughly 250 tribes, speaking many languages and dialects. They lived in social groups, in families, villages and clans, and within these spheres reared their offspring and wrested a living from the harsh environment. Those living in New England soon knew conflict born of animosity. The Puritans wanted them to disappear—or become "civilized." When some thousand Indians in eastern Massachusetts died of smallpox, Governor John Winthrop explained the result by finding, "The Lord hathe cleared our title to what we possess." The Puritans took advantage of traditional conflict between various Indian tribes when they did not slaughter those who stood in their way, and countless Indian wars were fought in the colonial period. In addition, extensive tribal alliances were formed, and heroic struggles went on with the settlers before the Indians were crushed, and similar guerrilla struggles went on in both North and South Carolina. In upstate New York, the Iroquois Confederacy, also known as the Five (later Six) Nations, dominated. Having an impressive governmental structure, the Confederacy was recommended by Benjamin Franklin as a model for the colonies, whereby separate states could coalesce into one powerful nation. The Iroquois Confederacy traded with Dutch settlers, largely in furs, and became embroiled in a growing conflict with the Hurons, who were backed by the French. It also clashed with settlers who were trying to move west out of the New England and Hudson River Valley regions, because it stood athwart the most advantageous route for those who wanted to move. Eventually, of course, no force could stop the settlers. Yet another source of conflict centered on clashing white versus Indian notions of property. For the Indians, land was not just to be used but a commodity to be bought and improved. They did not place a monetary value on land.

By the 1790s, most of the Indian tribes in the East had suffered drastic losses in people and territory, owing to battle, famine, and exposure to the harsh elements. Their cultures were increasingly sapped, their peoples reduced to indolence, drunkenness, social dereliction, and murderous in-fighting; whites perceived the Indians as inferior beings, incapable of change and unassimilable. On the frontier at the time, a dozen Indian tribes were forced to give up their lands by treaties and soon were driven off. The Battle of Tippecanoe, for instance, marked the beginning of the end for Tecumseh and the Shawnee.

By the time of President Monroe, the idea of a general removal of the eastern Indians to the Great Plains had surfaced. Indian lands in the older regions would be exchanged for those west of the Mississippi. The Indians of the Northeast were removed without difficulty, but many of those in the South, the so-called Five Civilized Tribes—the Creek, Choctaw, Chickasaw, Cherokee, and Seminole—had settled permanently on the lands, farmed them, built homes, erected gristmills, and educated their children in local missionary schools. But their lands were coveted by Southern planters and farmers; treaties were concluded, millions of acres relinquished, and they were unwillingly moved in the Jackson years. They traveled by wagon and on foot, suffered from hunger and diseases like cholera, and many died before they had been settled in the west. They were reduced to poverty, suffering intensely in improvised settlements; their armed resistance, when attempted by the Sauk and Fox tribes, resulted in their massacre. Of the Cherokee removal to the Indian Territory (Oklahoma), one observer lamented: "Such a dereliction of all faith and virtue, such a denial of justice, and such deafness to screams for mercy were never heard of in time of peace...since the earth was made."

Isolation, betrayal, and exile was their lot. Even in their new region, the long-term refuge was a pledge betrayed, as the government withdrew its promised protection and left the tribes without the ability to safeguard their interests. They were confined to increasingly smaller reservations, supplied with inferior goods by the Indian Bureau, exploited by greedy prospectors, and either starved on the reservations or were killed outside. After the Civil War, white settlers—miners, railroaders, and cattlemen—justified their actions with high-sounding rhetoric like "manifest destiny" or "civilization against savagery." Moving west along the rail lines, they came into conflict with the Native Americans. The U.S. Army fought pitched battles with the more combative Indian nations—the Comanche, Apache, Kiowa, Cheyenne, and Sioux. Occasionally, the whites lost, as in the Battle of the Little Bighorn, but generally the tribes were decimated by the Army's superior organization and firepower. With the slaughter of the vast buffalo herds upon which the Plains Indians depended for food, Indian survival was further endangered. Violent encounters with the Cheyenne and Arapaho also contributed. The last major clashes came with the butchery of Sioux at Wounded Knee, South Dakota, in 1890. It was the final tragic episode. The Indian lands were now expropriated. Under the Dawes Act, the Indian Bureau sought to encourage Native Americans to become farmers, but they were given the least fertile soil, and they were further vulnerable to cheating comparable to that which initially occurred when ante-bellum treaties were made. Being deprived of land and support resulted in further pauperization and dependency on government handouts. Congress belatedly granted Indians citizenship in 1924.

"Object of these laws is to establish peace"

THE IROQUOIS FEDERATION CONSTITUTION

c. 1570

The exact date of the founding of the remarkable Confederation of the Iroquois is not known: It might have been long before Europeans arrived, it might have been five centuries ago, it might have been as "recent" as 1570. According to Iroquois tradition, the holy man Deganawidah (c.1550–c.1600), said to be born of a virgin, decided that bloody and endless wars among tribes in the huge rectangle from the Hudson River to Lake Erie must cease. The tribes must try to live in harmony and justice in a government of law. He united the Seneca, Cayuga, Onondaga, Oneida, and Mohawk under the sheltering branches of a symbolic Tree of Great Peace. (The Tuscarora came aboard, as the sixth nation, in 1724.) Legislative, executive, and judicial powers were held by one body, the Council of the Forty-nine Sachems. Onondaga were the fire-keepers and the wampum-keepers. The Iroquois Constitution (which was not an influence in the composition of the U.S. Constitution) was known to the Iroquois as the Great Binding Law, or the Great Immutable Law. It was transmitted orally from one generation to the next until put into written form in the late 1800s.

This is wisdom and justice of the part of the Great Spirit to create and raise chiefs, give and establish unchangable laws, rules and customs between the Five Nation Indians, viz the Mohawks, Oneidas, Onondagas, Cayugas and Senecas and the other nations of Indians here in North America. The object of these laws is to establish peace between the numeras nations of Indians, hostility will be done away with, for the preservation and protection of life, property and liberty.

And the number of chiefs in this confederation of the five Nation Indians are fifty in number, no more and no less. They are the ones to arrange, to legislate and to look after the affairs of their people.

And the Mohawks, an Indian Nation, forms a part of the body of this Five Nation Indians con-federation, and their representatives in this con-federation is nine chiefs.

And the Oneidas, an Indian Nation, forms a party of the body of this Five Nation Indians confederation, and their representatives in this confederation is nine chiefs.

And the Onondagas, an Indian Nation, form a part of the body of this Five Nation Indians confederation, and their representatives in this confederation is fourteen chiefs.

And the Cayugas, an Indian Nation, forms a part of the body of this Five Nation Indians con-federation, and their representatives in this con-federation is ten chiefs.

And the Senecas, an Indian Nation, forms a part of the body of this Five Nation Indians con-federation, and their representatives in this con-federation is eight chiefs.

And when the Five Nation Indians confederation chiefs assemble to hold a council, the council shall be duly opened and closed by the Onondaga chiefs, the Firekeepers. They will offer thanks to the Great Spirit that dwells in heaven above: the source and ruler of our lives, and it is him that sends daily blessings upon us, our daily wants and daily health, and they will then declare the council open for the transaction of business, and give decisions of all that is done in the council.

And there are three totems or castes of the Mohawk Nation viz. the Tortoise, the Wolf and the Bear; each has 3 head chiefs, 9 in all. The chiefs of the Tortoise and Wolf castes are the council by themselves, and the chiefs of the Bear castes are to listen and watch the progress of the council or discussion of the two castes; and if they see any error they are to correct them, and explain, where they are wrong; and when they decide with the sanction of the Bear castes then their speaker will refer the matter to the other side of the council fire, to the second combination chiefs, viz The Oneidas and Cayugas.

And the council of the five Nations shall not be opened until all of the three castes of the Mohawk chiefs are present; and if they are not all present it shall be legal for them to transact the business of the council if all the three totems have one or more representatives present, and if not it shall not be legal except in small matters; for all the three castes of the Mohawk chiefs must be present to be called a full council. . . .

"Why do you white people differ so much about . . . the Book?"

RED JACKET ON RELIGION
1805

The Seneca chief Sagoyewatha (c.1758–1830), known as Red Jacket for the red coat he wore as an English ally in the American Revolution, opposed the white man's takeover of Iroquois lands. He addressed a council of Iroquois Confederation chiefs after a white missionary had spoken to the parley.

There was a time when our forefathers owned this great island. Their seats extended from the rising to the setting sun. The Great Spirit had made it for the use of Indians. He had created the buffalo, the deer, and other animals for food. He had made the bear and the beaver. Their skins served us for clothing. He had scattered them over the country and taught us how to take them. He had caused the earth to produce corn for bread. All this He had done for His red children because He loved them. If we had some disputes about our hunting-ground they were generally settled without the shedding of much blood.

But an evil day came upon us. Your forefathers crossed the great water and landed on this island. Their numbers were small. They found friends and not enemies. They told us they had fled from their own country for fear of wicked men and had come here to enjoy their religion. They asked for a small seat. We took pity on them, granted their request, and they sat down among us. We gave them corn and meat; they gave us poison in return.

The white people, brother, had now found our country. Tidings were carried back and more came among us. Yet we did not fear them. We took them to be friends. They called us brothers. We believed them and gave them a larger seat. At length their numbers had greatly increased. They wanted more land; they wanted our country. Our eyes were opened and our minds became uneasy. Wars took place. Indians were hired to fight against Indians, and many of our people were destroyed. They also brought strong liquor among us. It was strong and powerful, and has slain thousands.

Brother, our seats were once large and yours were small. You have now become a great people, and we have scarcely a place left to spread our blankets. You have got our country, but are not satisfied; you want to force your religion upon us. . . .

Brother, you say there is but one way to worship and serve the Great Spirit. If there is but one religion, why do you white people differ so much about it? Why not all agreed, as you can all read the Book?

Brother, we do not understand these things. We are told that your religion was given to your forefathers and has been handed down from father to son. We also have a religion which was given to our forefathers and has been handed down to us, their children. We worship in that way. It teaches us to be thankful for all the favors we receive, to love each other, and to be united. We never quarrel about religion.

Brother, the Great Spirit has made us all, but He has made a great difference between His white and His red children. He has given us different complexions and different customs. To you He has given the arts. To these He has not opened our eyes. We know these things to be true. Since He has made so great a difference between us in other things, why may we not conclude that He has given us a different religion according to our understanding? The Great Spirit does right. He knows what is best for His children; we are satisfied.

Brother, we do not wish to destroy your religion or take it from you. We only want to enjoy our own.

Brother, you say you have not come to get our land or our money, but to enlighten our minds. I will now tell you that I have been at your meetings and saw you collect money from the meeting. I can not tell what this money was intended for, but suppose that it was for your minister; and, if we should conform to your way of thinking, perhaps you may want some from us.

Brother, we are told that you have been preaching to the white people in this place. These people are our neighbors. We are acquainted with them. We will wait a little while and see what effect your preaching has upon them. If we find it does them good, makes them honest, and less disposed to cheat Indians, we will then consider again of what you have said. . . .

"War . . . shall forever cease"

THE TREATY OF FORT LARAMIE
1868

The first Treaty of Fort Laramie (1851) established boundaries for Indians hostile to one another. The Sioux and the Shoshone, among other tribes, agreed to permit construction of roads and forts in their territory. Seventeen years later, a new Laramie agreement was concluded by the U.S.'s Indian Peace Commission and duly authorized chiefs and headmen of bands of the Sioux Nation. The United States agreed to close the Rocky Mountain Bozeman Trail (which crossed the Oregon Trail at Fort Laramie and led to gold mines in Montana), withdraw military posts built to protect the trail, restrain settlement of unceded Indian territory, and establish a Sioux reservation west of the Missouri River, in South Dakota, with food, clothing, and other supplies. It also recognized the hunting rights of the Indians in the Powder River area (northern Wyoming, eastern Montana). The Indians agreed to halt their attacks on white settlers and railroad workers. Both parties desired peace and pledged their honor to keep it.

ARTICLE 1. From this day forward all war between the parties to this agreement shall forever cease. The Government of the United States desires peace, and its honor is hereby pledged to keep it. The Indians desire peace, and they now pledge their honor to maintain it.

If bad men among the whites, or among other people subject to the authority of the United States, shall commit any wrong upon the person or property of the Indians, the United States will, upon proof made to the agent and forwarded to the Commissioner of Indian Affairs at Washington City, proceed at once to cause the offender to be arrested and punished according to the laws of the United States, and also re-imburse the injured person for the loss sustained.

If bad men among the Indians shall commit a wrong or depredation upon the person or property of any one, white, black, or Indian, subject to the authority of the United States, and at peace therewith, the Indians herein named solemnly agree that they will, upon proof made to their agent and notice by him, deliver up the wrong-doer to the United States, to be tried and punished according to its laws; and in case they wilfully refuse so to do, the person injured shall be re-imbursed for his loss from the annuities or other moneys due or to become due to them under this or other treaties made with the United States. And the President, on advising with the Commissioner of Indian Affairs, shall prescribe such rules and regulations for ascertaining damages under the provisions of this article as in his judgment may be proper. But no one sustaining loss while violating the provisions of this treaty or the laws of the United States shall be re-imbursed therefor.

ARTICLE 2. The United States agrees that the following district of country, to wit, viz: commencing on the east bank of the Missouri River where the forty-sixth parallel of north latitude crosses the same, thence along low-water mark down said east bank to a point opposite where the northern line of the State of Nebraska strikes the river, thence west across said river, and along the northern line of Nebraska to the one hundred and fourth degree of longitude west from Greenwich, thence north on said meridian to a point where the forty-sixth parallel of north latitude intercepts the same, thence due east along said parallel to the place of beginning; and in addition thereto, all existing reservations on the east bank of said river shall be, and the same is, set apart for the absolute and undisturbed use and occupation of the Indians herein named, and for such other friendly tribes or individual Indians as from time to time they may be willing, with the consent of the United States, to admit amongst them; and the United States now solemnly agrees that no persons except those herein designated and authorized so to do, and except such officers, agents, and employés of the Government as may be authorized to enter upon Indian reservations in discharge of duties enjoined by law, shall ever be permitted to pass over, settle upon, or reside in the territory described in this article, or in such territory as may be added to this reservation for the use of said Indians, and henceforth they will and do hereby relinquish all claims or rights in and to any portion of the United States or Territories, except such as is embraced within the limits aforesaid, and except as hereinafter provided.

ARTICLE 3. If it should appear from actual survey or other satisfactory examination of said tract of land that it contains less than one hundred and sixty acres of tillable land for each person who, at the time, may be authorized to reside on it under the provisions of this treaty, and a very considerable number of such persons shall be disposed to commence cultivating the soil as farmers, the United States agrees to set apart, for the use of said Indians, as herein provided, such additional quantity of arable land, adjoining to said reservation, or as near to the same as it can be obtained, as may be required to provide the necessary amount.

ARTICLE 4. The United States agrees, at its own proper expense, to construct at some place on the Missouri River, near the center of said reservation, where timber and water may be convenient, the following buildings, to wit: a warehouse, a store-room for the use of the agent in storing goods belonging to the Indians, to cost not less than twenty-five hundred dollars; an agency-building for the residence of the agent, to cost not exceeding three thousand dollars; a residence for the physician, to cost not more than three thousand dollars; and five other buildings, for a carpenter, farmer, blacksmith, miller, and engineer, each to cost not exceeding two thousand dollars; also a schoolhouse or mission-building, so soon as a sufficient number of children can be induced by the agent to attend school, which shall not cost exceeding five thousand dollars.

The United States agrees further to cause to be erected on said reservation, near the other buildings herein authorized, a good steam circular-saw mill, with a grist-mill and shingle-machine attached to the same, to cost not exceeding eight thousand dollars. . . .

ARTICLE 9. At any time after ten years from the making of this treaty, the United States shall have the privilege of withdrawing the physician, farmer, blacksmith, carpenter, engineer, and miller herein provided for, but in case of such withdrawal, an additional sum thereafter of ten thousand dollars per annum shall be devoted to the education of said Indians, and the Commissioner of Indian Affairs shall, upon careful inquiry into their condition, make such rules and regulations for the expenditure of said sum as will best promote the educational and moral improvement of said tribes.

ARTICLE 10. In lieu of all sums of money or other annuities provided to be paid to the Indians herein named, under any treaty or treaties heretofore made, the United States agrees to deliver at the agency-house on the reservation herein named, on or before the first day of August of each year, for thirty years, the following articles, to wit:

For each male person over fourteen years of age, a suit of good substantial woolen clothing, consisting of coat, pantaloons, flannel shirt, hat, and a pair of home-made socks.

For each female over twelve years of age, a flannel skirt, or the goods necessary to make it, a pair of woolen hose, twelve yards of calico, and twelve yards of cotton domestics.

For the boys and girls under the ages named, such flannel and cotton goods as may be needed to make each a suit as aforesaid, together with a pair of woolen hose for each.

And in order that the Commissioner of Indian Affairs may be able to estimate properly for the articles herein named, it shall be the duty of the agent each year to forward to him a full and exact census of the Indians, on which the estimate from year to year can be based.

And in addition to the clothing herein named, the sum of ten dollars for each person entitled to the beneficial effects of this treaty shall be annually appropriated for a period of thirty years, while such persons roam and hunt, and twenty dollars for each person who engages in farming, to be used by the Secretary of the Interior in the purchase of such articles as from time to time the condition and necessities of the Indians may indicate to be proper. . . .

Article 11 . . . The tribes who are parties to this agreement hereby stipulate that they will relinquish all right to occupy permanently the territory outside their reservation as herein defined, but yet reserve the right to hunt on any lands north of North Platte, and on the Republican Fork of the Smoky Hill River, so long as the buffalo may range thereon in such numbers as to justify the chase. And they, the said Indians, further expressly agree:

1st. That they will withdraw all opposition to the construction of the railroads now being built on the plains.

2d. That they will permit the peaceful construction of any railroad not passing over their reservation as herein defined.

3d. That they will not attack any persons at home, or travelling, nor molest or disturb any wagon-trains, coaches, mules, or cattle belonging to the people of the United States, or to persons friendly therewith.

4th. They will never capture, or carry off from the settlements, white women or children.

5th. They will never kill or scalp white men, nor attempt to do them harm.

6th. They withdraw all pretence of opposition to the construction of the railroad now being built along the Platte River and westward to the Pacific Ocean, and they will not in future object to the construction of railroads, wagon-roads, mail-stations, or other works of utility or necessity, which may be ordered or permitted by the laws of the United States. But should such roads or other works be constructed on the lands of their reservation, the Government will pay the tribe whatever amount of damage may be assessed by three disinterested commissioners to be appointed by the President for that purpose, one of said commissioners to be a chief or head-man of the tribe.

7th. They agree to withdraw all opposition to the military posts or roads now established south of the North Platte River, or that may be established, not in violation of treaties heretofore made or hereafter to be made with any of the Indian tribes.

ARTICLE 12. No treaty for the cession of any portion or part of the reservation herein described which may be held in common shall be of any validity or force as against the said Indians, unless executed and signed by at least three-fourths of all the adult male Indians, occupying or interested in the same; and no cession by the tribe shall be understood or construed in such manner as to deprive, without his consent, any individual member of the tribe of his rights to any tract of land selected by him, as provided in article 6 of this treaty.

ARTICLE 13. The United States hereby agrees to furnish annually to the Indians the physician, teachers, carpenter, miller, engineer, farmer, and blacksmiths as herein contemplated, and that such appropriations shall be made from time to time, on the estimates of the Secretary of the Interior, as will be sufficient to employ such persons.

ARTICLE 14. It is agreed that the sum of five hundred dollars annually, for three years from date, shall be expended in presents to the ten persons of said tribe who in the judgment of the agent may grow the most valuable crops for the respective year.

ARTICLE 15. The Indians herein named agree that when the agency-house or other buildings shall be constructed on the reservation named, they will regard said reservation their permanent home, and they will make no permanent settlement elsewhere; but they shall have the right, subject to the conditions and modifications of this treaty, to hunt, as stipulated in Article 11 hereof.

ARTICLE 16. The United States hereby agrees and stipulates that the country north of the North Platte River and east of the summits of the Big Horn Mountains shall be held and considered to be unceded Indian territory, and also stipulates and agrees that no white person or persons shall be permitted to settle upon or occupy any portion of the same; or without the consent of the Indians first had and obtained, to pass through the same; and it is further agreed by the United States that within ninety days after the conclusion of peace with all the bands of the Sioux Nation, the military posts now established in the territory in this article named shall be abandoned, and that the road leading to them and by them to the settlements in the Territory of Montana shall be closed. . . .

"Eventually . . . acquire the arts of civilized life"

THE BLACK HILLS TREATY
1877

The dome-like, darkly wooded, mineral-rich Black Hills, in western South Dakota and northeastern Wyoming—the highest range of mountains between the Rockies and the Alleghenys—were the sacred Papa Sapa of the Sioux. White prospectors swarmed in after the discovery of gold there by an expedition (1874) led by Civil War hero General George A. Custer (1839–1876). The 1868 Fort Laramie Treaty had stipulated that Lakota would "own" the Black Hills (and all of Dakota west of the Missouri River) forever. In 1877, Congress forced an agreement on certain bands of the Sioux Nation and on Northern Arapaho and Cheyenne: The Indians would cede territory and rights in return for U.S. aid assisting "the said Indians in the work of civilization," furnishing "schools and instruction in mechanical and agricultural arts, as provided for by the treaty of 1868," . . . and aiding "said Indians as far as possible in finding a market for their surplus productions." For nearly a century, the Sioux have courted the U.S. justice system, demanding return of their 6,000 square miles. In 1980, the Lakota rejected an award of $105-million; they insist on return of the land.

Be it enacted by the Senate and House of Representatives of the United States of America in Congress assembled, That a certain agreement made by . . . commissioners on the part of the United States with the different bands of the Sioux Nation of Indians, and also the Northern Arapaho and Cheyenne Indians, be, and the same is hereby, ratified and confirmed: *Provided,* That nothing in this act shall be construed to authorize the removal of the Sioux Indians to the Indian Territory and the President of the United States is hereby directed to prohibit the removal of any portion of the Sioux Indians to the Indian Territory until the same shall be authorized by an act of Congress hereafter enacted, except article four, except also the following portion of article six: "And if said Indians shall remove to said Indian Territory as hereinbefore provided, the Government shall erect for each of the principal chiefs a good and comfortable dwelling-house" said article not having been agreed to by the Sioux Nation; said agreement is in words and figures following, namely: "Articles of agreement made pursuant to the provisions of an act of Congress entitled "An act making appropriations for the current and contingent expenses of the Indian Department, and for fulfilling treaty stipulations with various Indian tribes, for the year ending June thirtieth, eighteen hundred and seventy-seven, and for other purposes," approved August 15, 1876, by and between George W. Manypenny, Henry B. Whipple, Jared W. Daniels, Albert G. Boone, Henry C. Bulis, Newton Edmunds, and Augustine S. Gaylord, commissioners on the part of the United States, and the different bands of the Sioux Nation of Indians, and also the Northern Arapahoes and Cheyennes, by their chiefs and headmen, whose names are hereto subscribed, they being duly authorized to act in the premises.

"ARTICLE 1. The said parties hereby agree that the northern and western boundaries of the reservation defined by article 2 of the treaty between the United States and different tribes of Sioux Indians, concluded April 29, 1868, and proclaimed February 24, 1869, shall be as follows: The western boundaries shall commence at the intersection of the one hundred and third meridian of longitude with the northern boundary of the State of Nebraska; thence north along said meridian to its intersection with the South Fork of the Cheyenne River; thence down said stream to its junction with the North Fork; thence up the North Fork of said Cheyenne River to the said one hundred and third meridian; thence north along said meridian to the South Branch of Cannon Ball River or Cedar Creek; and the northern boundary of their said reservation shall follow the said South Branch to its intersection with the main Cannon Ball River, and thence down the said main Cannon Ball River to the Missouri River; and the said Indians do hereby relinquish and cede to the United States all the territory lying outside the said reservation, as herein modified and described, including all privileges of hunting; and article 16 of said treaty is hereby abrogated.

"ARTICLE 2. The said Indians also agree and consent that wagon and other roads, not exceeding three in number, may be constructed and maintained, from convenient and accessible points on the Missouri River, through said reservation, to the country lying immediately west thereof, upon such routes as shall be designated by the President of the United States; and they also consent and agree to the free navigation of the Missouri River.

"ARTICLE 3. The said Indians also agree that they will hereafter receive all annuities provided by the said treaty of 1868, and all subsistence and supplies which may be provided for them under the present or any future act of Congress, at such points and places on the said reservation, and in the vicinity of the Missouri River, as the President of the United States shall designate.

"ARTICLE 4. [The Government of the United States and the said Indians, being mutually desirous that the latter shall be located in a country where they may eventually become self-supporting and acquire the arts of civilized life, it is therefore agreed that the said Indians shall select a delegation of five or more chiefs and principal men from each band, who shall, without delay, visit the Indian Territory under the guidance and protection of suitable persons, to be appointed for that purpose by the Department of the Interior, with a view to selecting therein a permanent home for the said Indians. If such delegation shall make a selection which shall be satisfactory to themselves, the people whom they represent, and to the United States, then the said Indians agree that they will remove to the country so selected within one year from this date. And the said Indians do further agree in all things to submit themselves to such beneficent plans as the Government may provide for them in the selection of a country suitable for a permanent home, where they may live like white men.]

"ARTICLE 5. In consideration of the foregoing cession of territory and rights, and upon full compliance with each and every obligation assumed by the said Indians, the United States does agree to provide all necessary aid to assist the said Indians in the work of civilization; to furnish them schools and instruction in mechanical and agricultural arts, as provided for by the treaty of 1868. Also to provide the said Indians with subsistence consisting of a ration for each individual of a pound and a half of beef, (or in lieu thereof, one-half pound of bacon), one-half pound of flour, and one-half pound of corn; and for every one hundred rations, four pounds of coffee, eight pounds of sugar, and three pounds of beans, or in lieu of said articles the equivalent thereof, in the discretion of the Commissioner of Indian Affairs. Such rations, or so much thereof as may be necessary, shall be continued until the Indians are able to support themselves. Rations shall, in all cases, be issued to the head of each separate family; and whenever schools shall have been provided by the Government for said Indians, no rations shall be issued for children between the ages of six and fourteen years (the sick and infirm excepted) unless such children shall regularly attend school. Whenever the said Indians shall be located upon lands which are suitable for cultivation, rations shall be issued only to the persons and families of those persons who labor, (the aged, sick, and infirm excepted;) and as an incentive to industrious habits the Commissioner of Indian Affairs may provide that such persons be furnished in payment for their labor such other necessary articles as are requisite for civilized life. The Government will aid said Indians as far as possible in finding a market for their surplus productions, and in finding employment, and will purchase such surplus, as far as may be required, for supplying food to those Indians, parties to this agreement, who are unable to sustain themselves; and will also employ Indians, so far as practicable, in the performance of Government work upon their reservation.

"ARTICLE 6. Whenever the head of a family shall, in good faith, select an allotment of said land upon such reservation and engage in the cultivation thereof, the Government shall, with his aid, erect a comfortable house on such allotment; [and if said Indians shall remove to said Indian Territory as hereinbefore provided, the Government shall erect for each of the principal chiefs a good and comfortable dwelling-house.]

"ARTICLE 7. To improve the morals and industrious habits of said Indians, it is agreed that the agent, trader, farmer, carpenter, blacksmith, and other artisans employed or permitted to reside within the reservation belonging to the Indians, parties to this agreement, shall be lawfully married and living with their respective families on the reservation; and no person other than an Indian of full blood, whose fitness, morally or otherwise, is not, in the opinion of the Commissioner of Indian Affairs, conducive to the welfare of said Indians, shall receive any benefit from this agreement or former treaties, and may be expelled from the reservation.

"ARTICLE 8. The provisions of the said treaty of 1868, except as herein modified, shall continue in full force, and, with the provisions of this agreement, shall apply to any country which may hereafter be occupied by the said Indians as a home; and Congress shall, by appropriate legislation, secure to them an orderly government; they shall be subject to the laws of the United States, and each individual shall be protected in his rights of property, person, and life.

"ARTICLE 9. The Indians, parties to this agreement, do hereby solemnly pledge themselves, individually and collectively, to observe each and all of the stipulations herein contained, to select allotments of land as soon as possible after their removal to their permanent home, and to use their best efforts to learn to cultivate the same. And they do solemnly pledge themselves that they will at all times maintain peace with the citizens and Government of the United States; that they will observe the laws thereof and loyally endeavor to fulfill all the obligations assumed by them under the treaty of 1868 and the present agreement, and to this end will, whenever requested by the President of the United States, select so many suitable men from each band to co-operate with him in maintaining order and peace on the reservation as the President may deem necessary, who shall receive such compensation for their services as Congress may provide.

"ARTICLE 10. In order that the Government may faithfully fulfill the stipulations contained in this agreement, it is mutually agreed that a census of all Indians affected hereby shall be taken in the month of December of each year, and the names of each head of family and adult person registered; said census to be taken in such manner as the Commissioner of Indian Affairs may provide.

"ARTICLE 11. It is understood that the term reservation herein contained shall be held to apply to any country which shall be selected under the authority of the United States as the future home of said Indians. . . .

"I will fight no more forever"

CHIEF JOSEPH SURRENDERS
1877

United States soldiers pursued Chief Joseph's retreating band of Nez Perce ("pierced nose") out of Oregon's Wallowa Valley (coveted by whites) and across 1,500 miles of central Idaho, western Montana, Yellowstone National Park, and central and southern Montana. The troops finally forced surrender after a five-day battle 30 miles south of sanctuary in Canada. Joseph (c.1840–1904)—humane, philosophical, statesmanlike—a legendary Indian known to his people as Thunder Traveling to the Loftier Mountain Heights, declared that he would "fight no more forever." He then conducted an unremitting 26-year effort to get better treatment for his people.

Tell General Howard I know his heart. What he told me before, I have it in my heart. I am tired of fighting. Our chiefs are killed; Looking-Glass is dead, Ta-Hool-Hool-Shute is dead. The old men are all dead. It is the young men who say yes or no. He who led on the young men is dead. It is cold, and we have no blankets; the little children are freezing to death. My people, some of them, have run away to the hills, and have no blankets, no food. No one knows where they are—perhaps freezing to death. I want to have time to look for my children, and see how many of them I can find. Maybe I shall find them among the dead. Hear me, my chiefs! I am tired; my heart is sick and sad. From where the sun now stands I will fight no more forever.

"An Indian is a 'person'"

STANDING BEAR V. CROOK
1879

Sometimes, U.S.-Indian conflicts were resolved in a courtroom. By what right was U.S. Army General George Crook (1829–1890) holding under armed guard the 50-year-old Ponca Chief Standing Bear (1829–1908), or Mochunozhin, and his band of 66 followers? Why weren't they allowed to return to Indian Territory? Standing Bear declared that he wanted to save himself and his tribe: "If a white man had land, and someone should swindle him, that man would try to get it back, and you would not blame him . . . I need help." In a historic decision opposing the U.S. attorney's position, District Judge Elmer S. Dundy ruled that an Indian is a "person" within the meaning of habeas corpus; as such, he is entitled to sue out a writ of habeas corpus in the Federal courts when it is shown that the petitioner is deprived of liberty under color of authority of the United States, or is in custody of an officer in violation of the Constitution or a law of the United States, or in violation of a treaty made in pursuance thereof. The right of expatriation is a natural, inherent, and inalienable right, and extends to the Indian as well as to the white race. The military had no special privileges in peacetime to deny Indians the basic constitutional protection against imprisonment without due cause. The Commissioner of Indian Affairs declared, however, that Judge Dundy's ruling had no bearing on other tribes. The Ponca eventually were given a reservation on their former homeland in northern Nebraska.

During the fifteen years in which I have been engaged in administering the laws of my country, I have never been called upon to hear or decide a case that appealed so strongly to my sympathy as the one now under consideration. On the one side, we have a few of the remnants of a once numerous and powerful, but now weak, insignificant, unlettered, and generally despised race; on the other, we have the representative of one of the most powerful, most enlightened, and most Christianized nations of modern times. On the one side, we have the representatives of this wasted race coming into this national tribunal of ours, asking for justice and liberty to enable them to adopt our boasted civilization, and to pursue the arts of peace, which have made us great and happy as a nation; on the other side, we have this magnificent, if not magnanimous, government, resisting this application with the determination of sending these people back to the country which is to them less desirable than perpetual imprisonment in their own native land. But I think it is creditable to the heart and mind of the brave and distinguished officer who is made respondent herein to say that he has no sort of sympathy in the business in which he is forced by his position to bear a part so conspicuous; and, so far as I am individually concerned, I think it not improper to say that, if the strongest possible sympathy could give the relators title to freedom, they would have been restored to liberty the moment the arguments in their behalf were closed. No examination or further thought would then have been necessary or expedient. But in a country where liberty is regulated by law, something more satisfactory and enduring than mere sympathy must furnish and constitute the rule and basis of judicial action. It follows that this case must be examined and decided on principles of law, and that unless the relators are entitled to their discharge under the constitution or laws of the United States, or some treaty made pursuant thereto, they must be remanded to the custody of the officer who caused their arrest, to be returned to the Indian Territory, which they left without the consent of the government.

On the 8th of April, 1879, the relators, Standing Bear and twenty-five others, during the session of the court held at that time at Lincoln, presented their petition, duly verified, praying for the allowance of a writ of habeas corpus and their final discharge from custody thereunder.

The petition alleges, in substance, that the relators are Indians who have formerly belonged to the Ponca tribe of Indians, now located in the Indian Territory; that they had some time previously withdrawn from the tribe, and completely severed their tribal relations therewith, and had adopted the general habits of the whites, and were then endeavoring to maintain themselves by their own exertions, and without aid or assistance from the general government; that whilst they were thus engaged, and without being guilty of violating any of the laws of the United States, they were arrested and restrained of their liberty by order of the respondent, George Crook. . . . the writ was returned, and the authority for the arrest and detention is therein shown. The substance of the return to the writ, and the . . . additional statement since filed, is that the relators are individual members of, and connected with, the Ponca tribe of Indians; that they had fled or escaped from a reservation situated some place within the limits of the Indian Territory—had departed therefrom without permission from the government; and, at the request of the secretary of the interior, the general of the army had issued an order which required the respondent to arrest and return the relators to their tribe in the Indian Territory, and that, pursuant to the said order, he had caused the relators to be arrested on the Omaha Indian reservation, and that they were in his custody for the purpose of being returned to the Indian Territory.

It is claimed upon the one side, and denied upon the other, that the relators had withdrawn and severed, for all time, their connection with the tribe to which they belonged; and upon this point alone was there any testimony produced by either party hereto. The other matters stated in the petition and the return to the writ are conceded to be true; so that the questions to be determined are purely questions of law.

On the 8th of March, 1859, a treaty was made by the United States with the Ponca tribe of Indians, by which a certain tract of country, north of the Niobrara river and west of the Missouri, was set apart for the permanent home of the said Indians, in which the government agreed to protect them during their good behavior. But just when, or how, or why, or under what circumstances, the Indians left their reservation in Dakota and went to the Indian Territory, does not appear.

The district attorney very earnestly questions the jurisdiction of the court to issue the writ, and to hear and determine the case made herein, and has supported his theory with an argument of great ingenuity and much ability. But, nevertheless, I am of the opinion that his premises are erroneous, and his conclusions, therefore, wrong and unjust. The great respect I entertain for that officer, and the very able manner in which his views were presented, make it necessary for me to give somewhat at length the reasons which lead me to this conclusion.

The district attorney discussed at length the reasons which led to the origin of the writ of habeas corpus, and the character of the proceedings and practice in connection therewith in the parent country. It was claimed that the laws of the realm limited the right to sue out this writ to the free subjects of the kingdom, and that none others came within the benefits of such beneficent laws; and, reasoning from analogy, it is claimed that none but American citizens are entitled to sue out this high prerogative writ in any of the federal courts. I have not examined the English laws regulating the suing out of the writ, nor have I thought it necessary so to do. Of this I will only observe that if the laws of England are as they are claimed to be, they will appear at a disadvantage when compared with our own. This only proves that the laws of a limited monarchy are sometimes less wise and humane than the laws of our own republic—that whilst the parliament of Great Britain was legislating in behalf of the favored few, the congress of the United States was legislating in behalf of all mankind who come within our jurisdiction.

Section 751 of the Revised Statutes declares that "the supreme court and the circuit and district courts shall have power to issue writs of habeas corpus." Section 752 confers the power to issue writs on the judges of said courts, within their jurisdiction, and declares this to be "for the purpose of inquiry into the cause of restraint of liberty." Section 753 restricts the power, limits the jurisdiction, and defines the cases where the writ may properly issue. That may be done under this section where the prisoner "is in custody under or by color of authority of the United States, * * * or is in custody for an act done or omitted in pursuance of a law of the United States, * * * or in custody in violation of the constitution or of a law or treaty of the United States." Thus, it will be seen that when a person is in custody or deprived of his liberty under color of authority of the United States, or in violation of the constitution or laws or treaties of the United States, the federal judges have jurisdiction, and the writ can properly issue. I take it that the true construction to be placed upon this act is this, that in all cases where federal officers, civil or military, have the custody and control of a person claimed to be unlawfully restrained of liberty, they are then restrained of liberty under color of authority of the United States, and the federal courts can properly proceed to determine the question of unlawful restraint, because no other courts can properly do so. In the other instance, the federal courts and judges can properly issue the writ in all cases where the person is alleged to be in custody in violation of the constitution or a law or treaty of the United States. In such a case, it is wholly immaterial what officer, state or federal, has custody of the person seeking the relief. These relators may be entitled to the writ in either case. Under the first paragraph they certainly are—that is, if an Indian can be entitled to it at all—because they are in custody of a federal officer, under color of authority of the United States. And they may be entitled to the writ under the other paragraph, before recited, for the reason, as they allege, that they are restrained of liberty in violation of a provision of their treaty, before referred to. Now, it must be borne in mind that the habeas corpus act describes applicants for the writ as "persons," or "parties," who may be entitled thereto. It nowhere describes them as "citizens," nor is citizenship in any way or place made a qualification for suing out the writ, and, in the absence of express provision or necessary implication which would require the interpretation contended for by the district attorney, I should not feel justified in giving the words "person" and "party" such a narrow construction. The most natural, and therefore most reasonable, way is to attach the same meaning to words and phrases when found in a statute that is attached to them when and where found in general use. If we do so in this instance, then the question cannot be open to serious doubt. Webster describes a person as "a living soul; a self-conscious being; a moral agent; especially a living human being; a man, woman, or child; an individual of the human race." This is comprehensive enough, it would seem, to include even an Indian. In defining certain generic terms, the first section of the Revised Statutes, declares that the word "person" includes copartnerships and corporations. On the whole, it seems to me quite evident that the comprehensive language used in this section is intended to apply to all mankind—as well the relators as the more favored white race. This will be doing no violence to language, or to the spirit or letter of the law, nor to the intention, as it is believed, of the law-making power of the government. I must hold, then, that Indians, and consequently the relators, are "persons," such as are described by and included within the laws before quoted. It is said, however, that this is the first instance on record in which an Indian has been permitted to sue out and maintain a writ of habeas corpus in a federal court, and therefore the court must be without jurisdiction in the premises. This is a non sequitur. I confess I do not know of another instance where this has been done, but I can also say that the occasion for it perhaps has never before been so great. It may be that the Indians think it wiser and better, in the end, to resort to this peaceful process than it would be to undertake the hopeless task of redressing their own alleged wrongs by force of arms. Returning reason, and the sad experience of others similarly situated, have taught them the folly and madness of the arbitrament of the sword. They can readily see that any serious resistance on their part would be the signal for their utter extermination. Have they not, then, chosen the wiser part by resorting to the very tribunal erected by those they claim have wronged and oppressed them? This, however, is not the tribunal of their own choice, but it is the only one into which they can lawfully go for deliverance. It cannot, therefore, be fairly said that because no Indian ever before invoked the aid of this writ in a federal court, the rightful authority to issue it does not exist. Power and authority rightfully conferred do not necessarily cease to exist in consequence of long non-user. Though much time has elapsed, and many generations have passed away, since the passage of the original habeas corpus act, from which I have quoted, it will not do to say that these Indians cannot avail themselves of its beneficent provisions simply because none of their ancestors ever sought relief thereunder.

Every "person" who comes within our jurisdiction, whether he be European, Asiatic, African, or "native to the manor born," must obey the laws of the United States. Every one who violates them incurs the penalty provided thereby. When a "person" is charged, in a proper way, with the commission of crime, we do not inquire upon the trial in what country the accused was born, nor to what sovereign or government allegiance is due, nor to what race he belongs. The questions of guilt and innocence only form the subjects of inquiry. An Indian, then, especially off from his reservation, is amenable to the criminal laws of the United States, the same as all other persons. They being subject to arrest for the violation of our criminal laws, and being "persons" such as the law contemplates and includes in the description of parties who may sue out the writ, it would indeed be a sad commentary on the justice and impartiality of our laws to hold that Indians, though natives of our own country, cannot test the validity of an alleged illegal imprisonment in this manner, as well as a subject of a foreign government who may happen to be sojourning in this country, but owing it no sort of allegiance. I cannot doubt that congress intended to give to every person who might be unlawfully restrained of liberty under color of authority of the United States, the right to the writ and a discharge thereon. I conclude, then, that, so far as the issuing of the writ is concerned, it was properly issued, and that the relators are within the jurisdiction conferred by the habeas corpus act.

A question of much greater importance remains for consideration, which, when determined, will be decisive of this whole controversy. This relates to the right of the government to arrest and hold the relators for a time, for the purpose of being returned to a point in the Indian Territory from which it is alleged the Indians escaped. I am not vain enough to think that I can do full justice to a question like the one under consideration. But, as the matter furnishes so much valuable material for discussion, and so much food for reflection, I shall try to present it as viewed from my own standpoint, without reference to consequences or criticisms, which, though not specially invited, will be sure to follow.

A review of the policy of the government adopted in its dealings with the friendly tribe of Poncas, to which the relators at one time belonged, seems not only appropriate, but almost indispensable to a correct understanding of this controversy. The Ponca Indians have been at peace with the government, and have remained the steadfast friends of the whites, for many years. They lived peaceably upon the land and in the country they claimed and called their own.

On the 12th of March, 1858, they made a treaty with the United States, by which they ceded all claims to lands, except the following tract: "Beginning at a point on the Niobrara river, and running due north so as to intersect the Ponca river twenty-five miles from its mouth; thence from said point of intersection up and along the Ponca river twenty miles; thence due south to the Niobrara river; and thence down and along said river to the place of beginning; which tract is hereby reserved for the future homes of said Indians." In consideration of this cession, the government agreed "to protect the Poncas in the possession of the tract of land reserved for their future homes, and their persons and property thereon, during good behavior on their part." Annuities were to be paid them for thirty years, houses were to be built, schools were to be established, and other things were to be done by the government, in consideration of said cession. See 12 Stat. 997.

On the 10th of March, 1865, another treaty was made, and a part of the other reservation was ceded to the government. Other lands, however, were, to some extent, substituted therefor, "by way of rewarding them for their constant fidelity to the government, and citizens thereof, and with a view of returning to the said tribe of Ponca Indians their old burying-grounds and cornfields." This treaty also provides for paying $15,080 for spoliations committed on the Indians. See 14 Stat. 675.

On the 29th day of April, 1868, the government made a treaty with the several bands of Sioux Indians, which treaty was ratified by the senate on the 16th of the following February, in and by which the reservations set apart for the

Poncas under former treaties were completely absolved. 15 Stat. 635. This was done without consultation with, or knowledge or consent on the part of, the Ponca tribe of Indians.

On the 15th of August, 1876, congress passed the general Indian appropriation bill, and in it we find a provision authorizing the secretary of the interior to use $25,000 for the removal of the Poncas to the Indian Territory, and providing them a home therein, with consent of the tribe. 19 Stat. 192.

In the Indian appropriation bill passed by congress on the 27th day of May, 1878, we find a provision authorizing the secretary of the interior to expend the sum of $30,000 for the purpose of removing and locating the Ponca Indians on a new reservation, near the Kaw river.

No reference has been made to any other treaties or laws, under which the right to arrest and remove the Indians is claimed to exist.

The Poncas lived upon their reservation in southern Dakota, and cultivated a portion of the same, until two or three years ago, when they removed therefrom, but whether by force or otherwise does not appear. At all events, we find a portion of them, including the relators, located at some point in the Indian Territory. There, the testimony seems to show, is where the trouble commenced. Standing Bear, the principal witness, states that out of five hundred and eighty-one Indians who went from the reservation in Dakota to the Indian Territory, one hundred and fifty-eight died within a year or so, and a great proportion of the others were sick and disabled, caused, in a great measure, no doubt, from change of climate; and to save himself and the survivors of his wasted family, and the feeble remnant of his little band of followers, he determined to leave the Indian Territory and return to his old home, where, to use his own language, "he might live and die in peace, and be buried with his fathers." He also states that he informed the agent of their final purpose to leave, never to return, and that he and his followers had finally, fully, and forever severed his and their connection with the Ponca tribe of Indians, and had resolved to disband as a tribe, or band, of Indians, and to cut loose from the government, go to work, become self-sustaining, and adopt the habits and customs of a higher civilization. To accomplish what would seem to be a desirable and laudable purpose, all who were able to do so went to work to earn a living. The Omaha Indians, who speak the same language, and with whom many of the Poncas have long continued to intermarry, gave them employment and ground to cultivate, so as to make them self-sustaining. And it was when at the Omaha reservation, and when thus employed, that they were arrested by order of the government, for the purpose of being taken back to the Indian Territory. They claim to be unable to see the justice, or reason, or wisdom, or necessity, of removing them by force from their own native plains and blood relations to a far-off country, in which they can see little but new-made graves opening for their reception. The land from which they fled in fear has no attractions for them. The love of home and native land was strong enough in the minds of these people to induce them to brave every peril to return and live and die where they had been reared. The bones of the dead son of Standing Bear were not to repose in the land they hoped to be leaving forever, but were carefully preserved and protected, and formed a part of what was to them a melancholy procession homeward. Such instances of parental affection, and such love of home and native land, may be heathen in origin, but it seems to me that they are not unlike Christian in principle.

What is here stated in this connection is mainly for the purpose of showing that the relators did all they could to separate themselves from their tribe and to sever their tribal relations, for the purpose of becoming self-sustaining and living without support from the government. This being so, it presents the question as to whether or not an Indian can withdraw from his tribe, sever his tribal relation therewith, and terminate his allegiance thereto, for the purpose of making an independent living and adopting our own civilization.

If Indian tribes are to be regarded and treated as separate but dependent nations, there can be no serious difficulty about the question. If they are not to be regarded and treated as separate, dependent nations, then no allegiance is owing from an individual Indian to his tribe, and he could, therefore, withdraw therefrom at any time. The question of expatriation has engaged the attention of our government from the time of its very foundation. Many heated discussions have been carried on between our own and foreign governments on this great question, until diplomacy has triumphantly secured the right to every person found within our jurisdiction. This right has always been claimed and admitted by our government, and it is now no longer an open question. It can make but little difference, then, whether we accord to the Indian tribes a national character or not, as in either case I think the individual Indian possesses the clear and God-given right to withdraw from his tribe and forever live away from it, as though it had no further existence. If the right of expatriation was open to doubt in this country down to the year 1868, certainly since that time no sort of question as to the right can now exist. On the 27th of July of that year congress passed an act, now appearing as section 1999 of the Revised Statutes, which declares that: "Whereas, the right of expatriation is a natural and inherent right of all people, indispensable to the enjoyment of the rights of life,

liberty, and the pursuit of happiness; and, whereas, in the recognition of this principle the government has freely received emigrants from all nations, and invested them with the rights of citizenship. * * * Therefore, any declaration, instruction, opinion, order, or decision of any officer of the United States which denies, restricts, impairs, or questions the right of expatriation, is declared inconsistent with the fundamental principles of the republic."

This declaration must forever settle the question until it is reopened by other legislation upon the same subject. This is, however, only reaffirming in the most solemn and authoritative manner a principle well settled and understood in this country for many years past.

In most, if not all, instances in which treaties have been made with the several Indian tribes, where reservations have been set apart for their occupancy, the government has either reserved the right or bound itself to protect the Indians thereon. Many of the treaties expressly prohibit white persons being on the reservations unless specially authorized by the treaties or acts of congress for the purpose of carrying out treaty stipulations.

Laws passed for the government of the Indian country, and for the purpose of regulating trade and intercourse with the Indian tribes, confer upon certain officers of the government almost unlimited power over the persons who go upon the reservations without lawful authority. Section 2149 of the Revised Statutes authorizes and requires the commissioner of Indian affairs, with the approval of the secretary of the interior, to remove from any "tribal reservation" any person being thereon without authority of law, or whose presence within the limits of the reservation may, in the judgment of the commissioner, be detrimental to the peace and welfare of the Indians. The authority here conferred upon the commissioner fully justifies him in causing to be removed from Indian reservations all persons thereon in violation of law, or whose presence thereon may be detrimental to the peace and welfare of the Indians upon the reservations. This applies as well to an Indian as to a white person, and manifestly for the same reason, the object of the law being to prevent unwarranted interference between the Indians and the agent representing the government. Whether such an extensive discretionary power is wisely vested in the commissioner of Indian affairs or not, need not be questioned. It is enough to know that the power rightfully exists, and, where existing, the exercise of the power must be upheld. If, then, the commissioner has the right to cause the expulsion from the Omaha Indian reservation of all persons thereon who are there in violation of law, or whose presence may be detrimental to the peace and welfare of the Indians, then he must of necessity be authorized to use the necessary force to accomplish his purpose. Where, then, is he to look for this necessary force? The military arm of the government is the most natural and most potent force to be used on such occasions, and section 2150 of the Revised Statutes, specially authorizes the use of the army for this service. The army, then, it seems, is the proper force to employ when intruders and trespassers who go upon the reservations are to be ejected therefrom.

The first subdivision of the Revised Statutes last referred to provides that "the military forces of the United States may be employed, in such manner and under such regulations as the president may direct, in the apprehension of every person who may be in the Indian country in violation of law, and in conveying him immediately from the Indian country, by the nearest convenient and safe route, to the civil authority of the territory or judicial district in which such

person shall be found, to be proceeded against in due course of law." This is the authority under which the military can be lawfully employed to remove intruders from an Indian reservation. What may be done by the troops in such cases is here fully and clearly stated; and it is this authority, it is believed, under which the respondent acted.

All Indian reservations held under treaty stipulations with the government must be deemed and taken to be a part of the "Indian country," within the meaning of our laws on that subject. The relators were found upon the Omaha Indian reservation. That being a part of the Indian country, and they not being a part of the Omaha tribe of Indians, they were there without lawful authority, and if the commissioner of Indian affairs deemed their presence detrimental to the peace and welfare of the Omaha Indians, he had lawful warrant to remove them from the reservation, and to employ the necessary military force to effect this object in safety.

General Crook had the rightful authority to remove the relators from the reservation, and must stand justified in removing them therefrom. But when the troops are thus employed they must exercise the authority in the manner provided by the section of the law just read. This law makes it the duty of the troops to convey the parties arrested, by the nearest convenient and safe route, to the civil authority of the territory or judicial district in which such persons shall be found, to be proceeded against in due course of law. The duty of the military authorities is here very clearly and sharply defined, and no one can be justified in departing therefrom, especially in time of peace. As General Crook had the right to arrest and remove the relators from the Omaha Indian reservation, it follows, from what has been stated, that the law required him to convey them to this city and turn them over to the marshal and United States attorney, to be proceeded against in due course of law. Then proceedings could be instituted against them in either the circuit or district court, and if the relators had incurred a penalty under the law, punishment would follow; otherwise, they would be discharged from custody. But this course was not pursued in this case; neither was it intended to observe the laws in that regard, for General Crook's orders, emanating from higher authority, expressly required him to apprehend the relators and remove them by force to the Indian Territory, from which it is alleged they escaped. But in what General Crook has done in the premises no fault can be imputed to him. He was simply obeying the orders of his superior officers, but the orders, as we think, lack the necessary authority of law, and are, therefore, not binding on the relators.

I have searched in vain for the semblance of any authority justifying the commissioner in attempting to remove by force any Indians, whether belonging to a tribe or not, to any place, or for any other purpose than what has been stated. Certainly, without some specific authority found in an act of congress, or in a treaty with the Ponca tribe of Indians, he could not lawfully force the relators back to the Indian Territory, to remain and die in that country, against their will. In the absence of all treaty stipulations or laws of the United States authorizing such removal, I must conclude that no such arbitrary authority exists. It is true, if the relators are to be regarded as a part of the great nation of Ponca Indians, the government might, in time of war, remove them to any place of safety so long as the war should last, but perhaps no longer, unless they were charged with the commission of some crime. This is a war power merely, and exists in time of war only. Every nation exercises the right to arrest and detain an alien enemy during the existence of a war, and all subjects or citizens of the hostile nations are subject to be dealt with under this rule.

But it is not claimed that the Ponca tribe of Indians are at war with the United States, so that this war power might be used against them; in fact, they are amongst the most peaceable and friendly of all the Indian tribes, and have at times received from the government unmistakable and substantial recognition of their long-continued friendship for the whites. In time of peace the war power remains in abeyance, and must be subservient to the civil authority of the government until something occurs to justify its exercise. No fact exists, and nothing has occurred, so far as the relators are concerned, to make it necessary or lawful to exercise such an authority over them. If they could be removed to the Indian Territory by force and kept there in the same way, I can see no good reason why they might not be taken and kept by force in the penitentiary at Lincoln, or Leavenworth, or Jefferson City, or any other place which the commander of the forces might, in his judgment, see proper to designate. I cannot think that any such arbitrary authority exists in this country.

The reasoning advanced in support of my views, leads me to conclude:

1. That an Indian is a "person" within the meaning of the laws of the United States, and has, therefore, the right to sue out a writ of habeas corpus in a federal court, or before a federal judge, in all cases where he may be confined or in custody under color of authority of the United States, or where he is restrained of liberty in violation of the constitution or laws of the United States.

2. That General George Crook, the respondent, being commander of the military department of the Platte, has the custody of the relators, under color of authority of the United States, and in violation of the laws thereof.

3. That no rightful authority exists for removing by force any of the relators to the Indian Territory, as the respondent has been directed to do.

4. That the Indians possess the inherent right of expatriation, as well as the more fortunate white race, and have the inalienable right to "life, liberty, and the pursuit of happiness," so long as they obey the laws and do not trespass on forbidden ground. And,

5. Being restrained of liberty under color of authority of the United States, and in violation of the laws thereof, the relators must be discharged from custody, and it is so ordered.

Ordered accordingly.

"The government has never been intent upon robbing the Indians"

CARL SCHURZ ON THE INDIAN DILEMMA

1881

Carl Schurz (1829–1906) was born in Germany and involved in that country's revolutionary movement (1848–1849) before fleeing to the United States. He was a protean fellow: a lawyer (admitted to the Wisconsin bar, in 1859), a reformer, an abolitionist, briefly the U.S. minister to Spain during the Lincoln Administration (1861–1865), and a general (without military training) in the Union Army. After the Civil War (1861–1865), he toured the South and strongly recommended black suffrage and civil rights. He was a newspaper correspondent, an editor, a Missouri Senator, and an outspoken critic of President Ulysses S. Grant's Administration. Schurz sought a merit-based system of civil service and was the chief organizer of the Liberal Republican Party. It was as Secretary of the Interior for President Rutherford B. Hayes (1822–1893) that Schurz addressed the "Indian dilemma": the history of U.S.-Indian relations was a record of broken treaties, unjust wars, and cruel spoilation; government could fairly be held responsible for most of the Indian wars. Secretary Schurz urged an enlightened policy.

THAT THE HISTORY of our Indian relations presents, in great part, a record of broken treaties, of unjust wars, and of cruel spoliation is a fact too well known to require proof or to suffer denial. But it is only just to the government of the United States to say that its treaties with Indian tribes were, as a rule, made in good faith, and that most of our Indian wars were brought on by circumstances for which the government itself could not fairly be held responsible. Of the treaties, those were the most important by which the government guaranteed to Indian tribes certain tracts of land as reservations to be held and occupied by them forever under the protection of the United States, in the place of other lands ceded by the Indians. There is no reason to doubt that in most, if not all, of such cases those who conducted Indian affairs on the part of the government, not anticipating the rapid advance of settlement, sincerely believed in the possibility of maintaining those reservations intact for the Indians, and that, in this respect, while their intentions were honest, their foresight was at fault.

There are men still living who spent their younger days near the borders of "Indian country" in Ohio and Indiana; and it is a well-known fact that, when the Indian Territory was established west of the Mississippi, it was generally thought that the settlements of white men would never crowd into that region, at least not for many generations. Thus were such reservations guaranteed by the government with the honest belief that the Indians would be secure in their possession, which, as subsequent events proved, was a gross error of judgment.

It is also a fact that most of the Indian wars grew, not from any desire of the government to disturb the Indians in the territorial possessions guaranteed to them but from the restless and unscrupulous greed of frontiersmen who pushed their settlements and ventures into the Indian country, provoked conflicts with the Indians, and then called for the protection of the government against the resisting and retaliating Indians, thus involving it in the hostilities which they themselves had begun. It is true that in some instances Indian wars were precipitated by acts of rashness and violence on the part of military men without orders from the government, while the popular impression that Indian outbreaks were generally caused by the villainy of government agents, who defrauded and starved the Indians, is substantially unfounded. Such frauds and robberies have no doubt been frequently committed.

It has also happened that Indian tribes were exposed to great suffering and actual starvation in consequence of the neglect of Congress to provide the funds necessary to fulfill treaty stipulations. But things of this kind resulted but seldom in actual hostilities. To such wrongs the Indians usually submitted with a more enduring patience than they receive credit for, although, in some instances, it must be admitted, outrages were committed by Indians without provocation, which resulted in trouble on a large scale.

In mentioning these facts, it is not my purpose to hold the government entirely guiltless of the wrongs inflicted upon the Indians. It has, undoubtedly, sometimes lacked in vigor when Indian tribes needed protection. It has, in many cases, yielded too readily to the pressure of those who wanted to possess themselves of Indian lands. Still less would I justify some high-handed proceedings on the part of the government in moving peaceable Indian tribes from place to place without their consent, trying to rectify old blunders by new acts of injustice. But I desire to point out that by far the larger part of our Indian troubles have sprung from the greedy encroachments of white men upon Indian lands, and that, hostilities being brought about in this manner, in which the Indians uniformly succumbed, old treaties and arrangements were overthrown to be supplanted by new ones of a similar character, which eventually led to the same results.

In the light of events, the policy of assigning to the Indian tribes large tracts of land as permanent reservations, within the limits of which they might continue to roam at pleasure, with the expectation that they would never be disturbed thereon, appears as a grand mistake, a natural, perhaps even an unavoidable mistake in times gone by, but a mistake for all that; for that policy failed to take into account the inevitable pressure of rapidly and irresistibly advancing settlement and enterprise. While duly admitting and confessing the injustice done, we must understand the real nature of the difficulty if we mean to solve it. . . .

It is needless to say that the rights of the Indians are a matter of very small consideration in the eyes of those who covet their possessions. The average frontiersman looks upon the Indian simply as a nuisance that is in his way. There are certainly men among them of humane principles, but also many whom it would be difficult to convince that it is a crime to kill an Indian, or that to rob an Indian of his lands is not a meritorious act. This pressure grows in volume and intensity as the population increases, until finally, in some way or another, one Indian reservation after another falls into the hands of white settlers. . . .

The Western country is rapidly filling up. A

steady stream of immigration is following the railroad lines and then spreading to the right and left. The vacant places still existing are either worthless or will soon be exposed to the same invasion. The plains are being occupied by cattle raisers, the fertile valleys and bottomlands by agriculturists, the mountains by miners. What is to become of the Indians? . . .

We are sometimes told that ours is a powerful government which might accomplish such things if it would only put forth its whole strength. Is this so? The government is, indeed, strong in some respects, but weak in others. It may be truthfully said that the government has never been intent upon robbing the Indians. It has frequently tried, in good faith, to protect them against encroachment, and almost as frequently it has failed. It has simply yielded to the pressure exercised upon it by the people who were in immediate contact with the Indians. . . .

What we can and should do is, in general terms, to fit the Indians, as much as possible, for the habits and occupations of civilized life by work and education; to individualize them in the possession and appreciation of property by allotting to them lands in severalty, giving them a fee simple title individually to the parcels of land they cultivate, inalienable for a certain period, and to obtain their consent to a disposition of that part of their lands which they cannot use, for a fair compensation, in such a manner that they no longer stand in the way of the development of the country as an obstacle, but form part of it and are benefited by it.

The circumstances surrounding them place before the Indians this stern alternative—extermination or civilization. The thought of exterminating a race, once the only occupant of the soil upon which so many millions of our own people have grown prosperous and happy, must be revolting to every American who is not devoid of all sentiments of justice and humanity. To civilize them, which was once only a benevolent fancy, has now become an absolute necessity if we mean to save them.

Can Indians be civilized? This question is answered in the negative only by those who do not want to civilize them. My experience in the management of Indian affairs, which enabled me to witness the progress made even among the wildest tribes, confirms me in the belief that it is not only possible but easy to introduce civilized habits and occupations among Indians if only the proper means are employed. We are frequently told that Indians will not work. True, it is difficult to make them work as long as they can live upon hunting. But they will work when their living depends upon it, or when sufficient inducements are offered to them. Of this there is an abundance of proof. To be sure, as to Indian civilization, we must not expect too rapid progress or the attainment of too lofty a standard. We can certainly not transform them at once into great statesmen, or philosophers, or manufacturers, or merchants; but we can make them small farmers and herders. Some of them show even remarkable aptitude for mercantile pursuits on a small scale.

I see no reason why the degree of civilization attained by the Indians in the states of New York, Indiana, Michigan, and some tribes in the Indian Territory should not be attained in the course of time by all. I have no doubt that they can be sufficiently civilized to support themselves, to maintain relations of good neighborship with the people surrounding them, and altogether to cease being a disturbing element in society. The accomplishment of this end, however, will require much considerate care and wise guidance. That care and guidance is necessarily the task of the government which, as to the Indians at least, must exercise paternal functions until they are sufficiently advanced to take care of themselves. . . . When the wild Indian first turns his face from his old habits toward "the ways of the white man," his self-reliance is severely shaken. The picturesque and proud hunter and warrior of the plain or the forest gradually ceases to exist. In his new occupations, with his new aims and objects, he feels himself like a child in need of leading strings. Not clearly knowing where he is to go, he may be led in the right direction, and he may also be led astray.

He is apt to accept the vices as well as the virtues and accomplishments of civilization, and the former, perhaps, more readily than the latter. He is as accessible to bad as to good advice or example, and the class of people usually living in the immediate vicinity of Indian camps and reservations is frequently not such as to exercise upon him an elevating influence. He is in danger of becoming a drunkard before he has learned to restrain his appetites, and of being tricked out of his property before he is able to appreciate its value. He is overcome by a feeling of helplessness, and he naturally looks to the "Great Father" to take him by the hand and guide him on. That guiding hand must necessarily be one of authority and power to command confidence and respect. It can be only that of the government which the Indian is accustomed to regard as a sort of omnipotence on earth. Everything depends upon the wisdom and justice of that guidance.

To fit the Indians for their ultimate absorption in the great body of American citizenship, three things are suggested by common sense as well as philanthropy: (1) that they be taught to work by making work profitable and attractive to them; (2) that they be educated, especially the youth of both sexes; (3) that they be individualized in the possession of property by settlement in severalty with a fee simple title, after which the lands they do not use may be disposed of for general settlement and enterprise without danger and with profit to the Indians. . . .

The Indian, in order to be civilized, must not only learn how to read and write but how to live. On most of the Indian reservations he lives only among his own kind, excepting the teachers and the few white agency people. He may feel the necessity of changing his mode of life ever so strongly; he may hear of civilization ever so much; but as long as he has not with his own eyes seen civilization at work, it will remain to him only a vague, shadowy idea—a newfangled, outlandish contrivance, the objects of which cannot be clearly appreciated by him in detail.

He hears that he must accept "the white man's way," and, in an indistinct manner, he is impressed with the necessity of doing so. But what is the white man's way? What ends does it serve? What means does it employ? What is necessary to attain it? The teaching in a school on an Indian reservation, in the midst of Indian barbarism, answers these questions only from hearsay. The impressions it thus produces, whether in all things right or in some things wrong, will, in any event, be insufficient to give the mind of the Indian a clear conception of what "the white man's way" really is.

The school on the reservation undoubtedly does some good, but it does not enough. If the Indian is to become civilized, the most efficient method will be to permit him to see and watch civilization at work in its own atmosphere. In order to learn to live like the white man, he should see and observe how the white man lives in his own surroundings, what he is doing, and what he is doing it for. He should have an opportunity to observe, not by an occasional bewildering glimpse, like the Indians who now and then come to Washington to see the "Great Father," but observe with the eye of an interested party, while being taught to do likewise. . . .

Allotments of farm tracts to Indians and their settlement in severalty have already been attempted under special laws or treaties with a few tribes; in some instances, with success; in others, the Indians, when they had acquired individual title to their land, and before they had learned to appreciate its value, were induced to dispose of it, or were tricked out of it by unscrupulous white men who took advantage of their ignorance. They were thus impoverished again and some of them fell back upon the government for support. This should be guarded against, as much as it can be, by a legal provision making the title to their farm tracts inalienable for a certain period, say twenty-five years, during which the Indians will have sufficient opportunity to acquire more provident habits, to become somewhat acquainted with the ways of the world, and to learn to take care of themselves.

In some cases where the allotment of lands in severalty and the granting of patents conveying a fee simple title to Indians was provided for in Indian treaties, the Interior Department under the last administration saw fit to put off the full execution of this provision for the reason that the law did not permit the insertion in the patent of the inalienability clause, that without such a clause the Indians would be exposed to the kind of spoliation above mentioned, and that it was hoped Congress would speedily supply that deficiency by the passage of the general Severalty Bill then under discussion. Indeed, without such a clause in the land patents, it cannot be denied that the conveyance of individual fee simple title to Indians would be a hazardous experiment, except in the case of those most advanced in civilization. . . .

The policy here outlined is apt to be looked upon with disfavor by two classes of people: on the one hand, those who think that "the only good Indian is a dead Indian," and who denounce every recognition of the Indian's rights and every desire to promote his advancement in civilization as sickly sentimentality; and, on the other hand, that class of philanthropists who, in their treatment of the Indian question, pay no regard to surrounding circumstances and suspect every policy contemplating a reduction of the Indian reservations of being a scheme of spoliation and robbery gotten up by speculators and "land grabbers." With the first class it seems useless to reason. As to the second, they do not themselves believe, if they are sensible, that twenty-five years hence millions of acres of valuable land will, in any part of the country, still be kept apart as Indian hunting grounds.

The question is whether the Indians are to be exposed to the danger of hostile collisions, and of being robbed of their lands in consequence, or whether they are to be induced by proper and fair means to sell that which, as long as they keep it, is of no advantage to anybody, but which, as soon as they part with it for a just compensation, will be of great advantage to themselves and their white neighbors alike. No true friend of the Indian will hesitate to choose the latter line of policy as one in entire accord with substantial justice, humanity, the civilization and welfare of the red men, and the general interests of the country.

"All allotments shall be selected by the Indians"

THE DAWES ACT
1887

Complex problems surrounded the status of Indian tribes and lands in the 1880s. Could Indians be "civilized" and absorbed into the mainstream of American life? Could Indians establish agriculture along traditional European-American freehold lines? Should tribes be considered "domestic nations?" Responding to President Chester A. Arthur's proposal for land allotments "to such Indians . . . as desire it," Congress, in 1887 (during Grover Cleveland's first of two non-consecutive Presidential terms), legislated the allotment of lands in severalty on the various reservations. The Dawes Act granted to heads of Indian families 160 acres (twice as much if the land were fit only for grazing) and comparable allotments to unmarried Indians. (Grants were not extended to the Five Civilized Nations, in Oklahoma.) The Indians would be protected by the laws of the U.S. and the Territories. The Act, named for Senator Henry L. Dawes, of Massachusetts (1816–1903), was also called the General Allotment Act, or the Indian Homestead Act. After twenty-five years, the Indians were to be granted U.S. citizenship and could sell the land. The Indian Reorganization Act of 1934 overturned the Dawes Act, which was deemed a failure, because it had attempted to impose an alien culture on the Indian and generated a tangle of legalities.

Be it enacted &c. That in all cases where any tribe or band of Indians has been, or shall hereafter be, located upon any reservation created for their use, either by treaty stipulation or by virtue of an act of Congress or executive order setting apart the same for their use, the President of the United States be, and he hereby is, authorized, whenever in his opinion any reservation or any part thereof of such Indians is advantageous for agriculture and grazing purposes to cause said reservation, or any part thereof, to be surveyed, or resurveyed if necessary, and to allot the lands in said reservation in severalty to any Indian located thereon in quantities as follows:

To each head of a family, one-quarter of a section;

To each single person over eighteen years of age, one-eighth of a section; and,

To each other single person under eighteen years now living, or who may be born prior to the date of the order of the President directing an allotment of the lands embraced in any reservation, one-sixteenth of a section. . . .

Sec. 2. That all allotments set apart under the provisions of this act shall be selected by the Indians, heads of families selecting for their minor children, and the agents shall select for each orphan child, and in such manner as to embrace the improvements of the Indians making the selection. . . .

Provided, That if any one entitled to an allotment shall fail to make a selection within four years after the President shall direct that allotments may be made on a particular reservation, the Secretary of the Interior may direct the agent of such tribe or band, if such there be, and if there be no agent, then a special agent appointed for that purpose, to make a selection for such Indian, which selection shall be allotted as in cases where selections are made by the Indians, and patents shall issue in like manner. . . .

Sec. 4. That where any Indian not residing upon a reservation, or for whose tribe no reservation has been provided by treaty, act of Congress or executive order, shall make settlement upon any surveyed or unsurveyed lands of the United States not otherwise appropriated, he or she shall be entitled, upon application to the local land-office for the district in which the lands are located, to have the same allotted to him or her, and to his or her children, in quantities and manner as provided in this act for Indians residing upon reservations; and when such settlement is made upon unsurveyed lands, the grant to such Indians shall be adjusted upon the survey of the lands so as to conform thereto; and patents shall be issued to them for such lands in the manner and with the restrictions as herein provided. . . .

Sec. 5. . . . *And provided further,* That at any time after lands have been allotted to all the Indians of any tribe as herein provided, or sooner if in the opinion of the President it shall be for the best interests of said tribe, it shall be lawful for the Secretary of the Interior to negotiate with such Indian tribe for the purchase and release by said tribe in conformity with the treaty or statute under which such reservation is held, of such portions of its reservation not allotted as such tribe shall, from time to time, consent to sell. . . .

Sec. 6. . . . And every Indian born within the territorial limits of the United States to whom allotments shall have been made under the provisions of this act, or under any law or treaty, and every Indian born within the territorial limits of the United States who has voluntarily taken up, within said limits, his residence separate and apart from any tribe of Indians therein, and has adopted the habits of civilized life, is hereby declared to be a citizen of the United States, and is entitled to all the rights, privileges, and immunities of such citizens, whether said Indian has been or not, by birth or otherwise, a member of any tribe of Indians within the territorial limits of the United States without in any manner impairing or otherwise affecting the right of any such Indian to tribal or other property. . . .

AMENDMENT TO THE DAWES ACT,
FEBRUARY 28, 1891

Be it enacted, &c. [Section 1 of the Dawes Act is amended "to allot each Indian located thereon one-eighth of a section of land."]

Provided, That in case there is not sufficient land in any of said reservations to allot lands to each individual in quantity as above provided the land . . . shall be allotted to each individual pro rata, as near as may be, according to legal subdivisions: . . .

And provided further, That when the lands allotted, or any legal subdivision thereof, are only valuable for grazing purposes, such lands shall be allotted in double quantities. . . .

"Authorized to proclaim new Indian reservations"

THE INDIAN REORGANIZATION ACT
1934

Congress's Wheeler-Howard Act—the Indian Reorganization Act—marked a radical change in official treatment of Indians. It encouraged group progress and independence. The most important piece of Indian legislation in a half century culminated the reform movement set by corncob-pipe smoking, New Deal-Indian Affairs Commissioner John Collier (1884–1968). Wheeler-Howard repealed the Dawes Act (1887) with its train of evil consequences. Dawes's individual allotments had been an impossibly complex practice. Tribal lands would no longer be allotted to individuals. "Surplus" reservation lands not homesteaded would be recovered. Bans on traditional languages and religions were lifted.

No land of any Indian reservation, created or set apart by treaty or agreement with the Indians, Act of Congress, Executive order, purchase, or otherwise, shall be allotted in severalty to any Indian.

SEC. 2. The existing periods of trust placed upon any Indian lands and any restriction on alienation thereof are hereby extended and continued until otherwise directed by Congress.

SEC. 3. The Secretary of the Interior, if he shall find it to be in the public interest, is hereby authorized to restore to tribal ownership the remaining surplus lands of any Indian reservation heretofore opened, or authorized to be opened, to sale, or any other form of disposal by Presidential proclamation, or by any of the public land laws of the United States:

SEC. 4. Except as herein provided, no sale, devise, gift, exchange or other transfer of restricted Indian lands or of shares in the assets of any Indian tribe or corporation organized hereunder, shall be made or approved: . . .

SEC. 5. The Secretary of the Interior is hereby authorized, in his discretion, to acquire through purchase, relinquishment, gift, exchange, or assignment, any interest in lands, water rights or surface rights to lands, within or without existing reservations, including trust or otherwise restricted allotments whether the allottee be living or deceased, for the purpose of providing land for Indians. . . . Title to any lands or rights acquired pursuant to this Act shall be taken in the name of the United States in trust for the Indian tribe or individual Indian for which the land is acquired, and such lands or rights shall be exempt from State and local taxation.

SEC. 6. The Secretary of the Interior is directed to make rules and regulations for the operation and management of Indian forestry units on the principle of sustained-yield management, to restrict the number of livestock grazed on Indian range units to the estimated carrying capacity of such ranges, and to promulgate such other rules and regulations as may be necessary to protect the range from deterioration, to prevent soil erosion, to assure full utilization of the range, and like purposes.

Sec. 7. The Secretary of the Interior is hereby authorized to proclaim new Indian reservations on lands acquired pursuant to any authority conferred by this Act, or to add such lands to existing reservations: *Provided,* That lands added to existing reservations shall be designated for the exclusive use of Indians entitled by enrollment or by tribal membership to residence at such reservations. . . .

"The Indian future is determined by Indian acts . . . decisions."

PRESIDENT NIXON ON INDIAN AFFAIRS
1970

Calling Indians "the most deprived, most isolated group" in the United States, President Richard M. Nixon (1913–1994) believed that it was long past time that the government's Indian policies recognized and built "upon the capacities and insights of the Indian people." The time had come to "break decisively with the past and to create conditions for a new era in which the Indian future is determined by Indian acts and Indian decisions." Mr. Nixon set the stage for legislation and court decisions.

The first Americans—the Indians—are the most deprived and most isolated minority group in our nation. On virtually every scale of measurement—employment, income, education, health—the condition of the Indian people ranks at the bottom.

This condition is the heritage of centuries of injustice. From the time of their first contact with European settlers, the American Indians have been oppressed and brutalized, deprived of their ancestral lands and denied the opportunity to control their own destiny. Even the Federal programs which are intended to meet their needs have frequently proven to be ineffective and demeaning.

But the story of the Indian in America is something more than the record of the white man's frequent aggression, broken agreements, intermittent remorse and prolonged failure. It is a record also of endurance, of survival, of adaptation and creativity in the face of overwhelming obstacles. It is a record of enormous contributions to this country—to its art and culture, to its strength and spirit, to its sense of history and its sense of purpose.

It is long past time that the Indian policies of the Federal government began to recognize and build upon the capacities and insights of the Indian people. Both as a matter of justice and as a matter of enlightened social policy, we must begin to act on the basis of what the Indians themselves have long been telling us. The time has come to break decisively with the past and to create the conditions for a new era in which the Indian future is determined by Indian acts and Indian decisions.

The first and most basic question that must be answered with respect to Indian policy concerns the historic and legal relationship between the Federal government and Indian communities. In the past, this relationship has oscillated between two equally harsh and unacceptable extremes.

On the one hand, it has—at various times during previous Administrations—been the stated policy objective of both the Executive and Legislative branches of the Federal government eventually to terminate the trusteeship relationship between the Federal government and the Indian people. As recently as August of 1953, in House Concurrent Resolution 108, the Congress declared that termination was the long-range goal of its Indian policies. This would mean that Indian tribes would eventually lose any special standing they had under Federal law: the tax exempt status of their lands would be discontinued; Federal responsibility for their economic and social well-being would be repudiated; and the tribes themselves would be effectively dismantled. Tribal property would be divided among individual members who would then be assimilated into the society at large.

This policy of forced termination is wrong, in my judgment, for a number of reasons. First, the premises on which it rests are wrong. Termination implies that the Federal government has taken on a trusteeship responsibility for Indian communities as an act of generosity toward a disadvantaged people and that it can therefore discontinue this responsibility on a unilateral basis whenever it sees fit. But the unique status of Indian tribes does not rest on any premise such as this. The special relationship between Indians and the Federal government is the result instead of solemn obligations which have been entered into by the United States Government. Down through the years, through written treaties and through formal and informal agreements, our government has made specific commitments to the Indian people. For their part, the Indians have often surrendered claims to vast tracts of land and have accepted life on government reservations. In exchange, the government has agreed to provide community services such as health, education and public safety, services which would presumably allow Indian communities to enjoy a standard of living comparable to that of other Americans.

This goal, of course, has never been achieved. But the special relationship between the Indian tribes and the Federal government which arises from these agreements continues to carry immense moral and legal force. To terminate this relationship would be no more appropriate than to terminate the citizenship rights of any other American.

The second reason for rejecting forced termination is that the practical results have been clearly harmful in the few instances in which termination actually has been tried. The removal of Federal trusteeship responsibility has produced considerable disorientation among the affected Indians and has left them unable to relate to a myriad of Federal, State and local assistance efforts. Their economic and social condition has often been worse after termination than it was before.

The third argument I would make against forced termination concerns the effect it has had upon the overwhelming majority of tribes which still enjoy a special relationship with the Federal government. The very threat that this relationship may someday be ended has created a great deal of apprehension among Indian groups and this apprehension, in turn, has had a blighting effect on tribal progress. Any step that might result in greater social, economic or political autonomy is regarded with suspicion by many Indians who fear that it will only bring them closer to the day when the Federal government will disavow its responsibility and cut them adrift.

In short, the fear of one extreme policy, forced termination, has often worked to produce the opposite extreme: excessive dependence on the Federal government. In many cases this dependence is so great that the Indian community is almost entirely run by outsiders who are responsible and responsive to Federal officials in Washington, D.C., rather than to the communities they are supposed to be serving. This is the second of the two harsh approaches which have long plagued our Indian policies. . . .

I believe that both of these policy extremes are wrong. Federal termination errs in one direction, Federal paternalism errs in the other. Only by clearly rejecting both of these extremes can we achieve a policy which truly serves the best interests of the Indian people. Self-determination among the Indian people can and must be encouraged without the threat of eventual termination. In my view, in fact, that is the only way that self-determination can effectively be fostered.

This, then, must be the goal of any new national policy toward the Indian people; to strengthen the Indian's sense of autonomy without threatening his sense of community. We must assure the Indian that he can assume control of his own life without being separated involuntarily from the tribal group. And we must make it clear that Indians can become independent of Federal control without being cut off from Federal concern and Federal support. My specific recommendations to the Congress are designed to carry out this policy.

Because termination is morally and legally unacceptable, because it produces bad practical results, and because the mere threat of termination tends to discourage greater self-sufficiency among Indian groups, I am asking the Congress to pass a new Concurrent Resolution which would expressly renounce, repudiate and repeal the termination policy as expressed in House Concurrent Resolution 108 of the 83rd Congress. This resolution would explicitly affirm the integrity and right to continued existence of all Indian tribes and Alaska native governments, recognizing that cultural pluralism is a source of national strength. It would assure these groups that the United States Government would continue to carry out its treaty and trusteeship obligations to them as long as the groups themselves believed that such a policy was necessary or desirable. It would guarantee that whenever Indian groups decided to assume control or responsibility for government service programs, they could do so and still receive adequate Federal financial support. In short, such a resolution would reaffirm for the Legislative branch—as I hereby affirm for the Executive branch—that the historic relationship between the Federal government and the Indian communities cannot be abridged without the consent of the Indians.

Even as we reject the goal of forced termination, so must we reject the suffocating pattern of paternalism. But how can we best do this? There is no reason why Indian communities should be deprived of the privilege of self-determination merely because they receive monetary support from the Federal government. Nor should they lose Federal money because they reject Federal control.

. . . . it should be up to the Indian tribe to determine whether it is willing and able to assume administrative responsibility for a service program which is presently administered by a Federal agency. To this end, I am proposing legislation which would empower a tribe or a group of tribes or any other Indian community to take over the control or operation of Federally-funded and administered programs in the Department of the Interior and the Department of Health, Education and Welfare whenever the tribal council or comparable community government group voted to do so. . . .

Under the proposed legislation, Indian control of Indian programs would always be a wholly voluntary matter. It would be possible for an Indian group to select that program or that specified portion of a program that it wants to run without assuming responsibility for other components. The "right of retrocession" would also be guaranteed; this means that if the local community elected to administer a program and then later decided to give it back to the Federal government, it would always be able to do so.

Appropriate technical assistance to help local organizations successfully operate these programs would be provided by the Federal government. . . . The legislation I propose would include appropriate protections against any action which endangered the rights, the health, the safety or the welfare of individuals. It would also contain accountability procedures to guard against gross negligence or mismanagement of Federal funds.

This legislation would apply only to services which go directly from the Federal government to the Indian community; those services which are channeled through State or local governments could still be turned over to Indian control by mutual consent. To run the activities for which they have assumed control, the Indian groups could employ local people or outside experts. If they chose to hire Federal employees who had formerly administered these projects, those employees would still enjoy the privileges of Federal employee benefit programs—under special legislation which will also be submitted to the Congress.

Legislation which guarantees the right of Indians to contract for the control or operation of Federal programs would directly channel more money into Indian communities, ... A policy which encourages Indian administration of these programs will help build greater pride and resourcefulness within the Indian community. At the same time, programs which are managed and operated by Indians are likely to be more effective in meeting Indian needs. . . .

No government policy toward Indians can be fully effective unless there is a relationship of trust and confidence between the Federal government and the Indian people. Such a relationship cannot be completed overnight; it is inevitably the product of a long series of words and actions. But we can contribute significantly to such a relationship by responding to just grievances which are especially important to the Indian people.

One such grievance concerns the sacred Indian lands at and near Blue Lake in New Mexico. From the fourteenth century, the Taos Pueblo Indians used these areas for religious and tribal purposes. In 1906, however, the United States Government appropriated these lands for the creation of a national forest. According to a recent determination of the Indian Claims Commission, the government "took said lands from petitioner without compensation."

For 64 years, the Taos Pueblo has been trying to regain possession of this sacred lake and watershed area in order to preserve it in its natural condition and limit its non-Indian use. The Taos Indians consider such action essential to the protection and expression of their religious faith.

The restoration of the Blue Lake lands to the Taos Pueblo Indians is an issue of unique and critical importance to Indians throughout the country. I therefore take this opportunity wholeheartedly to endorse legislation which would restore 48,000 acres of sacred land to the Taos Pueblo people, with the statutory promise that they would be able to use these lands for traditional purposes and that except for such uses the lands would remain forever wild. . . .

One of the saddest aspects of Indian life in the United States is the low quality of Indian education. Drop-out rates for Indians are twice the national average and the average educational level for all Indians under Federal supervision is less than six school years. Again, at least a part of the problem stems from the fact that the Federal government is trying to do for Indians what many Indians could do better for themselves. . . .

Consistent with our policy that the Indian community should have the right to take over the control and operation of federally funded programs, we believe every Indian community wishing to do so should be able to control its own Indian schools. This control would be exercised by school boards selected by Indians and functioning much like other school boards throughout the nation. . . .

We must also take specific action to benefit Indian children in public schools.

Economic deprivation is among the most serious of Indian problems. Unemployment among Indians is ten times the national average; the unemployment rate runs as high as 80 percent on some of the poorest reservations. Eighty percent of reservation Indians have an income which falls below the poverty line; the average annual income for such families is only $1,500. . . . I am proposing the "Indian Financing Act of 1970."

. . . I also urge that legislation be enacted which would permit any tribe which chooses to do so to enter into leases of its land for up to 99 years. Indian people now own over 50 million acres of land that are held in trust by the Federal government. In order to compete in attracting investment capital for commercial, industrial and recreational development of these lands, it is essential that the tribes be able to offer long-term leases. Long-term leasing is preferable to selling such property since it enables tribes to preserve the trust ownership of their reservation homelands. . . .

Despite significant improvements in the past decade and a half, the health of Indian people still lags 20 to 25 years behind that of the general population. The average age at death among Indians is 44 years, about one-third less than the national average. Infant mortality is nearly 50% higher for Indians and Alaska natives than for the population at large; the tuberculosis rate is eight times as high and the suicide rate is twice that of the general population. Many infectious diseases such as trachoma and dysentery that have all but disappeared among other Americans continue to afflict the Indian people.

This Administration is determined that the health status of the first Americans will be improved. In order to initiate expanded efforts in this area, I will request the allocation of an additional $10 million for Indian health programs for the current fiscal year.

. . . Indian health programs will be most effective if more Indians are involved in running them. Yet—almost unbelievably—we are presently able to identify in this country only 30 physicians and fewer than 400 nurses of Indian descent. To meet this situation, we will expand our efforts to train Indians for health careers.

Our new census will probably show that a larger proportion of America's Indians are living off the reservation than ever before in our history. Some authorities even estimate that more Indians are living in cities and towns than are remaining on the reservation. Of those American Indians who are now dwelling in urban areas, approximately three-fourths are living in poverty.

The Bureau of Indian Affairs is organized to serve the 462,000 reservation Indians. The BIA's responsibility does not extend to Indians who have left the reservation, but this point is not always clearly understood. As a result of this misconception, Indians living in urban areas have often lost out on the opportunity to participate in other programs designed for disadvantaged groups. As a first step toward helping the urban Indians, I am instructing appropriate officials to do all they can to ensure that this misunderstanding is corrected.

But misunderstandings are not the most important problem confronting urban Indians. The biggest barrier faced by those Federal, State and local programs which are trying to serve urban Indians is the difficulty of locating and identifying them. Lost in the anonymity of the city, often cut off from family and friends, many urban Indians are slow to establish new community ties. Many drift from neighborhood to neighborhood; many shuttle back and forth between reservations and urban areas. Language and cultural differences compound these problems. As a result, Federal, State and local programs which are designed to help such persons often miss this most deprived and least understood segment of the urban poverty population. . . .

The United States Government acts as a legal trustee for the land and water rights of American Indians. These rights are often of critical economic importance to the Indian people; frequently they are also the subject of extensive legal dispute. In many of these legal confrontations, the Federal government is faced with an inherent conflict of interest. The Secretary of the Interior and the Attorney General must at the same time advance *both* the *national* interest in the use of land and water rights *and* the *private* interests of Indians in land which the government holds as trustee. . . .

I am calling on the Congress to establish an Indian Trust Counsel Authority to assure independent legal representation for the Indians' natural resource rights. . . . At least two of the board members would be Indian. . . .

To help guide the implementation of a new national policy concerning American Indians, I am recommending to the Congress the establishment of a new position in the Department of the Interior—Assistant Secretary for Indian and Territorial Affairs. . . .

Many of the new programs which are outlined in this message have grown out of this Administration's experience with other Indian projects that have been initiated or expanded during the last 17 months. The Office of Economic Opportunity has been particularly active in the development of new and experimental efforts. . . .

Because of the high rate of unemployment and underemployment among Indians, there is probably no other group in the country that would be helped as directly and as substantially by programs such as the new Family Assistance Plan and the proposed Family Health Insurance Plan. It is estimated, for example, that more than half of all Indian families would be eligible for Family Assistance benefits and the enactment of this legislation is therefore of critical importance to the American Indian. . . .

Power to the People

The complexities and contradictions that comprise the American mind, it is useful to remind us, at times have been expressed in diametrically opposed tendencies or simply dissonance between ideals and realities, rhetoric and practices. Words and formulas to the contrary, government has increasingly become central to the lives of Americans, notwithstanding glib phrases like "rugged individualism" and "free enterprise." The negative state has receded in practice and importance in the twentieth century; after 1900, the day was past when Yale's William Graham Sumner, the leading voice of a laissez-faire economic order, categorically repudiated all reform efforts. Beginning about 1902 and rising to a crescendo a decade later, the Muckrakers—that rough grouping of journalists, novelists, poets, and critics—attacked abuses in both government and business, and became integral to the Progressive period.

Corporations, trusts, and great wealth became subject to an intense scrutiny and criticism. Progressivism itself became a movement for reform ideas and advocated programs that emphasized social and political solutions to individual misfortune. Initiated first in the states, measures were passed that affected the way in which people lived and worked. Progressives sought to improve the lives of those adversely affected by industrialization. Prisons, reform schools, educational facilities, suffrage, municipal government, and public utility commissions were matters of state concern. State lawmakers pushed through laws reducing hours of labor, making the workplace safer, improving conditions in sweatshops and tenement houses. The Federal government, taking up the Progressive cause in this area, enacted workmen's compensation measures, passed laws prohibiting child labor and regulating hours of labor, and passed anti-trust measures and railroad and banking reform.

The interwar years did not see a relapse into the negative state. In the early 1930s, the Depression touched virtually all facets of national life. Unemployment rose, production declined sharply, crop prices tumbled, foreclosures on homes and farms became a daily feature of existence. Confronted by a social and economic crisis that gripped the country, President Franklin Roosevelt chose a continuation of the reforms of three decades earlier— and more than reforms, his Administration launched an unprecedented program of assistance to the poor and the unemployed. It did so to the end of feeding the hungry, clothing the naked, calming the economic panic, bringing relief and economic stabilization to the country. "Welfare," no longer a term of opprobrium, became conventional and respectable. President Herbert Hoover's arraignment of direct governmental responsibility for the individual was rejected by a growing majority of Americans. Roosevelt, taking a polar-opposite perspective, believed that ultimately—if all else failed—clothes, housing, food for the nation's poor were a governmental responsibility. Consequently, "welfare," like "relief," was no longer the monopoly of private charity. Endorsing long-range goals as well as the immediate objectives of relief and eco-

nomic stability, Roosevelt's Administration introduced fundamental and lasting changes. Thus the New Deal saw a quantum leap in government regulation and intervention, with the Social Security Act of 1935 becoming the supreme symbol of a welfare state. Perhaps even bolder, more original, was the Tennessee Valley Authority (TVA), which intended to salvage one of the poorest, most flood-prone regions of the country. TVA was a massive scheme of regional development. It built sixteen new dams, took over five existing ones, generated low-rate electric power for 40,000 rural homes, and redeemed the land from constant flooding. The capstone of a national economic and social policy that explicitly repudiated cherished individualistic values, the New Deal vastly enlarged the sphere of public action, created countless new governmental agencies, swelled existing government departments.

President Harry Truman's Fair Deal hardly represented the reversal of Roosevelt's program; though the McMahon Atomic Energy Act of July 1946 can hardly be considered a typical social welfare measure, it suggested that the President was not coy about extending government regulatory power. President Lyndon Johnson, a Chief Executive with large dreams, announced the Great Society in 1964, and his program can easily be seen as a continuation and enlargement of the liberal New Deal tradition. He promised to deal with the full range of social and economic problems confronting society in the mid-1960s—racism, poverty, decaying cities, the degraded quality of life—and he placed an extraordinary array of reform legislation before Congress. The legislature passed and funded Medicare, Medicaid, the 1965 Voting Rights Act, the Federal funding of urban transit, the Clean Air Act. The last, revised in 1970, suggests that even in the decade of President Richard Nixon, the momentum did not cease. The leader who introduced wage and price controls and would have signed a Family Assistance Plan measure could hardly repudiate the Great Society program and governmental assistance to the needy. Nor did that paradigm of a free market economy, President Ronald Reagan, entirely reverse the trend. His Administration represented some degree of popular disillusionment with the welfare state and presumably *excessive government involvement in social policy. He slowed the growth of certain Federal programs, such as welfare and food stamps. But a contradictory massive expenditure, namely defense spending, showed an enormous increase. Social Security and Medicare continued to grow.*

"Examinations of specimens shall be made"

The Pure Food and Drug Act
1906

At the beginning of the twentieth century, Congress enacted legislation for preventing the manufacture, sale, or transportation of adulterated or misbranded or poisonous or deleterious foods, drugs, medicine, and liquors, and for regulating traffic therein. Reform was in the air and even revealed itself in literature. Upton Sinclair's (1878–1968) sixth novel, *The Jungle,* exposed horrifying conditions in meat-packing plants. It told how rats and workers who had fallen into the vats were encased in sausages.

That it shall be unlawful for any person to manufacture within any Territory or the District of Columbia any article of food or drug which is adulterated or misbranded, within the meaning of this Act; and any person who shall violate any of the provisions of this section shall be guilty of a misdemeanor, and for each offense shall, upon conviction thereof, be fined not to exceed five hundred dollars or shall be sentenced to one year's imprisonment, or both such fine and imprisonment, in the discretion of the court, and for each subsequent offense and conviction thereof shall be fined not less than one thousand dollars or sentenced to one year's imprisonment, or both such fine and imprisonment, in the discretion of the court.

SEC. 2. That the introduction into any State or Territory or the District of Columbia from any other State or Territory or the District of Columbia, or from any foreign country, or shipment to any foreign country of any article of food or drugs which is adulterated or misbranded, within the meaning of this Act, is hereby prohibited; and any person who shall ship or deliver for shipment from any State or Territory or the District of Columbia to any other State or Territory or the District of Co-

lumbia, or to a foreign country, or who shall receive in any State or Territory or the District of Columbia from any other State or Territory or the District of Columbia, or foreign country, and having so received, shall deliver, in original unbroken packages, for pay or otherwise, or offer to deliver to any other person, any such article so adulterated or misbranded within the meaning of this Act, or any person who shall sell or offer for sale in the District of Columbia or the Territories of the United States any such adulterated or misbranded foods or drugs, or export or offer to export the same to any foreign country, shall be guilty of a misdemeanor, and for such offense be fined not exceeding two hundred dollars for the first offense, and upon conviction for each subsequent offense not exceeding three hundred dollars or be imprisoned not exceeding one year, or both, in the discretion of the court: *Provided,* That no article shall be deemed misbranded or adulterated within the provisions of this Act when intended for export to any foreign country and prepared or packed according to the specifications or directions of the foreign purchaser when no substance is used in the preparation or packing thereof in conflict with the laws of the foreign country to which said article is intended to be shipped; but if said article shall be in fact sold or offered for sale for domestic use or consumption, then this proviso shall not exempt said article from the operation of any of the other provisions of this Act. . . .

SEC. 4. That the examinations of specimens of foods and drugs shall be made in the Bureau of Chemistry of the Department of Agriculture, or under the direction and supervision of such Bureau, for the purpose of determining from such examinations whether such articles are adulterated or misbranded within the meaning of this Act; and if it shall appear from any such examination that any of such specimens is adulterated or misbranded within the meaning of this Act, the Secretary of Agriculture shall cause notice thereof to be given to the party from whom such sample was obtained. . . .

SEC. 6. That the term "drug," as used in this Act, shall include all medicines and preparations recognized in the United States Pharmacopœia or National Formulary for internal or external use, and any substance or mixture of substances intended to be used for the cure, mitigation, or prevention of disease of either man or other animals. The term "food," as used herein, shall include all articles used for food, drink, confectionery, or condiment by man or other animals, whether simple, mixed, or compound. . . .

SEC. 11. The Secretary of the Treasury shall deliver to the Secretary of Agriculture, upon his request from time to time, samples of foods and drugs which are being imported into the United States or offered for import, giving notice thereof to the owner or consignee, who may appear before the Secretary of Agriculture, and have the right to introduce testimony, and if it appear from the examination of such samples that any article of food or drug offered to be imported into the United States is adulterated or misbranded within the meaning of this Act, or is otherwise dangerous to the health of the people of the United States, or is of a kind forbidden entry into, or forbidden to be sold or restricted in sale in the country in which it is made or from which it is exported, or is otherwise falsely labeled in any respect, the said article shall be refused admission, and the Secretary of the Treasury shall refuse delivery to the consignee and shall cause the destruction of any goods refused delivery which shall not be exported by the consignee within three months from the date of notice of such refusal under such regulations as the Secretary of the Treasury may prescribe:

"Permits . . . for excavation . . . may be granted"

THE ANTIQUITIES ACT
1906

A growing interest in preserving not only the great scenic wonders of the American West but also the sites and structures associated with early American cultures led to the passage of the Antiquities Act authorizing the President "to declare by public proclamation historic landmarks, historic and prehistoric structures, and other objects of historic or scientific interest." With the creation of the National Park Service a decade later, Congress established a national conservation agency with the primary responsibility of promoting and regulating its federally-owned lands in a manner that would "leave them unimpaired for the enjoyment of future generations." With the enactment of the Historic Sites Act of 1935, the preservation mandate of the National Park Service was extended to include historic properties not owned or administered by the Federal government. Since 1966, when the seminal National Historic Preservation Act was passed, over a dozen major pieces of Federal preservation legislation have been enacted.

Any person who shall appropriate, excavate, injure, or destroy any historic or prehistoric ruin or monument, or any object of antiquity, situated on lands owned or controlled by the Government of the United States, without the permission of the Secretary of the Department of the Government having jurisdiction over the lands on which said antiquities are situated, shall upon conviction, be fined in a sum of not more than five hundred dollars or be imprisoned for a period of not more than ninety days, or shall suffer both fine and imprisonment, in the discretion of the court.

SEC. 2. That the President of the United States is hereby authorized, in his discretion, to declare by public proclamation historic landmarks, historic and prehistoric structures, and other objects of historic or scientific interest that are situated upon the lands owned or controlled by the Government of the United States to be national monuments, and may reserve as a part thereof parcels of land, the limits of which in all cases shall be confined to the smallest area compatible with the proper care and management of the objects to be protected: *Provided,* That when such objects are situated upon a tract covered by a bona fide unperfected claim or held in private ownership, the tract, or so much thereof as may be necessary for the proper care and management of the object, may be relinquished to the Government, and the Secretary of the Interior is hereby authorized to accept the relinquishment of such tracts in behalf of the Government of the United States.

SEC. 3. That permits for the examination of ruins, the excavation of archaeological sites, and the gathering of objects of antiquity upon the lands under their respective jurisdictions may be granted by the Secretaries of the Interior, Agriculture, and War to institutions which they may deem properly qualified to conduct such examination, excavation, or gathering, subject to such rules and regulations as they may prescribe: *Provided,* That the examinations, excavations, and gatherings are undertaken for the benefit of reputable museums, universities, colleges, or other recognized scientific or educational institutions, with a view to increasing the knowledge of such objects, and that the gatherings shall be made for permanent preservation in public museums. . . .

"Shall have power to construct such dams, and reservoirs"

THE TENNESSEE VALLEY AUTHORITY ACT
1933

Responding to President Franklin Delano Roosevelt's (1882–1945) New Deal declaration that the Tennessee River transcend mere power development, Congress acted to improve navigability and flood control, provide for reforestation, provide for the agricultural and industrial development of the valley, and provide for the national defense by the creation of a corporation for the operation of U.S. properties at and near Muscle Shoals, Alabama. The President said, "This development leads logically to national planning for a complete river watershed involving many states and the future lives and welfare of millions. It touches and gives life to all forms of human concerns." Eventually, there were five TVA dams, 20 other dams were improved, and a system of inland waterways constructed. TVA became one of the nation's largest and cheapest suppliers of power, channeling electricity to rural areas in seven states. In the 1950s, President Dwight D. Eisenhower (1890–1969) condemned TVA as an example of "creeping socialism."

Be it enacted by the Senate and House of Representatives of the United States of America in Congress assembled, That for the purpose of maintaining and operating the properties now owned by the United States in the vicinity of Muscle Shoals, Alabama, in the interest of the national defense and for agricultural and industrial development, and to improve navigation in the Tennessee River and to control the destructive flood water in the Tennessee River and Mississippi River Basins, there is hereby created a body corporate by the name of the "Tennessee Valley Authority" (hereinafter referred to as the "Corporation").

Sec. 2. (a) The board of directors of the Corporation (hereinafter referred to as the "board") shall be composed of three members, to be appointed by the President, by and with the advice and consent of the Senate. In appointing the members of the board, the President shall designate the chairman. All other officials, agents, and employees shall be designated and selected by the board. . . .

(j) Shall have power to construct such dams, and reservoirs, in the Tennessee River and its tributaries, as in conjunction with Wilson Dam, and Norris, Wheeler, and Pickwick Landing Dams, now under construction, will provide a nine-foot channel in the said river and maintain a water supply for the same, from Knoxville to its mouth, and will best serve to promote navigation on the Tennessee River and its tributaries and control destructive flood waters in the Tennessee and Mississippi River drainage basins; and shall have power to acquire or construct power houses, power structures, transmission lines, navigation projects, and incidental works in the Tennessee River and its tributaries, and to unite the various power installations into one or more systems by transmission lines. The directors of the Authority are hereby directed to report to Congress their recommendations not later than April 1, 1936, for the unified development of the Tennessee River system.

(k) Shall have power in the name of the United States—

(a) to convey by deed, lease, or otherwise, any real property in the possession of or under the control of the Corporation to any person or persons, for the purpose of recreation or use as a summer residence, or for the operation on such premises of pleasure resorts for boating, fishing, bathing, or any similar purpose; . . .

Sec. 5. The board is hereby authorized—

(a) To contract with commercial producers for the production of such fertilizers or fertilizer materials as may be needed in the Government's program of development and introduction in excess of that produced by Government plants. Such contracts may provide either for outright purchase of materials by the board or only for the payment of carrying charges on special materials manufactured at the board's request for its program.

(b) To arrange with farmers and farm organizations for large-scale practical use of the new forms of fertilizers under conditions permitting an accurate measure of the economic return they produce. . . .

(e) Under the authority of this Act the board may make donations or sales of the product of the plant or plants operated by it to be fairly and equitably distributed through the agency of county demonstration agents, agricultural colleges, or otherwise as the board may direct, for experimentation, education, and introduction of the use of such products in cooperation with practical farmers so as to obtain information as to the value, effect, and best methods of their use. . . .

(h) To establish, maintain, and operate laboratories and experimental plants, and to undertake experiments for the purpose of enabling the Corporation to furnish nitrogen products for military purposes, and nitrogen and other fertilizer products for agricultural purposes in the most economical manner and at the highest standard of efficiency. . . .

(j) Upon the requisition of the Secretary of War or the Secretary of the Navy to manufacture for and sell at cost to the United States explosives or their nitrogenous content.

(k) Upon the requisition of the Secretary of War the Corporation shall allot and deliver without charge to the War Department so much power as shall be necessary in the judgment of said Department for use in operation of all locks, lifts, or other facilities in aid of navigation.

(l) To produce, distribute, and sell electric power, as herein particularly specified. . . .

Sec. 7. In order to enable the Corporation to exercise the powers and duties vested in it by this Act—

(a) The exclusive use, possession, and control of the United States nitrate plants numbered 1 and 2, including steam plants, located, respectively, at Sheffield, Alabama, and Muscle Shoals, Alabama, together with all real estate and buildings connected therewith, all tools and machinery, equipment, accessories, and materials belonging thereto, and all laboratories and plants used as auxiliaries thereto; the fixed-nitrogen research laboratory, the Waco limestone quarry, in Alabama, and Dam Numbered 2, located at Muscle Shoals, its power house, and all hydroelectric and operating appurtenances (except the locks), and all machinery, lands, and buildings in connection therewith, and all appurtenances thereof, and all other property to be acquired by the Corporation in its own name or in the name of the United States of America, are hereby entrusted to the Corporation for the purposes of this Act.

(b) The President of the United States is authorized to provide for the transfer to the Corporation of the use, possession, and control of such other real or personal property of the United States as he may from time to time deem necessary and proper for the purposes of the Corporation as herein stated. . . .

Sec. 8 . . . . (c) Each member of the board, before entering upon the duties of his office, shall subscribe to an oath (or affirmation) to support the Constitution of the United States and to faithfully and impartially perform the duties imposed upon him by this Act. . . .

Sec. 11. It is hereby declared to be the policy of the Government so far as practical to distribute and sell the surplus power generated at Muscle Shoals equitably among the States, counties, and municipalities within transmission distance. This policy is further declared to be that the projects herein provided for shall be considered primarily as for the benefit of the people of the section as a whole and particularly the domestic and rural consumers to whom the power can economically be made available, and accordingly that sale to and use by industry shall be a secondary purpose, to be utilized principally to secure a sufficiently high load factor and revenue returns which will permit domestic and rural use at the lowest possible rates and in such manner as to encourage increased domestic and rural use of electricity. It is further hereby declared to be the policy of the Government to utilize the Muscle Shoals properties so far as may be necessary to improve, increase, and cheapen the production of fertilizer ingredients by carrying out the provisions of this Act [48 Stat. 65, 16 U.S.C. sec. 831j].

Sec. 12. In order to place the board upon a fair basis for making such contracts and for receiving bids for the sale of such power, it is hereby expressly authorized, either from appropriations made by Congress or from funds secured from the sale of such power, or from funds secured by the sale of bonds hereafter provided for, to construct, lease, purchase, or authorize the construction of transmission lines within transmission distance from the place where generated, and to interconnect with other systems. The board is also authorized to lease to any person, persons, or corporation the use of any transmission line owned by the Government and operated by the board, but no such lease shall be made that in any way interferes with the use of such transmission lines by the board: . . .

Sec. 14. The board shall make a thorough investigation as to the present value of Dam Numbered 2, and the steam plants at nitrate plant numbered 1, and nitrate plant numbered 2, and as to the cost of Cove Creek Dam, for the purpose of ascertaining how much of the value or the cost of said properties shall be allocated and charged up to (1) flood control, (2) navigation, (3) fertilizer, (4) national defense, and (5) the development of power. . . .

The board shall on or before January 1, 1937, file with Congress a statement of its allocation of the value of all such properties turned over to said board, and which have been completed prior to the end of the preceding fiscal year, and shall thereafter in its annual report to Congress file a statement of its allocation of the value of such properties as have been completed during the preceding fiscal year.

For the purpose of accumulating data useful to the Congress in the formulation of legislative policy in matters relating to the generation, transmission, and distribution of electric energy and the production of chemicals necessary to national defense and useful in agriculture, and to the Federal Power Commission and other Federal and State agencies, and to the public, the board shall keep complete accounts of its costs of generation, transmission, and distribution of electric energy and shall keep a complete account of the total cost of generating and transmission facilities constructed or otherwise acquired by the Corporation, and of producing such chemicals, and a description of the major components of such costs according to such uniform system of accounting for public utilities as the Federal Power Commission has, and if it has none, then it is hereby empowered and directed to prescribe such uniform system of accounting, together with records of such other physical data and operating statistics of the Authority as may be helpful in determining the actual cost and value of services, and the practices, methods, facilities, equipment, appliances, and standards and sizes, types, location, and geographical and economic integration of plants and systems best suited to promote the public interest, efficiency, and the wider and more economical use of electric energy. . . .

Nothing in this subsection shall prevent the Corporation or its distributors from supplying electric power to any customer within any area in which the Corporation or its distributors had generally established electric service on July 1, 1957, and to which electric service was not being supplied from any other source on the effective date of this Act.

Nothing in this subsection shall prevent the Corporation, when economically feasible, from making exchange power arrangements with other power-generating organizations with which the Corporation had such arrangements on July 1, 1957, nor prevent the Corporation from continuing to supply power to Dyersburg, Tennessee, and Covington, Tennessee, or from entering into

contracts to supply or from supplying power to the cities of Paducah, Kentucky; Princeton, Kentucky; Glasgow, Kentucky; Fulton, Kentucky; Monticello, Kentucky; Hickman, Kentucky; Chickamauga, Georgia; Ringgold, Georgia; Oak Ridge, Tennessee; and South Fulton, Tennessee; or agencies thereof; or from entering into contracts to supply or from supplying power for the Naval Auxiliary Air Station in Lauderdale and Kemper Counties, Mississippi, through the facilities of the East Mississippi Electric Power Association: *Provided further,* That nothing herein contained shall prevent the transmission of TVA power to the Atomic Energy Commission or the Department of Defense or any agency thereof, on certification by the President of the United States that an emergency defense need for such power exists. Nothing in this Act shall affect the present rights of the parties in any existing lawsuits involving efforts of towns in the same general area where TVA power is supplied to obtain TVA power. . . .

(h) It is hereby declared to be the intent of this section to aid the Corporation in discharging its responsibility for the advancement of the national defense and the physical, social and economic development of the area in which it conducts its operations by providing it with adequate authority and administrative flexibility to obtain the necessary funds with which to assure an ample supply of electric power for such purposes by issuance of bonds and as otherwise provided herein. . . .

Sec. 16. The board, whenever the President deems it advisable, is hereby empowered and directed to complete Dam Numbered 2 at Muscle Shoals, Alabama, and the steam plant at nitrate plant numbered 2, in the vicinity of Muscle Shoals, by installing in Dam Numbered 2 the additional power units according to the plans and specifications of said dam, and the additional power unit in the steam plant at nitrate plant numbered 2.

Sec. 17. The Secretary of War, or the Secretary of the Interior, is hereby authorized to construct, either directly or by contract to the lowest responsible bidder, after due advertisement, a dam in and across Clinch River in the State of Tennessee, which has by long custom become known and designated as the Cove Creek Dam, together with a transmission line from Muscle Shoals, according to the latest and most approved designs, including power house and hydroelectric installations and equipment for the generation of power, in order that the waters of the said Clinch River may be impounded and stored above said dam for the purpose of increasing and regulating the flow of the Clinch River and the Tennessee River below, so that the maximum amount of primary power may be developed at Dam Numbered 2 and at any and all other dams below the said Cove Creek Dam: *Provided, however,* That the President is hereby authorized by appropriate order to direct the employment by the Secretary of War, or by the Secretary of the Interior, of such engineer or engineers as he may designate, to perform such duties and obligations as he may deem proper, either in the drawing of plans and specifications for said dam, or to perform any other work in the building or construction of the same. The President may, by such order, place the control of the construction of said dam in the hands of such engineer or engineers taken from private life as he may desire: *And provided further,* That the President is hereby expressly authorized, without regard to the restriction or limitation of any other statute, to select attorneys and assistants for the purpose of making any investigation he may deem proper to ascertain whether, in the control and management of Dam Numbered 2, or any other dam or property owned by the Government in the Tennessee River Basin, or in the authorization of any improvement therein, there has been any undue or unfair advantage given to private persons, partnerships, or corporations, by any officials or employees of the Government, or whether in any such matters the Government has been injured or unjustly deprived of any of its rights.

Sec. 18. In order to enable and empower the Secretary of War, the Secretary of the Interior, or the board to carry out the authority hereby conferred, in the most economical and efficient manner, he or it is hereby authorized and empowered in the exercise of the powers of national defense in aid of navigation, and in the control of the flood waters of the Tennessee and Mississippi Rivers, constituting channels of interstate commerce, to exercise the right of eminent domain for all purposes of this Act, and to condemn all lands, easements, rights of way, and other area necessary in order to obtain a site for said Cove Creek Dam, and the flowage rights for the reservoir of water above said dam, and to negotiate and conclude contracts with States, counties, municipalities, and all State agencies and with railroads, railroad corporations, common carriers, and all public utility commissions and any other person, firm, or corporation, for the relocation of railroad tracks, highways, highway bridges, mills, ferries, electric-light plants, and any and all other properties, enterprises, and projects whose removal may be necessary in order to carry out the provisions of this Act. When said Cove Creek Dam, transmission line, and power house shall have been completed, the possession, use, and control thereof shall be entrusted to the Corporation for use and operation in connection with the general Tennessee Valley project, and to promote flood control and navigation in the Tennessee River. . . .

Sec. 20. The Government of the United States

hereby reserves the right, in case of war or national emergency declared by Congress, to take possession of all or any part of the property described or referred to in this Act for the purpose of manufacturing explosives or for other war purposes; but, if this right is exercised by the Government, it shall pay the reasonable and fair damages that may be suffered by any party whose contract for the purchase of electric power or fixed nitrogen or fertilizer ingredients is hereby violated, after the amount of the damages has been fixed by the United States Claims Court in proceedings instituted and conducted for that purpose under rules prescribed by the court. . . .

Sec. 22. To aid further the proper use, conservation, and development of the natural resources of the Tennessee River drainage basin and of such adjoining territory as may be related to or materially affected by the development consequent to this Act, and to provide for the general welfare of the citizens of said areas, the President is hereby authorized, by such means or methods as he may deem proper within the limits of appropriations made therefor by Congress, to make such surveys of and general plans for said Tennessee basin and adjoining territory as may be useful to the Congress and to the several States in guiding and controlling the extent, sequence, and nature of development that may be equitably and economically advanced through the expenditure of public funds, or through the guidance or control of public authority, all for the general purpose of fostering an orderly and proper physical, economic, and social development of said areas; and the President is further authorized in making said surveys and plans to cooperate maintenance shall have been submitted to and approved by the board; and the construction, commencement of construction, operation, or maintenance of such structures without such approval is hereby prohibited. When such plans shall have been approved, deviation therefrom either before or after completion of such structures is prohibited unless the modification of such plans has previously been submitted to and approved by the board. . . .

Sec. 31. This Act shall be liberally construed to carry out the purposes of Congress to provide for the disposition of and make needful rules and regulations respecting Government properties entrusted to the Authority, provide for the national defense, improve navigation, control destructive floods, and promote interstate commerce and the general welfare, but no real estate shall be held except what is necessary in the opinion of the board to carry out plans and projects actually decided upon requiring the use of such land: *Provided,* That any land purchased by the Authority and not necessary to carry out plans and projects actually decided upon shall be sold by the Authority as agent of the United States, after due advertisement, at public auction to the highest bidder, or at private sale as provided in section 4(k) of this Act.

"Unknown factors are involved"

DEVELOPING ATOMIC ENERGY
1946

A year after the U.S. atomic bombing of the Japanese cities Hiroshima and Nagasaki led to Japan's surrender (1945) and the end of the Second World War, but before development of the super H-bomb (an atomic bomb triggers a hydrogen bomb), Congress established the Atomic Energy Commission. It was believed that development and utilization of atomic energy would improve the public welfare, increase the standard of living, strengthen free competition in private enterprise, and promote world peace. Policy would be subject to the paramount objective of assuring the common defense and security of the nation.

DECLARATION OF POLICY

SECTION 1. (a) FINDINGS AND DECLARATION.—Research and experimentation in the field of nuclear chain reaction have attained the stage at which the release of atomic energy on a large scale is practical. The significance of the atomic bomb for military purposes is evident. The effect of the use of atomic energy for civilian purposes upon the social, economic, and political structures of today cannot now be determined. It is a field in which unknown factors are involved. Therefore, any legislation will necessarily be subject to revision from time to time. It is reasonable to anticipate, however, that tapping this new source of energy will cause profound changes in our present way of life. Accordingly, it is hereby declared to be the policy of the people of the United States that, subject at all times to the paramount objective of assuring the common defense and security, the development and utilization of atomic energy shall, so far as practicable, be directed toward improving the public welfare, increasing the standard of living, strengthening free competition in private enterprise, and promoting world peace.

(b) PURPOSE OF ACT.—It is the purpose of this Act to effectuate the policies set out in section 1(a) by providing, among others, for the following major programs relating to atomic energy:

(1) A program of assisting and fostering private research and development to encourage maximum scientific progress;

(2) A program for the control of scientific and technical information which will permit the dissemination of such information to encourage scientific progress, and for the sharing on a reciprocal basis of information concerning the practical industrial application of atomic energy as soon as effective and enforceable safeguards against its use for destructive purposes can be devised;

(3) A program of federally conducted research and development to assure the Government of adequate scientific and technical accomplishment;

(4) A program for Government control of the production, ownership, and use of fissionable material to assure the common defense and security and to insure the broadest possible exploitation of the fields; and

(5) A program of administration which will be consistent with the foregoing policies and with international arrangements made by the United States, and which will enable the Congress to be currently informed so as to take further legislative action as may hereafter be appropriate.

ORGANIZATION

SEC. 2. (a) ATOMIC ENERGY COMMISSION.—

(1) There is hereby established an Atomic Energy Commission (herein called the Commission), which shall be composed of five members. Three members shall constitute a quorum of the Commission. The President shall designate one member as Chairman of the Commission. . . .

RESEARCH

SEC. 3. (a) RESEARCH ASSISTANCE.— The Commission is directed to exercise its powers in such manner as to insure the continued conduct of research and development activities in the fields specified below by private or public institutions or persons and to assist in the acquisition of an ever-expanding fund of theoretical and practical knowledge in such fields. To this end the Commission is authorized and directed to make arrangements (including contracts, agreements, and loans) for the conduct of research and development activities relating to—

(1) nuclear processes;

(2) the theory and production of atomic energy, including processes, materials, and devices related to such production;

(3) utilization of fissionable and radioactive materials for medical, biological, health, or military purposes;

(4) utilization of fissionable and radioactive materials and processes entailed in the produc-

tion of such materials for all other purposes, including industrial uses; and

(5) the protection of health during research and production activities. . . .

(7) PUBLIC LANDS.—All uranium, thorium, and all other materials determined pursuant to paragraph (1) of this subsection to be peculiarly essential to the production of fissionable material, contained, in whatever concentration, in deposits in the public lands are hereby reserved for the use of the United States subject to valid claims, rights, or privileges existing on the date of the enactment of this Act: The Secretary of the Interior shall cause to be inserted in every patent, conveyance, lease, permit, or other authorization hereafter granted to use the public lands or their mineral resources, under any of which there might result the extraction of any materials so reserved, a reservation to the United States of all such materials, whether or not of commercial value, together with the right of the United States through its authorized agents or representatives at any time to enter upon the land and prospect for, mine, and remove the same, making just compensation for any damage or injury occasioned thereby.

MILITARY APPLICATIONS OF ATOMIC ENERGY

SEC. 6. (a) AUTHORITY.—The Commission is authorized to—

(1) conduct experiments and do research and development work in the military application of atomic energy; and

(2) engage in the production of atomic bombs, atomic bomb parts, or other military weapons utilizing fissionable materials; except that such activities shall be carried on only to the extent that the express consent and direction of the President of the United States has been ob-

tained, which consent and direction shall be obtained at least once each year. . . .

INTERNATIONAL ARRANGEMENTS

SEC. 8.

. . . (b) EFFECT OF INTERNATIONAL ARRANGEMENTS.—Any provision of this Act or any action of the Commission to the extent that it conflicts with the provisions of any international arrangement made after the date of enactment of this Act shall be deemed to be of no further force or effect.

PROPERTY OF THE COMMISSION

SEC. 9. (a) The President shall direct the transfer to the Commission of all interests owned by the United States or any Government agency in the following property:

(1) All fissionable material; all atomic weapons and parts thereof; all facilities, equipment and materials for the processing, production, or utilization of fissionable material or atomic energy; all processes and technical information of any kind, and the source thereof (including data, drawings, specifications, patents, patent applications, and other sources) relating to the processing, production, or utilization of fissionable material or atomic energy; and all contracts, agreements, leases, patents, applications for patents, inventions and discoveries (whether patented or unpatented), and other rights of any kind concerning any such items;

(2) All facilities, equipment, and materials, devoted primarily to atomic energy research and development; and

(3) Such other property owned by or in the custody or control of the Manhattan Engineer District or other Government agencies as the President may determine.

SEC 10. . . .

(2) That the dissemination of scientific and technical information relating to atomic energy should be permitted and encouraged so as to provide that free interchange of ideas and criticisms which is essential to scientific progress.

(3) Whoever, with intent to injure the United States or with intent to secure an advantage to any foreign nation, acquires or attempts or conspires to acquire any document, writing, sketch, photograph, plan, model, instrument, appliance, note or information involving or incorporating restricted data shall, upon conviction thereof, be punished by death or imprisonment for life (but the penalty of death or imprisonment for life may be imposed only upon recommendation of the jury and only in cases where the offense was committed with intent to injure the United States); or by a fine of not more than $20,000 or imprisonment for not more than twenty years, or both. . . .

"To promote the public health and welfare"

THE CLEAN AIR ACT
1970

Since 1970, each state has had primary responsibility for ensuring air quality within its borders. Emissions of all airborne microscopic particles under 10 microns in diameter (by comparison, a human hair is 100 microns in diameter) have had to be reduced. A governor of California (Ronald W. Reagan, born 1911) said that if he were to single out the one major issue that most likely would dominate the nation's political attention in the 1970s, "it would be environmental protection . . . What good is a booming economy," he asked, "if the air is too foul to breathe, the water too polluted to drink, and our cities too cluttered with ugly examples of environmental neglect to provide comfortable living?" Years of regional disputes were settled in 1990 when House and Senate negotiators strengthened and broadened the Government's authority: Stricter standards were set and timetables for cutting chemical contamination sharply were established. Too, production of chemicals that destroy the ozone layer was to cease. The quality of America's air has improved dramatically, thanks to cleaner cars, cleaner power plants, and cleaner fuels.

THE CONGRESS FINDS—
(1) that the predominant part of the Nation's population is located in its rapidly expanding metropolitan and other urban areas, which generally cross the boundary lines of local jurisdictions and often extend into two or more States;

(2) that the growth in the amount and complexity of air pollution brought about by urbanization, industrial development, and the increasing use of motor vehicles, has resulted in mounting dangers to the public health and welfare, including injury to agricultural crops and livestock, damage to and the deterioration of property, and hazards to air and ground transportation;

(3) that air pollution prevention (that is, the reduction or elimination, through any measures, of the amount of pollutants produced or created at the source) and air pollution control at its source is the primary responsibility of States and local governments; and

(4) that Federal financial assistance and leadership is essential for the development of cooperative Federal, State, regional, and local programs to prevent and control air pollution.

(b) Declaration.

The purposes of this subchapter are—

(1) to protect and enhance the quality of the Nation's air resources so as to promote the public health and welfare and the productive capacity of its population;

(2) to initiate and accelerate a national research and development program to achieve the prevention and control of air pollution;

(3) to provide technical and financial assistance to State and local governments in connec-

tion with the development and execution of their air pollution prevention and control programs; and

(4) to encourage and assist the development and operation of regional air pollution prevention and control programs.

(c) Pollution prevention

A primary goal of this chapter is to encourage or otherwise promote reasonable Federal, State, and local governmental actions, consistent with the provisions of this chapter, for pollution prevention.

"All possible sources of energy be developed"

THE ENERGY REORGANIZATION ACT
1974

In order to promote more efficient management of energy sources, Congress reorganized and consolidated certain functions of the Federal government in creating the Energy Research and Development Administration and Nuclear Regulatory Commission.

DECLARATION OF PURPOSE

SEC. 2. (a) The Congress hereby declares that the general welfare and the common defense and security require effective action to develop and increase the efficiency and reliability of use of, all energy sources to meet the needs of present and future generations, to increase the productivity of the national economy and strengthen its position in regard to international trade, to make the Nation self-sufficient in energy, to advance the goals of restoring, protecting, and enhancing environmental quality, and to assure public health and safety.

(b) The Congress finds that to best achieve these objectives, improve Government operations, and assure the coordinated and effective development of all energy sources, it is necessary to establish an Energy Research and Development Administration to bring together and direct Federal activities relating to research and development on the various sources of energy, to increase the efficiency and reliability in the use of energy, and to carry out the performance of other functions, including but not limited to the Atomic Energy Commission's military and production activities and its general basic research activities. In establishing an Energy Research

and Development Administration to achieve these objectives, the Congress intends that all possible sources of energy be developed consistent with warranted priorities.

(c) The Congress finds that it is in the public interest that the licensing and related regulatory functions of the Atomic Energy Commission be separated from the performance of the other functions of the Commission, and that this separation be effected in an orderly manner, pursuant to this Act, assuring adequacy of technical and other resources necessary for the performance of each.

(d) The Congress declares that it is in the public interest and the policy of Congress that small business concerns be given a reasonable opportunity to participate, insofar as is possible, fairly and equitably in grants, contracts, purchases, and other Federal activities relating to research, development and demonstration of sources of energy efficiency, and utilization and conservation of energy. In carrying out this policy, to the extent practicable, the Administrator shall consult with the Administrator of the Small Business Administration.

(e) Determination of priorities which are warranted should be based on such considerations as power-related values of an energy source, preservation of material resources, reduction of pollutants, export market potential (including reduction of imports), among others. On such a basis, energy sources warranting priority might include, but not be limited to, the various methods or utilizing solar energy. [42 U.S.C. 5801]

TITLE I—ENERGY RESEARCH AND DEVELOPMENT ADMINISTRATION

ABOLITION AND TRANSFERS

SEC. 104. (a) The Atomic Energy Commission is hereby abolished. Sections 21 and 22 of the Atomic Energy Act of 1954, as amended (42 U.S.C. 2031 and 2032) are repealed.

(b) All other functions of the Commission, the Chairman and members of the Commission, and the officers and components of the Commission are hereby transferred or allowed to lapse pursuant to the provisions of this Act.

(c) There are hereby transferred to and vested in the Administrator all functions of the Atomic Energy Commission, the Chairman and members of the Commission, and the officers and components of the Commission, except as otherwise provided in this Act.

"Ordered, adjudged, and decreed"
BREAKING UP AT&T
1982

In a landmark anti-trust decision that transformed the telephone industry, the United States dismantled the monopolistic American Telephone and Telegraph Company (AT&T). Ending a seven-year suit, AT&T gave up all of its twenty-two relatively low-profit, wholly-owned local telephone subsidiaries. It was, however, free to enter previously prohibited areas, such as data processing. AT&T got a green light to speed along the information superhighway. Sixteen years after the breakup, the 111-year-old, largest long-distance carrier and direct Internet access provider had 134,000 employees and annual revenues of $52.2-billion. (In 1911, in a monumental anti-trust case, the Rockefeller family's Standard Oil Company was divided into subsidiaries. The Supreme Court, finding that Standard had engaged in an unreasonable combination, ruled that the holding company was in restraint of trade and, as such, in violation of the Sherman Anti-trust Act.)

Plaintiff, United States of America, having filed its complaint herein on January 14, 1949; the defendants having appeared and filed their answer to such complaint denying the substantive allegations thereof; the parties, by their attorneys, having severally consented to a Final Judgment which was entered by the Court on January 24, 1956, and the parties having subsequently agreed that modification of such Final Judgment is required by the technological, economic and regulatory changes which have occurred since the entry of such Final Judgment;

Upon joint motion of the parties and after hearing by the Court, it is hereby

ORDERED, ADJUDGED, AND DE-CREED that the Final Judgment entered on January 24, 1956, is hereby vacated in its entirety and replaced by the following items and provisions:

A. Not later than six months after the effective date of this Modification of Final Judgment, defendant AT&T shall submit to the Department of Justice for its approval, and thereafter implement, a plan of reorganization. Such plan shall provide for the completion, within 18 months after the effective date of this Modification of Final Judgment, of the following steps:

1. The transfer from AT&T and its affiliates to the BOCs, or to a new entity subsequently to be separated from AT&T and to be owned by the BOCs, of sufficient facilities, personnel, systems, and rights to technical information to permit the BOCs to perform, independently of AT&T, exchange telecommunications and exchange access functions, including the procurement for, and engineering, marketing and management of, those functions, and sufficient to enable the BOCs to meet the equal exchange access requirements of Appendix B;

2. The separation within the BOCs of all facilities, personnel and books of account between those relating to the exchange telecommunications or exchange access functions and those relating to other functions (including the

provision of interexchange switching and transmission and the provision of customer premises equipment to the public); provided that there shall be no joint ownership of facilities, but appropriate provision may be made for sharing, through leasing or otherwise, of multifunction facilities so long as the separated portion of each BOC is ensured control over the exchange telecommunications and exchange access functions;

3. The termination of the License Contracts between AT&T and the BOCs and other subsidiaries and the Standard Supply Contract between Western Electric and the BOCs and other subsidiaries; and

4. The transfer of ownership of the separated portions of the BOCs providing local exchange and exchange access services from AT&T by means of a spin-off of stock of the separated BOCs to the shareholders of AT&T, or by other disposition; provided that nothing in this Modification of Final Judgment shall require or prohibit the consolidation of the ownership of the BOCs into any particular number of entities.

B. Notwithstanding separation of ownership, the BOCs may support and share the costs of a centralized organization for the provision of engineering, administrative and other services which can most efficiently be provided on a centralized basis. The BOCs shall provide, through a centralized organization, a single point of contact for coordination of BOCs to meet the requirements of national security and emergency preparedness.

C. Until September 1, 1987, AT&T, Western Electric, and the Bell Telephone Laboratories, shall, upon order of any BOC, provide on a priority basis all research, development, manufacturing, and other support services to enable the BOCs to fulfill the requirements of this Modification of Final Judgment. AT&T and its affili-

ates shall take no action that interferes with the BOCs' requirements of nondiscrimination established by section II.

D. After the reorganization specified in paragraph I(A)(4), AT&T shall not acquire the stock or assets of any BOC.

II BOC REQUIREMENTS

A. Subject to Appendix B, each BOC shall provide to all interexchange carriers and information service providers exchange access, information access, and exchange services for such access on an unbundled, tariffed basis, that is equal in type, quality, and price to that provided to AT&T and its affiliates.

B. No BOC shall discriminate between AT&T and its affiliates and their products and services and other persons and their products and services in the:

1. procurement of products and services;

2. establishment and dissemination of technical information and procurement and interconnection standards;

3. interconnection and use of the BOC's telecommunications service and facilities or in the charges for each element of service; and

4. provision of new services and the planning for and implementation of the construction or modification of facilities, used to provide exchange access and information access.

C. Within six months after the reorganization specified in paragraph I(A)4, each BOC shall submit to the Department of Justice procedures for ensuring compliance with the requirements of paragraph B.

D. After completion of the reorganization specified in section I, no BOC shall, directly or through any affiliated enterprise:

1. provide interexchange telecommunications services or information services;

2. manufacture or provide telecommunications products or customer premises equipment (except for provision of customer premises equipment for emergency services); or

3. provide any other product or service, except exchange telecommunications and exchange access service, that is not a natural monopoly service actually regulated by tariff.

For the purposes of this Modification of Final Judgment:

A. "Affiliate" means any organization or entity, including defendant Western Electric Company, Incorporated, and Bell Telephone Laboratories, Incorporated, that is under direct or indirect common ownership with or control by AT&T or is owned or controlled by another affiliate. For the purposes of this paragraph, the terms "ownership" and "owned" mean a direct or indirect equity interest (or the equivalent thereof) of more than fifty (50) percent of an entity. "Subsidiary" means any organization or entity in which AT&T has stock ownership, whether or not controlled by AT&T.

B. "AT&T" shall mean defendant American Telephone and Telegraph Company and its affiliates.

C. "Bell Operating Companies" and "BOCs" mean the corporations listed in Appendix A attached to this Modification of Final Judgment and any entity directly or indirectly owned or controlled by a BOC or affiliated through substantial common ownership.

D. "Carrier" means any person deemed a carrier under the Communications Act of 1934 or amendments thereto, or, with respect to intrastate telecommunications, under the laws of any State.

E. "Customer premises equipment" means equipment employed on the premises of a person (other than a carrier) to originate, route, or terminate telecommunications, but does not include equipment used to multiplex, maintain, or terminate access lines.

F. "Exchange access" means the provision of exchange services for the purpose of originating or terminating interexchange telecommunications. Exchange access services include any activity or function performed by a BOC in connection with the origination or termination of interexchange telecommunications, including but not limited to, the provision of network control signalling, answer supervision, automatic calling number identification, carrier access codes, directory services, testing and maintenance of facilities and the provision of information necessary to bill customers. Such services shall be provided by facilities in an exchange area for the transmission, switching, or routing, within the exchange area, of interexchange traffic originating or terminating within the exchange area, and shall include switching traffic within the exchange area above the end office and delivery and receipt of such traffic at a point or points within an exchange area designated by an interexchange carrier for the connection of its facilities with those of the BOC. Such connections, at the option of the interexchange carrier, shall deliver traffic with signal quality and characteristics equal to that provided similar traffic of AT&T, including equal probability of blocking, based on reasonable traffic estimates supplied by each interexchange carrier. Exchange services for exchange access shall not include the performance by any BOC of interexchange traffic routing for any interexchange carrier. In the reorganization specified in section I, trunks used to transmit AT&T's traffic between end offices and class 4 switches shall be exchange access facilities to be owned by the BOCs.

G. "Exchange area," or "exchange" means a geographic area established by a BOC in accordance with the following criteria:

1. any such area shall encompass one or more contiguous local exchange areas serving common social, economic, and other purposes, even where such configuration transcends municipal or other local governmental boundaries;

2. every point served by a BOC within a State shall be included within an exchange area;

3. no such area which includes part or all of one standard metropolitan statistical area (or a consolidated statistical area, in the case of densely populated States) shall include a substantial part of any other standard metropolitan statistical area (or a consolidated statistical area, in the case of densely populated States), unless the Court shall otherwise allow; and

4. except with approval of the Court, no exchange area located in one State shall include any point located within another State.

H. "Information" means knowledge or intelligence represented by any form of writing, signs, signals, pictures, sounds, or other symbols.

I. "Information access" means the provision of specialized exchange telecommunications services by a BOC in an exchange area in connection with the origination, termination, transmission, switching, forwarding or routing of telecommunications traffic to or from the facilities of a provider of information services. Such specialized exchange telecommunications services include, where necessary, the provision of network control signalling, answer supervision, automatic calling number identification, carrier access codes, testing and maintenance of facilities, and the provision of information necessary to bill customers.

J. "Information service" means the offering of a capability for generating, acquiring, storing, transforming, processing, retrieving, utilizing, or making available information which may be conveyed via telecommunications, except that such service does not include any use of any such capability for the management, control, or operation of a telecommunications system or the management of a telecommunications service.

K. "Interexchange telecommunications" means telecommunications between a point or points located in one exchange telecommunications area and a point or points located in one or more other exchange areas or a point outside an exchange area.

L. "Technical information" means intellectual property of all types, including, without limitation, patents, copyrights, and trade secrets, relating to planning documents, designs, specifications, standards, and practices and procedures, including employee training.

N. "Telecommunications equipment" means equipment, other than customer premises equipment, used by a carrier to provide telecommunications services.

O. "Telecommunications" means the transmission, between or among points specified by the user, of information of the user's choosing, without change in the form or content of the information as sent and received, by means of electromagnetic transmission, with or without benefit of any closed transmission medium, including all instrumentalities, facilities, apparatus, and services (including the collection, storage, forwarding, switching, and delivery of such information) essential to such transmission.

P. "Telecommunications service" means the offering for hire of telecommunications facilities, or of telecommunications by means of such facilities.

Q. "Transmission facilities" means equipment (including without limitation wire, cable, microwave, satellite, and fibre-optics) that transmit information by electromagnetic means or which directly support such transmission, but does not include customer premises equipment. . . .

"The task has fallen on my shoulders"

CORAZON C. AQUINO ADDRESSES THE CONGRESS
1986

The United States annexed the Philippines (500 miles off the southeast coast of Asia) in the Treaty of Paris (1899) ending the Spanish-American War and for decades poured aid into the 7,100-island archipelago. In 1946, a year after it had liberated the Philippines from four-year Japanese military occupation, the U.S. granted the islands their independence. In 1986, the president of the Philippines stirred a joint session of the U.S. Congress, "democracy's most famous home." Three years earlier, Corazon C. Aquino (born 1933) had buried her husband, Benigno S. Aquino (1932–1983), slain by political foes as he deplaned in Manila on his return from sanctuary in America. The murder began the revolution that ultimately brought Mrs. Aquino to the presidency and to Washington.

Three years ago, I left America in grief to bury my husband, Ninoy Aquino. I thought I had left it also to lay to rest his restless dream of Philippine freedom. Today, I have returned as the president of a free people.

In burying Ninoy, a whole nation honored him. By that brave and selfless act of giving honor, a nation in shame recovered its own. A country that had lost faith in its future found it in a faithless and brazen act of murder. So in giving, we receive. In losing we find; and out of defeat, we snatched our victory.

For the nation, Ninoy became the pleasing sacrifice that answered their prayers for freedom.

Fourteen years ago this month was the first time we lost him. A president-turned-dictator, and traitor to his oath, suspended the constitution and shut down the congress that was much like this one before which I am honored to speak. He detained my husband along with thousands of others—senators, publishers and anyone who had spoken up for the democracy as its end drew near. But for Ninoy, a long and cruel ordeal was reserved. The dictator already knew that Ninoy was not a body merely to be imprisoned but a spirit he must break. For even as the dictatorship demolished one by one the institutions of democracy—the press, the congress, the independence of the judiciary, the protection of the bill of rights—Ninoy kept their spirit alive in himself.

The government sought to break him by indignities and terror. They locked him up in a tiny, nearly airless cell in a military camp in the north. They stripped him naked and held the threat of sudden midnight execution over his head, Ninoy held up manfully under all of it. I barely did as well. For 43 days, the authorities would not tell me what had happened to him. This was the first time my children and I felt we had lost him.

When that didn't work, they put him on trial for subversion, murder and a host of other crimes before a military commission. Ninoy challenged its authority and went on a fast. If he survived it, then, he felt, God intended him for another fate. We had lost him again. For nothing would hold him back from his determination to see his fast through to the end. He stopped only when it dawned on him that the government would keep his body alive after the fast had destroyed his brain. And so, with barely any life in his body, he called off the fast on the fortieth day. God meant him for other things, he felt. He did not know that an early death would still be his fate, that only the timing was wrong.

At any time during his long ordeal, Ninoy could have made a separate peace with the dictatorship, as so many of his countrymen had done. But the spirit of democracy that inheres in our race and animates this chamber could not be allowed to die. He held out, in the loneliness of his cell and the frustration of exile, the democratic alternative to the insatiable greed and mindless cruelty of the right and the purging holocaust of the left.

And then, we lost him irrevocably and more painfully than in the past. The news came to us in Boston. It had to be after the three happiest years of our lives together. But his death was my country's resurrection in the courage and faith by which alone they could be free again. The dictator had called him a nobody. Two million people threw aside their passivity and fear and escorted him to his grave. And so began the revolution that has brought me to democracy's most famous home, the Congress of the United States.

The task had fallen on my shoulders to continue offering the democratic alternative to our people.

Archibald MacLeish had said that democracy must be defended by arms when it is attacked by arms and by truth when it is attacked by lies. He failed to say how it shall be won.

I held fast to Ninoy's conviction that it must be by the ways of democracy. I held out for participation in the 1984 election the dictatorship called even if I knew it would be rigged. I was warned by the lawyers of the opposition that I ran the grave risk of legitimizing the foregone results of elections that were clearly going to be fraudulent. But I was not fighting for lawyers but for the people in whose intelligence I had implicit faith. By the exercise of democracy, even in a dictatorship, they would be prepared for democracy when it came. And then, also, it was the only way I knew by which we could measure our power even in the terms dictated by the dictatorship.

The people vindicated me in an election shamefully marked by government thuggery and fraud. The opposition swept the elections, garnering a clear majority of the votes, even if they ended up, thanks to a corrupt commission on elections, with barely a third of the seats in parliament. Now, I knew our power.

Last year, in excess of arrogance, the dictatorship called for its doom in a snap election. The people obliged with over a million signatures, they drafted me to challenge the dictatorship. And I obliged them. The rest is the history that dramatically unfolded on your television screens and across the front pages of your newspapers.

You saw a nation, armed with courage and integrity, stand fast by democracy against threats and corruption. You saw women poll watchers break out in tears as armed goons crashed the polling places to steal the ballots, but just the same, they tied themselves to the ballot boxes. You saw a people committed to the ways of democracy that they were prepared to give their lives for its pale imitation. At the end of the day, before another wave of fraud could distort the results, I announced the people's victory. . . .

Many of you here today played a part in changing the policy of your country towards us. We, Filipinos, thank each of you for what you did: for, balancing America's strategic interest against human concerns, illuminates the American vision of the world.

Today, we face the aspirations of a people who had known so much poverty and massive unemployment for the past 14 years and yet offered their lives for the abstraction of democracy. Wherever I went in the campaign, slum area or impoverished village, they came to me with one cry: democracy! Not food, although they clearly needed it, but democracy not work, although they surely wanted it, but democracy, not money, for they gave what little they had to my campaign. They didn't expect me to work a miracle that would instantly put food into their mouths, clothes on their back, education in their children, and work that will put dignity in their lives. but I feel the pressing obligation to respond quickly as the leader of a people so deserving of all these things.

We face a communist insurgency that feeds on economic deterioration, even as we carry a great share of the free world defenses in the pacific. These are only two of the many burdens my people carry even as they try to build a worthy and enduring house for their new democracy, that may serve as well as a redoubt for freedom in Asia.

. . . . To all Americans, as the leader of a proud and free people, I address this question: has there been a greater test of national commitment to the ideals you hold dear than that my people have gone through? You have spent many lives and much treasure to bring freedom to many lands that were reluctant to receive it. And here you have a people who won it by themselves and need only the help to preserve it.

Three years ago, I said, thank you, America, for the haven from oppression, and the home you gave Ninoy, myself and our children, and for the three happiest years of our lives together. today, I say, join us, America, as we build a new home for democracy, another haven for the oppressed, so it may stand as a shining testament of our two nations' commitment to freedom.

"Some 43,000,000 Americans have . . . physical or mental disabilities."

THE AMERICANS WITH DISABILITIES ACT
1990

Because forms of discrimination against individuals with disabilities were a serious and pervasive social problem, Congress established a prohibition of discrimination on the basis of disability. Promoting legislation was Senator Bob Dole (born 1923), of Kansas, who had been severely injured during the Second World War and has little use of his right arm. The number of Americans with one or more physical or mental disabilities equals the population of six New York Cities.

Sec. 2. Findings and Purposes.
(a) FINDINGS.—The Congress finds that—

(1) some 43,000,000 Americans have one or more physical or mental disabilities, and this number is increasing as the population as a whole is growing older;

(2) historically, society has tended to isolate and segregate individuals with disabilities, and, despite some improvements, such forms of discrimination against individuals with disabilities continue to be a serious and pervasive social problem;

(3) discrimination against individuals with disabilities persists in such critical areas as employment, housing, public accommodations, education, transportation, communication, recreation, institutionalization, health services, voting, and access to public services;

(4) unlike individuals who have experienced discrimination on the basis of race, color, sex, national origin, religion, or age, individuals who have experienced discrimination on the basis of disability have often had no legal recourse to redress such discrimination;

(5) individuals with disabilities continually encounter various forms of discrimination, including outright intentional exclusion, the discriminatory effects of architectural, transportation, and communication barriers, overprotective rules and policies, failure to make modifications to existing facilities and practices, exclusionary qualification standards and criteria, segregation, and relegation to lesser services, programs, activities, benefits, jobs, or other opportunities;

(6) census data, national polls, and other studies have documented that people with disabilities, as a group, occupy an inferior status in our society, and are severely disadvantaged socially, vocationally, economically, and educationally;

(7) individuals with disabilities are a discrete and insular minority who have been faced with restrictions and limitations, subjected to a history of purposeful unequal treatment, and relegated to a position of political powerlessness in our society, based on characteristics that are beyond the control of such individuals and resulting from stereotypic assumptions not truly indicative of the individual ability of such indi-

viduals to participate in, and contribute to, society;

(8) the Nation's proper goals regarding individuals with disabilities are to assure equality of opportunity, full participation, independent living, and economic self-sufficiency for such individuals; and

(9) the continuing existence of unfair and unnecessary discrimination and prejudice denies people with disabilities the opportunity to compete on an equal basis and to pursue those opportunities for which our free society is justifiably famous, and costs the United States billions of dollars in unnecessary expenses resulting from dependency and nonproductivity.

(b) PURPOSE.—It is the purpose of this Act—

(1) to provide a clear and comprehensive national mandate for the elimination of discrimination against individuals with disabilities;

(2) to provide clear, strong, consistent, enforceable standards addressing discrimination against individuals with disabilities;

(3) to ensure that the Federal Government plays a central role in enforcing the standards established in this Act on behalf of individuals with disabilities; and

(4) to invoke the sweep of congressional authority, including the power to enforce the fourteenth amendment and to regulate commerce, in order to address the major areas of discrimination faced day-to-day by people with disabilities.

As used in this Act:

(1) AUXILIARY AIDS AND SERVICES.—The term "auxiliary aids and services" includes—

(A) qualified interpreters or other effective methods of making aurally delivered materials available to individuals with hearing impairments;

(B) qualified readers, taped texts, or other effective methods of making visually deliv-

ered materials available to individuals with visual impairments;

(C) acquisition or modification of equipment or devices; and

(D) other similar services and actions.

(2) DISABILITY.—The term "disability" means, with respect to an individual—

(A) a physical or mental impairment that substantially limits one or more of the major life activities of such individual;

(B) a record of such an impairment; or

(C) being regarded as having such an impairment.

(3) STATE.—The term "State" means each of the several States, the District of Columbia, the Commonwealth of Puerto Rico, Guam, American Samoa, the Virgin Islands, the Trust Territory of the Pacific Islands, and the Commonwealth of the Northern Mariana Islands.

. . . (A) IN GENERAL.—The term "employer" means a person engaged in an industry affecting commerce who has 15 or more employees for each working day in each of 20 or more calendar weeks in the current or preceding calendar year, and any agent of such person, except that, for two years following the effective date of this title, an employer means a person engaged in an industry affecting commerce who has 25 or more employees for each working day in each of 20 or more calendar weeks in the current or preceding year, and any agent of such person.

(B) EXCEPTIONS.—The term "employer" does not include—

(i) the United States, a corporation wholly owned by the government of the United States, or an Indian tribe; or

(ii) a bona fide private membership club (other than a labor organization) that is exempt from taxation under section 501(c) of the Internal Revenue Code of 1986.

(6) ILLEGAL USE OF DRUGS.—

(A) In general.—The term "illegal use of drugs" means the use of drugs, the possession or distribution of which is unlawful under the Controlled Substances Act (21 U.S.C. 812). Such term does not include the use of a drug taken under supervision by a licensed health care professional, or other uses authorized by the Controlled Substances Act or other provisions of Federal law.

(B) Drugs.—The term "drug" means a controlled substance, as defined in schedules I through V of section 202 of the Controlled Substances Act.

(7) Person, etc.—The terms "person," "labor organization," "employment agency," "commerce," and "industry affecting commerce," shall have the same meaning given such terms in section 701 of the Civil Rights Act of 1964 (42 U.S.C. 2000e).

(8) Qualified individual with a disability.—The term "qualified individual with a disability" means an individual with a disability who, with or without reasonable accommodation, can perform the essential functions of the employment position that such individual holds or desires. For the purposes of this title, consideration shall be given to the employer's judgment as to what functions of a job are essential, and if an employer has prepared a written description before advertising or interviewing applicants for the job, this description shall be considered evidence of the essential functions of the job.

(9) Reasonable accommodation.—The term "reasonable accommodation" may include—

(A) making existing facilities used by employees readily accessible to and usable by individuals with disabilities; and

(B) job restructuring, part-time or modified work schedules, reassignment to a vacant position, acquisition or modification of equipment or devices, appropriate adjustment or modifications of examinations, training materials or policies, the provision of qualified readers or interpreters, and other similar accommodations for individuals with disabilities.

(10) Undue hardship.—

(A) In general.—The term "undue hardship" means an action requiring significant difficulty or expense, when considered in light of the factors set forth in subparagraph (B).

(B) Factors to be considered.—In determining whether an accommodation would impose an undue hardship on a covered entity, factors to be considered include—

(i) the nature and cost of the accommodation needed under this Act;

(ii) the overall financial resources of the facility or facilities involved in the provision of the reasonable accommodation; the number of persons employed at such facility; the effect on expenses and resources, or the impact otherwise of such accommodation upon the operation of the facility;

(iii) the overall financial resources of the covered entity; the overall size of the business of a covered entity with respect to the number of its employees; the number, type, and location of its facilities; and

(iv) the type of operation or operations of the covered entity, including the composition, structure, and functions of the workforce of such entity; the geographic separateness, administrative, or fiscal relationship of the facility or facilities in question to the covered entity. . . .

THIS LAND IS YOUR LAND

Looking back over more than a century, it is clear that the Civil War marked a sea change in American life. In the North, hostilities accelerated a factory system already underway. It greatly stimulated the iron and steel industry, meat packing, shipping, banking, and railroad construction. The rapid extension of railroads, resolving the transportation problem, is inextricably enmeshed with westward migration. The High Plains eventually were brought under the plow, but before farmers could settle the land a number of obstacles had to be eliminated, including how to transport farm produce. Between the 1870s and 1890s, the settlement of public lands, the marketing of the products of agriculture, and the advance of the railroads were interlocked. Crossing the Continent along a half dozen lines over these two decades, the railroads carried miners into the mountains, cattlemen to the grasslands, farm produce to eastern urban markets. The need for railroads had been spurred by the Forty Niners journeying to California and by the discovery of gold in Colorado and silver in the rich strike at the Comstock Lode. The 1862 Pacific Railroad Act was the model for future railway legislation. Under its terms, Congress subsidized the construction of the transcontinental railways by extraordinarily generous land grants and government loans. As a consequence, the railway companies became—after the state and Federal governments—the largest landholders in the West, and whole territories such as the Dakotas owed their existence to them, as did scores of towns and cities. Moreover, the railway companies further contributed to settlement by selling land cheaply, thus creating and building up farm communities along the rights of way—and hauling their farm products to eastern urban markets. Ribboning the West after the Civil War, railroads were intimately linked to the development of the region.

The West and its growth had a profound impact on national development. Since Jefferson's faith in a sturdy yeomanry, the West had been considered essential space for the agrarian utopia. For over a century after the United States came into existence, its white inhabitants never ran out of land, and until the 1890s they were never confronted with the visible end of the frontier. But before the century ended, their picturesque mining and cattle regions and the old, romantic "Wild West" had fallen under the impact of farmers who swarmed out onto the vast grasslands and into the mountain valleys. And even earlier and certainly after the century had passed into the 1900s, nostalgia for a somehow wilder and freer frontier age grasped the national imagination. Before then, the West's existence prompted some highly important measures. One, the Morrill Act of 1862, changed the shape of higher education in America. Though at first having the goal of subsidizing agricultural education through donation of public lands to the states, it initiated and was responsible for the rapid growth of state universities, and it became the precedent for Federal aid to education in the twentieth century. It reflected the value of schools for Americans, the belief that democracy could not work without an enlightened electorate. The Homestead Act made available 160 acres of public land to those who would settle and cultivate it for five years, and homesteaders flooded western lands. It seemed to promise that an immense public domain—perhaps a billion acres at this time—would be thrown open to an independent yeomanry, but that did not happen. Though stimulating the opening of prairie wheat fields, implementation of the Homestead Act was riddled by incompetence and fraud; speculation resulted in a market rise in land prices that ultimately frustrated homesteaders.

Being a primary source of potential wealth until the late nineteenth century, public lands—as the fate of the Homestead Act indicates—fell victim to lumber companies, ranchers' associations, colonization companies, and naked, vulgar greed. Railroads bought and sold state legislatures, mining companies exploited immigrant labor, timber and cattle barons despoiled the public domain—and oil companies in the twentieth century ruled the states in which they had operations. Much as earlier vested interests had bribed corrupt public officials and greased their way to power, oil companies did the same in the 1920s, obtaining control of public lands that held immensely valuable naval oil reserves. With the eras of the two Roosevelts as exceptions, it was only after mid-century that the public became aware of environmental degradation and the pernicious mix of environmentalism and corporate rapacity. Only in the late 1960s did successive Administrations consider environmental protection statutes, such as hazardous waste and anti-pollution laws, and measures to discourage private development, such as wetlands restrictions. In effect, the public became increasingly concerned with the land and the creatures who lived off the land, recognizing that, unlike earlier views of the West, the great bounties of nature bestowed upon America were not limitless or renewable.

"Entitled to enter one quarter section"

THE HOMESTEAD ACT
1862

Before the Civil War (1861–1865), southern Congressmen, fearing the settlement of western territory and the formation of more non-slave states, blocked proposals offering free land to settlers. In 1858, the Senate defeated a homestead bill by one vote. One year later, President James Buchanan (1791–1868) vetoed a homestead bill that Congress had passed. A year into the Civil War, rebel-free Congress acted to secure homesteads on the public domain for loyal settlers. Any adult citizen (or person intending to become a citizen) who headed a family could qualify for a grant of 160 acres by paying a small registration fee and living on the land continuously for five years. If the settler was willing to pay $1.25 an acre, he could obtain the land after six months' residence. Settlers, mostly inept urban slum dwellers looking for a better life, set out for Kansas, Nebraska, the Dakotas, and the Great Plains, once considered uninhabitable. Speculators got their hands on much of the land granted under the Homestead Act.

That any person who is the head of a family, or who has arrived at the age of twenty-one years, and is a citizen of the United States, or who shall have filed his declaration of intention to become such, as required by the naturalization laws of the United States, and who has never borne arms against the United States Government or given aid and comfort to its enemies, shall, from and after the first January, eighteen hundred and sixty-three, be entitled to enter one quarter section or a less quantity of unappropriated public lands, upon which said person may have filed a preëmption claim, or which may, at the time the application is made, be subject to preëmption at one dollar and twenty-five cents, or less, per acre; or eighty acres or less of such unappropriated lands, at two dollars and fifty cents per acre, to be located in a body, in conformity to the legal subdivisions of the public lands, and after the same shall have been surveyed: *Pro-*

vided, That any person owning and residing on land may, under the provisions of this act, enter other land lying contiguous to his or her said land, which shall not, with the land already owned and occupied, exceed in the aggregate one hundred and sixty acres.

SEC. 2. *And be it further enacted,* That the person applying for the benefit of this act shall, upon application to the register of the land office in which he or she is about to make such entry, make affidavit before the said register or receiver that he or she is the head of a family, or is twenty-one years or more of age, or shall have performed service in the army or navy of the United States, and that he has never borne arms against the Government of the United States or given aid and comfort to its enemies, and that such application is made for his or her exclusive use and benefit, and that said entry is made for the purpose of actual settlement and cultivation, and not either directly or indirectly for the use or benefit of any other person or persons whomsoever; and upon filing the said affidavit with the register or receiver, and on payment of ten dollars, he or she shall thereupon be permitted to enter the quantity of land specified: *Provided, however,* That no certificate shall be given or patent issued therefor until the expiration of five years from the date of such entry; and if, at the expiration of such time, or at any time within two years thereafter, the person making such entry; or, if he be dead, his widow; or in case of her death, his heirs or devisee; or in case of a widow making such entry, her heirs or devisee, in case of her death; shall prove by two credible witnesses that he, she, or they have resided upon or cultivated the same for the term of five years immediately succeeding the time of filing the affidavit aforesaid, and shall make affidavit that no part of said land has been alienated, and that he has borne true allegiance to the Government of the United States; then, in such case, he, she, or they, if at that time a citizen of the United States, shall be entitled to a patent, as in other cases provided for by law: *And provided, further,* That in case of the death of both father and mother, leaving an infant child, or children, under twenty-one years of age, the right and fee shall ensure to the benefit of said infant child or children; and the executor, administrator, or guardian may, at any time within two years after the death of the surviving parent, and in accordance with the laws of the State in which such children for the time being have their domicil, sell said land for the benefit of said infants, but for no other purpose; and the purchaser shall acquire absolute title by the purchase, and be entitled to a patent from the United States, on payment of the office fees and sum of money herein specified. . . .

"U.S. shall extinguish . . . rapidly . . . Indian titles to all lands"

THE PACIFIC RAILWAY ACT
1862

In 1853, Congress authorized a survey of transcontinental railroad routes. The U.S. legislative body, with the power of the purse, was in the mood to provide for the completion of the most gigantic internal improvement the age had contemplated—a coast-to-coast railroad. During the second year of the Civil War (1861–1865), it enacted a bill to aid in the construction of a railroad and telegraph line from the Missouri River west to the Pacific Ocean, affording the enterprise liberal encouragement without placing the public land and treasure at the mercy of reckless speculators. A route chosen was called the "middle" route; namely, from western Kansas to western Nevada. In return for subsidies and grants, the government was to be given the usual preference in the transmission of troops and materiél and in the use of the telegraph, which was to be built collateral with the road. (Once again the impulse of war prompted the march of civilization.) On May 10, 1869, at Promontory, Utah Territory, a golden spike hammered to the yell of "DONE!" marked connection of eastbound and westbound, 3,250-mile-long track. It was hailed as the most important enterprise of the kind ever executed in any country.

The said corporation is hereby authorized and empowered to lay out, locate, construct, furnish, maintain and enjoy a continuous railroad and telegraph . . . from a point on the one hundredth meridian of longitude west from Greenwich, between the south margin of the valley of the Republican River and the north margin of the valley of the Platte River, to the western boundary of the Nevada Territory, upon the route and terms hereinafter provided. . . .

Sec. 2. That the right of way through the public lands be . . . granted to said company for the construction of said railroad and telegraph line; and the right . . . is hereby given to said company to take from the public lands adjacent to the line of said road, earth, stone, timber, and other materials for the construction thereof; . . . The United States shall extinguish as rapidly as may be the Indian titles to all lands falling under the operation of this act. . . .

Sec. 3. That there be . . . granted to the said company, for the purpose of aiding in the construction of said railroad and telegraph line, and to secure the safe and speedy transportation of mails, troops, munitions of war, and public stores thereon, every alternate section of public land, designated by odd numbers, to the amount of five alternate sections per mile on each side of said railroad. . . . *Provided* That all mineral lands shall be excepted from the operation of this act;

but where the same shall contain timber, the timber thereon is hereby granted to said company. . . .

Sec. 5. That for the purposes herein mentioned the Secretary of the Treasury shall . . . in accordance with the provisions of this act, issue to said company bonds of the United States of one thousand dollars each, payable in thirty years after date, paying six per centum per annum interest . . . to the amount of sixteen of said bonds per mile for each section of forty miles; . . . Sec. 9. That the Leavenworth, Pawnee and Western Railroad Company of Kansas are hereby authorized to construct a railroad and telegraph line . . . upon the same terms and conditions in all respects as are provided [for construction of the Union Pacific Railroad]. . . . The Central Pacific Railroad Company of California are hereby authorized to construct a railroad and telegraph line from the Pacific coast . . . to the eastern boundaries of California, upon the same terms and conditions in all respects [as are provided for the Union Pacific Railroad].

Sec. 10. . . . And the Central Pacific Railroad Company of California after completing its road across said State, is authorized to continue the construction of said railroad and telegraph through the Territories of the United States to the Missouri River . . .

Sec. 11. That for three hundred miles of said road most mountainous and difficult of construction, to wit: one hundred and fifty miles westerly from the eastern base of the Rocky Mountains, and one hundred and fifty miles eastwardly from the western base of the Sierra Nevada mountains . . . The bonds to be issued to aid in the construction thereof shall be treble the number per mile herein before provided . . .

"No mineral lands shall be selected or purchased"

PUBLIC LANDS FOR COLLEGES
1862

In 1862, Congress legislated the Morrill Land Grant Act, named for Vermont Congressman Justin Smith Morrill (1810–1898). Each state that remained in the Union was granted acres equivalent to the total number of members in its House and Senate delegations multiplied by 30,000. (Vermont, for example, with two Senators and one Representative, was granted 90,000 acres.) The state was to sell the land and use the proceeds for the endowment of at least one college offering courses related to agriculture and the mechanical arts, without excluding the general sciences and classical studies. From "land-grant colleges" grew the system of state universities (for example, the University of Vermont) and established the principle of Federal aid to education. In 1890, a second Morrill Act extended the land-grant provision to 16 southern states.

Be it enacted by the Senate and House of Representatives of the United States of America in Congress assembled, That there be granted to the several States, for the purposes hereinafter mentioned, an amount of public land, to be apportioned to each State a quantity equal to thirty thousand acres for each senator and representative in Congress to which the States are respectively entitled by the apportionment under the census of eighteen hundred and sixty: *Provided,* That no mineral lands shall be selected or purchased under the provisions of this act.

SEC. 2. *And be it further enacted,* That the land aforesaid, after being surveyed, shall be apportioned to the several States in sections or subdivisions of sections, not less than one quarter of a section; and whenever there are public lands in a State subject to sale at private entry at one dollar and twenty-five cents per acre, the quantity to which said State shall be entitled shall be selected from such lands within the limits of such State,

and the Secretary of the Interior is hereby directed to issue to each of the States in which there is not the quantity of public lands subject to sale at private entry at one dollar and twenty-five cents per acre, to which said State may be entitled under the provisions of this act, land scrip in the amount in acres for the deficiency of its distributive share: said scrip to be sold by said States and the proceeds thereof applied to the uses and purposes prescribed in this act, and for no other use or purpose whatsoever: *Provided,* That in no case shall any State to which land scrip may thus be issued be allowed to locate the same within the limits of any other State, or of any Territory of the United States, but their assignees may thus locate said land scrip upon any of the unappropriated lands of the United States subject to sale at private entry at one dollar and twenty-five cents, or less, per acre: *And provided, further,* That not more than one million acres shall be located by such assignees in any one of

THIS LAND IS YOUR LAND

the States: *And provided, further,* That no such location shall be made before one year from the passage of this act.

SEC. 3. *And be it further enacted,* That all the expenses of management, superintendence, and taxes from date of selection of said lands previous to their sales, and all expenses incurred in the management and disbursement of the moneys which may be received therefrom, shall be paid by the States to which they may belong, out of the treasury of said States, so that the entire proceeds of the sale of said lands shall be applied without any diminution whatever to the purposes hereinafter mentioned.

SEC. 4. *And be it further enacted,* That all moneys derived from the sale of the lands aforesaid by the States to which the lands are apportioned, and from the sales of land scrip hereinbefore provided for, shall be invested in stocks of the United States, or of the States, or some other safe stocks, yielding not less than five per centum upon the par value of said stocks; and that the moneys so invested shall constitute a perpetual fund, the capital of which shall remain forever undiminished, (except so far as may be provided in section fifth of this act,) and the interest of which shall be inviolably appropriated, by each State which may take and claim the benefit of this act, to the endowment, support, and maintenance of at least one college where the leading object shall be, without excluding other scientific and classical studies, and including military tactics, to teach such branches of learning as are related to agriculture and the mechanic arts, in such manner as the legislatures of the States may respectively prescribe, in order to promote the liberal and practical education of the industrial classes in the several pursuits and professions in life. . . .

"The first period of American history is closed"

THE END OF THE FRONTIER
1893

The U.S. Superintendent of the Census for 1890 reported, "Up to and including 1880 the country had a frontier of settlement . . . but at present the unsettled area has been so broken into by isolated bodies of settlement that there can hardly be said to be a frontier line. In the discussion of its extent, its westward movement, etc., it cannot, therefore, any longer have a place in the census reports." This brief official statement, in the scholarly view of University of Wisconsin history professor Frederick Jackson Turner (1861–1932), capped the closing of a great historic movement. American history, to a large degree, had been the history of the settlement of the West. Turner's thesis was revolutionary. Earlier historians had focused on religious liberty or nationalism or slavery or other issues and institutions; to Professor Turner, the frontier was the source of the individualism, restless energy, self-reliance, and inventiveness that were characteristically American.

So long as free land exists, the opportunity for a competency exists, and economic power secures political power. But the democracy born of free land, strong in selfishness and individualism, intolerant of administrative experience and education, and pressing individual liberty beyond its proper bounds, has its dangers as well as its benefits. Individualism in America has allowed a laxity in regard to governmental affairs which has rendered possible the spoils system and all the manifest evils that follow from the lack of a highly developed civic spirit. In this connection may be noted also the influence of frontier conditions in permitting lax business honor, inflated paper currency and wild-cat banking. The colonial and revolutionary frontier was the region whence emanated many of the worst forms of an evil currency. The West in the War of 1812 repeated the phenomenon on the frontier of that day, while the speculation and wild-cat banking of the period of the crisis of 1837 occurred on the new frontier belt of the next tier of States. Thus each one of the periods of lax financial integrity coincides with periods when a new set of frontier communities had arisen, and coincides in area with these successive frontiers, for the most part. The recent Populist agitation is a case in point. Many a State that now declines any connection with the tenets of the Populists, itself adhered to such ideas in an earlier stage of the development of the State. A primitive society can hardly be expected to show the intelligent appreciation of the complexity of business interests in a developed society. The continual recurrence of these areas of paper-money agitation is another evidence that the frontier can be isolated and studied as a factor in American history of the highest importance.

The East has always feared the result of an unregulated advance of the frontier, and has tried to check and guide it. The English authorities would have checked settlement at the headwaters of the Atlantic tributaries and allowed the "savages to enjoy their deserts in quiet lest the peltry trade should decrease. . . ."

. . . Tidewater Virginia and South Carolina gerrymandered those colonies to insure the dominance of the coast in their legislatures. Washington desired to settle a State at a time in the Northwest; Jefferson would reserve from settlement the territory of his Louisiana Purchase north of the thirty-second parallel, in order to offer it to the Indians in exchange for their settlements east of the Mississippi. "When we shall be full on this side," he writes, "we may lay off a range of States on the western bank from the head to the mouth, and so range after range, advancing compactly as we multiply." Madison went so far as to argue to the French minister that the United States had no interest in seeing population extend itself on the right bank of the Mississippi, but should rather fear it. When the Oregon question was under debate, in 1824, Smyth, of Virginia, would draw an unchangeable line for the limits of the United States at the outer limit of two tiers of States beyond the Mississippi, complaining that the seaboard States were being drained of the flower of their population by the bringing of too much land into market. Even Thomas Benton, the man of widest views of the destiny of the West, at this stage of his career declared that along the ridge of the Rocky mountains "the western limits of the Republic should be drawn, and the statue of the fabled god Terminus should be raised upon its highest peak, never to be thrown down." But the attempts to limit the boundaries, to restrict land sales and settlement, and to deprive the West of its share of political power were all in vain. Steadily the frontier of settlement advanced and carried with it individualism, democracy, and nationalism, and powerfully affected the East and the Old World.

The most effective efforts of the East to regulate the frontier came through its educational and religious activity, exerted by interstate migration and by organized societies. Speaking in 1835, Dr. Lyman Beecher declared: "It is equally plain that the religious and political destiny of our nation is to be decided in the West," and he pointed out that the population of the West "is assembled from all the States of the Union and from all the nations of Europe, and is rushing in like the waters of the flood, demanding for its moral preservation the immediate and universal action of those institutions which discipline the mind and arm the conscience and the heart. And so various are the opinions and habits, and so recent and imperfect is the acquaintance, and so sparse are the settlements of the West, that no homogeneous public sentiment can be formed to legislate immediately into being the requisite institutions. And yet they are all needed immediately in their utmost perfection and power. A nation is being 'born in a day.' . . . But what will become of the West if her prosperity rushes up to such a majesty of power, while those great institutions linger which are necessary to form the mind and the conscience and the heart of that vast world. It must not be permitted. . . . Let no man at the East quiet himself and dream of liberty, whatever may become of the West. . . . Her destiny is our destiny."

With the appeal to the conscience of New England, he adds appeals to her fears lest other religious sects anticipate her own. The New England preacher and school-teacher left their mark on the West. The dread of Western emancipation from New England's political and economic control was paralleled by her fears lest the West cut loose from her religion. Commenting in 1850 on reports that settlement was rapidly extending northward in Wisconsin, the editor of the *Home*

Missionary writes: "We scarcely know whether to rejoice or mourn over this extension of our settlements. While we sympathize in whatever tends to increase the physical resources and prosperity of our country, we can not forget that with all these dispersions into remote and still remoter corners of the land the supply of the means of grace is becoming relatively less and less." Acting in accordance with such ideas, home missions were established and Western colleges were erected. As seaboard cities like Philadelphia, New York, and Baltimore strove for the mastery of Western trade, so the various demoninations strove for the possession of the West. Thus an intellectual stream from New England sources fertilized the West. Other sections sent their missionaries; but the real struggle was between sects. The contest for power and the expansive tendency furnished to the various sects by the existence of a moving frontier must have had important results on the character of religious organization in the United States. The multiplication of rival churches in the little frontier towns had deep and lasting social effects. The religious aspects of the frontier make a chapter in our history which needs study.

From the conditions of frontier life came intellectual traits of profound importance. The works of travelers along each frontier from colonial days onward describe certain common traits, and these traits have, while softening down, still persisted as survivals in the place of their origin, even when a higher social organization succeeded. The result is that to the frontier the American intellect owes its striking characteristics. That coarseness and strength combined with acuteness and inquisitiveness; that practical, inventive turn of mind, quick to find expedients; that masterful grasp of material things, lacking in the artistic but powerful to effect great ends; that restless, nervous energy; that domi-

nant individualism, working for good and for evil, and withal that buoyancy and exuberance which comes with freedom—these are traits of the frontier, or traits called out elsewhere because of the existence of the frontier. Since the days when the fleet of Columbus sailed into the waters of the New World, America has been another name for opportunity, and the people of the United States have taken their tone from the incessant expansion which has not only been open but has even been forced upon them. He would be a rash prophet who should assert that the expansive character of American life has now entirely ceased. Movement has been its dominant fact, and, unless this training has no effect upon a people, the American energy will continually demand a wider field for its exercise. But never again will such gifts of free land offer themselves. For a moment, at the frontier, the bonds of custom are broken and unrestraint is triumphant. There is not *tabula rasa*. The stubborn American environment is there with its imperious summons to accept its conditions; the inherited ways of doing things are also there; and yet, in spite of environment, and in spite of custom, each frontier did indeed furnish a new field of opportunity, a gate of escape from the bondage of the past; and freshness, and confidence, and scorn of older society, impatience of its restraints and its ideas, and indifference to its lessons, have accompanied the frontier. What the Mediterranean Sea was to the Greeks, breaking the bond of custom, offering new experiences, calling out new institutions and activities, that, and more, the ever retreating frontier has been to the United States directly, and to the nations of Europe more remotely. And now, four centuries from the discovery of America, at the end of a hundred years of life under the Constitution, the frontier has gone, and with its going has closed the first period of American history.

"Immediately to cause suit to be instituted"

TEAPOT DOME

1924

It has been opined that no single incident in American history may more accurately demonstrate vulnerability to the excesses of greed and ignorance than the Teapot Dome-Elk Hills imbroglio of the 1920s. President Warren G. Harding's Secretary of the Interior, Albert Bacon Fall (1861–1944), received hundreds of thousands of dollars and a herd of cattle in bribes for granting leases in naval-oil reserves at Elk Hills, California, and Teapot Dome, Wyoming, without competitive bidding. The scandal broke in 1922 when Harry Slattery, a conservationist who had opposed Mr. Fall's nomination, provided investigators with the tips that convicted the cabinet officer for his Teapot Dome-lease arrangement with Harry F. Sinclair's Mammoth Oil Company. (Fall had leased the Elk Hills Reserve to Edward F. Doheny (1856–1935), of Pan-American Petroleum Company.) A hint that something was askew was the sudden rise in once dead-broke Fall's buying power. Fall was jailed for 10 months for misusing the President's trust—the only Cabinet officer before Watergate (1970s) to be imprisoned. Before the scandal erupted, President Harding (1865–1923) had died, mysteriously, on holiday in California. Congress, in joint resolution, directed Harding's successor, Calvin Coolidge (1872–1933), to institute and prosecute suits to cancel the leases.

WHEREAS IT APPEARS from evidence taken by the Committee on Public Lands and Surveys of the United States Senate that certain lease of Naval Reserve Numbered 3, in the State of Wyoming, bearing date April 7, 1922, made in form by the Government of the United States, through Albert B. Fall, Secretary of the Interior, and Edwin Denby, Secretary of the Navy, as lessor, to the Mammoth Oil Company, as lessee, and that certain contract between the Government of the United States and the Pan American Petroleum and Transport Company, dated April 25, 1922, signed by Edward C. Finney, Acting Secretary of the Interior, and Edwin Denby, Secretary of the Navy, relating among other things to the construction of oil tanks at Pearl Harbor, Territory of Hawaii, and that certain lease of Naval Reserve Numbered 1, in the State of California, bearing date December 11, 1922, made in form by the Government of the United States through Albert B. Fall, Secretary of the Interior, and Edwin Denby, Secretary of the Navy, as lessor, to the Pan American Petroleum Company, as lessee, were executed under circumstances indicating fraud and corruption; and

Whereas the said leases and contract were entered into without authority on the part of the officers purporting to act in the execution of the same for the United States and in violation of the laws of Congress; and

Whereas such leases and contract were made in defiance of the settled policy of the Government, adhered to through three successive administrations, to maintain in the ground a great reserve supply of oil adequate to the needs of the Navy in any emergency threatening the national security: Therefore be it

Resolved by the Senate and House of Representatives of the United States of America in Congress assembled, That the said leases and contract are against the public interest and that the lands embraced therein should be recovered and held for the purpose to which they were dedicated; and

Resolved further, That the President of the United States be, and he hereby is, authorized and directed immediately to cause suit to be instituted and prosecuted for the annulment and cancellation of the said leases and contract and all contracts incidental or supplemental thereto, to enjoin the further extraction of oil from the said reserves under said leases or from the territory covered by the same to secure any further appropriate incidental relief, and to prosecute such other actions or proceedings, civil and criminal, as may be warranted by the facts in relation to the making of the said leases and contract.

And the President is further authorized and directed to appoint, by and with the advice and consent of the Senate, special counsel who shall have charge and control of the prosecution of such litigation, anything in the statutes touching the powers of the Attorney General of the Department of Justice to the contrary notwithstanding.

"To promote the highest use of the public lands"

THE GRAZING ACT
1934

The Taylor Grazing Act, the "Magna Carta of conservation," is still the basis for grazing policies on public Federal land in the West and a prime example of democracy in action. Legislated in the second year of the New Deal, it established grazing as the dominant use for much of the public domain. More than 80,000,000 western acres (later increased to 142-million acres) were removed from potential sale and reserved for grazing under Federal control. It has been thought that virtually the entire remaining public domain should be set aside for Federal management rather than for sale; further settlement was all but out of the question. Local ranchers may graze an allotted number of animals on these lands.

*B*e it enacted by the Senate and House of Representatives of the United States of America in Congress assembled, That in order to promote the highest use of the public lands pending its final disposal, the Secretary of the Interior is authorized, in his discretion, by order to establish grazing districts or additions thereto and/or to modify the boundaries thereof, not exceeding in the aggregate an area of eighty million acres of vacant, unappropriated, and unreserved lands from any part of the public domain of the United States (exclusive of Alaska), which are not in national forests, national parks and monuments, Indian reservations, revested Oregon and California Railroad grant lands, or revested Coos Bay Wagon Road grant lands, and which in his opinion are chiefly valuable for grazing and raising forage crops: *Provided,* That no lands withdrawn or reserved for any other purpose shall be included in any such district except with the approval of the head of the department having jurisdiction thereof. Nothing in this Act shall be construed in any way to diminish, restrict, or impair any right which has been heretofore or may be hereafter initiated under existing law validly affecting the public lands, and which is maintained pursuant to such law except as otherwise expressly provided in this Act, nor to affect any land heretofore or hereafter surveyed which, except for the provisions of this Act, would be a part of any grant to any State, nor as limiting or restricting the power or authority of any State as to matters within its jurisdiction. Whenever any grazing district is established pursuant to this Act, the Secretary shall grant to owners of land adjacent to such district, upon application of any such owner, such rights-of-way over the lands included in such district for stock-driving purposes as may be necessary for the convenient access by any such owner to marketing facilities or to lands not within such district owned by such person or upon which such person has stock-grazing rights. . . . Nothing in this Act shall be construed as in any way altering or restricting the right to hunt or fish within a grazing district in accordance with the laws of the United States or of any State, or as vesting in any permittee any right whatsoever to interfere with hunting or fishing within a grazing district.

SEC. 2. The Secretary of the Interior shall make provision for the protection, administration, regulation, and improvement of such grazing districts as may be created under the authority of the foregoing section, and he shall make such rules and regulations and establish such service, enter into such cooperative agreements, and do any and all things necessary to accomplish the purposes of this Act and to insure the objects of such grazing districts, namely, to regulate their occupancy and use, to preserve the land and its resources from destruction or unnecessary injury, to provide for the orderly use, improvement, and development of the range; and the Secretary of the Interior is authorized to continue the study of erosion and flood control and to perform such work as may be necessary amply to protect and rehabilitate the areas subject to the provisions of this Act, through such funds as may be made available for that purpose, and any willful violation of the provisions of this Act or of such rules and regulations thereunder after actual notice thereof shall be punishable by a fine of not more than $500.

SEC. 3. That the Secretary of the Interior is hereby authorized to issue or cause to be issued permits to graze livestock on such grazing districts to such bona fide settlers, residents, and other stock owners as under his rules and regulations are entitled to participate in the use of the range, upon the payment annually of reasonable fees in each case to be fixed or determined from time to time: *Provided,* That grazing permits shall be issued only to citizens of the United States or to those who have filed the necessary declarations of intention to become such, as re-

quired by the naturalization laws and to groups, associations, or corporations authorized to conduct business under the laws of the State in which the grazing district is located. . . . *Provided further,* That nothing in this Act shall be construed or administered in any way to diminish or impair any right to the possession and use of water for mining, agriculture, manufacturing, or other purposes which has heretofore vested or accrued under existing law validly affecting the public lands or which may be hereafter initiated or acquired and maintained in accordance with such law. So far as consistent with the purposes and provisions of this Act, grazing privileges recognized and acknowledged shall be adequately safeguarded, but the creation of a grazing district or the issuance of a permit pursuant to the provisions of this Act shall not create any right, title, interest, or estate in or to the lands.

SEC. 4. Fences, wells, reservoirs, and other improvements necessary to the care and management of the permitted livestock may be constructed on the public lands within such grazing districts under permit issued by the authority of the Secretary, or under such cooperative arrangement as the Secretary may approve. . . .

SEC. 5. That the Secretary of the Interior shall permit, under regulations to be prescribed by him, the free grazing within such districts of livestock kept for domestic purposes; and provided that so far as authorized by existing law or laws hereinafter enacted, nothing herein contained shall prevent the use of timber, stone, gravel, clay, coal, and other deposits by miners, prospectors for mineral, bona fide settlers and residents, for firewood, fencing, buildings, mining, prospecting, and domestic purposes within areas subject to the provisions of this Act.

SEC. 6. Nothing herein contained shall restrict the acquisition, granting or use of permits or rights-of-way within grazing districts under existing law; or ingress or egress over the public lands in such districts for all proper and lawful purposes; and nothing herein contained shall restrict prospecting, locating, developing, mining, entering, leasing, or patenting the mineral resources of such districts under law applicable thereto. . . .

SEC. 8. . . . Where mineral reservations are made in lands conveyed by the United States, it shall be so stipulated in the patent, and any person who acquires the right to mine and remove the reserved mineral deposits may enter and occupy so much of the surface as may be required for all purposes incident to the mining and removal of the minerals therefrom, and may mine and remove such minerals, upon payment to the owner of the surface for damages caused to the land and improvements thereon. . . .

SEC. 11. That when appropriated by Congress, 25 per centum of all moneys received from each grazing district on Indian lands ceded to the United States for disposition under the public-land laws during any fiscal year is hereby made available for expenditure by the Secretary of the Interior for the construction, purchase, or maintenance of range improvements; and an additional 25 per centum of the money received from grazing during each fiscal year shall be paid at the end thereof by the Secretary of the Treasury to the State in which said lands are situated, to be expended as the State legislature may prescribe for the benefit of public schools and public roads of the county or counties in which such grazing lands are situated. And the remaining 50 per centum of all money received from such grazing lands shall be deposited to the credit of the Indians pending final disposition under applicable laws, treaties, or agreements. . . .

SEC. 13. That the President of the United States is authorized to reserve by proclamation and place under national-forest administration in any State where national forests may be created or enlarged by Executive order any unappropriated public lands lying within watersheds forming a part of the national forests which, in his opinion, can best be administered in connection with existing national-forest administration units, and to place under the Interior Department administration any lands within national forests, principally valuable for grazing, which, in his opinion, can best be administered under the provisions of this Act: *Provided,* That such reservations or transfers shall not interfere with legal rights acquired under any public-land laws so long as such rights are legally maintained. . . .

Sec. 14. . . . That any legal subdivisions of the public land, not exceeding one hundred and sixty acres, the greater part of which is mountainous or too rough for cultivation, may, in the discretion of the said Secretary, be ordered into the market and sold pursuant to this section upon the application of any person who owns land or holds a valid entry of lands adjoining such tract, regardless of the fact that such tract may not be isolated or disconnected within the meaning of this section. . . .

SEC. 15. The Secretary of the Interior is further authorized in his discretion, where vacant, unappropriated, and unreserved lands of the public domain are situated in such isolated or disconnected tracts of six hundred and forty acres or more as not to justify their inclusion in any grazing district to be established pursuant to this Act, to lease any such lands to owners of lands contiguous thereto for grazing purposes, upon application therefor by any such owner, and upon such terms and conditions as the Secretary may prescribe. . . .

"Stimulate the health and welfare of Man"

THE NATIONAL ENVIRONMENTAL POLICY ACT

1969

In 1969, when Congress enacted the National Environmental Policy Act, it established a Council on Environmental Quality—recognizing "that each person should enjoy a healthful environment . . ."

Sec. 2. The purposes of this Act are: To declare a national policy which will encourage productive and enjoyable harmony between man and his environment; to promote efforts which will prevent or eliminate damage to the environment and biosphere and stimulate the health and welfare of man; to enrich the understanding of the ecological systems and natural resources important to the Nation; and to establish a Council on Environment Quality.

TITLE I

DECLARATION OF NATIONAL ENVIRONMENTAL POLICY

Sec. 101(a) The Congress, recognizing the profound impact of man's activity on the interrelations of all components of the natural environment, particularly the profound influences of population growth, high-density urbanization, industrial expansion, resource exploitation, and new and expanding technological advances and recognizing further the critical importance of restoring and maintaining environmental quality to the overall welfare and development of man, declares that it is the continuing policy of the Federal Government, in cooperation with State and local governments, and other concerned public and private organizations, to use all practicable means and measures, including financial and technical assistance, in a manner calculated to foster and promote the general welfare, to create and maintain conditions under which man and nature can exist in productive harmony, and fulfill the social, economic, and other requirements of present and future generations of Americans.

(b) In order to carry out the policy set forth in this Act, it is the continuing responsibility of the Federal Government to use all practicable means, consistent with other essential considerations of national policy, to improve and coordinate Federal plans, functions, programs, and resources to the end that the Nation may

(1) fulfill the responsibilities of each generation as trustee of the environment for succeeding generations;

(2) assure for all Americans safe, healthful, productive, and esthetically and culturally pleasing surroundings;

(3) attain the widest range of beneficial uses of the environment without degradation, risk to health or safety, or other undesirable and unintended consequences;

(4) preserve important historic, cultural, and natural aspects of our national heritage, and maintain, whenever possible, an environment which supports diversity and variety of individual choice;

(5) achieve a balance between population and resource use which will permit high standards of living and a wide sharing of life's amenities; and

(6) enhance the quality of renewable resources and approach the maximum attainable recycling of depletable resources.

(c) The Congress recognizes that each person should enjoy a healthful environment and that each person has a responsibility to contribute to the preservation and enhancement of the environment.

Sec. 102. The Congress authorizes and directs that, to the fullest extent possible: (1) the policies, regulations, and public laws of the United States shall be interpreted and administered in accordance with the policies set forth in this Act, and (2) all agencies of the Federal Government shall

(A) utilize a systemic, interdisciplinary approach which will insure the integrated use of the natural and social sciences and the environmental design arts in planning and in decisionmaking which may have an impact on man's environment;

(B) identify and develop methods and procedures in consultation with the Council on Environmental Quality established by title II of this Act, which will insure that presently unquantified environmental amenities and values may be given appropriate consideration in decisionmaking along with economic and technical considerations;

(C) include in every recommendation or report on proposals for legislation and other major Federal actions significantly affecting the quality of the human environment, a detailed statement by the responsible official on

(i) the environment impact of the proposed action,

(ii) any adverse environmental effects which cannot be avoided should the proposal be implemented,

(iii) alternatives to the proposed action,

(iv) the relationship between local short-term uses of man's environment and the maintenance and enhancement of long-term productivity, and,

(v) any irreversible and irretrievable commitments of resources which would be involved in the proposed action should it be implemented.

FOREIGN AFFAIRS

T he rise to world power was surely one of the most remarkable developments in our history. A latecomer to the stage of international affairs, the U.S. devoted much energy to the elementary challenge of conquering a wilderness. Within a century and a half of undertaking this task, the United States emerged as the dominant world power. In this process of emergence, a few persistent themes are apparent. One is the relentless pursuit of overseas markets—which early-on produced a crisis. Anglo-French hostilities, beginning in 1793, stimulated a shipping boom for neutral countries, as France opened its commercial empire heretofore closed to non-French traders and trading vessels. Taking advantage of this opportunity, American frigates ran afoul of England, which wished to curtail any and all trade with its enemy. The British fleet, ruling the waves, seized about 300 U.S. vessels, confiscated their property, and forced many of their sailors into the English navy. By 1794, such practices aroused strong feelings in the United States, and even the pro-British Federalists expected war, which President Washington wisely sought to prevent by diplomatic negotiations.

Yet another equally constant theme became evident after the Civil War, graphically so in the 1890s. It was a difficult time: economic depression, labor struggles, divisive politics, "new" immigrants, racial violence, corporate abuses. Despite these dispiriting developments, or perhaps in need of distraction because of them, Americans turned away from their internal affairs. They looked outward—to other parts of the world. The business sector did likewise, because America now produced more manufactured goods than the domestic market could absorb; foreign markets—especially the China market—seemed most alluring. Expansionist sentiments were supported and rationalized by ideological convictions that were rooted in the Jacksonian period, if not at the outset of settlement, and were revitalized in the late nineteenth century—thus the belief that Americans were "destined" to conquer new lands because of the superiority of their institutions and biological stock; their special destiny owed to their racial and cultural heritage. Believing that the nation must spread its values and institutions more aggressively than in the past, a small but determined group of men like Congressman Henry Cabot Lodge, Theodore Roosevelt, Reverend Josiah Strong, and Captain Alfred Thayer Mahan challenged American insularity and public indifference and gave voice to a combined commercial missionary idealism. They provided the necessary direction and momentum, stimulating popular receptivity to schemes promoting overseas commercial and territorial interests. Focusing on Spanish-held Cuba as a country that best exemplified their concerns, they made an emotional appeal for the forceful end of Spain's tyranny on the island. "Our own interests [in Cuba] were great...," Roosevelt admitted. "But even greater were our interests from the standpoint of humanity. Cuba was at our very doors. It was a dreadful thing for us to sit supinely and watch her death agony." Americans could not do so. This appeal would wake the dead, and Cuban intervention was greeted enthusiastically. McKinley's accession to the executive office was a godsend for everyone concerned, and so was Teddy Roosevelt's "splendid little war." By the time it was over, the outlines of an American empire existed.

And by this time, the traditional American reluctance to enter into entangling alliances also was at an end. An informal agreement of Anglo-Saxon powers shortly emerged, with England supporting American efforts to discourage Japanese, German, and Russian attempts to carve enclaves out of the Chinese empire. This extension of the Monroe Doctrine into the Pacific continued a persistent expression of interest there ever since mid-century—and would be intermittently revived, by President Nixon in the Shanghai communiquè and with U.S. involvement in Vietnam. In 1899, in a dubious act of benevolence toward China, Secretary of State John Hay announced the Open Door policy, a bold stroke satisfying our commercial interests. By guaranteeing Chinese rights against foreign encroachments, the United States stood tall as a protector of the cause of freedom. Successive Administrations also made the American presence felt in the Caribbean and in Central America, by intervening in the internal affairs of nations in the region. Presidents Roosevelt, Taft, and Wilson undertook interventions to preserve stability and to counter the influence of rival big powers. Wilson, in the name of America's moral leadership, dispatched marines to Haiti in 1915, owing to domestic turbulence in that country; the troops remained until 1934. Even in the 1930s, then, notwithstanding the turn toward isolationism, foreign affairs were never completely neglected. The prospect of trade and the need for foreign markets dictated as much. The Franklin Roosevelt Administration recognized the Soviet Union in 1933, much to the delight of selected groups of businessmen and America's writers and intellectuals.

America's isolationist sentiment gradually eroded once the Second World War broke out in 1939. After German forces had crushed France in the summer of 1940, the Administration began to move toward support of the Allied forces as rapidly as public opinion allowed. With Wendell Wilkie *defeated in the 1940 election, Roosevelt promulgated a lend-lease system of economic aid to the beleaguered British government and, perceiving the conflict in ideological terms, asserted that United States policy was governed by the search for "four" essential freedoms. When hostilities ended, the uneasy Grand Alliances reverted to the ideological conflicts that characterized the interwar years, with the United States emerging as the greatest power in a bipolar world. President Truman moved toward an intractably hard-line policy vis-a-vis the Soviet Union and confrontation with what was perceived as an aggressive international communist threat to a free world.*

Successive American Chief Executives hewed to the same ideological line, which made involvement in the rice paddies of Southeast Asia a foregone and tragic outcome. Their actions in Vietnam, based on the assumption of a monolithic communist conspiracy, were exposed in the Pentagon Papers. Vietnam itself was no departure from U.S. foreign policy. It was no aberration. It was the result of twenty years of incremental decisions, each of which appeared justified by an immediate political or military crisis. Few officials asked the basic questions: Did we have any right to be in Vietnam? What was our policy in Vietnam? The war was America's longest. The United States poured vast amounts of both economic and military resources into that benighted country. It spent billions, and dropped more tonnage than was dropped by all belligerents in the Second World War—all aimed at a small, undeveloped society. Yet America's policies, practices, and views did not alter once hostilities ended—except in one respect, where a modest change occurred. The Tonkin Bay Resolution had been a full-dress defense of inherent Presidential power to wage war without looking to Congress for authorization; that is, the Resolution represented a Congressional delegation to the President of the power to declare war—which, as one Supreme Court Justice concluded, was an impermissible delegation. Reflecting this marked departure from the doctrine of separation of powers, Congress did move to limit Presidential power to wage war without its approval, but the statute's mandates could be easily evaded by a determined Chief Executive.

Richard Nixon retained the ideological imperatives that brought the United States into the incalculable disaster that was Vietnam. It made his move toward a detente with Russia and a rapprochement with the People's Republic of China a stunning surprise and an adroit diplomatic triumph. In no small measure it was made possible by his past skill in the art of anti-communism. His credentials were such that no one could accuse him of being "soft on communism." In any case, his was a flexibility, opportunism if you will, that was desolately lacking in the foreign policy of both Presidents Reagan and Bush, though changes in Soviet leadership made a settlement with the U.S.S.R. entirely feasible. Instead, Reagan and Bush retained the forty-year-old view of an evil and dangerous conspiratorial enemy. Both recognized the importance of the Middle East, with its vast oil reserves, and its strategic importance for Russia as well as the United States. Indeed, every modern Presidency has expended vast financial and political resources to maintain American influence, if not hegemony, in the region. Reagan's fixation on the Middle East was indirect and involved. His chief advisors allowed Colonel Oliver North to function, as the Tower Commission concluded, "largely outside the orbit of the U.S. government"—in an effort to use funds from Iranian arms sales to fund the Contras in Nicaragua. Bush's commitment to U.S. dominance in the region was obviously far more direct, because he persuaded the United Nations to approve a mission to drive Iraq out of small, oil-rich Kuwait, which it had invaded in the summer of 1990. The Soviet Union had unraveled by this time, the Cold War had come to an end, but a reason for earlier American concern about the Middle East still existed. The late nineteenth-century pursuit of overseas markets had, in this region at least, been replaced by fearful concern about control of oil fields.

"Inviolable . . . peace . . . sincere friendship"

THE JAY TREATY
1794

In the 28-article Jay Treaty (officially, the Treaty of Amity, Commerce, and Navigation) John Jay (1745–1829), on leave as Chief Justice of the United States, was able to dislodge British garrison troops from the triangular section south of the Great Lakes to the confluence of the Mississippi and Ohio rivers, reinforcing the integrity of the boundaries established in the Treaty of Paris of 1783, which ended the American War of Independence. In the 1780s, Jay had been U.S. Secretary for Foreign Affairs and a pseudonymous author of *The Federalist* papers vigorously supporting ratification of the Constitution. President George Washington (1732–1799) sent Jay to London as minister extraordinary to settle a number of U.S.-British disputes. Negotiators and principal signators of the Jay Treaty displayed mutual respect and amiability, but the treaty became a bitter partisan issue in the U.S., for it made no mention of England's violations of maritime law, particularly the impressment of U.S. sailors. Fifteen months passed between signing and promulgation. (The U.S. would consider the War of 1812 with Britain an abrogation of the Jay Treaty.)

His Britannic Majesty and the United States of America, being desirous, by a treaty of amity, commerce and navigation, to terminate their difference in such a manner, as, without reference to the merits of their respective complaints and pretentions, may be the best calculated to produce mutual satisfaction and good understanding; and also to regulate the commerce and navigation between their respective countries, territories and people, in such a manner as to render the same reciprocally beneficial and satisfactory; they have, respectively, named their Plenipotentiaries, and given them full powers to treat of, and conclude the said treaty, that is to say: . . .

ARTICLE I.

There shall be a firm, inviolable and universal peace, and a true and sincere friendship between His Britannic Majesty, his heirs and successors, and the United States of America; and between their respective countries, territories, cities, towns and people of every degree, without exception of persons or places.

ARTICLE II.

His Majesty will withdraw all his troops and garrisons from all posts and places within the boundary lines assigned by the treaty of peace to the United States. This evacuation shall take place on or before the first day of June, one thousand seven hundred and ninety-six, and all the proper measures shall in the interval be taken by concert between the Government of the United States and His Majesty's Governor-General in America for settling the previous arrangements which may be necessary respecting the delivery of the said posts: The United States in the mean time, at their discretion, extending their settlements to any part within the said boundary line, except within the precincts or jurisdiction of any of the said posts. All settlers and traders, within the precincts or jurisdiction of the said posts, shall continue to enjoy, unmolested, all their property of every kind, and shall be protected therein. They shall be at full liberty to remain there, or to remove with all or any part of their effects; and it shall also be free to them to sell their lands, houses or effects, or to retain the property thereof, at their discretion; such of them as shall continue to reside within the said boundary lines, shall not be compelled to become citizens of the United States, or to take any oath of allegiance to the Government thereof; but they shall be at full liberty so to do if they think proper, and they shall make and declare their election within one year after the evacuation aforesaid. And all persons who shall continue there after the expiration of the said year, without having declared their intention of remaining subjects of His Britannic Majesty, shall be considered as having elected to become citizens of the United States.

ARTICLE III.

It is agreed that it shall at all times be free to His Majesty's subjects, and to the citizens of the United States, and also to the Indians dwelling on either side of the said boundary line, freely to pass and repass by land or inland navigation, into the respective territories and countries of the two parties, on the continent of America, (the country within the limits of the Hudson's Bay Company only excepted.) and to navigate all the lakes, rivers and waters thereof, and freely to carry on trade and commerce with each other. But it is understood that this article does not extend to the admission of vessels of the United States into the sea-ports, harbours, bays or creeks of His Majesty's said territories; nor into such parts of the rivers in His Majesty's said territories as are between the mouth thereof, and the highest port of entry from the sea, except in small vessels trading bona fide between Montreal and Quebec, under such regulations as shall be established to prevent the possibility of any frauds in this respect. Nor to the admission of British vessels from the sea into the rivers of the United States, beyond the highest ports of entry for foreign vessels from the sea. The river Mississippi shall, however, according to the treaty of peace, be entirely open to both parties; and it is further agreed, that all the ports and places on its eastern side, to whichsoever of the parties belonging, may freely be resorted to and used by both parties, in as ample a manner as any of the Atlantic ports or places of the United States, or any of the ports or places of His Majesty in Great Britain.

All goods and merchandize whose importation into His Majesty's said territories in America shall not be entirely prohibited, may freely, for the purposes of commerce, be carried into the same in the manner aforesaid, by the citizens of the United States, and such goods and merchandize shall be subject to no higher or other duties than would be payable by His Majesty's subjects on the importation of the same from Europe into the said territories. And in like manner all goods and merchandize whose importation into the United States shall not be wholly prohibited, may freely, for the purposes of commerce, be carried into the same, in the manner aforesaid, by His Majesty's subjects, and such goods and merchandize shall be subject to no higher or other duties than would be payable by the citizens of the United States on the importation of the same in American vessels into the Atlantic ports of the said States. And all goods not prohibited to be exported from the said territories respectively, may in like manner be carried out of the same by the two parties respectively, paying duty as aforesaid.

No duty of entry shall ever be levied by either party on peltries brought by land or inland navigation into the said territories respectively, nor shall the Indians passing or repassing with their own proper goods and effects of whatever nature, pay for the same any impost or duty whatever. But goods in bales, or other large packages, unusual among Indians, shall not be considered as goods belonging bona fide to Indians.

No higher or other tolls or rates of ferriage than what are or shall be payable by natives, shall be demanded on either side; and no duties shall be payable on any goods which shall merely be carried over any of the portages or carrying-places on either side, for the purpose of being immediately re-embarked and carried to some other place or places. But as by this stipulation it is only meant to secure to each party a free passage across the portages on both sides, it is agreed that this exemption from duty shall extend only to such goods as are carried in the usual and direct road across the portage, and are not attempted to be in any manner sold or exchanged during their passage across the same, and proper regulations may be established to prevent the possibility of any frauds in this respect.

As this article is intended to render in a great degree the local advantages of each party common to both, and thereby to promote a disposition favorable to friendship and good neighborhood, it is agreed that the respective Governments will mutually promote this amicable intercourse, by causing speedy and impartial justice to be done, and necessary protection to be extended to all who may be concerned therein.

ARTICLE IV.

Whereas it is uncertain whether the river Mississippi extends so far to the northward as to be intersected by a line to be drawn due west from the Lake of the Woods, in the manner mentioned in the treaty of peace between His Majesty and the United States: it is agreed that measures shall be taken in concert between His Majesty's Government in America and the Government of the United States, for making a joint survey of the said river from one degree of latitude below the falls of St. Anthony, to the principal source or sources of the said river, and also of the parts adjacent thereto; and that if, on the result of such survey, it should appear that the said river would not be intersected by such a line as is above mentioned, the two parties will thereupon proceed, by amicable negotiation, to regulate the boundary line in that quarter, as well as all other points to be adjusted between the said parties, according to justice and mutual convenience, and in conformity to the intent of the said treaty.

"Sincere and cordial amity"

THE TREATY OF KANAGAWA

1854

Commodore Matthew Calbraith Perry (1794–1858), demanding respect, steamed into Yedo (Tokyo Bay) with four warships, "four black dragons." The Japanese, who had rebuffed earlier treaty proposals, were unable to turn back the American force. Perry carried instructions from President Millard Fillmore (1880–1874) to arrange a treaty that would: 1) afford hospitable treatment for American seamen and their ships if shipwrecked or driven into Japanese ports by storms; 2) open one or two ports for the purposes of provisioning and repairing ships; and 3) open one or more ports for trading purposes. For a time, the peerless, industrious, enterprising U.S. commander-in-chief of naval forces in Far East seas, envoy extraordinary, and minister plenipotentiary (and "father of the steam navy") was tested by the bellicose, feudal island kingdom's centuries-old isolation from the West. Japanese negotiators finally recognized that ancient laws might be *too* ancient. The spirit of the age called for change. The guarantee of "perfect, permanent, and universal peace, and a sincere and cordial amity" held until Pearl Harbor.

ARTICLE I

There shall be a perfect, permanent, and universal peace, and a sincere and cordial amity, between the United States of America on the one part, and the Empire of Japan on the other, and between their people, respectively, without exception of persons or places.

ARTICLE II

The port of Shimoda, in the principality of Izu, and the port of Hakodate, in the principality of Matsumae, are granted by the Japanese as ports for the reception of American ships, where they can be supplied with wood, water, provisions, and coal, and other articles their necessity may require, as far as the Japanese have them. The time for opening the first-named port is im-

mediately on signing this treaty; the last-named port is to be opened immediately after the same day in the ensuing Japanese year.

Note: A tariff of prices shall be given by the Japanese officers of the things which they can furnish, payment for which shall be in gold and silver coin.

ARTICLE III

Whenever ships of the United States are thrown or wrecked on the coast of Japan, the Japanese vessels will assist them, and carry their crews to Shimoda or Hakodate, and hand them over to their countrymen appointed to receive them. Whatever articles the shipwrecked men may have preserved shall likewise be restored, and the expenses incurred in the rescue and support of American and Japanese, who may thus be thrown upon the shores of either nation, are not to be refunded.

ARTICLE IV

Those shipwrecked persons and other citizens of the United States shall be free as in other countries, and not subjected to confinement, but shall be amenable to just laws.

ARTICLE V

Shipwrecked men, and other citizens of the United States, temporarily living at Shimoda and Hakodate, shall not be subject to such restrictions and confinements as the Dutch and Chinese are at Nagasaki; but shall be free at Shimoda to go where they please within the limits of seven Japanese miles [or ri] from a small island in the harbor of Shimoda, marked on the accompanying chart, hereto appended: and shall in like manner be free to go where they please at Hakodate, within limits to be defined after the visit of the United States squadron to that place.

ARTICLE VI

If there be any other sort of goods wanted, or any business which shall require to be arranged, there shall be careful deliberation between the parties in order to settle such matters.

ARTICLE VII

It is agreed that ships of the United States resorting to the ports open to them shall be permitted to exchange gold and silver coin, and articles of goods, for other articles of goods, under such regulations which shall be temporar-

ily established by the Japanese government for that purpose. It is stipulated, however, that the ships of the United States shall be permitted to carry away whatever articles they are unwilling to exchange.

ARTICLE VIII

Wood, water, provisions, coal, and goods required shall only be procured through the agency of Japanese officers appointed for that purpose, and in no other manner.

ARTICLE IX

It is agreed, that if, at any future day, the government of Japan shall grant to any other nation or nations privileges and advantages which are not herein granted to the United States and the citizens thereof, that the same privileges and advantages shall be granted likewise to the United States and to the citizens thereof without any consultation or delay.

ARTICLE X

Ships of the United States shall be permitted to resort to no other ports in Japan but Shimoda and Hakodate, unless in distress or forced by stress of weather.

ARTICLE XI

There shall be appointed by the government of the United States consuls or agents to reside in Shimoda at any time after the expiration of eighteen months from the date of the signing of this treaty; provided that either of the two governments deems such arrangement necessary. . . .

"Spain relinquishes . . . Cuba"

THE SPANISH-AMERICAN WAR TREATY
1899

In the treaty marking the end of both the "splendid little" four-month, two-ocean Spanish-American War and Spain's once imposing empire in the Western Hemisphere, the United States gained Cuba, Puerto Rico, the Pacific island of Guam, and the 7,100 islands of the Philippines. U.S. forces had captured revolution-shattered Cuba (of the 5,462 U.S. dead, only 379 were killed in combat; yellow fever was the principal enemy) and sank or destroyed all 10 ships of the Spanish fleet in Manila Bay, in the Philippines. U.S. public opinion had been inflamed by ruthless Spanish rule in Cuba, by the mysterious explosion that sank the U.S. battleship *Maine* in Havana harbor (260 sailors killed), and by sensational, jingoistic, war-mongering, page-wide "yellow-press" headlines promoting the U.S. as a global power armed with a potent navy and overseas bases. (Only the incredible ineptitude of the Spaniards and the phenomenal luck of the Americans kept the grim, dirty, and very bloody war from stretching into a struggle as long and as full of disaster as the Boer War in South Africa [1899–1902] would become for the British.) President William McKinley (1843–1901) told news reporters, "God told me to take the Philippines," but he confessed that he had had no idea where the islands were. Cuba became an independent republic, for a time under U.S. military occupation.

WHEREAS, a Treaty of Peace between the United States of America and Her Majesty the Queen Regent of Spain, in the name of her August Son, Don Alfonso XIII; was concluded and signed by their respective plenipotentiaries at Paris on the tenth day of December, 1898, the original of which Convention being in the English and Spanish languages, is word for word as follows: . . .

ARTICLE I.

Spain relinquishes all claim of sovereignty over and title to Cuba.

And as the island is, upon its evacuation by Spain, to be occupied by the United States, the United States will, so long as such occupation shall last, assume and discharge the obligations that may under international law result from the fact of its occupation, for the protection of life and property.

ARTICLE II.

Spain cedes to the United States the island of Porto Rico and other islands now under Spanish sovereignty in the West Indies, and the island of Guam in the Marianas or Ladrones.

ARTICLE III.

Spain cedes to the United States the archipelago known as the Philippine Islands, and comprehending the islands lying within the following line:

A line running from west to east along or near the twentieth parallel of north latitude, and through the middle of the navigable channel of Bachi, from the one hundred and eighteenth (118th) to the one hundred and twenty seventh (127th) degree meridian of longitude cast of Greenwich, thence along the one hundred and twenty seventh (127th) degree meridian of longitude east of Greenwich to the parallel of four degrees and forty five minutes (4° 45′) north latitude, thence along the parallel of four degrees and forty five degrees 4° 45′) north latitude to its intersection with the meridian of longitude one hundred and nineteen degrees and thirty five minutes (119° 35′) east of Greenwich, thence along the meridian of longitude one hundred and nineteen degrees and thirty five minutes (119° 35′) east of Greenwich to the parallel of latitude seven degrees and forty minutes (7° 40′) north, thence along the parallel of latitude seven degrees and forty minutes (7° 40′) north to its intersection with the one hundred and sixteenth (116th) degree meridian of longitude east of Greenwich, thence by a direct line to the intersection of the tenth (10th) degree parallel of north latitude with the one hundred and eighteenth (118th) degree meridian of longitude east of Greenwich, and thence along the one hundred and eighteenth (118th) degree meridian of longitude east of Greenwich to the point of beginning.

The United States will pay to Spain the sum of twenty million dollars ($20,000,000) within three months after the exchange of the ratifications of the present treaty.

ARTICLE IV.

The United States will, for the term of ten years from the date of the exchange of the ratifications of the present treaty, admit Spanish ships and merchandise to the ports of the Philippine Islands on the same terms as ships and merchandise of the United States.

ARTICLE V.

The United States will, upon the signature of the present treaty, send back to Spain, at its own cost, the Spanish soldiers taken as prisoners of war on the capture of Manila by the American forces. The arms of the soldiers in question shall be restored to them. . . .

ARTICLE XVI.

It is understood that any obligations assumed in this treaty by the United States with respect to Cuba are limited to the time of its occupancy thereof; but it will upon the termination of such occupancy, advise any Government established in the island to assume the same obligations. . . .

"We regard the condition at Pekin as one of virtual anarchy"

CHINA AND THE OPEN DOOR
1900

Secretary of State John Milton Hay (1838–1905), once private secretary to President Abraham Lincoln (1809–1865), telegraphed U.S. embassies and missions in Europe and the U.S. office in Tokyo with a statement declaring that the United States stood for the territorial and administrative integrity of all China and for commercial equality or freedom of trade with China by Western nations. Reformulating the U.S.'s open door, or equal opportunity, policy (1899), the communique was prompted by the uprising of the fanatical, violent, nationalistic Chinese "Boxers" (the secret society "Harmonious Fists"), threatening "foreign devils" (missionaries and Chinese converts to Christianity) and disruption of previously guaranteed rights.

DEPARTMENT OF STATE
Washington, July 3, 1990

In this critical posture of affairs in China it is deemed appropriate to define the attitude of the United States as far as present circumstances permit this to be done. We adhere to the policy initiated by us in 1857, of peace with the Chinese nation, of furtherance of lawful commerce, and of protection of lives and property of our citizens by all means guaranteed under extraterritorial treaty rights and by the law of nations. If wrong be done to our citizens we propose to hold the responsible authors to the uttermost accountability. We regard the condition at Pekin as one of virtual anarchy, whereby power and responsibility are practically devolved upon the local provincial authorities. So long as they are not in overt collusion with rebellion and use their power to protect foreign life and property we regard them as representing the Chinese people, with whom we seek to remain in peace and friendship. The purpose of the President is, as it has been heretofore, to act concurrently with the other powers, first, in opening up communication with Pekin and rescuing the American officials, missionaries, and other Americans who are in danger; secondly, in affording all possible protection everywhere in China to American life and property; thirdly, in guarding and protecting all legitimate American interests; and fourthly, in aiding to prevent a spread of the disorders to the other provinces of the Empire and a recurrence of such disasters. It is, of course, too early to forecast the means of attaining this last result; but the policy of the government of the United States is to seek a solution which may bring about permanent safety and peace to China, preserve Chinese territorial and administrative entity, protect all rights guaranteed to friendly powers by treaty and international law, and safeguard for the world the principle of equal and impartial trade with all parts of the Chinese Empire.

"I had . . . a swell racket"

General Butler: Racketeer for Capitalism
1931

Major General Smedley Darlington Butler (1881–1940) served in the U.S. Marine Corps for 35 years and twice won the Medal of Honor. In 1931, he stunned an American Legion convention in New England with this recitation of his history:

I spent 33 years . . . being a high-class muscle man for Big Business, for Wall Street and the bankers. In short, I was a racketeer for capitalism. . . .

I helped purify Nicaragua for the international banking house of Brown Brothers in 1909–1912. I helped make Mexico and especially Tampico safe for American oil interests in 1916. I brought light to the Dominican Republic for American sugar interests in 1916. I helped make Haiti and Cuba a decent place for the National City [Bank] boys to collect revenue in. I helped in the rape of half a dozen Central American republics for the benefit of Wall Street. . . .

In China in 1927 I helped see to it that Standard Oil went its way unmolested. . . . I had . . . a swell racket. I was rewarded with honors, medals, promotions. . . . I might have given Al Capone a few hints. The best he could do was to operate a racket in three cities. The Marines operated on three continents. . . .

We don't want any more wars, but a man is a damn fool to think there won't be any more of them. I am a peace-loving Quaker, but when war breaks out every damn man in my family goes. If we're ready, nobody will tackle us. Give us a club and we will face them all. . . .

No pacifists or Communists are going to govern this country. If they try it there will be seven million men like you rise up and strangle them. Pacifists? Hell, I'm a pacifist, but I always have a club behind my back!

Later, the arch-conservative American Liberty League tried to persuade General Butler to lead an army of war veterans in demonstration against President Franklin Delano Roosevelt's (1882–1945) silver standard. Butler determined that the League's goal was really a cover for marching against the nation's capital and, perhaps, overthrowing the government. He blew the whistle.

"*I trust that relations . . . may remain . . . friendly*"

THE U.S. RECOGNIZES THE U.S.S.R.
1933

Confident that the Soviet Union would cease support of subversive activities in the United States, President Franklin Delano Roosevelt (1882–1945) agreed to resume normal diplomatic relations with Moscow in letters addressed to Soviet Foreign Commissar Maxim Litvinov (1876–1951); he did not need Congressional approval. Recognition of the Soviet regime was the new U.S. Chief Executive's first venture into personal diplomacy. Every other major power had already recognized Russia, a potential ally against empire-aspiring Japan and an invaluable ally in case Hitler rampaged. It was also a potential buyer of American goods. Mr. Roosevelt, in a personal letter to the Soviet President, noted "the desirability" of ending "the present abnormal relations between the hundred and twenty-five million people of the United States and of the hundred and sixty million people of Russia." Within two years, the Third International, meeting in Moscow, targeted the U.S. for agitation and propaganda. Stalin's regime reneged on every promise.

My dear Mr. Litvinov:

I am very happy to inform you that as a result of our conversations the Government of the United States has decided to establish normal diplomatic relations with the Government of the Union of Soviet Socialist Republics and to exchange ambassadors.

I trust that the relations now established between our peoples may forever remain normal and friendly, and that our Nations henceforth may cooperate for their mutual benefit and for the preservation of the peace of the world.

———

My dear Mr. Litvinov:

I am glad to have received the assurance expressed in your note to me of this date that it will be the fixed policy of the Government of the Union of Soviet Socialist Republics:

1. To respect scrupulously the indisputable right of the United States to order its own life within its own jurisdiction in its own way and to refrain from interfering in any manner in the internal affairs of the United States, its territories or possessions.

2. To refrain, and to restrain all persons in Government service and all organizations of the Government or under its direct or indirect control, including organizations in receipt of any financial assistance from it, from any act overt or covert liable in any way whatsoever to injure the tranquillity, prosperity, order, or security of the whole or any part of the United States, its territories or possessions, and, in particular, from any act tending to incite or encourage armed intervention, or any agitation or propaganda having as an aim, the violation of the territorial

integrity of the United States, its territories or possessions, or the bringing about by force of a change in the political or social order of the whole or any part of the United States, its territories or possessions.

3. Not to permit the formation or residence on its territory of any organization or group—and to prevent the activity on its territory of any organization or group, or of representatives or officials of any organization or group—which makes claim to be the Government of, or makes attempt upon the territorial integrity of, the United States, its territories or possessions; not to form, subsidize, support or permit on its territory military organizations or groups having the aim of armed struggle against the United States, its territories or possessions, and to prevent any recruiting on behalf of such organizations and groups.

4. Not to permit the formation or residence on its territory or any organization or group—and to prevent the activity on its territory of any organization or group, or of representatives or officials of any organization or group—which has as an aim the overthrow or the preparation for the overthrow of, or the bringing about by force of a change in, the political or social order of the whole or any part of the United States, its territories or possessions.

It will be the fixed policy of the Executive of the United States within the limits of the powers conferred by the Constitution and the laws of the United States to adhere reciprocally to the engagements above expressed.

"Common principles in . . . national policies"

THE ATLANTIC CHARTER
1941

The United States, still not an active player, was standing like a reluctant brother on the brink as Nazi Germany conquered Poland, the Low Countries, and France, torpedoed North Atlantic shipping, and bombed Great Britain. Then President Franklin Delano Roosevelt (1882–1945) and British Prime Minister Winston Spencer Churchill (1874–1965) met on war vessels off the eastern tip of Newfoundland to outline a program for lasting peace. They called for the final destruction of Nazi tyranny and for the establishment of a wider and permanent system of general security (F.D.R. later suggested the name "the United Nations"). The British P.M. wanted to draw the U.S. Navy across the Atlantic as either a buffer or a combatant. The North Atlantic meeting was a success in personal terms, but the British steamed home believing that the Americans had a long way to go before playing a decisive part in the war.

The President of the United States of America and the Prime Minister, Mr. Churchill, representing His Majesty's Government in the United Kingdom, being met together, deem it right to make known certain common principles in the national policies of their respective countries on which they base their hopes for a better future for the world.

First, their countries seek no aggrandizement, territorial or other;

Second, they desire to see no territorial changes that do not accord with the freely expressed wishes of the peoples concerned;

Third, they respect the right of all peoples to choose the form of government under which they will live; and they wish to see sovereign rights and self government restored to those who have been forcibly deprived of them;

Fourth, they will endeavor, with due respect for their existing obligations, to further the en-joyment by all States, great or small, victor or vanquished, of access, on equal terms, to the trade and to the raw materials of the world which are needed for their economic prosperity;

Fifth, they desire to bring about the fullest collaboration between all nations in the economic field with the object of securing, for all, improved labor standards, economic advancement and social security;

Sixth, after the final destruction of the Nazi tyranny, they hope to see established a peace which will afford to all nations the means of dwelling in safety within their own boundaries, and which will afford assurance that all the men in all the lands may live out their lives in freedom from fear and want;

Seventh, such a peace should enable all men to traverse the high seas and oceans without hindrance;

Eighth, they believe that all of the nations of

the world, for realistic as well as spiritual reasons must come to the abandonment of the use of force. Since no future peace can be maintained if land, sea or air armaments continue to be employed by nations which threaten, or may threaten, aggression outside of their frontiers, they believe, pending the establishment of a wider and permanent system of general security, that the disarmament of such nations is essential. They will likewise aid and encourage all other practicable measures which will lighten for peace-loving peoples the crushing burden of armaments.

"From Stettin in the Baltic to Trieste in the Adriatic"

CHURCHILL'S IRON CURTAIN SPEECH
1946

It is a speech that resonates to this day. Less than a year after V-E Day, former British Prime Minister Winston Spencer Churchill (1874–1965), speaking at Westminster College, in Fulton, Missouri, broadcast the memorable "cold-war" geographical fact that the Soviet Union's post-war sphere of influence had imprisoned eastern Europe: "from Stettin in the Baltic to Trieste in the Adriatic, an iron curtain has descended across the Continent." The "war" went on for four decades, until East Germans hammered down the Berlin Wall in the late 1980s.

NEITHER THE SURE PREVENTION of war nor the continuous rise of world organization will be gained without what I have called the fraternal association of the English-speaking peoples. This means a special relationship between the British Commonwealth and Empire and the United States.

. . . Fraternal association requires not only the growing friendship and mutual understanding between our two vast but kindred systems of society but the continuance of the intimate relationships between our military advisers, leading to common study of potential dangers, similarity of weapons and manuals of instruction, and interchange of officers and cadets at colleges. It should carry with it the continuance of the present facilities for mutual security by the joint use of all naval and airforce bases in the possession of either country all over the world. . . .

. . . Eventually there may come the principle of common citizenship, but that we may be content to leave to destiny, whose outstretched arm so many of us can clearly see.

There is, however, an important question we must ask ourselves. Would a special relationship between the United States and the British Commonwealth be inconsistent with our overriding loyalties to the world organization? I reply that, on the contrary, it is probably the only means by which that organization will achieve its full stature and strength. . . . Special associations between members of the United Nations which have no aggressive point against any other country, which harbor no design incompatible with the Charter of the United Nations, far from being harmful, are beneficial and, as I believe, indispensable.

. . . The Dark Ages may return, the Stone Age may return on the gleaming wings of science, and what might now shower immeasurable material blessings upon mankind may even bring about its total destruction.

Beware, I say; time may be short. Do not let us take the course of letting events drift along till it is too late. If there is to be a fraternal association of the kind I have described, with all the extra strength and security which both our countries can derive from it, let us make sure that that great fact is known to the world, and that it plays its part in steadying and stabilizing the foundations of peace. Prevention is better than cure.

A shadow has fallen upon the scenes so lately lighted by the Allied victory. Nobody knows what Soviet Russia and its Communist international organization intends to do in the immediate future, or what are the limits, if any, to their expansive and proselytizing tendencies. I have a strong admiration and regard for the valiant Russian people and for my wartime comrade Marshal Stalin. There is sympathy and goodwill in Britain—and I doubt not here also—toward the peoples of all the Russias and a resolve to persevere through many differences and rebuffs in establishing lasting friendships.

We understand the Russians need to be secure on her western frontiers from all renewal of German aggression. We welcome her to her rightful place among the leading nations of the world. Above all we welcome constant, frequent, and growing contacts between the Russian people and our own people on both sides of the Atlantic. It is my duty, however, to place before you certain facts about the present position in Europe—I am sure I do not wish to, but it is my duty, I feel, to present them to you.

From Stettin in the Baltic to Trieste in the Adriatic, an iron curtain has descended across the Continent. Behind that line lie all the capitals of the ancient states of central and eastern Europe. Warsaw, Berlin, Prague, Vienna, Budapest, Belgrade, Bucharest, and Sofia, all these famous cities and the populations around them lie in the Soviet sphere and all are subject in one form or another, not only to Soviet influence but to a very high and increasing measure of control from Moscow. Athens alone, with its immortal glories, is free to decide its future at an election under British, American, and French observation. The Russian-dominated Polish govern-

ment has been encouraged to make enormous and wrongful inroads upon Germany, and mass expulsions of millions of Germans on a scale grievous and undreamed of are now taking place.

The Communist parties, which were very small in all these Eastern states of Europe, have been raised to preeminence and power far beyond their numbers and are seeking everywhere to obtain totalitarian control. Police governments are prevailing in nearly every case, and so far, except in Czechoslovakia, there is no true democracy. Turkey and Persia are both profoundly alarmed and disturbed at the claims which are made upon them and at the pressure being exerted by the Moscow government. An attempt is being made by the Russians in Berlin to build up a quasi-Communist Party in their zone of occupied Germany by showing special favors to groups of left-wing German leaders.

At the end of the fighting last June, the American and British armies withdrew westward in accordance with an earlier agreement to a depth, at some points, 150 miles on a front of nearly 400 miles to allow the Russians to occupy this vast expanse of territory which the Western democracies had conquered. If now the Soviet government tries, by separate action, to build up a pro-Communist Germany in their areas, this will cause new serious difficulties in the British and American zones and will give the defeated Germans the power of putting themselves up to auction between the Soviets and Western democracies. Whatever conclusions may be drawn from these facts—and facts they are—this is certainly not the liberated Europe we fought to build up. Nor is it one which contains the essentials of permanent peace.

The safety of the world, ladies and gentlemen, requires a new unity in Europe from which no nation should be permanently outcast. . . .

. . . I have felt bound to portray the shadow

which, alike in the West and in the East, falls upon the world. I was a minister at the time of the Versailles Treaty and a close friend of Mr. Lloyd George. I did not myself agree with many things that were done, but I have a very vague impression in my mind of that situation, and I find it painful to contrast it with that which prevails now. In those days there were high hopes and unbounded confidence that the wars were over and that the League of Nations would become all-powerful. I do not see or feel the same confidence or even the same hopes in the haggard world at this time.

On the other hand I repulse the idea that a new war is inevitable; still more that it is imminent. It is because I am so sure that our fortunes are in our own hands and that we hold the power to save the future that I feel the duty to speak out now that I have an occasion to do so. I do not believe that Soviet Russia desires war. What they desire is the fruits of war and the indefinite expansion of their power and doctrines. But what we have to consider here today, while time remains, is the permanent prevention of war and the establishment of conditions of freedom and democracy as rapidly as possible in all countries.

Our difficulties and dangers will not be removed by closing our eyes to them. They will not be removed by mere waiting to see what happens; nor will they be relieved by a policy of appeasement. What is needed is a settlement, and the longer this is delayed the more difficult it will be and the greater our dangers will become. From what I have seen of our Russian friends and allies during the war, I am convinced that there is nothing they admire so much as strength, and there is nothing for which they have less respect than for military weakness. For that reason the old doctrine of a balance of power is unsound. We cannot afford, if we can help it, to work on narrow margins, offering temptations to a trial of strength.

If the Western democracies stand together in strict adherence to the principles of the United Nations Charter, their influence for furthering these principles will be immense and no one is likely to molest them. If, however, they become divided or falter in their duty, and if these all-important years are allowed to slip away, then indeed catastrophe may overwhelm us all. . . .

"The rehabilitation of Europe"

THE MARSHALL PLAN
1947

Two years after V-E Day, Europe was still all rubble. On a flight home from the continent, the U.S. Assistant Secretary of State for Economic Affairs, Will Clayton, drafted the formulation and promotion of a recovery plan. Secretary of State George C. Marshall (1880–1959) proposed the rescue in a 12-minute, flat, vague speech delivered in a monotone at the Harvard University commencement in June, 1947, offering immense help to rehabilitate the ruined countries: "Whether we like it or not, we find ourselves, our Nation, in a world position of vast responsibility. We can act for our own good by acting for the world's good." News organizations mostly missed the import of General Marshall's speech; Harvard and State Department officials did not burnish the speech's significance. Eighteen European nations responded, assessing their resources and needs so that aid could be integrated on a broad scale; they worked up blueprints for reconstruction, improved standards of living, increased manufacturing production, new housing, and expanded agriculture. The Soviet Union and its satellites refused to participate, viewing the Marshall Plan as an anti-Russian force. Between 1948 and 1952, the U.S. poured $12-billion into the program. For helping to put Europe back on its feet, General Marshall was awarded the Nobel Peace Prize (1953). The Marshall Plan indeed thwarted the westward spread of Communism.

In considering the requirements for the rehabilitation of Europe, the physical loss of life, the visible destruction of cities, factories, mines, and railroads was correctly estimated, but it has become obvious during recent months that this visible destruction was probably less serious than the dislocation of the entire fabric of European economy. For the past 10 years conditions have been highly abnormal. The feverish preparation for war and the more feverish maintenance of the war effort engulfed all aspects of national economies. Machinery has fallen into disrepair or is entirely obsolete. Under the arbitrary and destructive Nazi rule, virtually every possible enterprise was geared into the German war machine. . . . The breakdown of the business structure of Europe during the war was complete. Recovery has been seriously retarded. . . . the rehabilitation of the economic structure of Europe quite evidently will require a much longer time and greater effort than had been foreseen.

There is a phase of this matter which is both interesting and serious. The farmer has always produced the foodstuffs to exchange with the city dweller for the other necessities of life. This division of labor is the basis of modern civilization. At the present time it is threatened with breakdown. The town and city industries are not producing adequate goods to exchange with the food-producing farmer. Raw materials and fuel are in short supply. Machinery is lacking or worn out. The farmer or the peasant cannot find the goods for sale which he desires to purchase. . . . He feeds more grain to stock and finds for himself and his family an ample supply of food, however short he may be on clothing and the other ordinary gadgets of civilization. Meanwhile people in the cities are short of food and fuel. So the governments are forced to use their foreign money and credits to procure these necessities abroad. This process exhausts funds which are urgently needed for reconstruction. Thus a very serious situation is rapidly developing which bodes no good for the world. The modern system of the division of labor upon which the exchange of products is based is in danger of breaking down.

The truth of the matter is that Europe's requirements for the next 3 or 4 years of foreign food and other essential products—principally from America—are so much greater than her present ability to pay that she must have substantial additional help, or face economic, social, and political deterioration of a very grave character.

The remedy lies in breaking the vicious circle and restoring the confidence of the European people in the economic future of their own countries and of Europe as a whole. The manufacturer and the farmer throughout wide areas must be able and willing to exchange their products for currencies the continuing value of which is not open to question.

Aside from the demoralizing effect on the world at large and the possibilities of disturbances arising as a result of the desperation of the people concerned, the consequences to the economy of the United States should be apparent to all. It is logical that the United States should do whatever it is able to do to assist in the return of normal economic health in the world, without which there can be no political stability and no assured peace. Our policy is directed not against any county or doctrine but against hunger, poverty, desperation, and chaos. Its purpose should be the revival of a working economy in the world so as to permit the emergence of political and social conditions in which free institutions can exist. Such assistance, I am convinced, must not be on a piecemeal basis as various crises develop. Any assistance that this Government may render in the future should provide a cure rather than a mere palliative. Any government that is willing to assist in the task of recovery will find full cooperation, I am sure, on the part of the United States Government. Any government which maneuvers to block the recovery of other countries cannot expect help from us. Furthermore, governments, political parties, or groups which seek to perpetuate human misery in order to profit therefrom politically or otherwise will encounter the opposition of the United States.

. . . It would be neither fitting nor efficacious for this Government to undertake to draw up unilaterally a program designed to place Europe on its feet economically. This is the business of the Europeans. The initiative, I think, must come from Europe. The role of this country should consist of friendly aid in the drafting of a European program and of later support of such a program so far as it may be practical for us to do so. The program should be a joint one, agreed to by a number, if not all European nations.

An essential part of any successful action on the part of the United States is an understanding on the part of the people of America of the character of the problem and the remedies to be applied. Political passion and prejudice should have no part. . . .

"To promote stability and well-being"

THE NORTH ATLANTIC TREATY
1949

Democratic nations of the North Atlantic community, driven by the accelerating stridency of the Cold War, organized a defensive alliance, the North Atlantic Treaty Organization (NATO), as a shield, a military trip-wire, providing collective security. An attack against one or more of the parties in Europe or North America would be considered as an attack against them all. The U.S. Senate ratified the treaty by a vote of 82 to 13. For the first time, the U.S. was in a peacetime alliance; it would not again stand neutral while Europe was overrun. Because NATO encourages political, social, and economic ties among its members, subversive opportunities for Soviet Communism were blocked. The dozen signatory countries, which had been divided by geography and history for at least 150 years, were the United States, the United Kingdom, Canada, France, Italy, the Netherlands, Norway, Belgium, Denmark, Luxembourg, Iceland, and Portugal. (A month after NATO was organized, the Soviet Union lifted its blockade of Berlin. The Allies had been airlifting supplies into West Berlin, the Allied section of the partitioned former German capital.) In the Spring of 1999, NATO-U.S. warplanes raided Yugoslavia during the search for a solution to a crisis in the province of Kosovo.

The Parties to this Treaty reaffirm their faith in the purposes and principles of the Charter of the United Nations and their desire to live in peace with all peoples and all governments.

They are determined to safeguard the freedom, common heritage and civilisation of their peoples, founded on the principles of democracy, individual liberty and the rule of law.

They seek to promote stability and well-being in the North Atlantic area.

They are resolved to unite their efforts for collective defence and for the preservation of peace and security.

They therefore agree to this North Atlantic Treaty:

ARTICLE 1

The Parties undertake, as set forth in the Charter of the United Nations, to settle any international dispute in which they may be involved by peaceful means in such a manner that international peace and security and justice are not endangered, and to refrain in their international relations from the threat or use of force in any manner inconsistent with the purposes of the United Nations.

ARTICLE 2

The Parties will contribute toward the further development of peaceful and friendly international relations by strengthening their free institutions, by bringing about a better understanding of the principles upon which these institutions are founded, and by promoting conditions of stability and well-being. They will seek to eliminate conflict in their international economic policies and will encourage economic collaboration between any or all of them.

ARTICLE 3

In order more effectively to achieve the objectives of this Treaty, the Parties, separately and jointly, by means of continuous and effective self-help and mutual aid, will maintain and develop their individual and collective capacity to resist armed attack.

ARTICLE 4

The Parties will consult together whenever, in the opinion of any of them, the territorial integrity, political independence or security of any of the Parties is threatened.

ARTICLE 5

The Parties agree that an armed attack against one or more of them in Europe or North America shall be considered an attack against them all, and consequently they agree that, if such an armed attack occurs, each of them, in exercise of the right of individual or collective self-defence recognised by Article 51 of the Charter of the United Nations, will assist the Party or Parties so attacked by taking forthwith, individually, and in concert with the other Parties, such action as it deems necessary, including the use of armed force, to restore and maintain the security of the North Atlantic area.

Any such armed attack and all measures taken as a result thereof shall immediately be reported to the Security Council. Such measures shall be terminated when the Security Council has taken the measures necessary to restore and maintain international peace and security.

ARTICLE 6(1)

For the purpose of Article 5, an armed attack on one or more of the Parties is deemed to include an armed attack:

—on the territory of any of the Parties in Europe or North America, on the Algerian Departments of France (2), on the territory of Turkey or on the islands under the jurisdiction of any of the Parties in the North Atlantic area north of the Tropic of Cancer;

—on the forces, vessels, or aircraft of any of the Parties, when in or over these territories or any area in Europe in which occupation forces of any of the Parties were stationed on the date when the Treaty entered into force or the Mediterranean Sea or the North Atlantic area north of the Tropic of Cancer.

ARTICLE 7

The Treaty does not effect, and shall not be interpreted as affecting, in any way the rights and obligations under the Charter of the Parties which are members of the United Nations, or the primary responsibility of the Security Council for the maintenance of international peace and security.

ARTICLE 8

Each Party declares that none of the international engagements now in force between it and any other of the Parties or any third State is in conflict with the provisions of this Treaty, and undertakes not to enter into any international engagement in conflict with this Treaty.

ARTICLE 9

The Parties hereby establish a Council, on which each of them shall be represented to consider matters concerning the implementation of this Treaty. The Council shall be so organised as to be able to meet promptly at any time. The Council shall set up such subsidiary bodies as may be necessary; in particular it shall establish immediately a defence committee which shall recommend measures for the implementation of Articles 3 and 5.

ARTICLE 10

The Parties may, by unanimous agreement, invite any other European State in a position to further the principles of this Treaty and to contribute to the security of the North Atlantic area to accede to this Treaty. Any State so invited may become a party to the Treaty by depositing its instrument of accession with the Government of the United States of America. The Government of the United States of America will inform each of the Parties of the deposit of each such instrument of accession.

ARTICLE 11

This Treaty shall be ratified and its provisions carried out by the Parties in accordance with their respective constitutional processes. The instruments of ratification shall be deposited as soon as possible with the Government of the United States of America, which will notify all the other signatories of each deposit. The Treaty shall enter into force between the States which have ratified it as soon as the ratification of the majority of the signatories, including the ratifications of Belgium, Canada, France, Luxembourg, the Netherlands, the United Kingdom and the United States, have been deposited and shall come into effect with respect to other States on the date of the deposit of their ratifications.

ARTICLE 12

After the Treaty has been in force for ten years, or at any time The Treaty came into force on 24 August 1949, after the deposition of the ratifications of all signatory states.

thereafter, the Parties shall, if any of them so requests, consult together for the purpose of reviewing the Treaty, having regard for the factors then affecting peace and security in the North Atlantic area including the development of universal as well as regional arrangements under the Charter of the United Nations for the maintenance of international peace and security.

ARTICLE 13

After the Treaty has been in force for twenty years, any Party may cease to be a Party one year after its notice of denunciation has been given to the Government of the United States of America, which will inform the Governments of the other Parties of the deposit of each notice of denunciation.

ARTICLE 14

This Treaty, of which the English and French texts are equally authentic, shall be deposited in the archives of the Government of the United States of America. Duly certified copies will be transmitted by that government to the governments of the other signatories.

(NOTE: article 6 is amended; original article 6 appears below:

ART. 6. For the purpose of Article 5 an armed attack on one or more of the Parties is deemed to include an armed attack on the territory of any of the Parties in Europe or North America, on the Algerian departments of France, on the occupation forces of any Party in Europe, on the islands under the jurisdiction of any Party in the North Atlantic area north of the Tropic of Cancer or on the vessels or aircraft in this area of any of the Parties.

"Importance of Southeast Asia to the security of the United States"

U.S. GOALS IN SOUTHEAST ASIA
1952

In early 1952, the National Security Council outlined U.S. objectives and a course of action with respect to Southeast Asia. The region was defined as that embracing Indochina, Thailand, Burma, Malaya, and Indonesia. Policy would be threefold: prevent those countries from passing into the communist orbit, assist them to develop the will and the ability to resist communism from within and without, and contribute to the strengthening of the free world. A decade later, the U.S., fearing that if one Southeast Asian nation fell, additional ones would fall (the "domino effect"), injected large-scale military forces into Vietnam.

OBJECTIVE

1. To prevent the countries of Southeast Asia from passing into the communist orbit, and to assist them to develop will and ability to resist communism from within and without and to contribute to the strengthening of the free world.

GENERAL CONSIDERATIONS

2. Communist domination, by whatever means, of all Southeast Asia would seriously endanger in the short term, and critically endanger in the longer term, United States security interests.

a. The loss of any of the countries of Southeast Asia to communist aggression would have critical psychological, political and economic consequences. In the absence of effective and timely counteraction, the loss of any single country would probably lead to relatively swift submission to or an alignment with communism by the remaining countries of this group. Furthermore, an alignment with communism of the rest of Southeast Asia and India, and in the longer term, of the Middle East (with the probable exceptions of at least Pakistan and Turkey) would in all probability progressively follow: Such widespread alignment would endanger the stability and security of Europe.

b. Communist control of all of Southeast Asia would render the U.S. position in the Pacific offshore island chain precarious and would seriously jeopardize fundamental U.S. security interests in the Far East.

c. Southeast Asia, especially Malaya and Indonesia, is the principal world source of natural rubber and tin, and a producer of petroleum and other strategically important commodities. The rice exports of Burma and Thailand are critically important to Malaya, Ceylon and Hong Kong and are of considerable significance to Japan and India, all important areas of free Asia.

d. The loss of Southeast Asia, especially of Malaya and Indonesia, could result in such economic and political pressures in Japan as to make it extremely difficult to prevent Japan's eventual accommodation to communism.

3. It is therefore imperative that an overt attack on Southeast Asia by the Chinese Communists be vigorously opposed. In order to pursue the military courses of action envisaged in this paper to a favorable conclusion within a reasonable period, it will be necessary to divert military strength from other areas thus reducing our military capability in those areas, with the recognized increased risks involved therein, or to increase our military forces in being, or both.

4. The danger of an overt military attack against Southeast Asia is inherent in the existence of a hostile and aggressive Communist China, but such an attack is less probable than continued communist efforts to achieve domination through subversion. The primary threat to Southeast Asia accordingly arises from the possibility that the situation in Indochina may deteriorate as a result of the weakening of the resolve of, or as a result of the inability of the governments of France and of the Associated States to continue to oppose the Viet Minh rebellion, the military strength of which is being steadily increased by virtue of aid furnished by the Chinese Communist regime and its allies.

5. The successful defense of Tonkin is critical to the retention in non-Communist hands of mainland Southeast Asia. However, should Burma come under communist domination, a communist military advance through Thailand might make Indochina, including Tonkin, militarily indefensible. The execution of the following U.S. courses of action with respect to individual countries of the area may vary depending upon the route of communist advance into Southeast Asia.

6. Actions designed to achieve our objectives in Southeast Asia require sensitive selection and application, on the one hand to assure the optimum efficiency through coordination of measures for the general area, and on the other, to accommodate to the greatest practicable extent to the individual sensibilities of the several governments, social classes and minorities of the area.

COURSES OF ACTION

SOUTHEAST ASIA

7. With respect to Southeast Asia, the United States should:

a. Strengthen propaganda and cultural activities, as appropriate, in relation to the area to foster increased alignment of the people with the free world.

b. Continue, as appropriate, programs of economic and technical assistance designed to strengthen the indigenous non-communist governments of the area.

c. Encourage the countries of Southeast Asia to restore and expand their commerce with each other and with the rest of the free world, and stimulate the flow of the raw material resources of the area to the free world.

d. Seek agreement with other nations, including at least France, the UK, Australia and New Zealand, for a joint warning to Communist China regarding the grave consequences of Chinese aggression against Southeast Asia, the issuance of such a warning to be contingent upon the prior agreement of France and the UK to participate in the courses of action set forth in paragraphs 10 c, 12, 14 f (1) and (2) and 15 c (1) and (2), and such others as are determined as a result of prior trilateral consultation, in the event such a warning is ignored.

e. Seek UK and French agreement in principle that a naval blockade of Communist China should be included in the minimum courses of action set forth in paragraph 10c below.

f. Continue to encourage and support closer cooperation among the countries of Southeast Asia, and between those countries and the United States, Great Britain, France, the Philippines, Australia, New Zealand, South Asia and Japan.

g. Strengthen, as appropriate, covert operations designed to assist in the achievement of U.S. objectives in Southeast Asia.

h. Continue activities and operations designed to encourage the overseas Chinese communities in Southeast Asia to organize and activate anti-communist groups and activities within their own communities, to resist the effects of parallel pro-communist groups and activities and, generally, to increase their orientation toward the free world.

i. Take measures to promote the coordinated defense of the area, and encourage and support the spirit of resistance among the peoples of Southeast Asia to Chinese Communist aggression and to the encroachments of local communists.

j. Make clear to the American people the importance of Southeast Asia to the security of the United States. . . .

"The Government had not met that burden"

THE PENTAGON PAPERS
1971

More than 45,000 Americans already had been killed fighting alongside the South Vietnamese in the civil war in the rice paddies and jungles of Vietnam when Secretary of Defense Robert S. McNamara (born 1916) commissioned a classified, "Top-Secret" history of the U.S. role in the conflict. When the 47 volumes (7,000 pages), dubbed "the Pentagon Papers," were leaked to the press, analysis challenging official truth concluded that "the history as a whole demonstrated that . . . four [Presidential] Administrations progressively developed a sense of commitment to a non-communist Vietnam, a readiness to fight the North to protect the South, and an ultimate frustration with this effort—to a much greater extent than their public statements acknowledged at the time." In 1967, U.S. General William Westmoreland (born 1914) had told Secretary McNamara, "With the optimum force," the U.S. would need "about three years" to wind down U.S. involvement in Vietnam, and "with the minimum force, at least five." Upon the advice of Pentagon public relations people and against his "better judgement," Westmoreland struck out a "prophetic sentence" in a speech to Congress: "We will not lose the war on the battlefield but it can be lost here in Washington." Vietnam was America's "living-room war," as coverage of front-line and aerial combat dominated network-television's nightly newscasts, bringing the war into every home. Seeing firefights, defoliation, and the futility of the grinding war turned many Americans toward the anti-war movement. U.S. troops left Vietnam in 1973 and the peace treaty was signed in 1975. The Supreme Court, by a 6–3 decision, had ruled that newspapers, accused in Federal court of treasonous defiance of the U.S., could publish the Pentagon Papers without causing grave and irreparable harm to the nation's security. Twenty years later, the U.S. attorney declared that no harm was done by publication. Six-million pages are stamped secret every year.

PER CURIAM.
We granted certiorari in these cases in which the United States seeks to enjoin The New York Times and The Washington Post from publishing the contents of a classified study entitled "History of U.S. Decision-Making Process on Viet Nam Policy."—U.S.—(1971).

"Any system of prior restraints of expression comes to this court bearing a heavy presumption against its constitutional validity." Bantam Books, Inc. v. Sullivan, 372 U.S. 58, 70 (1963); see also Near v. Minnesota, 283 U.S. 697 (1931). The Government "thus carries a heavy burden of showing justification for the enforcement of such a restraint." Organization for a Better Austin v. Keefe—U.S.—(1971). The District

Court for the Southern District of New York in The New York Times case and the District Court for the District of Columbia and the Court of Appeals for the District of Columbia Circuit in The Washington Post case held that the Government had not met that burden.

We agree.

The judgment of the Court of Appeals for the District of Columbia Circuit is therefore affirmed. The order of the Court of Appeals for the Second Circuit is reversed and the case is remanded with directions to enter a judgment affirming the judgment of the District Court for the Southern District of New York. The stays entered June 25, 1971, by the court are vacated. The mandates shall issue forthwith.

So ordered.

MR. JUSTICE DOUGLAS, *with whom* MR. JUSTICE BLACK *joins, concurring.*

It should be noted at the onset that the First Amendment provides that "Congress shall make no law . . . abridging the freedom of speech or of the press." That leaves, in my view, no room for governmental restraint on the press. . . .

MR. JUSTICE BLACK, *with whom* MR. JUSTICE DOUGLAS *joins, concurring.*

I adhere to the view that the Government's case against The Washington Post should have been dismissed and that the injunction against The New York Times should have been vacated without oral argument when the cases were first presented to this Court. I believe that every moment's continuance of the injunctions against these newspapers amounts to a flagrant, indefensible and continuing violation of the First Amendment. Furthermore, after oral arguments, I agree completely that we must affirm the judgment of the Court of Appeals for the District of Columbia and reverse the judgment of the Court of Appeals for the Second Circuit for the reasons stated by my brothers Douglas and Brennan. In my view it is unfortunate that some of my brethren are apparently willing to hold that the publication of news may sometimes be enjoined. Such a holding would make a shambles of the First Amendment.

Our Government was launched in 1789 with the adoption of the Constitution. The Bill of Rights, including the First Amendment, followed in 1791. Now, for the first time in the 182 years since the founding of the Republic, the Federal courts are asked to hold that the First Amendment does not mean what it says, but rather means that the Government can halt the publication of current news of vital importance to the people of this country.

In seeking injunctions against these newspapers and in its presentation to the Court, the executive branch seems to have forgotten the essential purpose and history of the First Amendment. When the Constitution was adopted, many people strongly opposed it because the document contained no bill of rights to safeguard certain basic freedoms. They especially feared that the new powers granted to a central government might be interpreted to permit the government to curtail freedom of religion, press, assembly and speech. In response to an overwhelming public clamor, James Madison offered a series of amendments to satisfy citizens that these great liberties would remain safe and beyond the power of government to abridge. Madison proposed what later became the First Amendment in three parts, two of which are set out below, and one of which proclaimed: "The people shall not be deprived or abridged of their right to speak, to write, or to publish their sentiments; and the freedom of the press, as one of the great bulwarks of liberty, shall be inviolable." The amendments were offered to curtail and restrict the general powers granted to the executive, legislative and judicial branches two years before in the original Constitution. The Bill of Rights changed the original Constitution into a new charter under which no branch of government could abridge the people's freedoms of press, speech, religion and assembly.

Yet the Solicitor General argues and some members of the Court appear to agree that the general powers of the Government adopted in the original Constitution should be interpreted to limit and restrict the specific and emphatic guarantees of the Bill of Rights adopted later. I can imagine no greater perversion of history. Madison and the other framers of the First Amendment, able men that they were, wrote in language they earnestly believed could never be misunderstood: "Congress shall make no law . . . abridging the freedom of the press." Both the history and language of the First Amendment support the view that the press must be left free to publish news, whatever the source, without censorship, injunctions or prior restraints.

In the First Amendment the Founding Fathers gave the free press the protection it must have to fulfill its essential role in our democracy. The press was to serve the governed, not the governors. The Government's power to censor the press was abolished so that the press would remain forever free to censure the Government. The press was protected so that it could bare the secrets of government and inform the people. Only a free and unrestrained press can effectively expose deception in government. And paramount among the responsibilities of a free press is the duty to prevent any part of the Government from deceiving the people and sending them off to distant lands to die of foreign fevers and foreign shot and shell. In my view, far from deserving condemnation for their courageous reporting, The New York Times, The Washington Post and other newspapers should be commended for serving the purpose that the Found-ing Fathers saw so clearly. In revealing the workings of government that led to the Vietnam war, the newspapers nobly did precisely that which the founders hoped and trusted they would do.

The Government's case here is based on premises entirely different from those that guided the framers of the First Amendment. The Solicitor General has carefully and emphatically stated:

"Now, Mr. Justice [Black], your construction of . . . [the First Amendment] is well known, and I certainly respect it. You say that no law means no law, and that should be obvious. I can only say, Mr. Justice, that to me it is equally obvious that 'no law,' and I would seek to persuade the Court that that is true . . . [t]here are other parts of the Constitution that grant power and responsibilities to the executive end . . . the First Amendment was not intended to make it impossible for the executive to function or to protect the security of the United States."

And the Government argues in its brief that in spite of the First Amendment, "the authority of the executive department to protect the nation against publication of information whose disclosure would endanger the national security stems from two interrelated sources: The constitutional power of the President over the conduct of foreign affairs and his authority as Commander in Chief."

In other words, we are asked to hold that despite the First Amendment's emphatic command, the executive branch, the Congress and the judiciary can make laws enjoining publication of current news and abridging freedom of the press in the name of "national security." The Government does not even attempt to rely on act of Congress. Instead it makes the bold and dangerously far-reaching contention that the courts should take it upon themselves to "make" a law abridging freedom of the press in the name of equity, Presidential power and national security, even when the representatives of the people in Congress have adhered to the command of the First Amendment and refused to make such a law. See concurring opinion of Mr. Justice Douglas, Post.

To find that the President has "inherent power" to halt the publication of news by resort to the courts would wipe out the First Amendment and destroy the fundamental liberty and security of the very people the Government hopes to make "secure." No one can read the history of the adoption of the First Amendment without being convinced beyond any doubt that it was injunctions like those sought here that Madison and his collaborators intended to outlaw in this nation for all time.

The word "security" is a broad, vague generality whose contours should not be invoked to abrogate the fundamental law embodied in the First Amendment. The guarding of military and diplomatic secrets at the expense of informed representative government provides no real security for our Republic.

The framers of the First Amendment, fully aware of both the need to defend a new nation and the abuses of the English and colonial Governments, sought to give this new society strength and security by providing that freedom of speech, press, religion and assembly should not be abridged. This thought was eloquently expressed in 1937 by Mr. Chief Justice Hughes— great man and great Chief Justice that he was— when the Court held a man could not be punished for attending a meeting run by Communists.

"The greater the importance of safeguarding the community from incitements to the overthrow of our institutions by force and violence, the more imperative is the need to preserve inviolate the constitutional rights of free speech, free press and free assembly in order to maintain the opportunity for free political discussion, to the end that government may be responsive to the will of the people and that changes, if desired, may be obtained by peaceful means. Therein lies the security of the Republic, the very foundation of constitutional government." . . .

"There are essential differences . . . in their social systems and foreign policies"

THE SHANGHAI COMMUNIQUE
1972

Long-time anti-communist Richard M. Nixon's unexpected Presidential "journey for peace" to the People's Republic of China prompted coinage of the "Nixon in China Syndrome": The ability to effect change by those appearing to have the greatest stake in the status quo. At the time, the U.S. and China did not have formal diplomatic relations; Mr. Nixon (1913–1994) had long urged containment of the most populated nation on the planet. The President and Chinese minister Chou En-lai (1898–1976) agreed in a joint communique that there was a need to normalize relations, to increase Sino-American talks, and for progressive reduction in U.S. forces and facilities on the island of Taiwan (Formosa) as tension in the area diminished. (The U.S. defense treaty with Taiwan ended in 1979.) The historic meeting gave both the U.S. and China some leverage with the Soviet Union, but it also prompted Beijing to begin complaining about every detail of its relationship with Washington.

THE U.S. SIDE STATED: Peace in Asia and peace in the world requires efforts both to reduce immediate tensions and to eliminate the basic causes of conflict. The United States will work for a just and secure peace: just, because it fulfills the aspirations of peoples and nations for freedom and progress; secure, because it removes the danger of foreign aggression. The United States supports individual freedom and social progress for all the peoples of the world, free of outside pressure or intervention. The United States believes that the effort to reduce tensions is served by improving communication between countries that have different ideologies so as to lessen the risks of confrontation through accident, miscalculation or misunderstanding. Countries should treat each other with mutual respect and be willing to compete peacefully, letting performance be the ultimate judge. No country should claim infallibility and each country should be prepared to re-examine its own attitudes for the common good. The United States stressed that the peoples of Indochina should be allowed to determine their destiny without outside intervention; its constant primary objective has been a negotiated solution; the eight-point proposal put forward by the Republic of Vietnam and the United States on January 27, 1972 represents a basis for the attainment of that objective; in the absence of a negotiated settlement the United States envisages the ultimate withdrawal of all U.S. forces from the region consistent with the aim of self-determination for each country of Indochina. The United States will maintain its close ties with and support for the Republic of Korea; the United States will support efforts of the Republic of Korea to seek a relaxation of tension and increased communication in the Korean peninsula. The United States places the highest value on its friendly relations with Japan; it will continue to develop the existing close bonds. Consistent with the United Nations Security Council Resolution of December 21, 1971, the United States favors the continuation of the ceasefire between India and Pakistan and the withdrawal of all military forces to within their own territories and to their own sides of the ceasefire line in Jammu and Kashmir; the United States supports the right of the peoples of South Asia to shape their own future in peace, free of military threat, and without having the area become the subject of great power rivalry.

The Chinese side stated: Wherever there is oppression, there is resistance. Countries want independence, nations want liberation and the people want revolution—this has become the irresistible trend of history. All nations, big or small, should be equal; big nations should not bully the small and strong nations should not bully the weak. China will never be a superpower and it opposes hegemony and power politics of any kind. The Chinese side stated that it firmly supports the struggles of all the oppressed people and nations for freedom and liberation and that the people of all countries have the right to choose their social systems according to their own wishes and the right to safeguard the independence, sovereignty and territorial integrity of their own countries and oppose foreign aggression, interference, control and subversion. All foreign troops should be withdrawn to their own countries.

The Chinese side expressed its firm support to the peoples of Vietnam, Laos and Cambodia in their efforts for the attainment of their goal and its firm support to the seven-point proposal of the Provisional Revolutionary Government of the Republic of South Vietnam and the elaboration of February this year on the two key prob-

lems in the proposal, and to the Joint Declaration of the Summit Conference of the Indochinese Peoples. It firmly supports the eight-point program for the peaceful unification of Korea put forward by the Government of the Democratic People's Republic of Korea on April 12, 1971, and the stand for the abolition of the "U.N. Commission for the Unification and Rehabilitation of Korea." It firmly opposes the revival and outward expansion of Japanese militarism and firmly supports the Japanese people's desire to build an independent, democratic, peaceful and neutral Japan. It firmly maintains that India and Pakistan should, in accordance with the United Nations resolutions on the India-Pakistan question, immediately withdraw all their forces to their respective territories and to their own sides of the ceasefire line in Jammu and Kashmir and firmly supports the Pakistan Government and people in their struggle to preserve their independence and sovereignty and the people of Jammu and Kashmir in their struggle for the right of self-determination.

There are essential differences between China and the United States in their social systems and foreign policies. However, the two sides agreed that countries, regardless of their social systems, should conduct their relations on the principles of respect for the sovereignty and territorial integrity of all states, non-aggression against other states, non-interference in the internal affairs of other states, equality and mutual benefit, and peaceful coexistence. International disputes should be settled on this basis, without resorting to the use or threat of force. The United States and the People's Republic of China are prepared to apply these principles to their mutual relations.

With these principles of international relations in mind the two sides stated that:

• progress toward the normalization of relations between China and the United States is in the interests of all countries;

- both wish to reduce the danger of international military conflict;
- neither should seek hegemony in the Asia-Pacific region and each is opposed to efforts by any other country or group of countries to establish such hegemony; and
- neither is prepared to negotiate on behalf of any third party or to enter into agreements or understandings with the other directed at other states.

Both sides are of the view that it would be against the interests of the peoples of the world for any major country to collude with another against other countries, or for major countries to divide up the world into spheres of interest.

The two sides reviewed the long-standing serious disputes between China and the United States. The Chinese side reaffirmed its position: The Taiwan question is the crucial question obstructing the normalization of relations between China and the United States; the Government of the People's Republic of China is the sole legal government of China; Taiwan is a province of China which has long been returned to the motherland; the liberation of Taiwan is China's internal affair in which no other country has the right to interfere; and all U.S. forces and military installations must be withdrawn from Taiwan. The Chinese Government firmly opposes any activities which aim at the creation of "one China, one Taiwan," "one China, two governments," "two Chinas," and "independent Taiwan" or advocate that "the status of Taiwan remains to be determined."

The U.S. side declared: The United States acknowledges that all Chinese on either side of the Taiwan Strait maintain there is but one China and that Taiwan is a part of China. The United States Government does not challenge that position. It reaffirms its interest in a peaceful settlement of the Taiwan question by the Chinese themselves. With this prospect in mind, it affirms the ultimate objective of the withdrawal of all U.S. forces and military installations from Taiwan. In the meantime, it will progressively reduce its forces and military installations on Taiwan as the tension in the area diminishes.

The two sides agreed that it is desirable to broaden the understanding between the two peoples. To this end, they discussed specific areas in such fields as science, technology, culture, sports and journalism, in which people-to-people contacts and exchanges would be mutually beneficial. Each side undertakes to facilitate the further development of such contacts and exchanges.

Both sides view bilateral trade as another area from which mutual benefit can be derived, and agreed that economic relations based on equality and mutual benefit are in the interest of the peoples of the two countries. They agree to facilitate the progressive development of trade between their two countries.

The two sides agreed that they will stay in contact through various channels, including the sending of a senior U.S. representative to Peking from time to time for concrete consultations to further the normalization of relations between the two countries and continue to exchange views on issues of common interest.

The two sides expressed the hope that the gains achieved during this visit would open up new prospects for the relations between the two countries. . . .

"The President . . . shall consult with Congress"

THE WAR POWERS RESOLUTION
1973

By overriding President Richard M. Nixon's veto of "clearly unconstitutional" legislation, Congress limited Presidential power to commit U.S. armed forces to hostilities abroad without Congressional approval. It was the most aggressive assertion of independence and power by the legislative branch against the executive branch in many years. Congress simply wanted to participate in any decision to use the armed forces. Supporters of the War Powers Resolution had waged a three-year battle.

SECTION I. This joint resolution may be cited as the "War Powers Resolution."

SEC. 2. (a) It is the purpose of this joint resolution to fulfill the intent of the framers of the Constitution of the United States and insure that the collective judgment of both the Congress and the President will apply to the introduction of United States Armed Forces into hostilities, or into situations where imminent involvement in hostilities is clearly indicated by the circumstances, and to the continued use of such forces in hostilities or in such situations.

(b) Under article I, section 8, of the Constitution, it is specifically provided that the Congress shall have the power to make all laws necessary and proper for carrying into execution, not only its own powers but also all other powers vested by the Constitution in the Government of the United States, or in any department or officer thereof.

(c) The constitutional powers of the President as Commander-in-Chief to introduce United States Armed Forces into hostilities, or into situations where imminent involvement in hostilities is clearly indicated by the circumstances, are

exercised only pursuant to (1) a declaration of war, (2) specific statutory authorization, or (3) a national emergency created by attack upon the United States, its territories or possessions, or its armed forces.

SEC. 3. The President in every possible instance shall consult with Congress before introducing United States Armed Forces into hostilities or into situation where imminent involvement in hostilities is clearly indicated by the circumstances, and after every such introduction shall consult regularly with the Congress until United States Armed Forces are no longer engaged in hostilities or have been removed from such situations.

SEC. 4. (a) In the absence of a declaration of war, in any case in which United States Armed Forces are introduced—

(1) into hostilities or into situations where imminent involvement in hostilities is clearly indicated by the circumstances;

(2) into the territory, airspace or waters of a foreign nation, while equipped for combat, except for deployments which relate solely to supply, replacement, repair, or training of such forces; or

(3) in numbers which substantially enlarge United States Armed Forces equipped for combat already located in a foreign nation; the President shall submit within 48 hours to the Speaker of the House of Representatives and to the President pro tempore of the Senate a report, in writing, setting forth—

(A) the circumstances necessitating the introduction of United States Armed Forces;

(B) the constitutional and legislative authority under which such introduction took place; and

(C) the estimated scope and duration of the hostilities or involvement.

(b) The President shall provide such other information as the Congress may request in the fulfillment of its constitutional responsibilities with respect to committing the Nation to war and to the use of United States Armed Forces abroad

(c) Whenever United States Armed Forces are introduced into hostilities or into any situation described in subsection (a) of this section, the President shall, so long as such armed to (a) Each report submitted pursuant to section 4(a)(1) shall be transmitted to the Speaker of the House of Representatives and to the President pro tempore of the Senate on the same calendar day. Each report so transmitted shall be referred to the Committee on Foreign Affairs of the House of Representatives and to the Committee on Foreign Relations of the Senate for appropriate action. If, when the report is transmitted, the Congress has adjourned sine die or has adjourned for any period in excess of three calendar days, the Speaker of the House of Representatives and the President pro tempore of the Senate, if they deem it advisable (or if petitioned by at least 30 percent of the membership of their respective Houses) shall jointly request the President to convene Congress in order that it may consider the report and take appropriate action pursuant to this section.

(b) Within sixty calendar days after a report is submitted or is required to be submitted pursuant to section 4(a)(1), whichever is earlier, the President shall terminate any use of United States Armed Forces with respect to which such report was submitted (or required to be submitted), unless the Congress (1) has declared war or has enacted a specific authorization for such use of United States Armed Forces, (2) has extended by law such sixty-day period, or (3) is physically unable to meet as a result of an armed attack upon the United States. Such sixty-day period shall be extended for not more than an additional thirty days if the President determines and certifies to the Congress in writing that unavoidable military necessity respecting the safety of United States Armed Forces requires the continued use of such armed forces in the course of bringing about a prompt removal of such forces.

(c) Notwithstanding subsection (b), at any time that United States Armed Forces are engaged in hostilities outside the territory of the United States, its possessions and territories without a declaration of war or specific statutory authorization, such forces shall be removed by the President if the Congress so directs by concurrent resolution. . . .

"Obtained the approval of the President"

OLIVER NORTH TESTIFIES

1987

The United States imposed an embargo on arms shipments to Iran in November, 1979. Seven years later, Americans learned that the Reagan Administration (1981–1989) had been selling arms to this Middle Eastern sponsor of international terrorism. In August, 1987, President Ronald W. Reagan (born 1911) confessed that "our original initiative got all tangled up in the sale of arms, and the sale of arms got tangled up with the hostages [several Americans held by Muslim radicals in Beirut, Lebanon] . . . I let my preoccupation with the hostages intrude into areas it didn't belong." The sales were to provide the "bona fide" necessary for a diplomatic opening to Iran. (Dealing with hostage-takers was a violation of longstanding U.S. policy.) One of the central players in the Iran-Contra affair (defined as hostility toward the rule of law), the charismatic Oliver North (born 1943), a ramrod-straight Marine, justified his own lies, telling Congressional investigators of secret military assistance to Iran and the Nicaraguan opposition (the Contras) and claimed that all covert operations are "at essence a lie." Like any good Marine, North was merely following orders. Criminal trials of "patriotic men of zeal encroaching a democratic government" sought to ferret out lies and contradictory testimony, and restore shredded evidence. Indictments were returned against North and three co-conspirators as "Olliemania" swept the nation.

I think it is very important for the American people to understand that this is a dangerous world; that we live at risk and that this nation is at risk in a dangerous world. And that they ought not to be led to believe, as a consequence of these hearings, that this nation cannot or should not conduct covert operations. By their very nature, covert operations or special activities are a lie. There is great deceit, deception practiced in the conduct of covert operations. They are at essence a lie.

. . . Throughout the conduct of my entire tenure at the National Security Council, I assumed that the President was aware of what I was doing and had, through my superiors, approved it. I sought approval of my superiors for every one of my actions and it is well-documented. I assumed when I had approval to proceed from either Judge Clark, Bud McFarlane or Admiral Poindexter, that they had indeed solicited and obtained the approval of the President.

"The targets being struck tonight"
THE GULF WAR
1991

Iraq invaded and annexed its oil-rich southern neighbor Kuwait in the summer of 1990. Through the end of the year, the United States and coalition partners built up a massive liberating force in the Middle East, particularly in the vast deserts of Saudi Arabia. Before taking military action against Iraq, President George W. Bush (born 1924) asked Congress for a declaration of support. (Like his predecessors, Mr. Bush refused to recognize the validity of the War Powers Resolution; Congress had overridden President Richard M. Nixon's veto.) Four days after Congress authorized the use of military force (Senate vote, 52–47; House, 250–183), the allied coalition launched Operation Desert Storm. The 100-hour assault drove the Iraqis out of Kuwait and running for their lives. It was a technological triumph (laser bombs, Patriot antiaircraft missiles, Tomahawk offensive missiles). Thousands of Allied troops may have suffered chemical contamination—"Gulf War syndrome"—when they blew up Iraqi munition dumps. Iraq's leader, Saddam Hussein (born 1937), remained a threat to peace in the region. In late 1998, President Bill Clinton (born 1946) launched missiles into Iraq again.

To AUTHORIZE THE USE OF United States Armed Forces pursuant to United Nations Security Council Resolution 678.

Whereas the Government of Iraq without provocation invaded and occupied the territory of Kuwait on August 2, 1990, and

Whereas both the House of Representatives (in H.J. Res. 658 of the 101st Congress) and the Senate (in S. Con. Res. 147 of the 101st Congress) have condemned Iraq's invasion of Kuwait and declared their support for international action to reverse Iraq's aggression; and

Whereas Iraq's conventional, chemical, biological, and nuclear weapons and ballistic missile programs and its demonstrated willingness to use weapons of mass destruction pose a grave threat to world peace; and

Whereas the international community has demanded that Iraq withdraw unconditionally and immediately from Kuwait and that Kuwait's independence and legitimate government be restored; and

Whereas the U.N. Security Council repeatedly affirmed the inherent right of individual or collective self-defense in response to the armed attack by Iraq against Kuwait in accordance with Article 51 of the U.N. Charter; and

Whereas in the absence of full compliance by Iraq with its resolutions, the U.N. Security Council in Resolution 678 has authorized member states of the United Nations to use all necessary means, after January 15, 1991, to uphold and implement all relevant Security Council resolutions and to restore international peace and security in the area; and

Whereas Iraq has persisted in its illegal occupation of, and brutal aggression against Kuwait; Now, therefore, be it

Resolved by the Senate and House of Representatives of the United States of America in Congress assembled,

SECTION 1.
SHORT TITLE

This joint resolution may be cited as the "Authorization for Use of Military Force Against Iraq Resolution."

SECTION 2.
AUTHORIZATION FOR USE OF U.S. ARMED FORCES

(a) *Authorization.*—The President is authorized, subject to subsection (b), to use United States Armed Forces pursuant to United Nations Security Council Resolution 678 (1990) in order to achieve implementation of Security Council Resolutions 660, 661, 662, 664, 665, 666, 667, 669, 670, 674, and 677.

(b) *Requirement for determination that use of military force is necessary.*—Before exercising the authority granted in subsection (a), the President shall make available to the Speaker of the House of Representatives and the President pro tempore of the Senate his determination that—

(1) the United States has used all appropriate diplomatic and other peaceful means to obtain compliance by Iraq with the United Nations Security Council resolutions cited in subsection (a); and (2) that those efforts have not been and would not be successful in obtaining such compliance.

(c) *War powers resolution requirements.*—

(1) *Specific statutory authorization.*—Consistent with section 8(a) of the War Powers Resolution, the Congress declares that this section is intended to constitute specific statutory authorization within the meaning of section 5(b) of the War Powers Resolution.

(2) *Applicability of other requirements.*—Nothing in this resolution supersedes any requirement of the War Powers Resolution.

SECTION 3.
REPORTS TO CONGRESS

At least once every 60 days, the President shall submit to the Congress a summary on the status of efforts to obtain compliance by Iraq with the resolutions adopted by the United Nations Security Council in response to Iraq's aggression.

―――――

At a news conference held at the Pentagon Secretary of Defense Dick Cheney (born 1941) delivered the following briefing: "At seven o'clock tonight, three o'clock Thursday morning in the gulf, the armed forces of the United States began an operation at the direction of the president to force Saddam Hussein to withdraw his troops from Kuwait and to end his occupation of that country. At the direction of the president, I signed the executive order yesterday afternoon to undertake this operation, subject to certain conditions. It was to begin only after we'd met the terms of the resolution passed last Saturday by the Congress. Those conditions have been complied with, and proper notice has been given, as required. And the operation was not to take place if there had been any last-minute diplomatic breakthroughs. The operation under way tonight, taking place in the predawn darkness of the Persian Gulf, involves allied forces of four nations: the United States, the United Kingdom, Saudi Arabia, and Kuwait.

"As they undertake their missions, they do so after months of careful planning. At the direction of the president, great care has been taken to focus on military targets, to minimize U.S. casualties, and to do everything possible to avoid injury to civilians in Iraq and Kuwait.

"The targets being struck tonight are located throughout Iraq and Kuwait. Our focus is on the destruction of Saddam Hussein's offensive military capabilities—the very capabilities that he used to seize control of Kuwait and that make him a continuing threat to the nations of the Middle East."

A FIRE WITHIN:
REALLY NEW IDEAS

The American mind, as some scholars have argued, is a divided mind, and the national creed cannot be reduced to a set of self-evident propositions. The spiritual mission of a Christian people, the moral primacy of the individual, equality of opportunity, localism and laissez faire the virtue of those who living close to the soil, may be useful myths but, as a number of the following sections suggest, they are not without contrary norms and practices. Consider, for example, Tocqueville's oft-cited comment that a "general equality of condition among the people" exists in America, a conclusion that fails to consider the condition of women, blacks, and Native Americans. Or his observations on the power of the majority: "The very essence of democratic government consists in the absolute sovereignty of the majority." Indeed, the Founding Fathers understood that democracy derives its authority from the people. They subscribed to two basic principles: All government derives from the people and all government is limited. Yet Tocqueville, arguing with himself, did not believe majority rule to be an unalloyed virtue. Majority rule, he feared, could devolve into majority tyranny. Majority will has, at times, treated minorities with an insouciant disregard for their rights that bordered on arbitrary use of power.

Consider, for instance, Thoreau's refusal to pay taxes, derived from the distinct possibility that the outcome of the Mexican War meant slavery extension, to which he profoundly objected. His essay first appeared under the title "Resistance to Civil Government," and resistance landed him in jail. Or consider the fate of Socialist Party leader Eugene V. Debs, who, in the Thoreau tradition, resisted the First World War and went to prison for a speech against the war. Or consider the legislation of that time which, complemented by extra-legal action of officials and mobs, outlawed criticism of the government, its leaders, and its national symbols—like the flag or army uniform—in wartime America, trends that accurately reflected the will of the majority. In effect, majoritarian witch-hunting in 1917–1919, triggered by hysterical fear of German and communist conspiracies, led to widespread censorship of the press and the mails and over 1500 prosecutions for "disloyalty," a flaccidly-defined term that was in the eye of the beholder. Or witness, for instance, the right to freedom of expression, to which the majority reputedly subscribes in the abstract at least. But, we may speculate, the majority that approved the imprisonment of Debs would endorse the press and theater censorship so doggedly pursued by Anthony Comstock. As Secretary of the Committee for the Suppression of Vice, which he helped found, Comstock crusaded against obscenity, pornography, birth control, abortion, and information on sexual reproduction. Indeed, he was the moving force behind passage of the 1873 anti-obscenity law, quite properly named after him, that would clean up art and literature by banning "obscene" materials from the mails. Regardless of the First Amendment, the majority, we may speculate, would readily agree to censorship of the "obscene," "indecent," "lewd," and "lascivious" books and pictures that were in vogue at the time. After all, the Comstock law remains on the books today.

"Comstockery," to borrow George Bernard Shaw's term, would surely apply to Walt Whitman in the antebellum decades. The sexual dalliance of Whitman's early years, his bisexuality, his belief that sexuality reflects a healthy body, not prurience or repression, spoke to a robust joy in living. An unashamed embrace of what was then thought "vulgar", and in Comstock's day would be thought "obscene," needed silencing. A repressive puritanism in sexual relationships dominated much of nineteenth-century popular thinking, and it targeted the homoerotic Calamus poems and Leaves of Grass. That the latter was banned in Boston is unsurprising, though Emerson, for all his New England cautiousness, correctness, and respectability, praised it. Emerson himself was a pivotal figure in the flowering of a distinctively American literature. He arrived on the literary landscape at a time when an explosion of literacy, complemented by a rising middle class, created a market for books, newspapers, and magazines. Yet Emerson can be set apart from the majority, given his frequent criticism of the gross materialism and commercialism of his times. Moreover, his belief in the oversoul and in a monism of man, nature, and God also placed him outside the perimeter of popular thinking.

In the post-Civil War decades, diametrically opposing tendencies can be found embedded in the actions, reactions, and interactions of the majority. Certainly most Americans still embraced "rugged individualism" and rejected governmental welfare measures—even if they lived off them—as "creeping socialism" or communism. Rather, they extolled self-reliance. Anything less—poverty, for example—was commonly thought to be a sign of vice, ignorance, improvidence, weakness. To take money from the government was to take "charity," and it connoted failure in life. Driven by Christian faith and the doctrine of stewardship, Andrew Carnegie and his fellow entrepreneurs gave large benefactions, to be sure, but these were purely private charities and generally given to institutions, to churches and to universities, rather *than to individuals. There is some paradox evident when the unconscionable Daniel Drew founded Drew Theological Seminary, and Leland Stanford, who bribed every legislator in sight, established the university bearing his name. Most industrial and financial barons did likewise, and they were the subjects of hero tales read avidly and admired by a public they fleeced. The Protestant ethic of thrift and industry continued to dominate the national mindset. Consequently, the majority would take exception to Edward Bellamy's arraignment of the competitive system and perhaps dismiss his vision of an ideal society in the year 2000.*

Furthermore, the public was fascinated by the Wright Brothers, much as they were later entranced by Charles Lindbergh, and by Einstein and other refugee scientists whose work with the atom, while something not popularly understood, piqued their interest. Challenges and high adventure had enormous appeal to Americans. Their fascination with both fads and new technology brought them into the late nineteenth-century movie houses in unprecedented numbers—whether neighborhood nickelodeons or the later "downtown" movie palaces—much as, nearly a century later, they would have a love affair with the computer. Moreover, unlike the radio and telephone, which were largely the property of the middle class in the 1920s, the silent screen had a cross-class audience. Indeed, it had mostly working-class patrons at the outset. Everyone, it seems, was drawn to the simple, naive heroes and the formulaic plots on the silent screen.

From the Victorians and Comstock to Ronald Reagan, concern with moral decline dominated popular thinking. After the turbulent political and social scenes of the 1960s and 1970s, when conservatives emerged victoriously over liberal Democrats, it became obvious that a "moral" agenda dominated majority thinking. Christians, Protestant and Catholic alike, perceived a degraded public and private morality. President Reagan promised voters an America of his own past, rooted in small-town, rural virtues—patriotism, self help, hard work, belief in God, the family, the flag. To him, and to the great majority of enterprising Americans, the nation held out unlimited opportunity. A historic antagonism to the Federal government and to liberal Federal activism peaked in the 1980s. It is ironic that this majority view was shared by a great many Americans—the poor, the undereducated, the unemployed, minorities, and others—who had been sustained by the liberal social policy of previous Administrations. Many of them now voted for an Administration that sought to rewrite the national agenda, reverse the role of government, dismantle most of the basic features of the New Deal, Fair Deal, and Great Society. Old articles of the antebellum faith, popular sovereignty on the local level unmolested by a distant Federal government, the moral certainties of competition, the myth of success—there is room at the top for those who are ambitious and hard-working—retained their currency, however much this mid-nineteenth century social philosophy was at variance with the realities of the new age.

"Unlimited power is in itself a bad and dangerous thing"

TOCQUEVILLE: DEMOCRACY IN AMERICA

1835

The French politician and writer Alexis de Tocqueville (1805–1859) traveled around America for nine months in the early 1830s. (His official mission was to examine the U.S. penal system.) Deeply committed to human freedom, he wrote one of the great studies of American institutions, the classic multivolume *Democracy in America*: Americans "are nearer equality than in any other country in the world"—that is, everyone has equality of opportunity. In his still-quoted portrait, Tocqueville addressed the unlimited power of the majority and its consequences.

The very essence of democratic government consists in the absolute sovereignty of the majority; for there is nothing in democratic states that is capable of resisting it. Most of the American constitutions have sought to increase this natural strength of the majority by artificial means.

Of all political institutions, the legislature is the one that is most easily swayed by the will of the majority. The Americans determined that the members of the legislature should be elected by the people *directly,* and for a *very brief term,* in order to subject them, not only to the general convictions, but even to the daily passions, of their constituents. The members of both houses are taken from the same classes in society and nominated in the same manner; so that the movements of the legislative bodies are almost as rapid, and quite as irresistible, as those of a single assembly. It is to a legislature thus constituted that almost all the authority of the government has been entrusted.

At the same time that the law increased the strength of those authorities which of themselves were strong, it enfeebled more and more those which were naturally weak. It deprived the representatives of the executive power of all stability and independence; and by subjecting them completely to the caprices of the legislature, it robbed them of the slender influence that the nature of a democratic government might have allowed them to exercise. In several states the judicial power was also submitted to the election of the majority; and in all of them its existence was made to depend on the pleasure of the legislative authority, since the representatives were empowered annually to regulate the stipend of the judges.

Custom has done even more than law. A proceeding is becoming more and more general in the United States which will, in the end, do away with the guarantees of representative government: it frequently happens that the voters, in electing a delegate, point out a certain line of conduct to him and impose upon him certain positive obligations that he is pledged to fulfill. With the exception of the tumult, this comes to the same thing as if the majority itself held its deliberations in the market-place.

Several particular circumstances combine to render the power of the majority in America not only preponderant, but irresistible. The moral authority of the majority is partly based upon the notion that there is more intelligence and wisdom in a number of men united than in a single individual, and that the number of the legislators is more important than their quality. The theory of equality is thus applied to the intellects of men; and human pride is thus assailed in its last retreat by a doctrine which the minority hesitate to admit, and to which they will but slowly assent. Like all other powers, and perhaps more than any other, the authority of the many requires the sanction of time in order to appear legitimate. At first it enforces obedience by constraint; and its laws are not *respected* until they have been long maintained.

The right of governing society, which the majority supposes itself to derive from its superior intelligence, was introduced into the United States by the first settlers; and this idea, which of itself would be sufficient to create a free nation, has now been amalgamated with the customs of the people and the minor incidents of social life.

The French under the old monarchy held it for a maxim that the king could do no wrong; and if he did do wrong, the blame was imputed to his advisers. This notion made obedience very easy; it enabled the subject to complain of the law without ceasing to love and honor the lawgiver. The Americans entertain the same opinion with respect to the majority.

The moral power of the majority is founded upon yet another principle, which is that the interests of the many are to be preferred to those of the few. It will readily be perceived that the respect here professed for the rights of the greater number must naturally increase or diminish according to the state of parties. When a nation is divided into several great irreconcilable interests, the privilege of the majority is often overlooked, because it is intolerable to comply with its demands.

If there existed in America a class of citizens whom the legislating majority sought to deprive of exclusive privileges which they had possessed for ages and to bring down from an elevated station to the level of the multitude, it is probable that the minority would be less ready to submit to its laws. But as the United States was colonized by men holding equal rank, there is as yet no natural or permanent disagreement between the interests of its different inhabitants.

There are communities in which the members of the minority can never hope to draw the majority over to their side, because they must then give up the very point that is at issue between them. Thus an aristocracy can never become a majority while it retains its exclusive privileges, and it cannot cede its privileges without ceasing to be an aristocracy.

In the United States, political questions cannot be taken up in so general and absolute a manner; and all parties are willing to recognize the rights of the majority, because they all hope at some time to be able to exercise them to their own advantage. The majority in that country, therefore, exercise a prodigious actual authority, and a power of opinion which is nearly as great; no obstacles exist which can impede or even retard its progress, so as to make it heed the complaints of those whom it crushes upon its path. This state of things is harmful in itself and dangerous for the future. . . .

I hold it to be an impious and detestable maxim that, politically speaking, the people have a right to do anything; and yet I have asserted that all authority originates in the will of the majority. Am I, then, in contradiction with myself?

A general law, which bears the name of justice, has been made and sanctioned, not only by a majority of this or that people, but by a majority of mankind. The rights of every people are therefore confined within the limits of what is just. A nation may be considered as a jury which is empowered to represent society at large and to apply justice, which is its law. Ought such a jury, which represents society, to have more power than the society itself whose laws it executes?

When I refuse to obey an unjust law, I do not contest the right of the majority to command, but I simply appeal from the sovereignty of the people to the sovereignty of mankind. Some have not feared to assert that a people can never outstep the boundaries of justice and reason in those affairs which are peculiarly its own; and that consequently full power may be given to the majority by which it is represented. But this is the language of a slave.

A majority taken collectively is only an individual, whose opinions, and frequently whose interests, are opposed to those of another individual, who is styled a minority. If it be admitted that a man possessing absolute power may misuse that power by wronging his adversaries, why should not a majority be liable to the same reproach? Men do not change their characters by uniting with one another; nor does their patience in the presence of obstacles increase with their strength. For my own part, I cannot believe it; the power to do everything, which I should refuse to one of my equals, I will never grant to any number of them.

I do not think that, for the sake of preserving liberty, it is possible to combine several principles in the same government so as really to oppose them to one another. The form of government that is usually termed *mixed* has always appeared to me a mere chimera. Accurately speaking, there is no such thing as a *mixed government,* in the sense usually given to that word, because in all communities some one principle of action may be discovered which preponderates over the others. England in the last century, which has been especially cited as an example of this sort of government, was essentially an aristocratic state, although it comprised some great elements of democracy; for the laws and customs of the country were such that the aristocracy could not but preponderate in the long run and direct public affairs according to its own will. The error arose from seeing the interests of the nobles perpetually contending with those of the people, without considering the issue of the contest, which was really the important point. When a community actually has a mixed government—that is to say, when it is equally divided between adverse principles—it must either experience a revolution or fall into anarchy.

I am therefore of the opinion that social power superior to all others must always be placed somewhere; but I think that liberty is endangered when this power finds no obstacle which can retard its course and give it time to moderate its own vehemence.

Unlimited power is in itself a bad and dangerous thing. Human beings are not competent to exercise it with discretion. God alone can be omnipotent, because his wisdom and his justice are always equal to his power. There is no power on earth so worthy of honor in itself or clothed with rights so sacred that I would admit its uncontrolled and all-predominant authority. When I see that the right and the means of absolute command are conferred on any power whatever, be it called a people or a king, an aristocracy or a democracy, a monarchy or a republic, I say there is the germ of tyranny, and I seek to live elsewhere, under other laws.

In my opinion, the main evil of the present democratic institutions of the United States does not raise, as is often asserted in Europe, from their weakness, but from their irresistible strength. I am not so much alarmed at the excessive liberty which reigns in that country as at the inadequate securities which one finds there against tyranny.

When an individual or a party is wronged in the United States, to whom can he apply for redress? If to public opinion, public opinion constitutes the majority; if to the legislature, it represents the majority and implicitly obeys it; if to the executive power, it is appointed by the majority and serves as a passive tool in its hands. The public force consists of the majority under arms; the jury is the majority invested with the right of hearing judicial cases; and in certain states even the judges are elected by the majority. However iniquitous or absurd the measure of which you complain, you must submit to it as well as you can.*

If, on the other hand, a legislative power could be so constituted as to represent the majority without necessarily being the slave of its passions, an executive so as to retain a proper share of authority, and a judiciary so as to remain independent of the other two powers, a government would be formed which would still be democratic while incurring scarcely any risk of tyranny.

I do not say that there is a frequent use of tyranny in America at the present day; but I maintain that there is no sure barrier against it, and that the causes which mitigate the government there are to be found in the circumstances and the manners of the country more than in its laws.

. . . . In that immense crowd which throngs the avenues to power in the United States, I found very few men who displayed that manly candor and masculine independence of opinion which frequently distinguished the Americans in former times, and which constitutes the leading feature in distinguished characters wherever they may be found. It seems at first sight as if all the minds of the Americans were formed upon one model, so accurately do they follow the same route. A stranger does, indeed, sometimes meet with Americans who dissent from the rigor of these formulas, with men who deplore the defects of the laws, the mutability and the ignorance of democracy, who even go so far as to observe the evil tendencies that impair the national character, and to point out such remedies as it might be possible to apply; but no one is

*A striking instance of the excesses that may be occasioned by the despotism of the majority occurred at Baltimore during the War of 1812. At that time the war was very popular in Baltimore. A newspaper that had taken the other side excited, by its opposition, the indignation of the inhabitants. The mob assembled, broke the printing-presses, and attacked the house of the editors. The militia was called out, but did not obey the call; and the only means of saving the wretches who were threatened by the frenzy of the mob was to throw them into prison as common malefactors. But even this precaution was ineffectual; the mob collected again during the night; the magistrates again made a vain attempt to call out the militia; the prison was forced, one of the newspaper editors was killed upon the spot, and the others were left for dead. The guilty parties, when they were brought to trial, were acquitted by the jury.

I said one day to an inhabitant of Pennsylvania: "Be so good as to explain to me how it happens that in a state founded by Quakers, and celebrated for its toleration, free blacks are not allowed to exercise civil rights. They pay taxes; is it not fair that they should vote?"

"You insult us," replied my informant, "if you imagine that our legislators could have committed so gross an act of injustice and intolerance."

"Then the blacks possess the right of voting in this country?"

"Without doubt."

"How comes it, then, that at the polling-booth this morning I did not perceive a single Negro?"

"That is not the fault of the law. The Negroes have an undisputed right of voting, but they voluntarily abstain from making their appearance."

"A very pretty piece of modesty on their part!" rejoined I.

"Why, the truth is that they are not disinclined to vote, but they are afraid of being maltreated; in this country the law is sometimes unable to maintain its authority without the support of the majority. But in this case the majority entertains very strong prejudices against the blacks, and the magistrates are unable to protect them in the exercise of their legal rights."

"Then the majority claims the right not only of making the laws, but of breaking the laws it has made?"

there to hear them except yourself, and you, to whom these secret reflections are confided, are a stranger and a bird of passage. They are very ready to communicate truths which are useless to you, but they hold a different language in public.

If these lines are ever read in America, I am well assured of two things: in the first place, that all who peruse them will raise their voices to condemn me; and, in the second place, that many of them will acquit me at the bottom of their conscience.

I have heard of patriotism in the United States, and I have found true patriotism among the people, but never among the leaders of the people. This may be explained by analogy: despotism debases the oppressed much more than the oppressor: in absolute monarchies the king often has great virtues, but the courtiers are invariably servile. It is true that American courtiers do not say "Sire," or "Your Majesty," a distinction without a difference. They are forever talking of the natural intelligence of the people whom they serve; they do not debate the question which of the virtues of their master is pre-eminently worthy of admiration, for they as-sure him that he possesses all the virtues without having acquired them, or without caring to acquire them; they do not give him their daughters and their wives to be raised at his pleasure to the rank of his concubines; but by sacrificing their opinions they prostitute themselves. Moralists and philosophers in America are not obliged to conceal their opinions under the veil of allegory; but before they venture upon a harsh truth, they say: "We are aware that the people whom we are addressing are too superior to the weaknesses of human nature to lose the command of their temper for an instant. We should not hold this language if we were not speaking to men whom their virtues and their intelligence render more worthy of freedom than all the rest of the world." The sycophants of Louis XIV could not flatter more dexterously.

For my part, I am persuaded that in all governments, whatever their nature may be, servility will cower to force, and adulation will follow power. The only means of preventing men from degrading themselves is to invest no one with that unlimited authority which is the sure method of debasing them. . . .

"Books are the best of things"

RALPH WALDO EMERSON: THE AMERICAN SCHOLAR

1837

Transcendentalist Ralph Waldo Emerson (1803–1882), the "Sage of Concord," was one of America's leading philosophical essayists and poets. Although his life was based on loss and facing up to loss (from time to time he opened his wife's coffin), he maintained an optimistic view of mankind and nature. Emerson was deeply religious. He believed everyone had "the universe inside" him. He reveled in the life of the mind: ideas tangible things, books were the best of things. It's been said that his adult life was half epiphany, half cordwood. In each of 25 years, he delivered 80 or so public lectures, each an hour or two long. Enthusiasm greeted Emerson's *American Scholar* speech at Harvard, where he had once been an undistinguished student.

We do not meet for games of strength or skill, for the recitation of histories, tragedies, and odes, like the ancient Greeks; for parliaments of love and poesy, like the Troubadours; nor for the advancement of science, like our contemporaries in the British and European capitals. Thus far, our holiday has been simply a friendly sign of the survival of the love of letters amongst a people too busy to give to letters any more. As such it is precious as the sign of an indestructible instinct. Perhaps the time is already come when it ought to be, and will be, something else; when the sluggard intellect of this continent will look from under its iron lids and fill the postponed expectation of the world with something better than the exertions of mechanical skill. Our day of dependence, our long apprenticeship to the learning of other lands, draws to a close. The millions that around us are rushing into life, cannot always be fed on the sere remains of foreign harvests. Events, actions arise, that must be sung, that will sing themselves. Who can doubt that poetry will revive and lead in a new age, as the star in the constellation Harp, which now flames in our zenith, astronomers announce, shall one day be the polestar for a thousand years?

In this hope I accept the topic which not only usage but the nature of our association seem to prescribe to this day—the AMERICAN SCHOLAR. Year by year we come up hither to read one more chapter of his biography. Let us inquire what light new days and events have thrown on his character and his hopes. . . .

I. The first in time and the first in importance of the influences upon the mind is that of nature. Every day, the sun; and, after sunset, Night and her stars. Ever the winds blow; ever the grass grows. Every day, men and women, conversing—beholding and beholden. The scholar is he of all men whom this spectacle most engages. He must settle its value in his mind. What is nature to him? There is never a beginning, there is never an end, to the inexplicable continuity of this web of God, but always circular power returning into itself. Therein it resembles his own spirit, whose beginning, whose ending, he never can find—so entire, so boundless. Far too as her splendors shine, system on system shooting like rays, upward, downward, without centre, without circumference—in the mass and in the particle, Nature hastens to render account of herself to the mind. Classification begins. To the young mind every thing is individual, stands by itself. By and by, it finds how to join two things and see in them one nature; then three, then three thousand; and so, tyrannized over by its own unifying instinct, it goes on tying things together, diminishing anomalies, discovering roots running under ground whereby contrary and remote things cohere and flower out from one stem. It presently learns that since the dawn of history there has been a constant accumulation and classifying of facts. But what is classification but the perceiving that these objects are not chaotic, and are not foreign, but have a law which is also a law of the human mind? The astronomer discovers that geometry, a pure abstraction of the human mind, is the measure of planetary motion. The chemist finds proportions and intelligible method throughout matter; and science is nothing but the finding of analogy, identity, in the most remote parts. The ambitious soul sits down before each refractory fact; one after another reduces all strange constitutions, all new powers, to their class and their law, and goes on forever to animate the last fibre of organization, the outskirts of nature, by insight.

Thus to him, to this schoolboy under the bending dome of day, is suggested that he and it proceed from one root; one is leaf and one is flower; relation, sympathy, stirring in every vein. And what is that root? Is not that the soul of his soul? A thought too bold; a dream too wild. Yet when this spiritual light shall have revealed the law of more earthly natures—when he has learned to worship the soul, and to see that the natural philosophy that now is, is only the first gropings of its gigantic hand, he shall look forward to an ever expanding knowledge as to a becoming creator. He shall see that nature is the opposite of the soul, answering to it part for part. One is seal and one is print. Its beauty is the beauty of his own mind. Its laws are the laws of his own mind. Nature then becomes to him the measure of his attainments. So much of nature as he is ignorant of, so much of his own mind does he not yet possess. And, in fine, the ancient precept, "Know thyself," and the modern precept, "Study nature," become at last one maxim.

II. The next great influence into the spirit of the scholar is the mind of the Past—in whatever form, whether of literature, of art, of institutions, that mind is inscribed. Books are the best type of the influence of the past, and perhaps we shall get at the truth—learn the amount of this influence more conveniently—by considering their value alone.

The theory of books is noble. The scholar of the first age received into him the world around; brooded thereon; gave it the new arrangement of his own mind, and uttered it again. It came into him life; it went out from him truth. It came to him short-lived actions; it went out from him immortal thoughts. It came to him business; it went from him poetry. It was dead fact; now, it is quick thought. It can stand, and it can go. It now endures, it now flies, it now inspires. Precisely in proportion to the depth of mind from which it issued, so high does it soar, so long does it sing. . . .

Books are the best of things, well used; abused, among the worst. What is the right use? What is the one end which all means go to effect? They are for nothing but to inspire. I had better never see a book than to be warped by its attraction clean out of my own orbit, and made a satellite instead of a system. The one thing in the world, of value, is the active soul. This every man is entitled to; this every man contains within him, although in almost all men obstructed and as yet unborn. The soul active sees absolute truth and utters truth, or creates. In this action it is genius; not the privilege of here and there a favorite, but the sound estate of every man. In its essence it is progressive. The book, the college, the school of art, the institution of any kind, stop with some past utterance of genius. This is good, say they—let us hold by this. . . .

It is remarkable, the character of the pleasure we derive from the best books. They impress us with the conviction that one nature wrote and the same reads. We read the verses of one of the great English poets, of Chaucer, of Marvell, of Dryden, with the most modern joy—with a pleasure, I mean, which is in great part caused by the abstraction of all *time* from their verses. There is some awe mixed with the joy of our surprise, when this poet, who lived in some past world, two or three hundred years ago, says that which lies close to my own soul, that which I also had well-nigh thought and said. . . .

I would not be hurried by any love of system, by any exaggeration of instincts, to underrate the Book. We all know, that as the human body can be nourished on any food, though it were boiled grass and the broth of shoes, so the human mind can be fed by any knowledge. And great and heroic men have existed who had almost no other information than by the printed page. I only would say that it needs a strong head to bear that diet. One must be an inventor to read well. As the proverb says, "He that would bring home the wealth of the Indies, must carry out the wealth of the Indies." . . .

Of course there is a portion of reading quite indispensable to a wise man. History and exact science he must learn by laborious reading. Colleges, in like manner, have their indispensable office—to teach elements. But they can only highly serve us when they aim not to drill, but to create; when they gather from far every ray of various genius to their hospitable halls, and by the concentrated fires, set the hearts of their youth on flame. Thought and knowledge are natures in which apparatus and pretension avail nothing. Gowns and pecuniary foundations, though of towns of gold, can never countervail the least sentence or syllable of wit. Forget this, and our American colleges will recede in their public importance, whilst they grow richer every year.

III. There goes in the world a notion that the scholar should be a recluse, a valetudinarian—as unfit for any handiwork or public labor as a penknife for an axe. The so-called "practical men" sneer at speculative men, as if, because they speculate or *see,* they could do nothing. I have heard it said that the clergy—who are always, more universally than any other class, the scholars of their day—are addressed as women; that the rough, spontaneous conversation of men they do not hear, but only a mincing and diluted speech. They are often virtually disfranchised; and indeed there are advocates for their celibacy. As far as this is true of the studious classes, it is not just and wise. Action is with the scholar subordinate, but it is essential. Without it he is not yet man. Without it thought can never ripen into truth. Whilst the world hangs before the eye as a cloud of beauty, we cannot even see its beauty. Inaction is cowardice, but there can be no scholar without the heroic mind. The preamble of thought, the transition through which it passes from the unconscious to the conscious, is action. Only so much do I know, as I have lived. Instantly we know whose words are loaded with life, and whose not. . . .

If it were only for a vocabulary, the scholar would be covetous of action. Life is our dictionary. Years are well spent in country labors; in town; in the insight into trades and manufactures; in frank intercourse with many men and women; in science; in art; to the one end of mastering in all their facts a language by which to illustrate and embody our perceptions. I learn immediately from any speaker how much he has already lived, through the poverty or the splendor of his speech. Life lies behind us as the quarry from whence we get tiles and copestones for the masonry of to-day. This is the way to learn grammar. Colleges and books only copy the language which the field and the work-yard made.

But the final value of action, like that of books, and better than books, is that it is a resource. That great principle of Undulation in nature, that shows itself in the inspiring and expiring of the breath; in desire and satiety; in the ebb and flow of the sea; in day and night; in heat and cold; and, as yet more deeply ingrained in every atom and every fluid, is known to us under the name of Polarity—these "fits of easy transmission and reflection," as Newton called them, are the law of nature because they are the law of spirit.

The mind now thinks, now acts, and each fit reproduces the other. When the artist has exhausted his materials, when the fancy no longer paints, when thoughts are no longer apprehended and books are a weariness—he has always the resources *to live*. Character is higher than intellect. Thinking is the function. Living is the functionary. The stream retreats to its source. A great soul will be strong to live, as well as strong to think. . . .

The office of the scholar is to cheer, to raise, and to guide men by showing them facts amidst appearances. He plies the slow, unhonored, and unpaid task of observation. Flamsteed and Herschel, in their glazed observatories, may catalogue the stars with the praise of all men, and the results being splendid and useful, honor is sure. But he, in his private observatory, cataloguing obscure and nebulous stars of the human mind, which as yet no man has thought of as such—watching days and months sometimes for a few facts; correcting still his old records; must relinquish display and immediate fame. . . . he must accept—how often!—poverty and solitude. For the ease and pleasure of treading the old . . . He is to find consolation in exercising the highest functions of human nature. He is one who raises himself from private considerations and breathes and lives on public and illustrious thoughts. He is the world's eye. He is the world's heart.

He and he only knows the world. The world of any moment is the merest appearance. . . . He learns that he who has mastered any law in his private thoughts, is master to that extent of all men whose language he speaks, and of all into whose language his own can be translated. The poet, in utter solitude remembering his spontaneous thoughts and recording them, is found to have recorded that which men in crowded cities find true for them also. The orator distrusts at first the fitness of his frank confessions, his want of knowledge of the persons he addresses, until he finds that he is the complement of his hearers; that they drink his words because he fulfils for them their own nature; the deeper he dives into his privatest, secretest presentiment, to his wonder he finds this is the most acceptable, most public, and universally true. The people delight in it; the better part of every man feels, This is my music; this is myself.

In self-trust all the virtues are comprehended. Free should the scholar be—free and brave. Free even to the definition of freedom, "without any hindrance that does not arise out of his own constitution." Brave; for fear is a thing which a scholar by his very function puts behind him. Fear always springs from ignorance. . . .

Yes, we are the cowed—we the trustless. It is a mischievous notion that we are come late into nature; that the world was . . . The great man makes the great thing. Wherever Macdonald sits, there is the head of the table. Linnæus makes botany the most alluring of studies, and wins it from the farmer and the herb-woman; Davy, chemistry; and Cuvier, fossils. The day is always his who works in it with serenity and great aims. The unstable estimates of men crowd to him whose mind is filled with a truth, as the heaped waves of the Atlantic follow the moon. . . .

Men, such as they are, very naturally seek money or power; and power because it is as good as money—the "spoils," so called, "of office." And why not? for they aspire to the highest, and this, in their sleep-walking, they dream is highest. Wake them and they shall quit the false good and leap to the true, and leave governments to clerks and desks. This revolution is to be wrought by the gradual domestication of the idea of Culture. The main enterprise of the world for splendor, for extent, is the upbuilding of a man. . . . The private life of one man shall be a more illustrious monarchy, more formidable to its enemy, more sweet and serene in its influence to its friend, than any kingdom in history. For a man, rightly viewed, comprehendeth the particular natures of all men. . . . The human mind cannot be enshrined in a person who shall set a barrier on any one side to this unbounded, unboundable empire. It is one central fire, which, flaming now out of the lips of Etna, lightens the capes of Sicily, and now out of the throat of Vesuvius, illuminates the towers and vineyards of Naples. It is one light which beams out of a thousand stars. It is one soul which animates all men. . . .

There is one man of genius who has done much for this philosophy of life, whose literary value has never yet been rightly estimated; I mean Emanuel Swedenborg. The most imaginative of men, yet writing with the precision of a mathematician, he endeavored to engraft a purely philosophical Ethics on the popular Christianity of his time. Such an attempt of course must have difficulty which no genius could surmount. But he saw and showed the connection between nature and the affections of the soul. He pierced the emblematic or spiritual character of the visible, audible, tangible word. Especially did his shade-loving muse hover over and interpret the lower parts of nature; he showed the mysterious bond that allies moral evil to the foul material forms, and has given in epical parables a theory of insanity, of beasts, of unclean and fearful things. . . .

"I learned," said the melancholy Pestalozzi, "that no man in God's wide earth is either willing or able to help any other man." Help must come from the bosom alone. The scholar is that man who must take up into himself all the ability of the time, all the contributions of the past, all the hopes of the future. He must be an university of knowledges. If there be one lesson more than another which should pierce his ear, it is, The world is nothing, the man is all; in yourself is the law of all nature, and you know not yet how a globule of sap ascends; in yourself slumbers the whole of Reason; it is for you to know all; it is for you to dare all. . . .

"That government is best which governs not at all"

THOREAU ON CIVIL DISOBEDIENCE
1846

Henry David Thoreau (1817–1862) was a pencil maker, a transcendentalist, an anarchist, an essayist, a poet, and a naturalist. In a two-year experiment, he lived the simple, self-reliant, contemplative life of a free spirit, fronting "only the essential facts of life . . . to drive life into a corner," in a one-room hut on the shore of Walden Pond, Massachusetts (on land provided by longtime companion Ralph Waldo Emerson [1803–1882]). Thoreau's "Civil Disobedience," a classic of individualism, inspires believers in passive resistance.

I HEARTILY accept the motto—"That government is best which governs least;" and I should like to see it acted up to more rapidly and systematically. Carried out, it finally amounts to this, which also I believe,—"That government is best which governs not at all;" and when men are prepared for it, that will be the kind of government which they will have. Government is at best but an expedient; but most governments are usually, and all governments are sometimes, inexpedient. The objections which have been brought against a standing army, and they are many and weighty, and deserve to prevail, may also at last be brought against a standing government. The standing army is only an arm of the standing government. The government itself, which is only the mode which the people have chosen to execute their will, is equally liable to be abused and perverted before the people can act through it. Witness the present Mexican war, the work of comparatively a few individuals using the standing government as their tool; for, in the outset, the people would not have consented to this measure.

This American government,—what is it but a tradition, though a recent one, endeavoring to transmit itself unimpaired to posterity, but each instant losing some of its integrity? It has not the vitality and force of a single living man; for a single man can bend it to his will. It is a sort of wooden gun to the people themselves; and, if ever they should use it in earnest as a real one against each other, it will surely split. But it is not the less necessary for this; for the people must have some complicated machinery or other, and hear its din, to satisfy that idea of government which they have. Governments show thus how successfully men can be imposed on, even impose on themselves, for their own advantage. It is excellent, we must all allow; yet this government never of itself furthered any enterprise, but by the alacrity with which it got out of its way. *It* does not keep the country free. *It* does not settle the West. *It* does not educate. The character inherent in the American people has done all that has been accomplished; and it would have done somewhat more, if the government had not sometimes got in its way. For government is an expedient by which men would fain succeed in letting one another alone; and, as has been said, when it is most expedient, the governed are most let alone by it. Trade and commerce, if they were not made of india rubber, would never manage to bounce over the obstacles which legislators are continually putting in their way; and, if one were to judge these men wholly by the effects of their actions, and not partly by their intentions, they would deserve to be classed and punished with those mischievous persons who put obstructions on the railroads.

But, to speak practically and as a citizen, unlike those who call themselves no-government men, I ask for, not at once no government, but *at once* a better government. Let every man make known what kind of government would command his respect, and that will be one step toward obtaining it.

"*An immense amount of reading matter*"

THE NEW-YORK DAILY TIMES
September 21, 1851

Henry Raymond's dream came true in September, 1851. The erstwhile Vermonter (1820–1869) was publishing a daily newspaper in New York City.

The carrier of The New-York Daily Times proposes to leave it at this house every morning for a week, for the perusal of the family, and to enable them, if they desire it, to receive it regularly. The Times is a very cheap paper, costing the subscriber only SIXPENCE a week, and contains an immense amount of reading matter for that price.

The proprietors have abundant capital, able assistants and every facility for making it as good a paper as there is in the City of New York. It will contain regularly all the news of the day, full telegraphic reports from all quarters of the country, full city news, correspondence, editorials, etc., etc.

At the end of the week the carrier will call for his pay; and a continuance of subscription is very respectfully solicited.

"So large a circulation in so short a time"

THE NEW-YORK DAILY TIMES
September 27, 1851

Within a week of startup, paid daily circulation of the *Times* boomed to over 10,000 copies.

This is the ninth number of the New York-York Daily Times, and it has now a regular paying circulation of over TEN THOUSAND copies. If any other newspaper in this or in any other part of the world ever reached so large a circulation in so short a time, we should be glad to be informed of the fact. It is taken by business men at their stores, and by the most respectable families in town.

"An extraordinary task"

The New-York Times
1896

In 1896, Adolph Ochs (1858–1935), son of German immigrants, bought the *Times* for $75,000. He eschewed popular yellow journalism, gave the news "impartially, without fear or favor, regardless of any party, sect, or interest involved," and made the newspaper one of the world's foremost dailies, the "newspaper of record" with all the news that's fit to print. Ochs's aim was to give the news "in language that is permissable in good society. . . . the *Times* is impressed with the responsibility of what it prints." Newspapers all over the U.S. reprinted Och's vow to maintain the Times' "great history for right-doing."

To undertake the management of The New-York Times, with its great history for right-doing, and to attempt to keep bright the lustre which Henry J. Raymond and George Jones have given it, is an extraordinary task. But if a sincere desire to conduct a high-standard newspaper, clean, dignified and trustworthy, requires honesty, watchfulness, earnestness, industry and practical knowledge applied with common sense, I enertain the hope that I can succeed in maintaining the high estimate that thoughtful, pure-mindedf people have ever had of The New-York Times.

It will be my earnest aim that The New-York Times give the news, all the news, in concise and attractive form, in language that is parliamentary in good society, and give it as early, if not earlier, than it can be learned through any other reliable medium; . . . to make the columns of The New-York Times a forum for the consideration of all questions of public importance, and to that end to invite intelligent discussion from all shades of opinion.

. . . nor will there be a departure freom the general tone and character and policies pursued with relation to public questions that have distinguished The New-York Times as a nonpartisan newspaper—unless it be, if possible, to intensify its devotion to the cause of sound money and tariff reform, opposition to wastfulness and peculation in administering the public affairs and its advocacy of the lowest tax consistent with good government, and no more government than is absolutely necessary to protect society, maintain individual vested rights and assure the free exercise of a sound conscience.

"'Leaves of Grass' . . . Extraordinary"

Emerson Writes Whitman
1855

Ralph Waldo Emerson (1803–1882), America's "literary banker," was an early booster of Walt Whitman. By letter, Emerson greeted Whitman (1819–1892) "at the beginning of a great career," hailing Whitman's *Leaves of Grass* as "the American poem," "a nondescript monster which yet had terrible eyes and buffalo strength." Whitman, supposing the "letter was meant to be blazoned," stamped the praise on the cover of the enlarged second edition (1856). Slavery was ripping the United States apart; Whitman believed that his epic poem could bring the divided nation together: "Me imperturbe, standing at ease in Nature, Master of all, or mistress of all, aplomb in the midst of irrational things." When the self-proclaimed national bard refused to remove his sexual poems from later editions of *Leaves of Grass*, Emerson turned away from the "good gray poet."

Concord Massachusetts 21 July 1855

DEAR SIR,

I am not blind to the worth of the wonderful gift of "Leaves of Grass." I find it the most extraordinary piece of wit & wisdom that America has yet contributed. I am very happy in reading it, as great power makes us happy. It meets the demand I am always making of what seemed the sterile & stingy Nature, as if too much handiwork or too much lymph in the temperament were making our western wits fat & mean.

I give you joy of your free & brave thought. I have great joy in it. I find incomparable things said incomparably well, as they must be. I find the courage of *treatment*, which so delights us, & which large perception only can inspire.

I greet you at the beginning of a great career, which yet must have had a long foreground somewhere, for such a start. I rubbed my eyes a little to see if this sunbeam were no illusion; but the solid sense of the book is a sober certainty. It has the best merits, namely, of fortifying & encouraging.

I did not know until I, last night, saw the book advertised in a newspaper, that I could trust the name as real & available for a Post-office. I wish to see my benefactor, & have felt much like striking my tasks, & visiting New York to pay you my respects.

R. W. EMERSON.

"Spend the surplus . . . for benevolent purposes"

The Carnegie Memorandum
1868

Andrew Carnegie (1835–1919) grew up in poverty, then made tons of money in the steel business after introducing the first Pullman railroad sleeping car. He believed in benevolence: "the amassing of wealth is one of the worst species of idolatry—no idol more debasing than the worship of money." He offered to pay for the construction of a public library building for any municipality that would guarantee funds for its operation. He financed approximately 1,681 libraries in the United States. After his death, more libraries (some abroad) were built under the terms of his will. Some communities rejected Carnegie's money as "tainted;" others debated long and hard before acceptance. Carnegie libraries became a feature of American life, a source of both pleasure and enlightenment.

Beyond this [$50,000 a year] never earn—make no effort to increase fortune, but spend the surplus each year for benevolent purposes. . . . Man must have an idol—the amassing of wealth is one of the worst species of idolatry—no idol more debasing than the worship of money. . . . To continue much longer . . . with most of my thoughts wholly upon the way to make more money in the shortest possible time, must degrade me beyond hopes of permanent recovery.

"No obscene . . . publication"

THE COMSTOCK ACTS
1873

Anthony Comstock (1844–1915) waged warfare upon publishers and vendors of printed matter that deviated from his saintly views. He lobbied for laws to prevent sending obscene literature through the mail, delivering to Congressmen satchelsful of "lewd, filthy" books, pictures, and devices he wanted banned. Comstock helped organize the New York Society for the Suppression of Vice. (He boasted of driving 15 people to suicide.) "Comstockery" became a disparaging label for puritanical crusading and overzealous moral censorship of the fine arts and literature, often mistaking outspokenly honest works for salacious ones. Many believed Comstock statutes were subversive of the principles of American liberty and destructive to individual rights guaranteed by the Constitution. In 1873, the morals crusader, who had been a Union soldier in the Civil War, secured stricter Federal postal legislation against obscene matter.

SEC. 3893. No obscene, lewd, or lascivious book, pamphlet, picture, paper, print, or other publication of an indecent character, or any article or thing designed or intended for the prevention of conception or procuring of abortion, nor any article or thing intended or adapted for any indecent or immoral use or nature, nor any written or printed card, circular, book, pamphlet, advertisement, or notice of any kind giving information, directly or indirectly, where or how, or of whom, or by what means either of the things before mentioned may be obtained or made, nor any letter upon the envelope of which, or postal card upon which indecent or scurrilous epithets may be written or printed, shall be carried in the mail; and any person who shall knowingly deposit, or cause to be deposited, for mailing or delivery, any of the herein beforementioned articles or things, or any notice or paper containing any advertisement relating to the aforesaid articles or things; and any person who, in pursuance of any plan or scheme for disposing of any of the herein before-mentioned articles or things, shall take or cause to be taken, from the mail any such letter or package, shall be deemed guilty of a misdemeanor, and shall, for every offense, be fined not less than one hundred dollars, nor more than five thousand dollars, or imprisoned at hard labor not less than one year, nor more than ten years, or both.

SEC. 5389. Every person who, within the District of Columbia, or any of the Territories of the United States, or other place within the exclusive jurisdiction of the United States, sells, or lends, or gives away, or in any manner exhibits or offers to sell, or to lend, or to give away, or in any manner to exhibit, or otherwise publishes or offers to publish in any manner, or has in his possession, for any such purpose, any obscene book, pamphlet, paper, writing, advertisement, circular, print, picture, drawing, or other representation, figure, or image on or of paper or other material, or any cast, instrument, or other article of an immoral nature, or any drug or medicine, or any article whatever, for the prevention of conception, or for causing unlawful abortion, or who advertises the same for sale, or writes or prints, or causes to be written or printed, any card, circular, book, pamphlet, advertisement, or notice of any kind, stating when, where, how, or of whom, or by what means, any of the articles in this section hereinbefore mentioned can be procured or obtained; or manufactures, draws, or prints, or in anywise makes any of such articles, shall be imprisoned at hard labor in the penitentiary for not less than six months, nor more than five years for each offense, or fined not less than one hundred dollars, nor more than two thousand dollars, with costs of court.

"Give free play to every instinct of human nature"

LOOKING BACKWARD
1888

Three prominent Americans, philosopher John Dewey (1859–1952), historian Charles Beard (1874–1948), and *Atlantic* magazine editor Edward Weeks (1898–1989), agreed that Edward Bellamy's *Looking Backward* was the most influential book by an American in the preceding half century, second only to *Das Kapital* as the most influential book published anywhere. The vivid, futuristic Utopian novel, in which a wealthy young Bostonian put into hypnotic sleep in 1887 wakes in the happy, peaceful land of state socialism of 2000, proposed the most revolutionary changes imaginable. Bellamy (1850–1898) conceived a society without lawyers, bankers, stockbrokers, and merchants. The concepts of rich and poor were eliminated. Everybody in the classless society had the inalienable right to a living wage. The wealth-producing power of the community would be increased enormously by the elimination of waste and the application of simple principles that elicited the best work from every citizen. Credit and debt disappeared, and the uncertainties of fortunes that impel men to struggle and contend for wealth were eliminated. Education was universal in Bellamy's Utopia. Ignorance, crime, and vice were unknown. *Looking Backward* helped to create a consciousness and a climate for "economic democratization," which culminated decades later in the New Deal—but not in the "classless society" that Bellamy claimed to desire.

"If I were to give you, in one sentence, a key to what may seem the mysteries of our civilization as compared with that of your age, I should say that it is the fact that the solidarity of the race and the brotherhood of man, which to you were but fine phrases, are, to our thinking and feeling, ties as real and as vital as physical fraternity.

"But even setting that consideration aside, I do not see why it so surprises you that those who cannot work are conceded the full right to live on the produce of those who can. Even in your day, the duty of military service for the protection of the nation, to which our industrial service corresponds, while obligatory on those able to discharge it, did not operate to deprive of the privileges of citizenship those who were unable. They stayed at home, and were protected by those who fought, and nobody questioned their right to be, or thought less of them. So, now, the requirement of industrial service from those able to render it does not operate to deprive of the privileges of citizenship, which now implies the citizen's maintenance, him who cannot work.

The worker is not a citizen because he works, but works because he is a citizen. As you recognize the duty of the strong to fight for the weak, we, now that fighting is gone by, recognize his duty to work for him.

"A solution which leaves an unaccounted-for residuum is no solution at all; and our solution of the problem of human society would have been none at all had it left the lame, the sick, and the blind outside with the beasts, to fare as they might. Better far have left the strong and well unprovided for than these burdened ones, toward whom every heart must yearn, and for whom ease of mind and body should be provided, if for no others. Therefore it is, as I told you this morning, that the title of every man, woman, and child to the means of existence rests on no basis less plain, broad, and simple than the fact that they are fellows of one race—members of one human family. The only coin current is the image of God, and that is good for all we have.

"I think there is no feature of the civilization of your epoch so repugnant to modern ideas as the neglect with which you treated your dependent classes. Even if you had no pity, no feeling of brotherhood, how was it that you did not see that you were robbing the incapable class of their plain right in leaving them unprovided for?"

———

"Emigration is another point I want to ask you about," said I. "With every nation organized as a close industrial partnership, monopolizing all means of production in the country, the emigrant, even if he were permitted to land, would starve. I suppose there is no emigration nowadays."

"On the contrary, there is constant emigration, by which I suppose you mean removal to foreign countries for permanent residence," replied Dr. Leete. "It is arranged on a simple in-ternational arrangement of indemnities. For example, if a man at twenty-one emigrates from England to America, England loses all the expense of his maintenance and education, and America gets a workman for nothing. America accordingly makes England an allowance. The same principle, varied to suit the case, applies generally. If the man is near the term of his labor when he emigrates, the country receiving him has the allowance. As to imbecile persons, it is deemed best that each nation should be responsible for its own, and the emigration of such must be under full guarantees of support by his own nation. Subject to these regulations, the right of any man to emigrate at any time is unrestricted."

———

"By the way," said I, "talking of literature, how are books published now? Is that also done by the nation?"

"Certainly."

"But how do you manage it? Does the government publish everything that is brought it as a matter of course, at the public expense, or does it exercise a censorship and print only what it approves?"

"Neither way. The printing department has no censorial powers. It is bound to print all that is offered it, but prints it only on condition that the author defray the first cost out of his credit. He must pay for the privilege of the public ear, and if he has any message worth hearing we consider that he will be glad to do it. Of course, if incomes were unequal, as in the old times, this rule would enable only the rich to be authors, but the resources of citizens being equal, it merely measures the strength of the author's motive. The cost of an edition of an average book can be saved out of a year's credit by the practice of economy and some sacrifices. The book, on being published, is placed on sale by the nation."

"The author receiving a royalty on the sales as with us, I suppose," I suggested.

"Not as with you, certainly," replied Dr. Leete, "but nevertheless in one way. The price of every book is made up of the cost of its publication with a royalty for the author. The author fixes this royalty at any figure he pleases. Of course if he puts it unreasonably high it is his own loss, for the book will not sell. The amount of this royalty is set to his credit and he is discharged from other service to the nation for so long a period as this credit at the rate of allowance for the support of citizens shall suffice to support him. If his book be moderately successful, he has thus a furlough for several months, a year, two or three years, and if he in the mean time produces other successful work, the remission of service is extended so far as the sale of that may justify. An author of much acceptance succeeds in supporting himself by his pen during the entire period of service, and the degree of any writer's literary ability, as determined by the popular voice, is thus the measure of the opportunity given him to devote his time to literature. In this respect the outcome of our system is not very dissimilar to that of yours, but there are two notable differences. In the first place, the universally high level of education nowadays gives the popular verdict a conclusiveness on the real merit of literary work which in your day it was as far as possible from having. In the second place, there is no such thing now as favoritism of any sort to interfere with the recognition of true merit. Every author has precisely the same facilities for bringing his work before the popular tribunal. To judge from the complaints of the writers of your day, this absolute equality of opportunity would have been greatly prized."

"In the recognition of merit in other fields of original genius, such as music, art, invention, design," I said, "I suppose you follow a similar principle."

"Yes," he replied, "although the details differ. In art, for example, as in literature, the people are the sole judges. They vote upon the acceptance of statutes and paintings for the public buildings, and their favorable verdict carries with it the artist's remission from other tasks to devote himself to his vocation. On copies of his work disposed of, he also derives the same advantage as the author on sales of his books. In all these lines of original genius the plan pursued is the same—to offer a free field to aspirants, and as soon as exceptional talent is recognized to release it from all trammels and let it have free course. The remission of other service in these cases is not intended as a gift or reward, but as the means of obtaining more and higher service. Of course there are various literary, art, and scientific institutes to which membership comes to the famous and is greatly prized. The highest of all honors in the nation, higher than the presidency, which calls merely for good sense and devotion to duty, is the red ribbon awarded by the vote of the people to the great authors, artists, engineers, physicians, and inventors of the generation. Not over a certain number wear it at any one time, though every bright young fellow in the country loses innumerable nights' sleep dreaming of it. I even did myself."

"Just as if mamma and I would have thought any more of you with it," exclaimed Edith; "not that it isn't, of course, a very fine thing to have."

"You had no choice, my dear, but to take your father as you found him and make the best of him," Dr. Leete replied; "but as for your mother, there, she would never have had me if I had not assured her that I was bound to get the red ribbon or at least the blue."

On this extravagance Mrs. Leete's only comment was a smile.

"How about periodicals and newspapers?" I said. "I won't deny that your book publishing system is a considerable improvement on ours, both as to its tendency to encourage a real literary vocation, and, quite as important, to discourage mere scribblers; but I don't see how it can be made to apply to magazines and newspapers. It is very well to make a man pay for publishing a book, because the expense will be only occasional; but no man could afford the expense of publishing a newspaper every day in the year. It took the deep pockets of our private capitalists to do that, and often exhausted even them before the returns came in. If you have newspapers at all, they must, I fancy, be published by the government at the public expense, with government editors, reflecting government opinions. Now, if your system is so perfect that there is never anything to criticise in the conduct of affairs, this arrangement may answer. Otherwise I should think the lack of an independent unofficial medium for the expression of public opinion would have most unfortunate results. Confess, Dr. Leete, that a free newspaper press, with all that it implies, was a redeeming incident of the old system when capital was in private hands, and that you have to set off the loss of that against your gains in other respects."

"I am afraid I can't give you even that consolation," replied Dr. Leete, laughing. "In the first place, Mr. West, the newspaper press is by no means the only or, as we look at it, the best vehicle for serious criticism of public affairs. To us, the judgments of your newspapers on such themes seem generally to have been crude and flippant, as well as deeply tinctured with prejudice and bitterness. In so far as they may be taken as expressing public opinion, they give an unfavorable impression of the popular intelligence, while so far as they may have formed public opinion, the nation was not to be felicitated.

Nowadays, when a citizen desires to make a serious impression upon the public mind as to any aspect of public affairs, he comes out with a book or pamphlet, published as other books are. But this is not because we lack newspapers and magazines, or that they lack the most absolute freedom. The newspaper press is organized so as to be a more perfect expression of public opinion than it possibly could be in your day, when private capital controlled and managed it primarily as a money-making business, and secondarily only as a mouthpiece for the people."

———

"However earnestly a man may long for leisure for purposes of study or meditation," I remarked, "he cannot get out of the harness, if I understand you rightly, except in these two ways you have mentioned. He must either by literary, artistic, or inventive productiveness indemnify the nation for the loss of his services, or must get a sufficient number of other people to contribute to such an indemnity."

"It is most certain," replied Dr. Leete, "that no able-bodied man nowadays can evade his share of work and live on the toil of others, whether he calls himself by the fine name of student or confesses to being simply lazy. At the same time our system is elastic enough to give free play to every instinct of human nature which does not aim at dominating others or living on the fruit of others' labor. There is not only the remission by indemnification but the remission by abnegation. Any man in his thirty-third year, his term of service being then half done, can obtain an honorable discharge from the army, provided he accepts for the rest of his life one half the rate of maintenance other citizens receive. It is quite possible to live on this amount, though one must forego the luxuries and elegancies of life, with some, perhaps, of its comforts."

"Longest 57 seconds"

THE WRIGHTS FLY
1903

One of America's most distinguished scientists, the astronomer and mathematician Simon Newcomb (1835–1909), predicted in 1901 that man would never fly.

> "The desire to fly like a bird is inborn in our race, and we can no more be expected to abandon the idea than the ancient mathematician could have been expected to give up the problem of squaring the circle . . . As the case stands, the first successful flyer will be the handiwork of a watchmaker and will carry nothing heavier than an insect. . . . The example of the bird does not prove that man can fly."

Two years later, the Wright brothers Orville (1871–1948) and Wilbur (1867–1912) flew in a power-driven airplane over the windswept sand dunes of Kitty Hawk, North Carolina. They telegraphed the historic news to their father, in Dayton, Ohio. The transmission was garbled. Wilbur had made a 59-second flight (not 57), and Orville's name was misspelled.

> Success four flights thursday morning all against twenty one mile wind started from Level with engine power alone average speed through air thirty one miles longest 57 seconds inform Press home #### Christmas.
>
> OREVELLE WRIGHT

(That distinguished scientist also had predicted that it would be impossible for an aeroplane to carry passengers; maybe "two or three buttons but will not carry more than four.")

"I am opposed to the social system"

EUGENE V. DEBS GOES TO PRISON
1918

Eugene Victor Debs (1855–1926), a Socialist labor leader and president of the American Railway Union, campaigned for the U.S. Presidency five times. In the 1912 election, the pacifist netted six percent of the votes (901,255). In the 1920 election, the first since the Nineteenth Amendment to the Constitution extended the vote to women, Debs was in prison, yet garnered three percent of the votes (915,490). He had been incarcerated for opposing (nonviolently) America's participation in the First World War and sentenced to ten years for violating the Espionage Act. Debs claimed that the Federal government was "undermining the very foundation of political liberty and economic rights." He was released on orders from President Warren G. Harding (1865–1923), who invited the period's most celebrated wartime protestor to the White House for a chat. Before he was sentenced. Debs had addressed the court.

Years ago I recognized my kinship with all living beings, and I made up my mind that I was not one bit better than the meanest on earth. I said then, and I say now, that while there is a lower class, I am in it; while there is a criminal element, I am of it; and while there is a soul in prison, I am not free.

I listened to all that was said in this court in support and justification of this prosecution, but my mind remains unchanged. I look upon the Espionage Law as a despotic enactment in flagrant conflict with democratic principles and with the spirit of free institutions. . . .

Your Honor, I have stated in this court that I am opposed to the social system in which we live, that I believe in a fundamental change—but if possible by peaceable and orderly means. . . .

Standing here this morning, I recall my boyhood. At fourteen I went to work in a railroad shop; at sixteen I was firing a freight engine on a railroad. I remember all the hardships and privations of that earlier day, and from that time until now my heart has been with the working class. I could have been in Congress long ago. I have preferred to go to prison. . . .

In this country—the most favored beneath the bending skies—we have vast areas of the richest and most fertile soil, material resources in inexhaustible abundance, the most marvelous productive machinery on earth, and millions of eager workers ready to apply their labor to that machinery to produce in abundance for every man, woman, and child—and if there are still vast numbers of our people who are the victims of poverty and whose lives are an unceasing struggle all the way from youth to old age, until at last death comes to their rescue and still their aching hearts and lulls these hapless victims to dreamless sleep, it is not the fault of the Almighty: it cannot be charged to nature, but it is due entirely to the outgrown social system in which we live, that ought to be abolished not only in the interest of the toiling masses but in the higher interest of all humanity. . . .

I believe, Your Honor, in common with all socialists, that this nation ought to own and control its own industries. I believe, as all socialists do, that all things that are jointly needed and used ought to be jointly owned—that industry, the basis of our social life, instead of being the private property of the few and operated for their enrichment, ought to be the common property of all, democratically administered in the interest of all. . . .

I am opposing a social order in which it is possible for one man who does absolutely nothing that is useful to amass a fortune of hundreds of millions of dollars, while millions of men and women who work all the days of their lives secure barely enough for a wretched existence.

This order of things cannot always endure . . . we shall have the universal commonwealth—the harmonious cooperation of every nation with every other nation on earth. . . .

I can see the dawn of the better day for humanity. The people are awakening. In due time they will and must come to their own. . . .

I am now prepared to receive your sentence.

"May also accept . . . motion-picture films"

THE NATIONAL ARCHIVES
1934

In the words of President Herbert C. Hoover (1874–1964), as he laid the building's cornerstone, in Washington, D.C., in February, 1933, the National Archives preserves the "records that bind State to State and the hearts of all our people in an indissoluble union." The Archives, "the heritage of the past that is the seed that brings forth the harvest of the future," houses the documentary record that captures the sweep of American history: from slave-ship manifests to captured Second World War records; from journals of polar expeditions to Indian treaties; from the 550 volumes of records of the Continental Congress to records of Watergate; from photographs of the Civil War and the Vietnam war to over 1.5-million maps, including the work of explorers Meriwether Lewis (1774–1809), William Clark (1770–1838), and Zebulon Pike (1779–1813); from over 150,000 reels of motion-picture film to footage of every President since Grover Cleveland; from hundreds of thousands of sound recordings to vast collections of computer tapes and microfilm. Annual operating expenses run to around $200-million.

Be it enacted by the Senate and House of Representatives of the United States of America in Congress assembled, That there is hereby created the Office of Archivist of the United States, the Archivist to be appointed by the President of the United States, by and with the advice and consent of the Senate.

SEC. 2. The salary of the Archivist shall be $10,000 annually. All persons to be employed in the National Archives Establishment shall be appointed by the Archivist solely with reference to their fitness for their particular duties and without regard to civil-service law; and the Archivist shall make rules and regulations for the government of the National Archives; . . .

SEC. 3. All archives or records belonging to the Government of the United States (legislative, executive, judicial, and other) shall be under the charge and superintendence of the Archivist to this extent: He shall have full power to inspect personally or by deputy the records of any agency of the United States Government whatsoever and wheresoever located, and shall have the full cooperation of any and all persons in charge of such records in such inspections, and to requisition for transfer to the National Archives Establishment such archives, or records as the National Archives Council, hereafter provided shall approve for such transfer, and he shall have authority to make regulations for the arrangement, custody, use, and withdrawal of material deposited in the National Archives Building: . . .

SEC. 4. The immediate custody and control of

the National Archives Building and such other buildings, grounds, and equipment as may from time to time become a part of the National Archives Establishment (except as the same is vested by law in the Director of National Buildings, Parks, and Reservations) and their contents shall be vested in the Archivist of the United States.

SEC. 5. That there is hereby created also a National Historical Publications Commission which shall make plans, estimates, and recommendations for such historical works and collections of sources as seem appropriate for publication and/or otherwise recording at the public expense, said Commission to consist of the Archivist of the United States, who shall be its chairman; the historical adviser of the Department of State; the chief of the historical section of the War Department, General Staff; the superintendent of naval records in the Navy Department; the Chief of the Division of Manuscripts in the Library of Congress; and two members of the American Historical Association appointed by the president thereof from among those persons who are or have been members of the executive council of the said association: *Provided,* That the preparation and publication of annual and special reports on the archives and records of the Government, guides, inventory lists, catalogs, and other instruments facilitating the use of the collections shall have precedence over detailed calendars and textual reproductions.

SEC. 6. That there is hereby further created a National Archives Council composed of the Secretaries of each of the executive departments of the Government (or an alternate from each department to be named by the Secretary thereof),

the Chairman of the Senate Committee on the Library, the Chairman of the House Committee on the Library, the Librarian of Congress, the Secretary of the Smithsonian Institution, and the Archivist of the United States. The said Council shall define the classes of material which shall be transferred to the National Archives Building and establish regulations governing such transfer; and shall have power to advise the Archivist in respect to regulations governing the disposition and use of the archives and records transferred to his custody.

SEC. 7. The National Archives may also accept, store, and preserve motion-picture films and sound recordings pertaining to and illustrative of historical activities of the United States, and in connection therewith maintain a projecting room for showing such films and reproducing such sound recordings for historical purposes and study. . . .

SEC. 9. That the Archivist shall make to Congress, at the beginning of each regular session, a report for the preceding fiscal year as to the National Archives, the said report including a detailed statement of all accessions and of all receipts and expenditures on account of the said establishment. He shall also transmit to Congress the recommendations of the Commission on National Historical Publications, and, on January 1 of each year, with the approval of the Council, a list or description of the papers, documents, and so forth (among the archives and records of the Government), which appear to have no permanent value or historical interest, and which, with the concurrence of the Government agency concerned, and subject to the approval of Congress, shall be destroyed or otherwise effectively disposed of. . . .

"It may become possible to set up a nuclear chain reaction"

EINSTEIN WRITES THE PRESIDENT
1939

Albert Einstein (1879–1955) put his name to a letter drafted by the physicist Leo Szilard (1898–1964) urging President Franklin Delano Roosevelt (1882–1945) to have the U.S. carry on nuclear research. Two months later, the letter was delivered by hand to the President by a vice president of a large Wall Street investment bank (and advisor to the New Deal). Germany had by then conquered Poland and was engaged in a "phony war" with western European nations. Although Einstein later said that he had "really only acted as a mailbox" for Szilard, he was held in such esteem at the highest level of the U.S. government that the communique got results: The U.S. began looking into development of atomic weapons. At the end of 1942, physicists in Chicago led by Enrico Fermi (1901–1954) achieved the first self-sustained nuclear chain reaction, then dispatched a coded telephone message: "You'll be interested to know that the Italian navigator has just landed in the new world. The Earth was not as large as he had estimated, and he arrived at the new world sooner than he had expected. Everyone landed safe and happy." Atomic bombs were possible.

SOME RECENT WORK by E. Fermi and L. Szilard, which has been communicated to me in manuscript, leads me to expect that the element uranium may be turned into a new and important source of energy in the immediate future. Certain aspects of the situation which has arisen seem to call for watchfulness and, if necessary, quick action on the part of the administration. I believe, therefore, that it is my duty to bring to your attention the following facts and recommendations.

In the course of the last four months it has been made probable—through the work of Joliot in France as well as Fermi and Szilard in America—that it may become possible to set up a nuclear chain reaction in a large mass of uranium, by which vast amounts of power and large quantities of new radium-like elements would be generated. Now it appears almost certain that this could be achieved in the immediate future.

This new phenomenon would also lead to the construction of bombs, and it is conceivable—though much less certain—that extremely powerful bombs of a new type may thus be constructed. A single bomb of this type, carried by boat and exploded in a port, might very well destroy the whole port together with some of the surrounding territory. However, such bombs might very well prove to be too heavy for transportation by air.

The United States has only very poor ores of uranium in moderate quantities. There is some good ore in Canada and the former Czechoslovakia, while the most important source of uranium is Belgian Congo.

In view of this situation you may think it desirable to have some permanent contact maintained between the administration and the group of physicists working on chain reactions in America. One possible way of achieving this might be for you to entrust with this task a person who has your confidence and who could perhaps serve in an unofficial capacity. His task might comprise the following:

(a) To approach government departments, keep them informed of the further development, and put forward recommendations for government action, giving particular attention to the problem of securing a supply of uranium ore for the United States.

(b) To speed up the experimental work, which is at present being carried on within the limits of the budgets of university laboratories, by providing funds, if such funds be required, through his contacts with private persons who are willing to make contributions for this cause, and perhaps also by obtaining the cooperation of industrial laboratories which have the necessary equipment.

I understand that Germany has actually stopped the sale of uranium from the Czechoslovakian mines which she has taken over. That she should have taken such early action might perhaps be understood on the ground that the son of the German undersecretary of state, Von Weizsacker, is attached to the Kaiser-Wilhelm-Institut in Berlin, where some of the American work on uranium is now being repeated.

"An impregnable defense for America"

AMERICA FIRST
1940

In the early 1940s, the America First Committee was the most powerful isolationist (non-interventionist) pressure group in the United States. Nurtured on the campus of Yale University, it wanted the U.S. to stay out of the war in Europe. The Committee's most popular speaker was America's most popular hero, the airman Charles A. Lindbergh (1902–1974), the first person to fly solo across the Atlantic Ocean (1927). In a 25-minute speech before 8,000 people crowded into the Des Moines (Iowa) Coliseum, pro-German "Lucky Lindy" declared that the "ever-increasing effort to force the United States" into the European conflict was "so successful that, today, our country stands on the verge of war." With "the utmost frankness," he named the groups he deemed "responsible for changing our national policy from one of neutrality and independence to one of entanglement in European affairs." Lindbergh, who had engendered great enmity with President Franklin Roosevelt, believed the U.S. should build its armed forces, especially its air force. Lindbergh's anti-Semitic and pro-Nazi stances led to much criticism of Lindbergh and to toppling of the "American God." (America First members included Norman Thomas, Gerald Ford, and Sargeant Shriver.)

The Committee issued four principles. "1. The United States must build an impregnable defense for America.

"2. No foreign power, nor group of powers, can successfully attack a *prepared* America.

"3. American democracy can be preserved only by keeping out of the European war.

"4. 'Aid short of war' weakens national defense at home and threatens to involve America in war abroad."

LINDBERGH CHARGES THREE GROUPS

"The three most important groups who have been pressing this country toward war are the British, the Jewish, and the Roosevelt Administration. Behind these groups, but of lesser importance, are a number of capitalists, anglophiles, and intellectuals, who believe that their future, and the future of mankind, depend upon the domination of the British Empire. Add to these the communistic groups who were opposed to intervention until a few weeks ago, and I believe I have named the major war agitators in this country."

"The most powerful voice in America"

A "VAST WASTELAND"

1961

The new chairman of the Federal Communications Commission, Newton N. Minow (born 1926), startled the National Association of Broadcasters when he described television at its worst a "vast wasteland," coinage that immediately entered the vernacular. Users of public airwaves, he asserted, were trustees for all Americans. Thirty years later, Mr. Minow worried that his grandchildren would actually be harmed by television: "A new generation has the chance to put the vision back into television, to travel from the wasteland to the promised land," to make television a saving radiance in the sky. Public television should become just as much a public commitment as public libraries, hospitals, parks, schools, and universities.

Your license lets you use the public's airwaves as trustees for 180 million Americans. The public is your beneficiary. If you want to stay on as trustees, you must deliver a decent return to the public—not only to your stockholders. So, as a representative of the public, your health and your product are among my chief concerns.

As to your health: Let's talk only of television today. In 1960 gross broadcast revenues of the television industry were over $1,268,000,000; profit before taxes was $243,900,000—an average return on revenue of 19.2 percent. Compare this with 1959, when gross broadcast revenues were $1,163,900,000 and profit before taxes was $222,300,000, an average return on revenue of 19.1 percent. So, the percentage increase of total revenues from 1959 to 1960 was 9 percent, and the percentage increase of profit was 9.7 percent. This, despite a recession. For your investors, the price has indeed been right.

I have confidence in your health.

But not in your product.

It is with this and much more in mind that I come before you today.

One editorialist in the trade press wrote that "the FCC of the New Frontier is going to be one of the toughest FCCs in the history of broadcast regulation." If he meant that we intend to enforce the law in the public interest, let me make it perfectly clear that he is right—we do.

. . . in today's world, with chaos in Laos and the Congo aflame, with Communist tyranny on our Caribbean doorstep and relentless pressure on our Atlantic alliance, with social and economic problems at home of the gravest nature, yes, and with technological knowledge that makes it possible, as our President has said, not only to destroy our world but to destroy poverty around the world—in a time of peril and opportunity, the old complacent, unbalanced fare of action-adventure and situation comedies is simply not good enough.

Your industry possesses the most powerful voice in America. It has an inescapable duty to make that voice ring with intelligence and with leadership. In a few years this exciting industry has grown from a novelty to an instrument of overwhelming impact on the American people.

It should be making ready for the kind of leadership that newspapers and magazines assumed years ago, to make our people aware of their world.

Ours has been called the jet age, the atomic age, the space age. It is also, I submit, the television age. And just as history will decide whether the leaders of today's world employed the atom to destroy the world or rebuild it for mankind's benefit, so will history decide whether today's broadcasters employed their powerful voice to enrich the people or debase them.

. . . . when television is bad, nothing is worse. I invite you to sit down in front of your television set when your station goes on the air and stay there without a book, magazine, newspaper, profit-and-loss sheet or rating book to distract you—and keep your eyes glued to that set until the station signs off. I can assure you that you will observe a vast wasteland.

You will see a procession of game shows, violence, audience participation shows, formula comedies about totally unbelievable families, blood and thunder, mayhem, violence, sadism, murder, western badmen, western good men, private eyes, gangsters, more violence and cartoons. And, endlessly, commercials—many screaming, cajoling and offending. And most of all, boredom. True, you will see a few things you will enjoy. But they will be very, very few. And if you think I exaggerate, try it.

Gentlemen, your trust accounting with your beneficiaries is overdue.

I do not accept the idea that the present overall programming is aimed accurately at the public taste. The ratings tell us only that some people have their television sets turned on, and of that number, so many are tuned to one channel and so many to another. They don't tell us what the public might watch if they were offered half a dozen additional choices. A rating, at best, is an indication of how many people saw what you gave them. Unfortunately it does not reveal the depth of the penetration, or the intensity of reaction, and it never reveals what the acceptance would have been if what you gave them had been better—if all the forces of art and creativity and daring and imagination had been unleashed. I believe in the people's good sense and good taste, and I am not convinced that the people's taste is as low as some of you assume. . . .

Let me make clear that what I am talking about is balance. I believe that the public interest is made up of many interests. There are many people in this great country, and you must serve all of us. You will get no argument from me if you say that, given a choice between a western and a symphony, more people will watch the western. I like westerns and private eyes too—but a steady diet for the whole country is obviously not in the public interest. We all know that people would more often prefer to be entertained than stimulated or informed. But your obligations are not satisfied if you look only to popularity as a test of what to broadcast. You are not only in show business; you are free to communicate ideas as well as relaxation. You must provide a wider range of choices, more diversity, more alternatives. It is not enough to cater to the nation's whims—you must also serve the nation's needs.

And I would add this—that if some of you persist in a relentless search for the highest rating and the lowest common denominator, you may very well lose your audience. Because, to paraphrase a great American who was recently my law partner, the people are wise, wiser than some of the broadcasters—and politicians—think. . . .

Television will rapidly join the parade into space. International television will be with us soon. No one knows how long it will be until a broadcast from a studio in New York will be viewed in India as well as in Indiana, will be seen in the Congo as it is seen in Chicago. But as surely as we are meeting here today, that day will come—and once again our world will shrink.

What will the people of other countries think of us when they see our western badmen and good men punching each other in the jaw in between the shooting? What will the Latin American or African child learn of America from our great communications industry? We cannot permit television in its present form to be our voice overseas.

There is your challenge to leadership. You must reexamine some fundamentals of your industry. You must open your minds and open your hearts to the limitless horizons of tomorrow. . . .

"Our liberal friends . . . know so much that isn't so!"

Ronald W. Reagan: "The Speech"
1964

The Presidential speechwriter Peggy Noonan (born 1950) believes that Ronald W. Reagan's speech for the 1964 Republican Presidential candidate Barry Goldwater (1909–1998) should be labeled "the Speech." It was the one, she says, that "proved" that Reagan (born 1911) could be President:

> "On one level it's a speech about freedom, about the relationship of the individual to the state. On another it's a speech about what works in government. But it's primarily a speech about money. It's a speech that reminds you he was a child of the Depression. He knew what it was not to have anything. When he looked at government, the bottom line shone through."

A few days before Reagan's speech, Goldwater mentioned canceling it because of a reference to social security; Goldwater had been "getting kicked all over the place on the issue." "The Speech" raised $8-million in contributions and changed Reagan's life. Sixteen years later, he would be elected President.

I have spent most of my life as a Democrat. I recently have seen fit to follow another course. I believe that the issues confronting us cross party lines. Now, one side in this campaign has been telling us that the issues of this election are the maintenance of peace and prosperity. The line has been used "We've never had it so good!"

But I have an uncomfortable feeling that this prosperity isn't something upon which we can base our hopes for the future. No nation in history has ever survived a tax burden that reached a third of its national income. Today thirty-seven cents out of every dollar earned in this country is the tax collector's share, and yet our government continues to spend 17 million dollars a day more than the government takes in. We haven't balanced our budget twenty-eight out of the last thirty-four years. We have raised our debt limit three times in the last twelve months, and now our national debt is one and a half times bigger than all the combined debts of all the nations of the world. . . .

There can be no real peace while one American is dying someplace in the world for the rest of us. We are at war with the most dangerous enemy that has ever faced mankind in his long climb from the swamp to the stars, and it has been said if we lose that war, and in so doing lose this way of freedom of ours, history will record with the greatest astonishment that those who had the most to lose did the least to prevent its happening. Well, I think it's time we ask ourselves if we still know the freedoms that were intended for us by the Founding Fathers.

Not too long ago two friends of mine were talking to a Cuban refugee, a businessman who had escaped from Castro, and in the midst of his story one of my friends turned to the other and said, "We don't know how lucky we are." And the Cuban stopped and said, "How lucky you are! I had someplace to escape to." In that sentence he told us the entire story. If we lose freedom here, there is no place to escape to. This is the last stand on earth.

And this idea that government is beholden to the people, that it has no other source of power except the sovereign people, is still the newest and most unique idea in all the long history of man's relation to man. Whether we believe in our capacity for self-government or whether we abandon the American Revolution and confess that a little intellectual elite in a far-distant capital can plan our lives for us better than we can plan them ourselves.

You and I are told increasingly that we have to choose between a left or right, but I would like to suggest that there is no such thing as a left or right. There is only an up or down—up to man's age-old dream—the ultimate in individual freedom consistent with law and order—or down to the ant heap of totalitarianism, and regardless of their sincerity, their humanitarian motives, those who would trade our freedom for security have embarked on this downward course.

Senator Clark of Pennsylvania defines liberalism as "meeting the material needs of the masses through the full power of centralized government." Well, I for one resent it when a representative of the people refers to you and me—the free men and women of this country—as "the masses." This is a term we haven't applied to ourselves in America. But beyond that, "the full power of centralized government"—this was the very thing the Founding Fathers sought to minimize. They knew that governments don't con-

trol *things.* A government can't control the economy without controlling people. And they knew when a government sets out to do that, it must use force and coercion to achieve its purpose. They also knew, those Founding Fathers, that outside of its legitimate functions, government does nothing as well or as economically as the private sector of the economy.

Now, we have no better example of this than the government's involvement in the farm economy over the last thirty years. Since 1955 the cost of this program has nearly doubled. One-fourth of farming in America is responsible for 85 percent of the farm surplus. Three-fourths of farming is out on the free market and has known a 21 percent increase in the per capita consumption of all its produce. You see, that one-fourth of farming is regulated and controlled by the federal government. In the last three years we have spent forty-three dollars in the feed grain program for every dollar bushel of corn we don't grow.

Meanwhile, back in the city, under urban renewal the assault on freedom carries on. Private property rights are so diluted that public interest is almost anything that a few government planners decide it should be. In a program that takes from the needy and gives to the greedy, we see such spectacles as in Cleveland, Ohio, a million-and-a-half-dollar building completed only three years ago must be destroyed to make way for what government officials call a "more compatible use of the land." The President tells us he is now going to start building public housing units in the thousands where heretofore we have only built them in the hundreds. But FHA and the Veterans Administration tell us that they have 120,000 housing units they've taken back through mortgage foreclosures.

For three decades we have sought to solve the problems of unemployment through government planning, and the more the plans fail, the more the planners plan. The latest is the Area Redevelopment Agency. They have just declared Rice County, Kansas, a depressed area. Rice County, Kansas, has two hundred oil wells, and the 14,000 people there have over thirty million dollars on deposit in personal savings in their banks. When the government tells you you are depressed, lie down and be depressed!

We have so many people who can't see a fat man standing beside a thin one without coming to the conclusion that the fat man got that way by taking advantage of the thin one! So they are going to solve all the problems of human misery through government and government planning. . . .

Anytime you and I question the schemes of the do-gooders, we are denounced as being against their humanitarian goals. They say we are always "against" things, never "for" anything. Well, the trouble with our liberal friends is not that they are ignorant, but that they know so much that isn't so! . . . can't we introduce voluntary features that would permit a citizen to do better on his own, to be excused upon presentation of evidence that he had made provisions for the nonearning years? Should we not allow a widow with children to work, and not lose the benefits supposedly paid for by her deceased husband? Shouldn't you and I be allowed to declare who our beneficiaries will be under these programs, which we cannot do? I think we are for telling our senior citizens that no one in this country should be denied medical care because of a lack of funds. . . .

I think we are for aiding our allies by sharing of our material blessings with those nations which share in our fundamental beliefs, but we are against doling out money government to government, creating bureaucracy, if not socialism, all over the world. We set out to help 19

countries. We are helping 107. We spent $146 billion. With that money, we bought a 2-million-dollar yacht for Haile Selassie. We bought dress suits for Greek undertakers, extra wives for Kenya government officials. We bought a thousand TV sets for a place where they have no electricity. In the last six years, fifty-two nations have bought $7 billion of our gold, and all fifty-two are receiving foreign aid from us. No government ever voluntarily reduces itself in size. Government programs, once launched, never disappear. Actually, a government bureau is the nearest thing to eternal life we'll ever see on this earth!

Federal employees number 2.5 million, and federal, state, and local, one out of six of the nation's work force is employed by government. These proliferating bureaus with their thousands of regulations have cost us many of our constitutional safeguards. How many of us realize that today federal agents can invade a man's property without a warrant? They can impose a fine without a formal hearing, let alone a trial by jury, and they can seize and sell his property in auction to enforce the payment of that fine. In Chicot County, Arkansas, James Wier overplanted his rice allotment. The government obtained a $17,000 judgment, and a U.S. marshal sold his 950-acre farm at auction. The government said it was necessary as a warning to others to make the system work! Last February 19th, at the University of Minnesota, Norman Thomas, six times candidate for president on the Socialist Party ticket, said, "If Barry Goldwater became president, he would stop the advance of socialism in the United States." I think that's exactly what he will do!

As a former Democrat, I can tell you Norman Thomas isn't the only man who has drawn this parallel to socialism with the present administration. Back in 1936, Mr. Democrat himself, Al

Smith, the great American, came before the American people and charged that the leadership of his party was taking the party of Jefferson, Jackson, and Cleveland down the road under the banners of Marx, Lenin, and Stalin. And he walked away from his party, and he never returned to the day he died, because to this day, the leadership of that party has been taking that party, that honorable party, down the road in the image of the labor socialist party of England. Now it doesn't require expropriation or confiscation of private property or business to impose socialism upon a people. What does it mean whether you hold the deed or the title to your business or property if the government holds the power of life and death over that business or property? Such machinery already exists. The government can find some charge to bring against any concern it chooses to prosecute. Every businessman has his own tale of harassment. Somewhere a perversion has taken place. Our natural, inalienable rights are now considered to be a dispensation from government, and freedom has never been so fragile, so close to slipping from our grasp as it is at this moment. Our Democratic opponents seem unwilling to debate these issues. . . .

Those who would trade our freedom for the soup kitchen of the welfare state have told us that they have a utopian solution of peace without victory. They call their policy "accommodation." And they say if we only avoid any direct confrontation with the enemy, he will forget his evil ways and learn to love us. All who oppose them are indicted as warmongers. They say we offer simple answers to complex problems. Well, perhaps there is a simple answer . . . not an easy one . . . but a simple one, if you and I have the courage to tell our elected officials that we want our *national* policy based upon what we know in our hearts is morally right.

We cannot buy our security, our freedom from the threat of the bomb by committing an immorality so great as saying to a billion human beings now in slavery behind the Iron Curtain, "Give up your dreams of freedom because to save our own skin, we are willing to make a deal with your slave-masters." Alexander Hamilton said, "A nation which can prefer disgrace to danger is prepared for a master, and deserves one!" Let's set the record straight. There is no argument over the choice between peace and war, but there is only one guaranteed way you can have peace . . . and you can have it in the next second . . . surrender!

Admittedly there is a risk in any course we follow other than this, but every lesson in history tells us that the greater risk lies in appeasement, and this is the specter our well-meaning liberal friends refuse to face . . . that their policy of accommodation is appeasement, and it gives no choice between peace and war, only between fight or surrender. If we continue to accommodate, continue to back and retreat, eventually we have to face the final demand—the ultimatum. And what then? When Nikita Khrushchev has told his people he knows what our answer will be? He has told them that we are retreating under the pressure of the cold war, and someday when the time comes to deliver the ultimatum, our surrender will be voluntary because by that time we will have been weakened from within spiritually, morally, and economically. He believes this because from our side he has heard voices pleading for "peace at any price" or "better Red than dead," or as one commentator put it, he would rather "live on his knees than die on his feet." And therein lies the road to war, because those voices don't speak for the rest of us. You and I know and do not believe that life is so dear and peace so sweet as to be purchased at the price of chains and slavery. If nothing in life is worth dying for, when did this begin—just in the face of this enemy?—or should Moses have told the children of Israel to live in slavery under the pharaohs? Should Christ have refused the cross? Should the patriots at Concord Bridge have thrown down their guns and refused to fire the shot heard round the world? The martyrs of history were not fools, and our honored dead who gave their lives to stop the advance of the Nazis didn't die in vain! Where, then, is the road to peace? Well, it's a simple answer after all.

You and I have the courage to say to our enemies, "There is a price we will not pay." There is a point beyond which they must not advance! This is the meaning in the phrase of Barry Goldwater's "peace through strength!" Winston Churchill said that "the destiny of man is not measured by material computation. When great forces are on the move in the world, we learn we are spirits—not animals." And he said, "There is something going on in time and space, and beyond time and space, which, whether we like it or not, spells duty." You and I have a rendezvous with destiny. We will preserve for our children this, the last best hope of man on earth, or we will sentence them to take the last step into a thousand years of darkness.

"Anxious to obtain a place for themselves"

THE KERNER REPORT
1968

There were race riots in at least 23 American cities during the long, hot summer of 1967. The worst came during a two-week period in July, first in Newark, New Jersey, then in Detroit, Michigan. President Lyndon B. Johnson (1908–1973) ordered the National Advisory Commission on Civil Disorders to "let your search be free . . . As best you can, find the truth and express it in your report." The Kerner Report (which was named for commission chairman Otto Kerner [1908–1976], governor of Illinois) did exactly that: There was an insidious and pervasive white sense of the inferiority of black men; the nation was moving toward two societies, one black, one white—separate and unequal. But the Kerner Report also declared,

> "We have uncovered no startling truths, no unique insights, no simple solutions. The deepening racial division is not inevitable. The movement apart can be reversed. Choice is still possible. Pursuing the present course will involve, ultimately, the destruction of basic democratic values."

The civil disorders of 1967 involved Negroes acting against local symbols of white American society, authority and property in Negro neighborhoods—rather than against white persons.

Of 164 disorders reported during the first nine months of 1967, eight (5 percent) were major in terms of violence and damage; 33 (20 percent) were serious but not major; 123 (75 percent) were minor and undoubtedly would not have received national attention as "riots" had the nation not been sensitized by the more serious outbreaks.

In the 75 disorders studied by a Senate subcommittee, 83 deaths were reported. Eighty-two percent of the deaths and more than half the injuries occurred in Newark and Detroit. About 10 percent of the dead and 38 percent of the injured were public employees, primarily law officers and firemen. The overwhelming majority of the persons killed or injured in all the disorders were Negro civilians.

Initial damage estimates were greatly exaggerated. In Detroit, newspaper damage estimates at first ranged from $200 million to $500 million; the highest recent estimate is $45 million. In Newark, early estimates ranged from $15 to $25 million. A month later damage was estimated at $10.2 million, over 80 percent in inventory losses.

In the 24 disorders in 23 cities that we surveyed:

The final incident before the outbreak of disorder, and the initial violence itself, generally took place in the evening or at night at a place in which it was normal for many people to be on the streets.

Violence usually occurred almost immediately following the occurrence of the final precipitating incident, and then escalated rapidly. With but few exceptions, violence subsided during the day, and flared rapidly again at night. The night-day cycles continued through the early period of the major disorders.

Disorder generally began with rock and bottle throwing and window breaking. Once store windows were broken, looting usually followed.

Disorder did not erupt as a result of a single "triggering" or "precipitating" incident. Instead, it was generated out of an increasingly disturbed social atmosphere, in which typically a series of tension-heightening incidents over a period of weeks or months became linked in the minds of many in the Negro community with a reservoir of underlying grievances. At some point in the mounting tension, a further incident—in itself often routine or trivial—became the breaking point and the tension spilled over into violence.

"Prior" incidents, which increased tensions and ultimately led to violence, were police actions in almost half the cases; police actions were "final" incidents before the outbreak of violence in 12 of the 24 surveyed disorders.

No particular control tactic was successful in every situation. The varied effectiveness of control techniques emphasizes the need for advance training, planning, adequate intelligence systems, and knowledge of the ghetto community.

Negotiations between Negroes—including your militants as well as older Negro leaders—and white officials concerning "terms of peace" occurred during virtually all the disorders surveyed. In many cases, these negotiations involved discussion of underlying grievances as well as the handling of the disorder by control authorities.

The typical rioter was a teenager or young adult, a lifelong resident of the city in which he rioted, a high school dropout; he was, neverthe-

less, somewhat better educated than his nonrioting Negro neighbor, and was usually underemployed or employed in a menial job. He was proud of his race, extremely hostile to both whites and middle-class Negroes and, although informed about politics, highly distrustful of the political system.

A Detroit survey revealed that approximately 11 percent of the total residents of two riot areas admitted participation in the rioting, 20 to 25 percent identified themselves as "bystanders," over 16 percent identified themselves as "counter-rioters" who urged rioters to "cool it," and the remaining 48 to 53 percent said they were at home or elsewhere and did not participate. In a survey of Negro males between the ages of 15 and 35 residing in the disturbance area in Newark, about 45 percent identified themselves as rioters, and about 55 percent as "noninvolved."

Most rioters were young Negro males. Nearly 53 percent of arrestees were between 15 and 24 years of age; nearly 81 percent between 15 and 35.

In Detroit and Newark about 74 percent of the rioters were brought up in the North. In contrast, of the noninvolved, 36 percent in Detroit and 52 percent in Newark were brought up in the North.

What the rioters appeared to be seeking was fuller participation in the social order and the material benefits enjoyed by the majority of American citizens. Rather than rejecting the American system, they were anxious to obtain a place for themselves in it.

Numerous Negro counter-rioters walked the streets urging rioters to "cool it." The typical counter-rioter was better educated and had higher income than either the rioter or the noninvolved.

The proportion of Negroes in local government was substantially smaller than the Negro proportion of population. Only three of the 20 cities studied had more than one Negro legislator; none had ever had a Negro mayor or city manager. In only four cities did Negroes hold other important policy-making positions or serve as heads of municipal departments.

Although almost all cities had some sort of formal grievance mechanism for handling citizen complaints, this typically was regarded by Negroes as ineffective and was generally ignored.

"Computer software company exceeds $1-billion in sales in year"

MICROSOFT TIMELINE
1975–1995

The world's leading computer software provider, Microsoft has had a long-held vision: A computer on every desk and in every home. And a long-held belief: Cyberspace is to America today what the frontier was a century ago—the engine driving an economic democracy. Headquartered in Washington State, Microsoft is an international company with offices in more than 48 countries. Net revenues in 1995 soared to nearly six-billion dollars and net income to one-billion, four hundred and fifty-three million dollars. Microsoft C.E.O. Bill Gates (born 1954), spearhead of the Information Age, is the world's richest person. In late 1998, the U.S. charged Microsoft with repeatedly using its market power for anticompetitive ends.

1/1/75 The MITS (Micro Instrumentation and Telemetry Systems) Altair 8800 appears on the cover of Popular Electronics. The article inspires Paul Allen and Bill Gates to develop a BASIC Interpreter for the Altair.

2/1/75 Bill Gates and Paul Allen complete BASIC and license it to their first customer, MITS of Albuquerque, New Mexico, the manufacturer of the Altair 8800 personal computer. This is the first computer language program written for a personal computer.

3/1/75 Paul Allen joins MITS (Micro Instrumentation and Telemetry Systems) as Director of Software.

7/1/75 Bill Gates' and Paul Allen's BASIC officially ships as version 2.0 in both 4K and 8K editions.

7/22/75 Paul Allen and Bill Gates sign a licensing agreement with MITS regarding the BASIC Interpreter. Microsoft is not yet an official partnership. In fact, the name has not even been chosen.

11/29/75 In a letter to Paul Allen, Bill Gates uses the name "Micro-soft" to refer to their Partnership. This is the earliest known written reference.

2/3/76 Bill Gates is one of the first programmers to raise the issue of software piracy. In his "An Open Letter to Hobbyists," first published in *Computer Notes*, Gates accuses hobbyists of stealing software and thus preventing ". . . good software from being written." He prophetically concludes with the line, ". . . Nothing would please me more than being able to hire ten programmers and deluge the hobby market with good software."

3/27/76 Twenty-year old Bill Gates gives the opening address at the First Annual World Altair Computer Convention (WACC) held in Albuquerque, New Mexico.

7/1/76 Microsoft refines and enhances BASIC

to sell to other customers including DTC, General Electric, NCR, and Citibank.

11/1/76 Paul Allen resigns from MITS to join Microsoft full time.

11/26/76 The tradename "Microsoft" is registered with the Office of the Secretary of the State of New Mexico "to identify computer programs for use in automatic data processing systems; pre-programming processing systems; and data processing services including computer programming services." The application says that the name has been in continuous use since November 11, 1975.

2/3/77 A partnership agreement between Paul Allen and Bill Gates is officially executed.

12/31/78 Microsoft's year end sales exceed $1 million dollars.

1/1/79 Microsoft moves its offices to Bellevue, Washington from Albuquerque, New Mexico.

4/4/79 Microsoft 8080 BASIC is the first microprocessor product to win the ICP Million Dollar Award.

6/18/79 Microsoft announces Microsoft BASIC for the 8086 16-bit microprocessor. This first release of a resident high-level language for use on 16-bit machines marks the beginning of widespread use of these processors.

11/29/79 Microsoft expands its service to the European market.

4/2/80 Microsoft announces the Microsoft Z-80 SoftCard, a microprocessor on a printed circuit board that plugs into the Apple II computer and allows owners to run thousands of programs available for the 8080/Z-80 class of computers with only minor modifications. Microsoft will provide BASIC, FORTRAN, and COBOL languages for the Z-80 SoftCard.

8/25/80 Microsoft announces Microsoft XENIX OS, a portable operating system for 16-bit microprocessors.

6/25/81 Microsoft reorganizes into a privately held corporation with Bill Gates as President and Chairman of the Board, and Paul Allen as Executive Vice President. Microsoft becomes Microsoft, Inc., an incorporated business in the State of Washington.

8/12/81 IBM introduces its Personal Computer, which uses Microsoft's 16-bit operating system, MS-DOS 1.0, plus Microsoft BASIC, COBOL, PASCAL, and other Microsoft products.

6/28/82 Microsoft announces a new corporate logo, new packaging, and a comprehensive set of retail dealer support materials.

7/16/82 The Microsoft Local Area Network (MILAN) is now fully functional, linking all of Microsoft's in-house development computers including a DEC 2060, two PDP-11/70s, a VAX 11/250 and many MC68000 machines running XENIX. This system will simplify e-mail delivery on-site.

5/2/83 Microsoft introduces the Microsoft Mouse, a low-cost, hand-held pointing device for use with the IBM PC, as well as, any MS-DOS-based personal computer.

9/29/83 Microsoft introduces its full-featured word processing program, Microsoft Word for MS-DOS 1.00.

11/10/83 Microsoft unveils Microsoft Windows, an extension of the MS-DOS operating system that provides a graphical operating environment. Windows features a window management capability that allows a user to view unrelated application programs simultaneously. It also provides the capability to transfer data from one application program to another.

1/24/84 Microsoft takes a leading role in developing software for the Apple Macintosh computer.

3/22/84 Microsoft Press introduces its first two titles, Cary Lu's "The Apple Macintosh

Book," and Peter Norton's "Exploring the IBM PCjr Home Computer."

4/1/84 Microsoft announces the creation of a new Hardware and Peripherals Division under the direction of William Roland.

8/14/84 Microsoft announces that IBM has chosen Microsoft XENIX and MS-DOS for its new generation personal computer, the IBM PC AT. The new PC sets a standard in multi-user systems by endorsing XENIX.

8/12/85 Microsoft celebrates its 10th anniversary with sales figures for the fiscal year of 1985 of $140 million. The company has 900 employees and a diverse product line including industry standards like operating systems, languages, business software, hardware, and computer "how-to" books.

9/3/85 Microsoft announces that it has selected the Republic of Ireland as the site of its first production facilty outside the U.S.

11/20/85 Microsoft announces the retail shipment of Microsoft Windows, an operating system, which extends the features of the DOS operating system. Windows provides users with the ability to work with several programs at the same time and easily switch between them without having to quit and restart individual applications.

3/13/86 Microsoft stock goes public at $21.00 per share, rising to $28.00 per share by the end of the first trading day. Initial public offering raises $61 million.

4/2/87 Microsoft announces Microsoft Operating System/2 (MS OS/2) a new personal computer operating system. It has been designed and developed specifically to harness the capabilities of personal computers based upon the Intel 80286 and 80386 microprocessors.

4/2/87 Microsoft announces Microsoft Windows 2.0, offering compatibility with existing Windows applications.

7/30/87 Microsoft announces that it has completed an agreement to acquire Forethought, Inc., an applications software company. Forethought develops and markets PowerPoint, a leading desktop presentation application.

9/8/87 Microsoft announces the shipment of its first CD-ROM application, Microsoft Bookshelf, a collection of 10 of the most popular and useful reference works on a single CD-ROM disk. Bookshelf is the first general purpose application to bring the benefits of CD-ROM technology to personal computer users.

1/13/88 Microsoft and Ashton-Tate announce the Microsoft SQL Server, a relational database server software product for Local Area Networks (LANs).

4/8/88 Microsoft moves into the new Manufacturing and Distribution site in Canyon Park, in Bothell, Washington.

6/5/89 Microsoft announces the formation of the Multimedia Division, dedicated to the development and marketing of multimedia systems software and consumer products. The division will be headed by Min Yee, Vice President. Yee will also continue as Publisher of Microsoft Press. He will report to Jon Shirley, President.

8/1/89 Microsoft announces that The Microsoft Office will soon be available on CD-ROM. This is the first general business software for Macintosh systems to be made available on CD-ROM.

11/13/89 Microsoft and IBM broaden the scope of their development agreement by agreeing to jointly develop a consistent, full range of systems software offerings for the 1990s.

12/27/89 Microsoft announces that Jon Shirley will retire as President and Chief Operating Officer on June 30, 1990.

4/2/90 Microsoft announces the appointment of Michael R. Hallman as Company President and Chief Operating Officer.

4/9/90 Microsoft introduces Russian MS-DOS 4.01. MS-DOS is the first Microsoft product localized for the Soviet market. The Russian version brings the total number of foreign-language versions to 13, including versions in Arabic, Chinese, Hebrew, Japanese (Kanji), and Korean (Hangeul).

5/22/90 Microsoft announces the immediate, worldwide availability of Microsoft Windows 3.0.

7/25/90 Kicking of its 15th anniversary celebration, Microsoft, with revenues of $1.18 billion, becomes the first personal computer software company to exceed $1 billion in sales in a single year.

1/1/91 Microsoft announces the availability of Microsoft Excel for Windows 3.0.

3/11/91 Microsoft announces the Microsoft BallPoint Mouse, designed especially for use with laptop computers.

3/18/91 Microsoft announces that it has purchased a 26 percent share of Dorling Kindersley, Ltd., a London-based book publisher and international packager. As part of the agreement, the Microsoft Multimedia Publishing Group gains the rights to license content from Dorling Kindersley for use in future Microsoft multimedia software titles.

5/20/91 Microsoft announces Microsoft Visual BASIC for Windows at Windows World '91 in Atlanta. It is a graphical application development system for Windows 3.0 that combines visual design tools with a powerful, general-purpose programming language and Windows.

11/14/91 Microsoft announces the Multimedia Edition of Microsoft Works for Windows 2.0. This is the first business productivity application from Microsoft to incorporate multimedia.

4/6/92 Microsoft ships Microsoft Windows 3.1 with over 1,000 enhancements. The new version created unprecedented user demand with over one million advance orders placed worldwide.

6/23/92 President George Bush awards Bill Gates the National Medal of Technology for Technological Achievement, at a White House Rose Garden ceremony. The President recognizes Gates "for his early vision of universal computing at home and in the office; for his technical and business management skills in creating a worldwide technology company; and for his contribution to the development of the personal computing industry."

10/27/92 Microsoft announces the worldwide availability of Microsoft Windows for Workgroups 3.1 which integrates networking and workgroup functionality directly into Windows 3.1.

4/14/93 Microsoft reports that the number of licensed users of Microsoft Windows now totals more than 25 million, making it the most popular graphical operating system in the world.

4/27/93 Microsoft announces the immediate availability of Microsoft Mouse 2.0, with a sophisticated new ergonometric design for maximum comfort. The new Mouse is equally effective for both right- and left-handed users.

6/1/93 Microsoft announces that Judge Vaughn R. Walker of the U.S. District Court of Northern California ruled today in Microsoft's favor in the Apple vs. Microsoft and Hewlett-Packard copyright suit. The judge granted Microsoft's and Hewlett-Packard's motions to dismiss the last remaining copyright infringement claims against Microsoft Windows 2.03 and 3.0, as well as, the HP NewWave.

12/6/93 Microsoft is named the "1993 Most Innovative Company Operating in the U.S." by *Fortune Magazine*, as part of its Fifth Annual Study of America's Best Cities for Business.

12/7/93 Microsoft announces its first software products designed especially for children: Creative Writer and Fine Artist.

4/18/94 Microsoft announces that Microsoft Windows for Workgroups 3.11 has become the world's best selling retail operating system, edging Windows 3.1 into the No. 2 spot. Sales totaled just over 300,000 copies worldwide in January 1994. International success has led the way, with some European markets such as Sweden and the United Kingdom seeing more than 70 percent of their retail volume of Windows move to Windows for Workgroups 3.11.

11/8/94 Bob Herbold joins Microsoft as a new Executive Vice President and the Chief Operating Officer. In this position, he will serve as a member of the Office of the President and report directly to Bill Gates.

1/7/95 Bill Gates announces Microsoft Bob for Windows, at the Consumer Electronics Show in Las Vegas. Bob is designed to provide the essential tools for home computing in eight interconnected programs that help users organize, communicate and play with their computer.

3/22/95 Microsoft and DreamWorks SKG announce that they have signed a joint-venture agreement to form a new software company designed to produce interactive and multimedia entertainment properties. Initially to be called DreamWorks Interactive, the newly formed company was announced jointly by Bill Gates and Patty Stonesifer, and DreamWorks principals Steven Spielberg, Jeffrey Katzenberg, and David Geffin. Microsoft and DreamWorks will each contribute 50 percent of the funding required to build the company. Separately, Microsoft announces that it will be a strategic investor and minority partner in DreamWorks SKG.

5/20/95 Microsoft and Intuit Inc. announce that they have agreed to terminate their planned merger.

6/16/95 The U.S. Court of Appeals reinstates a 1994 antitrust settlement between Microsoft and the Justice Department that was rejected by U.S. District Judge Stanley Sporkin in February 1995. The court's 26-page opinion delivers a harsh rebuke to the judge and grants Microsoft's request to remove him from the case.

"Pray . . . for those . . . struggling in poverty"

ECONOMIC JUSTICE FOR ALL
1986

On the tenth anniversary of the National Conference of Catholic Bishops' economic pastoral message challenging Reagan-era enthusiasm for an unrestrained market economy, the bishops offered suggestions to help parishes and individuals renew their commitment to an economic life subject to moral principles: people have the right to food, shelter, education, health care, and a safe environment.

IDEAS FOR INDIVIDUALS

- Pray for economic justice, for those who are struggling in poverty, for those whose decisions and behavior contribute to economic justice and injustice.
- Start a small group in your parish, or encourage a group to which you already belong (e.g., parish councils, RCIA, Sodality, social concerns committee, etc.), to read, reflect, and respond to the tenth anniversary message.
- Reflect on the economic choices your family makes and consider how they promote or diminish economic justice. Do they contribute to our growing culture of consumption? Do you patronize companies that treat their workers fairly? If you hire people to help with child care, housecleaning, or yard work, are they paid a living wage? As a manager or through your union or trade association, do you promote job creation, decent wages, good benefits, and other family-friendly policies?
- Become active in a political party, legislative network, or community organization and work to make it more responsive to economic justice issues in this country and around the world.

- During elections, evaluate how the positions of candidates advance or undermine human life and human dignity in our communities, nation, and world.
- Volunteer your time to serve the poor through a local social service program.

IDEAS FOR PARISHES

The following ideas and suggestions are intended to assist pastors and parish leadership to share the Church's teaching on economic justice. They follow the strategy and framework outlined in the bishops' statement on parish social ministry, *Communities of Salt and Light,* which encourages parishes to integrate social justice into all aspects of parish life.

GETTING STARTED

Like all parish events and programs, efforts to share the Church's teaching on economic justice during the tenth anniversary of *Economic Justice for All* must start with careful planning by the pastor and the parish leadership. You may want to use a staff meeting and/or a parish council meeting to consider how this theme could be integrated into the life of your parish. Are there events planned during the coming year where the homilist or speaker could address economic justice? You may want to consider the following suggestions for various ministries.

PRAYER AND WORSHIP

- As you plan for eucharistic liturgies, consider how the themes of economic justice and concern for the poor are reflected in the readings. Appropriately integrate these themes in the introductory comments, the general intercessions, the homily, the music, and the announcements.
- Make a commitment that parish activities—staff meetings, parish council meetings, other committee meetings—will be started with a prayer for the poor and for a recommitment to economic justice.

PREACHING AND EDUCATION

- Homilists can connect readings about how we treat "widows, orphans, and aliens" and "the least among us" to the decisions we make today. Point out that the work parishioners do every day in their businesses and communities provides many opportunities to promote economic justice. Do we use our voices and votes to protect the poor and to promote policies that broaden economic opportunities for all families? How do employers and supervisors treat their workers—especially their low-wage workers? Do we invest in and patronize companies that see people as a priority?
- Sponsor an adult education program, speaker, or discussion group that focuses on issues of economic justice.
- Encourage younger religious education students to promote economic justice by volun-

teering at a soup kitchen or other charitable organization to help those who are poor.

FAMILY, WORK, CITIZENSHIP

- Offer opportunities for families to participate in programs that help them make economic choices that promote justice.
- Sponsor a "business breakfast" or vocation reflection groups (i.e., groups organized by occupation—lawyers, doctors, construction workers, etc.—that meet to discuss how their faith shapes their work). Encourage these groups to explore how members promote economic justice in their work.
- Parishes can be models of economic justice that can inspire parishioners in their work lives.
- Conduct a nonpartisan voter registration drive and encourage parishioners to use the opportunities of our democracy to work for greater respect for human life and economic, tax, and social welfare policies that promote economic opportunity, provide decent jobs at decent wages, and protect the poor and vulnerable.
- Offer nonpartisan voter education, using your bulletin, education programs and other opportunities to share with parishioners how Catholic social teaching applies to the major economic issues of our day.

ADVOCATING FOR JUSTICE

- Organize a parish legislative network composed of people willing to call or write legislators regarding economic justice and other issues of human life and dignity.
- Contact your diocesan social action office, pro-life office, and state Catholic Conference to learn about economic justice and other issues under consideration by your state legislature or Congress.

- Identify other local advocacy groups and join in coalition with their efforts to work for justice.

ORGANIZING FOR JUSTICE

- Join or provide support for a local community organization that works for economic justice.
- Organize an exchange program among parishioners that encourages more modest consumption habits.

BUILDING SOLIDARITY BEYOND PARISH AND NATIONAL BOUNDARIES

- Invite parishioners and others who have recently visited or moved from another part of the world to speak to your religious education classes or other parish groups.
- Consider establishing a "sister parish" relationship with a parish in another country. This relationship can include "exchange" visits, written communication, as well as financial support.
- Organize parish participation in one of the international programs offered by Catholic Relief Services, the National Council of Catholic Women, the Catholic Near East Welfare Association (CNEWA), or the Holy Childhood Association.
- Activate your parish legislative network to work on international justice issues, encouraging legislators to focus our foreign policy on promoting economic development throughout the world.

Excerpts from "A Decade After Economic Justice for All," copyright 1995 by the United States Catholic Conference, Inc., Washington, D.C., used with permission.

"Copyright protects expression"

ASSOCIATION OF AMERICAN PUBLISHERS ON THE
NII COPYRIGHT PROTECTION ACT OF 1995
1996

The Association of American Publishers (AAP) represents publishers of print and electronic books and journals as well as other information, education, and entertainment materials. Before the U.S. House Subcommittee on Courts and Intellectual Property, the AAP supported National Information Infrastructure (NII) legislation for the purposes of making modest but necessary updating refinements in the copyright act to ensure protection of intellectual property on the NII. The group recommended that some portions of the bill be revised in order to achieve objectives and avoid potential unintended results. Disagreements derailed legislative movement.

The book, journal and new media publishers in the United States, represented by the Association of American Publishers ("AAP"), welcome the opportunity to address H.R. 2441, the NII Copyright Protection Act.

As Chairman Moorhead said in introducing this legislation: "With . . . evolutions in technology, the copyright law must change as well to protect one of our Nation's most valuable resources and exports, the products of our authors."

The members of this Association play a significant role in creating those resources and exports. Ensuring protection of copyright on the National Information Infrastructure (NII) is vital to our industry. It also is critical to our country if the U.S. is to maintain its preeminence as the world's leading creator and disseminator of ideas, information, entertainment and education. We need effective copyright laws if this crucial segment of our economy is to continue to thrive and grow, creating new jobs and generating new revenue.

INTRODUCTION

AAP's members are a diverse lot. We are large, multi-faceted corporations whose names are household words; we are also small literary presses, non-profit university presses, regional publishers, professional and scholarly societies. . . . we comprise some 300 companies publishing hardcover and paperback books in every field, including general fiction and non-fiction, poetry, children's books, textbooks, Bibles, reference works, scientific, medical, technical, professional and scholarly books and journals, materials for classroom instruction and testing. Members of our Association produce computer software and electronic products and services, such as CD-ROMs and online databases.

The publication of hardcover and paperback books in printed form and their distribution to the nation's bookstores will continue for a long time. But the computer age and, more recently, the explosive growth of the Internet and online services are creating a new electronic marketplace in which the product, the service and the mode of delivery are assuming new forms. AAP members are actively providing education, information and entertainment to consumers in new forms. Increasingly common today, portions of, supplements to and even entire copies of traditional print works are available in new media. In fact, some works are published by our members exclusively in digital format.

Moreover, these new products can be delivered to consumers both through a variety of commercial outlets and directly to their schools, offices and homes. They can be sent over copper wires, cables and through the air for capture by computers, terminals and television sets and most likely combination set/desk top devices. These transformations are occurring at a breathtaking pace; AAP members are leading participants in this exciting new marketplace.

But participation will be inhibited if legal protection for their creations is not available. Without an effective legal foundation for the protection of intellectual property, the most commercially valuable content will be withheld and the potential to create new first rate multimedia and digital content will simply not develop, let alone flourish. Copyright has always been the foundation of our vibrant intellectual property industries and the underlying tenet of the bill before you continues to support that critical premise.

The constitutional goal of promoting "the Progress of Science and useful Arts" remains a modern goal and the legal system of copyright protection remains the right way to achieve the goal. Indeed, the AAP concurs with the general view that, as it stands even without revision, copyright law currently covers expression that is created and disseminated in digital form over electronic networks. It is a testament to the Members of Congress who developed and passed copyright legislation in prior years that the statute works and has the flexibility to apply to forms of expression and distribution never contemplated at the time of passage.

However, by enacting modest and carefully-drawn amendments to the Copyright Act, Congress can provide greater certainty which stimulates investment and job creation and which will ensure continued U.S. leadership in the creation of intellectual property. Moreover, with changes that accommodate new technology, with the hallmark flexibility of the Act and without shifting the balance of interests and needs between owners and users of intellectual property, this Congress can set the path for the rest of the world to follow.

Finally, by way of introduction, it must be noted that filling gaps in the Copyright Act to meet new technology will not interfere with the robust free speech and exchange of ideas on which this country is built. Copyright protects expression, and only that expression over which the author has chosen to exercise some control. Those who want the world to make any and all use of their works remain unencumbered; they are as free to publish on the Internet as they are free to publish on paper. Nothing you are considering today changes that.

STATUTORY PROPOSALS

1. TRANSMISSION

In the interest of clarification, the AAP supports the inclusion of the word *transmission* in all of the proposals contained in Section 2 of the bill. These four small changes in the Copyright Act confirm application of the law, as it stands today, to expression that is published, distributed and imported electronically, rather than in hard copy. These proposals neither expand nor shrink rights nor do they create conflicts or confusion among licensors, licensees and consumers of any particular rights in a given work. . . .

The AAP believes that the analysis of whether or not a work has been published under the Copyright Act will remain subject to the same analysis as it is today, whether that work is delivered in hard copy or transmitted over wires. The touchstone is whether copies of the work are distributed to the public. Otherwise all online communication, even private e-mail, would be deemed published for mandatory deposit and other Copyright Act purposes. This is not, and should not be, the law.

Often AAP members, or more likely their authors, are using transmission to convey or share comments on a work-in-progress. Most likely, segments of scientific and professional publishing will use the NII increasingly to engage in collaborative research and writing and/or to seek peer review and commentary before the work is considered finished or, indeed, *published*. In short, transmission of a work does not and should not *ipso facto* constitute publication. We read the changes proposed by the bill to achieve the necessary result—to make clear that although publication can be achieved by transmission, not all transmissions will necessarily constitute publication. . . .

2. NEW SECTION 1201—CIRCUMVENTION OF COPYRIGHT PROTECTION SYSTEMS

It is the ease and speed of perfect reproduction, broad dissemination and undisclosed manipulation of works on the NII that make it imperative that the users obey, and understand they must obey, the rules of the road.

Too often there has been an unfortunate culture of adulation, rather than one of abhorrence,

when "hackers" break into systems and files thought to be secure; the law must support copyright proprietors who use technological tools to protect their works. This is an area where the law must be supplemented in order to accomplish its overall purpose.

New Section 1201 of the Copyright Act would prohibit, for the first time, the importation, manufacture or distribution of any product or device or performance of any service, designed to circumvent any technological copyright protection scheme. The importance of including such a provision in the law cannot be overstated. . . .

We fully support the position of the Register of Copyrights in her testimony to the effect that it seems inconsistent to provide criminal penalties for violation of the integrity of copyright management information but not for the circumvention of copyright protection systems. We agree with the Copyright Office that the greater potential threat to the economic interests of the owners comes from the interference with copyright protection systems.

It is wrong that the current laws do not suffice to hold the intentional activities of flagrant infringers to the test of criminal liability because they seek a perverse glory, rather than financial gain, from their hacking.

3. NEW SECTION 1202—INTEGRITY OF COPYRIGHT MANAGEMENT INFORMATION

AAP supports the intent of the proposed new Section 1202 which would establish a criminal offense for knowingly providing false copyright management information, for knowingly removing or altering copyright management information affixed by the copyright owner, or for distributing or importing works with removed or altered copyright management information.

As valuable and necessary as these provisions are in the electronic world, AAP members are concerned over their potential misapplication. Questions have been raised about whether they could lead to disputes or even criminal charges in connection with age-old business practices such as "ghost" writing, "as told to's" and other forms of collaborative and pseudonymous works. We also wonder how this proposal would affect legitimate disputes over the ownership of, or right to exercise one or more, but not all, of the exclusive rights in a work. These concerns are as real to producers and distributors of films, records, software and, particularly, multimedia works as they are to publishers. To address these questions and concerns, we recommend that proposed Sections 1202(a) and/or (c) be amended to clarify that the offense relates to parties intending to remove or alter pertinent ownership and licensing information, rather than the current catch-all language that may ensnare unwitting copyright proprietors in its net. . . .

AAP members are deeply engaged in developing their own copyright management systems—using new technology and exploring new ways of doing business. Unless there is useful legal protection for the variety of management and protection systems being developed to grant site licenses, provide controlled yet flexible access, to convey transmission or downloading permissions, in short to allow uses of all sorts, the multiplicity of opportunities to offer broad access to different markets will not happen. There are exciting opportunities for new ways of doing business and providing access that the interests and needs of the marketplace—both commercial and not-for-profit—will support, if indeed not mandate. But without the ability to maintain control which is a major, if not the, underlying tenet of our copyright law, the technology will become and remain a deterrent rather than a facilitator for creators, their publishers and, of course, for the public as well.

4. REVISED SECTION 108—LIBRARY EXEMPTIONS

. . . publishers recognize that the current practice of librarians is to make three facsimile copies, rather than one, for purposes of preservation and replacement. We understand that one of those is literally stored in "iron mountain" as a "doomsday" copy, that one is placed in the archive of the library collection as a master copy and used as needed and that only one copy is circulated. Although this practice does technically violate Section 108 of the law, the publishing community has accepted *de facto* the practice since its benefits to society clearly outweigh the potential harm so long as only one copy is allowed in circulation. Hence, we have no objection to the concept of three copies rather than one, provided only one is in use.

The concern arises with inclusion, for the first time, of the right to create *digital* copies for purposes of replacement and preservation. Recognizing the importance of and need for preservation and cognizant of the wonders of the new technology, publishers do not want to interfere with the best way to ensure preservation. We are prepared to support amending Section 108 to allow creation by libraries of digital versions of works for preservation, provided it does not allow the libraries to treat such digital version as part of its collection for the whole range of library activities. It is imperative that any digital copy so created, by definition without authority of the copyright proprietor and hence without the copyright protection scheme the proprietor might well employ, not be used for circulation. Once a work is launched into the

NII without such protection, its further reproduction and transmission potentially is without limit. Distribution is and must remain the exclusive right of the proprietor. . . .

As the capability of the hardware and software improves and/or the market shifts to new operating systems, computer languages or other variables, proprietors must continue to have the exclusive right to choose whether and when to provide their materials in the new versions. For years we have seen software developers serve different requirements and users by creating different versions of the same programs for DOS and MAC and now Windows95 machines. Likewise, the publisher of an electronic encyclopedia on CD-ROM updates, upgrades, and adapts to new technology on a regular basis. A library should not be allowed to create a new digital version from an older generation of digital work in order to use it on the newest equipment, all in the guise of preservation. If a library is concerned about the ability to access an old version of a product that cannot be used on the newest machinery, the solution is simple; keep the old machinery or get permission from the copyright proprietor to create the derivative work. This is not a question of preservation. . . .

The publishers fully endorse broad access to their materials; they want the public to read them. But, they cannot sanction a situation where they create the work, sell a copy and see the library become the publisher to the rest of the world.

With the advent of digital technology and networks, it would be a catastrophic mistake to permit the existing formulation to extend, even inadvertently, to digital versions created by a library. This is an issue being studied in many circles, including the Conference on Fair Use, and we believe it is premature to stick any toe into these waters until an assessment of the real-life impact of any changes is made. . . .

FAIR USE

Contrary to some press reports and commentary that has circulated, nothing in the legislative proposals before you changes the fair use provisions of Section 107 of the Copyright Act, and/or the decades of common law decisions from which it was developed. Moreover, our members want to be sure that the Association convey in our testimony the importance that we attach, both as publishers and on behalf of our authors, to the fair use defense contained in the copyright law. Indeed, publishers have previously come to Congress to ensure that fair use would apply to all works, including unpublished works. It is not our intention, nor our desire, to see the diminution of fair use principles in the digital world. The law, common and statutory, has accommodated changes in technology and in businesses and has worked reasonably well for all concerned. The publishing community believes there is no reason that we, our authors, our readers and others cannot continue to rely on the factual analysis process required by Section 107 for all types of works, including digital ones.

This does not mean that the application of fair use in the digital world is static or even capable of rigid definition. There is a digital difference and its impact is yet to be fully understood. . . . We have learned that comfortable words like "browsing" and "resource sharing" no longer mean the same thing to all who use them. In short, we have learned that in many of these areas, it is premature to write new rules.

ONLINE SERVICE PROVIDER LIABILITY

Another area where we believe Congress has been wise to defer any amendment to the Copyright Act is rules for assessing liability for those who provide online services and/or Internet access. We appreciate concerns about the risk of imposing strict liability for infringement of materials of which the provider was not and arguably could not have been aware. . . .

MANUFACTURER RESPONSIBILITY FOR ANALOG WORKS

AAP members have published, still do publish and probably always will publish on paper—in notebooks, textbooks, trade books and journals. While silicon chips may be as ground breaking as the Gutenberg printing press, we do not believe they will lead to the end of the printed page to supply education, entertainment, enlightenment and information through words, charts, graphs, photographs and other illustrations. Uncontrolled photocopying and scanning might.

In efforts to control the rapid spread of massive illegal photocopying, AAP members have successfully litigated against unlicensed copy shops. The Association and its members work with universities and bookstores, librarians and professors to spread knowledge of the law and good copyright practice to college campuses and corporate libraries. Our members have been active in the creation, development and growth of the Copyright Clearance Center to facilitate lawful photocopying.

Society has seen the disappearance of the sheet music business because of illegal photocopying. And while the book, journal and other publishers have survived the world of traditional photocopying, it is not altogether clear how well they will survive unregulated deployment of the new copying equipment. Although not wanting to be melodramatic, publishers do fear for their future, and the well-being of their authors, when looking at a world with low-cost, easy-to-use ubiquitous scanners, copiers, and binders.

Yesterday's slow one-copy-at-a-time process, where you had to stand by and feed in page-by-page, and which produced continually inferior copies is, indeed, yesterday's machine. In contrast, today's equipment allows the user to drop a thick pile of printed pages into a hopper whence they can be scanned, stored and digitized for future retrieval and searching and editing; they can be transmitted, downloaded, printed and bound, all without a human being standing by, without any diminution in quality, with unlimited quantities distributed via networks to any and every place on the globe, all without any authorization by, or even knowledge of, or compensation to the proprietor. Publishers believe that before it is too late and before this admittedly exciting technology swallows copyright protection altogether, the manufacturers of this equipment must be asked to work on solving the problems that their increasingly advanced machines are causing.

While holding that the use of VCRs to make time-shifting copies of broadcast TV programs for individual home viewing was a fair use, the Supreme Court plurality also noted that the VCR could be used for a range of lawful purposes, thereby suggesting its manufacturer should not be liable even for an infringing use. We do not believe manufacturers should hide behind this dictum. Simply because a machine can be used without infringing copyright should not lead policy makers to close their eyes to the purpose, design and broad anticipated uses of such devices to reproduce copyrighted works, or to the responsibility of the manufacturers of these devices to participate in the search for solutions to control copyright infringement.

We are distressed to see print and television advertising by major companies such as Xerox,

AT&T, HP, Ricoh, Canon and others inviting, presumably with lack rather than malice of forethought, the indiscriminate digitization, modification and transmission of materials, without regard to whether they are inducing and promoting copyright infringements.

We understand that yet another device is far along in development by manufacturers—the page-turner copier. Such a machine would do all of the scanning and storing and faxing and duplicating offered by the current devices. The added element of page-turning capability quite simply would allow the equipment to break what is today's most practical barrier against widespread copying of printed materials—namely, the binding.

. . . We think that awareness and increasing acceptance of the principle of manufacturer responsibility readily leads to acceptance of a relationship between the traditional principles of "vicarious liability" looking to the ability to control, and the logic and ethic of our belief that if the manufacturers of the new replicating and transmitting technologies have or can develop infringement-controlling technologies, they well ought deploy and pursue them as a matter of responsible business behavior, policy and law. . . .

CONCLUSION

. . . U.S. copyright industries are a vibrant sector of American business, culture, education and life and we appreciate the attention shown by Congress to making it possible for the creative process to flourish. We thank you for your understanding that protection of intellectual property is the surest way to nurture yet more creativity and to spread its benefits—material, as well as intellectual and spiritual—to all in society. We are eager to assist in the ongoing process in any way that we can and hope you will call on us as the process proceeds.

"I have done it the hard way"

SENATOR DOLE TAKES UP THE GAUNTLET
1996

Senator Robert Dole (born 1923), of Kansas, was President Gerald R. Ford's Vice Presidential running mate—and hatchet man—in the national election of 1976 (Jimmy Carter, 297 electoral votes to Ford's 240). Twenty years later, Mr. Dole abruptly ended his 35-year Congressional career and Senate majority leadership in hopes of recharging his campaign as the Republican Party's Presidential candidate in the 1996 election. The very emblem of a thoroughly unpopular Congress, "Beltway Bob" sought to expunge his image as the ultimate Washington insider and deal-maker. In his Senate resignation speech, crafted by the magic-realist novelist Mark Helprin (born 1947)—"staging lousy, writing terrific, delivery improving and moving" was pundit William Safire's verdict—Senator Dole declared that it was his obligation "to the Senate, and to the people of America . . . to leave behind all trappings of power, all comfort and all security" (but not his $107,000 annual pension) and to seek the Presidency as a "private citizen, a Kansan, an American, just a man," with "nowhere to go but the White House or home." Dole lost big to President Bill Clinton (born 1946), who in February, 1999, decisively survived a Senate trial on charges of perjury and obstruction of justice. Dole's spouse, Liddy, dubbed "Nurse Ratchet," said she would run for the Republican Presidential nomination in 2000. She was C.E.O. of the American Red Cross.

• • • One of the qualities of American politics that distinguishes us from other nations is that we judge our politicians as much by the manner in which they leave office as by the vigor with which they pursue it. You do not lay claim to the office you hold, it lays claim to you. Your obligation is to bring to it the gifts you can of labor and honesty and then to depart with grace. And my time to leave this office has come, and I will seek the Presidency with nothing to fall back on but the judgment of the people and nowhere to go but the White House or home.

Six times, six times, I've run for Republican leader of the United States Senate, and six times my colleagues, giving me their trust, have elected me, and I'm proud of that.

So my campaign for the President is not merely about obtaining office. It's about fundamental things, consequential things, things that are real. My campaign is about telling the truth, it's about doing what is right, it's about electing a President who's not attracted to the glories of the office but rather to its difficulties. It's about electing a President who, once he takes office, will keep his perspective and remain by his deepest nature and inclination one of the people. . . . I announce that I will forgo the privileges not only of the office of the majority leader but of the United States Senate itself, . . . And I will then stand before you without office or authority a private citizen, a Kansan, an American, just a man. But I will be the same man I was when I walked into the room, the same man I was yesterday and the day before, and a long time ago when I arose from my hospital bed and was permitted by the grace of God to walk again in the world. And I trust in the hard way, for little has come to me except in the hard way, which is good because we have a hard task ahead of us.

We are gaining but still behind in the polls. The press does not lean our way. And many Beltway pundits confidently dismiss my chances of victory. I do not find this disheartening, and I do not find it discouraging, for this is where I touch the ground, and it is in touching the ground in moments of difficulty that I've always found my strength. I have been there before, I have done it the hard way, and I will do it the hard way once again. . . .

Our campaign will leave Washington behind to look to America. As summer nears, I will seek the bright light and open spaces of this beautiful country and will ask for the wise counsel of its people, from the seacoasts of Maine and California to the old railroad towns in the Midwest to the verdant South, from the mountains of Colorado to the suburbs of Chicago, and in places in between known mainly to you who call them home.

I have absolute confidence in the victory that to some may seem unattainable. This is because I have seen victory and I have seen defeat, and I know when one is set to give way to the other. And to concentrate upon the campaign, giving all and risking all, I must leave Congress that I have loved, and which I have been honored to serve—many of my friends here today. And some might find it surprising, given the view that Congress has been my life, but that is not so. With all due respect to Congress, America has been my life. . . .

And the very least a Presidential candidate owes America is his full attention—everything he can give, everything he has—and that is what America shall receive from me. . . .

HOME OF THE BRAVE

O n April 15, 1865, Lincoln was assassinated. An almost limitless grief swept across the nation. Even those Northerners who had opposed or vilified him joined their countrymen in suddenly transforming their fallen chief into something of a saint. Crowds gathered in the cold wet rain outside the poor lodging house across from Ford's Theater, where the President lay unconscious and dying. One newspaper reported, "The tolling of bells announced to the lamenting people that he had ceased to breathe. His great and loving heart was still." Offices and stores closed, black crepe replaced the red, white, and blue bunting that had just been put up to celebrate Appomattox Courthouse and Northern victory. Six days later, Lincoln's funeral train departed on the mournful journey from the White House to Springfield, Illinois, with thousands gathered along the route as it passed. "Now he belongs to the ages," Secretary of War Edwin Stanton lamented.

Much the same popular reaction greeted news of President Kennedy's assassination. Millions of Americans again internalized the loss, making it a personal one. Watching the tragic end on television, they heard the drum beat as the honor guard accompanied the coffin. They saw Walter Cronkite, America's beloved anchorman, cry, and they collectively shared his grief at a loss that seemed as personal and immediate as which had occurred 98 years earlier. They had been drawn to Kennedy's youth, charm, intelligence, image of good looks, manly toughness, great promise of fulfillment. He had conveyed, almost in spite of himself, a sense of caring for those in need, a sense of commitment to those troubled by poverty or victimized by racism. Le Figaro accurately took the national pulse: "What remains as the loss...is a certain feeling of possibilities, of an élan, and—why not say it?—of an expression of beauty. These are not political qualities, but surely they are enduring legendary and mythological qualities." Now Kennedy, too, belonged to the ages; now he was a legend—the gallant, young, strangely star-crossed prince prematurely taken from his people. Thereafter, with shock and disbelief, they pondered the bizarre events that followed—the single assassin who was himself murdered. The detailed drawings of the gun, endless specifics about the trajectory of the bullets, the murderer and his past, and the penchant for sensational speculation that Lee Harvey Oswald could not alone have killed the President could not be put to rest by the report of the Warren Commission's investigation of Kennedy's assassination.

The nation was equally fascinated by another President, but for different reasons. Two especially notable events brought the public spotlight to bear upon Richard Nixon. The first occurred when, nominated as the Vice-Presidential running mate for Dwight Eisenhower in 1952, Nixon was questioned about his highly irregular personal political fund by which he paid debts accumulated during the years when he was a Congressman and Senator. Defending this slush fund on television, he invoked his debts, his wife's clothes, and his daughters' pet dog, and convinced critics that the charges had no foundation. Eisenhower thought it "the corniest thing" he had ever heard, but, given the positive popular reaction, could not drop Nixon from the ticket. The second event, growing out of the Watergate affair, which resulted in three articles of impeachment brought against Nixon by the House Judiciary Committee, was less easily disposed of. It involved a variety of charges—break-ins, cover-ups, illegal wire taps, perjury, and obstruction of justice. His own tapes spelled his doom. He resigned the Presidency on August 8, 1974, admitting only "bad judgment."

The political passions that Nixon loosed on the nation, specifically the conviction that communists had infiltrated the government, labor unions, schools, the media, and the field of entertainment, that they were part of an international conspiracy to subvert the republic, were embodied in the House Un-American Activities Committee. An investigatory committee established by Congress in 1938 and which later numbered Nixon as its ablest member, HUAC relentlessly searched out subversive activities. Focusing on Hollywood, the hearings established a characteristic ritual of favorable and unfavorable witnesses. The former, in this instance Hollywood directors, producers, and matinee idols, were adored by the public and committee members alike. Conversely, unfavorable witnesses usually "took the Fifth"—refusing to testify on the grounds that they might incriminate themselves or others whom the Committee asked about—or spent a year in jail for contempt of Congress. Often ex-New Dealers, these witnesses frequently provided a forum for the committee to attack Roosevelt and his Administration as guilty of treason and betrayal. Many felt they could not afford the luxury of refusing to testify, for the result, if not jail, meant the blacklist; that is, being named as a communist or communist sympathizer and effectively being denied work in their profession. HUAC and Senator Joseph McCarthy were one of a piece, both consumed by fantasies of subversion. A Senator in search of an issue that might appeal to Wisconsin's voters, McCarthy came up with the charge of communists in the State Department, and later he found them in other governmental agencies. Accusations led to further accusations and finally, in the summer of 1954, he recklessly attacked the United States Army for "coddling" security risks and communists. He did so on television before a large national audience, and so visibly bullied high officials and so obviously failed to sustain the charges of betrayal from within that a precipitate fall from grace followed.

More characteristically Republican than McCarthy, were affirmations to self-reliance and individualism, and tributes to those "making it" without governmental assistance. One could elevate himself, or herself, out of poverty by frugality, sobriety, hard work. The idea of success was a traditional, stubbornly held, consensually endorsed theme coming from mid-century America. Self-reliance, self-improvement, the self-made man who adhered to the Protestant work ethic and slowly climbed the ladder of success first appeared in Jackson's day. The surge of westward expansion, the emergence of a factory system and a wage-earning workforce, the growing impersonality of employer-employee relations—nothing seemingly altered popular beliefs in one's moral duties and in the pursuit of individual success. By the 1890s, Populists, Single Taxers, Greenbackers, socialists, both utopian and scientific, were challenging these assumptions, as were religious leaders, especially social gospelers, who rejected the gospel of competition and would instead apply the teachings of Jesus to labor-management relations. Nonetheless, the self-made man retained its hold on the national mind, and businessmen continued to look for men of character, that is, men who held ethical convictions, were self-reliant, undertook chores without shirking, and did not seek the easy road. Notwithstanding changes in the old order and a transformed social and economic landscape over a century, this view became an ideological fixture for Republicans and retained its vitality for many Americans.

"Fallen cold and dead"

"O CAPTAIN! MY CAPTAIN!"

1865

Walt Whitman (1819–1892) whined that he was made sick by having to read his most popular, and most conventional, poem so many times to meet audience requests and expectations. "It's 'My Captain!'" he complained, "always 'My Captain!' My God! When will they listen to me whole and good?" The dirge, which had "certain emotional immediate reasons for being," honored assassinated President Abraham Lincoln (1809–1865). The restlessly innovative Whitman revised the poem many times.

O Captain! my Captain! our fearful trip is done,
The ship has weather'd every rack, the prize we sought is won,
The port is near, the bells I hear, the people all exulting,

While follow eyes the steady keel, the vessel grim and daring;
But O heart! heart! heart!
O the bleeding drops of red,
Where on the deck my Captain lies,
Fallen cold and dead.

O Captain! my Captain! rise up and hear the bells;
Rise up—for you the flag is flung—for you the bugle trills,
For you bouquets and ribbon'd wreaths—for you the shores a-crowding,
For you they call, the swaying mass, their eager faces turning;
Here Captain! dear father!
The arm beneath your head!
It is some dream that on the deck,
You've fallen cold and dead.

My Captain does not answer, his lips are pale and still,
My father does not feel my arm, he has no pulse nor will,
The ship is anchor'd safe and sound, its voyage closed and done,
From fearful trip the victor ship comes in with object won:
Exult O shores, and ring O bells!
But I with mournful tread,
Walk the deck my Captain lies,
Fallen cold and dead.

"The world cries out for such..."

A Message to Garcia

1899

It is said that American companies have distributed to their employees more than 40,000,000 copies of Elbert G. Hubbard's brief essay on the importance of perseverance, "A Message to Garcia," which was inspired by an actual incident in the Spanish-American War (1898–1899). First Lieutenant Andrew S. Rowan (1857–1943), disguised as an English sportsman and using the Spanish he had learned while serving as a military attache in Chile, carried a diplomatic message from President William McKinley (1843–1901) to Cuban rebel leader Calixto Garcia y Iniguez, and carried back information on the state of the insurgent army. For his exploit, Lt. Rowan was decorated with the Distinguished Service Cross. Hubbard (1856–1915) sought to inspire loyalty and improve morale among workers: The world needs people who, against great odds, can carry a message to Garcia.

IN ALL THIS CUBAN BUSINESS there is one man stands out on the horizon of my memory like Mars at perihelion. When war broke out between Spain and the United States, it was very necessary to communicate quickly with the leader of the insurgents. Garcia was somewhere in the mountain fastnesses of Cuba—no one knew where. No mail nor telegraph message could reach him. The President must secure his cooperation, and quickly.

What to do!

Someone said to the President, "There's a fellow by the name of Rowan will find Garcia for you, if anybody can."

Rowan was sent for and given a letter to be delivered to Garcia. How "the fellow by the name of Rowan" took the letter, sealed it up in an oilskin pouch, strapped it over his heart, in four days landed by night off the coast of Cuba from an open boat, disappeared into the jungle, and in three weeks came out on the other side of the island, having traversed a hostile country on foot and delivered his letter to Garcia, are things I have no special desire now to tell in detail.

The point I wish to make is this: McKinley gave Rowan a letter to be delivered to Garcia; Rowan took the letter and did not ask, "Where is he at?" By the Eternal! there is a man whose form should be cast in deathless bronze and the statue placed in every college of the land. It is not book learning young men need, nor instruction about this and that, but a stiffening of the vertebrae which will cause them to be loyal to a trust, to act promptly, concentrate their energies; do the thing—"Carry a message to Garcia!"

General Garcia is dead now, but there are other Garcias.

No man who has endeavored to carry out an enterprise where many hands were needed, but has been well-nigh appalled at times by the imbecility of the average man—the inability or unwillingness to concentrate on a thing and do it. Slipshod assistance, foolish inattention, dowdy indifference, and half-hearted work seem the rule; and no man succeeds, unless by hook or crook, or threat, he forces or bribes other men to assist him; or, mayhap, God in His goodness performs a miracle and sends him an Angel of Light for an assistant.

You, reader, put this matter to a test: You are sitting now in your office—six clerks are within call. Summon any one and make this request: "Please look in the encyclopedia and make a brief memorandum for me concerning the life of Correggio."

Will the clerk quietly say, "Yes, sir," and go do the task?

He will look at you out of a fishy eye and ask one or more of the following questions:

Who was he?

Which encyclopedia?

Where is the encyclopedia?

Was I hired for that?

Don't you mean Bismarck?

What's the matter with Charlie doing it?

Is he dead?

Is there any hurry?

Shan't I bring you the book and let you look it up yourself?

What do you want to know for?

And I will lay you ten to one that after you have answered the questions, and explained how to find the information, and why you want it, the clerk will go off and get one of the other clerks to help him try to find Garcia—and then come back and tell you there is no such man. Of course I may lose my bet, but according to the law of average, I will not.

Now if you are wise you will not bother to explain to your "assistant" that Correggio is indexed under the C's, not in the K's, but you will smile sweetly and say, "Never mind," and go look it up yourself.

And this incapacity for independent action, this moral stupidity, this infirmity of the will, this unwillingness to cheerfully catch hold and lift are the things that put pure socialism so far into the future. If men will not act for themselves, what will they do when the benefit of their effort is for all? A first mate with knotted club seems necessary; and the dread of getting "the bounce" Saturday night holds many a worker to his place.

Advertise for a stenographer, and nine out of ten who apply can neither spell nor punctuate—and do not think it necessary to.

Can such a one write a letter to Garcia?

"You see that bookkeeper," said the foreman to me in a large factory.

"Yes, what about him?"

"Well, he's a fine accountant, but if I'd send him uptown on an errand, he might accomplish the errand all right, and, on the other hand, might stop at four saloons on the way, and when he got to Main Street would forget what he had been sent for."

Can such a man be entrusted to carry a message to Garcia?

We have recently been hearing much maudlin sympathy expressed for the "downtrodden denizen of the sweatshop" and the "homeless wanderer searching for honest employment," and with it all often go many hard words for the men in power.

Nothing is said about the employer who grows old before his time in a vain attempt to get frowsy ne'er-do-wells to do intelligent work; and his long, patient striving with "help" that does nothing but loaf when his back is turned. In every store and factory there is a constant weeding-out process going on. The employer is constantly sending away "help" that have shown their incapacity to further the interests of the business, and others are being taken on. No matter how good times are, this sorting continues, only if times are hard and work is scarce, the sorting is done finer—but out and forever out, the incompetent and unworthy go. It is the survival of the fittest. Self-interest prompts every employer to keep the best—those who can carry a message to Garcia.

I know one man of really brilliant parts who has not the ability to manage a business of his own, and yet who is absolutely worthless to anyone else because he carries with him constantly the insane suspicion that his employer is oppressing or intending to oppress him. He cannot give orders, and he will not receive them. Should a message be given him to take to Garcia, his answer would probably be, "Take it yourself, and be damned!"

Tonight this man walks the streets looking for work, the wind whistling through his threadbare coat. No one who knows him dare employ him, for he is a regular firebrand of discontent. He is impervious to reason, and the only thing that can impress him is the toe of a thick-soled No. 9 boot.

Of course, I know that one so morally deformed is no less to be pitied than a physical cripple; but in our pitying, let us drop a tear, too, for the men who are striving to carry on a great enterprise, whose working hours are not limited by the whistle, and whose hair is fast turning white through the struggle to hold in line dowdy indifference, slipshod imbecility, and the heartless ingratitude which, but for their enterprise, would be both hungry and homeless.

Have I put the matter too strongly? Possibly I have; but when all the world has gone a-slumming I wish to speak a word of sympathy for the man who succeeds—the man who, against great odds, has directed the efforts of others, and, having succeeded, finds there's nothing in it; nothing but bare board and clothes.

I have carried a dinner pail and worked for day's wages, and I have also been an employer of labor, and I know there is something to be said on both sides. There is no excellence, per se, in poverty; rages are no recommendation; and all employers are not rapacious and high-handed, any more than all poor men are virtuous.

My heart goes out to the man who does his work when the "boss" is away as well as when he is at home. And the man who, when given a letter for Garcia, quietly takes the missive, without asking any idiotic questions, and with no lurking intention of chucking it into the nearest sewer, or of doing aught else but deliver it, never gets "laid off," nor has to go on a strike for higher wages. Civilization is one long, anxious search for just such individuals. Anything such a man asks shall be granted; his kind is so rare that no employer can afford to let him go. He is wanted in every city, town, and village—in every office, shop, store, and factory. The world cries out for such; he is needed, and needed badly—the man who can carry a message to Garcia.

"A fair and just system"

THE PEACETIME DRAFT

1940

America's first peacetime military draft, described as "the greatest lottery in U.S. history," occurred nearly 14 months before the Japanese attack on U.S. facilities at the territory of Hawaii's Pearl Harbor and official U.S. entrance into the Second World War (1939–1945). The "winning" number, #158, plucked by a blindfolded Secretary of War from a 10-gallon glass globe of lottery slips, was announced by President Franklin D. Roosevelt (1882–1945). Every draft board with at least 158 eligible men had a #158; there were 6,175 "winners." The second number was #192, then on to #105, #679, #3508, #2441. The drawing went on for 17 hours, until all of the nearly 9,000 numbers in the bowl had been selected, establishing the order of the call-up. (Hitler had already conquered Europe and was pounding England from the sky.) The draft legislation provided for the common defense by increasing the personnel of the armed forces of the U.S. and providing for its training.

Be it enacted by the Senate and House of Representatives of the United States of America in Congress assembled, That (a) the Congress hereby declares that it is imperative to increase and train the personnel of the armed forces of the United States.

(b) The Congress further declares that in a free society the obligations and privileges of military training and service should be shared generally in accordance with a fair and just system of selective compulsory military training and service.

(c) The Congress further declares, in accordance with our traditional military policy as expressed in the National Defense Act of 1916, as amended, that it is essential that the strength and organization of the National Guard, as an integral part of the first-line defenses of this Nation, be at all times maintained and assured. To this end, it is the intent of the Congress that whenever the Congress shall determine that troops are

needed for the national security in excess of those of the Regular Army and those in active training and service under section 3 (b), the National Guard of the United States, or such part thereof as may be necessary, shall be ordered to active Federal service and continued therein so long as such necessity exists.

SEC. 2. Except as otherwise provided in this Act, it shall be the duty of every male citizen of the United States, and of every male alien residing in the United States, who, on the day or days fixed for the first or any subsequent registration, is between the ages of twenty-one and thirty-six, to present himself for and submit to registration at such time or times and place or places, and in such manner and in such age group or groups, as shall be determined by rules and regulations prescribed hereunder.

SEC. 3. (a) Except as otherwise provided in this Act, every male citizen of the United States, and every male alien residing in the United States who has declared his intention to become such a citizen, between the ages of twenty-one and thirty-six at the time fixed for his registration, shall be liable for training and service in the land or naval forces of the United States. The President is authorized from time to time, whether or not a state of war exists, to select and induct into the land and naval forces of the United States for training and service, in the manner provided in this Act, such number of men as in his judgment is required for such forces in the national interest: *Provided,* That within the limits of the quota determined under section 4 (b) for the subdivision in which he resides, any person, regardless of race or color, between the ages of eighteen and thirty-six, shall be afforded an opportunity to volunteer for induction into the land or naval forces of the United States for the training and service prescribed in subsection (b), but no person who so volunteers shall be inducted for such training and service so long as he is deferred after classification: *Provided further,* That no man shall be inducted for training and service under this Act unless and until he is acceptable to the land or naval forces for such training and service and his physical and mental fitness for such training and service has been satisfactorily determined: *Provided further,* That no men shall be inducted for such training and service until adequate provision shall have been made for such shelter, sanitary facilities, water supplies, heating and lighting arrangements, medical care, and hospital accommodations, for such men, as may be determined by the Secretary of War or the Secretary of the Navy, as the case may be, to be essential to public and personal health: *Provided further,* That except in time of war there shall not be in active training or service in the land forces of the United States at any one time under subsection (b) more than nine hundred thousand men inducted under the provisions of this Act.

The men inducted into the land or naval forces for training and service under this Act shall be assigned to camps or units of such forces.

(b) Each man inducted under the provisions of subsection (a) shall serve for a training and service period of twelve consecutive months, unless sooner discharged, except that whenever the Congress has declared that the national interest is imperiled, such twelve-month period may be extended by the President to such time as may be necessary in the interests of national defense.

(c) Each such man, after the completion of his period of training and service under subsection (b), shall be transferred to a reserve component of the land or naval forces of the United States; and until he attains the age of forty-five, or until the expiration of a period of ten years after such transfer, or until he is discharged from such reserve component, whichever occurs first, he shall be deemed to be a member of such reserve component and shall be subject to such additional training and service as may now or hereafter be prescribed by law: *Provided,* That any man who completes at least twelve months' training and service in the land forces under subsection (b), and who thereafter serves satisfactorily in the Regular Army or in the active National Guard for a period of at least two years, shall, in time of peace, be relieved from any liability to serve in any reserve component of the land or Naval forces of the United States and from further liability for the training and service under subsection (b), but nothing in this subsection shall be construed to prevent any such man, while in a reserve component of such forces, from being ordered or called to active duty in such forces.

(e) Persons inducted into the land forces of the United States under this Act shall not be employed beyond the limits of the Western Hemisphere except in the Territories and possessions of the United States, including the Philippine Islands. . . .

Sec. 4. (a) The selection of men for training and service under section 3 (other than those who are voluntarily inducted pursuant to this Act) shall be made in an impartial manner, under such rules and regulations as the President may prescribe, from the men who are liable for such training and service and who at the time of selection are registered and classified but not deferred or exempted: *Provided,* That in the selection and training of men under this Act, and in the interpretation and execution of the provisions of this Act, there shall be no discrimination against any person on account of race or color.

(b) Quotas of men to be inducted for training and service under this Act shall be determined for each State, Territory, and the District of Columbia, and for subdivisions thereof, on the basis of the actual number of men in the several States, Territories, and the District of Columbia, and the subdivisions thereof, who are liable for such training and service but who are not deferred after classification, except that credits shall be given in fixing such quotas for residents of such subdivisions who are in the land and naval forces of the United States on the date fixed for determing such quotas. After such quotas are fixed, credits shall be given in filling such quotas for residents of such subdivisions who subsequently become members of such forces. Until the actual numbers necessary for determining the quotas are known, the quotas may be based on estimates, and subsequent adjustments therein shall be made when such actual numbers are known. All computations under this subsection shall be made in accordance with such rules and regulations as the President may prescribe. . . .

(c) (1) The Vice President of the United States, the Governors of the several States and Territories, members of the legislative bodies of the United States and of the several States and Territories, judges of the courts of record of the United States and of the several States and Territories and the District of Columbia, shall, while holding such offices, be deferred from training and service under this Act in the land and naval forces of the United States.

(2) The President is authorized, under such rules and regulations as he may prescribe, to provide for the deferment from training and service under this Act in the land and naval forces of the United States, of any person holding an office (other than an office described in paragraph (1) of this subsection) under the United States or any State, Territory, or the District of Columbia, whose continued service in such office is found in accordance with section 10 (a) (2) to be necessary to the maintenance of the public health, safety, or interest.

(d) Regular or duly ordained ministers of religion, and students who are preparing for the ministry in theological or divinity schools recognized as such for more than one year prior to the date of enactment of this Act, shall be exempt from training and service (but not from registration) under this Act.

(e) The President is authorized, under such rules and regulations as he may prescribe, to provide for the deferment from training and service under this Act in the land and naval forces of the United States of those men whose employment in industry, agriculture, or other occupations or employment, or whose activity in other endeavors, is found in accordance with section 10 (a) (2) to be necessary to the maintenance of the national health, safety, or interest. The President is also authorized, under such rules and regulations as he may prescribe, to provide for the deferment from training and service under this Act in the land and naval forces of the United States (1) of those men in a status with respect to persons dependent upon them for support which renders their deferment advisable, and (2) of those men found to be physically, mentally, or morally deficient or defective. No deferment from such training and service shall be made in the case of any individual except upon the basis of the status of such individual, and no such deferment shall be made of individuals by occupational groups or of groups of individuals in any plant or institution.

(f) Any person who, during the year 1940, entered upon attendance for the academic year 1940–1941—

(1) at any college or university which grants a degree in arts or science, to pursue a course of instruction satisfactory completion of which is prescribed by such college or university as a prerequisite to either of such degrees; or

(2) at any university described in paragraph (1), to pursue a course of instruction to the pursuit of which a degree in arts or science is prescribed by such university as a prerequisite; and who, while pursuing such course of instruction at such college or university, is selected for training and service under this Act prior to the end of such academic year, or prior to July 1, 1941, whichever occurs first, shall, upon his request, be deferred from induction into the land or naval forces for such training and service until the end of such academic year, but in no event later than July 1, 1941.

(g) Nothing contained in this Act shall be construed to require any person to be subject to combatant training and service in the land or naval forces of the United States who, by reason of religious training and belief, is conscientiously opposed to participation in war in any form. . . .

SEC. 6. The President shall have authority to induct into the land and naval forces of the United States under this Act no greater number of men than the Congress shall hereafter make specific appropriation for from time to time.

SEC. 7. No bounty shall be paid to induce any person to enlist in or be inducted into the land or naval forces of the United States: *Provided,* That the clothing or enlistment allowances authorized by law shall not be regarded as bounties within the meaning of this section. No person liable for service in such forces shall be permitted or allowed to furnish a substitute for such service; no substitute as such shall be received, enlisted, enrolled, or inducted into the land or naval forces of the United States; and no person liable for training and service in such forces under section 3 shall be permitted to escape such training and service or be discharged therefrom prior to the expiration of his period of such training and service by the payment of money or any other valuable thing whatsoever as consideration for his release from such training and service or liability therefor. . . .

(h) Any person inducted into the land or naval forces for training and service under this Act shall, during the period of such training and service, be permitted to vote in person or by absentee ballot in any general, special, or primary election occurring in the State of which he is a resident, whether he is within or outside of such State at the time of such election, if under the laws of such State he is entitled so to vote in such election; but nothing in this subsection shall be construed to require granting to any such person a leave of absence for longer than one day in order to permit him to vote in person in any such election.

(i) It is the expressed policy of the Congress that whenever a vacancy is caused in the employment rolls of any business or industry by reason of induction into the service of the United States of an employee pursuant to the provisions of this Act such vacancy shall not be filled by any person who is a member of the Communist Party or the German-American Bund.

SEC. 9. The President is empowered, through the head of the War Department or the Navy Department of the Government, in addition to the present authorized methods of purchase or procurement, to place an order with any individual, firm, association, company, corporation, or organized manufacturing, industry for such product or material as may be required, and which is of the nature and kind usually produced or capable of being produced by such individual, firm, company, association, corporation, or organized manufacturing industry.

Compliance with all such orders for products or material shall be obligatory on any individual, firm, association, company, corporation, or organized manufacturing industry or the responsible head or heads thereof, and shall take precedence over all other orders and contracts theretofore placed with such individual, firm, company, association, corporation, or organized manufacturing industry, or the responsible head or heads thereof owning or operating any plant equipped for the manufacture of arms or ammunition or parts of ammunition, or any necessary supplies or equipment for the Army or Navy, and any individual, firm, association, company, corporation, or organized manufacturing industry or the responsible head or heads thereof owning or operating any plant equipped for the manufacture of arms or ammunition or parts of ammunition, or any necessary supplies or equipment for the Army or Navy, and any individual, firm, association, company, corporation, or organized manufacturing industry or the responsible head or heads thereof owning or operating any manufacturing plant, which, in the opinion of the Secretary of War or the Secretary of the Navy shall be capable of being readily transformed into a plant for the manufacture of arms or ammunition, or parts thereof, or other necessary supplies or equipment, who shall refuse to give to the United States such preference in the matter of the execution of orders, or who shall refuse to manufacture the kind, quantity, or quality of arms or ammunition, or the parts thereof, or any necessary supplies or equipment, as ordered by the Secretary of War or the Secretary of the Navy, or who shall refuse to furnish such arms, ammunition, or parts of ammunition, or other supplies or equipment, at a reasonable price as determined by the Secretary of War or the Secretary of the Navy, as the case may be, then, and in either such case, the President, through the head of the War or Navy Departments of the Government, in addition to the present authorized methods of purchase or procurement, is hereby authorized to take immediate possession of any such plant or plants, and through the appropriate branch, bureau, or department of the Army or Navy to manufacture therein such product or material as may be required, and any individual, firm, company, association, or corporation, or organized manufacturing industry, or the responsible head or heads thereof, failing to comply with the provisions of this section shall be deemed guilty of a felony, and upon conviction shall be punished by imprisonment for not more than three years and a fine not exceeding $50,000.

The first and second provisos in section 8 (b) of the Act entitled "An Act to expedite national defense, and for other purposes", approved June 28, 1940 (Public Act Numbered 671, Seventy-sixth Congress), are hereby repealed.

SEC. 10. (a) The President is authorized—

(1) to prescribe the necessary rules and regulations to carry out the provisions of this Act;

(2) to create and establish a Selective Service System, and shall provide for the classification of registrants and of persons who volunteer for induction under this Act on the basis of availability for training and service, and shall establish within the Selective Service System civilian local

boards and such other civilian agencies, including appeal boards and agencies of appeal, as may be necessary to carry out the provisions of this Act. There shall be created one or more local boards in each county or political subdivision corresponding thereto of each State, Territory, and the District of Columbia.

Sec. 12. (a) The monthly base pay of enlisted men of the Army and the Marine Corps shall be as follows: Enlisted men of the first grade, $126; enlisted men of the second grade, $84; enlisted men of the third grade, $72; enlisted men of the fourth grade, $60; enlisted men of the fifth grade, $54; enlisted men of the sixth grade, $36; enlisted men of the seventh grade, $30; except that the monthly base pay of enlisted men with less than four months' service during their first enlistment period and of enlisted men of the seventh grade whose inefficiency or other unfitness has been determined under regulations pre-scribed by the Secretary of War, and the Secretary of the Navy, respectively, shall be $21. The pay for specialists' ratings, which shall be in addition to monthly base pay, shall be as follows: First class, $30; second class, $25; third class, $20; fourth class, $15; fifth class, $6; sixth class, $3. Enlisted men of the Army and the Marine Corps shall receive, as a permanent addition to their pay, an increase of 10 per centum of their base pay and pay for specialists' ratings upon completion of the first four years of service, and an additional increase of 5 per centum of such base pay and pay for specialists' ratings for each four years of service thereafter, but the total of such increases shall not exceed 25 per centum. Enlisted men of the Navy shall be entitled to receive at least the same pay and allowances as are provided for enlisted men in similar grades in the Army and Marine Corps. . . .

Sec. 17. This Act shall take effect immediately.

"My side of the case"

RICHARD M. NIXON'S CHECKERS SPEECH
1952

After California Senator Richard M. Nixon (1913–1994) was nominated as Dwight D. Eisenhower's Vice Presidential running mate on the national Republican ticket in 1952, he had to defend himself against charges of having a "secret slush fund." In a televised speech, delivered without an official text, only with notes, Senator Nixon tugged emotions by referring to his wife's simple cloth coat to demonstrate that he was poor and by admitting that his family, in fact, had accepted a present: A cocker spaniel named Checkers. "The kids, like all kids, loved the dog, and . . . we are going to keep it." Senator Nixon's "side of the case" became known as the "Checkers Speech," a reference that now means any emotionally-charged and sympathy-seeking political address.

My fellow Americans: I come before you tonight as a candidate for the Vice Presidency and as a man whose honesty and integrity has been questioned.

Now, the usual political thing to do when charges are made against you is to either ignore them or to deny them without giving details. I believe we have had enough of that in the United States, particularly with the present Administration in Washington, D.C.

To me the office of the Vice Presidency of the United States is a great office, and I feel that the people have got to have confidence in the integrity of the men who run for that office and who might attain them.

I have a theory, too, that the best and only answer to a smear or to an honest misunderstanding of the facts is to tell the truth. And that is why I am here tonight. I want to tell you my side of the case.

I am sure that you have read the charge, and you have heard it, that I, Senator Nixon, took $18,000 from a group of my supporters.

Now, was that wrong? And let me say that it was wrong. I am saying it, incidentally, that it was wrong, not just illegal, because it isn't a question of whether it was legal or illegal, that isn't enough. The question is, was it morally wrong. I say that it was morally wrong—if any of that $18,000 went to Senator Nixon, for my personal use. I say that it was morally wrong if it was secretly given and secretly handled.

And I say that it was morally wrong if any of the contributors *got* special favors for the contributions that they made.

And now to answer those questions let me say this: not 1 cent of the $18,000 or any other money of that type ever went to me for my personal use. Every penny of it was used to pay for political expenses that I did not think should be charged to the taxpayers of the United States.

It was not a secret fund. As a matter of fact, when I was on "Meet the Press"—some of you may have seen it, last Sunday—Peter Edson came up to me, after the program, and he said, "Dick, what about this fund we hear about?" and

I said, "Well, there is no secret about it. Go out and see Dana Smith, who was the administrator of the fund," and I gave him his address. And I said "you will find that the purpose of the fund simply was to defray political expenses that I did not feel should be charged to the Government."

And, third, let me point out, and I want to make this particularly clear, that no contributor to this fund, no contributor to any of my campaigns, has ever received any consideration that he would not have received as an ordinary constituent.

I just don't believe in that, and I can say that never, while I have been in the Senate of the United States, as far as the people that contributed to this fund are concerned, have I made a telephone call for them to an agency, nor have I gone down to an agency in their behalf.

And the records will show that, the records which are in the hands of the Administration.

Well, then, some of you will say, and rightly, "Well, what did you use the fund for, Senator? Why did you have to have it?"

Let me tell you in just a word how a Senate office operates. First of all, the Senator gets $15,000 a year in salary. He gets enough money to pay for one trip a year, in salary. He gets enough money to pay for one trip a year, a round trip, that is, for himself and his family, between his home and Washington, D.C., and then he gets an allowance to handle the people that work in his office to handle his mail.

And the allowance for my State of California is enough to hire 13 people. And let me say, incidentally, that this allowance is not paid to the Senator.

It is paid directly to the individuals that the Senator puts on his pay roll, but all of these people and all of these allowances are for strictly official business; business, for example, when a constituent writes in and wants you to go down to the Veterans' Administration and get some information about his GI policy—items of that type, for example. But there are other expenses which are not covered by the Government. And I think I can best discuss those expenses by asking you some questions.

Do you think that when I or any other Senator makes a political speech, has it printed, should charge the printing of that speech and the mailing of that speech to the taxpayers?

Do you think, for example, when I or any other Senator makes a trip to his home State to make a purely political speech that the cost of that trip should be charged to the taxpayers?

Do you think when a Senator makes political broadcasts or political television broadcasts, radio or television, that the expense of those broadcasts should be charged to the taxpayers?

I know what your answer is; It is the same answer that audiences give me whenever I discuss this particular problem.

The answer is no. The taxpayers should not be required to finance items which are not official business but which are primarily political business.

Well, then the question arises, you say, "Well, how do you pay for these and how can you do it legally?" And there are several ways that it can be done, incidentally, and it is done legally in the United States Senate and in the Congress.

The first way is to be a rich man. I don't happen to be a rich man. So I couldn't use that.

Another way that is used is to put your wife on the pay roll. Let me say, incidentally, that my opponent, my opposite number for the Vice Presidency of the Democratic ticket, does have his wife on his pay roll and has had her on his pay roll for the past 10 years. Now just let me say this: That is his business, and I am not critical of him for doing that. You will have to pass judgment on that particular point, but I have never done that for this reason:

I have found that there are so many deserving stenographers and secretaries in Washington that needed the work that I just didn't feel it was right to put my wife on the pay roll—My wife sitting over here.

She is a wonderful stenographer. She used to teach stenography and she used to teach short-hand in high school. That was when I met her. And I can tell you folks that she has worked many hours nights and many hours on Saturdays and Sundays in my office, and she had done a fine job, and I am proud to say tonight that in the six years I have been in the House and in the Senate of the United States Pat Nixon has never been on the Government pay roll.

What are other ways that these finances can be taken care of? Some who are lawyers, and I happen to be a lawyer, continue to practice law, but I haven't been able to do that.

I am so far away from California and I have been so busy with my senatorial work that I have not engaged in any legal practice and, also, as far as law practice is concerned, it seemed to me that the relationship between an attorney and the client was so personal that you couldn't possibly represent a man as an attorney and then have an unbiased view when he presented his case to you in the event that he had one before the Government.

And so I felt that the best way to handle these necessary political expenses of getting my message to the American people and the speeches I made—the speeches that I had printed for the most part concerned this one message of exposing this Administration, the Communism in it, the corruption in it—the only way that I could do that was to accept the aid which people in my home State of California, who contributed to my campaign and who continued to make these contributions after I was elected, were glad to make.

And let me say I am proud of the fact that not one of them has ever asked me for a special favor. I am proud of the fact that not one of them has ever asked me to vote on a bill other than my own conscience would dictate. And I am proud of the fact that the taxpayers by subterfuge or otherwise have never paid one dime for expenses which I thought were political and should not be charged to the taxpayers.

Let me say, incidentally, that some of you may say, "Well, that is all right, Senator, that is your explanation, but have you got any proof?" And I would like to tell you this evening that just an hour ago we received an independent audit of this entire fund. I suggested to Governor Sherman Adams, who is the chief of staff of the Eisenhower campaign, that an independent audit and legal report be obtained, and I have that audit in my hand.

It is an audit made by Price Waterhouse & Co. firm, and the legal opinion by Gibson, Dunn & Crutcher, lawyers in Los Angeles, the biggest law firm, and incidentally one of the best ones in Los Angeles.

I am proud to report to you tonight that this audit and this legal opinion is being forwarded to General Eisenhower, and I would like to read to you the opinion that was prepared by Gibson, Dunn & Crutcher, based on all the pertinent laws and statutes, together with the audit report prepared by the certified public accountants.

It is our conclusion that Senator Nixon did not obtain any financial gain from the collection and disbursement of the funds by Dana Smith; that Senator Nixon did not violate any Federal or State law by reason of the operation of the fund; and that neither the portion of the fund paid by Dana Smith directly to third persons, nor the portion paid to Senator Nixon, to reimburse him for office expenses, constituted income in a sense which was either reportable or taxable as income under income tax laws.

(signed)
GIBSON, DUNN AND CRUTCHER,
BY ELMO H. CONLEY

That is not Nixon speaking, but that is an independent audit which was requested because I want the American people to know all the facts and I am not afraid of having independent people go in and check the facts, and that is exactly what they did.

But then I realized that there are still some who may say, and rightly so—and let me say that I recognize that some will continue to smear, regardless of what the truth may be—but that there has been understandably, some honest misunderstanding on this matter, and there are some that will say, "Well, maybe you were able, Senator, to fake this thing. How can we believe what you say—after all, is there a possibility that maybe you got some sums in cash? Is there a possibility that you might have feathered your own nest?" And so now what I am going to do—and, incidentally, this is unprecedented in the history of the American politics—I am going at this time to give to this television and radio audience a complete financial history, everything I have earned, everything I have spent, everything I own, and I want you to know the facts.

I will have to start early. I was born in 1913. Our family was one of modest circumstances, and most of my early life was spent in a store, out in East Whittier. It was a grocery store, one of those family enterprises.

The only reason we were able to make it go was because my Mother and Dad had five boys, and we all worked in the store. I worked my way through college and, to a great extent, through law school. And then, in 1940, probably the best thing that ever happened to me happened. I married Pat, who is sitting over here.

We had a rather difficult time, after we were married, like so many of the young couples who might be listening to us. I practiced law. She continued to teach school.

Then, in 1942, I went into the service. Let me say that my service record was not a particularly unusual one. I went to the South Pacific. I guess I'm entitled to a couple of battle stars. I got a couple of letters of commendation. But I was just there when the bombs were falling. And then I returned. I returned to the United States, and in 1946, I ran for the Congress. When we came out of the war, Pat and I—Pat during the war had worked as a stenographer, and in a bank, and as an economist for a Government agency—and, when we came out, the total of our savings, from both my law practice, her teaching, and all the time that I was in the war, the total for that entire period was just a little less than $10,000—every cent of that, incidentally, was in Government bonds—well, that's where we start, when I go into politics.

Now, whatever I earned since I went into politics—well, here it is. I jotted it down. Let me read the notes.

First of all I have had my salary as a Congressman and as a Senator.

Second, I have received a total in this past six years of $1,600 from estates which were in my law firm at the time that I severed my connection with it. And, incidentally, as I said before, I have not engaged in any legal practice, and have not accepted any fees from business that came into the firm after I went into politics.

I have made an average of approximately $1,500 a year, from nonpolitical speaking engagements and lectures.

And then, fortunately, we have inherited a little money. Pat sold her interest in her father's estate for $3,000, and I inherited $1,500 from my grandfather. We lived rather modestly.

For four years we lived in an apartment in Parkfairfax, Alexandria, Va. The rent was $80 a month. And we saved for the time that we could buy a house. Now, that was what we took in.

What did we do with this money? What do we have today to show for it? This will surprise you, because it is so little, I suppose, as standards generally go of people in public life.

First of all, we've got a house in Washington, which cost $41,000 and on which we owe $20,000. We have a house in Whittier, Calif., which cost $13,000, and on which we owe $10,000. My folks are living there at the present time.

I have just $4,000 in life insurance, plus my GI policy, which I have never been able to convert, and which will run out in two years.

I have no life insurance whatever on Pat. I have no life insurance on our two youngsters, Patricia and Julie.

I own a 1950 Oldsmobile car. We have our furniture. We have no stocks and bonds of any type. We have no interest of any kind, direct or indirect, in any business. Now, that is what we have. What do we owe?

Well, in addition to the mortgage, the $20,000 mortgage on the house in Washington, a $10,000 one on the house in Whittier, I owe $4,500 to the Riggs Bank, in Washington, D. C., with interest at 4 per cent.

I owe $3,500 to my parents, and the interest on that loan, which I pay regularly, because it is a part of the savings they made through the years they were working so hard—I pay regularly 4 per cent interest. And then I have a $500 loan, which I have on my life insurance.

Well, that's about it. That's what we have.

And that's what we owe. It isn't very much. But Pat and I have the satisfaction that every dime that we have got is honestly ours.

I should say this, that Pat doesn't have a mink coat. But she does have a respectable Republican cloth coat, and I always tell her that she would look good in anything.

One other thing I probably should tell you, because if I don't they will probably be saying this about me, too. We did get something, a gift, after the election.

A man down in Texas heard Pat on the radio mention the fact that our two youngsters would like to have a dog, and, believe it or not, the day before we left on this campaign trip we got a message from Union Station in Baltimore, saying they had a package for us. We went down to get it. You know what it was?

It was a little cocker spaniel dog, in a crate that he had sent all the way from Texas, black and white, spotted, and our little girl, Tricia, the six-year-old, named it Checkers.

And, you know, the kids, like all kids, loved the dog, and I just want to say this, right now, that regardless of what they say about it, we are going to keep it.

It isn't easy to come before a nation-wide audience and bare your life, as I have done. But I want to say some things before I conclude, that I think most of you will agree on.

Mr. Mitchell, the Chairman of the Democratic National Committee, made the statement that if a man couldn't afford to be in the United States Senate, he shouldn't run for the Senate. And I just want to make my position clear.

I don't agree with Mr. Mitchell when he says that only a rich man should serve his Government, in the United States Senate or in the Congress. I don't believe that represents the thinking of the Democratic Party, and I know it doesn't represent the thinking of the Republican Party.

I believe that it's fine that a man like Governor Stevenson, who inherited a fortune from his father, can run for President. But I also feel that it is essential in this country of ours that a man of modest means can also run for President, because, you know—remember Abraham Lincoln—you remember what he said—"God must have loved the common people, he made so many of them."

And now I'm going to suggest some courses of conduct.

First of all, you have read in the papers about other funds, now. Mr. Stevenson apparently had a couple. One of them in which a group of business people paid and helped to supplement the salaries of State employees. Here is where the money went directly into their pockets, and I think that what Mr. Stevenson should do should be to come before the American people, as I have, give the names of the people that contributed to that fund, give the names of the people who put this money into their pockets, at the same time that they were receiving money from their State government and see what favors, if any, they gave out for that.

I don't condemn Mr. Stevenson for what he did, but until the facts are in there is a doubt that would be raised. And as far as Mr. Sparkman is concerned, I would suggest the same thing. He's had his wife on the pay roll. I don't condemn him for that, but I think that he should come before the American people and indicate what outside sources of income he has had. I would suggest that under the circumstances both Mr. Sparkman and Mr. Stevenson should come before the American people, as I have, and make a complete financial statement as to their financial history, and if they don't it will be an admission that they have something to hide.

And I think you will agree with me—because, folks, remember, a man that's to be President of the United States, a man that is to be Vice President of the United States, must have the confidence of all the people. And that's why I'm doing what I'm doing, and that is why I suggest that Mr. Stevenson and Mr. Sparkman, if they are under attack, that should be what they are doing.

Now, let me say this: I know that this is not the last of the smears. In spite of my explanation tonight, other smears will be made. Others have been made in the past. And the purpose of the smears, I know, is this, to silence me, to make me let up.

Well, they just don't know who they are dealing with. I'm going to tell you this: I remember, in the dark days of the Hiss trial, some of the same columnists, some of the same radio commentators who are attacking me now and misrepresenting my position, were violently opposing me at the time I was after Alger Hiss. But I continued to fight, because I knew I was right, and I can say to this great television and radio audience that I have no apologies to the American people for my part in putting Alger Hiss where he is today. And as far as this is concerned, I intend to continue to fight.

Why do I feel so deeply? Why do I feel that in spite of the smears, the misunderstanding, the necessity for a man to come up here and bare his soul, as I have—why is it necessary for me to continue this fight? And I want to tell you why.

Because, you see, I love my country. And I think my country is in danger. And I think the only man that can save America at this time is the man that's running for President, on my ticket, Dwight Eisenhower.

You say, why do I think it is in danger? And I say, look at the record. Seven years of the Truman-Acheson Administration, and what's happened? Six hundred million people lost to the Communists.

And a war in Korea in which we have lost

117,000 American casualties, and I say to all of you that a policy that results in a loss of 600,000,000 people to the Communists and a war which costs us 117,000 American casualties isn't good enough for America, and I say that those in the State Department that made the mistakes which caused that war and which resulted in those losses should be kicked out of the State Department just as fast as we can get them out of there.

And let me say that I know Mr. Stevenson won't do that, because he defends the Truman policy, and I know that Dwight Eisenhower will do that, and that he will give America the leadership that it needs.

Take the problem of corruption. You have read about the mess in Washington. Mr. Stevenson can't clean it up because he was picked by the man, Truman under whose Administration the mess was made.

You wouldn't trust the man who made the mess to clean it up. That is Truman. And, by the same token you can't trust the man who was picked by the man who made the mess to clean it up, and that is Stevenson. And so I say, Eisenhower, who owes nothing to Truman, nothing to the big-city bosses—he is the man who can clean up the mess in Washington.

Take Communism. I say that as far as that subject is concerned the danger is great to America. In the Hiss case they got the secrets which enabled them to break the American secret State Department code.

They got secrets in the atomic-bomb case which enabled them to get the secret of the atomic bomb five years before they would have gotten it by their own devices. And I say that any man who called the Alger Hiss case a red herring isn't fit to be President of the United States.

I say that a man who, like Mr. Stevenson, has pooh-poohed and ridiculed the Communist threat in the United States—he said that they are phantoms among ourselves—he has accused us, that have attempted to expose the Communists, of looking for Communists in the Bureau of Fisheries and Wildlife. I say that a man who says that isn't qualified to be President of the United States.

And I say that the only man who can lead us into this fight to rid the Government of both those who are Communists and those who have corrupted this Government is Eisenhower, because General Eisenhower, you can be sure, recognizes the problem, and knows how to handle it.

Let me say this, finally. This evening I want to read to you just briefly excerpts from a letter that I received, a letter which after all this is over no one can take away from us. It reads as follows:

Dear Senator Nixon:

Since I am only 19 years of age, I can't vote in this presidential election, but believe me if I could you and General Eisenhower would certainly get my vote. My husband is in the Fleet Marines in Korea. He is in the front lines. And we have a two-month-old son he has never seen. And I feel confident that with great Americans like you and General Eisenhower in the White House, lonely Americans like myself will be united with their loved ones now in Korea. I only pray to God that you won't be too late. Enclosed is a small check to help you in your campaign. Living on $85 a month it is all I can afford at present, but let me know what else I can do.

Folks, it is a check for $10, and it is one that I shall never cash. And just let me say this: We hear a lot about prosperity these days, but I say why can't we have prosperity built on peace, rather than prosperity built on war? Why can't we have prosperity and an honest Government in Washington, D. C., at the same time?

Believe me, we can. And Eisenhower is the man that can lead the crusade to bring us that kind of prosperity.

And, now, finally, I know that you wonder whether or not I am going to stay on the Republican ticket or resign. Let me say this: I don't believe that I ought to quit, because I am not a quitter. And, incidentally, Pat is not a quitter. After all, her name was Patricia Ryan and she was born on St. Patrick's Day, and you know the Irish never quit.

But the decision, my friends, is not mine. I would do nothing that would harm the possibilities of Dwight Eisenhower to become President of the United States. And for that reason I am submitting to the Republican National Committee tonight through this television broadcast the decision which it is theirs to make. Let them decide whether my position on the ticket will help or hurt. And I am going to ask you to help them decide. Wire and write the Republican National Committee whether you think I should stay on or whether I should get off. And whatever their decision is, I will abide by it.

But just let me say this last word. Regardless of what happens, I am going to continue this fight. I am going to campaign up and down America until we drive the crooks and the Communists and those that defend them out of Washington, and remember, folks, Eisenhower is a great man. Folks, he is a great man, and a vote for Eisenhower is a vote for what is good for America.

"Liberals must speak out"

A STATEMENT BY ELIA KAZAN
1952

In his history of the House Committee on Un-American Activities' investigation of subversive activities in the entertainment industry during the Red Scare era, *Naming Names,* Victor S. Navasky (born 1932) noted that legendary film and stage director Elia Kazan's status and testimony, an apologetic curriculum vitae, and rumors of a big-money deal contingent on his naming names established Kazan (born 1909) as the ultimate betrayer, even as he was hailed on the political right as patriot and applauded by centrist liberals for doing the difficult but right thing. Kazan published an advertisement in *The New York Times* explaining his position and urging others to do what he had done: Inform on colleagues and friends. Because Kazan had informed on eight friends who were fellow members of the Communist Party in the 1930s, film groups denied him awards for lifetime achievement, until the Academy of Motion Picture Arts and Sciences in 1999 gave the ailing 89-year-old director of such classics as "On the Waterfront" and "A Streetcar Named Desire" an honorary Oscar for lifetime achievement.

In the past weeks intolerable rumors about my political position have been circulating in New York and Hollywood. I want to make my stand clear:

I believe that Communist activities confront the people of this country with an unprecedented and exceptionally tough problem. That is, how to protect ourselves from a dangerous and alien conspiracy and still keep the free, open, healthy way of life that gives us self-respect.

I believe that the American people can solve this problem wisely only if they have the facts about Communism. All the facts.

Now, I believe that any American who is in possession of such facts has the obligation to make them known, either to the public or to the appropriate Government agency.

Whatever hysteria exists—and there is some, particularly in Hollywood—is inflamed by mystery, suspicion and secrecy. Hard and exact facts will cool it.

The facts I have are sixteen years out of date, but they supply a small piece of background to the graver picture of Communism today.

I have placed these facts before the House Committee on Un-American Activities without reserve and I now place them before the public and before my co-workers in motion pictures and in the theatre.

Seventeen and a half years ago I was a twenty-four-year-old stage manager and bit actor, making $40 a week, when I worked.

At that time nearly all of us felt menaced by two things: the depression and the ever growing power of Hitler. The streets were full of unemployed and shaken men. I was taken in by the Hard Times version of what might be called the Communists' advertising or recruiting technique. They claimed to have a cure for depressions and a cure for Naziism and Fascism.

I joined the Communist Party late in the summer of 1934. I got out a year and a half later.

I have no spy stories to tell, because I saw no spies. Nor did I understand, at that time, any opposition between American and Russian national interest. It was not even clear to me in 1936 that the American Communist Party was abjectly taking its orders from the Kremlin.

What I learned was the minimum that anyone must learn who puts his head into the noose of party "discipline." The Communists automatically violated the daily practices of democracy to which I was accustomed. They attempted to control thought and to suppress personal opinion. They tried to dictate personal conduct. They habitually distorted and disregarded and violated the truth. All this was crudely opposite to their claims of "democracy" and "the scientific approach."

To be a member of the Communist Party is to have a taste of the police state. It is a diluted taste but it is bitter and unforgettable. It is diluted because you can walk out.

I got out in the spring of 1936.

The question will be asked why I did not tell this story sooner. I was held back, primarily, by concern for the reputations and employment of people who may, like myself, have left the Party many years ago.

I was also held back by a piece of specious reasoning which has silenced many liberals. It goes like this: "You may hate the Communists, but you must not attack them or expose them, because if you do you are attacking the right to hold unpopular opinions and you are joining the people who attack civil liberties."

I have thought soberly about this. It is, simply, a lie.

Secrecy serves the Communists. At the other pole, it serves those who are interested in silencing liberal voices. The employment of a lot of good liberals is threatened because they have allowed themselves to become associated with or silenced by the Communists.

Liberals must speak out.

I think it is useful that certain of us had this kind of experience with the Communists, for if we had not we should not know them so well. Today, when all the world fears war and they scream peace, we know how much their professions are worth. We know tomorrow they will have a new slogan.

Firsthand experience of dictatorship and thought control left me with an abiding hatred of these. It left me with an abiding hatred of Communist philosophy and methods and the conviction that these must be resisted always.

It also left me with the passionate conviction that we must never let the Communists get away with the pretense that they stand for the very things which they kill in their own countries.

I am talking about free speech, a free press, the rights of property, the rights of labor, racial equality and, above all, individual rights. I value these things. I take them seriously. I value peace, too, when it is not bought at the price of fundamental decencies.

I believe these things must be fought for wherever they are not fully honored and protected whenever they are threatened.

The motion pictures I have made and the plays I have chosen to direct represent my convictions.

I expect to continue to make the same kinds of pictures and to direct the same kinds of plays.

"Acted contrary to . . . ethics"

THE SENATE CENSURES SENATOR MCCARTHY
1954

The United States Senate censured Wisconsin's Joseph R. McCarthy (1908–1957)—
"Tail-Gunner Joe"—for conduct unbecoming a member, for refusing to explain a financial transaction of several years earlier, and for abusing colleagues. He had
accused the Army of coddling communists, distinguished Americans of treasonable
disloyalty, and former Presidents Franklin Delano Roosevelt (1882–1945) and Harry
S. Truman (1884–1972) of "twenty years of treason." He claimed that communists and
communist sympathizers infested the Department of State and were dictating policy.
McCarthy failed to present either an actionable or a plausible case against anyone. The
tail-gunner of a dive bomber during the Second World War, he went to high school at
the age of 20, completing four years of courses in nine months. After censure, McCarthy retreated to his rooms in Washington, D.C., watched soap operas on television,
stared into the fire, and became an acute alcoholic. *McCarthyism* has come to mean
reckless and indiscriminate attacks and charges of political disloyalty on persons innocent and defenseless.

Resolved, That the Senator from Wisconsin,
Mr. McCarthy, failed to cooperate with the
Subcommittee on Privileges and Elections of the
Senate Committee on Rules and Administration
in clearing up matters referred to that subcommittee which concerned his conduct as a Senator
and affected the honor of the Senate and, instead, repeatedly abused the subcommittee and
its members who were trying to carry out assigned duties, thereby obstructing the constitutional processes of the Senate, and that this
conduct of the Senator from Wisconsin, Mr.
McCarthy, is contrary to senatorial traditions
and is hereby condemned.

SEC. 2. The Senator from Wisconsin, Mr.
McCarthy, in writing to the chairman of the Select Committee To Study Censure Charges
(Mr. Watkins) after the Select Committee had
issued its report and before the report was presented to the Senate charging three members of
the Select Committee with "deliberate deception" and "fraud" for failure to disqualify themselves; in stating to the press on November 4,
1954, that the special Senate session that was to
begin November 8, 1954, was a "lynch party"; in
repeatedly describing this special Senate session
as a "lynch bee" in a nationwide television and
radio show on November 7, 1954; in stating to
the public press on November 13, 1954, that the
chairman of the Select Committee (Mr.
Watkins) was guilty of "the most unusual, most
cowardly thing I've heard of" and stating further: "I expected he would be afraid to answer
the questions, but didn't think he'd be stupid
enough to make a public statement"; and in
characterizing the said committee as the "unwitting handmaiden," "involuntary agent" and
"attorneys-in-fact" of the Communist Party and

in charging that the said committee in writing its report "imitated Communist methods—that it distorted, misrepresented, and omitted in its effort to manufacture a plausible rationalization" in support of its recommendations to the Senate, which characterizations and charges were contained in a statement released to the press and inserted in the Congressional Record of November 10, 1954, acted contrary to senatorial ethics and tended to bring the Senate into dishonor and disrepute, to obstruct the constitutional processes of the Senate, and to impair its dignity; and such conduct is hereby condemned.

"The shots . . . were fired by Lee Harvey Oswald"

THE WARREN COMMISSION REPORT
1964

Less than a year after President John F. Kennedy (1917–1963) was assassinated while riding in a motorcade in Dallas, Texas, the investigating commission headed by Chief Justice Earl Warren (1891–1974) concluded that a former Marine who had defected to the Soviet Union, twenty-four-year-old Lee Harvey Oswald (1939–1963)—acting alone—had been the gunman. The Warren Commission saw Oswald's act as the product of a life "characterized by isolation, frustration, and failure." More than 30 years later, most Americans did not believe the single-gunman verdict. A variety of conspiratorial theories were popular: "Cubans did it." "The C.I.A. did it." "Military-industrial corporations financed the plot." "Oil money was behind it." "Vice President Johnson had a hand in it." Oswald, who had denied shooting the President (whom he admired), "was a patsy." There even was speculation (published in at least five books) about an accidental assassination, that Oswald's misaligned rifle was aimed at the glamorous First Lady; Oswald's estranged, battered wife considered Jacqueline Kennedy "a goddess." (Gun experts informed the Warren Commission that Oswald's antiquated rifle shot high and to the right of the aiming point; the gun and its cheap mail-order sights could not be aligned properly. Jackie was at J.F.K.'s left.) Mr. Kennedy was the fourth President to be assassinated. Presidents Abraham Lincoln (in 1865), James Garfield (1881), and William McKinley (1901) also were murdered; their killers were swiftly executed (Lincoln's by a deranged soldier "on orders from God").

No limitations have been placed on the Commission's inquiry; it has conducted its own investigation, and all Government agencies have fully discharged their responsibility to cooperate with the Commission in its investigation. These conclusions represent the reasoned judgment of all members of the Commission and are presented after an investigation which has satisfied the Commission that it has ascertained the truth concerning the assassination of President Kennedy to the extent that a prolonged and thorough search makes this possible.

1. The shots which killed President Kennedy and wounded Governor Connally were fired from the sixth floor window at the southeast corner of the Texas School Book Depository. . . .

2. The weight of the evidence indicates that there were three shots fired.

3. Although it is not necessary to any essential findings of the Commission to determine just which shot hit Governor Connally, there is very

persuasive evidence from the experts to indicate that the same bullet which pierced the President's throat also caused Governor Connally's wounds. However, Governor Connally's testimony and certain other factors have given rise to some difference of opinion as to this probability but there is no question in the mind of any member of the Commission that all the shots which caused the President's and Governor Connally's wounds were fired from the sixth floor window of the Texas School Book Depository.

4. The shots which killed President Kennedy and wounded Governor Connally were fired by Lee Harvey Oswald. This conclusion is based upon the following:

(a) The Mannlicher-Carcano 6.5-millimeter Italian rifle from which the shots were fired was owned by and in the possession of Oswald.

(b) Oswald carried this rifle into the Depository Building on the morning of November 22, 1963.

(c) Oswald, at the time of the assassination, was present at the window from which the shots were fired.

(d) Shortly after the assassination, the Mannlicher-Carcano rifle belonging to Oswald was found partially hidden between some cartons on the sixth floor and the improvised paper bag in which Oswald brought the rifle to the Depository was found close by the window from which the shots were fired.

(e) Based on testimony of the experts and their analysis of films of the assassination, the Commission has concluded that a rifleman of Lee Harvey Oswald's capabilities could have fired the shots from the rifle used in the assassination within the elapsed time of the shooting. The Commission has concluded further that Oswald possessed the capability with a rifle which enabled him to commit the assassination.

(f) Oswald lied to the police after his arrest concerning important substantive matters.

(g) Oswald had attempted to kill Maj. Gen. Edwin A. Walker (Resigned, U.S. Army) on April 10, 1963, thereby demonstrating his disposition to take human life.

5. Oswald killed Dallas Police Patrolman J. D. Tippit approximately 45 minutes after the assassination. This conclusion upholds the finding that Oswald fired the shots which killed President Kennedy and wounded Governor Connally. . . .

6. Within 80 minutes of the assassination and 35 minutes of the Tippit killing Oswald resisted arrest at the theatre by attempting to shoot another Dallas police officer. . . .

9. The Commission has found no evidence that either Lee Harvey Oswald or Jack Ruby was part of any conspiracy, domestic or foreign, to assassinate President Kennedy.

10. In its entire investigation the Commission has found no evidence of conspiracy, subversion, or disloyalty to the U.S. Government by any Federal, State, or local official.

11. On the basis of the evidence before the Commission it concludes that Oswald acted alone. Therefore, to determine the motives for the assassination of President Kennedy, one must look to the assassin himself. Clues to Oswald's motives can be found in his family history, his education or lack of it, his acts, his writings, and the recollections of those who had close contacts with him throughout his life. The Commission has presented with this report all of the background information bearing on motivation which it could discover. Thus, others may study Lee Oswald's life and arrive at their own conclusions as to his possible motives.

The Commission could not make any definitive determination of Oswald's motives.

"Reason . . . must . . . guide our decision"

BARBARA JORDAN ON IMPEACHING PRESIDENT NIXON
1974

**Debate on articles of impeachment by the House of Representatives' Judiciary Com-
mittee addressed the resolution authorizing and directing the committee to investigate
whether sufficient grounds existed for the House to exercise its constitutional power
to impeach President Richard M. Nixon (1913–1994) for his involvement in Watergate. Texas Congresswoman Barbara Jordan (1936–1996), with a mesmerizing denunciation of the abuses, especially Mr. Nixon's distortion of the Constitution for political
reasons, argued for impeachment.**

I join my colleague, Mr. Rangel, in thanking
you for giving the junior members of this committee the glorious opportunity of sharing the
pain of this inquiry. Mr. Chairman, you are a
strong man and it has not been easy but we have
tried as best we can to give you as much assistance as possible.

Earlier today, we heard the beginning of the
Preamble to the Constitution of the United
States, We, the people. It is a very eloquent beginning. But when that document was completed on the 17th of September in 1787 I was not
included in that "We, the people." I felt somehow for many years that George Washington
and Alexander Hamilton just left me out by mistake. But through the process of amendment, interpretation and court decision I have finally
been included in "We, the people."

Today, I am an inquisitor, I believe hyperbole
would not be fictional and would not overstate
the solemness that I feel right now. My faith in
the Constitution is whole, it is complete, it is
total. I am not going to sit here and be an idle
spectator to the diminution, the subversion, the
destruction of the Constitution.

"Who can so properly be the inquisitors for
the nation as the representatives of the nation
themselves?" (Federalist No. 65) The subject of
its jurisdiction are those offenses which proceed
from the misconduct of public men. That is
what we are talking about. In other words, the
jurisdiction comes from the abuse of violation of
some public trust. It is wrong, I suggest, it is a
misreading of the Constitution for any member
here to assert that for a member to vote for an Article of Impeachment means that that member
must be convinced that the President should be
removed from office. The Constitution doesn't
say that. The powers relating to impeachment
are an essential check in the hands of this body,
the legislature, against and upon the encroachment of the Executive. In establishing the division between the two branches of the legislature,
the House and the Senate, assigning to the one
the right to accuse and to the other the right to
judge, the Framers of this Constitution were
very astute. They did not make the accusers and
the judges the same person.

We know the nature of impeachment. We
have been talking about it awhile now. "It is
chiefly designed for the President and his high
ministers" to somehow be called into account. It

is designed to "bridle" the Executive if he engages in excesses. "It is designed as a method of national inquest into the conduct of public men." (Hamilton, Federalist No. 65) The Framers confined in the Congress the power if need be, to remove the President in order to strike a delicate balance between a President swollen with power and grown tyrannical; and preservation of the independence of the Executive. The nature of impeachment is a narrowly channeled exception to the separation of powers maxim, the Federal Convention of 1787 said that. It limited impeachment to high crimes and misdemeanors and discounted and opposed the term, "maladministration." "It is to be used only for great misdemeanors," so it was said in the North Carolina ratification convention. And in the Virginia ratification convention: "We do not trust our liberty to a particular branch. We need one branch to check the others."

The North Carolina Ratification Convention: "No one need be afraid that officers who commit oppression will pass with immunity."

"Prosecutions of impeachments will seldom fail to agitate the passions of the whole community," said Hamilton in the Federalist Papers No. 65. "And to divide it into parties more or less friendly or inimical to the accused," I do not mean political parties in that sense.

The drawing of political lines goes to the motivation behind impeachment; but impeachment must proceed within the confines of the constitutional term, "high crime and misdemeanors."

Of the impeachment process, it was Woodrow Wilson who said that "nothing short of the grossest offenses against the plain law of the land will suffice to give them speed and effectiveness. Indignation so great as to overgrow party interest may secure a conviction; but nothing else can."

Commonsense would be revolted if we engaged upon this process for petty reasons. Congress has a lot to do. Appropriations, tax reform, health insurance, campaign finance reform, housing, environmental protection, energy sufficiency, mass transportation. Pettiness cannot be allowed to stand in the face of such overwhelming problems. So today we are not being petty. We are trying to be big because the task we have before us is a big one.

This morning in a discussion of the evidence we were told that the evidence which purports to support the allegations of misuse of the CIA by the President is thin. We are told that that evidence is insufficient. What that recital of the evidence this morning did not include is what the President did know on June 23, 1972. The President did know that it was Republican money, that it was money from the Committee for the Re-Election of the President, which was found in the possession of one of the burglars arrested on June 17.

What the President did know on June 23 was the prior activities of E. Howard Hunt, which included his participation in the break-in of Daniel Ellsberg's psychiatrist, which included Howard Hunt's participation in the Dita Beard ITT affair, which included Howard Hunt's fabrication of cables designed to discredit the Kennedy administration.

We were further cautioned today that perhaps these proceedings ought to be delayed because certainly there would be new evidence forthcoming from the President of the United States. There has not even been an obfuscated indication that this committee would receive any additional materials from the President. The committee subpena is outstanding and if the President wants to supply that material, the committee sits here.

The fact is that on yesterday, the American

people waited with great anxiety for 8 hours, not knowing whether their President would obey an order of the Supreme Court of the United States.

At this point I would like to juxtapose a few of the impeachment criteria with some of the President's actions.

Impeachment criteria: James Madison, from the Virginia Ratification Convention. "If the President be connected in any suspicious manner with any person and there be grounds to believe that he will shelter him, he may be impeached."

We have heard time and time again that the evidence reflects payment to the defendants of money. The President had knowledge that these funds were being paid and that these were funds collected for the 1972 Presidential campaign.

We know that the President met with Mr. Henry Petersen 27 times to discuss matters related to Watergate and immediately thereafter met with the very persons who were implicated in the information Mr. Petersen was receiving and transmitting to the President. The words are, "if the President be connected in any suspicious manner with any person and there be grounds to believe that he will shelter that person, he may be impeached."

Justice Story: "Impeachment is intended for occasional and extraordinary cases where a superior power acting for the whole people is put into operation to protect their rights and rescue their liberties from violations."

We know about the Huston plan. We know about the break-in of the psychiatrist's office. We know that there was absolute complete direction in August 1971 when the President instructed Ehrlichman to "do whatever is necessary." This instruction led to a surreptitious entry into Dr. Fielding's office.

"Protect their rights." "Rescue their liberties from violation."

The South Carolina Ratification Convention impeachment criteria: Those are impeachable "who behave amiss or betray their public trust."

Beginning shortly after the Watergate break-in and continuing to the present time the President has engaged in a series of public statements and actions designed to thwart the lawful investigation by Government prosecutors. Moreover, the President has made public announcements and assertions bearing on the Watergate case which the evidence will show he knew to be false.

These assertions, false assertions, impeachable, those who misbehave. Those who "behave amiss or betray their public trust."

James Madison again at the Constitutional Convention: "A President is impeachable if he attempts to subvert the Constitution."

The Constitution charges the President with the task of taking care that the laws be faithfully executed, and yet the President has counseled his aides to commit perjury, willfully disregarded the secrecy of grand jury proceedings, concealed surreptitious entry, attempted to compromise a Federal judge while publicly displaying his cooperation with the processes of criminal justice.

"A President is impeachable if he attempts to subvert the Constitution."

If the impeachment provision in the Constitution of the United States will not reach the offenses charged here, then perhaps that 18th century Constitution should be abandoned to a 20th century paper shredder. Has the President committed offenses and planned and directed and acquiesced in a course of conduct which the Constitution will not tolerate? That is the question. We know that. We know the question. We should now forthwith proceed to answer the question. It is reason, and not passion, which must guide our deliberations, guide our debate, and guide our decision.

Index

Pacific Ocean, Monroe Doctrine extended into, 437
Pacific Railway Act of 1862, 416, 420–421
Pacifism, 148
Palestine, partition of, 307
Pan-African movement, 225
Panama, 326–327
  U.S. troops ordered to, 269
Panama Canal, 326–327
Panama Canal Treaty of 1903, 326
Papa Sapa, 353
Paris Peace Treaty, 27–29, 86, 440
Parker, Theodore, 105
Passports, 131–132
Patriotism, 486
Peace Corps, formation of, 316
Pearl Harbor, 250–255, 299–300
Pennsylvania, Annapolis Convention and, 30–31
Pentagon Papers, 438, 464–467
People, power as vested in, 15
People's Party of America. See Populist Party
Perry, Matthew Calbraith, 443
Persian Gulf, military action in, 269
Person, definition of, 358–367
Philadelphia, Constitutional Congress at, 34
Philippines, U.S. annexation of, 408, 445
Phillips, Wendell, 105
Photo-spy planes, 317
Pierce, Franklin, 211
Pinkerton system, 235
Planned Parenthood, 260
Plessy, Homer Adolph, 126
Plessy v. Ferguson, 105, 126–127
  overturning of, 133–134
Plimoth Plantation, 4
Political parties, George Washington on, 275–276
Polk, James K., 92, 94, 95, 283
Ponca Indians, 358
  forcible relocation of, 363–366
Poor. See also Poverty
  assistance programs for, 384–385
Popular culture, 223
Population, explosive post-Revolution growth in, 222
Populist movement, 225
Populist Party, 225, 544
  platform of, 233–236

Pornography. See also Sexuality in the media
  suppression of, 478–479
Poverty. See also Poor
  combating, 529–531
Power
  limiting presidential, 438, 471–472
  politics of, 225–226, 267–269, 484–485
Powered flight, 505
Pregnancy, 139–143
Presidency, under Articles of Confederation, 21
President
  of the Confederacy, 203–204, 206–207, 207–208
  constitutional duties and powers of, 38–39, 40–42
  election of, 46
  executive powers of, 267–269
  limiting power of, 438, 471–472
  line item veto power granted to, 339–340
  term of office of, 48–49, 49, 236
President's Committee on Equality of Treatment and Opportunity in the Armed Forces, 308
President-General, 6–7
Privacy, right of, 140–141, 226, 260
Progressivism, period of, 384
Promontory, Utah, 420
Property
  under G.I. Bill, 247–249
  Indian notions of, 342
  preservation of historic, 167–169
  restoration of confiscated, 28–29
  slaves as, 120–121, 127
Prosperity, 158
Protestant ethic, 480, 544
Provisional Government of the Confederate States of America, 210
Public debt, 234
  George Washington on, 276–277
Public lands
  for colleges, 422–423
  grazing on, 429–431
  Homestead Act and, 417
  misuse of, 417
  settlement of, 415
Public opinion, 485
Public schools. See also Education
  increasing role of, 222–223
  racial segregation in, 133–134

Public television, 513–515
Puerto Rico, U.S. annexation of, 445
Pure Food and Drug Act of 1906, 387–388
Puritans, 2, 4, 5
  "civilization" of Indians by, 342
  as immigrants, 173–174

Quotas, abolition of, 256–258

Race riots, 521–523
Racism, 126–127, 521–523. See also Anti-Asian sentiments; Blacks; Discrimination; Indians; Segregation
  in baseball, 162–163
  civil rights and, 135–136, 137–138
  Constitution and, 119
  equality of races and, 132
  following the Civil War, 104–105, 123–125
  "I have a dream" speech and, 164–166
  immigration and, 175
  measures to combat, 149–150
  military, 297–298, 308
  the "Negro problem" and, 242
  slavery and, 71–72, 103–104
  William Clinton on, 335–338
Railroads
  advance of, 415–416
  legislation promoting development of, 420–421
  misuse of public lands by, 417
  popular ownership of, 235
Randolph, A. Philip, 297
Raymond, Henry J., 494, 496
Reagan, Ronald Wilson, 269, 439, 480
  on environmental protection, 400
  Iran-Contra Affair and, 473
  social policy of government under, 385–386
  speech to Republican Party by, 516–520
Red Jacket, 347–348
Red River, Florida Territory and, 87
Reform movement, 147–150, 383–384
Relief, 384–385
Religion
  denial of freedom to exercise, 71
  economic justice and, 529–531

Supreme Court (*cont.*).
  civil rights legislation and, 149–150
  creation and empowerment of, 34–35, 64–65
  Dred Scott decision by, 116–121, 192–193
  female suffrage ruling by, 122
  "Jim Crow" laws and, 126
  Marbury v. Madison decision by, 66–67
  organization and powers of, 42
  Plessy v. Ferguson decision by, 126–127
  on regulating sexual indecency, 261–263
  Roe v. Wade decision by, 139–143
  ruling on birth control by, 260
  school segregation struck down by, 149
  women's rights and, 105–106
Surrender of Japan after World War II, 305–306
Szilard, Leo, 510

Taft, William Howard, 437
"Tail-Gunner Joe," 565
Taiwan, U.S. defense treaty with, 468–470
Taney, Roger Brooke, 116, 196
Taxation
  colonial resistance to, 8–9
  in the Confederacy, 204
  congressional power of, 39–40
  federal powers of, 23
  Henry Thoreau on, 478
  of income, 47
  in Northwest Ordinance of 1787, 76
  Populist Party and, 235
  Republican stand on, 155
  Ronald Reagan on, 516
  Townsend Plan and, 160
Taylor Grazing Act of 1934, 429–431
Teapot Dome-Elk Hills imbroglio, 427–428
Technology
  Eisenhower's warning against government funding of, 313
  improved lifestyle resulting from, 222–223
Tecumseh, 342
Teheran rescue operation, 268–269

Telecommunications industry, reorganization of, 404–407
Telegraph, cross-country, 420
Television, as a "vast wasteland," 513–515
Tennessee Valley Authority (TVA), 385
  act creating, 391–396
Tenth Amendment, 46, 149
Term limitations, 266
Territories, addition of western, 70–72
Texas
  admission to the Union of, 189
  annexation of, 92–93, 283
  restrictive abortion law in, 139, 140–141, 141–142
  Treaty of Guadalupe-Hidalgo and, 95, 283
Third International of the Communist Party, 449
Thirteenth Amendment, 47, 110, 126, 214
Thomas, Norman M., 130, 518
Thoreau, Henry David
  on civil disobedience, 492–493
  refusal to pay taxes by, 478
Tippecanoe, Battle of, 342
Tocqueville, Alexis de, 34, 477–478
Tonkin Bay Resolution, 438
Tower Commission, 439
Townsend, Francis Everett, 160
Townsend Plan, 160
Transcendentalism, 151
Transportation, Populist Party and, 235
Treason, 42
Treaty of Amity, Commerce, and Navigation, 440–442
Treaty of Fort Laramie, 349–352, 353
Treaty of Guadalupe-Hidalgo, 95–96, 283
Treaty of Kanagawa, 443–444
Treaty of Paris of 1783. *See* Paris Peace Treaty
Treaty of Paris of 1899, 408
Trieste, Iron Curtain extending to, 453–455
Trimesters, 141–142
Trist, Nicholas, 95
Truman, Harry S, 268, 305, 385
  elimination of military segregation by, 308

firing of Douglas MacArthur by, 311
  Joseph McCarthy's accusations against, 565
  Korean War initiated by, 309–310
  policy toward Soviet Union, 438
  U.S. recognition of Israel and, 307
Turner, Frederick Jackson, 424
Tuscarora Indians, 345
Tuskegee Institute, 123
Twain, Mark, 211
Two-party system, 234
Tyranny, 484–485

Unconstitutionality of congressional acts, 66–67
Unemployed, assistance programs for, 384–385
Unemployment
  under G.I. Bill, 249
  Ronald Reagan on, 517–518
Union
  Abraham Lincoln's arguments for preservation of, 196–200
  formation of, 33–35, 51–53, 54–59
  Franklin's plan of, 6–7
  preservation of, 214
  social forces jeopardizing, 70–72
United Nations, 268, 309, 311, 451, 455
United Nations Security Council, 268
  Korean War and, 309
United States
  as an "arsenal of democracy," 296
  boundaries of, 27–28
  conflicts between Indians and, 358, 368–372
  as constructed and shaped through immigration, 173–175
  development of, 416
  establishment of rights of, 28
  formation of, 21–22
  Japan's attack against, 250–255
  "malaise" in, 328–330
  post-Revolution population growth of, 222
  protection of states by, 43
  revision of policies toward Indians of, 377–382
  southeast Asia and, 461–463
  Tocqueville on, 482–486
  Vietnam War and, 438–439

war between Mexico and, 283–285
as a world power, 435–439
United States Marines, 448
Urban League, 150
Utah
female suffrage in, 122
slavery and, 187, 189
Utopian experiments, 147–148,
151–152
Utopian society, 501–504, 544

"Vast wasteland," television as,
513–515
Vermont, entry into the Union of,
70, 78–79
Veterans Administration, 243
Vice President
of the Confederacy, 202, 207–208
Constitutional duties and powers
of, 37
constitutional duties and powers of,
40–42
election of, 40–41, 46
term of office of, 48–49, 49–50,
236
Vietnam, 461
U.S. involvement in, 464
Vietnam War, 438–439
Pentagon Papers and, 464
Violence, 137–138
Virginia, 4, 13, 30
Annapolis Convention and, 30–31
legal rights and liberties in, 1–2,
15–16
opposition to Constitution by, 34
Patrick Henry and, 10
Thomas Jefferson and, 279
Virginia Convention of Delegates, 10
Virginia Declaration of Rights, 15–16
Virginia Resolution, 185
V-J Day, 305–306
Voting age, 50
Voting Rights Act of 1965, 135–136,
150, 385

Wade, Henry, 139
Wages, 152, 158
Wampanoag Indians, 4
War, declaration and waging of, 23,
39

Ward, Samuel A., 179
War for Independence. *See* Revolutionary War
War of 1812, 174, 175, 440
War Powers Resolution, 471–472,
474
Warren, Earl, 133, 567
Warren, Mercy Otis, 60–63
Warren Commission, 542
report on Kennedy assassination
by, 567–568
Washington, Booker Taliaferro,
123–125
Washington, George, 27, 30, 78, 440
on arts and sciences, 259
as Constitutional Convention pres-
ident, 36
farewell address of, 273–278
first inaugural address by, 270–272
on his own presidency, 267
Watergate scandal, 319, 323, 543,
569
Wealth, 235
Franklin Roosevelt on, 289
stewardship of, 479–480
Weaver, James B., 233
Webster, Noah, 174
Weeks, Edward, 501
Weights and measures, federal stan-
dards of, 24–25
Weizmann, Chaim, 307
Welfare
government programs of, 384–385
Indians on, 344
West
American expansion into, 70–72,
84–85, 222, 418–419
George Washington on, 274–275
growth and development of,
416–417
Western Electric Company, Inc., 405,
406
Westmoreland, William, 464
Wheeler-Howard Act, 375–376
White America, need for coexistence
with blacks by, 335–338
White supremacy, 105
Whitman, Walt, 479, 545
letter from Ralph Waldo Emerson
to, 497

Wilkie, Wendell, 437–438
Wills, Garry, 216
Wilson, Woodrow, 149, 437
Fourteen Points of, 286–287
Windows (Microsoft), 526–528
Winthrop, John, 174
on Indians, 342
Women, emancipation of, 112
Women's rights, 105–106, 112–115,
144–145
Works Progress Administration
(W.P.A.), 223, 239–241
World Heritage List, 169
World War I
American recovery following,
154–159
majoritarian witch hunting during,
478
Woodrow Wilson and, 286
World War II
American isolationism and,
437–438
the Atlantic Charter and, 451
atomic research and, 510
attack against Pearl Harbor and,
250–255, 299–300
Dwight Eisenhower in, 312
Franklin Roosevelt's death before
the end of, 303
government support for the arts
following, 223–224
keeping America out of, 512
Lend-Lease legislation during, 295
peacetime draft before, 549–544
reconstruction of Europe following, 456–457
Robert Dole's injury in, 411
U.S. recognition of Israel following, 307
U.S. role in, 296
Wounded Knee, South Dakota,
slaughter of Indians at, 344
Wright, Orville and Wilbur, 480, 505
Wyoming Territory, female suffrage
in, 122

Yamamoto, Isoroku, 250

Zenger, John Peter, 107
"Zones of privacy," 260

JEROME AGEL has written and/or produced more than fifty major books, including collaborations with Marshall McLuhan, Carl Sagan, Isaac Asimov, R. Buckminster Fuller, and Stanley Kubrick. Titles include *The Medium is the Massage, I Seem to Be a Verb, The Cosmic Connection, The Making of Kubrick's* 2001, *Why in the World,* and *Predicting the Past.* United States histories include *The U.S. Constitution for Everyone* (20 printings!), *America at Random, A World Without: What Our Presidents Didn't Know,* and (with Richard B. Bernstein) *Amending America* and *Of the People, By the People, For the People.*

MILTON J. CANTOR, Ph.D., who contributed the section introductions, is professor of history at the University of Massachusetts, Amherst. He has written or edited eight books about American History, including *Main Problems in American History* and *The Divided Left: American Radicalism 1900–1975.*